HALSBURY'S Laws of England

Volume 40

2014

Editors of this Volume

MARTIN COOK, BA

CAROL MARSH, LLB, MA

MOHINI TULLOCH, LLM

AMANDA WRIGHT, LLB

Commissioning Editor

CLAIRE TURPIN, LLB, MSc

Indexer

JAMES A. WARD, BA, LLB,
a Solicitor of the Senior Courts of England and Wales

Managing Editor

HELEN HALVEY, LLB

TABLE OF CONTENTS

PAGE

Volume 41A

HOW TO USE HALSBURY'S LAWS OF ENGLAND

Volumes

Each text volume of Halsbury's Laws of England contains the law on the titles contained in it as at a date stated at the front of the volume (the operative date).

Information contained in Halsbury's Laws of England may be accessed in several ways.

First, by using the tables of contents.

Each volume contains both a general Table of Contents, and a specific Table of Contents for each title contained in it. From these tables you will be directed to the relevant part of the work.

Readers should note that the current arrangement of titles can be found in the Current Service.

Secondly, by using tables of statutes, statutory instruments, cases or other materials.

If you know the name of the Act, statutory instrument or case with which your research is concerned, you should consult the Consolidated Tables of statutes, cases and so on (published as separate volumes) which will direct you to the relevant volume and paragraph. The Consolidated Tables will indicate if the volume referred to is a Fifth Edition volume.

(Each individual text volume also includes tables of those materials used as authority in that volume.)

Thirdly, by using the indexes.

If you are uncertain of the general subject area of your research, you should go to the Consolidated Index (published as separate volumes) for reference to the relevant volume(s) and paragraph(s). The Consolidated Index will indicate if the volume referred to is a Fifth Edition volume.

(Each individual text volume also includes an index to the material contained therein.)

Additional Materials

The reorganisation of the title scheme of Halsbury's Laws for the Fifth Edition means that from time to time Fourth Edition volumes will be *partially* replaced by Fifth Edition volumes.

In certain instances an Additional Materials softbound book will be issued, in which will be reproduced material which has not yet been replaced by a Fifth Edition title. This will enable users to remove specific Fourth Edition volumes from the shelf and save valuable space pending the replacement of that material in the Fifth Edition. These softbound books are supplied to volumes subscribers free of charge. They continue to form part of the set of Halsbury's Laws Fourth Edition Reissue, and will be updated by the annual Cumulative Supplement and monthly Noter-Up in the usual way.

Updating publications

The text volumes of Halsbury's Laws should be used in conjunction with the annual Cumulative Supplement and the monthly Noter-Up.

The annual Cumulative Supplement

The Supplement gives details of all changes between the operative date of the text volume and the operative date of the Supplement. It is arranged in the same volume, title and paragraph order as the text volumes. Developments affecting particular points of law are noted to the relevant paragraph(s) of the text volumes. As from the commencement of the Fifth Edition, the Supplement will clearly distinguish between Fourth and Fifth Edition titles.

For narrative treatment of material noted in the Cumulative Supplement, go to the Annual Abridgment volume for the relevant year.

Destination Tables

In certain titles in the annual *Cumulative Supplement*, reference is made to Destination Tables showing the destination of consolidated legislation. Those Destination Tables are to be found either at the end of the titles within the annual *Cumulative Supplement*, or in a separate *Destination Tables* booklet provided from time to time with the *Cumulative Supplement*.

The Noter-Up

The Noter-Up is contained in the Current Service Noter-Up booklet, issued monthly and noting changes since the publication of the annual Cumulative Supplement. Also arranged in the same volume, title and paragraph order as the text volumes, the Noter-Up follows the style of the Cumulative Supplement. As from the commencement of the Fifth Edition, the Noter-Up will clearly distinguish between Fourth and Fifth Edition titles.

For narrative treatment of material noted in the Noter-Up, go to the relevant Monthly Review.

REFERENCES AND ABBREVIATIONS

ACT	Australian Capital Territory
A-G	Attorney General
Admin	Administrative Court
Admlty	Admiralty Court
Adv-Gen	Advocate General
affd	affirmed
affg	affirming
Alta	Alberta
App	Appendix
art	article
Aust	Australia
B	Baron
BC	British Columbia
C	Command Paper (of a series published before 1900)
c	chapter number of an Act
CA	Court of Appeal
CAC	Central Arbitration Committee
CA in Ch	Court of Appeal in Chancery
CB	Chief Baron
CCA	Court of Criminal Appeal
CCR	County Court Rules 1981 (as subsequently amended)
CCR	Court for Crown Cases Reserved
C-MAC	Courts-Martial Appeal Court
CO	Crown Office
COD	Crown Office Digest
CPR	Civil Procedure Rules
Can	Canada
Cd	Command Paper (of the series published 1900–18)
Cf	compare
Ch	Chancery Division
ch	chapter
cl	clause
Cm	Command Paper (of the series published 1986 to date)

Cmd	Command Paper (of the series published 1919–56)
Cmnd	Command Paper (of the series published 1956–86)
Comm	Commercial Court
Comr	Commissioner
Court Forms (2nd Edn)	Atkin's Encyclopaedia of Court Forms in Civil Proceedings, 2nd Edn. See note 2 post.
CrimPR	Criminal Procedure Rules
DC	Divisional Court
DPP	Director of Public Prosecutions
EAT	Employment Appeal Tribunal
EC	European Community
ECJ	Court of Justice of the European Community
EComHR	European Commission of Human Rights
ECSC	European Coal and Steel Community
ECtHR Rules of Court	Rules of Court of the European Court of Human Rights
EEC	European Economic Community
EFTA	European Free Trade Association
EWCA Civ	Official neutral citation for judgments of the Court of Appeal (Civil Division)
EWCA Crim	Official neutral citation for judgments of the Court of Appeal (Criminal Division)
EWHC	Official neutral citation for judgments of the High Court
Edn	Edition
Euratom	European Atomic Energy Community
Ex Ch	Court of Exchequer Chamber
ex p	ex parte
Fam	Family Division
Fed	Federal
Forms & Precedents (5th Edn)	Encyclopaedia of Forms and Precedents other than Court Forms, 5th Edn. See note 2 post.
GLC	Greater London Council
HC	High Court
HC	House of Commons
HK	Hong Kong
HL	House of Lords
IAT	Immigration Appeal Tribunal
ILM	International Legal Materials
INLR	Immigration and Nationality Law Reports
IRC	Inland Revenue Commissioners
Ind	India

Int Rels	International Relations
Ir	Ireland
J	Justice
JA	Judge of Appeal
Kan	Kansas
LA	Lord Advocate
LC	Lord Chancellor
LCC	London County Council
LCJ	Lord Chief Justice
LJ	Lord Justice of Appeal
LoN	League of Nations
MR	Master of the Rolls
Man	Manitoba
n	note
NB	New Brunswick
NI	Northern Ireland
NS	Nova Scotia
NSW	New South Wales
NY	New York
NZ	New Zealand
OHIM	Office for Harmonisation in the Internal Market
OJ	The Official Journal of the European Community published by the Office for Official Publications of the European Community
Ont	Ontario
P	President
PC	Judicial Committee of the Privy Council
PEI	Prince Edward Island
Pat	Patents Court
q	question
QB	Queen's Bench Division
QBD	Queen's Bench Division of the High Court
Qld	Queensland
Que	Quebec
r	rule
RDC	Rural District Council
RPC	Restrictive Practices Court
RSC	Rules of the Supreme Court 1965 (as subsequently amended)
reg	regulation
Res	Resolution
revsd	reversed

Rly	Railway
s	section
SA	South Africa
S Aust	South Australia
SC	Supreme Court
SI	Statutory Instruments published by authority
SR & O	Statutory Rules and Orders published by authority
SR & O Rev 1904	Revised Edition comprising all Public and General Statutory Rules and Orders in force on 31 December 1903
SR & O Rev 1948	Revised Edition comprising all Public and General Statutory Rules and Orders and Statutory Instruments in force on 31 December 1948
SRNI	Statutory Rules of Northern Ireland
STI	Simon's Tax Intelligence (1973–1995); Simon's Weekly Tax Intelligence (1996-current)
Sask	Saskatchewan
Sch	Schedule
Sess	Session
Sing	Singapore
TCC	Technology and Construction Court
TS	Treaty Series
Tanz	Tanzania
Tas	Tasmania
UDC	Urban District Council
UKHL	Official neutral citation for judgments of the House of Lords
UKPC	Official neutral citation for judgments of the Privy Council
UN	United Nations
V-C	Vice-Chancellor
Vict	Victoria
W Aust	Western Australia
Zimb	Zimbabwe

NOTE 1. A general list of the abbreviations of law reports and other sources used in this work can be found at the beginning of the Consolidated Table of Cases.

NOTE 2. Where references are made to other publications, the volume number precedes and the page number follows the name of the publication; eg the reference '12 Forms & Precedents (5th Edn) 44' refers to volume 12 of the Encyclopaedia of Forms and Precedents, page 44.

NOTE 3. An English statute is cited by short title or, where there is no short title, by regnal year and chapter number together with the name by which it is commonly known or a description of its subject matter and date. In the case of a foreign statute, the mode of citation generally follows the style of citation in use in the country concerned with the addition, where necessary, of the name of the country in parentheses.

NOTE 4. A statutory instrument is cited by short title, if any, followed by the year and number, or, if unnumbered, the date.

TABLE OF STATUTES

TABLE OF STATUTORY INSTRUMENTS

TABLE OF CIVIL PROCEDURE

Civil Procedure Rules 1998, SI 1998/3132 (CPR)

Practice Directions

TABLE OF EUROPEAN UNION LEGISLATION

TABLE OF NON-STATUTORY MATERIAL

TABLE OF CASES

PARA

A

B

PARA

B & S Contracts and Design Ltd v Victor Green Publications Ltd [1984] ICR 419, 128 Sol Jo 279, [1984] LS Gaz R 893, CA 1344
Babar Indian Restaurant v Rawat [1985] IRLR 57, EAT 769, 782, 870
Babcock FATA Ltd v Addison. See Addison v Babcock FATA Ltd
Babula v Waltham Forest College [2007] EWCA Civ 174, [2007] IRLR 346, [2007] ICR 1026, (2007) Times, 17 April, 151 Sol Jo LB 396, [2007] All ER (D) 98 (Mar) 70
Bache v Essex County Council [2000] 2 All ER 847, [2000] ICR 313, [2000] IRLR 251, [2000] 05 LS Gaz R 33, [2000] NLJR 99, CA 1522–1523
Bailey v BP Oil (Kent Refinery) Ltd [1980] IRLR 287, [1980] ICR 642, CA 708, 768, 1445
Bailey v Rimmell (1836) 5 LJ Ex 192, sub nom Bayley v Rimmell 2 Gale 60, 1 M & W 506, Tyr & Gr 806 723
Baillie v Kell (1838) 4 Bing NC 638, 7 LJCP 249, 6 Scott 379 .... 745, 825
Bainbridge v Westinghouse Brake and Signal Co Ltd (1966) 1 KIR 88, 1 ITR 55, Ind Trib 874
Baker v Superite Tools Ltd [1986] ICR 189, [1985] LS Gaz R 2906, EAT 1428
Baker v T E Hopkins & Son Ltd [1959] 3 All ER 225, [1959] 1 WLR 966, 103 Sol Jo 812, CA 32
Baker Perkins Ltd v Melone [2009] All ER (D) 202 (Jan), EAT 757
Bakers' Union v Clarks of Hove Ltd [1977] IRLR 167, Ind Trib; on appeal sub nom Clarks of Hove Ltd v Bakers' Union [1978] 2 All ER 15, [1978] 1 WLR 563, [1977] ICR 838, [1977] IRLR 264, 121 Sol Jo 528, EAT; revsd [1979] 1 All ER 152, [1978] 1 WLR 1207, [1978] ICR 1076, 13 ITR 356, sub nom Bakers' Union v Clarks of Hove Ltd [1978] IRLR 366, 122 Sol Jo 643, CA 1185, 1188
Bakhsh v UNISON (2009) UKEAT/0375/08, [2009] IRLR 418, [2009] All ER (D) 169 (Apr), EAT 916
Baldwin v Brighton and Hove City Council [2007] ICR 680, [2007] IRLR 232, [2006] All ER (D) 220 (Dec), EAT 48
Baldwin v British Coal Corpn [1995] IRLR 139 735
Balfour v Foreign and Commonwealth Office [1994] 2 All ER 588, [1994] 1 WLR 681, [1994] ICR 277, [1994] 2 LRC 48, CA 1466
Balfour Beatty Engineering Services Ltd v Unite the Union [2012] EWHC 267 (QB), [2012] IRLR 452, [2012] ICR 822 .... 1377, 1439
Balfour Beatty Power Networks v Wilcox [2006] EWCA Civ 1240, [2007] IRLR 63, [2006] All ER (D) 275 (Jul) 1530
Balmoral Group Ltd v Rae (2000) Times, 25 January, EAT 818
Balston Ltd v Headline Filters Ltd [1987] FSR 330 71
Bamsey v Albon Engineering & Manufacturing plc [2004] EWCA Civ 359, [2004] 2 CMLR 1353, [2004] ICR 1083, [2004] IRLR 457, [2004] 17 LS Gaz R 31, (2004) Times, 15 April, 148 Sol Jo LB 389, [2004] All ER (D) 482 (Mar) 142, 295
Banerjee v City and East London Area Health Authority [1979] IRLR 147, ECJ 802
Bangs v Connex South Eastern Ltd [2005] EWCA Civ 14, [2005] 2 All ER 316, [2005] IRLR 389, (2005) Times, 15 February, 149 Sol Jo LB 148, [2005] All ER (D) 263 (Jan), sub nom Connex South Eastern Ltd v Bangs [2005] ICR 763 1429
Bank of Credit and Commerce International SA (in liquidation) v Ali [1999] 4 All ER 83, [1999] 30 LS Gaz R 28, sub nom Bank of Credit and Commerce International SA (in liquidation) v Ali (No 3) [1999] IRLR 508; affd sub nom Bank of Credit and Commerce International SA (in liquidation) v Ali (No 2) [2002] EWCA Civ 82, [2002] 3 All ER 750, [2002] ICR 1258, [2002] IRLR 460, (2002) Times, 15 February, [2002] All ER (D) 308 (Jan) 829, 833
Bank of Credit and Commerce International SA (in liquidation) v Ali [2000] 3 All ER 51, [2000] ICR 1410, [2000] IRLR 398, CA; affd on other grounds [2001] UKHL 8, [2002] 1 AC 251, [2001] 1 All ER 961, [2001] 2 WLR 735, [2001] ICR 337, [2001] IRLR 292, 145 Sol Jo LB 67, [2001] NLJR 351, (2001) Times, 6 March, [2001] All ER (D) 06 (Mar) 151, 153, 809
Bank Voor Handel en Scheepvaart NV v Slatford [1953] 1 QB 248, [1952] 2 All ER 956, 31 ATC 535, 46 R & IT 120, [1952] TR 493, 96 Sol Jo 784, [1952] 2 TLR 861, CA; revsd sub nom Bank voor Handel en Scheepvaart NV v Administrator of Hungarian Property [1954] AC 584, [1954] 1 All ER 969, [1954] 2 WLR 867, 35 TC 311, 33 ATC 102, 47 R & IT 373, [1954] TR 115, 98 Sol Jo 301, HL 4
Banking Insurance and Finance Union v Barclays Bank plc [1987] ICR 495, [1987] LS Gaz R 901, EAT 137, 1200

L

PARA

National Union of General and Municipal Workers v Gillian [1946] KB 81, [1945] 2 All ER 593, 115 LJKB 43, 89 Sol Jo 543, 174 LT 8, 62 TLR 46, CA 897
National Union of Gold, Silver and Allied Trades v Albury Bros Ltd [1979] ICR 84, [1978] IRLR 504, 122 Sol Jo 662, CA 116, 1094
National Union of Mineworkers v Scargill [2012] EWHC 3750 (Ch), [2013] All ER (D) 197 (Feb) 25
National Union of Mineworkers (Yorkshire Area) v Millward [1995] IRLR 411, [1995] ICR 482, EAT 1005
National Union of Rail, Maritime and Transport Workers v United Kingdom (Application 31045/10) [2014] IRLR 467, (2014) Times, 30 April, [2014] ECHR 31045/10, [2014] All ER (D) 101 (Jun), ECtHR 1339, 1367, 1372
National Union of Tailors and Garment Workers v Charles Ingram & Co Ltd [1978] 1 All ER 1271, [1977] ICR 530, [1977] IRLR 147, 12 ITR 285, EAT 1094
National Union of Teachers v Avon County Council (1978) 76 LGR 403, [1978] ICR 626, [1978] IRLR 55, EAT 1185
Nationwide Building Society v Benn (2010) UKEAT/0273/09/JOJ, [2010] IRLR 922, [2010] All ER (D) 104 (Aug), EAT 139, 803
Naylor v Orton and Smith Ltd [1983] ICR 665, [1983] IRLR 233, EAT 772, 1340, 1351, 1429
Ndeze v Horizon Security Services Ltd (2014) UKEAT/0071/14, [2014] ICR D31, [2014] All ER (D) 72 (Aug), EAT 137
Neads v CAV Ltd [1983] IRLR 360 .... 28–29, 116, 746, 875, 1347
Neal v Freightliner Ltd (12 July 2013, unreported), EAT 295
Neale v Hereford and Worcester County Council [1986] ICR 471, sub nom Hereford and Worcester County Council v Neale [1986] IRLR 168, CA 1428–1429
Neary v Dean of Westminster [1999] IRLR 288, SCD 743–744
Neary v Governing Body of St Albans Girls' School [2009] EWCA Civ 1190, [2010] ICR 473, [2010] IRLR 124, (2009) Times, 23 November, [2009] All ER (D) 144 (Nov) 1465
Neepsend Steel and Tool Corpn Ltd v Vaughan [1972] 3 All ER 725, [1972] ICR 278, NIRC 878
Neidel v Stadt Frankfurt am Main: C-337/10 [2012] 3 CMLR 92, [2012] ICR 1201, [2012] IRLR 607, ECJ 267, 293
Neil v Strathclyde Borough Council. See Strathclyde Regional Council v Neil
Nelson v BBC [1977] ICR 649, [1977] IRLR 148, CA 113, 870
Nelson v BBC (No 2) [1979] IRLR 346, 123 Sol Jo 552, CA 821, 870
Nerva v RL & G Ltd [1997] ICR 11, [1996] IRLR 461, [1996] 23 LS Gaz R 35, 140 Sol Jo LB 140, CA 144
Nerva v United Kingdom (Application 42295/98) (2002) 36 EHRR 31, [2002] IRLR 815, 13 BHRC 246, (2002) Times, 10 October, [2002] ECHR 42295/98, [2002] All ER (D) 137 (Sep), ECtHR 144
Nesbitt v Secretary of State for Trade and Industry [2007] IRLR 847, [2007] All ER (D) 23 (Sep), EAT 2, 9
Nethermere (St Neots) Ltd v Gardiner [1984] ICR 612, sub nom, Nethermere (St Neots) Ltd v Taverna and Gardiner [1984] IRLR 240 CA 4, 1429
Netjets Management Ltd v Central Arbitration Committee [2012] EWHC 2685 (Admin), [2013] 1 All ER 288, [2012] IRLR 986, [2012] NLJR 1323, [2012] All ER (D) 57 (Oct) 1103
Neufeld v Secretary of State for Business, Enterprise and Regulatory Reform [2009] EWCA Civ 280, [2009] 3 All ER 790, [2009] ICR 1183, [2009] IRLR 475, [2009] 2 BCLC 273, [2009] BCC 687, (2009) Times, 10 April, [2009] BPIR 909, [2009] All ER (D) 40 (Apr) 9, 628
New Centurion Trust v Welch [1990] ICR 383, [1990] IRLR 123, [1990] 20 LS Gaz R 35, EAT 255, 734
New Century Cleaning Co Ltd v Church [2000] IRLR 27, [1999] All ER (D) 345, CA 254
New Horizon, The. See Tramp Shipping Corpn v Greenwich Marine Inc, The New Horizon
New ISG Ltd v Vernon [2007] EWHC 2665 (Ch), [2008] ICR 319, [2008] IRLR 115, (2007) Times, 12 December, [2007] All ER (D) 220 (Nov) 141
New Southern Railways Ltd (formerly South Central Trains) v Rodway. See South Central Trains v Rodway
Newham London Borough Council v National and Local Government Officers' Association [1993] ICR 189, [1993] IRLR 83, CA 1380

PARA

Stapp v Shaftesbury Society [1982] IRLR 326, CA 764, 830
Stavely v Uzielli (1860) 2 F & F 30 60
Steele v William Hill Organisation Ltd [2008] All ER (D) 80 (Aug), EAT 702, 708, 776
Steen v ASP Packaging Ltd (2013) UKEAT/23/13, [2014] ICR 56, EAT 821
Stekel v Ellice [1973] 1 All ER 465, [1973] 1 WLR 191, 117 Sol Jo 126 13
Stephen (Harold) & Co Ltd v Post Office [1978] 1 All ER 939, [1977] 1 WLR 1172, 121 Sol Jo 707, CA 1440
Stephens v Bower [2004] EWCA Civ 496, [2004] ICR 1582, [2004] IRLR 957, (2004) Times, 24 May, 148 Sol Jo LB 475, [2004] All ER (D) 106 (Apr) 135
Stephens (GW) & Son v Fish [1989] ICR 324, EAT 763–764
Stephenson v Delphi Diesel Systems Ltd [2003] ICR 471, [2003] All ER (D) 84 (Mar), EAT 95
Stephenson (SBJ) Ltd v Mandy [2000] FSR 286, [2000] IRLR 233 71
Stephenson & Co (Oxford) Ltd v Austin [1990] ICR 609, CA 763
Sterling Engineering Co Ltd v Patchett Ltd [1955] AC 534, [1955] 1 All ER 369, [1955] 2 WLR 424, 72 RPC 50, 99 Sol Jo 129, HL 72, 115
Stern v Simpson [1983] IRLR 52, EAT 762
Stevedoring and Haulage Services Ltd v Fuller [2001] EWCA Civ 651, [2001] IRLR 627, [2001] All ER (D) 106 (May) 4, 114
Stevens v Bexley Health Authority [1989] ICR 224, [1989] IRLR 240, EAT 888
Stevenson v Golden Wonder Ltd [1977] IRLR 474, EAT 776
Stevenson v Teesside Bridge and Engineering Ltd [1971] 1 All ER 296, 10 KIR 53, 6 ITR 44, 114 Sol Jo 907, DC 870
Stevenson v United Road Transport Union [1977] 2 All ER 941, [1977] ICR 893, CA 827, 1019, 1024
Stevenson (or Stephenson) Jordan and Harrison Ltd v MacDonald and Evans (1952) 69 RPC 10, [1952] 1 TLR 101, CA 4
Stewart v Amalgamated Union of Engineering Workers [1973] ICR 128, [1973] IRLR 57, NIRC 1362
Stewart v Glentaggart (1963) 42 ATC 318, [1963] TR 345, 1963 SC 300, 1963 SLT 119, Ct of Sess 831
Stewart v Moray Council [2006] ICR 1253, [2006] IRLR 592, EAT 1093, 1295
Stewart v New Testament Church of God [2007] EWCA Civ 1004, [2008] ICR 282, [2008] IRLR 134, [2007] All ER (D) 285 (Oct) 4
Stewart v Western SMT Co Ltd [1978] IRLR 553, EAT 776
Stewart (Rex) Jeffries Parker Ginsberg Ltd v Parker [1988] IRLR 483, CA 19, 733, 828
Stocker v Lancashire County Council [1992] IRLR 75, CA 768
Stocks v Magna Merchants Ltd [1973] 2 All ER 329, [1973] 1 WLR 1505, [1973] ICR 530, 117 Sol Jo 760 831
Stokes v Guest, Keen and Nettlefold (Bolts and Nuts) Ltd [1968] 1 WLR 1776, 5 KIR 401, 112 Sol Jo 821 33
Stokes v Hampstead Wine Co Ltd [1979] IRLR 298, EAT 763, 1472
Stone v Charrington & Co Ltd [1977] ICR 248, 12 ITR 255, EAT 1058
Storer v British Gas plc [2000] 2 All ER 440, [2000] 1 WLR 1237, [2000] ICR 603, [2000] IRLR 495, CA 1472
Storey v Fulham Steel Works Co (1907) 24 TLR 89, CA 744
Stowe-Woodward BTR Ltd v Beynon [1978] ICR 609, EAT 858
Strange (SW) Ltd v Mann [1965] 1 All ER 1069, [1965] 1 WLR 629, 109 Sol Jo 352 730
Stratford (J T) & Son Ltd v Lindley [1965] AC 269, [1964] 2 All ER 209, [1964] 2 WLR 1002, [1964] 1 Lloyd's Rep 237, 108 Sol Jo 298, CA; revsd [1965] AC 269, [1964] 3 All ER 102, [1964] 3 WLR 541, [1964] 2 Lloyd's Rep 133, 108 Sol Jo 636, HL 1212, 1342, 1360–1362
Strathclyde Regional Council v Neil [1984] IRLR 11, Sh Ct; affd sub nom Neil v Strathclyde Borough Council [1984] IRLR 14, 1983 SLT (Sh Ct) 89, Sh Ct 20
Street v Derbyshire Unemployed Workers' Centre [2004] EWCA Civ 964, [2004] 4 All ER 839, [2005] ICR 97, [2004] IRLR 687, (2004) Times, 6 September, [2004] All ER (D) 377 (Jul) 69
Stringer v Revenue and Customs Comrs: C-520/06 and C-350/06 [2009] All ER (EC) 906, [2009] ECR I-179, [2009] 2 CMLR 657, [2009] ICR 932, [2009] IRLR 214, Times, 28 January, [2009] All ER (D) 147 (Jan), ECJ 267, 291
Strongman (1945) Ltd v Sincock [1955] 2 QB 525, [1955] 3 All ER 90, [1955] 3 WLR 360, 99 Sol Jo 540, CA 31

V

Decisions of the European Court of Justice are listed below numerically. These decisions are also included in the preceding alphabetical list.

PARA

C-48/94: Ledernes Hovedorganisation (acting for Rygard) v Dansk Arbejdsgiverforening (acting for Sto Molle Akustik A/S) [1995] ECR I-2745, [1996] 3 CMLR 45, [1996] ICR 333, [1996] IRLR 51, ECJ 137
C-171/94 and C-172/94: Merckx v Ford Motors Co Belgium SA [1996] All ER (EC) 667, [1996] ECR I-1253, [1997] ICR 352, [1996] IRLR 467, ECJ 141
C-298/94: Henke v Gemeinde Schierke and Verwaltungsgemeinschaft Brocken [1997] All ER (EC) 173, [1996] ECR I-4989, [1997] 1 CMLR 373, [1997] ICR 746, [1996] IRLR 701, ECJ 137
C-319/94: Dethier (Jules) Equipement SA v Dassy and Sovam SPRL (in liquidation) [1998] All ER (EC) 346, [1998] ECR I-1061, [1998] 2 CMLR 611, [1998] ICR 541, [1998] IRLR 266, ECJ 138, 803
C-127/96, C-229/96 and C-74/97: Vidal (Francisco Hernandez) SA v Gomez Perez [1998] ECR I-8179, [1999] IRLR 132, ECJ 137
C-173/96: Sanchez Hidalgo v Asociacion de Servicios Aser and Sociedad Cooperativa Minerva [1998] ECR I-8237, [2002] ICR 73, [1999] IRLR 136, ECJ 137
C-399/96: Europièces SA (in liquidation) v Sanders [1999] All ER (EC) 831, [1998] ECR I-6965, [2001] 1 CMLR 667, [1998] All ER (D) 574, ECJ 138
C-167/97: R v Secretary of State for Employment, ex p Seymour-Smith [1999] 2 AC 554, [1999] All ER (EC) 97, [1999] 3 WLR 460, [1999] ECR I-623, [1999] 2 CMLR 273, [1999] ICR 447, [1999] IRLR 253, ECJ; apld sub nom R v Secretary of State for Employment, ex p Seymour-Smith (No 2) [2000] 1 All ER 857, [2000] 1 WLR 435, [2000] 1 CMLR 770, [2000] ICR 244, [2000] IRLR 263, [2000] 09 LS Gaz R 40, HL 758
C-185/97: Coote v Granada Hospitality Ltd [1998] All ER (EC) 865, [1998] ECR I-5199, [1998] 3 CMLR 958, [1999] ICR 100, [1998] IRLR 656, [1998] All ER (D) 423, ECJ 724
C-198/98: Everson v Secretary of State for Trade and Industry [2000] All ER (EC) 29, [1999] ECR I-8903, [2000] 1 CMLR 489, [2000] IRLR 202, ECJ 628
C-234/98: Allen v Amalgamated Construction Co Ltd [2000] All ER (EC) 97, [1999] ECR I-8643, [2000] 1 CMLR 1, [2000] IRLR 119, 632 IRLB 2, ECJ 137
C-303/98: Sindicato de Médicos de Asistencia Pública (Simap) v Conselleria de Sanidad y Consumo de la Generalidad Valenciana [2001] All ER (EC) 609, [2000] ECR I-7963, [2001] 3 CMLR 932, [2001] ICR 1116, [2000] IRLR 845, [2000] All ER (D) 1236, ECJ 267, 272
C-343/98: Collino v Telecom Italia SpA [2001] All ER (EC) 405, [2000] ECR I-6659, [2002] 3 CMLR 997, [2002] ICR 38, [2000] IRLR 788, [2000] All ER (D) 1196, ECJ 137, 139
C-172/99: Oy Liikenne Ab v Liskojärvi [2001] All ER (EC) 544, [2001] ECR I-745, [2001] 3 CMLR 807, [2002] ICR 155, [2001] IRLR 171, [2001] All ER (D) 168 (Jan), ECJ 137
C-173/99: R (on the application of the Broadcasting, Entertainment, Cinematographic and Theatre Union) v Secretary of State for Trade and Industry [2001] All ER (EC) 647, [2001] 1 WLR 2313, [2001] ECR I-4881, [2001] 3 CMLR 109, [2001] ICR 1152, [2001] IRLR 559, [2001] All ER (D) 272 (Jun), ECJ 267, 291
C-175/99: Mayeur v Association Promotion de l'information messine (APIM) [2000] ECR I-7755, [2002] 3 CMLR 564, [2002] ICR 1316, ECJ 137
C-350/99: Lange v Georg Schünemann GmbH [2001] All ER (EC) 481, [2001] ECR I-1061, [2001] IRLR 244, [2001] All ER (D) 90 (Feb), ECJ 119
C-133/00: Bowden v Tuffnells Parcels Express Ltd [2001] All ER (EC) 865, [2001] ECR I-7031, [2001] 3 CMLR 1342, [2001] IRLR 838, [2001] All ER (D) 32 (Oct), ECJ 267
C-164/00: Beckmann v Dynamco Whicheloe MacFarlane Ltd [2002] All ER (EC) 865, [2002] ECR I-4893, [2002] 2 CMLR 1152, [2003] ICR 50, [2002] IRLR 578, [2002] OPLR 289, (2002) Times, 17 June, [2002] All ER (D) 05 (Jun), ECJ 139
C-440/00: Gesamtbetriebsrat Der Kühne & Nagel AG & Co KG v Kühne & Nagel AG & Co KG [2004] ECR I-787, [2004] 2 CMLR 1242, [2004] IRLR 332, [2004] All ER (D) 31 (Jan), ECJ 1236
C-4/01: Martin v South Bank University [2003] ECR I-12859, [2004] 1 CMLR 472, [2004] ICR 1234, [2004] IRLR 74, [2003] OPLR 317, [2003] All ER (D) 85 (Nov), ECJ 139
C-201/01: Walcher v Bundesamt fur Soziales und Behindertenwesen Steiermark [2003] ECR I-8827, [2003] 3 CMLR 534, [2003] All ER (D) 66 (Sep), ECJ 628

PARA

C-342/01: Merino Gómez v Continental Industrias del Caucho SA [2004] ECR I-2605, [2004] 2 CMLR 38, [2005] ICR 1040, [2004] IRLR 407, [2004] All ER (D) 350 (Mar), ECJ 267
C-397/01 to C-403/01: Pfeiffer v Deutsches Rotes Kreuz, Kreisverband Waldshut eV [2004] ECR I-8835, [2005] ICR 1307, [2005] IRLR 137, [2004] All ER (D) 52 (Oct), ECJ 267
C-147/02: Alabaster v Woolwich plc [2005] All ER (EC) 490, [2004] ECR I-3101, [2004] 2 CMLR 186, [2005] ICR 695, [2004] IRLR 486, [2004] All ER (D) 558 (Mar), ECJ 429
C-151/02: Landeshauptstadt Kiel v Jaeger [2004] All ER (EC) 604, [2003] ECR I-8389, [2003] 3 CMLR 493, [2004] ICR 1528, [2003] IRLR 804, 75 BMLR 201, (2003) Times, 26 September, [2003] All ER (D) 72 (Sep), ECJ 267, 304
C-285/02: Elsner-Lakeberg v Land Nordrhein-Westfalen [2004] ECR I-5861, [2004] 2 CMLR 874, [2005] IRLR 209, [2004] All ER (D) 423 (May), ECJ 73
C-313/02: Wippel v Peek & Cloppenburg Gmbh & Co Kg [2004] ECR I-9483, [2005] IRLR 211, ECJ 75
C-425/02: Delahaye v Ministre de la Fonction publique et de la Réforme administrative [2005] All ER (EC) 575, [2004] ECR I-10823, [2005] IRLR 61, [2004] All ER (D) 196 (Nov), ECJ 137
C-188/03: Junk v Kuhnel [2005] ECR I-885, [2005] IRLR 310, [2005] All ER (D) 264 (Jan), ECJ 1185
C-478/03: Celtec Ltd v Astley [2005] ECR I-4389, [2005] ICR 1409, [2005] IRLR 647, (2005) Times, 9 June, [2005] All ER (D) 400 (May), ECJ 137
C-52/04: Personalrat der Feuerwehr Hamburg v Leiter der Feuerwehr Hamburg [2005] ECR I-7111, ECJ 267
C-53/04: Marrousu v Azienda Ospedaliera Ospedale San Martino di Genova e Cliniche Universitarie Convenzionate [2006] ECR I-7213, [2006] All ER (D) 36 (Sep), ECJ 84
C-131/04 and C-257/04: Caulfield v Marshalls Clay Products Ltd [2006] All ER (EC) 749, [2006] ECR I-2531, [2006] ICR 932, [2006] IRLR 386, (2006) Times, 22 March, [2006] All ER (D) 238 (Mar), ECJ 267, 295
C-131/04 and C-257/04: Clarke v Frank Staddon Ltd [2006] All ER (EC) 749, [2006] ECR I-2531, [2006] ICR 932, [2006] IRLR 386, (2006) Times, 22 March, [2006] All ER (D) 238 (Mar), ECJ 267, 295
C-131/04 and C-257/04: Robinson-Steele v RD Retail Services Ltd [2006] All ER (EC) 749, [2006] ECR I-2531, [2006] ICR 932, [2006] IRLR 386, (2006) Times, 22 March, [2006] All ER (D) 238 (Mar), ECJ 267, 295
C-180/04: Vassallo v Azienda Ospedaliera Ospedale San Martino di Genova e Cliniche Universitarie Convenzionate [2006] ECR I-7251, [2006] All ER (D) 45 (Sep), ECJ 84
C-212/04: Adeneler v Ellinikos Organismos Galaktos [2007] All ER (EC) 82, [2006] ECR I-6057, [2006] 3 CMLR 867, [2006] IRLR 716, [2006] All ER (D) 25 (Jul), ECJ 84
C-484/04: EC Commissionv United Kingdom [2006] ECR I-7471, [2006] 3 CMLR 1322, [2006] IRLR 888, [2007] ICR 592, (2006) Times, 21 September, [2006] All ER (D) 32 (Sep), ECJ 284, 300
C-499/04: Werhof v Freeway Traffic Systems GmbH & Co KG [2005] ECR I-2397, [2006] IRLR 400, [2006] All ER (D) 145 (Mar), ECJ 139
C-124/05: Federatie Nederlandse Vakbeweging v Netherlands State [2006] All ER (EC) 913, [2006] ECR I-3423, [2006] ICR 962, [2006] IRLR 561, [2006] All ER (D) 69 (Apr), ECJ 267
C-270/05: Athinaiki Chartopoiia AE v Panagiotidis [2007] ECR I-1499, [2007] IRLR 284, [2007] All ER (D) 186 (Feb), ECJ 1185
C-307/05: Del Cerro Alonso v Osakidetza-Servicio Vasco de Salud [2007] ECR I-7109, [2007] 3 CMLR 1492, [2008] ICR 145, [2007] IRLR 911, [2007] All ER (D) 87 (Sep), ECJ 87
C-341/05: Laval un Partneri Ltd v Svenska Byggnadsarbetareforbundet [2008] All ER (EC) 166, [2007] ECR I-11767, [2008] IRLR 160, [2007] All ER (D) 278 (Dec), ECJ 1344
C-385/05: Confederation general du travail v Premier ministre [2007] ECR I-611, [2007] 2 CMLR 163, [2007] All ER (D) 92 (Jan), ECJ 1185
C-438/05: International Transport Workers' Federation v Viking Line ABP [2008] All ER (EC) 127, [2007] ECR I-10779, [2008] 1 CMLR 1372, [2008] ICR 741, [2008] IRLR 143, (2007) Times, 14 December, [2007] All ER (D) 158 (Dec), ECJ 1344

EMPLOYMENT

VOLUME 39

2. RIGHTS ARISING IN THE COURSE OF EMPLOYMENT

(10) MATERNITY, PATERNITY, ADOPTION AND PARENTAL LEAVE

(i) Statutory Rights to Leave and Pay for Family or Domestic Reasons

354. Development of statutory rights to leave and pay for family or domestic reasons. A statutory right to return to work after maternity leave was first introduced in the Employment Protection Act 1975, under which payment during such leave was effectively split between the employer and the state[1]. A standardised form of statutory maternity pay was subsequently introduced by the Social Security Act 1986, payable through the employer but with recoupment of the cost from the state[2]. Major changes were subsequently required in order to comply with Council Directive (EC) 92/85 of 19 October 1992 on the introduction of measures to encourage improvements in the safety and health at work of pregnant workers and workers who have recently given birth or are breastfeeding[3]. For the purposes of implementing Council Directive (EC) 92/85 of 19 October 1992, a basic right to maternity leave was introduced (for all employees, not only those with the minimum service qualification required by domestic law) together with compulsory leave over the actual time of birth[4].

By this time, the law relating to maternity rights was of great complexity, and widely criticised both for that and for being too harsh, given that the penalty for failure to comply with the complex requirements (especially on the notices to be given by the employee) was often loss of rights altogether. In addition, there was a difficulty over the status of the employee's contract of employment during the period of maternity leave; the original aim had been to enact a purely statutory scheme, not reliant on the underlying contract, but this led to uncertainties as to whether an employee who did not have the statutory right could claim some sort of contractual right to return to work. Thus, when further amendment of the law was required, in order to comply with Council Directive (EC) 96/34 of 3 June 1996 on the framework agreement on parental leave[5], the opportunity was taken to reform the maternity provisions, rationalising them, and also reducing complexity and lessening the penalties for failure to comply with formalities. While the law on statutory maternity pay remained unaltered, the whole of the existing law on maternity leave was repealed and replaced[6]. The right to time off work to care for dependants was introduced at the same time (by way of amendment to the primary legislation)[7]. The called-for right to parental leave (exercisable by either parent) was introduced by way of making provision (as in the case of maternity leave) for the Secretary of State to exercise a power so conferred on him to make regulations[8], the result being that the substantive law on these matters is now to be found in the Maternity and Parental Leave etc Regulations 1999[9]. As now enacted, rights to maternity leave operate on different principles from the original scheme, in particular, by providing for the continuation of the contract of employment (for stipulated purposes), and simply permitting a qualifying employee to be 'absent from work' for the stipulated periods[10]. The result is that the present statutory scheme should be approached *de novo* and that case law on the old scheme is unlikely in most cases to be relevant.

Over time, rights to maternity leave and pay have been increased and extended[11], and these have been complemented by similar regimes giving rights to paternity leave and pay[12] and to paid leave for adoptive parents[13]. Accordingly, the following basic rights to parental leave now exist:

(1) the right to ordinary, compulsory and additional maternity leave[14];

(2) the right to ordinary and additional adoption leave[15];

(3) the right to paternity leave on the birth or adoption of a child[16]; and

(4) the right to parental leave for the purpose of caring for a child (including shared parental leave on the birth or adoption of a child)[17].

This is in addition to the right of employees generally (which could be used for these purposes) to apply to work flexibly[18]; and the right to take time off work:

(a) for ante-natal care[19];

(b) for adoption appointments[20]; and

(c) to care for dependants[21].

There is also statutory protection for the right not to be subjected to a detriment[22] or dismissed[23] for taking time off for family or domestic reasons.

1 See the Employment Protection Act 1975 ss 35(1)(b), 48–50, Sch 3 (repealed).

2 See the Social Security Act 1986 Pt V (ss 46–50) (repealed).

3 Ie Council Directive (EC) 92/85 of 19 October 1992 (OJ L348, 28.11.1992, p 1) on the introduction of measures to encourage improvements in the safety and health at work of pregnant workers and workers who have recently given birth or are breastfeeding: see **HEALTH AND SAFETY AT WORK** vol 52 (2014) PARA 311.

4 See the Trade Union Reform and Employment Rights Act 1993 ss 23–25 (repealed).

5 Ie Council Directive (EC) 96/34 of 3 June 1996 (OJ L145, 19.6.96, p 4) on the framework agreement on parental leave concluded by UNICE, CEEP and the ETUC (repealed): see now Council Directive (EU) 2010/18 of 8 March 2010 (OJ L68, 18.03.2010, p 13) implementing the revised Framework Agreement on parental leave concluded by BUSINESSEUROPE, UEAPME, CEEP and ETUC and repealing Directive (EC) 96/34.

6 See the Employment Relations Act 1999 ss 7–9, Sch 4 (amending the Employment Rights Act 1996 with consequential amendments).

7 See the Employment Rights Act 1996 ss 57A, 57B; and PARAS 347–348.

8 See the Employment Rights Act 1996 Pt VIII Ch I (ss 71–75) (maternity leave: see PARA 355 et seq) and Pt VIII Ch II (ss 76–80) (parental leave: see PARAS 390, 397). The new right to maternity leave came into force on 15 December 1999; it applies where the expected week of childbirth begins on or after 30 April 2000 (see the Employment Relations Act 1999 (Commencement No 2 and Transitional and Saving Provisions) Order 1999, SI 1999/2830, art 3, Sch 3 para 10; and the Maternity and Parental Leave etc Regulations 1999, SI 1999/3312, reg 3(1)). The new right to parental leave came into force on 15 December 1999, and only applies to a child born or adopted on or after that date (ie with no back-dating, even though the right lasts for the child's first five years): see reg 13(3) (revoked). As to the Secretary of State see PARA 5 note 21.

9 Ie the Maternity and Parental Leave etc Regulations 1999, SI 1999/3312: see PARA 356 et seq.

10 See the Employment Rights Act 1996 s 71(1) (ordinary maternity leave: cited in PARA 355) and s 73(1) (additional maternity leave: cited in PARA 355). Similar wording is used for parental leave: see s 76(1); and PARA 390. Two important results of this are that: (1) it is no longer correct (or, indeed, necessary) to talk of a 'right to return to work' because the return is automatic once the period of absence ends; and (2) where an employee is ill at the normal date for resumption of work, she no longer potentially loses her employment, but instead is in effect deemed to resume work, only to go off on the employer's normal sickness rules (the new statutory scheme adopts the solution to this often encountered problem devised by the Court of Appeal in *Crees v Royal London Mutual Insurance Society Ltd, Kwik Save Stores Ltd v Greaves* [1998] ICR 848, [1998] IRLR 245, CA, shortly before the reforms effected by the Employment Relations Act 1999).

11 Ie by amendments made to the Employment Rights Act 1996 Pt VIII Ch I (maternity leave: see PARA 355 et seq) by the Employment Act 2002 and by the Maternity and Parental Leave (Amendment) Regulations 2002, SI 2002/2789; and the Maternity and Parental Leave etc and the Paternity and Adoption Leave (Amendment) Regulations 2008, SI 2008/1966: see PARA 355. As to statutory maternity pay see PARA 401 et seq.

12 See the Employment Rights Act 1996 Pt VIII Ch III (ss 80A–80E); the Paternity and Adoption Leave Regulations 2002, SI 2002/2788; the Paternity and Adoption Leave (Adoption from Overseas) Regulations 2003, SI 2003/921; and PARA 368 et seq. As to statutory paternity pay see PARA 443 et seq.
13 See the Employment Rights Act 1996 Pt VIII Ch IA (ss 75A–75D) (adoption leave); the Paternity and Adoption Leave Regulations 2002, SI 2002/2788; the Paternity and Adoption Leave (Adoption from Overseas) Regulations 2003, SI 2003/921; and PARA 378 et seq. As to statutory adoption pay see PARA 488 et seq.
14 See PARA 355 et seq. As to shared parental leave see the Employment Rights Act 1996 Pt 8 Ch 1B (ss 75E–75K) (added by the Children and Families Act 2014 s 117); and PARA 398.
15 See PARA 377 et seq.
16 See PARA 368 et seq.
17 See PARA 390 et seq. Shared parental leave supersedes the provision previously made for additional paternity leave under the Employment Rights Act 1996 ss 80AA, 80BB (repealed).
18 See the Employment Rights Act 1996 Pt VIIIA (ss 80F–80I); and PARA 108 et seq.
19 See PARA 333 et seq.
20 See PARA 341 et seq.
21 See PARAS 347–348.
22 See PARA 620.
23 See PARA 784.

(ii) Maternity Leave

A. POWER TO MAKE REGULATIONS

355. Power to make regulations in relation to ordinary, compulsory, and additional maternity leave. The Secretary of State[1] may make regulations[2]:

(1) in relation to ordinary maternity leave[3]:
  (a) prescribing conditions which an employee[4] must satisfy to be absent from work at any time during an ordinary maternity leave period[5];
  (b) for calculating an ordinary maternity leave period[6];
  (c) providing that an employee who exercises her right to be absent from work at any time during an ordinary maternity leave period[7] is entitled, for such purposes and to such extent as may be prescribed, to the benefit of the terms and conditions of employment[8] which would have applied if she had not been absent[9]; is bound, for such purposes and to such extent as may be prescribed, by any obligations arising[10] under those terms and conditions[11]; and is entitled to return from leave to a job[12] of such kind as may be prescribed[13];
  (d) specifying matters which are, or are not, to be treated as remuneration for the purposes of ordinary maternity leave[14];

(2) in relation to compulsory maternity leave[15]:
  (a) prescribing conditions which an employee must satisfy if her employer[16] is not to permit her to work at any time during a compulsory maternity leave period[17];
  (b) for calculating a compulsory maternity leave period[18];

(3) in relation to additional maternity leave[19]:
  (a) prescribing conditions which an employee must satisfy to be absent from work at any time during an additional maternity leave period[20];
  (b) for calculating an additional maternity leave period[21];
  (c) allowing an employee to bring forward the date on which an additional maternity leave period ends, subject to prescribed

restrictions and subject to satisfying prescribed conditions[22]; allowing an employee in prescribed circumstances to revoke, or to be treated as revoking, the bringing forward of that date[23]; and specifying circumstances in which an employee may work for her employer during an additional maternity leave period without bringing the period to an end[24];

(d) providing that an employee who exercises her right to be absent from work at any time during an additional maternity leave period[25] is entitled, for such purposes and to such extent as may be prescribed, to the benefit of the terms and conditions of employment[26] which would have applied if she had not been absent[27]; is bound, for such purposes and to such extent as may be prescribed, by any obligations arising[28] under those terms and conditions[29]; and is entitled to return from leave[30] to a job of such kind as may be prescribed[31];

(e) specifying matters which are, or are not, to be treated as remuneration for the purposes of additional maternity leave[32].

Such regulations:

(i) may[33] make provision about redundancy[34] during an ordinary or additional maternity leave period[35];

(ii) may[36] make provision about dismissal, other than by reason of redundancy, during an ordinary or additional maternity leave period[37];

(iii) may[38] make provision disapplying certain statutory provisions[39] in specified cases and about dismissal at the conclusion of an ordinary or additional maternity leave period[40].

Such regulations[41] may also:

(A) make provision about notices to be given, evidence to be produced and other procedures to be followed by employees and employers;

(B) make provision for the consequences of failure to give notices, to produce evidence or to comply with other procedural requirements;

(C) make provision for the consequences of failure to act in accordance with a notice given by virtue of head (A) above;

(D) make special provision for cases where an employee has a right which corresponds to a right relating to maternity leave[42] and which arises under her contract of employment or otherwise;

(E) make provision modifying the effect of the statutory provisions relating to calculating a week's pay[43] in relation to an employee who is or has been absent from work on ordinary or additional maternity leave;

(F) make provision applying, modifying or excluding an enactment, in such circumstances as may be specified and subject to any conditions specified, in relation to a person entitled to ordinary, compulsory or additional maternity leave;

(G) make different provision for different cases or circumstances[44].

1 As to the Secretary of State see PARA 5 note 21.

2 As to the making of regulations under the Employment Rights Act 1996 generally see PARA 162. In exercise of the powers conferred by ss 71(1)–(3), (6), 72(1), (2), 73(1), (2), (4), (7), 74(1), (3), (4), and 75(1), amongst other provisions, the Secretary of State has made the Maternity and Parental Leave etc Regulations 1999, SI 1999/3312, regs 1–2, 3(1), 4–11, 12A, 17–22 (see PARA 356 et seq). As to the power to make regulations in relation to shared parental leave on birth see PARA 398.

3 As to ordinary maternity leave see PARAS 356–361.

4 As to the meaning of 'employee' see PARA 2.

5 Employment Rights Act 1996 s 71(1) (ss 71–75 substituted by the Employment Relations Act 1999 Sch 4 Pt I). As to the modification of the Employment Rights Act 1996 s 71 in relation to governing bodies of schools having a right to a delegated budget, acting in the exercise of their employment powers, see EDUCATION vol 35 (2011) PARA 355 et seq.

6 Employment Rights Act 1996 s 71(2) (as substituted: see note 5). Regulations under s 71(2):
   (1) must secure that, where an employee has a right to leave under s 71, she is entitled to an ordinary maternity leave period of at least 26 weeks (s 71(3)(a) (s 71 as so substituted; s 71(3) further substituted by the Work and Families Act 2006 s 11(1), Sch 1 para 31));
   (2) may allow an employee to choose, subject to prescribed restrictions, the date on which an ordinary maternity leave period starts (s 71(3)(b) (as so substituted));
   (3) may allow an employee to bring forward the date on which an ordinary maternity leave period ends, subject to prescribed restrictions and subject to satisfying prescribed conditions (s 71(3)(ba) (s 71(3) as so substituted; s 71(3)(ba), (bb) added by the Children and Families Act 2014 s 118(1), (2)(a)));
   (4) may allow an employee in prescribed circumstances to revoke, or to be treated as revoking, the bringing forward of that date (Employment Rights Act 1996 s 71(3)(bb) (s 71(3) as so substituted; s 71(3)(bb) as so added));
   (5) may specify circumstances in which an employee may work for her employer during an ordinary maternity leave period without bringing the period to an end (s 71(3)(c) (as so substituted))).

   Provision under head (3) above is to secure that an employee may bring forward the date on which an ordinary maternity leave period ends only if the employee or another person has taken, or is taking, prescribed steps as regards leave under the Employment Rights Act 1996 s 75E or statutory shared parental pay in respect of the child (see PARA 398): see s 71(3A) (s 71 as so substituted; s 71(3A) added by the Children and Families Act 2014 s 118(1), (2)(b)). For the purposes of the Employment Rights Act 1996 ss 71–73, 'prescribed' means prescribed by regulations made by the Secretary of State: s 75(2) (as so substituted). As to the meaning of 'week' see PARA 126 note 13. See also note 5.

7 Ie under the Employment Rights Act 1996 s 71(1) (see the text and notes 1–5), but subject to s 74 (redundancy and dismissal: see the text and notes 33–40).

8 For these purposes, 'terms and conditions of employment' includes matters connected with an employee's employment, whether or not they arise under her contract of employment, but does not include terms and conditions about remuneration: Employment Rights Act 1996 s 71(5). As to the meaning of 'employment' see PARA 2; and as to the meaning of 'contract of employment' see PARA 2.

9 Employment Rights Act 1996 s 71(4)(a) (s 71 as substituted (see note 5); s 71(4)(a), (b) amended, s 71(4)(c) further substituted, by the Employment Act 2002 s 17(1), (2)). See also note 5.

10 Ie except in so far as they are inconsistent with the Employment Rights Act 1996 s 71(1) (see the text and notes 1–5).

11 Employment Rights Act 1996 s 71(4)(b) (s 71 as substituted (see note 5); s 71(4)(b) as amended (see note 9)). See also note 5.

12 As to the meaning of 'job' see PARA 119 note 17.

13 Employment Rights Act 1996 s 71(4)(c) (s 71 as substituted (see note 5); s 71(4)(c) further substituted (see note 9)). The Secretary of State may make regulations making provision, in relation to the right under s 71(4)(c) to return after ordinary maternity leave, about seniority, pension rights and similar rights (see s 71(7)(a) (s 71 as substituted (see note 5); s 71(7) further substituted by the Employment Act 2002 s 17(1), (3))); and about terms and conditions of employment on return (see the Employment Rights Act 1996 s 71(7)(b) (as so substituted)). See also note 5.

14 Employment Rights Act 1996 s 71(6) (as substituted: see note 5). Accordingly, for the purposes of s 71 and s 73 (see head (3) in the text), only sums payable to an employee by way of wages or salary are to be treated as remuneration: see the Maternity and Parental Leave etc Regulations 1999, SI 1999/3312, reg 9(3); and PARA 359. See also note 5.

15 As to compulsory maternity leave see PARA 363. These provisions were made for the purposes of implementing Council Directive (EC) 92/85 of 19 October 1992 (OJ L348, 28.11.1992, p 1) art 8: see PARA 354.

16 As to the meaning of 'employer' see PARA 2.

17 Employment Rights Act 1996 s 72(1) (as substituted: see note 5). Any provision of, or made under, the Health and Safety at Work etc Act 1974 applies in relation to the prohibition under the Employment Rights Act 1996 s 72(1) as if it were imposed by regulations under the Health and Safety at Work etc Act 1974 s 15 (see HEALTH AND SAFETY AT WORK vol 52 (2014) PARA 388 et seq): Employment Rights Act 1996 s 72(4) (as so substituted). In exercise of the powers

conferred by virtue of s 72(4), the Secretary of State has made the Health and Safety at Work etc Act 1974 (Civil Liability) (Exceptions) Regulations 2013, SI 2013/1667, which came into force on 1 October 2013 (see reg 1). Accordingly, breach of a duty imposed by the Employment Rights Act 1996 s 72(1) (which by virtue of s 72(4) is for these purposes treated as imposed by health and safety regulations) is, so far as it causes damage, actionable (see the Health and Safety at Work etc Act 1974 (Civil Liability) (Exceptions) Regulations 2013, SI 2013/1667, reg 2(1)); and any term of an agreement which purports to exclude or restrict any liability for such a breach is void (reg 2(2)).

The Health and Safety at Work etc Act 1974 s 33(1)(c) (ie it is an offence to contravene any health and safety regulations or any requirement or prohibition imposed under any such regulations: see **HEALTH AND SAFETY AT WORK** vol 53 (2014) PARA 805) does not apply in relation to the prohibition under the Employment Rights Act 1996 s 72(1) and an employer who contravenes s 72(1) is guilty of an offence and liable on summary conviction to a fine not exceeding level 2 on the standard scale: Employment Rights Act 1996 s 72(5) (as so substituted). As to the standard scale see **SENTENCING AND DISPOSITION OF OFFENDERS** vol 92 (2010) PARA 142.

18 Employment Rights Act 1996 s 72(2) (as substituted: see note 5). Regulations under s 72(2) must secure that: (1) no compulsory maternity leave period is less than two weeks (s 72(3)(a) (as so substituted)); and every compulsory maternity leave period falls within an ordinary maternity leave period (s 72(3)(b) (as so substituted)).

19 As to additional maternity leave see PARA 356 et seq. The Maternity and Parental Leave etc Regulations 1999, SI 1999/3312, regs 5–7, 9–11, 12A, 17–18A, 21–22, which relate to additional maternity leave, replace the Employment Rights Act 1996 ss 79–85 (as originally enacted).

20 Employment Rights Act 1996 s 73(1) (as substituted: see note 5).

21 Employment Rights Act 1996 s 73(2) (as substituted: see note 5).

22 Employment Rights Act 1996 s 73(3)(a) (s 73 as substituted (see note 5); s 73(3) further substituted by the Work and Families Act 2006 Sch 1 para 32; the Employment Rights Act 1996 s 73(3)(a) amended by the Children and Families Act 2014 s 118(1), (3)(a)). Provision under the Employment Rights Act 1996 s 73(3)(a) is to secure that an employee may bring forward the date on which an additional maternity leave period ends only if the employee or another person has taken, or is taking, prescribed steps as regards leave under s 75E or statutory shared parental pay in respect of the child (see PARA 398): see s 73(3A) (s 73 as so substituted; s 73(3A) added by the Children and Families Act 2014 s 118(1), (3)(c)).

23 Employment Rights Act 1996 s 73(3)(aa) (s 73 as substituted (see note 5); s 73(3) as further substituted (see note 22); s 73(3)(aa) added by the Children and Families Act 2014 s 118(1), (3)(b)).

24 Employment Rights Act 1996 s 73(3)(b) (s 73 as substituted (see note 5); s 73(3) as further substituted (see note 22)).

25 Ie under the Employment Rights Act 1996 s 73(1): see the text and notes 19–20.

26 For these purposes, 'terms and conditions of employment' includes: (1) matters connected with an employee's employment, whether or not they arise under a contract of employment (Employment Rights Act 1996 s 73(5)(a) (as substituted: see note 5)); but (2) does not include terms and conditions about remuneration (s 73(5)(b) (as so substituted)). As to the meanings of 'employment' and 'contract of employment' see PARA 2.

27 Employment Rights Act 1996 s 73(4)(a) (as substituted: see note 5). Section 73(4) is subject to s 74 (see heads (i)–(iii) in the text): see s 73(4) (as so substituted).

28 Ie except in so far as they are inconsistent with the Employment Rights Act 1996 s 73(1): see the text and notes 19–20.

29 Employment Rights Act 1996 s 73(4)(b) (as substituted: see note 5). See also note 27.

30 For these purposes, the reference to return from leave includes, where appropriate, a reference to a continuous period of absence attributable partly to additional maternity leave and partly to ordinary maternity leave: Employment Rights Act 1996 s 73(5A) (s 73 as substituted (see note 5); s 73(5A) added by the Employment Act 2002 s 17(1), (4)).

31 Employment Rights Act 1996 s 73(4)(c) (as substituted: see note 5). The Secretary of State may make regulations making provision, in relation to the right under s 73(4)(c) to return after additional maternity leave, about seniority, pension rights and similar rights (see s 73(7)(a) (as so substituted)); and about terms and conditions of employment on return (see s 73(7)(b) (as so substituted)). See also note 27.

32 Employment Rights Act 1996 s 73(6) (as substituted: see note 5). See note 14.

33 Ie in the case of regulations under the Employment Rights Act 1996 s 71 (see heads (1)(a)–(d) in the text) or s 73 (see heads 3(a)–(e) in the text).

34 As to the meaning of 'redundancy' see PARA 870.

35 Employment Rights Act 1996 s 74(1) (as substituted: see note 5). Regulations made by virtue of s 74(1) or s 74(2) (see head (ii) in the text) may include:
 (1) provision requiring an employer to offer suitable alternative employment (s 74(3)(a) (as so substituted));
 (2) provision for the consequences of failure to comply with the regulations, which may include provision for a dismissal to be treated as unfair for the purposes of Pt X (ss 94–134A) (unfair dismissal: see PARA 757 et seq) (s 74(3)(b) (as so substituted)).
36 Ie in the case of regulations under the Employment Rights Act 1996 s 71 (see heads (1)(a)–(d) in the text) or s 73 (see heads 3(a)–(e) in the text).
37 Employment Rights Act 1996 s 74(2) (as substituted: see note 5). See also note 35.
38 Ie in the case of regulations under the Employment Rights Act 1996 s 71 (see heads (1)(a)–(d) in the text) or s 73 (see heads 3(a)–(e) in the text).
39 Ie provision for the Employment Rights Act 1996 s 71(4)(c) (see head (1)(c) in the text) or s 73(4)(c) (see head (3)(d) in the text) not to apply in specified cases.
40 See the Employment Rights Act 1996 s 74(4) (s 74 as substituted (see note 5); s 74(4) amended by the Employment Act 2002 s 17(1), (5)).
41 Ie regulations under the Employment Rights Act 1996 s 71 (see heads (1)(a)–(d) in the text), s 72 (see heads (2)(a), (b) in the text) or s 73 (see heads (3)(a)–(e) in the text).
42 Ie a right under the Employment Rights Act 1996 Pt VIII Ch I (ss 71–75) (maternity leave: see PARA 355 et seq).
43 Ie modifying the effect of the Employment Rights Act 1996 Pt XIV Ch II (ss 220–229) (calculation of a week's pay: see PARA 143 et seq).
44 See the Employment Rights Act 1996 s 75(1) (as substituted: see note 5).

B. ORDINARY MATERNITY LEAVE AND ADDITIONAL MATERNITY LEAVE

356. Entitlement to ordinary maternity leave and to additional maternity leave. An employee[1] is entitled to ordinary maternity leave and to additional maternity leave[2] provided that she satisfies the following conditions[3]:
 (1) no later than the end of the fifteenth week before her expected week of childbirth[4] or, if that is not reasonably practicable, as soon as is reasonably practicable, she notifies her employer[5] of: (a) her pregnancy; (b) the expected week of childbirth; and (c) the date on which she intends her ordinary maternity leave period to start[6]; and
 (2) if requested to do so by her employer, she produces for his inspection a certificate from either a registered medical practitioner or a registered midwife[7], stating the expected week of childbirth[8].

1 For these purposes, 'employee' means an individual who has entered into or works under, or, where the employment has ceased, worked under, a contract of employment; and 'contract of employment' means a contract of service or apprenticeship, whether express or implied and, if it is express, whether oral or in writing: Maternity and Parental Leave etc Regulations 1999, SI 1999/3312, reg 2(1). As to the meanings of 'employee', 'contract of employment' and related expressions in relation to employment rights generally see PARA 2 et seq. As to the meaning of 'contract of service' see PARA 1 note 1; and as to the meaning of 'writing' see PARA 2 note 8. As to the position of apprentices and youth trainees at common law see PARAS 112, 128–129, 636, 747–754. As to the statutory law on apprenticeships see EDUCATION vol 35 (2011) PARA 682 et seq.
2 For these purposes, 'ordinary maternity leave' means leave as provided for under the Employment Rights Act 1996 s 71 (see PARA 355); and 'additional maternity leave' means leave under s 73 (see PARA 355): see the Maternity and Parental Leave etc Regulations 1999, SI 1999/3312, reg 2(1).
3 See the Maternity and Parental Leave etc Regulations 1999, SI 1999/3312, reg 4(1) (amended by SI 2006/2014).
4 For these purposes, 'expected week of childbirth' means the week, beginning with midnight between Saturday and Sunday, in which it is expected that childbirth will occur; and 'childbirth' means the birth of a living child or the birth of a child whether living or dead after 24 weeks of pregnancy: Employment Rights Act 1996 s 235(1); Maternity and Parental Leave etc Regulations 1999, SI 1999/3312, reg 2(1). 'Week of childbirth' means the week, beginning with midnight between Saturday and Sunday, in which childbirth occurs: reg 2(1).

5 For these purposes, 'employer' means the person by whom an employee is, or, where the employment has ceased, was employed: Maternity and Parental Leave etc Regulations 1999, SI 1999/3312, reg 2(1). As to the meaning of 'employer' and related expressions in relation to employment rights generally see PARA 2.

6 Maternity and Parental Leave etc Regulations 1999, SI 1999/3312, reg 4(1)(a) (amended by SI 2002/2789). An employee who has notified her employer under the Maternity and Parental Leave etc Regulations 1999, SI 1999/3312, reg 4(1)(a)(iii) (see head (1)(c) in the text) of the date on which she intends her ordinary maternity leave period to start may subsequently vary that date, provided that she notifies her employer of the variation at least 28 days before the date varied, or 28 days before the new date, whichever is the earlier, or, if that is not reasonably practicable, as soon as is reasonably practicable: reg 4(1A) (reg 4(1A) added, reg 4(2) amended, by SI 2002/2789). The notification provided for in either the Maternity and Parental Leave etc Regulations 1999, SI 1999/3312, reg 4(1)(a)(iii) or in reg 4(1A) must be given in writing, if the employer so requests, and must not specify a date earlier than the beginning of the eleventh week before the expected week of childbirth: reg 4(2) (as so amended).

7 As to the meaning of 'registered medical practitioner' see **MEDICAL PROFESSIONS** vol 74 (2011) PARA 176; and as to the meaning of 'registered', in relation to midwives, see **MEDICAL PROFESSIONS** vol 74 (2011) PARA 713.

8 Maternity and Parental Leave etc Regulations 1999, SI 1999/3312, reg 4(1)(b).

357. Ordinary maternity leave period. An employee's[1] ordinary maternity leave[2] period commences with the earlier of:

(1) the date which she notifies to her employer[3] as the date on which she intends her ordinary maternity leave period to start, or, if by virtue of the provision for variation[4] she has notified more than one such date, the last date she notifies[5]; and

(2) the day which follows the first day after the beginning of the fourth week before the expected week of childbirth[6] on which she is absent from work wholly or partly because of pregnancy[7],

but, where the employee's ordinary maternity leave period has not so commenced when childbirth occurs, her ordinary maternity leave period commences on the day which follows the day on which childbirth occurs[8].

An employee's ordinary maternity leave period continues for a period of 26 weeks from its commencement, or until the end of the compulsory maternity leave period[9], if later[10].

An employer who is notified in this way[11] of the date on which[12] an employee's ordinary maternity leave period will commence or has commenced must notify the employee of the date on which her additional maternity leave period will end[13].

1 As to the meaning of 'employee' for these purposes see PARA 356 note 1.

2 As to the meaning of 'ordinary maternity leave' see PARA 356 note 2.

3 Ie in accordance with the Maternity and Parental Leave etc Regulations 1999, SI 1999/3312, reg 4 (see notes 7, 8; and PARA 356).

4 Ie by virtue of the provision for variation in the Maternity and Parental Leave etc Regulations 1999, SI 1999/3312, reg 4 (see reg 4(1A); and PARA 356 note 6).

5 Maternity and Parental Leave etc Regulations 1999, SI 1999/3312, reg 6(1)(a) (reg 6(1)(a), (b) amended by SI 2002/2789).

6 As to the meaning of 'expected week of childbirth' see PARA 356 note 4.

7 Maternity and Parental Leave etc Regulations 1999, SI 1999/3312, reg 6(1)(b) (as amended: see note 5). Where, by virtue of reg 6(1)(b), an employee's ordinary maternity leave period commences with the day which follows the first day after the beginning of the fourth week before the expected week of childbirth on which she is absent from work wholly or partly because of pregnancy: (1) reg 4(1) (see PARA 356) does not require her to notify her employer of the date specified in reg 4(1); but (2) whether or not she has notified him of that date, she is not entitled to ordinary maternity leave or to additional maternity leave unless she notifies him as soon as is reasonably practicable that she is absent from work wholly or partly because of pregnancy and of the date on which her absence on that account began: see reg 4(3) (amended

by SI 2002/2789; SI 2006/2014). The notification provided for in head (2) above must be given in writing, if the employer so requests: see the Maternity and Parental Leave etc Regulations 1999, SI 1999/3312, reg 4(5).

8 Maternity and Parental Leave etc Regulations 1999, SI 1999/3312, reg 6(2) (amended by SI 2002/2789). Where, by virtue of the Maternity and Parental Leave etc Regulations 1999, SI 1999/3312, reg 6(2), an employee's ordinary maternity leave period commences on the day which follows the day on which childbirth occurs: (1) reg 4(1) (see PARA 356) does not require her to notify her employer of the date specified in reg 4(1) (see PARA 356); but (2) whether or not she has notified him of that date, she is not entitled to ordinary maternity leave or to additional maternity leave unless she notifies him as soon as reasonably practicable after the birth that she has given birth and of the date on which the birth occurred: see reg 4(4) (amended by SI 2002/2789; SI 2006/2014). The notification provided for in head (2) above must be given in writing, if the employer so requests: see the Maternity and Parental Leave etc Regulations 1999, SI 1999/3312, reg 4(5).

9 Ie the period provided for in the Maternity and Parental Leave etc Regulations 1999, SI 1999/3312, reg 8: see PARA 363.

10 Maternity and Parental Leave etc Regulations 1999, SI 1999/3312, reg 7(1) (amended by SI 2002/2789). Where, however, any requirement imposed by or under any relevant statutory provision prohibits the employee from working for any period after the end of the period determined under the Maternity and Parental Leave etc Regulations 1999, SI 1999/3312, reg 7(1) by reason of her having recently given birth, her ordinary maternity leave period continues until the end of that later period: reg 7(2). For these purposes, 'relevant statutory provision' means a provision of an enactment or a provision of an instrument under an enactment, other than a provision for the time being specified in an order under the Employment Rights Act 1996 s 66(2) (suspension on maternity grounds: see PARA 598 note 7): Maternity and Parental Leave etc Regulations 1999, SI 1999/3312, reg 7(3).

Where the employee is dismissed after the commencement of an ordinary maternity leave period but before the time when that period would otherwise end, the period ends at the time of the dismissal: reg 7(5). As to redundancy during the maternity leave period see PARA 364; and as to the unfair dismissal provisions relating to pregnancy and maternity see PARA 784.

11 Ie under any provision of the Maternity and Parental Leave etc Regulations 1999, SI 1999/3312, reg 4 (see notes 7, 8; and PARA 356).

12 Ie by virtue of any provision of the Maternity and Parental Leave etc Regulations 1999, SI 1999/3312, reg 6: see the text and notes 1–8.

13 Maternity and Parental Leave etc Regulations 1999, SI 1999/3312, reg 7(6) (added by SI 2002/2789; and amended by SI 2006/2014). Such notification must be given to the employee: (1) where the employer is notified under the Maternity and Parental Leave etc Regulations 1999, SI 1999/3312, reg 4(1)(a)(iii) (see PARA 356), reg 4(3)(b) (see note 7 head (2)) or reg 4(4)(b) (see note 8 head (2)), within 28 days of the date on which he received the notification; (2) where the employer is notified under reg 4(1A) (see PARA 356 note 6), within 28 days of the date on which the employee's ordinary maternity leave period commenced: reg 7(7) (added by SI 2002/2789). As to the meaning of 'additional maternity leave' see PARA 356 note 2. As to notification provisions in the event of the employee being entitled to additional maternity leave see PARA 358.

358. Additional maternity leave period. Previously there were conditions to be satisfied before an employee[1] was entitled to additional maternity leave[2] but those conditions are no longer in force[3].

An employee's additional maternity leave period commences on the day after the last day of her ordinary maternity leave period[4]; and it continues until the end of the period 26 weeks from the day on which it commenced[5].

An employer[6] who is notified[7] of the date on which[8] an employee's ordinary maternity leave period will commence or has commenced must notify the employee of the date on which her additional maternity leave period will end[9].

1 As to the meaning of 'employee' for these purposes see PARA 356 note 1.

2 As to the meaning of 'additional maternity leave' see PARA 356 note 2.

3 See the Maternity and Parental Leave etc Regulations 1999, SI 1999/3312, reg 5 (repealed). The effect of the repeal is that an employee who qualifies for ordinary maternity leave will also qualify for additional maternity leave: see PARA 356. As to the meaning of 'ordinary maternity

leave' see PARA 356 note 2. As to the contractual provisions that continue to apply during additional maternity leave see PARA 359; and as to the right to return after additional maternity leave see PARA 362.

4 Maternity and Parental Leave etc Regulations 1999, SI 1999/3312, reg 6(3). As to the duration of ordinary maternity leave see PARA 357.

5 Maternity and Parental Leave etc Regulations 1999, SI 1999/3312, reg 7(4) (amended by SI 2002/2789). Where the employee is dismissed after the commencement of an additional maternity leave period but before the time when that period would otherwise end, the period ends at the time of the dismissal: Maternity and Parental Leave etc Regulations 1999, SI 1999/3312, reg 7(5). As to redundancy during the maternity leave period see PARA 364; and as to the unfair dismissal provisions relating to pregnancy and maternity see PARA 784.

6 As to the meaning of 'employer' for these purposes see PARA 356 note 5.

7 Ie under any provision of the Maternity and Parental Leave etc Regulations 1999, SI 1999/3312, reg 4: see PARA 356.

8 Ie by virtue of any provision of the Maternity and Parental Leave etc Regulations 1999, SI 1999/3312, reg 6: see PARA 357.

9 Maternity and Parental Leave etc Regulations 1999, SI 1999/3312, reg 7(6) (reg 7(6) added by SI 2002/2789; and amended by SI 2006/2014). Such notification must be given to the employee: (1) where the employer is notified under the Maternity and Parental Leave etc Regulations 1999, SI 1999/3312, reg 4(1)(a)(iii) (see PARA 356 text head (1)(c)), reg 4(3)(b) (see PARA 357 note 7 head (2)) or reg 4(4)(b) (see PARA 357 note 8 head (2)), within 28 days of the date on which he received the notification; (2) where the employer is notified under reg 4(1A) (see PARA 356 note 6), within 28 days of the date on which the employee's ordinary maternity leave period commenced: reg 7(7) (added by SI 2002/2789).

359. Contractual rights in relation to ordinary maternity leave and additional maternity leave. An employee[1] who takes ordinary maternity leave[2] or additional maternity leave[3]: (1) is entitled, during the period of leave[4], to the benefit of all of the terms and conditions of employment[5] which would have applied if she had not been absent[6]; and (2) is bound[7], during that period, by any obligations arising under those terms and conditions[8].

1 As to the meaning of 'employee' for these purposes see PARA 356 note 1.

2 As to the meaning of 'ordinary maternity leave' see PARA 356 note 2.

3 See the Maternity and Parental Leave etc Regulations 1999, SI 1999/3312, reg 9(1) (reg 9 substituted by SI 2002/2789; and the Maternity and Parental Leave etc Regulations 1999, SI 1999/3312, reg 9(1)–(3) amended, reg 9(4) added, by SI 2008/1966). As to the meaning of 'additional maternity leave' see PARA 356 note 2.

4 As to the duration of ordinary maternity leave see PARA 357; and as to the duration of additional maternity leave see PARA 358.

5 For these purposes, 'terms and conditions of employment' has the meaning given by the Employment Rights Act 1996 s 71(5) (see PARA 355 note 8) and s 73(5) (see PARA 355 note 26), and accordingly does not include terms and conditions about remuneration: Maternity and Parental Leave etc Regulations 1999, SI 1999/3312, reg 9(2) (as substituted and amended: see note 3). For the purposes of the Employment Rights Act 1996 ss 71, 73 (see PARA 355), only sums payable to an employee by way of wages or salary are to be treated as remuneration: Maternity and Parental Leave etc Regulations 1999, SI 1999/3312, reg 9(3) (as so substituted and amended). The term 'remuneration' under the Employment Rights Act 1996 s 71(5)(b), read with the Maternity and Parental Leave etc Regulations 1999, SI 1999/3312, reg 9(3), includes sick pay, so that entitlement to sick pay during maternity leave is excluded: see *Sutcliffe v Department of Work and Pensions* [2008] All ER (D) 171 (Feb), EAT.

6 Maternity and Parental Leave etc Regulations 1999, SI 1999/3312, reg 9(1)(a) (as substituted: see note 3). In the case of accrual of rights under an employment-related benefit scheme within the meaning given by the Social Security Act 1989 Sch 5 (see **PERSONAL AND OCCUPATIONAL PENSIONS** vol 80 (2013) PARA 303), nothing in the Maternity and Parental Leave etc Regulations 1999, SI 1999/3312, reg 9(1)(a) concerning the treatment of additional maternity leave is to be taken to impose a requirement which exceeds the requirements of the Social Security Act 1989 Sch 5 para 5 (repealed): Maternity and Parental Leave etc Regulations 1999, SI 1999/3312, reg 9(4) (as added: see note 3).

7 Ie subject only to the exceptions in the Employment Rights Act 1996 ss 71(4)(b), 73(4)(b): see PARA 355.

8 Maternity and Parental Leave etc Regulations 1999, SI 1999/3312, reg 9(1)(b) (as substituted and amended: see note 3).

360. Application of terms and conditions during ordinary maternity leave and additional maternity leave. Where an employee[1] is entitled to:

(1) ordinary maternity leave[2];

(2) additional maternity leave[3]; and

also to a right which corresponds to that right and which arises under the employee's contract of employment or otherwise[4]:

(a) the employee may not exercise the statutory right and the corresponding right separately but may, in taking the leave for which the two rights provide, take advantage of whichever right is, in any particular respect, the more favourable[5]; and

(b) the provisions[6] relating to the statutory right apply, subject to any modifications necessary to give effect to any more favourable contractual terms, to the exercise of the composite right described in head (a) above as they apply to the exercise of the statutory right[7].

1 As to the meaning of 'employee' for these purposes see PARA 356 note 1.
2 Maternity and Parental Leave etc Regulations 1999, SI 1999/3312, reg 21(1)(a). For the purposes of reg 21(2) (see heads (a), (b) in the text), the right to leave mentioned in head (1) in the text is referred to as a 'statutory right': see reg 21(1). As to the meaning of 'ordinary maternity leave' see PARA 356 note 2.
3 Maternity and Parental Leave etc Regulations 1999, SI 1999/3312, reg 21(1)(b). For the purposes of reg 21(2) (see heads (a), (b) in the text), the right to leave mentioned in head (2) in the text is referred to as a 'statutory right': see reg 21(1). As to the meaning of 'additional maternity leave' see PARA 356 note 2.
4 See the Maternity and Parental Leave etc Regulations 1999, SI 1999/3312, reg 21(1). As to the meaning of 'contract of employment' for these purposes see PARA 356 note 1. See also PARA 358.
5 Maternity and Parental Leave etc Regulations 1999, SI 1999/3312, reg 21(2)(a). Under the Employment Protection Act 1975 s 50(2), Sch 3 para 5 (repealed), which was in similar terms to the Maternity and Parental Leave etc Regulations 1999, SI 1999/3312, reg 21(1), (2), it was held that, in spite of the apparently wide drafting of the provision, there had to be limits to the extent to which any particular aspect of the maternity scheme might be sub-divided at the option of the employee: *Bovey v Board of Governors of the Hospital for Sick Children* [1978] ICR 934, [1978] IRLR 241, EAT (employee not allowed to combine an offer of return part-time at a basic grade with her statutory right to return to her previous full-time job on a higher grade); *sed quaere* whether this approach will continue to be taken.
6 Ie the provisions of the Employment Rights Act 1996 and of the Maternity and Parental Leave etc Regulations 1999, SI 1999/3312.
7 Maternity and Parental Leave etc Regulations 1999, SI 1999/3312, reg 21(2)(b).

361. Right to return after ordinary maternity leave. An employee[1] who returns to work after a period of ordinary maternity leave[2] which was:

(1) an isolated period of leave[3]; or

(2) the last of two or more consecutive periods of statutory leave[4] which did not include any period of additional maternity leave[5] or additional adoption leave[6], or a period of parental leave[7] of more than four weeks[8],

is entitled to return to the job in which she was employed before her absence[9]. An employee who returns to work after a period of ordinary maternity leave, not falling within the description in head (1) or head (2) above[10], is entitled to return from leave to the job in which she was employed before her absence, or, if it is not reasonably practicable for the employer[11] to permit her to return to that job, to another job which is both suitable for her and appropriate for her to do in the circumstances[12].

In these circumstances, the employee's right to return is a right to return: (a) with her seniority, pension rights and similar rights as they would have been if she had not been absent[13]; and (b) on terms and conditions not less favourable than those which would have applied if she had not been absent[14].

1 As to the meaning of 'employee' for these purposes see PARA 356 note 1.
2 As to the meaning of 'ordinary maternity leave' see PARA 356 note 2. As to the duration of ordinary maternity leave see PARA 357.
3 Maternity and Parental Leave etc Regulations 1999, SI 1999/3312, reg 18(1)(a) (reg 18 substituted, reg 18A added, by SI 2002/2789).
4 For these purposes, 'statutory leave' means leave provided for in the Employment Rights Act 1996 Pt VIII (ss 71–80I) (see PARAS 355 et seq, 368 et seq): see the Maternity and Parental Leave etc Regulations 1999, SI 1999/3312, reg 2(1) (definition added by SI 2002/2789). As to the right to return after periods of statutory leave see also PARAS 362, 373, 382, 383, 395.
5 As to the meaning of 'additional maternity leave' see PARA 356 note 2.
6 For these purposes, 'additional adoption leave' means leave under the Employment Rights Act 1996 s 75B (see PARA 377): see the Maternity and Parental Leave etc Regulations 1999, SI 1999/3312, reg 2(1) (definition added by SI 2002/1789).
7 For these purposes, 'parental leave' means leave under the Maternity and Parental Leave etc Regulations 1999, reg 13(1) (see PARA 391): see reg 2(1).
8 Maternity and Parental Leave etc Regulations 1999, SI 1999/3312, reg 18(1)(b) (as substituted: see note 3).
9 See the Maternity and Parental Leave etc Regulations 1999, SI 1999/3312, reg 18(1) (as substituted: see note 3). For these purposes, 'job', in relation to an employee returning after maternity leave or parental leave, means the nature of the work which the employee is employed to do in accordance with the employee's contract and the capacity and place in which the employee is so employed: see the Maternity and Parental Leave etc Regulations 1999, reg 2(1) (definition amended by SI 2002/2789). Allowance must be made for changes in the nature of the job occurring during the course of a person's absence: *Blundell v Governing Body of St Andrews Catholic Primary School* [2007] ICR 1451, [2007] IRLR 652, EAT.
The reference to the job in which an employee was employed before her absence is a reference to the job in which she was employed: (1) if her return is from an isolated period of statutory leave, immediately before that period began; (2) if her return is from consecutive periods of statutory leave, immediately before the first such period: see the Maternity and Parental Leave etc Regulations 1999, SI 1999/3312, reg 18(3) (as so substituted). Regulation 18(3) does not apply where reg 10 (redundancy during maternity leave: see PARA 364) applies, however: see reg 18(4) (as so substituted).
10 Maternity and Parental Leave etc Regulations 1999, SI 1999/3312, reg 18(2)(b) (as substituted: see note 3).
11 As to the meaning of 'employer' for these purposes see PARA 356 note 5.
12 Maternity and Parental Leave etc Regulations 1999, SI 1999/3312, reg 18(2) (as substituted: see note 3). Regulation 18(2) does not apply where reg 10 (redundancy during maternity leave: see PARA 364) applies, however: see reg 18(4) (as so substituted).
13 Maternity and Parental Leave etc Regulations 1999, SI 1999/3312, reg 18A(1)(a) (reg 18A as added (see note 3); reg 18A(1)(a) substituted by SI 2008/1966). The provision in the Maternity and Parental Leave etc Regulations 1999, SI 1999/3312, reg 18A(1) for an employee to be treated as if she had not been absent refers to her absence: (1) if her return is from an isolated period of statutory leave, since the beginning of that period; (2) if her return is from consecutive periods of statutory leave, since the beginning of the first such period: see reg 18A(3) (reg 18A as so added; reg 18A(3) amended by SI 2008/1966).
14 Maternity and Parental Leave etc Regulations 1999, SI 1999/3312, reg 18A(1)(b) (as added: see note 3). See note 13.

362. Right to return after additional maternity leave. An employee[1] who returns to work after a period of additional maternity leave[2], whether or not preceded by another period of statutory leave[3], is entitled to return from leave to the job in which she was employed before her absence, or, if it is not reasonably practicable for the employer[4] to permit her to return to that job[5], to another job which is both suitable for her and appropriate for her to do in the circumstances[6].

In these circumstances, the employee's right to return is a right to return: (1) with her seniority, pension rights and similar rights as they would have been if she had not been absent[7]; and (2) on terms and conditions not less favourable than those which would have applied if she had not been absent[8].

1 As to the meaning of 'employee' for these purposes see PARA 356 note 1.
2 As to the meaning of 'additional maternity leave' see PARA 356 note 2. As to the duration of additional maternity leave see PARA 358.
3 Maternity and Parental Leave etc Regulations 1999, SI 1999/3312, reg 18(2)(a) (reg 18 substituted, reg 18A added, by SI 2002/2789). The Maternity and Parental Leave etc Regulations 1999, SI 1999/3312, reg 18(2) does not apply where reg 10 (redundancy during maternity leave: see PARA 364) applies, however: see reg 18(4) (as so substituted). As to the meaning of 'statutory leave' see PARA 361 note 4. As to the right to return after periods of statutory leave see also PARAS 361, 373, 382, 383, 395. See also note 7.
4 As to the meaning of 'employer' for these purposes see PARA 356 note 5.
5 The reference to the job in which an employee was employed before her absence is a reference to the job in which she was employed: (1) if her return is from an isolated period of statutory leave, immediately before that period began; (2) if her return is from consecutive periods of statutory leave, immediately before the first such period: see the Maternity and Parental Leave etc Regulations 1999, SI 1999/3312, reg 18(3) (as substituted: see note 3). Regulation 18(3) does not apply where reg 10 (redundancy during maternity leave: see PARA 364) applies: see reg 18(4) (as so substituted). As to the meaning of 'job' see PARA 361 note 9.
6 Maternity and Parental Leave etc Regulations 1999, SI 1999/3312, reg 18(2) (as substituted: see note 3). See note 3.
7 Maternity and Parental Leave etc Regulations 1999, SI 1999/3312, reg 18A(1)(a) (reg 18A as added (see note 3); reg 18A(1)(a) substituted by SI 2008/1966). In the case of accrual of rights under an employment-related benefit scheme within the meaning of the Social Security Act 1989 Sch 5 (see **PERSONAL AND OCCUPATIONAL PENSIONS** vol 80 (2013) PARA 303), nothing in the Maternity and Parental Leave etc Regulations 1999, SI 1999/3312, reg 18(1)(a) concerning the treatment of additional maternity leave is to be taken to impose a requirement which exceeds the requirements of the Social Security Act 1989 Sch 5 para 5 (repealed) and Sch 5 para 6 (unfair family leave provisions): Maternity and Parental Leave etc Regulations 1999, SI 1999/3312, reg 18A(2) (reg 18A as so added; reg 18A(2) substituted by SI 2008/1966). The provision in the Maternity and Parental Leave etc Regulations 1999, SI 1999/3312, reg 18A(1) for an employee to be treated as if she had not been absent refers to her absence: (1) if her return is from an isolated period of statutory leave, since the beginning of that period; (2) if her return is from consecutive periods of statutory leave, since the beginning of the first such period: see reg 18A(3) (reg 18A as so added; reg 18A(3) amended by SI 2008/1966).
8 Maternity and Parental Leave etc Regulations 1999, SI 1999/3312, reg 18A(1)(b) (as added: see note 3). See note 7.

C. COMPULSORY MATERNITY LEAVE

363. Compulsory maternity leave. Compulsory maternity leave, that is the prohibition[1] against an employer[2] permitting an employee[3] who satisfies prescribed conditions to work during a particular period (the 'compulsory maternity leave period'), applies in relation to an employee who is entitled to ordinary maternity leave[4] and in respect of the period of two weeks commencing with the day on which childbirth[5] occurs[6].

1 Ie the prohibition in the Employment Rights Act 1996 s 72: see PARA 355.
2 As to the meaning of 'employer' for these purposes see PARA 356 note 5.
3 As to the meaning of 'employee' for these purposes see PARA 356 note 1.
4 As to the meaning of 'ordinary maternity leave' see PARA 356 note 2.
5 As to the meaning of 'childbirth' see PARA 356 note 4.
6 Maternity and Parental Leave etc Regulations 1999, SI 1999/3312, reg 8.

D. PROVISIONS COMMON TO ORDINARY, ADDITIONAL AND COMPULSORY MATERNITY LEAVE

364. Redundancy during maternity leave. Where, during an employee's[1] ordinary or additional maternity leave period[2], it is not practicable by reason of redundancy[3] for her employer[4] to continue to employ her under her existing contract of employment[5], but where there is a suitable available vacancy[6], the employee is entitled to be offered, before the end of her employment under her existing contract, alternative employment with her employer or his successor[7] or an associated employer[8] under a new contract of employment which complies with heads (1) and (2) below, and which takes effect immediately on the ending of her employment under the previous contract[9]. The new contract of employment must be such that: (1) the work to be done under it is of a kind which is both suitable in relation to the employee and appropriate for her to do in the circumstances[10]; and (2) its provisions as to the capacity and place in which she is to be employed, and as to the other terms and conditions of her employment, are not substantially less favourable to her than if she had continued to be employed under the previous contract[11].

1 As to the meaning of 'employee' for these purposes see PARA 356 note 1.

2 As to the meanings of 'ordinary maternity leave' and 'additional maternity leave' see PARA 356 note 2. As to the duration of ordinary maternity leave see PARA 357; and as to the duration of additional maternity leave see PARA 358.

3 As to the meaning of 'redundancy' see PARA 870.

4 As to the meaning of 'employer' for these purposes see PARA 356 note 5.

5 See the Maternity and Parental Leave etc Regulations 1999, SI 1999/3312, reg 10(1). As to the meaning of 'contract of employment' for these purposes see PARA 356 note 1.

6 Under the Employment Rights Act 1996 s 77(2) (repealed), which was in similar terms to the Maternity and Parental Leave etc Regulations 1999, SI 1999/3312, reg 10(1), (2), it was held that the availability of a suitable vacancy is a question of fact; and that a post may be available even if there are economic reasons for the employer not wishing to offer it to the employee in question: *Community Task Force v Rimmer* [1986] ICR 491, [1986] IRLR 203, EAT.

7 As to the meaning of 'successor' see PARA 133 note 10.

8 For these purposes, any two employers are to be treated as associated if one is a company of which the other, directly or indirectly, has control or if both are companies of which a third person, directly or indirectly, has control; and 'associated employer' is to be construed accordingly: Maternity and Parental Leave etc Regulations 1999, SI 1999/3312, reg 2(3). As to the meaning of 'associated employer' see also PARA 3.

9 See the Maternity and Parental Leave etc Regulations 1999, SI 1999/3312, reg 10(2). In order to establish that it was not practicable for the previous employment to continue, the employer must satisfy an employment tribunal that it was necessary to implement the redundancy during the period of maternity leave: *Bray v Calor Gas Ltd* [2005] All ER (D) 54 (Sep), EAT.

10 Maternity and Parental Leave etc Regulations 1999, SI 1999/3312, reg 10(3)(a). See *Simpson v Endsleigh Insurance Services Ltd* [2011] ICR 75, [2010] All ER (D) 95 (Sep), EAT (Regulations should not be interpreted as creating a two-staged process whereby at the first stage reg 10(3)(a) was satisfied and 10(3)(b) (see head (2) in the text) then became part of the negotiating process).

11 Maternity and Parental Leave etc Regulations 1999, SI 1999/3312, reg 10(3)(b). See note 10.

365. Notices to be given by the employee entitled to maternity leave. An employee[1] is entitled to ordinary maternity leave[2], provided that she has (*inter alia*) given the requisite notice to her employer[3]. Once that notice has been given, an employee need give no further notice in order to take additional maternity leave[4], if the employee qualifies for it[5]; nor need the employee give any notices to resume work at the end of the additional maternity leave period[6].

However, an employee who intends to return to work earlier than the end of her additional maternity leave period, must give to her employer not less than eight weeks' notice of the date on which she intends to return[7].

The consequence of not giving the above notices is no longer that the employee loses her statutory maternity rights; instead, if an employee attempts to return to work earlier than the end of her additional maternity leave period without complying with the requirement to give due notice[8], her employer is entitled to postpone her return to a date such as will secure that he has eight weeks' notice of her return[9].

An employee who complies with her obligations as to notice[10], or whose employer has postponed her return for want of the requisite notice[11], and who then decides to return to work: (1) earlier than the original return date[12], must give her employer not less than eight weeks' notice of the date on which she now intends to return[13]; and (2) later than the original return date, she must give her employer not less than eight weeks' notice ending with the original return date[14].

1 As to the meaning of 'employee' for these purposes see PARA 356 note 1.
2 As to the meaning of 'ordinary maternity leave' see PARA 356 note 2.
3 See PARA 356. As to the meaning of 'employer' for these purposes see PARA 356 note 5.
4 As to the meaning of 'additional maternity leave' see PARA 356 note 2. See also PARA 358.
5 See PARA 356.
6 This was a major change effected by the Employment Relations Act 1999, since much of the criticism of the previous maternity leave provisions centred on the ease with which an employee could lose her rights entirely by a failure (even technical) to comply with the complex notice provisions: see eg *Lavery v Plessey Telecommunications Ltd* [1983] ICR 534, [1983] IRLR 202, CA.

There is no provision in the Maternity and Parental Leave etc Regulations 1999, SI 1999/3312, specifically covering the position if the employee is ill at the due date for return or simply does not return; given that the contract continues throughout the relevant leaves (ie for certain purposes: see PARAS 359, 360), the employer's normal rules on sickness and unauthorised absence respectively will apply. As to the duration of ordinary maternity leave see PARA 357; and as to the duration of additional maternity leave see PARA 358. As to working during the maternity leave period see PARA 366.
7 Maternity and Parental Leave etc Regulations 1999, SI 1999/3312, reg 11(1) (substituted by SI 2006/2014). The Maternity and Parental Leave etc Regulations 1999, SI 1999/3312, reg 11 does not apply in a case where the employer did not notify the employee in accordance with reg 7(6), (7) (see PARAS 357, 358) of the date on which her additional maternity leave period would end: reg 11(5) (added by SI 2002/2789; and amended by SI 2006/2014).

In the case of an employee who is an employee shareholder (see PARA 154), the Maternity and Parental Leave etc Regulations 1999, SI 1999/3312, reg 11 must be read as if references to '8 weeks' notice' are, in each case, a reference to '16 weeks' notice': see the Employment Rights Act 1996 s 205A(3)(a); and PARA 154 note 14.
8 Ie without complying with the Maternity and Parental Leave etc Regulations 1999, SI 1999/3312, reg 11(1): see the text and note 7.
9 Maternity and Parental Leave etc Regulations 1999, SI 1999/3312, reg 11(2) (amended by SI 2006/2014). See also note 7. An employer is not, however, entitled under the Maternity and Parental Leave etc Regulations 1999, SI 1999/3312, reg 11(2) to postpone an employee's return to work to a date after the end of the relevant maternity leave period: reg 11(3). If an employee whose return to work has been postponed under reg 11(2) has been notified that she is not to return to work before the date to which her return was postponed, the employer is under no contractual obligation to pay her remuneration until the date to which her return was postponed if she returns to work before that date: reg 11(4).
10 Ie who complies with her obligations in the Maternity and Parental Leave etc Regulations 1999, SI 1999/3312, reg 11(1): see the text and note 7.
11 Ie in the circumstances described in the Maternity and Parental Leave etc Regulations 1999, SI 1999/3312, reg 11(2): see the text and notes 8–9.
12 For these purposes, the 'original return date' means the date which the employee notified to her employer as the date of her return to work under the Maternity and Parental Leave etc Regulations 1999, SI 1999/3312, reg 11(1) (see the text and note 7), or the date to which her return was postponed by her employer under reg 11(2) (see the text and notes 8–9): see reg 11(2B) (reg 11(2A), (2B) added by SI 2006/2014).
13 Maternity and Parental Leave etc Regulations 1999, SI 1999/3312, reg 11(2A)(a) (as added: see note 12). See also note 7.

14 Maternity and Parental Leave etc Regulations 1999, SI 1999/3312, reg 11(2A)(b) (as added: see note 12). See also note 7.

366. Work during maternity leave period. An employee[1] may carry out up to ten days' work for her employer[2] during her statutory maternity leave period[3] without bringing her maternity leave to an end[4]. For these purposes[5], any work[6] carried out on any day constitutes a day's work[7]. This restricted allowance for an employee to work during her statutory maternity leave period[8] does not confer any right on an employer to require that any work be carried out during the statutory maternity leave period, nor any right on an employee to work during the statutory maternity leave period[9].

Any days' work carried out in this way[10] do not have the effect of extending the total duration of the statutory maternity leave period[11].

1 As to the meaning of 'employee' for these purposes see PARA 356 note 1.

2 As to the meaning of 'employer' for these purposes see PARA 356 note 5.

3 For these purposes, 'statutory maternity leave period' means the period during which the employee is on statutory maternity leave; and 'statutory maternity leave' means ordinary maternity leave and additional maternity leave: see the Maternity and Parental Leave etc Regulations 1999, SI 1999/3312, reg 2(1) (both definitions added by SI 2006/2014). As to the meanings of 'ordinary maternity leave' and 'additional maternity leave' see PARA 356 note 2. See also PARA 358.

4 Maternity and Parental Leave etc Regulations 1999, SI 1999/3312, reg 12A(1) (reg 12A added by SI 2006/2014). The Maternity and Parental Leave etc Regulations 1999, SI 1999/3312, reg 12A(1) does not apply, however, in relation to any work carried out by the employee at any time from childbirth to the end of the period of two weeks which commences with the day on which childbirth occurs: reg 12A(5) (as so added). As to the meaning of 'childbirth' see PARA 356 note 4.

5 Ie for the purposes of the Maternity and Parental Leave etc Regulations 1999, SI 1999/3312, reg 12A.

6 For the purposes of the Maternity and Parental Leave etc Regulations 1999, SI 1999/3312, reg 12A, work means any work done under the contract of employment and may include training or any activity undertaken for the purposes of keeping in touch with the workplace: reg 12A(3) (as added: see note 4). However, reasonable contact from time to time between an employee and her employer which either party is entitled to make during a maternity leave period (for example to discuss an employee's return to work) does not bring that period to an end: reg 12A(4) (as so added). As to the meaning of 'contract of employment' for these purposes see PARA 356 note 1.

7 Maternity and Parental Leave etc Regulations 1999, SI 1999/3312, reg 12A(2) (as added: see note 4).

8 Ie the Maternity and Parental Leave etc Regulations 1999, SI 1999/3312, reg 12A.

9 Maternity and Parental Leave etc Regulations 1999, SI 1999/3312, reg 12A(6) (as added: see note 4).

10 Ie under the Maternity and Parental Leave etc Regulations 1999, SI 1999/3312, reg 12A.

11 Maternity and Parental Leave etc Regulations 1999, SI 1999/3312, reg 12A(7) (as added: see note 4).

367. Calculation of a week's pay in maternity leave cases. Where:

(1) under the provisions of the Employment Rights Act 1996 that relate to calculating a week's pay[1], the amount of a week's pay of an employee[2] falls to be calculated by reference to the average rate of remuneration, or the average amount of remuneration, payable to the employee in respect of a period of 12 weeks ending on a particular date (the 'calculation date')[3];

(2) during a week in that period, the employee was absent from work on ordinary or additional maternity leave[4]; and

(3) remuneration is payable to the employee in respect of that week under

her contract of employment[5], but the amount payable is less than the amount that would be payable if she were working[6],

that week is to be disregarded for the purpose of the calculation and account is to be taken of remuneration in earlier weeks so as to bring up to 12 the number of weeks of which account is taken[7].

1 Ie under the Employment Rights Act 1996 Pt XIV Ch II (ss 220–229) (calculation of a week's pay: see PARA 143 et seq).
2 As to the meaning of 'employee' for these purposes see PARA 356 note 1.
3 Maternity and Parental Leave etc Regulations 1999, SI 1999/3312, reg 22(a).
4 Maternity and Parental Leave etc Regulations 1999, SI 1999/3312, reg 22(b). As to the meanings of 'ordinary maternity leave' and 'additional maternity leave' see PARA 356 note 2. See also PARA 358.
5 As to the meaning of 'contract of employment' for these purposes see PARA 356 note 1.
6 Maternity and Parental Leave etc Regulations 1999, SI 1999/3312, reg 22(c).
7 See the Maternity and Parental Leave etc Regulations 1999, SI 1999/3312, reg 22.

(iii) Paternity Leave

A. POWER TO MAKE REGULATIONS

368. Power to make regulations in relation to paternity leave upon birth. The Secretary of State[1] must make regulations[2], in relation to paternity leave upon the birth of a child[3]:

(1) specifying conditions as to:
  (a) duration of employment[4];
  (b) relationship with a newborn, or expected child[5]; and
  (c) relationship with the child's mother,

  which an employee[6] must satisfy entitling him to be absent from work on leave for the purpose of caring for the child or supporting the mother[7];

(2) including provision for determining:
  (a) the extent of an employee's entitlement to such leave in respect of a child[8]; and
  (b) when such leave may be taken[9]; and

(3) providing:
  (a) that an employee who is absent on such leave is entitled, for such purposes and to such extent as the regulations may prescribe, to the benefit of the terms and conditions of employment[10] which would have applied if he had not been absent[11];
  (b) that an employee who is absent on such leave is bound, for such purposes and to such extent as the regulations may prescribe, by obligations arising[12] under those terms and conditions[13]; and
  (c) that an employee who is absent on such leave[14] is entitled to return from leave[15] to a job[16] of a kind prescribed by regulations, subject to head (v) below[17].

Such regulations may:

(i) specify things which are, or are not, to be taken as done for the purpose of caring for a child or supporting the child's mother[18];
(ii) make provision excluding the right to be absent in respect of a child where more than one child is born as a result of the same pregnancy[19];
(iii) make provision about how leave may be taken[20];
(iv) specify matters which are, or are not, to be treated as remuneration for the purposes of heads (3)(a) to (3)(c) above[21];

(v) make provision about redundancy[22], or dismissal other than by reason of redundancy, during a period of paternity leave upon the birth of a child[23];
(vi) make provision about notices to be given, evidence to be produced and other procedures to be followed by employees and employers[24];
(vii) make provision requiring employers or employees to keep records[25];
(viii) make provision for the consequences of failure to give notices, to produce evidence, to keep records or to comply with other procedural requirements[26];
(ix) make provision for the consequences of failure to act in accordance with a notice given by virtue of head (vi) above[27];
(x) make special provision for cases where an employee has a right which corresponds to a right to paternity leave upon the birth of a child[28] and which arises under his contract of employment or otherwise[29];
(xi) make provision modifying the effect of the statutory provisions relating to the calculation of a week's pay[30] in relation to an employee who is or has been absent from work under the statutory provisions[31] relating to paternity leave upon the birth of a child[32];
(xii) make provision applying, modifying or excluding an enactment, in such circumstances as may be specified and subject to any conditions which may be specified, in relation to a person entitled to take paternity leave upon the birth of a child[33];
(xiii) make different provision for different cases or circumstances[34].

1 As to the Secretary of State see PARA 5 note 21.
2 As to the making of regulations under the Employment Rights Act 1996 generally see PARA 162. In exercise of the powers conferred by ss 80A(1), (2), (5), 80C(1), (6), 80D(1), 80E, 99(1), the Secretary of State has made the Paternity and Adoption Leave Regulations 2002, SI 2002/2788 (see PARA 370 et seq).
3 See PARA 370 et seq. As to the power to make regulations in relation to shared parental leave on birth see PARA 398.
4 As to the meaning of 'employment' see PARA 2.
5 For these purposes, 'newborn child' includes a child stillborn after 24 weeks of pregnancy: see the Employment Rights Act 1996 s 80A(7) (ss 80A, 80C–80E added by the Employment Act 2002 s 1).
6 As to the meaning of 'employee' see PARA 2.
7 Employment Rights Act 1996 s 80A(1) (as added: see note 5).
8 Employment Rights Act 1996 s 80A(2)(a) (as added: see note 5). Provision under s 80A(2)(a) must secure that where an employee is entitled to leave under s 80A in respect of a child he is entitled to at least two weeks' leave: s 80A(3) (as so added). For these purposes, 'week' means any period of seven days: see s 80A(7) (as so added).
9 Employment Rights Act 1996 s 80A(2)(b) (as added: see note 5). Provision under s 80A(2)(b) must secure that:
(1) leave under s 80A must be taken before the end of a period of at least 56 days beginning with the date of the child's birth (s 80A(4) (as so added)); and
(2) once an employee takes leave under s 75E (shared parental leave on birth: see PARA 398) in respect of a child, the employee may not take leave under s 80A in respect of the child (s 80A(4A) (s 80A as so added; s 80A(4A) added by the Children and Families Act 2014 s 118(1), (6))).
Where more than one child is born as a result of the same pregnancy, the reference in head (1) above to the date of the child's birth must be read as a reference to the date of birth of the first child born as a result of the pregnancy: s 80A(6) (as so added).
10 For this purpose, 'terms and conditions of employment' includes matters connected with an employee's employment whether or not they arise under his contract of employment, but does not include terms and conditions about remuneration: see the Employment Rights Act 1996 s 80C(5) (as added: see note 5). Regulations under s 80A may specify matters which are, or are not, to be treated as remuneration for these purposes: see head (iv) in the text. See eg PARA 372 note 3.

11 Employment Rights Act 1996 s 80C(1)(a) (as added: see note 5). Section 80C(1) applies to regulations under s 80B (see PARA 369) as it applies to regulations under s 80A (see the text and notes 1–9): s 80C(3) (s 80C as so added; s 80C(3) amended by the Work and Families Act 2006 s 5(1), (2), (4); and the Children and Families Act 2014 Sch 7 paras 29, 34(1), (4)).
12 Ie except in so far as the obligations are inconsistent with the Employment Rights Act 1996 s 80A(1) (see head (1) in the text): s 80C(1)(b) (as added: see note 5).
13 Employment Rights Act 1996 s 80C(1)(b) (as added: see note 5).
14 The reference in head (3)(c) in the text to absence on leave under the Employment Rights Act 1996 s 80A (see heads (1), (2), (i)–(iii) in the text) includes, where appropriate, a reference to a continuous period of absence attributable partly to leave under s 80A and partly to any one or more of maternity leave, adoption leave, shared parental leave, and parental leave: s 80C(2) (s 80C as added (see note 5); s 80C(2) amended by the Work and Families Act 2006 s 5(1), (3); and the Children and Families Act 2014 Sch 7 paras 29, 34(1), (3)). As to maternity leave see PARA 355 et seq; as to adoption leave see PARA 377 et seq; as to parental leave see PARA 390 et seq; and as to shared parental leave see PARA 398 et seq.
15 Regulations under the Employment Rights Act 1996 s 80A (see heads (1), (2), (i)–(iii) in the text) may make provision, in relation to the right to return, about seniority, pension rights and similar rights, and about terms and conditions of employment on return: s 80C(7) (s 80C as added (see note 5); s 80C(7) amended by the Work and Families Act 2006 s 5(1), (6); and the Children and Families Act 2014 Sch 7 paras 29, 34(1), (7)).
16 As to the meaning of 'job' see PARA 119 note 17.
17 Employment Rights Act 1996 s 80C(1)(c) (as added: see note 5).
18 Employment Rights Act 1996 s 80A(5)(a) (as added: see note 5).
19 Employment Rights Act 1996 s 80A(5)(b) (as added: see note 5).
20 Employment Rights Act 1996 s 80A(5)(c) (as added: see note 5).
21 Employment Rights Act 1996 s 80C(6) (s 80C as added (see note 5); s 80C(6) amended by the Work and Families Act 2006 s 5(1), (6); and the Children and Families Act 2014 Sch 7 paras 29, 34(1), (6)).
22 As to the meaning of 'redundancy' see PARA 870.
23 Employment Rights Act 1996 s 80D(1) (s 80D as added (see note 5); s 80D(1) amended by the Work and Families Act 2006 Sch 1 para 37; and the Children and Families Act 2014 Sch 7 paras 29, 35). Such provision may include provision requiring an employer to offer alternative employment, and may include provision for the consequences of failure to comply with the regulations (which may include provision for a dismissal to be treated as unfair for the purposes of the Employment Rights Act 1996 Pt X (ss 94–134A) (unfair dismissal: see PARA 757 et seq)): s 80D(2) (as so added).
24 Employment Rights Act 1996 s 80E(1)(a) (s 80E as added (see note 5); amended by the Work and Families Act 2006 Sch 1 paras 38(1)–(3); and the Children and Families Act 2014 Sch 7 paras 29, 36).
25 Employment Rights Act 1996 s 80E(1)(b) (as added and amended: see note 24).
26 Employment Rights Act 1996 s 80E(1)(c) (as added and amended: see note 24).
27 Employment Rights Act 1996 s 80E(1)(d) (as added and amended: see note 24).
28 Ie a right under the Employment Rights Act 1996 s 80A: see heads (1), (2), (i)–(iii) in the text.
29 Employment Rights Act 1996 s 80E(1)(e) (as added and amended: see note 24).
30 Ie the Employment Rights Act 1996 Pt XIV Ch II (ss 220–229): see PARA 143 et seq.
31 Ie under the Employment Rights Act 1996 s 80A: see heads (1), (2), (i)–(iii) in the text.
32 Employment Rights Act 1996 s 80E(1)(f) (as added and amended: see note 24).
33 Employment Rights Act 1996 s 80E(1)(g) (as added and amended: see note 24). The text refers to a person entitled to take leave under s 80A (see heads (1), (2), (i)–(iii) in the text): see s 80E(1)(g) (as so added and amended).
34 Employment Rights Act 1996 s 80E(1)(h) (as added and amended: see note 24).

369. Power to make regulations in relation to paternity leave upon adoption. The Secretary of State[1] must make regulations[2], in relation to paternity leave upon the adoption of a child[3]:

(1) specifying conditions as to:
   (a) duration of employment[4];
   (b) relationship with a child placed, or expected to be placed, for adoption under the law of any part of the United Kingdom[5]; and
   (c) relationship with a person with whom the child is, or is expected to be, so placed for adoption[6],

which an employee must satisfy entitling him to be absent from work on leave for the purpose of caring for the child or supporting that person[7];

(2) including provision for determining:

(a) the extent of an employee's entitlement to such leave in respect of a child[8]; and

(b) when such leave may be taken[9]; and

(3) providing:

(a) that an employee who is absent on leave is entitled, for such purposes and to such extent as the regulations may prescribe, to the benefit of the terms and conditions of employment[10] which would have applied if he had not been absent[11];

(b) that an employee who is absent on leave is bound, for such purposes and to such extent as the regulations may prescribe, by obligations arising[12] under those terms and conditions[13]; and

(c) that an employee who is absent on leave[14] is entitled to return from leave[15] to a job[16] of a kind prescribed by regulations, subject to head (vi) below[17].

Such regulations may:

(i) specify things which are, or are not, to be taken as done for the purpose of caring for a child or supporting a person with whom a child is placed for adoption[18];

(ii) make provision excluding the right to be absent on paternity leave upon adoption in the case of an employee: (A) who[19] has already exercised a right to be absent on such leave in connection with the same child[20]; (B) who exercises a right to be absent from work on adoption leave[21]; (C) who has exercised a right to take paid time off to attend adoption appointments[22];

(iii) make provision excluding the right to be absent on such leave in respect of a child where more than one child is placed for adoption as part of the same arrangement[23];

(iv) make provision about how such leave may be taken[24];

(v) specify matters which are, or are not, to be treated as remuneration for the purposes of heads (3)(a) to (3)(c) above[25];

(vi) make provision about redundancy[26], or dismissal other than by reason of redundancy, during a period of paternity leave upon the adoption of a child[27];

(vii) make provision about notices to be given, evidence to be produced and other procedures to be followed by employees and employers[28];

(viii) make provision requiring employers or employees to keep records[29];

(ix) make provision for the consequences of failure to give notices, to produce evidence, to keep records or to comply with other procedural requirements[30];

(x) make provision for the consequences of failure to act in accordance with a notice given by virtue of head (vii) above[31];

(xi) make special provision for cases where an employee has a right which corresponds to a right to paternity leave upon the adoption of a child[32] and which arises under his contract of employment or otherwise[33];

(xii) make provision modifying the effect of the statutory provision concerning the calculation of a week's pay[34] in relation to an employee who is or has been absent from work under the statutory provisions[35] relating to paternity leave upon the adoption of a child[36];

(xiii) make provision applying, modifying or excluding an enactment, in such circumstances as may be specified and subject to any conditions which may be specified, in relation to a person entitled to take paternity leave upon the adoption of a child[37];

(xiv) make different provision for different cases or circumstances[38].

1 As to the Secretary of State see PARA 5 note 21.

2 As to the making of regulations under the Employment Rights Act 1996 generally see PARA 162. In exercise of the power conferred by ss 80B(1), (2), (5), 80C(1), (6), 80D(1), 80E, 99(1), the Secretary of State has made the Paternity and Adoption Leave Regulations 2002, SI 2002/2788 (see PARA 370 et seq) and the Paternity and Adoption Leave (Adoption from Overseas) Regulations 2003, SI 2003/921 (see PARAS 375–376).

3 See PARA 371 et seq. See also note 5. As to the power to make regulations in relation to shared parental leave on adoption see PARA 399.

4 Employment Rights Act 1996 s 80B(1)(a) (ss 80B–80E added by the Employment Act 2002 s 1). As to the meaning of 'employment' see PARA 2.

5 Employment Rights Act 1996 s 80B(1)(b) (as added: see note 4). Regulations under s 80B(1) must include provision for leave in respect of a child placed, or expected to be placed, under the Children Act 1989 s 22C (local authority's duty to provide child is in its care with accommodation: see **CHILDREN AND YOUNG PERSONS** vol 10 (2012) PARA 858) by a local authority in England with a local authority foster parent who has been approved as a prospective adopter: Employment Rights Act 1996 s 80B(6A) (s 80B as so added; s 80B(6A), (6B) added by the Children and Families Act 2014 s 121(2)(b)). In relation to regulations made by virtue of the Employment Rights Act 1996 s 80B(6A), s 80B has effect as if references to being placed for adoption were references to being placed under the Children Act 1989 s 22C with a local authority foster parent who has been approved as a prospective adopter, references to placement for adoption were references to placement under s 22C with such a person, and the Employment Rights Act 1996 s 80B(5)(aa) (see head (ii) in the text) is omitted: s 80B(6B) (as so added). The Secretary of State may by regulations provide for s 80B to have effect in relation to:

(1) cases which involve adoption, but not the placement of a child for adoption under the law of any part of the United Kingdom, with such modifications as the regulations may prescribe (s 80B(8) (as so added));

(2) cases which involve an employee who has applied, or intends to apply, with another person for a parental order under the Human Fertilisation and Embryology Act 2008 s 54 (parental orders: see **CHILDREN AND YOUNG PERSONS** vol 9 (2012) PARA 129) and a child who is, or will be, the subject of the order, with such modifications as the regulations may prescribe (Employment Rights Act 1996 s 80B(9) (s 80B as so added; s 80B(9) added by the Children and Families Act 2014 s 122(4))).

Further to head (1) above, see PARA 375. As to the meaning of 'employee' see PARA 2. As to the meanings of 'England' and 'United Kingdom' see PARA 2 note 12. As to the law relating to child adoption see **CHILDREN AND YOUNG PERSONS** vol 9 (2012) PARA 360 et seq. Children who are adopted from overseas are not placed for adoption but are and have been treated as privately fostered under the Children Act 1989 s 66 (see **CHILDREN AND YOUNG PERSONS** vol 10 (2012) PARA 1056 et seq) or as protected children under the Adoption Act 1976 ss 32–37 (now repealed). As to paternity leave provisions relating to adoptions from overseas see PARAS 375–376.

6 Employment Rights Act 1996 s 80B(1)(c) (as added: see note 4).

7 See the Employment Rights Act 1996 s 80B(1) (as added: see note 4).

8 Employment Rights Act 1996 s 80B(2)(a) (as added: see note 4). Provision under s 80B(2)(a) must secure that where an employee is entitled to leave under s 80B in respect of a child he is entitled to at least two weeks' leave: s 80B(3) (as so added). For these purposes, 'week' means any period of seven days: see s 80B(7) (as so added).

9 Employment Rights Act 1996 s 80B(2)(b) (as added: see note 4). Provision under s 80B(2)(b) must secure that:

(1) leave under s 80B must be taken before the end of a period of at least 56 days beginning with the date of the child's placement for adoption (s 80B(4) (as so added)); and

(2) once an employee takes leave under s 75G (shared parental leave on adoption : see PARA 399) in respect of a child, the employee may not take leave under s 80B in respect of the child (s 80B(4A) (s 80B as so added; s 80B(4A) added by the Children and Families Act 2014 s 118(1), (7))).

Where more than one child is placed for adoption as part of the same arrangement, the reference in head (1) above to the date of the child's placement must be read as a reference to the date of placement of the first child to be placed as part of the arrangement: Employment Rights Act 1996 s 80B(6) (as so added).

10 As to the meaning of 'terms and conditions of employment' see PARA 368 note 10. Regulations under the Employment Rights Act 1996 s 80B may specify matters which are, or are not, to be treated as remuneration for these purposes: see head (v) in the text. See eg PARA 372 note 3.

11 Employment Rights Act 1996 s 80C(1)(a) (as added: see note 4). Section 80C(1) applies to regulations under s 80B (see the text and notes 1–9) as it applies to regulations under s 80A (see PARA 368): s 80C(3) (s 80C as so added; s 80C(3) amended by the Work and Families Act 2006 s 5(1), (2), (4); and the Children and Families Act 2014 Sch 7 paras 29, 34(1), (4)).

12 Ie except in so far as the obligations are inconsistent with the Employment Rights Act 1996 s 80B(1) (see head (1) in the text): s 80C(1)(b) (as added: see note 4).

13 Employment Rights Act 1996 s 80C(1)(b) (as added: see note 4).

14 In the application of head (3)(c) in the text to regulations under the Employment Rights Act 1996 s 80B (see note 11), the reference to absence on leave under s 80B (see heads (1), (2), (i)–(iv) in the text) includes, where appropriate, a reference to a continuous period of absence attributable partly to leave under s 80B and partly to any one or more of maternity leave, adoption leave, shared parental leave, parental leave, and leave under s 80A (see PARA 368): s 80C(4) (s 80C as added (see note 4); s 80C(4) amended by the Work and Families Act 2006 s 5(1), (5); and the Children and Families Act 2014 Sch 7 paras 29, 34(1), (5)). As to maternity leave see PARA 355 et seq; as to adoption leave see PARA 377 et seq; as to parental leave see PARA 390 et seq; and as to shared parental leave see PARA 398 et seq.

15 Regulations under the Employment Rights Act 1996 s 80B (see heads (1), (2), (i)–(iv) in the text) may make provision, in relation to the right to return mentioned in head (3)(c) in the text, about seniority, pension rights and similar rights, and about terms and conditions of employment on return: s 80C(7) (s 80C as added (see note 4); s 80C(7) amended by the Work and Families Act 2006 s 5(1), (6); and the Children and Families Act 2014 Sch 7 paras 29, 34(1), (7)).

16 As to the meaning of 'job' see PARA 119 note 17.

17 Employment Rights Act 1996 s 80C(1)(c) (as added: see note 4).

18 Employment Rights Act 1996 s 80B(5)(a) (as added: see note 4).

19 Ie by virtue of provision under the Employment Rights Act 1996 s 80B(6A) (see note 5): see s 80B(5)(aa) (s 80B as added (see note 4); s 80B(5)(aa) added by the Children and Families Act 2014 s 121(2)(a)).

20 Employment Rights Act 1996 s 80B(5)(aa) (as added: see note 20).

21 Employment Rights Act 1996 s 80B(5)(b) (as added: see note 4).

22 Employment Rights Act 1996 s 80B(5)(ba) (s 80B as added (see note 4); s 80B(5)(ba) added by the Children and Families Act 2014 s 128(2)(b)). The text refers to a right to take time off under the Employment Rights Act 1996 s 57ZJ (see PARA 341): see s 80B(5)(ba) (as so added).

23 Employment Rights Act 1996 s 80B(5)(c) (as added: see note 4).

24 Employment Rights Act 1996 s 80B(5)(d) (as added: see note 4).

25 Employment Rights Act 1996 s 80C(6) (s 80C as added (see note 4); s 80C(6) amended by the Work and Families Act 2006 s 5(1), (6); and the Children and Families Act 2014 Sch 7 paras 29, 34(1), (6)).

26 As to the meaning of 'redundancy' see PARA 870.

27 Employment Rights Act 1996 s 80D(1) (s 80D as added (see note 4); s 80D(1) amended by the Work and Families Act 2006 Sch 1 para 37; and the Children and Families Act 2014 Sch 7 paras 29, 35). Such provision may include provision requiring an employer to offer alternative employment, and may include provision for the consequences of failure to comply with the regulations (which may include provision for a dismissal to be treated as unfair for the purposes of the Employment Rights Act 1996 Pt X (ss 94–134A) (unfair dismissal: see PARA 757 et seq)): s 80D(2) (as so added).

28 Employment Rights Act 1996 s 80E(1)(a) (s 80E as added (see note 4); amended by the Work and Families Act 2006 Sch 1 paras 38(1)–(3); and the Children and Families Act 2014 Sch 7 paras 29, 36).

29 Employment Rights Act 1996 s 80E(1)(b) (as added and amended: see note 28).

30 Employment Rights Act 1996 s 80E(1)(c) (as added and amended: see note 28).

31 Employment Rights Act 1996 s 80E(1)(d) (as added and amended: see note 28).

32 Ie a right under the Employment Rights Act 1996 s 80B: see heads (1), (2), (i)–(iv) in the text.

33 Employment Rights Act 1996 s 80E(1)(e) (as added and amended: see note 28).

34 Ie the Employment Rights Act 1996 Pt XIV Ch II (ss 220–229): see PARA 143 et seq.

35 Ie under the Employment Rights Act 1996 s 80B: see heads (1), (2), (i)–(iv) in the text.

36 Employment Rights Act 1996 s 80E(1)(f) (as added and amended: see note 28).

37 Employment Rights Act 1996 s 80E(1)(g) (as added and amended: see note 28). The text refers to a person entitled to take leave under s 80B (see heads (1), (2), (i)–(iv) in the text): see s 80E(1)(g) (as so added and amended).
38 Employment Rights Act 1996 s 80E(1)(h) (as added and amended: see note 28).

B. PATERNITY LEAVE UPON BIRTH

370. Entitlement to paternity leave upon the birth of a child. An employee[1] is entitled to be absent from work on leave for the purpose of caring for a child[2] or supporting the child's mother if:

(1) he satisfies the following conditions[3], being that:
 (a) he has been continuously employed[4] for a period of not less than 26 weeks ending with the week immediately preceding the fourteenth week before the expected week[5] of the child's birth[6];
 (b) he is either the father of the child or married to, the civil partner or the partner[7] of the child's mother, but not the child's father[8];
 (c) he has, or expects to have: (i) if he is the child's father, responsibility for the upbringing of the child; or (ii) if he is the mother's husband, civil partner or partner but not the child's father, the main responsibility, apart from any responsibility of the mother, for the upbringing of the child[9]; and
(2) he has complied with the following requirements as to notice and, where applicable, as to evidence[10], being that:
 (a) he must give his employer[11] notice[12] of his intention to take leave in respect of a child, specifying[13]: (i) the expected week of the child's birth[14]; (ii) the length of the period of leave that[15] the employee has chosen to take[16]; and (iii) the date on which[17] the employee has chosen that his period of leave should begin[18]; and
 (b) where the employer requests it, the employee must also give his employer a declaration, signed by the employee, to the effect that the purpose of his absence from work is to care for a child or to support the child's mother and that he satisfies the conditions[19] of entitlement[20].

An employee may choose[21] to take either one week's leave or two consecutive weeks' leave in respect of a child[22]. The leave may only be taken during the period which begins with the date on which the child is born and ends 56 days after that date (except in a case where the child is born before the first day of the expected week of its birth, when the period ends 56 days after that day)[23]. Within this period, an employee may choose to begin his period of leave on[24]:

(A) the date on which the child is born[25];
(B) the date falling such number of days after the date on which the child is born as the employee may specify[26] in a notice[27]; or
(C) a predetermined date, specified in a notice[28], which is later than the first day of the expected week of the child's birth[29].

An employee's period of paternity leave begins on the date specified in his notice[30] (or, where he has varied his choice of date[31], on the date specified in his notice, or the last such notice if he has varied his choice more than once)[32]. However, in a case where the employee has chosen to begin his period of leave on the date on which the child is born, and where he is at work on that date, his period of leave begins on the day after that date[33].

An employee must give his employer a further notice, as soon as is reasonably practicable after the child's birth, of the date on which the child was born[34].

1 For these purposes, 'employee' means an individual who has entered into or works under, or, where the employment has ceased, worked under, a contract of employment; and 'contract of employment' means a contract of service or apprenticeship, whether express or implied, and, if it is express, whether oral or in writing: see the Paternity and Adoption Leave Regulations 2002, SI 2002/2788, reg 2(1). As to the meanings of 'employee', 'contract of employment' and related expressions in relation to employment rights generally see PARA 2 et seq. As to the meaning of 'contract of service' see PARA 1 note 1; and as to the meaning of 'writing' see PARA 2 note 8. As to the position of apprentices and youth trainees at common law see PARAS 112, 128–129, 636, 747–754. As to the statutory law on apprenticeships see **EDUCATION** vol 35 (2011) PARA 682 et seq.

2 Ie subject to the Paternity and Adoption Leave Regulations 2002, SI 2002/2788, reg 4(1A): see reg 4(1) (reg 4(1) amended, reg 4(1A) added, by SI 2014/2112). Accordingly, an employee is not entitled to be absent from work under the Paternity and Adoption Leave Regulations 2002, SI 2002/2788, reg 4(1) if the employee has taken any shared parental leave in respect of the child: reg 4(1A) (as so added). For these purposes, 'shared parental leave' means leave under the Employment Rights Act 1996 s 75E (shared parental leave on birth: see PARA 398) or s 75G (shared parental leave on adoption : see PARA 399): see the Paternity and Adoption Leave Regulations 2002, SI 2002/2788, reg 2(1) (definition added by SI 2014/2112).

For these purposes, 'child' means a person who is, or when placed with an adopter for adoption was, under the age of 18; and 'adopter', in relation to a child, means a person who has been matched with the child for adoption, or, in a case where two people have been matched jointly, whichever of them has elected to be the child's adopter for the purposes of the Paternity and Adoption Leave Regulations 2002, SI 2002/2788: see reg 2(1). A person is matched with a child for adoption when an adoption agency decides that that person would be a suitable adoptive parent for the child, either individually or jointly with another person (reg 2(4)(a)); and a person elects to be a child's adopter, in a case where the child is matched with him and another person jointly, if he and that person agree, at the time at which they are matched, that he and not the other person will be the adopter (reg 2(4)(c)). 'Adoption agency' has the meaning given by the Adoption and Children Act 2002 s 2(1) (see **CHILDREN AND YOUNG PERSONS** vol 9 (2012) PARAS 432–433): see the Paternity and Adoption Leave Regulations 2002, SI 2002/2788, reg 2(1) (definition amended by SI 2014/2112). A person attains a particular age expressed in years at the commencement of the relevant anniversary of the date of his birth: see the Family Law Reform Act 1969 s 9; and **CHILDREN AND YOUNG PERSONS** vol 9 (2012) PARA 2.

3 See the Paternity and Adoption Leave Regulations 2002, SI 2002/2788, reg 4(1)(a). The text refers to the conditions specified in reg 4(2) (see heads (1)(a) to (1)(c) in the text): see reg 4(1)(a). An employee's entitlement to paternity leave under reg 4 is not affected by the birth, or expected birth, of more than one child as a result of the same pregnancy: reg 4(6). As to the power to make regulations in relation to shared parental leave on birth see PARA 398.

4 For these purposes, a reference in any provision of the Paternity and Adoption Leave Regulations 2002, SI 2002/2788, to a period of continuous employment is a reference to a period computed in accordance with the Employment Rights Act 1996 Pt XIV Ch I (ss 210–219) (continuous employment: see PARAS 130 et seq, 861 et seq), as if that provision were a part of the Employment Rights Act 1996: see the Paternity and Adoption Leave Regulations 2002, SI 2002/2788, reg 2(5).

5 For these purposes, 'expected week', in relation to the birth of a child, means the week, beginning with midnight between Saturday and Sunday, in which it is expected that the child will be born: see the Paternity and Adoption Leave Regulations 2002, SI 2002/2788, reg 2(1).

6 Paternity and Adoption Leave Regulations 2002, SI 2002/2788, reg 4(2)(a). An employee is to be treated as having satisfied the condition in reg 4(2)(a) on the date of the child's birth notwithstanding the fact that he has not then been continuously employed for a period of not less than 26 weeks, where: (1) the date on which the child is born is earlier than the fourteenth week before the week in which its birth is expected (reg 4(3)(a)); and (2) the employee would have been continuously employed for such a period if his employment had continued until that fourteenth week (reg 4(3)(b)).

7 For these purposes, 'partner', in relation to a child's mother or adopter, means a person, whether of a different sex or the same sex, who lives with the mother or adopter and the child in an enduring family relationship but is not the mother's or adopter's parent, grandparent, sister, brother, aunt or uncle: see the Paternity and Adoption Leave Regulations 2002, SI 2002/2788, reg 2(1), (2). The references to relationships are references to relationships of the full blood or half blood or, in the case of an adopted person, such of those relationships as would exist but for the adoption, and include the relationship of a child with his adoptive, or former adoptive, parents, but do not include any other adoptive relationships: see reg 2(3).

8 Paternity and Adoption Leave Regulations 2002, SI 2002/2788, reg 4(2)(b) (reg 4(2)(b), (c) amended by SI 2005/2114). An employee is to be treated as having satisfied the condition in the Paternity and Adoption Leave Regulations 2002, SI 2002/2788, reg 4(2)(b)(ii) concerning his relationship to the mother (not being the child's father) if he would have satisfied it but for the fact that the child's mother has died: reg 4(4).

Marriage of same sex couples is lawful in the law of England and Wales, and such marriages have the same effect as marriages of opposite sex couples: see the Marriage (Same Sex Couples) Act 2013 s 1(1), 11(1); and MATRIMONIAL AND CIVIL PARTNERSHIP LAW vol 72 (2009) PARA 1 et seq.

9 Paternity and Adoption Leave Regulations 2002, SI 2002/2788, reg 4(2)(c) (as amended: see note 8). An employee is to be treated as having satisfied the condition in reg 4(2)(c) if he would have satisfied it but for the fact that the child was stillborn after 24 weeks of pregnancy or has died: reg 4(5).

10 See the Paternity and Adoption Leave Regulations 2002, SI 2002/2788, reg 4(1)(b). Head (2) in the text refers to the notice requirements in reg 6 (see heads (2)(a), (b) in the text): see reg 4(1)(b).

11 For these purposes, 'employer' means the person by whom an employee is, or, where the employment has ceased, was, employed: see the Paternity and Adoption Leave Regulations 2002, SI 2002/2788, reg 2(1). As to the meaning of 'employer' and related expressions in relation to employment rights generally see PARA 2.

12 The notice so provided for must be given to the employer: (1) in or before the fifteenth week before the expected week of the child's birth (Paternity and Adoption Leave Regulations 2002, SI 2002/2788, reg 6(2)(a)); or (2) in a case where it was not reasonably practicable for the employee to give the notice in accordance with head (1) above, as soon as is reasonably practicable (reg 6(2)(b)).

13 See the Paternity and Adoption Leave Regulations 2002, SI 2002/2788, reg 6(1).

14 Paternity and Adoption Leave Regulations 2002, SI 2002/2788, reg 6(1)(a).

15 Ie in accordance with the Paternity and Adoption Leave Regulations 2002, SI 2002/2788, reg 5(1): see the text and notes 21–22.

16 Paternity and Adoption Leave Regulations 2002, SI 2002/2788, reg 6(1)(b).

17 Ie in accordance with the Paternity and Adoption Leave Regulations 2002, SI 2002/2788, reg 5(3): see heads (A)–(C) in the text.

18 Paternity and Adoption Leave Regulations 2002, SI 2002/2788, reg 6(1)(c). An employee who has given notice under reg 6(1) may vary the date he has chosen as the date on which his period of leave will begin, provided that he gives his employer notice of the variation:

(1) where the variation is to provide for the employee's period of leave to begin on the date on which the child is born, at least 28 days before the first day of the expected week of the child's birth (reg 6(4)(a));

(2) where the variation is to provide for the employee's period of leave to begin on a date that is a specified number of days (or a different specified number of days) after the date on which the child is born, at least 28 days before the date falling that number of days after the first day of the expected week of the child's birth (reg 6(4)(b));

(3) where the variation is to provide for the employee's period of leave to begin on a predetermined date (or a different predetermined date), at least 28 days before that date (reg 6(4)(c)),

or, if it is not reasonably practicable to give the notice at least 28 days before whichever day or date is relevant, as soon as is reasonably practicable (see reg 6(4)). In a case where:

(a) the employee has chosen to begin his period of leave on a particular predetermined date (reg 6(6)(a)); and

(b) the child is not born on or before that date (reg 6(6)(b)),

the employee must vary his choice of date, by substituting a later predetermined date or exercising an alternative option under reg 5(3) (see heads (A)–(C) in the text), and give his employer notice of the variation as soon as is reasonably practicable (see reg 6(6)). Notices under reg 6(1), (4), (6) must be given in writing, if the employer so requests: see reg 6(8). As to the meaning of 'writing' see PARA 2 note 8.

19 Ie in the Paternity and Adoption Leave Regulations 2002, SI 2002/2788, reg 4(2)(b), (c): see heads (1)(b), (c) in the text.

20 Paternity and Adoption Leave Regulations 2002, SI 2002/2788, reg 6(3).

21 Ie under the Paternity and Adoption Leave Regulations 2002, SI 2002/2788, reg 4: see the text and notes 1–10.

22 Paternity and Adoption Leave Regulations 2002, SI 2002/2788, reg 5(1).

23 See the Paternity and Adoption Leave Regulations 2002, SI 2002/2788, reg 5(2).

24 See the Paternity and Adoption Leave Regulations 2002, SI 2002/2788, reg 5(3).

25 Paternity and Adoption Leave Regulations 2002, SI 2002/2788, reg 5(3)(a).
26 Ie in a notice under the Paternity and Adoption Leave Regulations 2002, SI 2002/2788, reg 6: see heads (2)(a), (b) in the text.
27 Paternity and Adoption Leave Regulations 2002, SI 2002/2788, reg 5(3)(b).
28 See note 26.
29 Paternity and Adoption Leave Regulations 2002, SI 2002/2788, reg 5(3)(c).
30 Ie under the Paternity and Adoption Leave Regulations 2002, SI 2002/2788, reg 6(1): see head (2)(a) in the text.
31 Ie under the Paternity and Adoption Leave Regulations 2002, SI 2002/2788, reg 6(4) or reg 6(6): see note 18.
32 Paternity and Adoption Leave Regulations 2002, SI 2002/2788, reg 7(1).
33 See the Paternity and Adoption Leave Regulations 2002, SI 2002/2788, reg 7(2).
34 Paternity and Adoption Leave Regulations 2002, SI 2002/2788, reg 6(7). Notices under reg 6(7) must be given in writing, if the employer so requests: see reg 6(8).

C. PATERNITY LEAVE UPON ADOPTION

371. Entitlement to paternity leave upon the adoption of a child. An employee[1] is entitled to be absent from work for the purpose of caring for a child[2] or supporting the child's adopter[3] if:

(1) he satisfies the following conditions[4], being that:
 (a) he has been continuously employed[5] for a period of not less than 26 weeks[6] ending with the week in which the child's adopter is notified of having been matched with the child[7];
 (b) he is either married to, the civil partner or the partner[8] of the child's adopter[9]; and
 (c) he has, or expects to have, the main responsibility, apart from the responsibility of the adopter, for the upbringing of the child[10]; and

(2) he has complied with the following requirements as to notice and, where applicable, as to evidence[11], being that:
 (a) he must give his employer[12] notice[13] of his intention to take leave in respect of a child, specifying[14]: (i) the date on which the adopter was notified of having been matched with the child[15]; (ii) the date on which the child is expected to be placed with the adopter[16]; (iii) the length of the period of leave that[17] the employee has chosen to take[18]; and (iv) the date on which[19] the employee has chosen that his period of leave should begin[20]; and
 (b) where the employer requests it, the employee must also give his employer a declaration, signed by the employee, to the effect that the purpose of his absence from work will be for the purpose of caring for a child or supporting the child's adopter and that he satisfies the conditions[21] of entitlement[22].

An employee may choose to take either one week's leave or two consecutive weeks' leave in respect of a child[23]. The leave may only be taken during the period of 56 days beginning with the date on which the child is placed with the adopter[24]. Within this period, an employee may choose to begin a period of leave on[25]:

(A) the date on which the child is placed with the adopter[26];
(B) the date falling such number of days after the date on which the child is placed with the adopter as the employee may specify[27] in a notice[28]; or
(C) a predetermined date, specified in a notice[29], which is later than the date on which the child is expected to be placed with the adopter[30].

An employee's period of paternity leave begins on the date specified in his notice[31], or, where he has varied his choice of date[32], on that date specified in his notice, or the last such date if he has varied his choice more than once[33]. However, in a case where the employee has chosen to begin his period of leave on the date on which the child is placed with the adopter, and where he is at work on that date, the employee's period of leave begins on the day after that date[34].

An employee must give his employer a further notice, as soon as is reasonably practicable after the child's placement, of the date on which the child was placed[35].

1 As to the meaning of 'employee' for these purposes see PARA 370 note 1.

2 Ie subject to the Paternity and Adoption Leave Regulations 2002, SI 2002/2788, reg 8(1A): see reg 8(1) (reg 8(1) amended, reg 8(1A) added, by SI 2014/2112). Accordingly, an employee is not entitled to be absent from work under the Paternity and Adoption Leave Regulations 2002, SI 2002/2788, reg 8(1) if the employee has taken any shared parental leave in respect of the child, or has exercised a right to take time off under the Employment Rights Act 1996 s 57ZJ (right to paid time off work to attend adoption appointments: see PARA 341) in respect of the child: Paternity and Adoption Leave Regulations 2002, SI 2002/2788, reg 8(1A) (as so added). The reference to shared parental leave has effect only from 5 April 2015, however: see the Paternity and Adoption Leave (Amendment) Regulations 2014, SI 2014/2112, reg 1(4). As to the meaning of 'child' see PARA 370 note 2. An employee's entitlement to leave under the Paternity and Adoption Leave Regulations 2002, SI 2002/2788, reg 8 is not affected by the placement for adoption of more than one child as part of the same arrangement: reg 8(6). The provisions relating to paternity leave under reg 8 have effect only in relation to children matched with a person who is notified of having been matched on or after 6 April 2003, or placed for adoption on or after that date: see reg 3(2). As to the date on which a person is notified of having been matched with a child see PARA 370 note 2.

3 As to the meaning of 'adopter' see PARA 370 note 2.

4 Paternity and Adoption Leave Regulations 2002, SI 2002/2788, reg 8(1)(a). The text refers to the conditions specified in reg 8(2) (see heads (1)(a) to (1)(c) in the text): see reg 8(1)(a). See also note 2. As to paternity leave regulations relating to adoptions from overseas see PARA 376. As to the power to make regulations in relation to shared parental leave on adoption see PARA 399.

5 As to the meaning of references to a period of continuous employment see PARA 370 note 4.

6 For this purpose, 'week' means the period of seven days beginning with Sunday: see the Paternity and Adoption Leave Regulations 2002, SI 2002/2788, reg 8(3). See also note 2.

7 Paternity and Adoption Leave Regulations 2002, SI 2002/2788, reg 8(2)(a). See also note 2.

8 As to the meaning of 'partner', in relation to a child's mother or adopter, see PARA 370 note 7.

9 Paternity and Adoption Leave Regulations 2002, SI 2002/2788, reg 8(2)(b) (amended by SI 2005/2114). An employee is to be treated as having satisfied the condition in the Paternity and Adoption Leave Regulations 2002, SI 2002/2788, reg 8(2)(b) concerning his relationship to the child's adopter if he would have satisfied it but for the fact that the child's adopter died during the child's placement: reg 8(4). See also note 2.

Marriage of same sex couples is lawful in the law of England and Wales, and such marriages have the same effect as marriages of opposite sex couples: see the Marriage (Same Sex Couples) Act 2013 s 1(1), 11(1); and **MATRIMONIAL AND CIVIL PARTNERSHIP LAW** vol 72 (2009) PARA 1 et seq.

10 Paternity and Adoption Leave Regulations 2002, SI 2002/2788, reg 8(2)(c). An employee is to be treated as having satisfied the condition in reg 8(2)(c) concerning his responsibility for the upbringing of the child if he would have satisfied it but for the fact that the child's placement with the adopter has ended: reg 8(5). See also note 2.

11 Paternity and Adoption Leave Regulations 2002, SI 2002/2788, reg 8(1)(b). The text refers to the notice requirements in reg 10 and, where applicable, the evidential requirements in reg 10 (see heads (2)(a), (b) in the text): see reg 8(1)(b). See also note 2.

12 As to the meaning of 'employer' for these purposes see PARA 370 note 11.

13 The notice so provided for must be given to the employer: (1) no more than seven days after the date on which the adopter is notified of having been matched with the child (Paternity and Adoption Leave Regulations 2002, SI 2002/2788, reg 10(2)(a)); or (2) in a case where it was not reasonably practicable for the employee to give notice in accordance with head (1) above, as soon as is reasonably practicable (reg 10(2)(b)).

14 Paternity and Adoption Leave Regulations 2002, SI 2002/2788, reg 10(1).

15 Paternity and Adoption Leave Regulations 2002, SI 2002/2788, reg 10(1)(a).

16 Paternity and Adoption Leave Regulations 2002, SI 2002/2788, reg 10(1)(b).

17 Ie in accordance with the Paternity and Adoption Leave Regulations 2002, SI 2002/2788, reg 9(1): see the text and note 23.

18 Paternity and Adoption Leave Regulations 2002, SI 2002/2788, reg 10(1)(c). An employee who has given notice under reg 10(1) may vary the date he has chosen as the date on which his period of leave will begin, provided that he gives his employer notice of the variation:

(1) where the variation is to provide for the employee's period of leave to begin on the date on which the child is placed with his adopter, at least 28 days before the date specified in the employee's notice under reg 10(1) as the date on which the child is expected to be placed with the adopter (reg 10(4)(a));

(2) where the variation is to provide for the employee's period of leave to begin on a date that is a specified number of days (or a different specified number of days) after the date on which the child is placed with the adopter, at least 28 days before the date falling that number of days after the date specified in the employee's notice under reg 10(1) as the date on which the child is expected to be placed with the adopter (reg 10(4)(b));

(3) where the variation is to provide for the employee's period of leave to begin on a predetermined date, at least 28 days before that date (reg 10(4)(c)),

or, if it is not reasonably practicable to give the notice at least 28 days before whichever date is relevant, as soon as is reasonably practicable (see reg 10(4)). In a case where:

(a) the employee has chosen to begin his period of leave on a particular predetermined date (reg 10(6)(a)); and

(b) the child is not placed with the adopter on or before that date (reg 10(6)(b)),

the employee must vary his choice of date, by substituting a later predetermined date or exercising an alternative option under reg 9(3) (see heads (A)–(C) in the text), and give his employer notice of the variation as soon as is reasonably practicable (see reg 10(6)). Notices under reg 10(1), (4), (6) must be given in writing, if the employer so requests: see reg 10(8). As to the meaning of 'writing' see PARA 2 note 8.

19 Ie in accordance with the Paternity and Adoption Leave Regulations 2002, SI 2002/2788, reg 9(3): see heads (A)–(C) in the text.

20 Paternity and Adoption Leave Regulations 2002, SI 2002/2788, reg 10(1)(d).

21 Ie in the Paternity and Adoption Leave Regulations 2002, SI 2002/2788, reg 8(2)(b), (c): see heads (1)(b), (c) in the text.

22 Paternity and Adoption Leave Regulations 2002, SI 2002/2788, reg 10(3).

23 Paternity and Adoption Leave Regulations 2002, SI 2002/2788, reg 9(1).

24 Paternity and Adoption Leave Regulations 2002, SI 2002/2788, reg 9(2).

25 See the Paternity and Adoption Leave Regulations 2002, SI 2002/2788, reg 9(3).

26 Paternity and Adoption Leave Regulations 2002, SI 2002/2788, reg 9(3)(a).

27 Ie under the Paternity and Adoption Leave Regulations 2002, SI 2002/2788, reg 10: see head (2)(a) in the text.

28 Paternity and Adoption Leave Regulations 2002, SI 2002/2788, reg 9(3)(b).

29 See note 27.

30 Paternity and Adoption Leave Regulations 2002, SI 2002/2788, reg 9(3)(c).

31 See note 27.

32 Ie under the Paternity and Adoption Leave Regulations 2002, SI 2002/2788, reg 10(4) or (6): see note 18.

33 Paternity and Adoption Leave Regulations 2002, SI 2002/2788, reg 11(1).

34 Paternity and Adoption Leave Regulations 2002, SI 2002/2788, reg 11(2).

35 Paternity and Adoption Leave Regulations 2002, SI 2002/2788, reg 10(7). Notices under reg 10(7) must be given in writing, if the employer so requests: see reg 10(8).

D. COMMON PROVISIONS

372. Application of terms and conditions during paternity leave. An employee[1] who takes paternity leave[2]:

(1) is entitled, during the period of leave, to the benefit of all of the terms and conditions of employment[3] which would have applied if he had not been absent[4]; and

(2) is bound, during that period, by any obligations arising[5] under those terms and conditions[6].

Where an employee is entitled to paternity leave[7] (the 'statutory right'), and also to a right which corresponds to that right and which arises under the employee's contract of employment or otherwise[8]:

(a) the employee may not exercise the statutory right and the corresponding right separately but may, in taking the leave for which the two rights provide, take advantage of whichever right is, in any particular respect, the more favourable[9]; and

(b) the provisions relating to the statutory right[10] apply, subject to any modifications necessary to give effect to any more favourable contractual terms, to the exercise of the composite right described in head (a) above as they apply to the exercise of the statutory right[11].

1 As to the meaning of 'employee' for these purposes see PARA 370 note 1.
2 For these purposes, 'paternity leave' means leave under the Paternity and Adoption Leave Regulations 2002, SI 2002/2788, reg 4 (see PARA 370) or reg 8 (see PARA 371): see reg 2(1). As to the power to make regulations in relation to shared parental leave on adoption see PARA 399.
3 For these purposes, 'terms and conditions of employment' has the meaning given by the Employment Rights Act 1996 s 80C(5) (see PARA 368 note 10), and accordingly does not include terms and conditions about remuneration: see the Paternity and Adoption Leave Regulations 2002, SI 2002/2788, reg 12(2). For the purposes of the Employment Rights Act 1996 s 80C, only sums payable to an employee by way of wages or salary are to be treated as remuneration: see the Paternity and Adoption Leave Regulations 2002, SI 2002/2788, reg 12(3).
4 Paternity and Adoption Leave Regulations 2002, SI 2002/2788, reg 12(1)(a).
5 Ie subject only to the exception in the Employment Rights Act 1996 s 80C(1)(b): see PARAS 368, 369.
6 Paternity and Adoption Leave Regulations 2002, SI 2002/2788, reg 12(1)(b).
7 See the Paternity and Adoption Leave Regulations 2002, SI 2002/2788, reg 30(1)(a).
8 See the Paternity and Adoption Leave Regulations 2002, SI 2002/2788, reg 30(1). As to the meaning of 'contract of employment' see PARA 370 note 1.
9 Paternity and Adoption Leave Regulations 2002, SI 2002/2788, reg 30(2)(a).
10 Ie the provisions of the Employment Rights Act 1996 and of the Paternity and Adoption Leave Regulations 2002, SI 2002/2788.
11 Paternity and Adoption Leave Regulations 2002, SI 2002/2788, reg 30(2)(b).

373. Right to return after paternity leave. An employee[1] who returns to work after a period of paternity leave[2] which was:

(1) an isolated period of leave[3]; or

(2) the last of two or more consecutive periods of statutory leave[4] which did not include any period of parental leave[5] of more than four weeks[6], or any period of statutory leave which when added to any other periods of statutory leave (excluding parental leave) taken in relation to the same child means that the total amount of statutory leave taken in relation to that child totals more than 26 weeks[7],

is entitled to return from leave to the job in which he was employed before his absence[8]. An employee who returns to work after a period of paternity leave not falling within head (1) or head (2) above is entitled to return from leave to the job in which he was employed before his absence (or, if it is not reasonably practicable for the employer to permit him to return to that job, to another job which is both suitable for him and appropriate for him to do in the circumstances)[9].

In these circumstances, an employee's right to return[10] is a right to return:

(a) with his seniority, pension rights and similar rights: (i) in a case where the employee is returning from consecutive periods of statutory leave which included a period of additional adoption leave or additional maternity leave, as they would have been if the period or periods of his employment prior to the additional adoption leave or, as the case may be, additional maternity leave were continuous with the period of employment following it[11]; and (ii) in any other case, as they would have been if he had not been absent[12]; and

(b) on terms and conditions not less favourable than those which would have applied if he had not been absent[13].

1 As to the meaning of 'employee' for these purposes see PARA 370 note 1.
2 As to the meaning of 'paternity leave' see PARA 372 note 2. As to the power to make regulations in relation to shared parental leave on adoption see PARA 399.
3 Paternity and Adoption Leave Regulations 2002, SI 2002/2788, reg 13(1)(a).
4 For these purposes, 'statutory leave' means leave provided for in the Employment Rights Act 1996 Pt VIII (ss 71–80I) (see PARA 355 et seq): see the Paternity and Adoption Leave Regulations 2002, SI 2002/2788, reg 2(1). As to the right to return after periods of statutory leave see also PARAS 361, 362, 382, 383, 395.
5 For these purposes, 'parental leave' means leave under the Maternity and Parental Leave etc Regulations 1999, SI 1999/3312, reg 13(1) (see PARA 391): see the Paternity and Adoption Leave Regulations 2002, SI 2002/2788, reg 2(1).
6 Paternity and Adoption Leave Regulations 2002, SI 2002/2788, reg 13(1)(b)(i) (reg 13(1)(b) substituted by SI 2014/2112).
7 Paternity and Adoption Leave Regulations 2002, SI 2002/2788, reg 13(1)(b)(ii) (as substituted: see note 6).
8 See the Paternity and Adoption Leave Regulations 2002, SI 2002/2788, reg 13(1). The reference in reg 13(1), (2) (see also the text and note 9) to the job in which an employee was employed before his absence is a reference to the job in which he was employed: (1) if his return is from an isolated period of paternity leave, immediately before that period began (reg 13(3)(a)); (2) if his return is from consecutive periods of statutory leave, immediately before the first such period (reg 13(3)(b)).
9 Paternity and Adoption Leave Regulations 2002, SI 2002/2788, reg 13(2). See note 8.
10 Ie under the Paternity and Adoption Leave Regulations 2002, SI 2002/2788, reg 13: see the text and notes 1–9.
11 Paternity and Adoption Leave Regulations 2002, SI 2002/2788, reg 14(1)(a)(i). The provision in reg 14(a)(i) concerning the treatment of periods of additional maternity leave or additional adoption leave is subject to the requirements of the Social Security Act 1989 Sch 5 para 5 (repealed), Sch 5 para 5B (unfair adoption leave provisions), Sch 5 para 6 (unfair family leave provisions) (see **PERSONAL AND OCCUPATIONAL PENSIONS** vol 80 (2013) PARA 303): Paternity and Adoption Leave Regulations 2002, SI 2002/2788, reg 14(2) (amended by SI 2005/275).
12 Paternity and Adoption Leave Regulations 2002, SI 2002/2788, reg 14(1)(a)(ii). The provisions in reg 14(1)(a)(ii) and reg 14(1)(b) (see head (b) in the text) for an employee to be treated as if he had not been absent refers to his absence: (1) if his return is from an isolated period of paternity leave, since the beginning of that period (reg 14(3)(a)); (2) if his return is from consecutive periods of statutory leave, since the beginning of the first such period (reg 14(3)(b)).
13 Paternity and Adoption Leave Regulations 2002, SI 2002/2788, reg 14(1)(b). See note 12.

374. Calculation of a week's pay in paternity leave cases. Where:

(1) under the provisions of the Employment Rights Act 1996 that relate to the calculation of a week's pay[1], the amount of a week's pay of an employee[2] falls to be calculated by reference to the average rate of remuneration, or the average amount of remuneration, payable to the employee in respect of a period of 12 weeks ending on a particular date (the 'calculation date')[3];

(2) during a week in that period, the employee was absent from work on paternity leave[4]; and

(3) remuneration is payable to the employee in respect of that week under his contract of employment[5], but the amount payable is less than the amount that would be payable if he were working[6],

by the Paternity and Adoption Leave (Adoption from Overseas) Regulations 2003, SI 2003/921, reg 4(1), (2)(a)). For these purposes, 'enters Great Britain' means to enter Great Britain from outside the United Kingdom in connection with or for the purposes of adoption; and cognate expressions must be construed accordingly: Paternity and Adoption Leave Regulations 2002, SI 2002/2788, reg 2(1) (definition added by the Paternity and Adoption Leave (Adoption from Overseas) Regulations 2003, SI 2003/921, reg 4(1), (2)(b)). For these purposes, in a case where a child is to be adopted by two people jointly, a person elects to be a child's adopter, if he and the other person agree, at the time when the official notification is received, that he and not the other person will be the adopter: Paternity and Adoption Leave Regulations 2002, SI 2002/2788, reg 2(4) (substituted by the Paternity and Adoption Leave (Adoption from Overseas) Regulations 2003, SI 2003/921, reg 4(1), (3)). 'Official notification' means written notification, issued by or on behalf of the relevant domestic authority, that it is prepared to issue a certificate to the overseas authority concerned with the adoption of the child, or has issued a certificate and sent it to that authority, confirming, in either case, that the adopter is eligible to adopt and has been assessed and approved as being a suitable adoptive parent; and 'relevant domestic authority' means: (1) in the case of an adopter to whom the Intercountry Adoption (Hague Convention) Regulations 2003, SI 2003/118 (see now the Adoptions with a Foreign Element Regulations 2005, SI 2005/392) apply (see **CHILDREN AND YOUNG PERSONS** vol 9 (2012) PARA 529 et seq) and who is habitually resident in Wales, the National Assembly for Wales; and (2) in any other case, the Secretary of State: Paternity and Adoption Leave Regulations 2002, SI 2002/2788, reg 2(1) (definitions added by the Paternity and Adoption Leave (Adoption from Overseas) Regulations 2003, SI 2003/921, reg 4(1), (2)(b)). As to habitual residence see **CONFLICT OF LAWS** vol 19 (2011) PARA 360 et seq. As to the meaning of 'Wales' see PARA 2 note 12. As to the National Assembly for Wales see **CONSTITUTIONAL AND ADMINISTRATIVE LAW** vol 20 (2014) PARA 351 et seq. As to the Secretary of State see PARA 5 note 21.

Marriage of same sex couples is lawful in the law of England and Wales, and such marriages have the same effect as marriages of opposite sex couples: see the Marriage (Same Sex Couples) Act 2013 s 1(1), 11(1); and **MATRIMONIAL AND CIVIL PARTNERSHIP LAW** vol 72 (2009) PARA 1 et seq.

16 Paternity and Adoption Leave Regulations 2002, SI 2002/2788, reg 8(1)(a) (as substituted: see note 15). The text refers to the conditions specified in reg 8(2) (see heads (a)(i) to (a)(iv) in the text): see reg 8(1)(a) (as so substituted).

17 Paternity and Adoption Leave Regulations 2002, SI 2002/2788, reg 8(2)(a) (as substituted: see note 15).

18 As to the meaning of references to a period of continuous employment see PARA 370 note 4.

19 For these purposes, 'week' means the period of seven days beginning with Sunday: Paternity and Adoption Leave Regulations 2002, SI 2002/2788, reg 8(3) (as substituted: see note 15).

20 As to the meaning of 'employer' for these purposes see PARA 370 note 11.

21 Paternity and Adoption Leave Regulations 2002, SI 2002/2788, reg 8(2)(b) (as substituted: see note 15).

22 Paternity and Adoption Leave Regulations 2002, SI 2002/2788, reg 8(2)(c) (reg 8 as substituted (see note 15); reg 8(2)(c) amended by SI 2005/2114). An employee is treated as having satisfied the condition in the Paternity and Adoption Leave Regulations 2002, SI 2002/2788, reg 8(2)(c) if he would have satisfied it but for the fact that the child's adopter died during the period of 56 days commencing with the date on which the child entered Great Britain: reg 8(4) (as so substituted). See note 16.

23 Paternity and Adoption Leave Regulations 2002, SI 2002/2788, reg 8(2)(d) (as substituted: see note 15). An employee is treated as having satisfied the condition in reg 8(2)(d) if he would have satisfied it but for the fact that the child has ceased to live with the adopter: reg 8(5) (as so substituted).

24 Paternity and Adoption Leave Regulations 2002, SI 2002/2788, reg 8(1)(b) (as substituted: see note 15). The text refers to the notice requirements in reg 10 and, where applicable, the evidential requirements in reg 10 (see heads (b)(i), (b)(ii) in the text): see reg 8(1)(b) (as so substituted).

25 See the Paternity and Adoption Leave Regulations 2002, SI 2002/2788, reg 10(1) (as substituted: see note 15). Notice provided for:

(1) in heads (b)(i)(A), (B) in the text must be given to the employer no more than 28 days after the date on which the adopter of the child receives the official notification or the date on which he completes 26 weeks' continuous employment with the employer, whichever is later (reg 10(2)(a) (as so substituted));

(2) in head (b)(i)(C) in the text must be given to the employer at least 28 days prior to the

date which the employee has chosen as the date on which his period of paternity leave should begin (reg 10(2)(b) (as so substituted)); and
(3) in head (b)(i)(D) in the text must be given to the employer no more than 28 days after the date on which the child enters Great Britain (reg 10(2)(c) (as so substituted)).
Such notice must be given in writing, if the employer so requests: reg 10(5) (as so substituted). As to the meaning of 'writing' see PARA 2 note 8.

26 Ie in the Paternity and Adoption Leave Regulations 2002, SI 2002/2788, reg 8(2)(c) (see head (a)(iii) in the text) and reg 8(2)(d) (see head (a)(iv) in the text).
27 Paternity and Adoption Leave Regulations 2002, SI 2002/2788, reg 10(3) (reg 10 as substituted (see note 15); reg 10(3) amended by SI 2005/2114).
28 Paternity and Adoption Leave Regulations 2002, SI 2002/2788, reg 9(1) (as substituted: see note 15).
29 Paternity and Adoption Leave Regulations 2002, SI 2002/2788, reg 9(2) (as substituted: see note 15).
30 Ie under the Paternity and Adoption Leave Regulations 2002, SI 2002/2788, reg 10: see head (b)(i) in the text.
31 Paternity and Adoption Leave Regulations 2002, SI 2002/2788, reg 9(3) (as substituted: see note 15). A choice made under reg 9(3) is not irrevocable but where an employee subsequently makes a different choice the notification requirements contained in reg 10(1)(c) (see head (b)(i)(C) in the text) and reg 10(2)(b) (see note 25) apply to that choice: reg 10(4) (as so substituted). In a case where the employee receives an official notification before 6 April 2003 and the adopter's child enters Great Britain on or after that date, the employee may choose to begin a period of paternity leave only on a predetermined date, specified in a notice under reg 10, which is later than the date of entry, and (unless the employer agrees to an earlier commencement of the leave period) is at least 28 days after the date on which that notice was given: reg 9(4) (as so substituted).
32 Paternity and Adoption Leave Regulations 2002, SI 2002/2788, reg 10(6) (as substituted: see note 15).
33 Ie the Paternity and Adoption Leave Regulations 2002, SI 2002/2788, reg 11: see PARA 371.
34 Accordingly, an employee's period of paternity leave under the Paternity and Adoption Leave Regulations 2002, SI 2002/2788, reg 8 (see the text and notes 15–24) begins on the date specified in his notice under reg 10(1) (see head (b)(i) in the text), or, where he has varied his choice of date under reg 10(4) or (6) (see the text and notes 30–32), on that date specified in his notice, or the last such date if he has varied his choice more than once: reg 11(1). However, in a case where the employee has chosen to begin his period of leave on the date on which the child enters Great Britain, and where he is at work on that date, the employee's period of leave begins on the day after that date: reg 11(2) (modified by the Paternity and Adoption Leave (Adoption from Overseas) Regulations 2003, SI 2003/921, reg 8).
35 Ie the Paternity and Adoption Leave Regulations 2002, SI 2002/2788, regs 4–7: see PARA 370.
36 Paternity and Adoption Leave (Adoption from Overseas) Regulations 2003, SI 2003/921, reg 6.

(iv) Adoption Leave

A. POWER TO MAKE REGULATIONS

377. Power to make regulations in relation to ordinary and additional adoption leave. The Secretary of State[1] may make regulations[2] in relation to ordinary adoption leave[3]:

(1) setting prescribed[4] conditions which an employee must satisfy to be absent from work at any time during an ordinary adoption leave period[5];
(2) for calculating an ordinary adoption leave period[6];
(3) providing that[7] an employee who exercises his right to be absent from work at any time during an ordinary adoption leave period[8]:
    (a) is entitled, for such purposes and to such extent as may be prescribed, to the benefit of the terms and conditions of employment[9] which would have applied if he had not been absent[10];

(b) is bound, for such purposes and to such extent as may be prescribed, by any obligations arising[11] under those terms and conditions[12]; and

(c) is entitled to return from leave[13] to a job[14] of such kind as may be prescribed[15];

(4) specifying matters which are, or are not, to be treated as remuneration for the purposes of ordinary adoption leave[16].

The Secretary of State may make regulations in relation to additional adoption leave[17]:

(i) setting prescribed conditions which an employee must satisfy to be absent from work at any time during an additional adoption leave period[18];

(ii) for calculating an additional adoption leave period[19];

(iii) allowing an employee to bring forward the date on which an additional adoption leave period ends, subject to prescribed restrictions and subject to satisfying prescribed conditions[20]; allowing an employee in prescribed circumstances to revoke, or to be treated as revoking, the bringing forward of that date[21]; and specifying circumstances in which an employee may work for his employer during an additional adoption leave period without bringing the period to an end[22];

(iv) providing that[23] an employee who exercises his right to be absent from work at any time during an additional adoption leave period[24]:

(A) is entitled, for such purposes and to such extent as may be prescribed, to the benefit of the terms and conditions of employment[25] which would have applied if he had not been absent[26];

(B) is bound, for such purposes and to such extent as may be prescribed, by any obligations arising[27] under those terms and conditions[28]; and

(C) is entitled to return from leave[29] to a job of such kind as may be prescribed[30];

(v) specifying matters which are, or are not, to be treated as remuneration for the purposes of additional adoption leave[31].

Such regulations[32] may:

(aa) make provision about redundancy[33] during an ordinary or additional adoption leave period[34];

(bb) make provision about dismissal (other than by reason of redundancy) during an ordinary or additional adoption leave period[35];

(cc) make provision disapplying the entitlement to return from leave to a similar job[36] in specified cases, and about dismissal at the conclusion of an ordinary or additional adoption leave period[37];

(dd) make provision about notices to be given, evidence to be produced and other procedures to be followed by employees and employers[38];

(ee) make provision requiring employers or employees to keep records[39];

(ff) make provision for the consequences of failure to give notices, to produce evidence, to keep records or to comply with other procedural requirements[40];

(gg) make provision for the consequences of failure to act in accordance with a notice given by virtue of head (dd) above[41];

(hh) make special provision for cases where an employee has a right which corresponds to a right relating to adoption leave[42] and which arises under his contract of employment or otherwise[43];

(ii) make provision modifying the effect of the statutory provisions relating to calculating a week's pay[44] in relation to an employee who is or has been absent from work on ordinary or additional adoption leave[45];

(jj) make provision applying, modifying or excluding an enactment, in such circumstances as may be specified and subject to any conditions specified, in relation to a person entitled to ordinary or additional adoption leave[46];

(kk) make different provision for different cases or circumstances[47].

1 As to the Secretary of State see PARA 5 note 21.

2 As to the making of regulations under the Employment Rights Act 1996 generally see PARA 162. In exercise of the powers conferred by ss 75A(1)–(3), (6), (7), 75B(1), (2), (4), (8), 75C(1), (2), 75D(1), the Secretary of State has made the Paternity and Adoption Leave Regulations 2002, SI 2002/2788 (see PARA 378 et seq) and the Paternity and Adoption Leave (Adoption from Overseas) Regulations 2003, SI 2003/921 (see PARA 389). As to the power to make regulations in relation to shared parental leave on adoption see PARA 399.

3 As to ordinary adoption leave see PARA 378.

4 For the purposes of the Employment Rights Act 1996 s 75A (see heads (1)–(4) in the text) and s 75B (see heads (i)–(v) in the text), 'prescribed' means prescribed by regulations made by the Secretary of State: s 75D(2) (ss 75A–75D added by the Employment Act 2002 s 3). The conditions that may be prescribed under the Employment Rights Act 1996 s 75A(1) include conditions as to:

(1) being a local authority foster parent (s 75A(1A)(a) (s 75A as so added; s 75A(1A) added by the Children and Families Act 2014 s 121(1)));

(2) being approved as a prospective adopter (Employment Rights Act 1996 s 75A(1A)(b) (as so added));

(3) being notified by a local authority in England that a child is to be, or is expected to be, placed with the employee under the Children Act 1989 s 22C (local authority's duty to provide child is in its care with accommodation: see **CHILDREN AND YOUNG PERSONS** vol 10 (2012) PARA 858) (Employment Rights Act 1996 s 75A(1A)(c) (as so added)).

The Secretary of State may by regulations provide for s 75A to have effect in relation to cases which involve an employee who has applied, or intends to apply, with another person for a parental order under the Human Fertilisation and Embryology Act 2008 s 54 (parental orders: see **CHILDREN AND YOUNG PERSONS** vol 9 (2012) PARA 129) and a child who is, or will be, the subject of the order, with such modifications as the regulations may prescribe: Employment Rights Act 1996 s 75A(8) (s 75A as so added; s 75A(8) added by the Children and Families Act 2014 s 122(1)). Where the Employment Rights Act 1996 s 75A has effect in relation to such cases as are described in s 75A(8), regulations under s 75A about evidence to be produced may require statutory declarations as to eligibility to apply for a parental order or intention to apply for such an order: s 75D(1A) (s 75D as so added; s 75D(1A) added by the Children and Families Act 2014 s 122(3)). As to the meaning of 'employee' see PARA 2. As to the meaning of 'England' see PARA 2 note 12. As to the meaning of 'local authority foster parent' see **CHILDREN AND YOUNG PERSONS** vol 10 (2012) PARA 845.

5 See the Employment Rights Act 1996 s 75A(1) (as added: see note 4).

6 See the Employment Rights Act 1996 s 75A(2) (as added: see note 4). Regulations under s 75A(2) may:

(1) allow an employee to bring forward the date on which an ordinary adoption leave period ends, subject to prescribed restrictions and subject to satisfying prescribed conditions (s 75A(2A)(a) (s 75A as so added; s 75A(2A) added by the Work and Families Act 2006 Sch 1 para 33; and amended by the Children and Families Act 2014 s 118(1), (4)(a), (b)));

(2) allow an employee in prescribed circumstances to revoke, or to be treated as revoking, the bringing forward of that date (Employment Rights Act 1996 s 75A(2A)(b) (as so added and amended));

(3) specify circumstances in which an employee may work for his employer during an ordinary adoption leave period without bringing the period to an end (s 75A(2A)(c) (as so added and amended)).

Provision under head (1) above is to secure that an employee may bring forward the date on which an ordinary adoption leave period ends only if the employee or another person has taken, or is taking, prescribed steps as regards leave under s 75G (see PARA 399) or statutory shared parental pay (see PARA 534) in respect of the child: s 75A(2B) (s 75A as so added; s 75A(2B) added by the Children and Families Act 2014 s 118(1), (4)(c))).

7 Ie subject to the Employment Rights Act 1996 s 75C: see heads (aa)–(cc) in the text.

8 Ie under the Employment Rights Act 1996 s 75A(1): see head (1) in the text.

9 For the purposes of head (3)(a) in the text, 'terms and conditions of employment' includes matters connected with an employee's employment, whether or not they arise under a contract of employment, but does not include terms and conditions about remuneration: see the Employment Rights Act 1996 s 75A(4) (as added: see note 4). As to the meanings of 'employment' and 'contract of employment' see PARA 2.

10 Employment Rights Act 1996 s 75A(3)(a) (as added: see note 4).

11 Ie except in so far as they are inconsistent with the Employment Rights Act 1996 s 75A(1): see head (1) in the text.

12 Employment Rights Act 1996 s 75A(3)(b) (as added: see note 4).

13 For the purposes of head (3)(c) in the text, the reference to return from leave includes, where appropriate, a reference to a continuous period of absence attributable partly to ordinary adoption leave and partly to maternity leave: see the Employment Rights Act 1996 s 75A(5) (as added: see note 4). As to maternity leave see PARA 355 et seq.

14 As to the meaning of 'job' see PARA 119 note 17.

15 Employment Rights Act 1996 s 75A(3)(c) (as added: see note 4). The Secretary of State may make regulations making provision, in relation to the right to return under s 75A(3)(c) about seniority, pension rights and similar rights and terms and conditions of employment on return: s 75A(7) (as so added).

16 Employment Rights Act 1996 s 75A(6) (as added: see note 4).

17 As to entitlement to additional adoption leave see PARA 379. The Secretary of State may by regulations provide for the Employment Rights Act 1996 s 75B to have effect in relation to cases which involve an employee who has applied, or intends to apply, with another person for a parental order under the Human Fertilisation and Embryology Act 2008 s 54 (parental orders: see **CHILDREN AND YOUNG PERSONS** vol 9 (2012) PARA 129) and a child who is, or will be, the subject of the order, with such modifications as the regulations may prescribe: Employment Rights Act 1996 s 75B(9) (s 75B as added (see note 4); s 75B(9) added by the Children and Families Act 2014 s 122(2)). Where the Employment Rights Act 1996 s 75B has effect in relation to such cases as are described in s 75B(9), regulations under s 75B about evidence to be produced may require statutory declarations as to eligibility to apply for a parental order or intention to apply for such an order: s 75D(1A) (as added: see note 4).

18 Employment Rights Act 1996 s 75B(1) (as added: see note 4).

19 Employment Rights Act 1996 s 75B(2) (as added: see note 4).

20 Employment Rights Act 1996 s 75B(3)(a) (s 75B as added (see note 4); s 75B(3) substituted by the Work and Families Act 2006 Sch 1 para 34; the Employment Rights Act 1996 s 75B(3)(a) amended by the Children and Families Act 2014 s 118(1), (5)(a)). Provision under the Employment Rights Act 1996 s 75B(3)(a) is to secure that an employee may bring forward the date on which an additional adoption leave period ends only if the employee or another person has taken, or is taking, prescribed steps as regards leave under s 75G (see PARA 399) or statutory shared parental pay (see PARA 534) in respect of the child: s 75B(3A) (s 75B as so added; s 75B(3A) added by the Children and Families Act 2014 s 118(1), (5)(c)).

21 Employment Rights Act 1996 s 75B(3)(aa) (s 75B as added (see note 4); s 75B(3) as substituted (see note 20); s 75B(3)(aa) added by the Children and Families Act 2014 s 118(1), (5)(b)).

22 Employment Rights Act 1996 s 75B(3)(b) (s 75B as added (see note 4); s 75B(3) as substituted (see note 20)).

23 Ie subject to the Employment Rights Act 1996 s 75C: see heads (aa)–(cc) in the text.

24 Ie under the Employment Rights Act 1996 s 75B(1): see head (i) in the text.

25 For the purposes of head (iv)(A) in the text, 'terms and conditions of employment' includes matters connected with an employee's employment, whether or not they arise under a contract of employment, but does not include terms and conditions about remuneration: see the Employment Rights Act 1996 s 75B(5) (as added: see note 4).

26 Employment Rights Act 1996 s 75B(4)(a) (as added: see note 4).

27 Ie except in so far as they are inconsistent with the Employment Rights Act 1996 s 75B(1): see head (i) in the text.

28 Employment Rights Act 1996 s 75B(4)(b) (as added: see note 4).

29 For the purposes of head (iv)(C) in the text, the reference to return from leave includes, where appropriate, a reference to a continuous period of absence attributable partly to additional adoption leave and partly to maternity leave, or to ordinary adoption leave, or to both: see the Employment Rights Act 1996 s 75B(6) (as added: see note 4).

30 Employment Rights Act 1996 s 75B(4)(c) (as added: see note 4). The Secretary of State may make regulations making provision, in relation to the right to return under s 75B(4)(c) about seniority, pension rights and similar rights and about terms and conditions of employment on return: see s 75B(8) (as so added).
31 Employment Rights Act 1996 s 75B(7) (as added: see note 4).
32 Ie regulations under the Employment Rights Act 1996 s 75A (see heads (1)–(4) in the text) or s 75B (see heads (i)–(v) in the text).
33 As to the meaning of 'redundancy' see PARA 870.
34 Employment Rights Act 1996 s 75C(1)(a) (as added: see note 4). Regulations made by virtue of the Employment Rights Act 1996 s 75C(1) may include provision requiring an employer to offer suitable alternative employment, and may include provision for the consequences of failure to comply with the regulations (which may include provision for a dismissal to be treated as unfair for the purposes of Pt X (ss 94–134A) (unfair dismissal: see PARA 757 et seq)): see s 75C(2) (as so added).
35 Employment Rights Act 1996 s 75C(1)(b) (as added: see note 4). See also note 34.
36 Ie to make provision for the Employment Rights Act 1996 s 75A(3)(c) (see head (3)(c) in the text) or s 75B(4)(c) (see head (iv)(C) in the text) not to apply in specified cases.
37 Employment Rights Act 1996 s 75C(3) (as added: see note 4).
38 Employment Rights Act 1996 s 75D(1)(a) (as added: see note 4).
39 Employment Rights Act 1996 s 75D(1)(b) (as added: see note 4).
40 Employment Rights Act 1996 s 75D(1)(c) (as added: see note 4).
41 Employment Rights Act 1996 s 75D(1)(d) (as added: see note 4).
42 Ie a right under the Employment Rights Act 1996 Pt VIII Ch IA (ss 75A–75D): see heads (1)–(4), (i)–(v), (aa)–(kk) in the text.
43 Employment Rights Act 1996 s 75D(1)(e) (as added: see note 4).
44 Ie modifying the effect of the Employment Rights Act 1996 Pt XIV Ch II (ss 220–229): see PARA 143 et seq.
45 Employment Rights Act 1996 s 75D(1)(f) (as added: see note 4).
46 Employment Rights Act 1996 s 75D(1)(g) (as added: see note 4).
47 Employment Rights Act 1996 s 75D(1)(h) (as added: see note 4).

B. ORDINARY AND ADDITIONAL ADOPTION LEAVE

378. Entitlement to ordinary adoption leave. An employee[1] is entitled to ordinary adoption leave[2] in respect of a child[3] if:

(1) he satisfies the following conditions[4], being that:
   (a) he is the child's adopter[5]; and
   (b) he has notified the agency that he agrees that the child should be placed with him and on the date of placement[6]; and
(2) he has complied with the following requirements as to notice and, where applicable, as to evidence[7], being that:
   (a) he must give his employer[8] notice[9] of his intention to take ordinary adoption leave in respect of a child, specifying[10] the date on which the child is expected to be placed with him for adoption[11], and the date on which[12] the employee has chosen that his period of leave should begin[13]; and
   (b) where the employer requests it, the employee must also provide his employer with evidence, in the form of one or more documents issued by the adoption agency that matched the employee with the child, of: (i) the name and address of the agency; (ii) the date on which the employee was notified that he had been matched with the child; and (iii) the date on which the agency expects to place the child with the employee[14].

An employee may choose to begin a period of ordinary adoption leave on the date on which the child is placed with him for adoption, or on a predetermined date, specified in a notice[15], which is no more than 14 days before the date on which the child is expected to be placed with the employee and no later than that date[16].

An employee's ordinary adoption leave period is[17] a period of 26 weeks[18]. An employee's ordinary adoption leave period begins on the date specified[19] in his notice[20], except where the employee has chosen to begin his period of leave on the date on which the child is placed with him, and he is at work on that date, in which case the employee's period of leave begins on the day after that date[21].

An employer who is given notice[22] of the date on which an employee has chosen that his period of ordinary adoption leave should begin must notify the employee, within 28 days of his receipt of the notice, of the date on which the period of additional adoption leave[23] to which the employee will be entitled[24] after his period of ordinary adoption leave ends[25].

Where an employee is dismissed after an ordinary adoption leave period has begun, but before the time when that period would otherwise[26] end, the period ends at the time of the dismissal[27].

1 As to the meaning of 'employee' for these purposes see PARA 370 note 1.

2 For these purposes, 'ordinary adoption leave' means leave under the Employment Rights Act 1996 s 75A (see PARA 377): see the Paternity and Adoption Leave Regulations 2002, SI 2002/2788, reg 2(1). As to ordinary adoption leave in relation to overseas adoptions see PARA 389.

3 See the Paternity and Adoption Leave Regulations 2002, SI 2002/2788, reg 15(1). An employee's entitlement to leave under reg 15 (see heads (1), (2) in the text) is not affected by the placement for adoption of more than one child as part of the same arrangement: reg 15(4). As to the meaning of 'child' see PARA 370 note 2.

The provisions relating to adoption leave under reg 15 have effect only in relation to children matched with a person who is notified of having been matched on or after 6 April 2003, or placed for adoption on or after that date: see reg 3(2). For these purposes, a person is notified of having been matched with a child on the date on which he receives notification of the agency's decision under the Adoption Agencies Regulations 2005, SI 2005/389, reg 33(3)(a) or the Adoption Agencies (Wales) Regulations 2005, SI 2005/1313, reg 28(3) (see **CHILDREN AND YOUNG PERSONS** vol 9 (2012) PARAS 478–482): Paternity and Adoption Leave Regulations 2002, SI 2002/2788, reg 2(4)(b) (amended by SI 2014/2112). As to the meaning of references to a person being matched with a child for adoption see PARA 370 note 2. As to the modification of the Paternity and Adoption Leave Regulations 2002, SI 2002/2788, regs 15–17 in relation to overseas adoption see PARA 389.

4 Paternity and Adoption Leave Regulations 2002, SI 2002/2788, reg 15(1)(a). The text refers to the conditions specified in reg 15(2) (see heads (1)(a), (1)(b) in the text): see reg 15(1)(a).

5 Paternity and Adoption Leave Regulations 2002, SI 2002/2788, reg 15(2)(a). As to the meaning of 'adopter', in relation to a child, see PARA 370 note 2. The provision made by reg 15(2)(b), (3) continues to have effect until 5 April 2015, however: see the Paternity and Adoption Leave (Amendment) Regulations 2014, SI 2014/2112, reg 1(4).

6 Paternity and Adoption Leave Regulations 2002, SI 2002/2788, reg 15(2)(c). As to the meaning of 'adoption agency' see PARA 370 note 2.

7 Paternity and Adoption Leave Regulations 2002, SI 2002/2788, reg 15(1)(b). The text refers to the notice requirements in reg 17 and, where applicable, the evidential requirements in reg 17 (see heads (2)(a), (2)(b) in the text): see reg 15(1)(b).

8 As to the meaning of 'employer' for these purposes see PARA 370 note 11.

9 The notice provided for under head (2)(a) in the text must be given to the employer:

(1) no more than seven days after the date on which the employee is notified of having been matched with the child for the purposes of adoption (Paternity and Adoption Leave Regulations 2002, SI 2002/2788, reg 17(2)(a)); or

(2) in a case where it was not reasonably practicable for the employee to give notice in accordance with head (1) above, as soon as is reasonably practicable (reg 17(2)(b)).

Such notice must be given in writing, if the employer so requests: see reg 17(6). See note 3.

10 Paternity and Adoption Leave Regulations 2002, SI 2002/2788, reg 17(1).

11 Paternity and Adoption Leave Regulations 2002, SI 2002/2788, reg 17(1)(a).

12 Ie in accordance with the Paternity and Adoption Leave Regulations 2002, SI 2002/2788, reg 16(1) or (2) (see the text and notes 15–16).

13 Paternity and Adoption Leave Regulations 2002, SI 2002/2788, reg 17(1)(b). An employee who has given notice under reg 17(1) may vary the date he has chosen as the date on which his period of leave will begin, provided that he gives his employer notice of the variation:
 (1) where the variation is to provide for the employee's period of leave to begin on the date on which the child is placed with him for adoption, at least 28 days before the date specified in his notice under reg 17(1) as the date on which the child is expected to be placed with him (reg 17(4)(a));
 (2) where the variation is to provide for the employee's period of leave to begin on a predetermined date (or a different predetermined date), at least 28 days before that date (reg 17(4)(b)),

or, if it is not reasonably practicable to give the notice 28 days before whichever date is relevant, as soon as is reasonably practicable (see reg 17(4)). However, in a case where reg 16(2) applies (ie where the employee was notified of having been matched with a child before 6 April 2003: see note 16), he may only vary the date which he has chosen as the date on which his period of leave will begin by substituting a different predetermined date: reg 17(5). Notice under reg 17(4) must be given in writing, if the employer so requests: see reg 17(6).

14 See the Paternity and Adoption Leave Regulations 2002, SI 2002/2788, reg 17(3) (amended by SI 2004/923).

15 Ie a notice under the Paternity and Adoption Leave Regulations 2002, SI 2002/2788, reg 17 (see the text and notes 8–14).

16 See the Paternity and Adoption Leave Regulations 2002, SI 2002/2788, reg 16(1). See note 3. In a case where the employee was notified of having been matched with the child before 6 April 2003, the employee may choose to begin a period of leave only on a predetermined date, specified in a notice, which is after 6 April 2003 and at least 28 days after the date on which that notice is given: reg 16(2).

17 Ie subject to the Paternity and Adoption Leave Regulations 2002, SI 2002/2788, reg 22 (disrupted placement in the course of adoption leave: see PARA 385) and reg 24 (dismissal during adoption leave) (see the text and notes 26–27).

18 Paternity and Adoption Leave Regulations 2002, SI 2002/2788, reg 18(1).

19 Ie in his notice under the Paternity and Adoption Leave Regulations 2002, SI 2002/2788, reg 17(1) (see head (2)(a) in the text), or, where he has varied his choice of date, his notice under reg 17(4) (see note 13) (or the last such date if he has varied his choice more than once): see reg 18(2).

20 See the Paternity and Adoption Leave Regulations 2002, SI 2002/2788, reg 18(2).

21 See the Paternity and Adoption Leave Regulations 2002, SI 2002/2788, reg 18(3).

22 Ie under the Paternity and Adoption Leave Regulations 2002, SI 2002/2788, reg 17(1) (see head (2)(a) in the text) or reg 17(4) (see note 13).

23 As to entitlement to additional adoption leave see PARA 379.

24 Ie if he satisfies the conditions in the Paternity and Adoption Leave Regulations 2002, SI 2002/2788, reg 20(1): see PARA 379.

25 Paternity and Adoption Leave Regulations 2002, SI 2002/2788, reg 17(7). Such notification must be given to the employee: (1) where the employer is given notice under reg 17(1) (see head (2)(a) in the text), within 28 days of the date on which he received that notice (reg 17(8)(a)); (2) where the employer is given notice under reg 17(4) (see note 13), within 28 days of the date on which the employee's ordinary adoption leave period began (reg 17(8)(b)).

26 Ie apart from the Paternity and Adoption Leave Regulations 2002, SI 2002/2788, reg 24.

27 Paternity and Adoption Leave Regulations 2002, SI 2002/2788, reg 24.

379. Entitlement to additional adoption leave. An employee[1] is entitled to additional adoption leave[2] in respect of a child[3] if:

 (1) the child was placed with him for adoption[4];
 (2) he took ordinary adoption leave[5] in respect of the child[6]; and
 (3) his ordinary adoption leave period did not[7] end prematurely[8].

An employee's additional adoption leave period is[9] a period of 26 weeks beginning on the day after the last day of his ordinary adoption leave period[10].

Where an employee is dismissed after an additional adoption leave period has begun, but before the time when that period would otherwise[11] end, the period ends at the time of the dismissal[12].

1 As to the meaning of 'employee' for these purposes see PARA 370 note 1.
2 As to the meaning of 'additional adoption leave' see PARA 373 note 6.
3 As to the meaning of 'child' see PARA 370 note 2. As to overseas adoptions see PARA 389.
4 Paternity and Adoption Leave Regulations 2002, SI 2002/2788, reg 20(1)(a).
5 As to the meaning of 'ordinary adoption leave' see PARA 378 note 2.
6 Paternity and Adoption Leave Regulations 2002, SI 2002/2788, reg 20(1)(b).
7 Ie under the Paternity and Adoption Leave Regulations 2002, SI 2002/2788, reg 22(2)(a) (disrupted placement in the course of adoption leave: see PARA 385) and reg 24 (dismissal during adoption leave: see the text and notes 11–12).
8 Paternity and Adoption Leave Regulations 2002, SI 2002/2788, reg 20(1)(c).
9 Ie subject to the Paternity and Adoption Leave Regulations 2002, SI 2002/2788, reg 22 (disrupted placement in the course of adoption leave: see PARA 385) and reg 24 (dismissal during adoption leave: see the text and notes 11–12).
10 Paternity and Adoption Leave Regulations 2002, SI 2002/2788, reg 20(2).
11 Ie apart from the Paternity and Adoption Leave Regulations 2002, SI 2002/2788, reg 24.
12 Paternity and Adoption Leave Regulations 2002, SI 2002/2788, reg 24.

380. Contractual rights in relation to ordinary adoption leave and additional adoption leave. An employee[1] who takes ordinary adoption leave or additional adoption leave[2]:

(1) is entitled, during the period of leave, to the benefit of all of the terms and conditions of employment[3] which would have applied if he had not been absent[4]; and
(2) is bound[5], during that period, by any obligations arising under those terms and conditions[6].

1 As to the meaning of 'employee' for these purposes see PARA 370 note 1.
2 See the Paternity and Adoption Leave Regulations 2002, SI 2002/2788, reg 19(1) (amended by SI 2008/1966). As to the meaning of 'ordinary adoption leave' see PARA 378 note 2; and as to the meaning of 'additional adoption leave' see PARA 373 note 6.
3 For the purposes of head (1) in the text, 'terms and conditions of employment' has the meaning given by the Employment Rights Act 1996 ss 75A(4), 75B(5) (see PARA 377) and accordingly does not include terms and conditions about remuneration: see the Paternity and Adoption Leave Regulations 2002, SI 2002/2788, reg 19(2) (reg 19(2), (3) amended by SI 2008/1966). For the purposes of the Employment Rights Act 1996 ss 75A, 75B (see PARA 377) only sums payable to an employee by way of wages or salary are to be treated as remuneration: see the Paternity and Adoption Leave Regulations 2002, SI 2002/2788, reg 19(3) (as so amended).
4 Paternity and Adoption Leave Regulations 2002, SI 2002/2788, reg 19(1)(a).
5 Ie subject only to the exceptions in the Employment Rights Act 1996 s 75A(3)(b) and s 75B(4)(b): see PARA 377.
6 Paternity and Adoption Leave Regulations 2002, SI 2002/2788, reg 19(1)(b) (amended by SI 2008/1966).

381. Application of terms and conditions during ordinary adoption leave and additional adoption leave. Where an employee[1] is entitled to:

(1) ordinary adoption leave[2];
(2) additional adoption leave[3]; and

also to a right which corresponds to that right and which arises under the employee's contract of employment or otherwise[4]:

(a) the employee may not exercise the statutory right and the corresponding right separately but may, in taking the leave for which the two rights provide, take advantage of whichever right is, in any particular respect, the more favourable[5]; and
(b) the provisions[6] relating to the statutory right apply, subject to any modifications necessary to give effect to any more favourable contractual terms, to the exercise of the composite right described in head (a) above as they apply to the exercise of the statutory right[7].

1 As to the meaning of 'employee' for these purposes see PARA 370 note 1.
2 Paternity and Adoption Leave Regulations 2002, SI 2002/2788, reg 30(1)(b). For the purposes of reg 30(2) (see heads (a), (b) in the text), the right to leave mentioned in head (1) in the text is referred to as a 'statutory right': see reg 30(1). As to the meaning of 'ordinary adoption leave' see PARA 378 note 2.
3 Paternity and Adoption Leave Regulations 2002, SI 2002/2788, reg 30(1)(c). For the purposes of reg 30(2) (see heads (a), (b) in the text), the right to leave mentioned in head (2) in the text is referred to as a 'statutory right': see reg 30(1). As to the meaning of 'additional adoption leave' see PARA 373 note 6.
4 See the Paternity and Adoption Leave Regulations 2002, SI 2002/2788, reg 30(1). As to the meaning of 'contract of employment' for these purposes see PARA 370 note 1.
5 Paternity and Adoption Leave Regulations 2002, SI 2002/2788, reg 30(2)(a).
6 Ie the provisions of the Employment Rights Act 1996 and of the Maternity and Parental Leave etc Regulations 1999, SI 1999/3312.
7 Paternity and Adoption Leave Regulations 2002, SI 2002/2788, reg 30(2)(b).

382. Right to return after ordinary adoption leave. An employee[1] who returns to work after a period of ordinary adoption leave[2] which was:

(1) an isolated period of leave[3]; or
(2) the last of two or more consecutive periods of statutory leave[4] which did not include any period of parental leave[5] of more than four weeks[6], or any period of statutory leave which when added to any other periods of statutory leave (excluding parental leave) taken in relation to the same child means that the total amount of statutory leave taken in relation to that child totals more than 26 weeks[7],

is entitled to return from leave to the job in which he was employed before his absence[8]. An employee who returns to work after a period of ordinary adoption leave not falling within head (1) or head (2) above[9] is entitled to return from leave to the job in which he was employed before his absence (or, if it is not reasonably practicable for the employer to permit him to return to that job, to another job which is both suitable for him and appropriate for him to do in the circumstances)[10].

In these circumstances, an employee's right to return[11] is to return:

(a) with his seniority, pension rights and similar rights as they would have been if he had not been absent[12]; and
(b) on terms and conditions not less favourable than those which would have been applied to him if he had not been absent[13].

1 As to the meaning of 'employee' for these purposes see PARA 370 note 1.
2 As to the meaning of 'ordinary adoption leave' see PARA 378 note 2. As to ordinary adoption leave in relation to overseas adoptions see PARA 389.
3 Paternity and Adoption Leave Regulations 2002, SI 2002/2788, reg 26(1)(a).
4 As to the meaning of 'statutory leave' see PARA 373 note 4. As to the right to return after periods of statutory leave see also PARAS 361, 362, 373, 383, 395.
5 As to the meaning of 'parental leave' see PARA 373 note 7.
6 Paternity and Adoption Leave Regulations 2002, SI 2002/2788, reg 26(1)(b)(i) (reg 26(1)(b) substituted by SI 2014/2112).
7 Paternity and Adoption Leave Regulations 2002, SI 2002/2788, reg 26(1)(b)(ii) (as substituted: see note 6).
8 See the Paternity and Adoption Leave Regulations 2002, SI 2002/2788, reg 26(1). The reference in reg 26(1) and reg 26(2) (see the text and notes 9–10; and PARA 383) to the job in which an employee was employed before his absence is a reference to the job in which he was employed: (1) if his return is from an isolated period of adoption leave, immediately before that period began (reg 26(3)(a)); (2) if his return is from consecutive periods of statutory leave, immediately before the first such period (reg 26(3)(b)). Regulation 26 does not apply where reg 23 (redundancy and dismissal during adoption leave: see PARA 386) applies: reg 26(4). For these purposes, 'adoption leave' means ordinary or additional adoption leave: see reg 2(1).
9 See the Paternity and Adoption Leave Regulations 2002, SI 2002/2788, reg 26(2)(b).

388. Work during adoption leave period. An employee[1] may carry out up to ten days' work for his employer[2] during his statutory adoption leave period[3] without bringing his statutory adoption leave to an end[4]. For these purposes[5], any work[6] carried out on any day constitutes a day's work[7].

These provisions[8] do not confer any right on an employer to require that any work be carried out during the statutory adoption leave period, nor any right on an employee to work during the statutory adoption leave period[9]. Any day's work carried out under these provisions does not have the effect of extending the total duration of the statutory adoption leave period[10].

1 As to the meaning of 'employee' for these purposes see PARA 370 note 1.
2 As to the meaning of 'employer' for these purposes see PARA 370 note 11.
3 For these purposes, 'statutory adoption leave period' means the period during which the employee is on statutory adoption leave; and 'statutory adoption leave' means ordinary adoption leave and additional adoption leave: see the Paternity and Adoption Leave Regulations 2002, SI 2002/2788, reg 2(1) (both definitions added by SI 2006/2014). As to the meaning of 'ordinary adoption leave' see PARA 378 note 2. As to the meaning of 'additional adoption leave' see PARA 373 note 6.
4 Paternity and Adoption Leave Regulations 2002, SI 2002/2788, reg 21A(1) (reg 21A added by SI 2006/2014).
5 Ie for the purposes of the Paternity and Adoption Leave Regulations 2002, SI 2002/2788, SI 1999/3312, reg 21A.
6 For the purposes of the Paternity and Adoption Leave Regulations 2002, SI 2002/2788, reg 21A, work means any work done under the contract of employment and may include training or any activity undertaken for the purposes of keeping in touch with the workplace: reg 21A(3) (as added: see note 4). However, reasonable contact from time to time between an employee and his employer which either party is entitled to make during an adoption leave period (for example to discuss an employee's return to work) does not bring that period to an end: reg 21A(4) (as so added). As to the meaning of 'contract of employment' for these purposes see PARA 370 note 1.
7 Paternity and Adoption Leave Regulations 2002, SI 2002/2788, reg 21A(2) (as added: see note 4).
8 Ie the Paternity and Adoption Leave Regulations 2002, SI 2002/2788, reg 21A.
9 Paternity and Adoption Leave Regulations 2002, SI 2002/2788, reg 21A(5) (as added: see note 4).
10 Paternity and Adoption Leave Regulations 2002, SI 2002/2788, reg 21A(6) (as added: see note 4).

D. ADOPTIONS FROM OVERSEAS

389. Application of adoption leave regulations to adoptions from overseas. In cases of adoption from overseas[1], the adoption leave regulations[2] apply with some modifications[3].

The regulations apply in such cases without modification in relation to:

(1) the application of terms and conditions during ordinary adoption leave[4];
(2) the application of terms and conditions during additional adoption leave[5];
(3) redundancy during adoption leave[6];
(4) dismissal during adoption leave[7];
(5) the requirement to notify intention to return during the adoption leave period[8];
(6) the right to return after adoption leave[9];
(7) incidents of the right to return from adoption leave[10];
(8) protection from detriment[11];
(9) unfair dismissal[12];
(10) contractual rights to adoption leave[13]; and

(11) calculation of a week's pay[14].

However, the regulations governing entitlement to ordinary adoption leave[15], the start date for a period of such leave[16], and the associated notice and evidential requirements[17], are substituted so that an employee[18] is entitled to ordinary adoption leave in respect of a child[19] if:

(a) he satisfies the following conditions[20], being that:
   (i) he is the child's adopter[21];
   (ii) he has been continuously employed[22] for a period of not less than 26 weeks[23] either ending with the week in which he received an official notification[24], or commencing with the week in which the employee's employment with the employer[25] began[26]; and
(b) he has complied with the following requirements as to notice and, where applicable, as to evidence[27], being that:
   (i) he must give his employer notice of the date on which he received an official notification, the date on which the child is expected to enter Great Britain, the date which he has chosen as the date on which his period of adoption leave should begin[28] and the date on which the child enters Great Britain[29]; and
   (ii) where the employer requests it, the employee must also provide his employer with a copy of the official notification together with evidence of the date of the entry of the child into Great Britain[30].

An employee may choose to begin such a period of ordinary adoption leave on the date on which the child enters Great Britain, or on a predetermined date, specified in such a notice[31], which is no later than 28 days after the date on which the child enters Great Britain[32]. An employer who is given notice[33] of the date on which an employee has chosen that his period of ordinary adoption leave should begin must notify the employee, within 28 days of his receipt of the notice, of the date on which the period of additional adoption leave to which the employee will be entitled[34] after his period of ordinary adoption leave ends[35].

Where it becomes known to the employee that the child will not enter Great Britain, he must notify the employer of the fact as soon as is reasonably practicable[36].

The regulation which governs the duration and commencement of ordinary adoption leave[37] is modified accordingly[38].

The regulation which specifies the conditions of entitlement to additional adoption leave[39] is modified to reflect the fact that an employee's entitlement is in respect of a child who has entered Great Britain[40].

The regulation specifying what happens when a placement in the course of adoption leave is disrupted[41] is modified so that where the child dies[42] or ceases to live with the adopter[43], then[44]:

(A) except in the circumstances referred to in heads (B) and (C) below, the employee's adoption leave period ends eight weeks after the end of the relevant week[45];
(B) where the employee is taking ordinary adoption leave and the period of 26 weeks[46] ends within eight weeks of the end of the relevant week, the employee's ordinary adoption leave period ends on the expiry of the 26-week period, the employee is entitled to additional adoption leave and the employee's additional adoption leave period ends eight weeks after the end of the relevant week[47];
(C) where the employee is taking additional adoption leave and the period

of 26 weeks[48] ends within eight weeks of the end of the relevant week, the employee's additional adoption leave period ends on the expiry of the 26-week period[49].

1 As to the meaning of 'adoption from overseas' see PARA 376 note 1.

2 Ie the Paternity and Adoption Leave Regulations 2002, SI 2002/2788, Pt 1 (regs 1–3) (general), Pt 3 (regs 15–27) (adoption leave), Pt 4 (regs 28–31) (common provisions): see PARA 378 et seq.

3 Paternity and Adoption Leave (Adoption from Overseas) Regulations 2003, SI 2003/921, reg 3. Children who are adopted from overseas are not placed for adoption but are or have been treated as privately fostered under the Children Act 1989 s 66 (see **CHILDREN AND YOUNG PERSONS** vol 10 (2012) PARA 1056 et seq) or as protected children under the Adoption Act 1976 ss 32–37 (repealed).

4 Ie the Paternity and Adoption Leave Regulations 2002, SI 2002/2788, reg 19: see PARA 380. As to the meaning of 'ordinary adoption leave' see PARA 378 note 2.

5 Ie the Paternity and Adoption Leave Regulations 2002, SI 2002/2788, reg 19: see PARA 380. As to the meaning of 'additional adoption leave' see PARA 373 note 6.

6 Ie the Paternity and Adoption Leave Regulations 2002, SI 2002/2788, reg 23: see PARA 386.

7 Ie the Paternity and Adoption Leave Regulations 2002, SI 2002/2788, reg 24: see PARAS 378, 379.

8 Ie the Paternity and Adoption Leave Regulations 2002, SI 2002/2788, reg 25: see PARA 384.

9 Ie the Paternity and Adoption Leave Regulations 2002, SI 2002/2788, reg 26: see PARAS 382, 383.

10 Ie the Paternity and Adoption Leave Regulations 2002, SI 2002/2788, reg 27: see PARAS 382, 383.

11 Ie the Paternity and Adoption Leave Regulations 2002, SI 2002/2788, reg 28: see PARA 620.

12 Ie the Paternity and Adoption Leave Regulations 2002, SI 2002/2788, reg 29: see PARA 784.

13 Ie the Paternity and Adoption Leave Regulations 2002, SI 2002/2788, reg 30: see PARAS 372, 381.

14 Ie the Paternity and Adoption Leave Regulations 2002, SI 2002/2788, reg 31: see PARAS 374, 387.

15 Ie the Paternity and Adoption Leave Regulations 2002, SI 2002/2788, reg 15: see PARA 378.

16 Ie the Paternity and Adoption Leave Regulations 2002, SI 2002/2788, reg 16: see PARA 378.

17 Ie the Paternity and Adoption Leave Regulations 2002, SI 2002/2788, reg 17: see PARA 378.

18 As to the meaning of 'employee' for these purposes see PARA 370 note 1.

19 As to the meaning of 'child' see PARA 370 note 2.

20 Paternity and Adoption Leave Regulations 2002, SI 2002/2788, reg 15(1)(a) (regs 15–17 substituted by the Paternity and Adoption Leave (Adoption from Overseas) Regulations 2003, SI 2003/921, reg 9). The text refers to the conditions specified in the Paternity and Adoption Leave Regulations 2002, SI 2002/2788, reg 15(2) (see heads (a)(i), (ii) in the text): see reg 15(1)(a) (as so substituted).

The provisions relating to adoption leave under reg 15 have effect only where the adopter's child enters Great Britain on or after 6 April 2003: reg 3(1) (substituted by the Paternity and Adoption Leave (Adoption from Overseas) Regulations 2003, SI 2003/921, reg 5(1), (2)). As to the meanings of 'adopter', in relation to a child, and 'enters Great Britain' for these purposes see PARA 376 note 15. As to the meaning of 'Great Britain' see PARA 2 note 12.

21 Paternity and Adoption Leave Regulations 2002, SI 2002/2788, reg 15(2)(a) (as substituted: see note 20).

22 As to the meaning of references to a period of continuous employment see PARA 370 note 4.

23 For the purposes of head (a)(ii) in the text, 'week' means the period of seven days beginning with Sunday: see the Paternity and Adoption Leave Regulations 2002, SI 2002/2788, reg 15(3) (as substituted: see note 20).

24 Paternity and Adoption Leave Regulations 2002, SI 2002/2788, reg 15(2)(b)(i) (as substituted: see note 20). As to the meaning of 'official notification' see PARA 376 note 15.

25 As to the meaning of 'employer' for these purposes see PARA 370 note 11.

26 Paternity and Adoption Leave Regulations 2002, SI 2002/2788, reg 15(2)(b)(ii) (as substituted: see note 20).

27 Paternity and Adoption Leave Regulations 2002, SI 2002/2788, reg 15(1)(b) (as substituted: see note 20). The text refers to the notice requirements in reg 17 and, where applicable, the evidential requirements in reg 17 (see heads (b)(i), (b)(ii) in the text): see reg 15(1)(b) (as so substituted).

28 An employee who has given notice under head (b)(i) in the text, as to the date which he has chosen as the date on which his period of adoption leave should begin, may vary the date he has chosen as the date on which his leave will begin, provided that he gives his employer notice of the variation:
   (1) where the variation is to provide for the employee's period of leave to begin on the date on which the child enters Great Britain, at least 28 days before the date specified in his notice under head (b)(i) in the text as the date on which the child is expected to enter Great Britain (Paternity and Adoption Leave Regulations 2002, SI 2002/2788, reg 17(4)(a) (as substituted: see note 20));
   (2) where the variation is to provide for the employee's period of leave to begin on a predetermined date (or a different predetermined date), at least 28 days before that date (reg 17(4)(b) (as so substituted)),

   or, if it is not reasonably practicable to give the notice 28 days before whichever date is relevant, as soon as is reasonably practicable (see reg 17(4) (as so substituted))). However, in a case where reg 16(2) applies (ie where the employee was notified of having been matched with a child before 6 April 2003: see note 32), he may only vary the date which he has chosen as the date on which his period of leave will begin by substituting a different predetermined date: reg 17(5) (as so substituted). Notice under reg 17(4) must be given in writing, if the employer so requests: see reg 17(6) (as so substituted).

29 See the Paternity and Adoption Leave Regulations 2002, SI 2002/2788, reg 17(1) (as substituted: see note 20). The notice provided for:
   (1) in relation to the date on which the employee received an official notification (ie in reg 17(1)(a)) or the date on which the child is expected to enter Great Britain (ie in reg 17(1)(b)), must be given to the employer no more than 28 days after the date on which the employee receives the official notification or the date on which he completes 26 weeks' continuous employment with the employer, whichever is later (reg 17(2)(a) (as so substituted));
   (2) in relation to the date which the employee has chosen as the date on which his period of adoption leave should begin (ie in reg 17(1)(c)), must be given to the employer at least 28 days prior to the date which the employee has so chosen (reg 17(2)(b) (as so substituted)); and
   (3) in relation to the date on which the child enters Great Britain (ie in reg 17(1)(d)), must be given to the employer no more than 28 days after that date (reg 17(2)(c) (as so substituted)).

   Such notice must be given in writing, if the employer so requests: see reg 17(6) (as so substituted).

30 Paternity and Adoption Leave Regulations 2002, SI 2002/2788, reg 17(3) (as substituted: see note 20).

31 Ie a notice under the Paternity and Adoption Leave Regulations 2002, SI 2002/2788, reg 17.

32 See the Paternity and Adoption Leave Regulations 2002, SI 2002/2788, reg 16(1) (as substituted: see note 20).

   In a case where the employee receives an official notification before 6 April 2003 and the adopter's child enters Great Britain on or after that date, the employee may choose to begin a period of ordinary adoption leave only on a predetermined date, specified in a notice, which is later than the date of entry, and, unless the employer agrees to an earlier commencement of the leave period, is at least 28 days after the date on which that notice was given: reg 16(2) (as so substituted).

33 Ie under the Paternity and Adoption Leave Regulations 2002, SI 2002/2788, reg 17(1) (see head (b)(i) in the text) or reg 17(4) (see note 28).

34 Ie if he satisfies the conditions in the Paternity and Adoption Leave Regulations 2002, SI 2002/2788, reg 20(1) (see the text and note 40).

35 Paternity and Adoption Leave Regulations 2002, SI 2002/2788, reg 17(7) (as substituted: see note 20). Such notification must be given to the employee: (1) where the employer is given notice under reg 17(1)(c) (ie specifying the date which the employee has chosen as the date on which his period of adoption leave should begin), within 28 days of the date on which he received that notice (reg 17(8)(a) (as so substituted)); (2) where the employer is given notice under reg 17(4) (see note 28), within 28 days of the date on which the employee's ordinary adoption leave period began (reg 17(8)(b) (as so substituted)).

36 Paternity and Adoption Leave Regulations 2002, SI 2002/2788, reg 17(9) (as substituted: see note 20).

37 Ie the Paternity and Adoption Leave Regulations 2002, SI 2002/2788, reg 18: see PARA 378.

38 Accordingly, subject to the Paternity and Adoption Leave Regulations 2002, SI 2002/2788, reg 22 (disrupted placement in the course of adoption leave) (see the text and notes 41–49) and

reg 24 (dismissal during adoption leave) (see head (4) in the text), an employee's ordinary adoption leave period is a period of 26 weeks: reg 18(1). An employee's ordinary adoption leave period begins on the date specified in his notice under reg 17(1)(c) (see head (b)(i) in the text) or, where he varied his choice of date under reg 17(4) (see note 28) on the date so specified, except where the employee has chosen to begin his period of leave on the date on which the child enters Great Britain, and where he is at work on that date, in which case the employee's period of leave begins on the day after that date: see reg 18(2), (3) (modified by the Paternity and Adoption Leave (Adoption from Overseas) Regulations 2003, SI 2003/921, reg 10).

39 Ie the Paternity and Adoption Leave Regulations 2002, SI 2002/2788, reg 20.

40 Accordingly, an employee is entitled to additional adoption leave in respect of a child if: (1) the child has entered Great Britain; (2) he took ordinary adoption leave in respect of the child; and (3) his ordinary adoption leave period did not end prematurely: under the Paternity and Adoption Leave Regulations 2002, SI 2002/2788, reg 22(2)(a) (see head (A) in the text) or reg 24 (dismissal during adoption leave) (see head (4) in the text): see reg 20(1) (modified by the Paternity and Adoption Leave (Adoption from Overseas) Regulations 2003, SI 2003/921, reg 11). Subject to the Paternity and Adoption Leave Regulations 2002, SI 2002/2788, reg 22 and reg 24, an employee's additional adoption leave period is a period of 26 weeks beginning on the day after the last day of his ordinary adoption leave period: reg 20(2).

41 Ie the Paternity and Adoption Leave Regulations 2002, SI 2002/2788, reg 22: see PARA 385.

42 See the Paternity and Adoption Leave Regulations 2002, SI 2002/2788, reg 22(1)(a) (reg 22(1), (3) substituted by the Paternity and Adoption Leave (Adoption from Overseas) Regulations 2003, SI 2003/921, reg 12).

43 See the Paternity and Adoption Leave Regulations 2002, SI 2002/2788, reg 22(1)(b) (as substituted: see note 42).

44 Ie subject to the Paternity and Adoption Leave Regulations 2002, SI 2002/2788, reg 24: see PARAS 378, 379.

45 Paternity and Adoption Leave Regulations 2002, SI 2002/2788, reg 22(2)(a). For these purposes, the relevant week is:

(1) in a case falling within reg 22(1)(a) (see the text and note 42), the week during which the child dies (reg 22(3)(a) (as substituted: see note 42));

(2) in a case falling within reg 22(1)(b) (see the text and note 43), the week during which the child ceased to live with the adopter (reg 22(3)(b) (as so substituted)).

For this purpose, 'week' means the period of seven days beginning with Sunday: see reg 22(4).

46 Ie provided for in the Paternity and Adoption Leave Regulations 2002, SI 2002/2788, reg 18: see PARA 378.

47 Paternity and Adoption Leave Regulations 2002, SI 2002/2788, reg 22(2)(b).

48 Ie provided for in the Paternity and Adoption Leave Regulations 2002, SI 2002/2788, reg 20: see PARA 379.

49 Paternity and Adoption Leave Regulations 2002, SI 2002/2788, reg 22(2)(c).

(v) Parental Leave

A. POWER TO MAKE REGULATIONS

390. Power to make regulations in relation to parental leave. The Secretary of State[1] must make regulations[2] entitling an employee who satisfies specified conditions as to duration of employment[3], and as to having, or expecting to have, responsibility for a child, to be absent from work on parental leave for the purpose of caring for a child[4]. The regulations must include provision for determining the extent of an employee's entitlement to parental leave in respect of a child[5], and for determining when parental leave may be taken[6]. Such regulations may:

(1) specify things which are, or are not, to be taken as done for the purpose of caring for a child;

(2) require parental leave to be taken as a single period of absence in all cases or in specified cases;

(3) require parental leave to be taken as a series of periods of absence in all cases or in specified cases;

(4) require all or specified parts of a period of parental leave to be taken at or by specified times;
(5) make provision about the postponement by an employer[7] of a period of parental leave which an employee wishes to take;
(6) specify a minimum or maximum period of absence which may be taken as part of a period of parental leave;
(7) specify a maximum aggregate of periods of parental leave which may be taken during a specified period of time[8].

Such regulations must also provide:
(a) that an employee who is absent on parental leave is entitled, for such purposes and to such extent as may be prescribed, to the benefit of the terms and conditions of employment[9] which would have applied if the employee had not been absent[10];
(b) that an employee who is absent on parental leave is bound, for such purposes and to such extent as may be prescribed, by any obligations arising[11] under those terms and conditions[12]; and
(c) that an employee who is absent on parental leave[13] is entitled[14] to return from leave to a job[15] of such kind as the regulations may specify[16].

Such regulations may also:
(i) make provision about redundancy[17] during a period of parental leave and about dismissal (other than by reason of redundancy) during a period of parental leave[18];
(ii) provide for an employee to be entitled to choose to exercise all or part of the entitlement to parental leave by varying the terms of his contract of employment as to hours of work, or by varying his normal working practice as to hours of work, in a way specified in or permitted by the regulations for a period specified in the regulations[19];
(iii) make provision permitting all or part of an employee's entitlement to parental leave in respect of a child to be transferred to another employee in specified circumstances[20];
(iv) provide for specified provisions of the regulations not to apply in relation to an employee if any provision of his contract of employment confers an entitlement to absence from work for the purpose of caring for a child and incorporates or operates by reference to all or part of a collective agreement[21] or workforce agreement[22] of a kind specified in the regulations[23];
(v) make provision modifying the effect of the statutory provisions relating to the calculation of a week's pay[24] in relation to an employee who is or has been absent from work on parental leave[25];
(vi) make[26] any provision which appears to the Secretary of State to be necessary or expedient for the purpose of implementing the EU Council Directive on the framework agreement for parental leave[27] or for the purpose of dealing with any matter arising out of or related to the United Kingdom's obligations under it[28].

Such regulations may, in particular:
(A) make provision about notices to be given and evidence to be produced by employees to employers, by employers to employees, and by employers to other employers;
(B) make provision requiring employers or employees to keep records;
(C) make provision about other procedures to be followed by employees and employers;

(D) make provision, including provision creating criminal offences, specifying the consequences of failure to give notices, to produce evidence, to keep records or to comply with other procedural requirements;
(E) make provision specifying the consequences of failure to act in accordance with a notice given by virtue of head (A) above;
(F) make special provision for cases where an employee has a right which corresponds to a right conferred by the regulations and which arises under his contract of employment or otherwise;
(G) make provision applying, modifying or excluding an enactment, in such circumstances as may be specified and subject to any conditions specified, in relation to a person entitled to parental leave;
(H) make different provision for different cases or circumstances[29].

1 As to the Secretary of State see PARA 5 note 21.
2 As to the making of regulations under the Employment Rights Act 1996 generally see PARA 162. In exercise of the powers conferred by ss 76(1), (2), (5), 77(1), (4), 78(1), (2), (7), 79(1), (2), 99(1), the Secretary of State has made the Maternity and Parental Leave etc Regulations 1999, SI 1999/3312, regs 1, 2, 12A, 13–17, 18, 20–22 (see PARA 391 et seq). As to the power to make regulations in relation to shared parental leave on birth see PARA 398; and in relation to shared parental leave on adoption see PARA 399.
3 As to the meanings of 'employee' and 'employment' see PARA 2.
4 See the Employment Rights Act 1996 s 76(1) (ss 76–79 substituted by the Employment Relations Act 1999 Sch 4 Pt I).
5 Employment Rights Act 1996 s 76(2)(a) (as substituted: see note 4). Provision under s 76(2)(a) must secure that, where an employee is entitled to parental leave in respect of a child, he is entitled to a period or total period of leave of at least three months; but this is without prejudice to any provision which may be made by the regulations for cases in which a person ceases to satisfy conditions under s 76(1) (see the text and notes 1–4) or in which an entitlement to parental leave is transferred: see s 76(3) (as so substituted).
6 Employment Rights Act 1996 s 76(2)(b) (as substituted: see note 4). Provision under s 76(2)(b) may, in particular, refer to a child's age, or to a specified period of time starting from a specified event: see s 76(4) (as so substituted).
7 As to the meaning of 'employer' see PARA 2.
8 See the Employment Rights Act 1996 s 76(5) (as substituted: see note 4).
9 For the purposes of head (a) in the text, 'terms and conditions of employment' includes: (1) matters connected with an employee's employment, whether or not they arise under a contract of employment; but (2) does not include terms and conditions about remuneration: see the Employment Rights Act 1996 s 77(2) (as substituted: see note 4). Regulations under s 76 (see the text and notes 1–8) may specify matters which are, or are not, to be treated as remuneration for the purposes of head (2) above: s 77(3) (as so substituted). As to the meaning of 'contract of employment' see PARA 2.
10 Employment Rights Act 1996 s 77(1)(a) (as substituted: see note 4).
11 Ie except in so far as they are inconsistent with the Employment Rights Act 1996 s 76(1): see the text and notes 1–4.
12 Employment Rights Act 1996 s 77(1)(b) (as substituted: see note 4).
13 For the purposes of head (c) in the text, the reference to absence on parental leave includes, where appropriate, a reference to a continuous period of absence attributable partly to parental leave and partly to: (1) maternity leave; or (2) adoption leave, or to both: see the Employment Rights Act 1996 s 78(6) (s 78 as substituted (see note 4); s 78(6) amended by the Employment Act 2002 Sch 7 paras 24, 28). As to maternity leave see PARA 355 et seq; and as to adoption leave see PARA 377 et seq.
14 Ie subject to the Employment Rights Act 1996 s 78(1): see the text and notes 17–18.
15 As to the meaning of 'job' see PARA 119 note 17.
16 Employment Rights Act 1996 s 77(1)(c) (as substituted: see note 4). The regulations may make provision, in relation to the right to return mentioned in s 77(1)(c) about seniority, pension rights and similar rights and about terms and conditions of employment on return: s 77(4) (as so substituted).
17 As to the meaning of 'redundancy' see PARA 870.

18 See the Employment Rights Act 1996 s 78(1) (as substituted: see note 4). Provision made by virtue of s 78(1) may include: (1) provision requiring an employer to offer alternative employment (s 78(2)(a) (as so substituted)); (2) provision for the consequences of failure to comply with the regulations, which may include provision for a dismissal to be treated as unfair for the purposes of Pt X (ss 94–134A) (unfair dismissal: see PARA 757 et seq) (s 78(2)(b) (as so substituted)).

19 See the Employment Rights Act 1996 s 78(3) (as substituted: see note 4). Provision by virtue of s 78(3): (1) may restrict an entitlement to specified circumstances (s 78(4)(a) (as so substituted)); (2) may make an entitlement subject to specified conditions, which may include conditions relating to obtaining the employer's consent (s 78(4)(b) (as so substituted)); (3) may include consequential and incidental provisions (s 78(4)(c) (as so substituted)).

20 Employment Rights Act 1996 s 78(5) (as substituted: see note 4).

21 As to the meaning of 'collective agreement' see PARA 119 note 21.

22 As to the meaning of 'workforce agreement' see PARA 393.

23 See the Employment Rights Act 1996 s 78(7) (as substituted: see note 4).

24 Ie modifying the effect of the Employment Rights Act 1996 Pt XIV Ch II (ss 220–229): see PARA 143 et seq.

25 Employment Rights Act 1996 s 79(2) (as substituted: see note 4).

26 Ie without prejudice to the generality of the Employment Rights Act 1996 s 76.

27 See now Council Directive (EU) 2010/18 of 8 March 2010 (OJ L68, 18.03.2010, p 13) implementing the revised Framework Agreement on parental leave concluded by BUSINESSEUROPE, UEAPME, CEEP and ETUC (and repealing Council Directive (EC) 96/34 of 3 June 1996 (OJ L145, 19.6.96, p 4) on the framework agreement on parental leave concluded by UNICE, CEEP and the ETUC); and see PARA 354.

28 See the Employment Rights Act 1996 s 79(3) (as substituted: see note 4). See especially the Maternity and Parental Leave etc Regulations 1999, SI 1999/3312, regs 13–16, Sch 2; and PARAS 391, 392.

29 See the Employment Rights Act 1996 s 79(1) (as substituted: see note 4).

B. PARENTAL LEAVE

391. Entitlement to parental leave. An employee[1] who:

(1) has been continuously employed[2] for a period of not less than a year or is to be treated[3] as having been so employed[4]; and

(2) has, or expects to have, responsibility for a child[5],

is entitled[6] to be absent from work on parental leave for the purpose of caring for that child[7]. An employee is entitled to 18 weeks' leave in respect of any individual child[8].

An employee may not exercise any entitlement to parental leave in respect of a child:

(a) except in the cases referred to in heads (b) to (d) below, after the date of the child's fifth birthday or, in the case of a child placed with the employee for adoption by him, on or after the fifth anniversary of the date on which the placement began, or on or after the date of the child's eighteenth birthday, whichever is the earlier[9];

(b) in a case where the child:

  (i) was born before 15 December 1999, and whose fifth birthday was on or after that date[10]; or

  (ii) was placed with the employee for adoption by him before 15 December 1999, the fifth anniversary of whose placement was on or after that date[11],

  (not being a case to which head (c) or head (d) below applies) after 31 March 2005[12];

(c) in a case entitled to a disability living allowance[13], an armed forces independence payment[14], or a personal independence payment[15], after the date of the child's eighteenth birthday[16];

23 Maternity and Parental Leave etc Regulations 1999, SI 1999/3312, Sch 2 para 6(c)(iii) (as added: see note 21).
24 Maternity and Parental Leave etc Regulations 1999, SI 1999/3312, Sch 2 para 6(d)(i).
25 Maternity and Parental Leave etc Regulations 1999, SI 1999/3312, Sch 2 para 6(d)(ii).
26 Maternity and Parental Leave etc Regulations 1999, SI 1999/3312, Sch 2 para 6(e).
27 Ie under the Maternity and Parental Leave etc Regulations 1999, SI 1999/3312, reg 14: see PARA 391.
28 Maternity and Parental Leave etc Regulations 1999, SI 1999/3312, Sch 2 para 7 (amended by SI 2013/388, SI 2013/591). On its true construction, the Maternity and Parental Leave etc Regulations 1999, SI 1999/3312, Sch 2 para 7 does not permit parental leave to be taken for one day only as the phrase 'in a period' means 'for a period': *South Central Trains Ltd v Rodway* [2005] ICR 75, [2004] IRLR 777, EAT; affd sub nom *Rodway v New Southern Railways Ltd* [2005] EWCA Civ 443, [2005] ICR 1162, [2005] IRLR 583 (under the default provisions parental leave could only be taken for one week or in blocks of one week).
29 Maternity and Parental Leave etc Regulations 1999, SI 1999/3312, Sch 2 para 8. For these purposes, a year is the period of 12 months beginning:
   (1) except where head (2) below applies, on the date on which the employee first became entitled to take parental leave in respect of the child in question (Sch 2 para 9(a)); or
   (2) in a case where the employee's entitlement has been interrupted at the end of a period of continuous employment, on the date on which the employee most recently became entitled to take parental leave in respect of that child (Sch 2 para 9(b)),

   and each successive period of 12 months beginning on the anniversary of that date (see Sch 2 para 9). As to the meaning of references to a period of continuous employment for these purposes see PARA 391 note 2.

393. Workforce agreements used to replace the default provisions for parental leave. A workforce agreement, which may be used to replace the default provisions for parental leave[1], is an agreement between an employer[2] and his employees[3] or their representatives, in respect of which the following conditions are satisfied[4]:

(1) the agreement is in writing[5];
(2) it has effect for a specified period not exceeding five years[6];
(3) it applies either: (a) to all of the relevant members of the workforce[7]; or (b) to all of the relevant members of the workforce who belong to a particular group[8];
(4) the agreement is signed:
   (a) in the case of an agreement of the kind referred to in head (3)(a) above, by the representatives of the workforce[9], and in the case of an agreement of the kind referred to in head (3)(b) above, by the representatives of the group[10] to which the agreement applies (excluding, in either case, any representative not a relevant member of the workforce on the date on which the agreement was first made available for signature)[11]; or
   (b) if the employer employed 20 or fewer employees on the date referred to in head (4)(a) above, either by the appropriate representatives in accordance with that head or by the majority of the employees employed by him[12]; and
(5) before the agreement was made available for signature, the employer provided all the employees to whom it was intended to apply on the date on which it came into effect with copies of the text of the agreement and such guidance as those employees might reasonably require in order to understand it in full[13].

1 See PARA 392. As to the meaning of 'parental leave' see PARA 361 note 7.
2 As to the meaning of 'employer' for these purposes see PARA 356 note 5.
3 As to the meaning of 'employee' for these purposes see PARA 356 note 1.

4 See the Maternity and Parental Leave etc Regulations 1999, SI 1999/3312, reg 2(1), Sch 1 para 1.

5 Maternity and Parental Leave etc Regulations 1999, SI 1999/3312, Sch 1 para 1(a).

6 Maternity and Parental Leave etc Regulations 1999, SI 1999/3312, Sch 1 para 1(b).

7 Maternity and Parental Leave etc Regulations 1999, SI 1999/3312, Sch 1 para 1(c)(i). For these purposes, 'relevant members of the workforce' are all of the employees employed by a particular employer, excluding any employee whose terms and conditions of employment are provided for, wholly or in part, in a collective agreement: see Sch 1 para 2. As to the meaning of 'collective agreement' see PARA 392 note 4.

8 Maternity and Parental Leave etc Regulations 1999, SI 1999/3312, Sch 1 para 1(c)(ii). For these purposes, a 'particular group' is a group of the relevant members of a workforce who undertake a particular function, work at a particular workplace or belong to a particular department or unit within their employer's business: see Sch 1 para 2. As to the meaning of 'business' see PARA 392 note 19.

9 For these purposes, 'representatives of the workforce' are employees duly elected to represent the relevant members of the workforce: Maternity and Parental Leave etc Regulations 1999, SI 1999/3312, Sch 1 para 2. Representatives are 'duly elected' if the election at which they were elected satisfied the following requirements (see Sch 1 para 2):

   (1) the number of representatives to be elected is determined by the employer (Sch 1 para 3(a));
   (2) the candidates for election as representatives of the workforce are relevant members of the workforce, and the candidates for election as representatives of a group are members of the group (Sch 1 para 3(b));
   (3) no employee who is eligible to be a candidate is unreasonably excluded from standing for election (Sch 1 para 3(c));
   (4) all the relevant members of the workforce are entitled to vote for representatives of the workforce, and all the members of a particular group are entitled to vote for representatives of the group (Sch 1 para 3(d));
   (5) the employees entitled to vote may vote for as many candidates as there are representatives to be elected (Sch 1 para 3(e)); and
   (6) the election is conducted so as to secure that, so far as is reasonably practicable, those voting do so in secret, and that the votes given at the election are fairly and accurately counted (Sch 1 para 3(f)).

10 For these purposes, 'representatives of the group' are employees duly elected to represent the members of a particular group: see the Maternity and Parental Leave etc Regulations 1999, SI 1999/3312, Sch 1 para 2.

11 Maternity and Parental Leave etc Regulations 1999, SI 1999/3312, Sch 1 para 1(d)(i).

12 Maternity and Parental Leave etc Regulations 1999, SI 1999/3312, Sch 1 para 1(d)(ii).

13 Maternity and Parental Leave etc Regulations 1999, SI 1999/3312, Sch 1 para 1(e).

394. Application of terms and conditions during periods of parental leave. An employee[1] who takes parental leave[2]:

(1) is entitled, during the period of leave[3], to the benefit of his employer's[4] implied obligation to him of trust and confidence[5] and of any terms and conditions of his employment relating to[6]:
   (a) notice of the termination of the employment contract by his employer[7];
   (b) compensation in the event of redundancy[8]; or
   (c) disciplinary or grievance procedures[9];
(2) is bound, during that period, by his implied obligation to his employer of good faith[10] and by any terms and conditions of his employment relating to[11]:
   (a) notice of the termination of the employment contract by him[12];
   (b) the disclosure of confidential information[13];
   (c) the acceptance of gifts or other benefits[14]; or
   (d) the employee's participation in any other business[15].

Where an employee is entitled to parental leave[16] (the 'statutory right'), and also to a right which corresponds to that right and which arises under the employee's contract of employment or otherwise[17]:

(i) the employee may not exercise the statutory right and the corresponding right separately but may, in taking the leave for which the two rights provide, take advantage of whichever right is, in any particular respect, the more favourable[18]; and

(ii) the provisions[19] relating to the statutory right apply, subject to any modifications necessary to give effect to any more favourable contractual terms, to the exercise of the composite right described in head (i) above as they apply to the exercise of the statutory right[20].

1 As to the meaning of 'employee' for these purposes see PARA 356 note 1.
2 See the Maternity and Parental Leave etc Regulations 1999, SI 1999/3312, reg 17 (amended by SI 2008/1966). As to the meaning of 'parental leave' see PARA 361 note 7.
3 As to the duration of parental leave see PARA 391.
4 As to the meaning of 'employer' for these purposes see PARA 356 note 5.
5 As to the implied obligation of trust and confidence see PARA 48.
6 See the Maternity and Parental Leave etc Regulations 1999, SI 1999/3312, reg 17(a).
7 Maternity and Parental Leave etc Regulations 1999, SI 1999/3312, reg 17(a)(i).
8 Maternity and Parental Leave etc Regulations 1999, SI 1999/3312, reg 17(a)(ii). As to the meaning of 'redundancy' see PARA 870.
9 Maternity and Parental Leave etc Regulations 1999, SI 1999/3312, reg 17(a)(iii).
10 As to the implied obligation of good faith during employment ee PARA 67.
11 See the Maternity and Parental Leave etc Regulations 1999, SI 1999/3312, reg 17(b).
12 Maternity and Parental Leave etc Regulations 1999, SI 1999/3312, reg 17(b)(i).
13 Maternity and Parental Leave etc Regulations 1999, SI 1999/3312, reg 17(b)(ii).
14 Maternity and Parental Leave etc Regulations 1999, SI 1999/3312, reg 17(b)(iii).
15 Maternity and Parental Leave etc Regulations 1999, SI 1999/3312, reg 17(b)(iv). As to the meaning of 'business' see PARA 392 note 19.
16 See the Maternity and Parental Leave etc Regulations 1999, SI 1999/3312, reg 21(1)(c).
17 See the Maternity and Parental Leave etc Regulations 1999, SI 1999/3312, reg 21(1). As to the meaning of 'contract of employment' for these purposes see PARA 356 note 1.
18 Maternity and Parental Leave etc Regulations 1999, SI 1999/3312, reg 21(2)(a). Under the Employment Protection Act 1975 s 50(2), Sch 3 para 5 (repealed), which was in similar terms to the Maternity and Parental Leave etc Regulations 1999, SI 1999/3312, reg 21(1), (2), it was held that, in spite of the apparently wide drafting of the provision, there had to be limits to the extent to which any particular aspect of the maternity scheme might be sub-divided at the option of the employee: *Bovey v Board of Governors of the Hospital for Sick Children* [1978] ICR 934, [1978] IRLR 241, EAT (employee not allowed to combine an offer of return part-time at a basic grade with her statutory right to return to her previous full-time job on a higher grade); *sed quaere* whether this approach will continue to be taken.
19 Ie the provisions of the Employment Rights Act 1996 and of the Maternity and Parental Leave etc Regulations 1999, SI 1999/3312.
20 Maternity and Parental Leave etc Regulations 1999, SI 1999/3312, reg 21(2)(b).

395. Right to return after parental leave. An employee[1] who returns to work after a period of parental leave[2] of four weeks or less, which was:

(1) an isolated period of leave[3]; or

(2) the last of two or more consecutive periods of statutory leave[4] which did not include any period of additional maternity leave[5], or additional adoption leave[6], or a period of parental leave of more than four weeks[7],

is entitled to return to the job[8] in which he was employed before his absence[9]. An employee who returns to work after:

(a) a period of parental leave of more than four weeks, whether or not preceded by another period of statutory leave[10]; or

(b) a period of parental leave of four weeks or less, not falling within the description in head (1) or head (2) above[11], is entitled to return from leave to the job in which he was employed before his absence, or, if it is not reasonably practicable for the employer[12] to permit him to return to that job, to another job which is both suitable for him and appropriate for him to do in the circumstances[13].

In these circumstances, the employee's right to return is a right to return: (i) with his seniority, pension rights and similar rights as they would have been if he had not been absent[14]; and (ii) on terms and conditions not less favourable than those which would have applied if he had not been absent[15].

1 As to the meaning of 'employee' for these purposes see PARA 356 note 1.
2 As to the meaning of 'parental leave' see PARA 361 note 7.
3 Maternity and Parental Leave etc Regulations 1999, SI 1999/3312, reg 18(1)(a) (reg 18 substituted, reg 18A added, by SI 2002/2789).
4 As to the meaning of 'statutory leave' see PARA 361 note 4. As to the right to return after periods of statutory leave see also PARAS 361, 362, 373, 382, 383.
5 As to the meaning of 'additional maternity leave' see PARA 356 note 2.
6 As to the meaning of 'additional adoption leave' see PARA 361 note 6.
7 Maternity and Parental Leave etc Regulations 1999, SI 1999/3312, reg 18(1)(b) (as substituted: see note 3).
8 As to the meaning of 'job' see PARA 361 note 9.
9 See the Maternity and Parental Leave etc Regulations 1999, SI 1999/3312, reg 18(1) (as substituted: see note 3). Allowance must be made for changes in the nature of the job occurring during the course of a person's absence: *Blundell v Governing Body of St Andrews Catholic Primary School* [2007] ICR 1451, [2007] IRLR 652, EAT.

The reference to the job in which an employee was employed before his absence is a reference to the job in which he was employed: (1) if his return is from an isolated period of statutory leave, immediately before that period began; (2) if his return is from consecutive periods of statutory leave, immediately before the first such period: see the Maternity and Parental Leave etc Regulations 1999, SI 1999/3312, reg 18(3) (as so substituted). Regulation 18(3) does not apply where reg 10 (redundancy during maternity leave: see PARA 364) applies, however: see reg 18(4) (as so substituted).
10 Maternity and Parental Leave etc Regulations 1999, SI 1999/3312, reg 18(2)(a) (as substituted: see note 3).
11 Maternity and Parental Leave etc Regulations 1999, SI 1999/3312, reg 18(2)(b) (as substituted: see note 3).
12 As to the meaning of 'employer' for these purposes see PARA 356 note 5.
13 Maternity and Parental Leave etc Regulations 1999, SI 1999/3312, reg 18(2) (as substituted: see note 3). Regulation 18(2) does not apply where reg 10 (redundancy during maternity leave: see PARA 364) applies, however: see reg 18(4) (as so substituted).
14 Maternity and Parental Leave etc Regulations 1999, SI 1999/3312, reg 18A(1)(a) (reg 18A as added (see note 3); reg 18A(1)(a) substituted by SI 2008/1966). The provision in the Maternity and Parental Leave etc Regulations 1999, SI 1999/3312, reg 18A(1) for an employee to be treated as if he had not been absent refers to his absence: (1) if his return is from an isolated period of statutory leave, since the beginning of that period; (2) if his return is from consecutive periods of statutory leave, since the beginning of the first such period: see reg 18A(3) (reg 18A as so added; reg 18A(3) amended by SI 2008/1966).
15 Maternity and Parental Leave etc Regulations 1999, SI 1999/3312, reg 18A(1)(b) (as added: see note 3). See note 14.

396. Calculation of a week's pay in parental leave cases. Where:

(1) under the provisions of the Employment Rights Act 1996 that relate to calculating a week's pay[1], the amount of a week's pay of an employee[2] falls to be calculated by reference to the average rate of remuneration, or the average amount of remuneration, payable to the employee in respect of a period of 12 weeks ending on a particular date (the 'calculation date')[3];
(2) during a week in that period, the employee was absent from work on parental leave[4]; and
(3) remuneration is payable to the employee in respect of that week under

16 Employment Rights Act 1996 s 75E(4)(a) (as added: see note 4).
17 Employment Rights Act 1996 s 75E(4)(b) (as added: see note 4). Regulations under s 75E(4) may provide that the employee's entitlement is subject to the satisfaction by the child's mother of specified conditions:
  (1) as to employment or self-employment (s 75E(5)(a) (as so added));
  (2) as to having earnings of a specified amount for a specified period (s 75E(5)(b) (as so added));
  (3) as to caring or intending to care, with the employee, for the child (s 75E(5)(c) (as so added));
  (4) as to entitlement (or lack of entitlement) to maternity leave, statutory maternity pay or maternity allowance (s 75E(5)(d) (as so added)); and
  (5) as to the exercise of any such entitlement and the extent of any such exercise (s 75E(5)(e) (as so added)).

  The conditions as to employment or self-employment that may be specified in provision under s 75E(5) include conditions as to being in employed or self-employed earner's employment: see s 75K(4) (as so added); and see note 7. The Secretary of State may by regulations provide that s 75E(4)(b), (5) does not have effect, or has effect with modifications specified by the regulations, in a case where the mother of a child dies before another person has become entitled to leave under s 75E in respect of the child: s 75F(16)(a), (b) (as so added). As to statutory maternity pay see PARA 401 et seq.
18 Employment Rights Act 1996 s 75E(4)(c) (as added: see note 4). The Secretary of State may by regulations provide that s 75E(4)(c) does not have effect, or has effect with modifications specified by the regulations, in a case where the mother of a child dies before another person has become entitled to leave under s 75E in respect of the child: s 75F(16)(a) (as so added).
19 Employment Rights Act 1996 s 75E(4)(d) (as added: see note 4). The text refers to an entitlement to leave under s 75E(4): see s 75E(4)(d) (as so added). Provision under s 75E(4)(d) may require the employee to give notice to the employer about:
  (1) the amount of leave to which the employee would be entitled if the entitlement were fully exercised (disregarding for these purposes any intention of the child's mother to exercise an entitlement to leave under s 75E(1) (see the text and notes 1–14) or to statutory shared parental pay) (s 75E(6)(a) (as so added));
  (2) how much of the entitlement to leave the employee intends to exercise (s 75E(6)(b) (as so added));
  (3) the extent to which the child's mother intends to exercise an entitlement to leave under s 75E(1) or to statutory shared parental pay (s 75E(6)(c) (as so added)).

  The Secretary of State may by regulations provide that s 75E(6)(c) does not have effect, or has effect with modifications specified by the regulations, in a case where the mother of a child dies before another person has become entitled to leave under s 75E in respect of the child: s 75F(16)(c) (as so added).
20 Ie the amount of leave under the Employment Rights Act 1996 s 75E(4): see s 75E(4)(e) (as added: see note 4).
21 Employment Rights Act 1996 s 75E(4)(e) (as added: see note 4). The Secretary of State may by regulations provide that s 75E(4)(e) does not has effect, or have effect with modifications specified by the regulations, in a case where the mother of a child dies before another person has become entitled to leave under s 75E in respect of the child: s 75F(16)(a) (as so added).
22 Ie absent from work on leave under the Employment Rights Act 1996 s 75E(4): see s 75E(4) (as added: see note 4).
23 See the Employment Rights Act 1996 s 75E(4) (as added: see note 4).
24 Ie regulations under the Employment Rights Act 1996 s 75E (see the text and notes 1–23).
25 Ie under the Employment Rights Act 1996 s 75E(1) (see the text and notes 1–14) or s 75E(4) (see the text and notes 15–23): see s 75F(1)(a) (as added: see note 4).
26 Employment Rights Act 1996 s 75F(1)(a) (as added: see note 4). Provision under s 75F(1)(a) is to secure that the amount of leave to which an employee is entitled in respect of a child does not exceed:
  (1) in a case where the child's mother became entitled to maternity leave, the relevant amount of time reduced by: (a) where her maternity leave ends without her ordinary or additional maternity leave period having been curtailed by virtue of s 71(3)(ba) (see PARA 355 note 6) or s 73(3)(a) (see PARA 355), the amount of maternity leave taken by the child's mother (s 75F(2)(a)(i) (as so added)); or (b) except where head (a) above applies, the amount of time between the beginning of her maternity leave and the time when her ordinary or additional maternity leave period, as curtailed by virtue of s 71(3)(ba) or s 73(3)(a), comes to an end (s 75F(2)(a)(ii) (as so added));
  (2) in a case where the child's mother became entitled to statutory maternity pay or

maternity allowance but not maternity leave, the relevant amount of time reduced by an amount determined in accordance with the Social Security Contributions and Benefits Act 1992 s 171ZU(6)(a) or, as the case may be, s 171ZU(6)(b) (statutory shared parental pay on birth: see PARA 547) (Employment Rights Act 1996 s 75F(2)(b) (as so added)).

For the purposes of s 75F(2), the 'relevant amount of time' means an amount of time specified in or determined in accordance with regulations under s 75E (see the text and notes 1–23) (see s 75F(3) (as so added)); and, in reckoning, for the purposes of s 75F(2), the amount of maternity leave taken, a part of a week is to be treated as a full week (see s 75F(5) (as so added)). For these purposes, 'week' means any period of seven days: s 75F(15) (as so added). As to the meanings of 'ordinary maternity leave' and 'additional maternity leave' see PARA 356 note 2. As to the duration of ordinary maternity leave see PARA 357; and as to the duration of additional maternity leave see PARA 358.

Provision under s 75F(1)(a) is to secure also that the amount of leave to which an employee is entitled in respect of a child takes into account:

(i) in a case where another person is entitled to leave under s 75E in respect of the child, the amount of such leave taken by the other person (s 75F(4)(a) (as so added));

(ii) in a case where another person is entitled to statutory shared parental pay in respect of the child but not leave under s 75E, the number of weeks in respect of which such pay is payable to the other person (s 75F(4)(b) (as so added)).

In reckoning, for the purposes of s 75F(4), the amount of leave under s 75E taken during a period of such leave, a part of a week is to be treated as a full week: s 75F(6) (as so added).

27 Ie leave under the Employment Rights Act 1996 s 75E(1) (see the text and notes 1–14) or s 75E(4) (see the text and notes 15–23): see s 75F(1)(b) (as added: see note 4).

28 Employment Rights Act 1996 s 75F(1)(b) (as added: see note 4). Provision under s 75F(1)(b) is to secure that leave under s 75E (see the text and notes 1–23) must be taken before the end of such period as may be specified by the regulations: s 75F(7) (as so added).

29 Ie leave under the Employment Rights Act 1996 s 75E (see the text and notes 1–23): see s 75F(8) (as added: see note 4).

30 Employment Rights Act 1996 s 75F(8) (as added: see note 4).

31 Ie leave under the Employment Rights Act 1996 s 75E (see the text and notes 1–23): see s 75I(1)(a) (as added: see note 4).

32 Employment Rights Act 1996 s 75I(1)(a) (as added: see note 4). For the purposes of head (iii) in the text, 'terms and conditions of employment' includes matters connected with an employee's employment whether or not they arise under the employee's contract of employment, but does not include terms and conditions about remuneration: see s 75I(2) (as so added). Regulations under s 75E (see the text and notes 1–23) may specify matters which are, or are not, to be treated as remuneration for the purposes of s 75I: see s 75I(4) (as so added).

33 Ie leave under the Employment Rights Act 1996 s 75E (see the text and notes 1–23): see s 75I(1)(b) (as added: see note 4).

34 Ie except in so far as they are inconsistent with the Employment Rights Act 1996 s 75E(1) (see the text and notes 1–14) or s 75E(4) (see the text and notes 15–23): see s 75H(1)(b) (as added: see note 4).

35 Employment Rights Act 1996 s 75I(1)(b) (as added: see note 4).

36 Ie leave under the Employment Rights Act 1996 s 75E (see the text and notes 1–23): see s 75I(1)(c) (as added: see note 4). See note 37.

37 Employment Rights Act 1996 s 75I(1)(c) (as added: see note 4). The reference in head (v) in the text to absence on leave under s 75E includes, where appropriate, a reference to a continuous period of absence attributable partly to leave under s 75E and partly to any one or more periods of leave under s 75G (see PARA 399), maternity leave, paternity leave, adoption leave, and parental leave: see s 75I(3) (as so added). Regulations under s 75E may make provision, in relation to the right to return mentioned in head (v) in the text, about seniority, pension rights and similar rights, and about terms and conditions of employment on return: see s 75I(5) (as so added). As to adoption leave see PARA 377 et seq; as to paternity leave see PARA 368 et seq; and as to parental leave see PARA 390 et seq.

38 Ie regulations under the Employment Rights Act 1996 s 75E (see the text and notes 1–23).

39 Ie non-consecutive periods of leave under the Employment Rights Act 1996 s 75E (see the text and notes 1–23).

40 Employment Rights Act 1996 s 75F(9)(a) (as added: see note 4).

41 Employment Rights Act 1996 s 75F(9)(b) (as added: see note 4).

42 Employment Rights Act 1996 s 75F(10)(a) (as added: see note 4). The text refers to an amount of leave under s 75E (see the text and notes 1–23): see s 75F(10)(a) (as so added). Provision

under s 75F(10)(a) may provide for variation to be subject to the consent of an employer in circumstances specified by the regulations: s 75F(11) (as so added).

43 Ie in accordance with provision under the Employment Rights Act 1996 s 75E(3)(b) (see note 10) or s 75E(6)(b) (see note 19) or s 75F(13)(b) (see note 44): see s 75F(10)(b) (as added: see note 4).

44 Employment Rights Act 1996 s 75F(10)(b) (as added: see note 4). Provision under s 75F(10)(b) may require an employee to satisfy specified conditions:
- (1) as to giving notice of an intention to vary the amount of leave under s 75E (see the text and notes 1–23) to be taken by the employee (s 75F(12)(a) (as so added));
- (2) if the employee proposes to vary the amount of leave under s 75E(1) (see the text and notes 1–14) to be taken by the employee, as to the consent of P to that variation (s 75F(12)(b) (as so added));
- (3) if the employee proposes to vary the amount of leave under s 75E(4) (see the text and notes 15–23) to be taken by the employee, as to the consent of the child's mother to that variation (s 75F(12)(c) (as so added)).

Provision under head (1) above may require an employee to give notice to the employer about:
- (a) the extent to which the employee has exercised an entitlement to leave under s 75E(1) or s 75E(4) in respect of the child (s 75F(13)(a) (as so added));
- (b) how much of the entitlement to leave the employee intends to exercise (s 75F(13)(b) (as so added));
- (c) the extent to which a person other than the employee has exercised an entitlement to leave under s 75E or to statutory shared parental pay in respect of the child (s 75F(13)(c) (as so added));
- (d) the extent to which a person other than the employee intends to exercise such an entitlement (s 75F(13)(d) (as so added)).

The Secretary of State may by regulations provide that s 75F(12)(c) (see head (3) above) or s 75F(13)(c), (d) (see heads (c), (d) above) does not have effect, or has effect with modifications specified by the regulations, in a case where the mother of a child dies before another person has become entitled to leave under s 75E in respect of the child: see s 75F(16)(d), (e) (as so added).

45 Employment Rights Act 1996 s 75F(14)(a) (as added: see note 4).

46 Ie leave under the Employment Rights Act 1996 s 75E (see the text and notes 1–23).

47 Employment Rights Act 1996 s 75F(14)(b) (as added: see note 4).

48 Ie leave under the Employment Rights Act 1996 s 75E (see the text and notes 1–23).

49 Employment Rights Act 1996 s 75F(14)(c) (as added: see note 4).

50 Ie leave under the Employment Rights Act 1996 s 75E (see the text and notes 1–23).

51 Employment Rights Act 1996 s 75F(14)(d) (as added: see note 4).

52 Ie leave under the Employment Rights Act 1996 s 75E (see the text and notes 1–23).

53 Employment Rights Act 1996 s 75F(14)(e) (as added: see note 4).

54 Ie leave under the Employment Rights Act 1996 s 75E (see the text and notes 1–23).

55 Employment Rights Act 1996 s 75F(14)(f) (as added: see note 4).

56 Employment Rights Act 1996 s 75J(1) (as added: see note 4). The text refers to a period of leave under s 75E (see the text and notes 1–23): see s 75J(1) (as so added). Provision made by virtue of s 75J(1) may include provision requiring an employer to offer alternative employment, and provision for the consequences of failure to comply with the regulations (which may include provision for a dismissal to be treated as unfair for the purposes of Pt X (ss 94–134A) (unfair dismissal: see PARA 757 et seq)): see s 75J(2) (as so added).

57 Employment Rights Act 1996 s 75K(1)(a) (as added: see note 4). For these purposes, 'relevant person' means:
- (1) a person who, in connection with an employee's claim to be entitled to leave under section 75E (see the text and notes 1–23), is required to satisfy conditions specified in provision under s 75E(2) (see note 7) or s 75E(5) (see note 17) (s 75K(2)(a) (as so added)); or
- (2) a person who is an employer or former employer of such a person (s 75K(2)(b) (as so added)).

Under head (2) above, 'employer', in relation to a person falling within head (1) above who is an employed earner, includes a person who is a secondary contributor as regards that employed earner: see s 75K(3) (as so added). 'Secondary contributor', as regards an employed earner, means a person who is indicated by the Social Security Contributions and Benefits Act 1992 s 7(1), as s 7(1) has effect subject to s 7(2), as being a secondary contributor as regards the earner, or who is indicated by regulations under s 7(2) as being a person to be treated as a secondary contributor as regards the earner (see **WELFARE BENEFITS AND STATE PENSIONS** vol 104 (2014) PARA 385): Employment Rights Act 1996 s 75K(5) (as so added).

58 Employment Rights Act 1996 s 75K(1)(b) (as added: see note 4).

59 Employment Rights Act 1996 s 75K(1)(c) (as added: see note 4).
60 Employment Rights Act 1996 s 75K(1)(d) (as added: see note 4).
61 Ie leave under the Employment Rights Act 1996 s 75E (see the text and notes 1–23).
62 Employment Rights Act 1996 s 75K(1)(e) (as added: see note 4). As to the meaning of 'contract of employment' see PARA 2.
63 Ie the Employment Rights Act 1996 Pt XIV Ch II (ss 220–229) (calculation of a week's pay: see PARA 143 et seq).
64 Employment Rights Act 1996 s 75K(1)(f) (as added: see note 4). The text refers to absence from work on leave under s 75E (see the text and notes 1–23): see s 75K(1)(f) (as so added).
65 Employment Rights Act 1996 s 75K(1)(g) (as added: see note 4). The text refers to a person entitled to take leave under s 75E (see the text and notes 1–23): see s 75K(1)(g) (as so added).

B. SHARED PARENTAL LEAVE ON ADOPTION

399. Power to make regulations in relation to shared parental leave on adoption. The Secretary of State[1] may make regulations[2] in relation to shared parental leave on adoption, entitling an employee[3] who satisfies specified conditions[4]:

(1) as to duration of employment[5];
(2) as to being a person with whom a child is, or is expected to be, placed for adoption under the law of any part of the United Kingdom[6];
(3) as to caring or intending to care, with another person ('P'), for the child[7];
(4) as to entitlement to adoption leave[8];
(5) as to the exercise of that entitlement and the extent of any such exercise[9];
(6) as to giving notice of an intention to exercise an entitlement to shared parental leave on adoption[10]; and
(7) as to the consent of P to the amount of shared parental leave on adoption[11] that the employee intends to take[12],

to be absent from work on such leave[13] for the purpose of caring for the child[14].

The Secretary of State also may make regulations entitling an employee who satisfies specified conditions[15]:

(a) as to duration of employment[16];
(b) as to relationship with a child placed, or expected to be placed, for adoption under the law of any part of the United Kingdom or with a person ('A') with whom the child is, or is expected to be, so placed[17];
(c) as to caring or intending to care, with A, for the child[18];
(d) as to giving notice of an intention to exercise an entitlement to shared parental leave on adoption[19]; and
(e) as to the consent of A to the amount of shared parental leave on adoption[20] that the employee intends to take[21],

to be absent from work on such leave[22] for the purpose of caring for the child[23].

Such regulations[24] must:

(i) include provision for determining the amount of shared parental leave on adoption[25] to which an employee is entitled in respect of a child[26], and for determining when such leave[27] may be taken[28];
(ii) provide for the taking of such leave[29] in a single period or in non-consecutive periods[30];
(iii) provide that an employee who is absent on such leave[31] is entitled, for such purposes and to such extent as the regulations may prescribe, to the benefit of the terms and conditions of employment which would have applied if the employee had not been absent[32];

(iv) provide that an employee who is absent on such leave[33] is bound, for such purposes and to such extent as the regulations may prescribe, by obligations arising under those terms and conditions, except in so far as they are inconsistent with the provisions[34] that confer rights to such leave[35]; and

(v) provide that an employee who is absent on such leave[36] is entitled to return from leave to a job of a kind prescribed by the regulations, subject to head (J) below[37].

Such regulations[38] may:

(A) provide for an employer, subject to such restrictions as may be specified, to require an employee who proposes to take non-consecutive periods of shared parental leave on adoption[39] to take that amount of leave as a single period of leave[40];

(B) provide for a single period of shared parental leave on adoption that is so imposed on an employee to start with a day proposed by the employee or, if no day is proposed, with the first day of the first period of such leave proposed by the employee[41];

(C) provide for the variation, subject to such restrictions as may be specified, of the period or periods during which an amount of shared parental leave on adoption may be taken[42], and the amount of such leave that the employee previously[43] specified[44];

(D) specify things which are, or are not, to be taken as done for the purpose of caring for a child[45];

(E) make provision excluding the right to be absent on shared parental leave on adoption[46] in respect of a child where more than one child is placed for adoption as part of the same arrangement[47];

(F) specify a minimum amount of shared parental leave on adoption[48] which may be taken[49];

(G) make provision about how shared parental leave on adoption[50] may be taken[51];

(H) specify circumstances in which an employee may work for the employer during a period of shared parental leave on adoption[52] without bringing the particular period of leave, or the employee's entitlement to such leave, to an end[53];

(I) specify circumstances in which an employee may be absent on shared parental leave on adoption[54] otherwise than for the purpose of caring for a child without bringing the person's entitlement to such leave to an end[55];

(J) make provision about redundancy, or dismissal (other than by reason of redundancy), during a period of shared parental leave on adoption[56];

(K) make provision about notices to be given, evidence to be produced and other procedures to be followed by employees, employers, and relevant persons[57];

(L) make provision requiring such persons to keep records[58];

(M) make provision for the consequences of failure to give notices, to produce evidence, to keep records or to comply with other procedural requirements[59];

(N) make provision for the consequences of failure to act in accordance with a notice given by virtue of head (K) above[60];

(O) make special provision for cases where an employee has a right which corresponds to a right to shared parental leave on adoption[61] and which arises under the employee's contract of employment or otherwise[62];

(P) make provision modifying the effect of the provisions of the Employment Rights Act 1996 that relate to calculating a week's pay[63] in relation to an employee who is or has been absent from work on shared parental leave on adoption[64];

(Q) make provision applying, modifying or excluding an enactment, in such circumstances as may be specified and subject to any conditions which may be specified, in relation to a person entitled to take shared parental leave on adoption[65].

1 As to the Secretary of State see PARA 5 note 21.

2 As to the making of regulations under the Employment Rights Act 1996 generally see PARA 162. At the date at which this volume states the law, no such regulations had been made.

3 As to the meaning of 'employee' see PARA 2.

4 See the Employment Rights Act 1996 s 75G(1) (ss 75G–75K added by the Children and Families Act 2014 s 117(1)). Regulations under any of the Employment Rights Act 1996 ss 75G, 75H may make different provision for different cases or circumstances: s 75K(6) (as so added).

5 Employment Rights Act 1996 s 75G(1)(a) (as added: see note 4).

6 Employment Rights Act 1996 s 75G(1)(b) (as added: see note 4). Regulations under s 75G(1) are to provide for leave in respect of a child placed, or expected to be placed, under the Children Act 1989 s 22C (local authority's duty to provide child is in its care with accommodation: see CHILDREN AND YOUNG PERSONS vol 10 (2012) PARA 858) by a local authority in England with a local authority foster parent who has been approved as a prospective adopter: Employment Rights Act 1996 s 75G(7) (as so added). The provision made by s 75G and s 75H (see the text and notes 24–55) have effect in relation to regulations made by virtue of s 75G(7) as if references to a child being placed for adoption under the law of any part of the United Kingdom were references to being placed under the Children Act 1989 s 22C with a local authority foster parent who has been approved as a prospective adopter: Employment Rights Act 1996 s 75G(8) (as so added). The Secretary of State may by regulations provide for s 75G and s 75H to have effect in relation to:

(1) cases which involve adoption, but not the placement of a child for adoption under the law of any part of the United Kingdom, with such modifications as the regulations may prescribe (s 75H(17) (as so added)); and

(2) cases which involve an employee who has applied, or intends to apply, with another person for a parental order under the Human Fertilisation and Embryology Act 2008 s 54 (parental orders: see CHILDREN AND YOUNG PERSONS vol 9 (2012) PARA 129) and a child who is, or will be, the subject of the order, with such modifications as the regulations may prescribe (Employment Rights Act 1996 s 75H(18) (as so added)).

Where s 75G and s 75H have effect in relation to such cases as are described in s 75H(18), regulations under s 75G about evidence to be produced (see head (M) in the text) may require statutory declarations as to eligibility to apply for a parental order, and intention to apply for such an order: s 75K(7) (as so added). As to the meanings of 'England' and 'United Kingdom' see PARA 2 note 12. As to the law relating to child adoption see CHILDREN AND YOUNG PERSONS vol 9 (2012) PARA 360 et seq.

7 Employment Rights Act 1996 s 75G(1)(c) (as added: see note 4). Regulations under s 75G(1) may provide that the employee's entitlement is subject to the satisfaction by P of specified conditions:

(1) as to employment or self-employment (s 75G(2)(a) (as so added));

(2) as to having earnings of a specified amount for a specified period (s 75G(2)(b) (as so added));

(3) as to caring or intending to care, with the employee, for the child (s 75G(2)(c) (as so added)); and

(4) as to relationship with the child or the employee (s 75G(2)(d) (as so added)).

The conditions as to employment or self-employment that may be specified in provision under s 75G(2) include conditions as to being in employed or self-employed earner's employment: see s 75K(4) (as so added). As to the meanings of 'employment', 'employed earner' and 'self-employed earner' for these purposes see PARA 398 note 7.

8 Employment Rights Act 1996 s 75G(1)(d) (as added: see note 4). As to adoption leave see PARA 377 et seq.

9 Employment Rights Act 1996 s 75G(1)(e) (as added: see note 4).

10 Employment Rights Act 1996 s 75G(1)(f) (as added: see note 4). The text refers to an entitlement to leave under s 75G(1): see s 75G(1)(f) (as so added). Provision under s 75G(1)(f) may require the employee to give notice to the employer about:
  (1) the amount of leave to which the employee would be entitled if the entitlement were fully exercised (disregarding for these purposes any intention of P to exercise an entitlement to leave under s 75G(4) (see the text and notes 15–23) or to statutory shared parental pay) (s 75G(3)(a) (as so added));
  (2) how much of the entitlement to leave the employee intends to exercise (s 75G(3)(b) (as so added));
  (3) the extent to which P intends to exercise an entitlement to leave under s 75G(4) or to statutory shared parental pay (s 75G(3)(c) (as so added)).

  As to the meaning of 'employer' see PARA 2. As to statutory shared parental pay see PARA 534.
11 Ie the amount of leave under the Employment Rights Act 1996 s 75G(1): see s 75G(1)(g) (as added: see note 4).
12 Employment Rights Act 1996 s 75G(1)(g) (as added: see note 4).
13 Ie absent from work on leave under the Employment Rights Act 1996 s 75G(1): see s 75G(1) (as added: see note 4).
14 See the Employment Rights Act 1996 s 75G(1) (as added: see note 4).
15 See the Employment Rights Act 1996 s 75G(4) (as added: see note 4).
16 Employment Rights Act 1996 s 75G(4)(a) (as added: see note 4).
17 Employment Rights Act 1996 s 75G(4)(b) (as added: see note 4). Regulations under s 75G(4) are to provide for leave in respect of a child placed, or expected to be placed, under the Children Act 1989 s 22C (local authority's duty to provide child is in its care with accommodation: see CHILDREN AND YOUNG PERSONS vol 10 (2012) PARA 858) by a local authority in England with a local authority foster parent who has been approved as a prospective adopter: Employment Rights Act 1996 s 75G(7) (as so added). See also note 6.

  Regulations under s 75G(4) may provide that the employee's entitlement is subject to the satisfaction by A of specified conditions:
  (1) as to employment or self-employment (s 75G(5)(a) (as so added));
  (2) as to having earnings of a specified amount for a specified period (s 75G(5)(b) (as so added));
  (3) as to caring or intending to care, with the employee, for the child (s 75G(5)(c) (as so added));
  (4) as to entitlement (or lack of entitlement) to adoption leave or statutory adoption pay (s 75G(5)(d) (as so added)); and
  (5) as to the exercise of any such entitlement and the extent of any such exercise (s 75G(5)(e) (as so added)).

  The conditions as to employment or self-employment that may be specified in provision under s 75G(5) include conditions as to being in employed or self-employed earner's employment: see s 75K(4) (as so added); and see note 7. The Secretary of State may by regulations provide that s 75G(4)(b), (5) does not have effect, or has effect with modifications specified by the regulations, in a case where a person who is taking adoption leave, or is entitled to be paid statutory adoption pay in respect of a child, dies before another person has become entitled to leave under s 75G in respect of the child: s 75H(16)(a), (b) (as so added). As to statutory adoption pay see PARA 488 et seq.
18 Employment Rights Act 1996 s 75G(4)(c) (as added: see note 4). The Secretary of State may by regulations provide that s 75G(4)(c) does not have effect, or has effect with modifications specified by the regulations, in a case where a person who is taking adoption leave, or is entitled to be paid statutory adoption pay in respect of a child, dies before another person has become entitled to leave under s 75G in respect of the child: s 75H(16)(a) (as so added).
19 Employment Rights Act 1996 s 75G(4)(d) (as added: see note 4). The text refers to an entitlement to leave under s 75G(4): see s 75G(4)(d) (as so added). Provision under s 75G(4)(d) may require the employee to give notice to the employer about:
  (1) the amount of leave to which the employee would be entitled if the entitlement were fully exercised (disregarding for these purposes any intention of A to exercise an entitlement to leave under s 75G(1) (see the text and notes 1–14) or to statutory shared parental pay) (s 75G(6)(a) (as so added));
  (2) how much of the entitlement to leave the employee intends to exercise (s 75G(6)(b) (as so added));
  (3) the extent to which A intends to exercise an entitlement to leave under s 75G(1) or to statutory shared parental pay (s 75G(6)(c) (as so added)).

  The Secretary of State may by regulations provide that s 75G(6)(c) does not have effect, or has effect with modifications specified by the regulations, in a case where a person who is taking adoption leave, or is entitled to be paid statutory adoption pay in respect of a child, dies before another person has become entitled to leave under s 75G in respect of the child: s 75H(16)(c) (as so added).

20 Ie the amount of leave under the Employment Rights Act 1996 s 75G(4): see s 75G(4)(e) (as added: see note 4).

21 Employment Rights Act 1996 s 75G(4)(e) (as added: see note 4). The Secretary of State may by regulations provide that s 75G(4)(e) does not have effect, or has effect with modifications specified by the regulations, in a case where a person who is taking adoption leave, or is entitled to be paid statutory adoption pay in respect of a child, dies before another person has become entitled to leave under s 75G in respect of the child: s 75H(16)(a) (as so added).

22 Ie absent from work on leave under the Employment Rights Act 1996 s 75G(4): see s 75G(4) (as added: see note 4).

23 See the Employment Rights Act 1996 s 75G(4) (as added: see note 4).

24 Ie regulations under the Employment Rights Act 1996 s 75G (see the text and notes 1–23). As to the effect of s 75H in relation to regulations made by virtue of s 75G(7) and in relation to such cases as are described in s 75H(18) see note 6.

25 Ie under the Employment Rights Act 1996 s 75G(1) (see the text and notes 1–14) or s 75G(4) (see the text and notes 15–23): see s 75H(1)(a) (as added: see note 4).

26 Employment Rights Act 1996 s 75H(1)(a) (as added: see note 4). Provision under s 75H(1)(a) is to secure that the amount of leave to which an employee is entitled in respect of a child does not exceed:

(1) in a case where a person with whom the child is, or is expected to be, placed for adoption became entitled to adoption leave, the relevant amount of time reduced by: (a) where the person's adoption leave ends without the person's ordinary or additional adoption leave period having been curtailed by virtue of s 75A(2A)(a) (see PARA 377 note 6) or s 75B(3)(a) (see PARA 377), the amount of adoption leave taken by that person (s 75H(2)(a)(i) (as so added)); or (b) except where head (a) above applies, the amount of time between the beginning of the person's adoption leave and the time when the person's ordinary or additional adoption leave period, as curtailed by virtue of s 75A(2A)(a) or s 75B(3)(a), comes to an end (s 75H(2)(a)(ii) (as so added));

(2) in a case where a person with whom the child is, or is expected to be, placed for adoption became entitled to statutory adoption pay but not adoption leave, the relevant amount of time reduced by an amount determined in accordance with the Social Security Contributions and Benefits Act 1992 s 171ZV(6)(a) or, as the case may be, s 171ZV(6)(b) (statutory shared parental pay on adoption: see PARA 547) (Employment Rights Act 1996 s 75H(2)(b) (as so added)).

For the purposes of s 75H(2), the 'relevant amount of time' means an amount of time specified in or determined in accordance with regulations under s 75G (see the text and notes 1–23) (see s 75H(3) (as so added)); and, in reckoning, for the purposes of s 75H(2), the amount of adoption leave taken, a part of a week is to be treated as a full week (see s 75H(5) (as so added)). For these purposes, 'week' means any period of seven days: s 75H(15) (as so added). As to the meanings of 'ordinary adoption leave' and 'additional adoption leave' see PARA 377. As to the duration of ordinary adoption leave see PARA 378; and as to the duration of additional adoption leave see PARA 379.

Provision under s 75H(1)(a) is to secure also that the amount of leave to which an employee is entitled in respect of a child takes into account:

(i) in a case where another person is entitled to leave under s 75G in respect of the child, the amount of such leave taken by the other person (s 75H(4)(a) (as so added));

(ii) in a case where another person is entitled to statutory shared parental pay in respect of the child but not leave under s 75G, the number of weeks in respect of which such pay is payable to the other person (s 75H(4)(b) (as so added)).

In reckoning, for the purposes of s 75H(4), the amount of leave under s 75G taken during a period of such leave, a part of a week is to be treated as a full week: s 75H(6) (as so added).

27 Ie leave under the Employment Rights Act 1996 s 75G(1) (see the text and notes 1–14) or s 75G(4) (see the text and notes 15–23): see s 75H(1)(b) (as added: see note 4).

28 Employment Rights Act 1996 s 75H(1)(b) (as added: see note 4). Provision under s 75H(1)(b) is to secure that leave under s 75G (see the text and notes 1–23) must be taken before the end of such period as may be prescribed by the regulations: s 75H(7) (as so added).

29 Ie leave under the Employment Rights Act 1996 s 75G (see the text and notes 1–23): see s 75H(8) (as added: see note 4).

30 Employment Rights Act 1996 s 75H(8) (as added: see note 4).

31 Ie leave under the Employment Rights Act 1996 s 75G (see the text and notes 1–23): see s 75I(1)(a) (as added: see note 4).

32 Employment Rights Act 1996 s 75I(1)(a) (as added: see note 4). For the purposes of head (iii) in the text, 'terms and conditions of employment' includes matters connected with an employee's employment whether or not they arise under the employee's contract of employment, but does not include terms and conditions about remuneration: see s 75I(2) (as so added). Regulations under s 75G may specify matters which are, or are not, to be treated as remuneration for the purposes of s 75I: see s 75I(4) (as so added).
33 Ie leave under the Employment Rights Act 1996 s 75G (see the text and notes 1–23): see s 75I(1)(b) (as added: see note 4).
34 Ie except in so far as they are inconsistent with the Employment Rights Act 1996 s 75G(1) (see the text and notes 1–14) or s 75G(4) (see the text and notes 15–23): see s 75H(1)(b) (as added: see note 4).
35 Employment Rights Act 1996 s 75I(1)(b) (as added: see note 4).
36 Ie leave under the Employment Rights Act 1996 s 75G (see the text and notes 1–23): see s 75I(1)(c) (as added: see note 4). See note 37.
37 Employment Rights Act 1996 s 75I(1)(c) (as added: see note 4). The reference in head (v) in the text to absence on leave under s 75G includes, where appropriate, a reference to a continuous period of absence attributable partly to leave under s 75G and partly to any one or more of leave under s 75E (see PARA 398), maternity leave, paternity leave, adoption leave, and parental leave: see s 75I(3) (as so added). Regulations under s 75G may make provision, in relation to the right to return mentioned in head (v) in the text, about seniority, pension rights and similar rights, and terms and conditions of employment on return: see s 75I(5) (as so added). As to maternity leave see PARA 355 et seq; as to paternity leave see PARA 368 et seq; and as to parental leave see PARA 390 et seq.
38 Ie regulations under the Employment Rights Act 1996 s 75G (see the text and notes 1–23).
39 Ie non-consecutive periods of leave under the Employment Rights Act 1996 s 75G (see the text and notes 1–23).
40 Employment Rights Act 1996 s 75H(9)(a) (as added: see note 4).
41 Employment Rights Act 1996 s 75H(9)(b) (as added: see note 4).
42 Employment Rights Act 1996 s 75H(10)(a) (as added: see note 4). The text refers to an amount of leave under s 75G (see the text and notes 1–23): see s 75H(10)(a) (as so added). Provision under s 75H(10)(a) may provide for variation to be subject to the consent of an employer in circumstances specified by the regulations: s 75H(11) (as so added).
43 Ie in accordance with provision under the Employment Rights Act 1996 s 75G(3)(b) (see note 10) or s 75G(6)(b) (see note 19) or s 75H(13)(b) (see note 44): see s 75H(10)(b) (as added: see note 4).
44 Employment Rights Act 1996 s 75H(10)(b) (as added: see note 4). Provision under s 75H(10)(b) may require an employee to satisfy specified conditions:
    (1) as to giving notice of an intention to vary the amount of leave under s 75G (see the text and notes 1–23) to be taken by the employee (s 75H(12)(a) (as so added));
    (2) if the employee proposes to vary the amount of leave under s 75G(1) (see the text and notes 1–14) to be taken by the employee, as to the consent of P to that variation (s 75H(12)(b) (as so added));
    (3) if the employee proposes to vary the amount of leave under s 75G(4) (see the text and notes 15–23) to be taken by the employee, as to the consent of A to that variation (s 75H(12)(c) (as so added)).

    Provision under head (1) above may require an employee to give notice to the employer about:
    (a) the extent to which the employee has exercised an entitlement to leave under s 75G(1) or s 75G(4) in respect of the child (s 75H(13)(a) (as so added));
    (b) how much of the entitlement to leave the employee intends to exercise (s 75H(13)(b) (as so added));
    (c) the extent to which a person other than the employee has exercised an entitlement to leave under s 75G or to statutory shared parental pay in respect of the child (s 75H(13)(c) (as so added));
    (d) the extent to which a person other than the employee intends to exercise such an entitlement (s 75H(13)(d) (as so added)).

    The Secretary of State may by regulations provide that s 75H(12)(c) (see head (3) above) or s 75H(13)(c), (d) (see heads (c), (d) above) does not have effect, or has effect with modifications specified by the regulations, in a case where a person who is taking adoption leave, or is entitled to be paid statutory adoption pay in respect of a child, dies before another person has become entitled to leave under s 75G in respect of the child: see s 75H(16)(d), (e) (as so added).
45 Employment Rights Act 1996 s 75H(14)(a) (as added: see note 4).
46 Ie leave under the Employment Rights Act 1996 s 75G (see the text and notes 1–23).
47 Employment Rights Act 1996 s 75H(14)(b) (as added: see note 4).

48 Ie leave under the Employment Rights Act 1996 s 75G (see the text and notes 1–23).
49 Employment Rights Act 1996 s 75H(14)(c) (as added: see note 4).
50 Ie leave under the Employment Rights Act 1996 s 75G (see the text and notes 1–23).
51 Employment Rights Act 1996 s 75H(14)(d) (as added: see note 4).
52 Ie leave under the Employment Rights Act 1996 s 75G (see the text and notes 1–23).
53 Employment Rights Act 1996 s 75H(14)(e) (as added: see note 4).
54 Ie leave under the Employment Rights Act 1996 s 75G (see the text and notes 1–23).
55 Employment Rights Act 1996 s 75H(14)(f) (as added: see note 4).
56 Employment Rights Act 1996 s 75J(1) (as added: see note 4). The text refers to a period of leave under s 75G (see the text and notes 1–23): see s 75J(1) (as so added). Provision made by virtue of s 75J(1) may include provision requiring an employer to offer alternative employment, and provision for the consequences of failure to comply with the regulations (which may include provision for a dismissal to be treated as unfair for the purposes of Pt X (ss 94–134A) (unfair dismissal: see PARA 757 et seq)): see s 75J(2) (as so added).
57 Employment Rights Act 1996 s 75K(1)(a) (as added: see note 4). For these purposes, 'relevant person' means:
(1) a person who, in connection with an employee's claim to be entitled to leave under section 75G (see the text and notes 1–23), is required to satisfy conditions specified in provision under s 75G(2) (see note 7) or s 75G(5) (see note 17) (s 75K(2)(a) (as so added)); or
(2) a person who is an employer or former employer of such a person (s 75K(2)(b) (as so added)).
Under head (2) above, 'employer', in relation to a person falling within head (1) above who is an employed earner, includes a person who is a secondary contributor as regards that employed earner: see s 75K(3) (as so added).
As to the meaning of 'secondary contributor', as regards an employed earner, for these purposes see PARA 398 note 57.
58 Employment Rights Act 1996 s 75K(1)(b) (as added: see note 4).
59 Employment Rights Act 1996 s 75K(1)(c) (as added: see note 4).
60 Employment Rights Act 1996 s 75K(1)(d) (as added: see note 4).
61 Ie leave under the Employment Rights Act 1996 s 75G (see the text and notes 1–23).
62 Employment Rights Act 1996 s 75K(1)(e) (as added: see note 4). As to the meaning of 'contract of employment' see PARA 2.
63 Ie the Employment Rights Act 1996 Pt XIV Ch II (ss 220–229) (calculation of a week's pay: see PARA 143 et seq).
64 Employment Rights Act 1996 s 75K(1)(f) (as added: see note 4). The text refers to absence from work on leave under s 75G (see the text and notes 1–23): see s 75K(1)(f) (as so added).
65 Employment Rights Act 1996 s 75K(1)(g) (as added: see note 4). The text refers to a person entitled to take leave under s 75G (see the text and notes 1–23): see s 75K(1)(g) (as so added).

(11) STATUTORY PAYMENTS FOR FAMILY LEAVE

(i) Statutory Rights to Leave and Pay for Family Reasons

400. Development of statutory rights to remuneration for leave taken for family reasons. The development, over time, of rights to leave for family reasons has been accompanied by associated rights to remuneration for the leave so taken[1]. Accordingly, the following basic rights to statutory pay on such grounds now exist:
(1) the right to Statutory Maternity Pay[2];
(2) the right to Statutory Adoption Pay[3];
(3) the right to Statutory Paternity Pay[4]; and
(4) the right to Statutory Shared Parental Pay on Birth or Adoption[5].
This is in addition to the right of employees to take paid time off work:
(a) for ante-natal care[6];
(b) for adoption appointments[7]; and
(c) to care for dependants[8].

There is also statutory protection for the right not to be subjected to a detriment[9] or dismissed[10] for taking time off for family or domestic reasons.

1 See PARA 354.
2 See PARA 401 et seq.
3 See PARA 488 et seq.
4 See PARA 443 et seq.
5 See PARA 534 et seq.
6 See PARA 333 et seq.
7 See PARA 341 et seq.
8 See PARAS 347–348.
9 See PARA 620.
10 See PARA 784.

(ii) Statutory Maternity Pay

A. IN GENERAL

401. Liability of employer for payment of statutory maternity pay. Where a woman who is or has been an employee[1] satisfies the prescribed conditions[2], she is entitled[3] to payments (known as 'statutory maternity pay')[4]. The liability to make payments of statutory maternity pay to a woman is a liability of any person of whom she has been an employee[5] for the continuous period of employment that is prescribed[6].

Any agreement is void to the extent that it purports:

(1) to exclude, limit or otherwise modify any of statutory maternity pay provisions that are set out in Part XII of the Social Security Contributions and Benefits Act 1992[7]; or

(2) to require an employee or former employee to contribute, whether directly or indirectly, towards any costs incurred by her employer or former employer under Part XII[8],

but, for the avoidance of doubt, any agreement between an employer and an employee authorising any deductions from statutory maternity pay which the employer is liable to pay to an employee in respect of any period is not void by virtue of head (1) above if the employer: (a) is authorised by that or another agreement to make the same deductions from any contractual remuneration which he is liable to pay in respect of the same period[9]; or (b) would be so authorised if he were liable to pay contractual remuneration in respect of that period[10].

1 As to the meaning of 'employee' for these purposes see PARA 406.
2 Ie the conditions set out in the Social Security Contributions and Benefits Act 1992 s 164: see PARA 415.
3 Ie in accordance with the provisions of the Social Security Contributions and Benefits Act 1992 Pt XII (ss 164–171) (statutory maternity pay).
4 See the Social Security Contributions and Benefits Act 1992 s 164(1). Statutory maternity pay under Pt XII constitutes 'wages' for the purposes of the Employment Rights Act 1996 Pt II (ss 13–27) (protection of wages): see s 27(1); and PARA 254. Payments of statutory maternity pay under the Social Security Contributions and Benefits Act 1992 Pt XII are charged to income tax under the Income Tax (Earnings and Pensions) Act 2003 Pts 2–7 (ss 3–554): see **INCOME TAXATION** vol 58 (2014) PARA 730 et seq.
5 Ie as mentioned in the Social Security Contributions and Benefits Act 1992 s 164(2)(a): see PARA 415.
6 Social Security Contributions and Benefits Act 1992 s 164(3). As to the time limit for paying statutory maternity pay see PARA 431. As to the liability of the Commissioners for Revenue and Customs for payments of statutory maternity pay see PARA 403.

7 Social Security Contributions and Benefits Act 1992 s 164(6)(a). Head (1) in the text refers to any of the provisions of Pt XII (ss 164–171) (statutory maternity pay): see s 164(6)(a).
8 Social Security Contributions and Benefits Act 1992 s 164(6)(b). As to the meaning of 'employer' for these purposes see PARA 414.
9 Social Security Contributions and Benefits Act 1992 s 164(7)(a).
10 Social Security Contributions and Benefits Act 1992 s 164(7)(b).

402. General power to make regulations in relation to statutory maternity pay. The Secretary of State[1] may by regulations[2]:

(1) specify circumstances in which[3] there is to be no liability to pay statutory maternity pay[4] in respect of a week[5];
(2) specify circumstances in which[6] the liability to make payments of statutory maternity pay is to be a liability of the Commissioners for Revenue and Customs[7];
(3) specify in what circumstances employment is to be treated[8] as continuous[9];
(4) provide that a woman is to be treated as being employed for a continuous period of at least 26 weeks where: (a) she has been employed by the same employer for at least 26 weeks under two or more separate contracts of service[10]; and (b) those contracts were not continuous[11];
(5) provide that specified provisions[12] are to have effect subject to prescribed modifications[13] in such cases as may be prescribed[14];
(6) provide that the provisions relating to notice[15] are not to have effect, or are to have effect subject to prescribed modifications, in such cases as may be prescribed[16];
(7) provide for amounts earned by a woman under separate contracts of service with the same employer to be aggregated[17]; and
(8) provide that the amount of a woman's earnings for any period, or the amount of her earnings to be treated as comprised in any payment made to her or for her benefit, is to be calculated or estimated in such manner and on such basis as may be prescribed and that for that purpose payments of a particular class or description made or falling to be made to or by a woman are, to such extent as may be prescribed, to be disregarded or, as the case may be, to be deducted from the amount of her earnings[18].

Such regulations are subject to annulment in pursuance of a resolution of either House of Parliament[19].

1 As to the Secretary of State see PARA 5 note 21.
2 See the Social Security Contributions and Benefits Act 1992 s 164(9). As to the making of regulations under the Social Security Contributions and Benefits Act 1992 see PARA 407 note 3. At the date at which this volume states the law no such regulations had been made but, by virtue of the Interpretation Act 1978 s 17(2)(b), the Statutory Maternity Pay (General) Regulations 1986, SI 1986/1960, have effect as if made under the Social Security Contributions and Benefits Act 1992 s 164(9).
3 Ie notwithstanding the Social Security Contributions and Benefits Act 1992 s 164(1)–(8): see PARAS 401, 405, 415, 420.
4 As to the meaning of 'statutory maternity pay' see PARA 401.
5 Social Security Contributions and Benefits Act 1992 s 164(9)(a). As to circumstances in which there is no liability to pay statutory maternity pay see PARA 404. In Pt XVII (ss 164–171), except s 165(1), (4) and (6) (see PARA 424), s 166(1) (see PARA 428) and Sch 13 para 3(2) (see PARA 433), 'week' means a period of seven days beginning with Sunday or such other period as may be prescribed in relation to any particular case or class of case: see s 171(1A) (added by the Work and Families Act 2006 Sch 1 para 9(3)). 'Prescribed' means specified in or determined in accordance with regulations: see the Social Security Contributions and Benefits Act 1992 s 171(1).

6 Ie notwithstanding the Social Security Contributions and Benefits Act 1992 s 164(1)–(8): see PARAS 401, 405, 415, 420.

7 Social Security Contributions and Benefits Act 1992 s 164(9)(b) (s 164(9)(b) amended, s 164(11) added, by the Social Security Contributions (Transfer of Functions, etc) Act 1999 Sch 1 para 12(1)–(3)). Any regulations under the Social Security Contributions and Benefits Act 1992 s 164(9) which are made by virtue of s 164(9)(b) must be made with the concurrence of the Commissioners for Revenue and Customs: s 164(11) (as so added). As to the Commissioners for Her Majesty's Revenue and Customs see **INCOME TAXATION** vol 58 (2014) PARAS 33–34. As to the regulations so made see PARA 403.

8 Ie for the purposes of the Social Security Contributions and Benefits Act 1992 Pt XII (ss 164–171).

9 Social Security Contributions and Benefits Act 1992 s 164(9)(c). As to continuity of employment for these purposes see PARAS 416–419.

10 Social Security Contributions and Benefits Act 1992 s 164(9)(d)(i). As to the meaning of 'employer' for these purposes see PARA 414.

As from a day to be appointed under the Welfare Reform Act 2012 s 150(3), the Social Security Contributions and Benefits Act 1992 s 164(9)(da) is added allowing for regulations to provide for circumstances in which s 164(2)(aa) (not yet in force) (ie that a woman, at the end of the week immediately preceding the fourteenth week mentioned in s 164(2)(a), was entitled to be in that employment: see PARA 415) does not apply: see s 164(9)(da) (prospectively added by the Welfare Reform Act 2012 s 63(1), (3)(b)). However, at the date at which this volume states the law, no such day had been appointed.

11 Social Security Contributions and Benefits Act 1992 s 164(9)(d)(ii). As to continuity of employment see note 9.

12 Ie any of the provisions specified in the Social Security Contributions and Benefits Act 1992 s 164(10). The provisions specified are s 164(2)(a), (b) (see PARA 415) and s 166(1), (2) (see PARA 428): see s 164(10) (amended by the Employment Act 2002 Sch 7 paras 2, 6; and SI 1994/1230).

13 For these purposes, 'modifications' includes additions, omissions and amendments; and related expressions are to be construed accordingly: see the Social Security Contributions and Benefits Act 1992 s 171(1).

14 Social Security Contributions and Benefits Act 1992 s 164(9)(e) (s 164(9)(e) amended, s 164(9)(ea) added, by the Employment Act 2002 s 20(c), (d)). As to the modifications specified see PARA 415 note 14.

15 Ie the Social Security Contributions and Benefits Act 1992 s 164(4): see PARA 420.

16 Social Security Contributions and Benefits Act 1992 s 164(9)(ea) (as added: see note 14). As to notice see PARA 420 et seq.

17 Social Security Contributions and Benefits Act 1992 s 164(9)(f). As to the treatment of two or more employers as one see PARA 414.

18 Social Security Contributions and Benefits Act 1992 s 164(9)(g).

19 See the Social Security Contributions and Benefits Act 1992 s 176(3); and PARA 407 note 3.

403. Liability of the Commissioners for Revenue and Customs for payment of statutory maternity pay. Where:

(1) an adjudicating authority[1] has determined that an employer[2] is liable to make payments of statutory maternity pay to a woman[3]; and

(2) the time for appealing against that determination has expired[4]; and

(3) no appeal against the determination has been lodged or leave to appeal against the determination is required and has been refused[5],

then for any week in respect of which the employer was liable to make payments of statutory maternity pay but did not do so, and for any subsequent weeks in the maternity pay period[6], the liability to make those payments is[7] that of the Commissioners for Revenue and Customs[8] and not the employer[9].

Liability to make payments of statutory maternity pay is[10] a liability of the Commissioners and not the employer as from the week in which the employer first becomes insolvent[11] until the end of the maternity pay period[12].

1 For these purposes, 'adjudicating authority' means, as the case may be, the chief or any other adjudication officer, the First-tier Tribunal or the Upper Tribunal: Statutory Maternity Pay (General) Regulations 1986, SI 1986/1960, reg 7(2) (amended by SI 2008/2683). As to

adjudication officers see WELFARE BENEFITS AND STATE PENSIONS vol 104 (2014) PARA 575; and as to the First-tier Tribunal and the Upper Tribunal see COURTS AND TRIBUNALS vol 24 (2010) PARA 874 et seq.

2 As to the meaning of 'employer' for these purposes see PARA 414.

3 Statutory Maternity Pay (General) Regulations 1986, SI 1986/1960, reg 7(1)(a). As to the meaning of 'statutory maternity pay' see PARA 401.

4 Statutory Maternity Pay (General) Regulations 1986, SI 1986/1960, reg 7(1)(b).

5 Statutory Maternity Pay (General) Regulations 1986, SI 1986/1960, reg 7(1)(c).

6 As to the meaning of 'maternity pay period' see PARA 424.

7 Ie notwithstanding the Social Security Contributions and Benefits Act 1992 s 164(3): see PARA 401.

8 As to the Commissioners for Her Majesty's Revenue and Customs see INCOME TAXATION vol 58 (2014) PARAS 33–34. In connection with the payment of statutory maternity pay or of any other sum in connection with that pay the Commissioners may use electronic communications: see the Statutory Payment Schemes (Electronic Communications) Regulations 2002, SI 2002/3047; and INCOME TAXATION.

9 See the Statutory Maternity Pay (General) Regulations 1986, SI 1986/1960, reg 7(1) (reg 7(1), (3) amended by the Social Security Contributions (Transfer of Functions, etc) Act 1999 s 1(2), Sch 2); and see the Interpretation Act 1978 s 17(2)(a). As to the time limit for paying statutory maternity pay see PARA 432.

10 Ie notwithstanding the Social Security Contributions and Benefits Act 1992 s 164(3): see PARA 401.

11 For these purposes, an employer is to be taken to be insolvent if, and only if, in England and Wales:

(1) he has been adjudged bankrupt or has made a composition or arrangement with his creditors (Statutory Maternity Pay (General) Regulations 1986, SI 1986/1960, reg 7(4)(a)(i));

(2) he has died and his estate falls to be administered in accordance with an order under the Insolvency Act 1986 s 421 (insolvent estates of deceased persons: see BANKRUPTCY AND INDIVIDUAL INSOLVENCY vol 5 (2013) PARA 830 et seq) (Statutory Maternity Pay (General) Regulations 1986, SI 1986/1960, reg 7(4)(a)(ii)); or

(3) where an employer is a company, a winding-up order is made or a resolution for voluntary winding up is passed with respect to it or it enters administration, or a receiver or manager of its undertaking is duly appointed, or possession is taken, by or on behalf of the holders of any debentures secured by a floating charge, of any property of the company comprised in or subject to the charge or a voluntary arrangement proposed for the purposes of the Insolvency Act 1986 Pt I (ss 1–7B) (company voluntary arrangements: see COMPANY AND PARTNERSHIP INSOLVENCY vol 16 (2011) PARA 83 et seq) is approved under Pt I (Statutory Maternity Pay (General) Regulations 1986, SI 1986/1960, reg 7(4)(a)(iii) (amended by SI 2003/2096)).

As to the meanings of 'England' and 'Wales' see PARA 2 note 12. As to compositions or arrangements with creditors see BANKRUPTCY AND INDIVIDUAL INSOLVENCY vol 5 (2013) PARA 43 et seq; and as to bankruptcy generally see BANKRUPTCY AND INDIVIDUAL INSOLVENCY vol 5 (2013) PARA 129 et seq. As to winding-up orders see COMPANY AND PARTNERSHIP INSOLVENCY vol 16 (2011) PARA 386 et seq. As to voluntary winding-up see COMPANY AND PARTNERSHIP INSOLVENCY vol 17 (2011) PARA 898 et seq. As to administration orders see COMPANY AND PARTNERSHIP INSOLVENCY vol 16 (2011) PARA 159 et seq. As to the appointment of receivers and managers see COMPANY AND PARTNERSHIP INSOLVENCY vol 16 (2011) PARA 340 et seq. As to the taking of possession by or on behalf of the holders of debentures secured by a floating charge see COMPANIES vol 15 (2009) PARA 1333 et seq.

12 Statutory Maternity Pay (General) Regulations 1986, SI 1986/1960, reg 7(3) (as amended: see note 9); and see the Interpretation Act 1978 s 17(2)(a).

404. Circumstances in which liability to pay statutory maternity pay does not arise. No liability to make payments of statutory maternity pay[1] to a woman arises[2] in respect of a week within the maternity pay period[3] for any part of which she is detained in legal custody or sentenced to a term of imprisonment (except where the sentence is suspended), or of any subsequent week within that period[4].

An employer is not liable to make payments of statutory maternity pay in respect of a woman for any week within the maternity pay period which falls after the week in which she dies[5].

1 As to the meaning of 'statutory maternity pay' see PARA 401.
2 Ie notwithstanding the Social Security Contributions and Benefits Act 1992 s 164(1): see PARA 401.
3 As to the meaning of 'maternity pay period' see PARA 424.
4 Statutory Maternity Pay (General) Regulations 1986, SI 1986/1960, reg 9; and see the Interpretation Act 1978 s 17(2)(a).
5 Statutory Maternity Pay (General) Regulations 1986, SI 1986/1960, reg 10.

405. Contract of service ended for the purpose of avoiding liability for statutory maternity pay. Regulations under the Social Security Contributions and Benefits Act 1992[1] must make provision as to a former employer's[2] liability to pay statutory maternity pay[3] to a woman in any case where the former employer's contract of service with her has been brought to an end by the former employer solely, or mainly, for the purpose of avoiding liability for statutory maternity pay[4].

Accordingly, a former employer is liable to make payments of statutory maternity pay to any woman who was employed by him for a continuous period of at least eight weeks and whose contract of service with him was brought to an end by the former employer solely or mainly for the purpose of avoiding liability for statutory maternity pay[5]. In order to determine the amount payable by the former employer:

(1) the woman is deemed[6] to have been employed by him from the date her employment with him ended until the end of the week immediately preceding the fourteenth week before the expected week of confinement on the same terms and conditions of employment as those subsisting immediately before her employment ended[7]; and

(2) her normal weekly earnings for the period of eight weeks immediately preceding the fourteenth week before the expected week of confinement are to be calculated by reference to her normal weekly earnings for the period of eight weeks ending with the last day in respect of which she was paid under her former contract of service[8].

1 As to the making of regulations under the Social Security Contributions and Benefits Act 1992 see PARA 407 note 3. As to the general power to make regulations under the Social Security Contributions and Benefits Act 1992 in relation to statutory maternity pay see PARA 402.
2 As to the meaning of 'employer' for these purposes see PARA 414.
3 As to the meaning of 'statutory maternity pay' see PARA 401.
4 Social Security Contributions and Benefits Act 1992 s 164(8). Although 'contract of service' is defined for the purposes of statutory sick pay (see PARA 558 note 2), it is not so defined under the other statutory pay provisions (for which purposes see generally PARA 1 note 1). At the date at which this volume states the law, no such regulations had been made but, by virtue of the Interpretation Act 1978 s 17(2)(b), the Statutory Maternity Pay (General) Regulations 1986, SI 1986/1960, have effect as if made under the Social Security Contributions and Benefits Act 1992 s 164(8).
5 Statutory Maternity Pay (General) Regulations 1986, SI 1986/1960, reg 3(1). As to continuity of employment see PARAS 416–419.
6 Ie for the purposes of the Social Security Contributions and Benefits Act 1992 Pt XII (ss 164–171).
7 Statutory Maternity Pay (General) Regulations 1986, SI 1986/1960, reg 3(2)(a); and see the Interpretation Act 1978 s 17(2)(a).
8 Statutory Maternity Pay (General) Regulations 1986, SI 1986/1960, reg 3(2)(b). As to the calculation of normal weekly earnings for the purposes of statutory maternity pay see PARA 429.

B. MEANING OF 'EMPLOYEE' AND 'EMPLOYER'

406. Meaning of 'employee' for purposes of statutory maternity pay; treatment of two or more contracts of service as one. For the purposes of the statutory maternity pay provisions that are set out in Part XII of the Social Security Contributions and Benefits Act 1992[1], 'employee' means a woman who is gainfully employed in Great Britain[2] either under a contract of service[3] or in an office (including elective office) with earnings (as defined)[4], but subject to regulations made with the concurrence of the Her Majesty's Revenue and Customs[5] which may provide for cases where any such woman is not to be treated as an employee for those purposes, and for cases where a woman who would not otherwise be an employee for those purposes is to be treated as an employee for those purposes[6].

In a case where, and in so far as, a woman is treated as an employed earner[7], she is to be treated as an employee for the purposes of Part XII of the Social Security Contributions and Benefits Act 1992[8]; and, in a case where, and in so far as, such a woman is treated otherwise than as an employed earner, she is not to be treated for those purposes as an employee[9].

Any woman who is in employed earner's employment[10] under a contract of apprenticeship[11] is to be treated as an employee for the purposes of Part XII of the Social Security Contributions and Benefits Act 1992[12].

A woman who is in employed earner's employment[13] but:

(1) whose employer does not fulfil the prescribed conditions[14] as to residence or presence in Great Britain[15]; or

(2) is a woman who, by reason of any international treaty to which the United Kingdom[16] is a party or of any international convention binding the United Kingdom[17]:

  (a) is exempt from the provisions of the Social Security Contributions and Benefits Act 1992[18]; or

  (b) is a woman against whom the provisions of that Act are not enforceable[19],

is not to be treated[20] as an employee[21].

Without prejudice to any other power to make regulations under Part XII of the Social Security Contributions and Benefits Act 1992[22], regulations may specify cases in which[23] two or more contracts of service in respect of which the same woman is an employee are to be treated as one[24]. Accordingly, where two or more contracts of service exist concurrently between one employer and one employee, they are to be treated[25] as one except where[26] the earnings from those contracts of service are not aggregated for the purposes of earnings-related contributions[27].

1 Ie the Social Security Contributions and Benefits Act 1992 Pt XII (ss 164–171).

2 As to the meaning of 'Great Britain' for these purposes see PARA 407 note 7.

3 Although 'contract of service' is defined for the purposes of statutory sick pay (see PARA 558 note 2), it is not so defined under the other statutory pay provisions (for which purposes see generally PARA 1 note 1).

4 Ie earnings within the meaning of the Social Security Contributions and Benefits Act 1992 Pts I–V (ss 1–110) (see ss 3, 4, 112, 122; and **WELFARE BENEFITS AND STATE PENSIONS** vol 104 (2014) PARAS 381, 382).

5 As to the making of regulations under the Social Security Contributions and Benefits Act 1992 generally see PARA 407 note 3. As to the Commissioners for Her Majesty's Revenue and Customs see **INCOME TAXATION** vol 58 (2014) PARAS 33–34.

6 See the Social Security Contributions and Benefits Act 1992 s 171(1) (definition amended by the Social Security Contributions (Transfer of Functions, etc) Act 1999 Sch 1 para 15(1), (2); the

Income Tax (Earnings and Pensions) Act 2003 Sch 6 Pt 2 paras 169, 182; the Commissioners for Revenue and Customs Act 2005 Sch 4 para 43; the National Insurance Contributions Act 2014 s 15(3), Sch 2 paras 1, 4; and SI 2006/1031). As to the meaning of 'employee' and related expressions in relation to employment rights generally see PARA 2 et seq.

7 Ie by virtue of the Social Security (Categorisation of Earners) Regulations 1978, SI 1978/1689: see **WELFARE BENEFITS AND STATE PENSIONS** vol 104 (2014) PARA 381.

8 Ie for the purposes of the Social Security Contributions and Benefits Act 1992 Pt XII.

9 Statutory Maternity Pay (General) Regulations 1986, SI 1986/1960, reg 17(1) (reg 17(1) amended, reg 17(1A) added, by SI 2006/1031); and see the Interpretation Act 1978 s 17(2)(a). The Statutory Maternity Pay (General) Regulations 1986, SI 1986/1960, reg 17(1) has effect in relation to a woman who:

(1) is under the age of 16 (reg 17(1A)(a) (reg 17(1A) as so added; substituted by SI 2007/825)); and

(2) would or, as the case may be, would not have been treated as an employed earner by virtue of the Social Security (Categorisation of Earners) Regulations 1978, SI 1978/1689 (see **WELFARE BENEFITS AND STATE PENSIONS** vol 104 (2014) PARA 381) had she been over that age (Statutory Maternity Pay (General) Regulations 1986, SI 1986/1960, reg 17(1A)(b) (as so added and substituted)),

as it has effect in relation to a woman who is, or, as the case may be, is not so treated (see reg 17(1A) (as so added and substituted)). No woman who, by virtue of reg 17, would be treated as not being an employee for the purposes of the Social Security Contributions and Benefits Act 1992 Pt XII if her employment were in Great Britain is to be treated as an employee by virtue of the Statutory Maternity Pay (Persons Abroad and Mariners) Regulations 1987, SI 1987/418: see reg 3; and see the Interpretation Act 1978 s 17(2)(a).

10 Ie within the meaning of the Social Security Contributions and Benefits Act 1992: see **WELFARE BENEFITS AND STATE PENSIONS** vol 104 (2014) PARA 176.

11 As to the position of apprentices and youth trainees at common law see PARAS 112, 128–129, 636, 747–754. As to the statutory law on apprenticeships see **EDUCATION** vol 35 (2011) PARA 682 et seq.

12 Statutory Maternity Pay (General) Regulations 1986, SI 1986/1960, reg 17(2); and see the Interpretation Act 1978 s 17(2)(a).

13 Ie within the meaning of the Social Security Contributions and Benefits Act 1992: see **WELFARE BENEFITS AND STATE PENSIONS** vol 104 (2014) PARA 176.

14 Ie the conditions prescribed in the Social Security (Contributions) Regulations 2001, SI 2001/1004, reg 145 (conditions as to residence or presence in Great Britain: see **WELFARE BENEFITS AND STATE PENSIONS** vol 104 (2014) PARA 406).

15 Statutory Maternity Pay (General) Regulations 1986, SI 1986/1960, reg 17(3)(a); and see the Interpretation Act 1978 s 17(2)(a).

16 As to the meaning of 'United Kingdom' for these purposes see PARA 407 note 7.

17 Statutory Maternity Pay (General) Regulations 1986, SI 1986/1960, reg 17(3)(b).

18 Statutory Maternity Pay (General) Regulations 1986, SI 1986/1960, reg 17(3)(b)(i); and see the Interpretation Act 1978 s 17(2)(a).

19 Statutory Maternity Pay (General) Regulations 1986, SI 1986/1960, reg 17(3)(b)(ii); and see the Interpretation Act 1978 s 17(2)(a).

20 Ie for the purposes of the Social Security Contributions and Benefits Act 1992 Pt XII.

21 See the Statutory Maternity Pay (General) Regulations 1986, SI 1986/1960, reg 17(3); and see the Interpretation Act 1978 s 17(2)(a).

22 Ie under the Social Security Contributions and Benefits Act 1992 Pt XII (see PARA 402).

23 Ie for the purposes of the Social Security Contributions and Benefits Act 1992 Pt XII or of such provisions of Pt XII as may be prescribed.

24 See the Social Security Contributions and Benefits Act 1992 s 171(2)(b). Regulations under s 171(2) must be made with the concurrence of the Commissioners for Revenue and Customs: s 171(7) (added by the Social Security Contributions (Transfer of Functions, etc) Act 1999 Sch 1 para 15(1), (3)). At the date at which this volume states the law, no such regulations had been made but, by virtue of the Interpretation Act 1978 s 17(2)(b), the Statutory Maternity Pay (General) Regulations 1986, SI 1986/1960, reg 5 (see the text and notes 25–27) has effect as if made under the Social Security Contributions and Benefits Act 1992 s 171(2).

25 Ie for the purposes of the Social Security Contributions and Benefits Act 1992 Pt XII.

26 Ie by virtue of the Social Security (Contributions) Regulations 2001, SI 2001/1004, reg 14 (aggregation of earnings paid in respect of separate employed earner's employments under the same employer: see **WELFARE BENEFITS AND STATE PENSIONS** vol 104 (2014) PARA 382).

27 Statutory Maternity Pay (General) Regulations 1986, SI 1986/1960, reg 5; and see the Interpretation Act 1978 s 17(2)(a).

407. Modification of statutory provisions relating to statutory maternity pay to accommodate special classes of person. The Secretary of State[1] may, with the concurrence of the Treasury[2], make regulations[3] modifying the statutory maternity pay provisions that are set out in Part XII of the Social Security Contributions and Benefits Act 1992[4], in such manner as he thinks proper, in their application to any person who is, has been or is to be[5]:

(1) employed on board any ship, vessel, hovercraft or aircraft[6];
(2) outside Great Britain[7] at any prescribed[8] time or in any prescribed circumstances[9]; or
(3) in prescribed employment in connection with continental shelf operations[10].

Such regulations may, in particular, provide:

(a) for any of the statutory maternity pay provisions that are set out in Part XII of the Social Security Contributions and Benefits Act 1992[11] to apply to any such person, notwithstanding that it would not otherwise apply[12];
(b) for any such provision not to apply to any such person, notwithstanding that it would otherwise apply[13];
(c) for excepting any such person from the application of any such provision where she neither is domiciled[14] nor has a place of residence in any part of Great Britain[15];
(d) for the taking of evidence, for the purposes of the determination of any question arising under any such provision, in a country or territory outside Great Britain, by a British consular official or such other person as may be determined in accordance with the regulations[16].

1 As to the Secretary of State see PARA 5 note 21.

2 As to the Treasury see CONSTITUTIONAL AND ADMINISTRATIVE LAW vol 20 (2014) PARAS 262–265.

3 Regulations and orders under the Social Security Contributions and Benefits Act 1992 are made by the Secretary of State, subject to any provision providing for regulations or an order to be made by the Treasury or by the Commissioners for Revenue and Customs: see s 175(1), (1A) (s 175(1) amended, s 175(1A) added, by the Social Security Contributions (Transfer of Functions, etc) Act 1999 Sch 3 para 29(1)–(3); the Social Security Contributions and Benefits Act 1992 s 175(1A) amended by the Tax Credits Act 2002 Sch 6). As to the Commissioners for Her Majesty's Revenue and Customs see INCOME TAXATION vol 58 (2014) PARAS 33–34.

Powers under the Social Security Contributions and Benefits Act 1992 to make regulations or orders are exercisable by statutory instrument (s 175(2)), and any statutory instrument which:

(1) contains (whether alone or with other provisions) any order or regulations made under the Social Security Contributions and Benefits Act 1992 by the Secretary of State, the Treasury or the Commissioners for Revenue and Customs (s 176(3)(a) (amended by the Social Security Contributions (Transfer of Functions, etc) Act 1999 Sch 3 para 30)); and
(2) is not subject to any requirement that a draft of the instrument must be laid before and approved by a resolution of each House of Parliament (Social Security Contributions and Benefits Act 1992 s 176(3)(b)),

is subject to annulment in pursuance of a resolution of either House of Parliament (see s 176(3)). As to the Secretary of State's general power to make regulations relating to statutory maternity pay see PARA 402.

4 Ie the Social Security Contributions and Benefits Act 1992 Pt XII (ss 164–171). As to the meaning of 'statutory maternity pay' see PARA 401.

5 See the Social Security Contributions and Benefits Act 1992 s 170(1) (amended by the Social Security Contributions (Transfer of Functions, etc) Act 1999 Sch 1 para 14).

6 Social Security Contributions and Benefits Act 1992 s 170(1)(a).

7 For the purposes of the Social Security Contributions and Benefits Act 1992, any reference to 'Great Britain' includes a reference to the territorial waters of the United Kingdom adjacent to Great Britain; and any reference to 'the United Kingdom' includes a reference to the territorial

waters of the United Kingdom: see s 172. As to the meanings of 'Great Britain' generally and 'United Kingdom' see PARA 2 note 12. As to the territorial sea (or waters) of the United Kingdom see the Territorial Sea Act 1987 s 1; and INTERNATIONAL RELATIONS LAW vol 61 (2010) PARA 123 et seq; WATER AND WATERWAYS vol 100 (2009) PARA 31.

8 For these purposes, 'prescribed' means specified in or determined in accordance with regulations: see the Social Security Contributions and Benefits Act 1992 s 171(1).

9 Social Security Contributions and Benefits Act 1992 s 170(1)(b).

10 Social Security Contributions and Benefits Act 1992 s 170(1)(c). 'Continental shelf operations' means any activities which, if the Petroleum Act 1998 s 11(8)(a), (d) (application of civil law to certain offshore activities) were omitted, would nevertheless fall within s 11(2) (see ENERGY AND CLIMATE CHANGE vol 44 (2011) PARA 1080): see the Social Security Contributions and Benefits Act 1992 s 120(2) (amended by the Petroleum Act 1998 Sch 4 para 30); definition applied by the Social Security Contributions and Benefits Act 1992 170(1)(c). At the date at which this volume states the law, no such regulations had been made under head (3) in the text but, by virtue of the Interpretation Act 1978 s 17(2)(b), the Statutory Maternity Pay (Persons Abroad and Mariners) Regulations 1987, SI 1987/418 (see PARA 408 et seq) have effect as if made under the Social Security Contributions and Benefits Act 1992 ss 170, 171(1).

11 Ie the Social Security Contributions and Benefits Act 1992 Pt XII (ss 164–171).

12 Social Security Contributions and Benefits Act 1992 s 170(2)(a).

13 Social Security Contributions and Benefits Act 1992 s 170(2)(b).

14 As to domicile see CONFLICT OF LAWS vol 19 (2011) PARA 336 et seq.

15 Social Security Contributions and Benefits Act 1992 s 170(2)(c).

16 Social Security Contributions and Benefits Act 1992 s 170(2)(d).

408. Time for compliance with provisions relating to statutory maternity pay; employee outside the United Kingdom. Where:

(1) a woman is outside the United Kingdom[1];

(2) any act is required[2] to be done forthwith or on the happening of a certain event or within a specified time[3]; and

(3) because the woman is outside the United Kingdom, she or her employer[4] cannot comply with the requirement[5],

the woman or the employer, as the case may be, is deemed to have complied with it if the act is performed as soon as reasonably practicable[6].

1 Statutory Maternity Pay (Persons Abroad and Mariners) Regulations 1987, SI 1987/418, reg 6(a). As to the meaning of 'United Kingdom' for these purposes see PARA 407 note 7.

2 Ie by the Social Security Contributions and Benefits Act 1992 Pt XII (ss 164–171) or regulations made under that Act.

3 Statutory Maternity Pay (Persons Abroad and Mariners) Regulations 1987, SI 1987/418, reg 6(b); and see the Interpretation Act 1978 s 17(2)(a).

4 As to the meaning of 'employer' for these purposes see PARA 414.

5 Statutory Maternity Pay (Persons Abroad and Mariners) Regulations 1987, SI 1987/418, reg 6(c).

6 See the Statutory Maternity Pay (Persons Abroad and Mariners) Regulations 1987, SI 1987/418, reg 6.

409. Treatment of persons in other member states or absent from Great Britain for purposes of statutory maternity pay. A woman who is:

(1) gainfully employed in a member state other than the United Kingdom[1] in such circumstances that, if her employment were in Great Britain[2], she would be an employee[3] for the purposes of the statutory maternity pay provisions that are set out in Part XII of the Social Security Contributions and Benefits Act 1992[4] or a woman treated[5] as such an employee[6]; and

(2) subject[7] to the legislation of the United Kingdom[8],

is to be treated[9] as an employee for those purposes notwithstanding that she is not employed in Great Britain[10].

Where a woman, while absent from Great Britain for any purpose, is gainfully employed by an employer who is liable to pay in respect of her employment secondary Class 1 contributions[11], she is to be treated[12] as an employee[13].

1 As to the meaning of 'United Kingdom' for these purposes see PARA 407 note 7.
2 As to the meaning of 'Great Britain' for these purposes see PARA 407 note 7.
3 As to the meaning of 'employee' for these purposes see PARA 406.
4 Ie the Social Security Contributions and Benefits Act 1992 Pt XII (ss 164–171).
5 Ie under the Statutory Maternity Pay (General) Regulations 1986, SI 1986/1960, reg 17: see PARA 406.
6 Statutory Maternity Pay (Persons Abroad and Mariners) Regulations 1987, SI 1987/418, reg 2(a).
7 Ie under Council Regulation (EC) 1408/71 (OJ L149, 5.7.71, p 2) on the application of social security schemes to employed persons and their families moving within the Community (repealed: see now Council Regulation (EC) 883/2004 of 29 April 2004 (OJ L166, 30.4.2004, p 1) on the coordination of social security systems; and **WELFARE BENEFITS AND STATE PENSIONS** vol 104 (2014) PARA 600 et seq).
8 Statutory Maternity Pay (Persons Abroad and Mariners) Regulations 1987, SI 1987/418, reg 2(b).
9 Ie subject to the Statutory Maternity Pay (Persons Abroad and Mariners) Regulations 1987, SI 1987/418, reg 3: see PARA 406 note 9.
10 See the Statutory Maternity Pay (Persons Abroad and Mariners) Regulations 1987, SI 1987/418, reg 2.
11 Ie under the Social Security Contributions and Benefits Act 1992 s 6 (see **WELFARE BENEFITS AND STATE PENSIONS** vol 104 (2014) PARA 385) or the Social Security (Contributions) Regulations 2001, SI 2001/1004, reg 146 (payment of contributions for periods abroad: see **WELFARE BENEFITS AND STATE PENSIONS** vol 104 (2014) PARA 380).
12 Ie for the purposes of the Social Security Contributions and Benefits Act 1992 Pt XII but subject to the Statutory Maternity Pay (Persons Abroad and Mariners) Regulations 1987, SI 1987/418, reg 2 (see the text and notes 1–10), reg 3 (see PARA 406 note 9) and reg 7(3) (see PARA 410).
13 Statutory Maternity Pay (Persons Abroad and Mariners) Regulations 1987, SI 1987/418, reg 2A (added by SI 1996/777).

410. Treatment of mariners for purposes of statutory maternity pay. A mariner[1] engaged in employment on board a home-trade ship[2] with an employer[3] who has a place of business within the United Kingdom is to be treated[4] as an employee[5] for the purposes of the statutory maternity pay provisions that are set out in Part XII of the Social Security Contributions and Benefits Act 1992[6], notwithstanding that she may not be employed in Great Britain[7].

However, a mariner who is engaged in employment: (1) on a foreign-going ship[8]; or (2) on a home-trade ship with an employer who does not have a place of business within the United Kingdom[9], is not to be treated as an employee for the purposes of Part XII of the Social Security Contributions and Benefits Act 1992, notwithstanding that she may have been employed in Great Britain[10].

1 For these purposes, 'mariner' means a person who is or has been in employment under a contract of service either as a master or member of the crew of any ship or vessel, or in any other capacity on board any ship or vessel where: (1) the employment in that other capacity is for the purposes of that ship or vessel or her crew or any passengers or cargo or mails carried thereby; and (2) the contract is entered into in the United Kingdom with a view to its performance, in whole or in part, while the ship or vessel is on her voyage, but does not include a person in so far as her employment is as a serving member of the forces: see the Social Security (Contributions) Regulations 2001, SI 2001/1004, reg 115; definition applied by the Statutory Maternity Pay (Persons Abroad and Mariners) Regulations 1987, SI 1987/418, reg 7(1); and see the Interpretation Act 1978 s 17(2)(a). The expressions 'ship' and 'ship or vessel', except in the Statutory Maternity Pay (Persons Abroad and Mariners) Regulations 1987, SI 1987/418, reg 7(3) (see the text and notes 8–10), include hovercraft: see reg 7(1); and see the Interpretation Act 1978 s 17(2)(a). As to the meaning of 'United Kingdom' for these purposes see PARA 407

note 7. Although 'contract of service' is defined for the purposes of statutory sick pay (see PARA 558 note 2), it is not so defined under the other statutory pay provisions (for which purposes see generally PARA 1 note 1).

2 For these purposes, 'home-trade ship' includes: (1) every ship or vessel employed in trading or going within the following limits, ie the United Kingdom, including for this purpose the Republic of Ireland, the Channel Islands, the Isle of Man, and the continent of Europe between the river Elbe and Brest inclusive; (2) every fishing vessel not proceeding beyond the following limits: on the South, Latitude 48° 30' N; on the West, Longitude 12° W; on the North, Latitude 61° N: see the Social Security (Contributions) Regulations 2001, SI 2001/1004, reg 115; definition applied by the Statutory Maternity Pay (Persons Abroad and Mariners) Regulations 1987, SI 1987/418, reg 7(1); and see the Interpretation Act 1978 s 17(2)(a).

3 As to the meaning of 'employer' for these purposes see PARA 414.

4 Ie subject to the Statutory Maternity Pay (Persons Abroad and Mariners) Regulations 1987, SI 1987/418, reg 3: see PARA 406 note 9.

5 As to the meaning of 'employee' for these purposes see PARA 406.

6 Ie the Social Security Contributions and Benefits Act 1992 Pt XII (ss 164–171).

7 Statutory Maternity Pay (Persons Abroad and Mariners) Regulations 1987, SI 1987/418, reg 7(2). As to the meaning of 'Great Britain' for these purposes see PARA 407 note 7.

8 Statutory Maternity Pay (Persons Abroad and Mariners) Regulations 1987, SI 1987/418, reg 7(3)(a). For these purposes, 'foreign-going ship' means any ship or vessel which is not a home-trade ship: see the Social Security (Contributions) Regulations 2001, SI 2001/1004, reg 115; definition applied by the Statutory Maternity Pay (Persons Abroad and Mariners) Regulations 1987, SI 1987/418, reg 7(1); and see the Interpretation Act 1978 s 17(2)(a).

9 Statutory Maternity Pay (Persons Abroad and Mariners) Regulations 1987, SI 1987/418, reg 7(3)(b).

10 See the Statutory Maternity Pay (Persons Abroad and Mariners) Regulations 1987, SI 1987/418, reg 7(3).

411. Treatment of persons employed in operations on the continental shelf for purposes of statutory maternity pay. A woman in prescribed employment[1] is to be treated[2] as an employee for the purposes of the statutory maternity pay provisions that are set out in Part XII of the Social Security Contributions and Benefits Act 1992[3], notwithstanding that she may not be employed in Great Britain[4].

1 For these purposes, 'prescribed employment' means employment in a designated area or prescribed area in connection with any activity mentioned in the Petroleum Act 1998 s 11(2) (see ENERGY AND CLIMATE CHANGE vol 44 (2011) PARA 1080) in any designated area or in any prescribed area; 'designated area' means any area which may from time to time be designated by Order in Council under the Continental Shelf Act 1964 (see ENERGY AND CLIMATE CHANGE vol 44 (2011) PARAS 1033, 1040; INTERNATIONAL RELATIONS LAW vol 61 (2010) PARA 172) as an area within which the rights of the United Kingdom with respect to the sea bed and subsoil and their natural resources may be exercised; and 'prescribed area' means an area over which Norway or any member state other than the United Kingdom exercises sovereign rights for the purpose of exploring the sea bed and subsoil and exploiting their natural resources, being an area outside the territorial seas of Norway or that member state or any other area which is from time to time specified under the Petroleum Act 1998 s 10(8) (see ENERGY AND CLIMATE CHANGE vol 44 (2011) PARA 1080): see the Statutory Maternity Pay (Persons Abroad and Mariners) Regulations 1987, SI 1987/418, reg 8(1); and see the Interpretation Act 1978 s 17(2)(a). As to the meaning of 'United Kingdom' for these purposes see PARA 407 note 7.

2 Ie subject to the Statutory Maternity Pay (Persons Abroad and Mariners) Regulations 1987, SI 1987/418, reg 3: see PARA 406 note 9.

3 Ie for the purposes of the Social Security Contributions and Benefits Act 1992 Pt XII (ss 164–171). As to the meaning of 'employee' for these purposes see PARA 406.

4 Statutory Maternity Pay (Persons Abroad and Mariners) Regulations 1987, SI 1987/418, reg 8(2); and see the Interpretation Act 1978 s 17(2)(a). As to the meaning of 'Great Britain' for these purposes see PARA 407 note 7.

412. Crown employment for purposes of statutory maternity pay. The statutory maternity pay provisions that are set out in Part XII of the Social Security Contributions and Benefits Act 1992[1] apply in relation to persons employed by or under the Crown as they apply in relation to persons employed otherwise than by or under the Crown[2].

1 Ie the Social Security Contributions and Benefits Act 1992 Pt XII (ss 164–171). As to the meaning of 'statutory maternity pay' see PARA 401.
2 Social Security Contributions and Benefits Act 1992 s 169.

413. Treatment of National Health Service employees for purposes of statutory maternity pay. Where, in consequence of the establishment of one or more National Health Service trusts[1], a woman's contract of employment is treated by a scheme[2] as divided so as to constitute two or more contracts, or where an order[3] provides that a person's contract of employment is so divided, regulations[4] may make provision enabling her to elect for all of those contracts to be treated as one contract for the purposes of the statutory maternity pay provisions that are set out in Part XII of the Social Security Contributions and Benefits Act 1992[5] or such of those provisions as may be prescribed[6]. Any such regulations may prescribe:

(1) the conditions that must be satisfied if a woman is to be entitled to make such an election[7];
(2) the manner in which, and the time within which, such an election is to be made[8];
(3) the persons to whom, and the manner in which, notice of such an election is to be given[9];
(4) the information which a woman who makes such an election is to provide, and the persons to whom, and the time within which, she is to provide it[10];
(5) the time for which such an election is to have effect[11];
(6) which one of the woman's employers[12] under the two or more contracts is to be regarded for the purposes of statutory maternity pay as her employer under the one contract[13],

and the powers so conferred are without prejudice to any other power[14] to make regulations[15].

Accordingly, where, in consequence of the establishment of one or more National Health Service trusts[16], a woman's contract of employment is treated by a scheme[17] as divided so as to constitute two or more contracts, she may elect for all those contracts to be treated as one contract for the purposes of Part XII of the Social Security Contributions and Benefits Act 1992[18]. A woman who makes such an election must:

(a) give written notification of that election to each of her employers under the two or more contracts of service at least 28 days before the first day she is going to be absent from work with any of her employers, wholly or partly because of pregnancy, or if in the particular circumstances that is not practicable, as soon as is reasonably practicable[19];
(b) within 28 days of giving notice of that election (or, if in the particular circumstances that is not practicable, as soon as is reasonably practicable thereafter), provide each of her employers under the two or more contracts of service with the following information[20]:
    (i) the name and address of each of those employers[21]; and
    (ii) the date her employment with each of those employers commenced[22]; and
    (iii) details of her earnings[23] during the relevant period[24] from each employer[25].

An election so made lapses at the end of the maternity pay period[26].

1 Ie under the National Health Service Act 2006 or the National Health Service (Wales) Act 2006: see HEALTH SERVICES vol 54 (2008) PARA 155 et seq.
2 See note 1.
3 Ie an order under the National Health Service Act 2006 Sch 3 para 26(1) (repealed): see HEALTH SERVICES vol 54 (2008) PARA 125.
4 As to the making of regulations under the Social Security Contributions and Benefits Act 1992 generally see PARA 407 note 3.
5 Ie the Social Security Contributions and Benefits Act 1992 Pt XII (ss 164–171).
6 See the Social Security Contributions and Benefits Act 1992 s 171(3) (amended by the National Health Service (Consequential Provisions) Act 2006 Sch 1 paras 142, 148; and SI 2000/90). For these purposes, 'prescribed' means specified in or determined in accordance with regulations: see the Social Security Contributions and Benefits Act 1992 s 171(1). Regulations under s 171(3) must be made with the concurrence of the Commissioners for Revenue and Customs: see s 171(7) (added by the Social Security Contributions (Transfer of Functions, etc) Act 1999 Sch 1 para 15(1), (3)). At the date at which this volume states the law, no such regulations had been made but, by virtue of the Interpretation Act 1978 s 17(2)(b), the Statutory Maternity Pay (National Health Service Employees) Regulations 1991, SI 1991/590 (see the text and notes 16–26) have effect as if so made. As to the Commissioners for Her Majesty's Revenue and Customs see INCOME TAXATION vol 58 (2014) PARAS 33–34.
   As from a day to be appointed under the Health and Social Care Act 2012 s 306(4), the reference to 'the National Health Service Act 2006' in the Social Security Contributions and Benefits Act 1992 s 171(3) is repealed: see s 171(3) (as so amended; prospectively further amended by the Health and Social Care Act 2012 s 179(6), Sch 14 Pt 2 paras 58, 60). However, at the date at which this volume states the law, no such day had been appointed.
7 Social Security Contributions and Benefits Act 1992 s 171(3)(a).
8 Social Security Contributions and Benefits Act 1992 s 171(3)(b).
9 Social Security Contributions and Benefits Act 1992 s 171(3)(c).
10 Social Security Contributions and Benefits Act 1992 s 171(3)(d).
11 Social Security Contributions and Benefits Act 1992 s 171(3)(e).
12 As to the meaning of 'employer' for these purposes see PARA 414.
13 Social Security Contributions and Benefits Act 1992 s 171(3)(f).
14 Ie under the Social Security Contributions and Benefits Act 1992 Pt XII.
15 See the Social Security Contributions and Benefits Act 1992 s 171(3) (as amended: see note 6).
16 See note 1. For these purposes, 'NHS trust' is to be construed to include a reference to an NHS foundation trust within the meaning of the Health and Social Care (Community Health and Standards) Act 2003 s 1(1) (see HEALTH SERVICES vol 54 (2008) PARA 75 et seq) where the application for authorisation to become an NHS foundation trust was made by an NHS trust: see the Statutory Maternity Pay (National Health Service Employees) Regulations 1991, SI 1991/590, reg 1(5) (added by SI 2004/696).
17 See note 1.
18 Statutory Maternity Pay (National Health Service Employees) Regulations 1991, SI 1991/590, reg 2 (amended by SI 2013/235); and see the Interpretation Act 1978 s 17(2)(a). As to the employer to be regarded for the purposes of statutory maternity pay as the employer under the one contract where two or more contracts of service are so treated as one see the Statutory Maternity Pay (National Health Service Employees) Regulations 1991, SI 1991/590, reg 5 (amended by SI 2000/694; SI 2013/235); and see the Interpretation Act 1978 s 17(2)(a). Although 'contract of service' is defined for the purposes of statutory sick pay (see PARA 558 note 2), it is not so defined under the other statutory pay provisions (for which purposes see generally PARA 1 note 1).
19 See the Statutory Maternity Pay (National Health Service Employees) Regulations 1991, SI 1991/590, reg 3 (regs 3, 4 amended by SI 2002/2690).
20 See the Statutory Maternity Pay (National Health Service Employees) Regulations 1991, SI 1991/590, reg 4 (as amended: see note 19).
21 Statutory Maternity Pay (National Health Service Employees) Regulations 1991, SI 1991/590, reg 4(a).
22 Statutory Maternity Pay (National Health Service Employees) Regulations 1991, SI 1991/590, reg 4(b).
23 For these purposes, 'earnings' has the same meaning as it has for the purposes of the Social Security Contributions and Benefits Act 1992 s 171(5) (see PARA 429 note 2): see the Statutory Maternity Pay (National Health Service Employees) Regulations 1991, SI 1991/590, reg 4(c); and see the Interpretation Act 1978 s 17(2)(a).

24 For these purposes, 'relevant period' has the same meaning as it has for the purposes of the Social Security Contributions and Benefits Act 1992 s 171(5) (see PARA 429 note 3): see the Statutory Maternity Pay (National Health Service Employees) Regulations 1991, SI 1991/590, reg 4(c); and see the Interpretation Act 1978 s 17(2)(a).

25 Statutory Maternity Pay (National Health Service Employees) Regulations 1991, SI 1991/590, reg 4(c); and see the Interpretation Act 1978 s 17(2)(a).

26 Statutory Maternity Pay (National Health Service Employees) Regulations 1991, SI 1991/590, reg 6. As to the meaning of 'maternity pay period' see PARA 424.

414. Meaning of 'employer' for purposes of statutory maternity pay; treatment of two or more employers as one. For the purposes of the statutory maternity pay provisions that are set out in Part XII of the Social Security Contributions and Benefits Act 1992[1], 'employer', in relation to a woman who is an employee[2], means a person who is[3], or would be[4], liable to pay secondary Class 1 contributions in relation to any of her earnings[5].

Without prejudice to any other power to make regulations under Part XII of the Social Security Contributions and Benefits Act 1992[6], regulations may specify cases in which[7] two or more employers are to be treated as one[8]. Accordingly, in a case where the earnings paid to a woman in respect of two or more employments are aggregated and treated as a single payment of earnings[9] the employers of the woman in respect of those employments are to be treated for these purposes as one[10].

1 Ie the Social Security Contributions and Benefits Act 1992 Pt XII (ss 164–171).

2 As to the meaning of 'employee' for these purposes see PARA 406.

3 Ie under the Social Security Contributions and Benefits Act 1992 s 6: see WELFARE BENEFITS AND STATE PENSIONS vol 104 (2014) PARA 385.

4 Ie but for the condition in the Social Security Contributions and Benefits Act 1992 s 6(1)(b) (exclusion of liability where earnings are below lower earnings limit: see WELFARE BENEFITS AND STATE PENSIONS vol 104 (2014) PARA 385), or but for the employee being under the age of 16.

5 See the Social Security Contributions and Benefits Act 1992 s 171(1) (definition substituted by SI 2006/1031). As to the meaning of 'earnings' see PARA 430. As to secondary Class 1 contributions see WELFARE BENEFITS AND STATE PENSIONS vol 104 (2014) PARA 385. As to the meaning of 'employer' and related expressions in relation to employment rights generally see PARA 2 et seq.

6 Ie under the Social Security Contributions and Benefits Act 1992 Pt XII (see PARA 402). As to the making of regulations under the Social Security Contributions and Benefits Act 1992 see PARA 407 note 3.

7 Ie for the purposes of the Social Security Contributions and Benefits Act 1992 Pt XII or such provisions of Pt XII as may be prescribed. As to the meaning of 'prescribed' see PARA 407 note 8.

8 See the Social Security Contributions and Benefits Act 1992 s 171(2)(a). Regulations under s 171(2)(a) must be made with the concurrence of the Commissioners for Revenue and Customs: see s 171(7) (added by the Social Security Contributions (Transfer of Functions, etc) Act 1999 Sch 1 para 15(1), (3)). At the date at which this volume states the law, no such regulations had been made but, by virtue of the Interpretation Act 1978 s 17(2)(b), the Statutory Maternity Pay (General) Regulations 1986, SI 1986/1960, reg 18 (see the text and notes 9–10; and PARA 428) has effect as if made under the Social Security Contributions and Benefits Act 1992 s 171(2). As to the Commissioners for Her Majesty's Revenue and Customs see INCOME TAXATION vol 58 (2014) PARAS 33–34.

9 Ie under the Social Security (Contributions) Regulations 2001, SI 2001/1004, reg 15 (aggregation of earnings paid in respect of different employed earner's employments by different persons and apportionment of contribution liability: see WELFARE BENEFITS AND STATE PENSIONS vol 104 (2014) PARA 382).

10 Statutory Maternity Pay (General) Regulations 1986, SI 1986/1960, reg 18(1); and see the Interpretation Act 1978 s 17(2)(a).

C. CONDITIONS FOR ENTITLEMENT TO MATERNITY PAY; CONTINUOUS EMPLOYMENT

415. Conditions for entitlement to statutory maternity pay. The conditions[1] whose fulfilment entitles a woman to statutory maternity pay[2] are that:

(1) she has been in employed earner's[3] employment with an employer[4] for a continuous period of at least 26 weeks[5] ending with the week immediately preceding the fourteenth week before the expected week of confinement[6] but has ceased to work for him[7];

(2) as from a day to be appointed[8], at the end of the week immediately preceding the fourteenth week mentioned in head (1) in the text, she was entitled to be in that employment[9];

(3) her normal weekly earnings[10] for the period of eight weeks ending with the week immediately preceding the fourteenth week before the expected week of confinement are not less than the lower earnings limit in force[11] immediately before the commencement of the fourteenth week before the expected week of confinement[12]; and

(4) she has become pregnant and has reached, or been confined before reaching, the commencement of the eleventh week before the expected week of confinement[13].

In relation to a woman in employed earner's employment who was confined before the fourteenth week before the expected week of confinement, the conditions set out in head (1) and head (3) above also have effect with specified[14] modifications[15].

A woman who is an employee or treated as an employee for the purposes of the statutory provisions relating to persons abroad[16] and who:

(a) in the week immediately preceding the fourteenth week before the expected week of confinement was in employed earner's employment with an employer in Great Britain[17]; and

(b) had in any week within the period of 26 weeks immediately preceding that week been employed by the same employer in another member state[18],

is to be treated for these purposes[19] as having been employed in employed earner's employment in those weeks in which she was so employed in the other member state[20].

1 Ie the conditions mentioned in the Social Security Contributions and Benefits Act 1992 s 164(1): see PARA 401.

2 As to the meaning of 'statutory maternity pay' see PARA 401.

3 As to the meaning of 'employed earner' see the Social Security Contributions and Benefits Act 1992 s 2(1)(a), (3); and **WELFARE BENEFITS AND STATE PENSIONS** vol 104 (2014) PARA 381.

4 As to the meaning of 'employer' for these purposes see PARA 414.

5 As to the meaning of 'week' for these purposes see PARA 402 note 5.

6 For these purposes, 'confinement' means: (1) labour resulting in the issue of a living child; or (2) labour after 24 weeks of pregnancy resulting in the issue of a child whether alive or dead, and 'confined' is to be construed accordingly; and where a woman's labour begun on one day results in the issue of a child on another day, she is to be taken to be confined on the day of the issue of the child or, if labour results in the issue of twins or a greater number of children, she is to be taken to be confined on the day of the issue of the last of them: see the Social Security Contributions and Benefits Act 1992 s 171(1) (definition amended by the Still-Birth (Definition) Act 1992 ss 2(1), 4(2)).

7 Social Security Contributions and Benefits Act 1992 s 164(2)(a) (amended by the Employment Act 2002 ss 20(a), 54, Sch 8).

8 As from a day to be appointed under the Welfare Reform Act 2012 s 150(3), the Social Security Contributions and Benefits Act 1992 s 164(2)(aa) is added by the Welfare Reform Act 2012 s 63(1), (3)(a). However, at the date at which this volume states the law, no such day had been appointed.

9 Social Security Contributions and Benefits Act 1992 s 164(2)(aa) (prospectively added: see note 8).
10 As to the meaning of 'normal weekly earnings' see PARA 429.
11 Ie under the Social Security Contributions and Benefits Act 1992 s 5(1)(a) (earnings limits and thresholds for Class 1 contributions: see WELFARE BENEFITS AND STATE PENSIONS vol 104 (2014) PARA 384).
12 Social Security Contributions and Benefits Act 1992 s 164(2)(b).
13 Social Security Contributions and Benefits Act 1992 s 164(2)(c).
14 The modifications specified are that the conditions set out in head (1) and head (3) in the text are substituted by the following conditions (see the Statutory Maternity Pay (General) Regulations 1986, SI 1986/1960, reg 4(2) (amended by SI 1994/1367)), namely that:
    (1) she would, but for her confinement, have been in employed earner's employment with an employer for a continuous period of at least 26 weeks ending with the week immediately preceding the fourteenth week before the expected week of confinement (Statutory Maternity Pay (General) Regulations 1986, SI 1986/1960, reg 4(2)(a)); and
    (2) her normal weekly earnings for the period of eight weeks ending with the week immediately preceding the week of her confinement are not less than the lower earnings limit in force under the Social Security Contributions and Benefits Act 1992 s 5(1)(a) (see note 11) immediately before the commencement of the week of her confinement (reg 4(2)(b) (amended by SI 1994/1367)).

    As to the modification of the Social Security Contributions and Benefits Act 1992 s 166 (rates of payment) in relation to a woman to whom the Statutory Maternity Pay (General) Regulations 1986, SI 1986/1960, reg 4(2) applies see the Statutory Maternity Pay (General) Regulations 1986, SI 1986/1960, reg 4(3); and PARA 428 note 2.

    As to employed earner's employment within the meaning of the Social Security Contributions and Benefits Act 1992 see WELFARE BENEFITS AND STATE PENSIONS vol 104 (2014) PARA 176.
15 Statutory Maternity Pay (General) Regulations 1986, SI 1986/1960, reg 4(2) (as amended: see note 14).
16 Ie under the Statutory Maternity Pay (Persons Abroad and Mariners) Regulations 1987, SI 1987/418, reg 2: see PARA 409.
17 Statutory Maternity Pay (Persons Abroad and Mariners) Regulations 1987, SI 1987/418, reg 5(1)(a).
18 Statutory Maternity Pay (Persons Abroad and Mariners) Regulations 1987, SI 1987/418, reg 5(1)(b) (amended by SI 1996/777).
19 Ie for the purposes of the Social Security Contributions and Benefits Act 1992 s 164(2) (see the text and notes 1–13) and s 166 (see PARA 428).
20 See the Statutory Maternity Pay (Persons Abroad and Mariners) Regulations 1987, SI 1987/418, reg 5(1); and see the Interpretation Act 1978 s 17(2)(a).

416. Continuous employment; in general. Where in any week[1] a woman is, for the whole or part of the week:

(1) incapable of work in consequence of sickness or injury[2]; or
(2) absent from work on account of a temporary cessation of work[3]; or
(3) absent from work in circumstances such that, by arrangement or custom, she is regarded as continuing in the employment of her employer for all purposes or for any purpose[4]; or
(4) absent from work wholly or partly because of pregnancy or confinement[5]; or
(5) absent from work in consequence of taking paternity leave[6], adoption leave[7] or parental leave[8],

and returns to work for her employer after the incapacity for or absence from work, that week is to be treated for the purpose of the statutory maternity pay provisions that are set out in Part XII of the Social Security Contributions and Benefits Act 1992[9] as part of a continuous period of employment with that employer, notwithstanding that a contract of service does not exist with that employer in respect of that week[10].

Where a woman is employed under a contract of service for part only of the week immediately preceding the fourteenth week before the expected week of confinement, the whole of that week counts in computing[11] any period of continuous employment[12].

Where a woman who is pregnant:

(a) is an employee in an employed earner's employment[13] in which the custom is for the employer[14]:
  (i) to offer work for a fixed period of not more than 26 consecutive weeks[15];
  (ii) to offer work for such period on two or more occasions in a year for periods which do not overlap[16]; and
  (iii) to offer the work available to those persons who had worked for him during the last or a recent such period[17]; but
(b) is absent from work[18]:
  (i) wholly or partly because of the pregnancy or her confinement[19]; or
  (ii) because of incapacity arising from some specific disease or bodily or mental disablement[20],

then in her case these provisions[21] apply subject to specified[22] modifications[23].

Where a woman has been in employed earner's employment with the same employer in each of 26 consecutive weeks, but no more than 26 weeks, ending with the week immediately preceding the fourteenth week before the expected week of confinement, then, for the purpose of determining whether that employment amounts to a continuous period of at least 26 weeks, the first of those 26 weeks is a period commencing on the first day of her employment with the employer and ending at midnight on the first Saturday thereafter or on that day where her first day is a Saturday[24].

1 As to the meaning of 'week' for these purposes see PARA 402 note 5. See also the text and note 24.
2 Statutory Maternity Pay (General) Regulations 1986, SI 1986/1960, reg 11(1)(a). Incapacity for work which lasts for more than 26 consecutive weeks does not count for the purposes of head (1) in the text: reg 11(2).
3 Statutory Maternity Pay (General) Regulations 1986, SI 1986/1960, reg 11(1)(b).
4 Statutory Maternity Pay (General) Regulations 1986, SI 1986/1960, reg 11(1)(c).
5 Statutory Maternity Pay (General) Regulations 1986, SI 1986/1960, reg 11(1)(d) (reg 11(1)(d) amended, reg 11(1)(e) added, by SI 2002/2690). Head (4) in the text only applies to a woman who:
  (1) has a contract of service with the same employer both before and after her confinement but not during any period of absence from work due to her confinement and the period between those contracts does not exceed 26 weeks (Statutory Maternity Pay (General) Regulations 1986, SI 1986/1960, reg 11(3)(a)); or
  (2) returned to work in accordance with the Employment Protection (Consolidation) Act 1978 s 45(1) (repealed) or in pursuance of an offer made in circumstances described in s 56A(2) (repealed) after a period of absence from work wholly or partly occasioned by pregnancy or confinement (Statutory Maternity Pay (General) Regulations 1986, SI 1986/1960, reg 11(3)(b)).

As to the meaning of 'employer' for these purposes see PARA 414. As to the meaning of 'confinement' see PARA 415 note 6. Although 'contract of service' is defined for the purposes of statutory sick pay (see PARA 558 note 2), it is not so defined under the other statutory pay provisions (for which purposes see generally PARA 1 note 1).

Regulation 11(1)(d), (3) is effectively spent: reg 11(3)(b) (see head (2) above) refers to repealed provisions of the Employment Protection (Consolidation) Act 1978; the Employment Rights Act 1996 now contains no exact equivalent provisions (although, in relation to suspension from work on maternity grounds, see s 66; and PARA 598); the reform of maternity rights by the Employment Relations Act 1999 and the changes in 1999 continuing the employment contract during maternity leave (see PARA 359) make special provision unnecessary;

and the general continuity provision on which the Statutory Maternity Pay (General) Regulations 1986, SI 1986/1960, reg 11(1)(d) was modelled (ie the Employment Rights Act 1996 s 212(3)(d)) has been repealed.

6 Ie under the Employment Rights Act 1996 Pt VIII Ch III (ss 80A–80E): see PARA 368 et seq.

7 Ie under the Employment Rights Act 1996 Pt VIII Ch IA (ss 75A–75D): see PARA 377 et seq.

8 Statutory Maternity Pay (General) Regulations 1986, SI 1986/1960, reg 11(1)(e) (as added: see note 5). Parental leave is taken under the Employment Rights Act 1996 Pt VIII Ch II (ss 76–80): see PARA 390 et seq.

9 Ie for the purposes of the Social Security Contributions and Benefits Act 1992 Pt XII (ss 164–171), but subject to the Statutory Maternity Pay (General) Regulations 1986, SI 1986/1960, reg 11(2)–(4) (see notes 2, 5; and the text and notes 11–23): see reg 11(1); and see the Interpretation Act 1978 s 17(2)(a).

10 See the Statutory Maternity Pay (General) Regulations 1986, SI 1986/1960, reg 11(1); and see the Interpretation Act 1978 s 17(2)(a).

11 Ie for the purposes of the Social Security Contributions and Benefits Act 1992 Pt XII.

12 See the Statutory Maternity Pay (General) Regulations 1986, SI 1986/1960, reg 11(4); and see the Interpretation Act 1978 s 17(2)(a).

13 As to employed earner's employment within the meaning of the Social Security Contributions and Benefits Act 1992 see WELFARE BENEFITS AND STATE PENSIONS vol 104 (2014) PARA 176.

14 See the Statutory Maternity Pay (General) Regulations 1986, SI 1986/1960, reg 11(3A)(a) (regs 11(3A), 16A added by SI 1990/622).

15 Statutory Maternity Pay (General) Regulations 1986, SI 1986/1960, reg 11(3A)(a)(i) (as added: see note 14).

16 Statutory Maternity Pay (General) Regulations 1986, SI 1986/1960, reg 11(3A)(a)(ii) (as added: see note 14).

17 Statutory Maternity Pay (General) Regulations 1986, SI 1986/1960, reg 11(3A)(a)(iii) (as added: see note 14).

18 See the Statutory Maternity Pay (General) Regulations 1986, SI 1986/1960, reg 11(3A)(b) (as added: see note 14).

19 Statutory Maternity Pay (General) Regulations 1986, SI 1986/1960, reg 11(3A)(b)(i) (as added: see note 14).

20 Statutory Maternity Pay (General) Regulations 1986, SI 1986/1960, reg 11(3A)(b)(ii) (as added: see note 14).

21 Ie the Statutory Maternity Pay (General) Regulations 1986, SI 1986/1960, reg 11(1): see the text and notes 1–10.

22 The modifications specified are that the Statutory Maternity Pay (General) Regulations 1986, SI 1986/1960, reg 11(1) (see the text and notes 1–10) applies: (1) as if the words 'and returns to work for an employer after the incapacity for or absence from work' were omitted; and (2) reg 11(4) (see the text and notes 11–12) does not apply: see reg 11(3A) (as added: see note 14).

23 See the Statutory Maternity Pay (General) Regulations 1986, SI 1986/1960, reg 11(3A) (as added: see note 14).

24 Statutory Maternity Pay (General) Regulations 1986, SI 1986/1960, reg 16A (as added: see note 14).

417. Continuous employment and unfair dismissal. A woman in relation to whose dismissal an action is commenced which consists of:

(1) the presentation by her of a complaint[1] of unfair dismissal[2]; or

(2) her making a claim in accordance with a dismissal procedures agreement[3] designated[4] by an order[5]; or

(3) any action taken[6] by a conciliation officer[7]; or

(4) a decision arising out of the use of a statutory dispute resolution procedure[8] in a case where[9] such a procedure applies[10],

has the continuity of her employment preserved[11] if, in consequence of such action, she is reinstated or re-engaged by her employer[12] or by a successor[13] or associated employer[14] of that employer; and any week which falls within the interval beginning with the effective date of termination and ending with the date of reinstatement or re-engagement, as the case may be, counts in the computation of her period of continuous employment[15].

1 Ie under the Employment Rights Act 1996 s 111(1): see PARA 804.

2 Statutory Maternity Pay (General) Regulations 1986, SI 1986/1960, reg 12(1)(a); and see the Interpretation Act 1978 s 17(2)(a).
3 The Statutory Maternity Pay (General) Regulations 1986, SI 1986/1960, reg 12(1)(b) refers to a 'dismissals procedure agreement'; and, by virtue of reg 12(3), 'dismissals procedure agreement' has the same meaning as in the Trade Union and Labour Relations Act 1974 s 30(3), (4) (sic) (repealed). It is submitted that the reference to a 'dismissals procedure agreement' is intended to be a reference to a 'dismissal procedures agreement' as defined by s 30(1) (repealed). As to the meaning of 'dismissal procedures agreement' see now the Employment Rights Act 1996 s 235(1); and PARA 150 note 9. Cf the definition of 'dismissals procedure agreement' applied in the Statutory Paternity Pay and Statutory Adoption Pay (General) Regulations 2002, SI 2002/2822, reg 34 (see PARA 459 note 2).
4 Ie under the Employment Rights Act 1996 s 110: see PARAS 759–760.
5 Statutory Maternity Pay (General) Regulations 1986, SI 1986/1960, reg 12(1)(b); and see the Interpretation Act 1978 s 17(2)(a).
6 Ie under the Employment Tribunals Act 1996 s 18(5) (repealed).
7 Statutory Maternity Pay (General) Regulations 1986, SI 1986/1960, reg 12(1)(c) (reg 12(1)(c) amended, reg 12(1)(d) added, by SI 2005/358); and see the Interpretation Act 1978 s 17(2)(a).
8 Ie contained in the Employment Act 2002 Sch 2 (repealed).
9 Ie in accordance with the Employment (Dispute Resolution) Regulations 2004, SI 2004/752 (revoked).
10 Statutory Maternity Pay (General) Regulations 1986, SI 1986/1960, reg 12(1)(d) (as added: see note 7); and see the Interpretation Act 1978 s 17(2)(a).
11 Ie for the purposes of the Social Security Contributions and Benefits Act 1992 Pt XII (ss 164–171).
12 As to the meaning of 'employer' for these purposes see PARA 414.
13 For these purposes, 'successor' has the same meaning as in the Employment Rights Act 1996 s 235(1) (see PARA 133 note 10): see the Statutory Maternity Pay (General) Regulations 1986, SI 1986/1960, reg 12(3); and see the Interpretation Act 1978 s 17(2)(a).
14 For these purposes, 'associated employer' is to be construed in accordance with the Employment Rights Act 1996 s 231 (see PARA 3): see the Statutory Maternity Pay (General) Regulations 1986, SI 1986/1960, reg 12(3); and see the Interpretation Act 1978 s 17(2)(a).
15 See the Statutory Maternity Pay (General) Regulations 1986, SI 1986/1960, reg 12(2); and see the Interpretation Act 1978 s 17(2)(a).

418. Continuous employment and stoppages of work. Where for any week[1] or part of a week a woman does no work because there is a stoppage of work due to a trade dispute[2] at her place of employment, the continuity of her employment is to be treated[3] as continuing throughout the stoppage; but no such week counts[4] in the computation of her period of employment[5].

1 As to the meaning of 'week' for these purposes see PARA 402 note 5.
2 Ie a trade dispute within the meaning of the Jobseekers Act 1995 s 35(1): see **WELFARE BENEFITS AND STATE PENSIONS** vol 104 (2014) PARA 438.
3 Ie subject to the Statutory Maternity Pay (General) Regulations 1986, SI 1986/1960, reg 13(2): see note 5.
4 Ie subject to the Statutory Maternity Pay (General) Regulations 1986, SI 1986/1960, reg 13(3): see note 5.
5 Statutory Maternity Pay (General) Regulations 1986, SI 1986/1960, reg 13(1); and see the Interpretation Act 1978 s 17(2)(a). Where during the stoppage of work a woman is dismissed from her employment, the continuity of her employment is not to be treated, in accordance with the Statutory Maternity Pay (General) Regulations 1986, SI 1986/1960, reg 13(1), as continuing beyond the commencement of the day she stopped work: reg 13(2). The provisions of reg 13(1), to the extent that they provide that a week in which a stoppage of work occurred does not count in the computation of a period of employment, and reg 13(2) do not apply to a woman who proves that at no time did she have a direct interest in the trade dispute in question: reg 13(3).

419. Change of employer; reinstatement after service with armed forces etc. A woman's employment is to be treated, notwithstanding a change of employer[1], as continuous employment with the second employer where[2]:

(1) the employer's trade or business or an undertaking, whether or not it is

an undertaking established by or under an Act of Parliament, is transferred from one person to another[3];

(2) by or under an Act of Parliament, whether public or local and whenever passed, a contract of employment between any body corporate and the woman is modified and some other body corporate is substituted as her employer[4];

(3) on the death of her employer, the woman is taken into the employment of the personal representatives or trustees of the deceased[5];

(4) the woman is employed by partners, personal representatives or trustees and there is a change in the partners, or, as the case may be, personal representatives or trustees[6];

(5) the woman is taken into the employment of an employer who is, at the time she entered his employment, an associated employer[7] of her previous employer[8];

(6) on the termination of her employment with an employer she is taken into the employment of another employer and those employers are the governors of a school maintained by a local authority and that authority[9].

If a woman who is entitled to apply to her former employer under the Reserve Forces (Safeguard of Employment) Act 1985[10] enters the employment of that employer not later than the statutory six-month period[11], her previous period of employment with that employer, or, if there was more than one such period, the last of those periods, and the period of employment beginning in that period of six months are to be treated as continuous[12].

1 As to the meaning of 'employer' for these purposes see PARA 414.
2 See the Statutory Maternity Pay (General) Regulations 1986, SI 1986/1960, reg 14.
3 Statutory Maternity Pay (General) Regulations 1986, SI 1986/1960, reg 14(a).
4 Statutory Maternity Pay (General) Regulations 1986, SI 1986/1960, reg 14(b).
5 Statutory Maternity Pay (General) Regulations 1986, SI 1986/1960, reg 14(c).
6 Statutory Maternity Pay (General) Regulations 1986, SI 1986/1960, reg 14(d).
7 For these purposes, 'associated employer' is to be construed in accordance with the Employment Rights Act 1996 s 231 (see PARA 3): see the Statutory Maternity Pay (General) Regulations 1986, SI 1986/1960, reg 14(e); and see the Interpretation Act 1978 s 17(2)(a).
8 Statutory Maternity Pay (General) Regulations 1986, SI 1986/1960, reg 14(e).
9 Statutory Maternity Pay (General) Regulations 1986, SI 1986/1960, reg 14(f) (amended by SI 1990/622; SI 2010/1172). Head (6) in the text refers to a local authority within the meaning of the Education Act 1996 (see s 579(1); and **EDUCATION** vol 35 (2011) PARA 24): see the Statutory Maternity Pay (General) Regulations 1986, SI 1986/1960, reg 14(f) (as so amended).
10 As to the right to reinstatement under the Reserve Forces (Safeguard of Employment) Act 1985 see **ARMED FORCES** vol 3 (2011) PARA 370.
11 Ie the six-month period mentioned in the Reserve Forces (Safeguard of Employment) Act 1985 s 1(4)(b). A former employer's obligation under s 1 is discharged if after giving reasonable notice to the applicant he makes appropriate employment available to him at that first opportunity, except that:
   (1) an opportunity for taking the applicant into his former employer's employment is not to be deemed for the purposes of s 1(3), (4) (see **ARMED FORCES** vol 3 (2011) PARA 370) to have arisen if the former employer makes employment available to the applicant, but the applicant has, or reasonably believes that he has, reasonable cause for not taking it, and if the facts on which the applicant relies as constituting the reasonable cause are notified in writing to the former employer by him or by some person acting with his authority as soon as may be after he has been notified by the former employer that the employment is being made available to him (see s 1(4)(a)); and
   (2) in no case is the former employer to be under any obligation under s 1 to take the applicant into his employment after six months have elapsed from the end of the applicant's whole-time service (see s 1(4)(b)).
12 Statutory Maternity Pay (General) Regulations 1986, SI 1986/1960, reg 15.

D. NOTICE OF ABSENCE; EVIDENCE OF CONFINEMENT

420. Notice of absence from work for purposes of entitlement to statutory maternity pay. A woman is entitled to payments of statutory maternity pay[1] only if[2]:

(1) she gives the person who will be liable to pay it notice of the date from which she expects his liability to pay her statutory maternity pay to begin[3]; and

(2) the notice is given at least 28 days before that date or, if that is not reasonably practicable, as soon as is reasonably practicable[4].

The notice must be in writing[5] if the person who is liable to pay the woman statutory maternity pay so requests[6].

However, these provisions governing entitlement and liability[7] do not have effect in the case of a woman who leaves her employment with the person who will be liable to pay her statutory maternity pay after the beginning of the week immediately preceding the fourteenth week before the expected week of confinement[8]; and a woman who is so exempted[9] but who is confined before the eleventh week before the expected week of confinement is entitled to statutory maternity pay only if she gives the person who will be liable to pay it notice specifying the date she was confined[10].

1 As to the meaning of 'statutory maternity pay' see PARA 401.
2 See the Social Security Contributions and Benefits Act 1992 s 164(4) (substituted by the Employment Act 2002 s 20(b)). At the date at which this volume states the law, the Statutory Maternity Pay (General) Regulations 1986, SI 1986/1960, have effect as if made under the Social Security Contributions and Benefits Act 1992 s 164(4) (see the text and notes 7–10).
3 Social Security Contributions and Benefits Act 1992 s 164(4)(a) (as substituted: see note 2).
4 Social Security Contributions and Benefits Act 1992 s 164(4)(b) (as substituted: see note 2). As to the time for compliance where an employee is outside the United Kingdom see PARA 408.
5 As to the meaning of 'writing' see PARA 2 note 8.
6 Social Security Contributions and Benefits Act 1992 s 164(5).
7 Ie the Social Security Contributions and Benefits Act 1992 s 164(4): see the text and notes 1–4.
8 Statutory Maternity Pay (General) Regulations 1986, SI 1986/1960, reg 23(4) (substituted by SI 1994/1367; and further substituted by SI 2002/2690). As to the meaning of 'confinement' see PARA 415 note 6.
9 Ie from the Social Security Contributions and Benefits Act 1992 s 164(4): see the text and notes 1–4.
10 Statutory Maternity Pay (General) Regulations 1986, SI 1986/1960, reg 23(5) (substituted by SI 1994/1367).

421. Notice requirements in special cases for purposes of entitlement to statutory maternity pay. Where a woman is confined before the beginning of the fourteenth week[1] before the expected week of confinement[2], she is entitled to payments of statutory maternity pay[3] only if[4]:

(1) she gives notice to the person who will be liable to pay it of the date on which she was confined[5]; and

(2) that notice is given within 28 days of the date she was confined or, if in the particular circumstances that is not practicable, as soon as is reasonably practicable thereafter[6]; and

(3) where the person so requests, the notice is in writing[7].

Where a woman is confined before the date stated in the notice required by the statutory provisions governing entitlement and liability[8] as being the date her absence from work is due to begin, she is entitled to payments of statutory maternity pay only if[9]:

(a) she gives a further notice to the person who will be liable to pay it specifying the date she was confined and the date her absence from work began[10]; and

(b) that further notice is given within 28 days of the date she was confined or, if in the particular circumstances that is not practicable, as soon as is reasonably practicable thereafter[11]; and

(c) where the person so requests, the notice is in writing[12].

1 As to the meaning of 'week' for these purposes see PARA 402 note 5.
2 As to the meaning of 'confinement' see PARA 415 note 6.
3 As to the meaning of 'statutory maternity pay' see PARA 401.
4 See the Statutory Maternity Pay (General) Regulations 1986, SI 1986/1960, reg 23(1).
5 Statutory Maternity Pay (General) Regulations 1986, SI 1986/1960, reg 23(1)(a) (reg 23(1)(a), (b) amended by SI 2002/2690).
6 Statutory Maternity Pay (General) Regulations 1986, SI 1986/1960, reg 23(1)(b) (as amended: see note 5). For these purposes, a notice contained in an envelope which is properly addressed and sent by prepaid post is deemed to be given on the date on which it is posted: see reg 23(3). As to the time for compliance where an employee is outside the United Kingdom see PARA 408.
7 Statutory Maternity Pay (General) Regulations 1986, SI 1986/1960, reg 23(1)(c). As to the meaning of 'writing' see PARA 2 note 8.
8 Ie a notice provided in accordance with the Social Security Contributions and Benefits Act 1992 s 164(4): see PARA 420.
9 See the Statutory Maternity Pay (General) Regulations 1986, SI 1986/1960, reg 23(2) (amended by SI 1994/1367).
10 Statutory Maternity Pay (General) Regulations 1986, SI 1986/1960, reg 23(2)(a) (reg 23(2)(a), (b) amended by SI 2002/2690).
11 Statutory Maternity Pay (General) Regulations 1986, SI 1986/1960, reg 23(2)(b) (as amended: see note 10).
12 Statutory Maternity Pay (General) Regulations 1986, SI 1986/1960, reg 23(2)(c).

422. Evidence of expected week of confinement or of confinement in general for purposes of entitlement to statutory maternity pay. A woman must provide the person who is liable to pay her statutory maternity pay[1] with evidence as to her pregnancy and the expected date of confinement[2] in such form and at such time as may be prescribed[3].

Accordingly, a woman must provide the person who is liable to pay her statutory maternity pay with evidence as to[4]:

(1) the week in which the expected date of confinement occurs[5]; and

(2) where her entitlement to statutory maternity pay depends on the fact of her confinement, the week in which she was confined[6].

The evidence must be submitted to the person who will be liable to make payments of statutory maternity pay not later than the end of the third week of the maternity pay period[7]; but, where the woman has good cause, the evidence may be submitted later than that date but not later than the end of the thirteenth week of the maternity pay period[8].

1 As to the meaning of 'statutory maternity pay' see PARA 401; and as to the persons liable to make payments see PARA 401 et seq.
2 As to the meaning of 'confinement' see PARA 415 note 6.
3 See the Social Security Administration Act 1992 s 15(1)(a). For the purposes of the Social Security Administration Act 1992, 'prescribe' means prescribe by regulations; and 'prescribed' must be construed accordingly: see s 191 (definition amended by the Welfare Reform Act 2007 Sch 5 paras 2, 10). As to the making of regulations under the Social Security Administration Act 1992 generally see WELFARE BENEFITS AND STATE PENSIONS vol 104 (2014) PARA 400. Any regulations for the purposes of s 15(1) must be made with the concurrence of the Revenue and Customs: s 15(1A) (added by the Social Security Contributions (Transfer of Functions, etc) Act 1999 Sch 3 para 43). As to the Commissioners for Her Majesty's Revenue and Customs see INCOME TAXATION vol 58 (2014) PARAS 33–34. At the date at which this volume states the law,

no such regulations had been made under s 15(1) but, by virtue of the Interpretation Act 1978 s 17(2)(b), the Statutory Maternity Pay (Medical Evidence) Regulations 1987, SI 1987/235 (see PARA 423), have effect as if made under the Social Security Administration Act 1992 s 15(1).

4 See the Statutory Maternity Pay (General) Regulations 1986, SI 1986/1960, reg 22(1).

5 Statutory Maternity Pay (General) Regulations 1986, SI 1986/1960, reg 22(1)(a).

6 Statutory Maternity Pay (General) Regulations 1986, SI 1986/1960, reg 22(1)(b). For the purposes of head (2) in the text, a certificate of birth is sufficient evidence that the woman was confined in the week in which the birth occurred: reg 22(2).

7 As to the meaning of 'maternity pay period' see PARA 424.

8 Statutory Maternity Pay (General) Regulations 1986, SI 1986/1960, reg 22(3). For these purposes, evidence contained in an envelope which is properly addressed and sent by prepaid post is deemed to have been submitted on the day on which it was posted: see reg 22(4). As to the time for compliance where an employee is outside the United Kingdom see PARA 408.

423. Maternity certificates for purposes of entitlement to statutory maternity pay. The evidence as to pregnancy and the expected date of confinement[1] which a woman is required to provide to a person who is liable to pay her statutory maternity pay[2] must be furnished in the form of a maternity certificate in the prescribed form[3] given by a doctor[4] or by a registered midwife[5], not earlier than the beginning of the twentieth week before the expected week of confinement, in accordance with the following rules[6]:

(1) a maternity certificate must be given by a doctor or registered midwife attending the woman[7] and must not be given by the woman herself[8];

(2) the maternity certificate must be on a form provided by the Secretary of State[9] for the purpose and the wording must be that set out in the appropriate part of the prescribed form[10];

(3) every maternity certificate must be completed in ink or other indelible substance, and must contain the following particulars[11]:

  (a) the woman's name[12];

  (b) the week in which the woman is expected to be confined or, if the maternity certificate is given after confinement, the date of that confinement and the date the confinement was expected to take place[13];

  (c) the date of the examination on which the maternity certificate is based[14];

  (d) the date on which the maternity certificate is signed[15]; and

  (e) the address of the doctor or, where the maternity certificate is signed by a registered midwife, the personal identification number given to her on her registration[16] and the expiry date of that registration[17],

  and it must bear opposite the word 'signature' the signature of the person giving the maternity certificate written after there has been entered on it the woman's name and the expected date or, as the case may be, the date of the confinement[18];

(4) after a maternity certificate has been given, no further maternity certificate based on the same examination may be furnished other than a maternity certificate by way of replacement of an original which has been lost or mislaid, in which case it must be clearly marked 'duplicate'[19].

1 As to the meaning of 'confinement' see PARA 415 note 6. As to the requirement to provide evidence of confinement see PARA 422.

2 As to the meaning of 'statutory maternity pay' see PARA 401. As to provisions governing entitlement and liability to statutory maternity pay see PARAS 401, 403.

3 The maternity certificate must be:

(1) in the appropriate form as set out in the Statutory Maternity Pay (Medical Evidence) Regulations 1987, SI 1987/235, Schedule Pt II (substituted by SI 1991/2284; amended by SI 2001/2931; SI 2004/865; SI 2004/1016; SI 2004/1771; SI 2013/235) (Statutory Maternity Pay (Medical Evidence) Regulations 1987, SI 1987/235, reg 2(a)); or
(2) in a form substantially to the like effect with such variations as the circumstances may require (reg 2(b)).

4 For these purposes, 'doctor' means a registered medical practitioner: see the Statutory Maternity Pay (Medical Evidence) Regulations 1987, SI 1987/235, reg 1(2). As to the meaning of 'registered medical practitioner' see MEDICAL PROFESSIONS vol 74 (2011) PARA 176.
5 For these purposes, 'registered midwife' means a midwife who is registered with the Nursing and Midwifery Council under the Nursing and Midwifery Order 2001, SI 2002/253 (see MEDICAL PROFESSIONS vol 74 (2011) PARA 713): see the Statutory Maternity Pay (Medical Evidence) Regulations 1987, SI 1987/235, reg 1(2) (definition substituted by SI 2002/881).
6 Statutory Maternity Pay (Medical Evidence) Regulations 1987, SI 1987/235, reg 2 (amended by SI 2001/2931). The text refers to the rules set out in the Statutory Maternity Pay (Medical Evidence) Regulations 1987, SI 1987/235, Schedule Pt I (see the text and notes 7–19): see reg 2 (as so amended).
7 For these purposes, any reference to a woman is a reference to the woman in respect of whom a maternity certificate is given in accordance with the Statutory Maternity Pay (Medical Evidence) Regulations 1987, SI 1987/235, Schedule Pt I (see also the text and notes 9–19): see Schedule Pt I r 1.
8 Statutory Maternity Pay (Medical Evidence) Regulations 1987, SI 1987/235, Schedule Pt I r 2.
9 As to the Secretary of State see PARA 5 note 21.
10 Statutory Maternity Pay (Medical Evidence) Regulations 1987, SI 1987/235, Schedule Pt I r 3. The text refers to the appropriate part of the form specified in Schedule Pt II (see note 3): see Schedule Pt I r 3.
11 See the Statutory Maternity Pay (Medical Evidence) Regulations 1987, SI 1987/235, Schedule Pt I r 4.
12 Statutory Maternity Pay (Medical Evidence) Regulations 1987, SI 1987/235, Schedule Pt I r 4(a).
13 Statutory Maternity Pay (Medical Evidence) Regulations 1987, SI 1987/235, Schedule Pt I r 4(b) (amended by SI 1991/2284).
14 Statutory Maternity Pay (Medical Evidence) Regulations 1987, SI 1987/235, Schedule Pt I r 4(c).
15 Statutory Maternity Pay (Medical Evidence) Regulations 1987, SI 1987/235, Schedule Pt I r 4(d). For these purposes, 'signature' means, in relation to any statement or certificate given in accordance with the Statutory Maternity Pay (Medical Evidence) Regulations 1987, SI 1987/235, the name by which the person giving that statement or certificate, as the case may be, is usually known (any name other than the surname being either in full or otherwise indicated) written by that person in his own handwriting; and 'signed' is to be construed accordingly: see reg 1(2).
16 Ie on her registration in the register maintained by the Nursing and Midwifery Council under the Nursing and Midwifery Order 2001, SI 2002/253, art 5 (see MEDICAL PROFESSIONS vol 74 (2011) PARA 713).
17 Statutory Maternity Pay (Medical Evidence) Regulations 1987, SI 1987/235, Schedule Pt I r 4(e) (substituted by SI 2002/881; amended by SI 2004/1771).
18 See the Statutory Maternity Pay (Medical Evidence) Regulations 1987, SI 1987/235, Schedule Pt I r 4.
19 Statutory Maternity Pay (Medical Evidence) Regulations 1987, SI 1987/235, Schedule Pt I r 5.

E. THE MATERNITY PAY PERIOD

424. General provision for the maternity pay period. Statutory maternity pay[1] is payable[2] in respect of each week[3] during a prescribed[4] period (the 'maternity pay period') of a duration not exceeding 52 weeks[5]. At the date this volume states the law, the prescribed period is set at 39 consecutive weeks[6]. The maternity pay periods begins with the eleventh week before the expected week of confinement[7]. Cases may, however, be prescribed in which the first day of the period is to be a prescribed day after the beginning of the eleventh week before the expected week of confinement, but not later than the day immediately following the day in which she is confined[8].

Except in such cases as may be prescribed, statutory maternity pay is not payable to a woman:

(1) by a person in respect of any week during any part of which she works under a contract of service with him[9];

(2) in respect of any week after she has been confined and during any part of which she works for any employer who is not liable to pay her statutory maternity pay[10].

Regulations may provide that these provisions are to have effect subject to prescribed modifications[11] in relation to cases in which[12]:

(a) a woman is confined before the eleventh week before the expected week of confinement[13]; and

(b) a woman is confined at any time after the end of the week immediately preceding the eleventh week before the expected week of confinement, and the maternity pay period has not then commenced for her[14].

1 As to the meaning of 'statutory maternity pay' see PARA 401.

2 Ie subject to the provisions of the Social Security Contributions and Benefits Act 1992 Pt XII (ss 164–171).

3 In the Social Security Contributions and Benefits Act 1992 s 165(1), (4), (6) (see also heads (1), (2) in the text), 'week' means a period of seven days beginning with the day of the week on which the maternity pay period begins: see s 165(8) (added by the Work and Families Act 2006 Sch 1 para 7(1), (4)).

4 For these purposes, 'prescribed' means specified in or determined in accordance with regulations: see the Social Security Contributions and Benefits Act 1992 s 171(1). As to the making of regulations under the Social Security Contributions and Benefits Act 1992 generally see PARA 407 note 3. At the date at which this volume states the law, no such regulations had been made but, by virtue of the Interpretation Act 1978 s 17(2)(b), the Statutory Maternity Pay (General) Regulations 1986, SI 1986/1960, have effect (see PARA 425 et seq) as if made under the Social Security Contributions and Benefits Act 1992 s 165(1), (3), (6), (7).

5 Social Security Contributions and Benefits Act 1992 s 165(1) (amended by the Work and Families Act 2006 s 1). In the Social Security Contributions and Benefits Act 1992,'maternity pay period' has the meaning assigned to it by s 165(1): see s 171(1).

Where a woman asks an employer or former employer of hers to provide her with a written statement, in respect of a period before the request is made, of one or more of the following:

(1) the weeks within that period which he regards as weeks in respect of which he is liable to pay statutory maternity pay to the woman (Social Security Administration Act 1992 s 15(2)(a));

(2) the reasons why he does not so regard the other weeks in that period (s 15(2)(b)); and

(3) his opinion as to the amount of statutory maternity pay to which the woman is entitled in respect of each of the weeks in respect of which he regards himself as liable to make a payment (s 15(2)(c)),

the employer or former employer shall, to the extent to which the request was reasonable, comply with it within a reasonable time (see s 15(2)).

6 See the Statutory Maternity Pay (General) Regulations 1986, SI 1986/1960, reg 2(2); and PARA 425.

7 Social Security Contributions and Benefits Act 1992 s 165(2) (s 165(2), (3) substituted by the Work and Families Act 2006 Sch 1 para 7(1), (2)). The provision made by the Social Security Contributions and Benefits Act 1992 s 165(2) is subject to s 165(3), (7): see the text and notes 8, 11–14. As to the meaning of 'confinement' see PARA 415 note 6.

8 Social Security Contributions and Benefits Act 1992 s 165(3) (as substituted: see note 7).

Regulations may provide for the duration of the maternity pay period as it applies to a woman to be reduced, subject to prescribed restrictions and conditions: s 165(3A) (s 165(3A)–(3D) added by the Children and Families Act 2014 s 120(1), (4)). Such regulations must secure that the reduced period ends at a time:

(1) after a prescribed period beginning with the day on which the woman is confined (Social Security Contributions and Benefits Act 1992 s 165(3B)(a) (as so added)); and

(2) when at least a prescribed part of the maternity pay period remains unexpired (s 165(3B)(b) (as so added)).

Such regulations may, in particular, prescribe restrictions and conditions relating to:

(a) the end of the woman's entitlement to maternity leave (s 165(3C)(a) (as so added));

(b) the doing of work by the woman (s 165(3C)(b) (as so added));
(c) the taking of prescribed steps by the woman or another person as regards leave under the Employment Rights Act 1996 s 75E (shared parental leave on birth: see PARA 398) in respect of the child (Social Security Contributions and Benefits Act 1992 s 165(3C)(c) (as so added));
(d) the taking of prescribed steps by the woman or another person as regards statutory shared parental pay (see PARA 534) in respect of the child (s 165(3C)(d) (as so added)).

Regulations also may provide for a reduction in the duration of the maternity pay period as it applies to a woman to be revoked, or to be treated as revoked, subject to prescribed restrictions and conditions: s 165(3D) (as so added).

9 Social Security Contributions and Benefits Act 1992 s 165(4) (amended by the Work and Families Act 2006 Sch 1 paras 7(1), (3)). See note 3. It is immaterial for these purposes whether the work referred to in the text is work under a contract of service which existed immediately before the maternity pay period or a contract of service which did not so exist: Social Security Contributions and Benefits Act 1992 s 165(5). Although 'contract of service' is defined for the purposes of statutory sick pay (see PARA 558 note 2), it is not so defined under the other statutory pay provisions (for which purposes see generally PARA 1 note 1).

10 Social Security Contributions and Benefits Act 1992 s 165(6). See note 3. As to the meaning of 'employer' for these purposes see PARA 414. As to the persons liable to make payments of statutory maternity pay see PARA 401 et seq. Where in the week immediately preceding the fourteenth week before the expected week of confinement a woman had two or more employers, but one or more of them was or were not liable to make payments to her of statutory maternity pay (a 'non-liable employer'), s 165(6) does not apply in respect of any week after the week of confinement but within the maternity pay period in which she works only for a non-liable employer: Statutory Maternity Pay (General) Regulations 1986, SI 1986/1960, reg 8(1); and see the Interpretation Act 1978 s 17(2)(a).

11 As to the making of regulations which modify provisions relating to statutory maternity pay see PARA 407.

12 See the Social Security Contributions and Benefits Act 1992 s 165(7).

13 Social Security Contributions and Benefits Act 1992 s 165(7)(a).

14 Social Security Contributions and Benefits Act 1992 s 165(7)(b) (amended by SI 1994/1230).

425. Prescribed modifications of statutory provisions relating to the maternity pay period. Where a woman gives notice to her employer[1] of the date from which she expects his liability to pay her statutory maternity pay to begin[2], and where, in conformity with that notice, she ceases to work for him in a week[3] which is later than the twelfth week before the expected week of confinement[4], the first day of the maternity pay period is[5] the day on which she expects his liability to pay her statutory maternity pay to begin in conformity with that notice provided that day is not later than the day immediately following the day on which she is confined[6]. The maternity pay period is a period of 39 consecutive weeks[7].

Where a woman is confined:

(1) before the eleventh week before the expected week of confinement[8]; or
(2) after the twelfth week before the expected week of confinement, and the confinement occurs on a day which precedes that mentioned in a notice given to her employer as being the day on which week she expects his liability to pay her statutory maternity pay to begin[9],

the first day of the maternity pay period is the day following the day on which she is so confined[10].

Where a woman is absent from work wholly or partly because of pregnancy or confinement on any day:

(a) which falls on or after the beginning of the fourth week before the expected week of confinement[11]; but
(b) not later than the day immediately following the day on which she is confined[12],

the first day of the maternity pay period is the day following the day on which she is so absent[13].

Where a woman leaves her employment:

(i) at any time falling after the beginning of the eleventh week before the expected week of confinement and before the start of the maternity pay period[14]; but

(ii) not later than the day on which she is confined[15],

the first day of the maternity pay period is the day following the day on which she leaves her employment[16].

1 As to the meaning of 'employer' for these purposes see PARA 414.
2 See the Statutory Maternity Pay (General) Regulations 1986, SI 1986/1960, reg 2(1)(a) (reg 2 substituted by SI 2006/2379). As to the meaning of 'statutory maternity pay' see PARA 401. As to liability to make payments of statutory maternity pay see PARA 401 et seq.
3 As to the meaning of 'week' for these purposes see PARA 402 note 5.
4 See the Statutory Maternity Pay (General) Regulations 1986, SI 1986/1960, reg 2(1)(b) (as substituted: see note 2). As to the meaning of 'confinement' see PARA 415 note 6.
5 Ie subject to the Statutory Maternity Pay (General) Regulations 1986, SI 1986/1960, reg 2(3)–(5) (see the text and notes 8–16): see reg 2(1) (as substituted: see note 2). As to the meaning of 'maternity pay period' see PARA 424.
6 See the Statutory Maternity Pay (General) Regulations 1986, SI 1986/1960, reg 2(1) (as substituted: see note 2). See *Wade v North Yorkshire Police Authority* [2011] IRLR 393, UKUT (an interpretation under which a woman could nominate a date from which she wished to claim statutory maternity pay produces clarity for both employer and employee: hence, the preferred construction, especially given the symmetries between the regimes for statutory maternity pay and statutory maternity leave, is that a woman may cease to work 'in conformity with [a] notice' for the purposes of the Statutory Maternity Pay (General) Regulations 1986, SI 1986/1960, reg 2(1), even if she has previously ceased to work on some other basis).
7 Statutory Maternity Pay (General) Regulations 1986, SI 1986/1960, reg 2(2) (as substituted: see note 2).
8 Statutory Maternity Pay (General) Regulations 1986, SI 1986/1960, reg 2(3)(a) (as substituted: see note 2).
9 Statutory Maternity Pay (General) Regulations 1986, SI 1986/1960, reg 2(3)(b) (as substituted: see note 2).
10 See the Statutory Maternity Pay (General) Regulations 1986, SI 1986/1960, reg 2(3) (as substituted: see note 2). This provision gives effect to the Social Security Contributions and Benefits Act 1992 s 165 (see PARA 424).
11 Statutory Maternity Pay (General) Regulations 1986, SI 1986/1960, reg 2(4)(a) (as substituted: see note 2).
12 Statutory Maternity Pay (General) Regulations 1986, SI 1986/1960, reg 2(4)(b) (as substituted: see note 2).
13 See the Statutory Maternity Pay (General) Regulations 1986, SI 1986/1960, reg 2(4) (as substituted: see note 2).
14 Statutory Maternity Pay (General) Regulations 1986, SI 1986/1960, reg 2(5)(a) (as substituted: see note 2).
15 Statutory Maternity Pay (General) Regulations 1986, SI 1986/1960, reg 2(5)(b) (as substituted: see note 2).
16 See the Statutory Maternity Pay (General) Regulations 1986, SI 1986/1960, reg 2(5) (as substituted: see note 2).

426. Liability to make payments of statutory maternity pay where woman works after confinement. Where, after her confinement[1], a woman:

(1) works for an employer[2] who is not liable to pay her statutory maternity pay[3] and is not a non-liable employer[4]; but

(2) before the end of her maternity pay period[5] ceases to work for that employer[6],

the person who, before she commenced work, was liable to make payments of statutory maternity pay to her is not liable[7] to make such payments to her for any weeks in the maternity pay period after she ceases work[8].

A woman must provide the person who is liable to pay her statutory maternity pay, where she commences work after her confinement but within the maternity pay period, with such additional information[9] as may be prescribed[10]. Accordingly, a woman who after the date of confinement but within the maternity pay period commences work in employed earner's[11] employment with a person who is not liable to make payments of statutory maternity pay to her and is not a non-liable employer[12] must, within seven days of the day she commenced work, inform any person who is so liable of the date she commenced work[13].

1 As to the meaning of 'confinement' see PARA 415 note 6.
2 As to the meaning of 'employer' for these purposes see PARA 414.
3 As to the meaning of 'statutory maternity pay' see PARA 401. As to liability to make payments of statutory maternity pay see PARA 401 et seq.
4 Statutory Maternity Pay (General) Regulations 1986, SI 1986/1960, reg 8(2)(a). As to the meaning of 'non-liable employer' for these purposes see PARA 424 note 10.
5 As to the meaning of 'maternity pay period' see PARA 424.
6 Statutory Maternity Pay (General) Regulations 1986, SI 1986/1960, reg 8(2)(b).
7 Ie notwithstanding the Social Security Contributions and Benefits Act 1992 s 164: see PARA 401.
8 See the Statutory Maternity Pay (General) Regulations 1986, SI 1986/1960, reg 8(2); and see the Interpretation Act 1978 s 17(2)(a).
9 Ie information additional to the medical evidence required under the Social Security Administration Act 1992 s 15(1)(a): see PARA 422.
10 See the Social Security Administration Act 1992 s 15(1)(b). For the purposes of the Social Security Administration Act 1992, 'prescribe' means prescribe by regulations; and 'prescribed' must be construed accordingly: see s 191 (definition amended by the Welfare Reform Act 2007 Sch 5 paras 2, 10). As to the making of regulations under the Social Security Administration Act 1992 generally see **WELFARE BENEFITS AND STATE PENSIONS** vol 104 (2014) PARA 400. Any regulations for the purposes of s 15(1) must be made with the concurrence of the Revenue and Customs: s 15(1A) (added by the Social Security Contributions (Transfer of Functions, etc) Act 1999 Sch 3 para 43). As to the Commissioners for Her Majesty's Revenue and Customs see **INCOME TAXATION** vol 58 (2014) PARAS 33–34.
11 As to the meaning of 'employed earner' see the Social Security Contributions and Benefits Act 1992 s 2(1)(a), (3); and **WELFARE BENEFITS AND STATE PENSIONS** vol 104 (2014) PARA 381.
12 Ie for the purposes of the Statutory Maternity Pay (General) Regulations 1986, SI 1986/1960, reg 8(1): see PARA 424 note 10.
13 Statutory Maternity Pay (General) Regulations 1986, SI 1986/1960, reg 24. As to the time for compliance where an employee is outside the United Kingdom see PARA 408.

427. Working in the maternity pay period. Where a woman does any work under a contract of service[1] with her employer[2] on any day, but for not more than ten days (whether consecutive or not), during her maternity pay period[3], statutory maternity pay[4] continues to be payable to the employee[5] by the employer[6].

1 Although 'contract of service' is defined for the purposes of statutory sick pay (see PARA 558 note 2), it is not so defined under the other statutory pay provisions (for which purposes see generally PARA 1 note 1).
2 As to the meaning of 'employer' for these purposes see PARA 414.
3 As to the meaning of 'maternity pay period' see PARA 424.
4 As to the meaning of 'statutory maternity pay' see PARA 401. As to liability to make payments of statutory maternity pay see PARA 401 et seq.
5 As to the meaning of 'employee' see PARA 406.
6 Statutory Maternity Pay (General) Regulations 1986, SI 1986/1960, reg 9A (added by SI 2006/2379).

F. PAYMENT OF MATERNITY PAY

428. Rates of payment for statutory maternity pay. Statutory maternity pay[1] is payable to a woman:

(1) at the earnings-related rate[2], in respect of the first six weeks in respect of which it is payable[3]; and

(2) at whichever is the lower of the earnings-related rate and such weekly rate as may be prescribed[4], in respect of the remaining portion of the maternity pay period[5].

Where two or more employers are treated as one[6], liability for statutory maternity pay payable by them[7] to a woman must be apportioned between them in such proportions as they may agree or, in default of agreement, in the proportions which the woman's earnings from each employment bear to the amount of the aggregated earnings[8].

1 As to the meaning of 'statutory maternity pay' see PARA 401.

2 The earnings-related rate is a weekly rate equivalent to 90% of a woman's normal weekly earnings for the period of eight weeks immediately preceding the fourteenth week before the expected week of confinement: Social Security Contributions and Benefits Act 1992 s 166(2) (s 166 substituted by the Employment Act 2002 s 19). As to the meaning of 'normal weekly earnings' for these purposes see PARA 429; and as to the meaning of 'week' generally see PARA 402 note 5; but see also note 3. As to the meaning of 'confinement' see PARA 415 note 6.

In relation to a woman to whom the Statutory Maternity Pay (General) Regulations 1986, SI 1986/1960, reg 4(2) applies (i e a woman in employed earner's employment who was confined before the fourteenth week before the expected week of confinement: see PARA 415 note 14), the Social Security Contributions and Benefits Act 1992 s 166 is modified so that s 166(2) has effect as if the reference to the period of eight weeks immediately preceding the fourteenth week before the expected week of confinement were a reference to the period of eight weeks immediately preceding the week in which her confinement occurred: Statutory Maternity Pay (General) Regulations 1986, SI 1986/1960, reg 4(3) (added by SI 1988/532; substituted by SI 1994/1367).

3 Social Security Contributions and Benefits Act 1992 s 166(1)(a) (as substituted: see note 2). In s 166(1) 'week' means any period of seven days: see s 166(1A) (added by the Work and Families Act 2006 Sch 1 para 8(1), (2)).

4 The weekly rate prescribed under the Social Security Contributions and Benefits Act 1992 s 166(1)(b) must not be less than the weekly rate of statutory sick pay for the time being specified in s 157(1) (see PARA 581) or, if two or more such rates are for the time being specified, the higher or highest of those rates: s 166(3) (as substituted: see note 2). For these purposes, 'prescribed' means specified in or determined in accordance with regulations: see s 171(1). As to the making of regulations under the Social Security Contributions and Benefits Act 1992 see PARA 407 note 3. At the date at which this volume states the law, no such regulations had been made but, by virtue of the Interpretation Act 1978 s 17(2)(b), the Statutory Maternity Pay (General) Regulations 1986, SI 1986/1960, have effect as if made under the Social Security Contributions and Benefits Act 1992 s 166(3). Accordingly, at the date at which this volume states the law, the rate of statutory maternity pay prescribed under s 166(1)(b) is a weekly rate of £138.18: Statutory Maternity Pay (General) Regulations 1986, SI 1986/1960, reg 6 (substituted by SI 2002/2690; amended by SI 2014/147). Where any payment of statutory maternity pay is paid for any week or part of a week, and the amount due includes a fraction of a penny, the payment must be rounded up to the next whole number of pence: Statutory Maternity Pay (General) Regulations 1986, SI 1986/1960, reg 28 (substituted by SI 2006/2379).

5 Social Security Contributions and Benefits Act 1992 s 166(1)(b) (as substituted: see note 2). Where, for any purpose of Pt XII (ss 164–171) or of regulations, it is necessary to calculate the daily rate of statutory maternity pay, the amount payable by way of statutory maternity pay for any day must be taken as one-seventh of the weekly rate: s 166(4) (added by the Work and Families Act 2006 Sch 1 para 8(1), (3)). As to the meaning of 'maternity pay period' see PARA 424.

6 Ie under the provisions of the Statutory Maternity Pay (General) Regulations 1986, SI 1986/1960, reg 18(1): see PARA 414.

7 As to liability to make payments of statutory maternity pay see PARA 401 et seq.

8 Statutory Maternity Pay (General) Regulations 1986, SI 1986/1960, reg 18(2).

429. Calculation of normal weekly earnings for purposes of statutory maternity pay. For the purposes of the statutory maternity pay provisions that are set out in Part XII of the Social Security Contributions and Benefits Act 1992[1], a woman's normal weekly earnings[2] are to be taken to be the average weekly earnings which in the relevant period[3] have been paid to her or paid for her benefit under the contract of service with the employer in question[4]. However, in such cases as may be prescribed[5] a woman's normal weekly earnings are to be calculated in accordance with regulations[6].

In a case where a woman has normal pay days at intervals of or approximating to one or more calendar months, including intervals of or approximating to a year, her normal weekly earnings must be calculated by dividing her earnings in the relevant period by the number of calendar months in that period, or, if it is not a whole number, the nearest whole number, multiplying the result by 12 and dividing by 52[7]. In cases where a woman does not have normal pay days at intervals of or approximating to one or more calendar month[8], and where the relevant period is not an exact number of weeks, the woman's normal weekly earnings must be calculated by dividing her earnings in the relevant period by the number of days in the relevant period and multiplying the result by seven[9].

In any case where:

(1) a woman is awarded a pay increase (or would have been awarded such an increase had she not then been absent on statutory maternity leave)[10]; and
(2) that pay increase applies to the whole or any part of the period between the beginning of the relevant period and the end of her period of statutory maternity leave[11],

her normal weekly earnings are to be calculated as if such an increase applied in each week of the relevant period[12].

1 Ie for the purposes of the Social Security Contributions and Benefits Act 1992 Pt XII (ss 164–171).

2 For these purposes, 'earnings' has the meaning given to it by regulations (see PARA 430): see the Social Security Contributions and Benefits Act 1992 s 171(5). Regulations under s 171(5) must be made with the concurrence of the Commissioners for Revenue and Customs: see s 171(7) (added by the Social Security Contributions (Transfer of Functions, etc) Act 1999 Sch 1 para 15(1), (3)). As to the making of regulations under the Social Security Contributions and Benefits Act 1992 see PARA 407 note 3. As to the Commissioners for Her Majesty's Revenue and Customs see INCOME TAXATION vol 58 (2014) PARAS 33–34. At the date at which this volume states the law, no such regulations had been made but, by virtue of the Interpretation Act 1978 s 17(2)(b), the Statutory Maternity Pay (General) Regulations 1986, SI 1986/1960, have effect as if made under the Social Security Contributions and Benefits Act 1992 s 171(5).

3 For these purposes, 'relevant period' has the meaning given to it by regulations (see note 2): see the Social Security Contributions and Benefits Act 1992 s 171(5). For the purposes of Pt XII (ss 164–171), a woman's normal weekly earnings are calculated in accordance with the Statutory Maternity Pay (General) Regulations 1986, SI 1986/1960, reg 21(2)–(7) (see also the text and notes 7–12): reg 21(1) (reg 21(1)–(3) amended by SI 1994/1367). Accordingly, the relevant period for these purposes is the period between (see the Statutory Maternity Pay (General) Regulations 1986, SI 1986/1960, reg 21(3) (as so amended)):

(1) the last normal pay day to fall before the appropriate date (reg 21(3)(a)); and
(2) the last normal pay day to fall at least eight weeks earlier than the normal pay day mentioned in head (1) above (reg 21(3)(b)),

including the normal pay day mentioned in head (1) above, but excluding that first mentioned in head (2) above (see reg 21(3)). The 'appropriate date' means the first day of the fourteenth week before the expected week of confinement, or the first day in the week in which the woman is confined, whichever is the earlier: see the Statutory Maternity Pay (General) Regulations 1986, SI 1986/1960, reg 21(2) (definition as so amended). 'Normal pay day' means a day on which the

the employer is not liable to make payments of statutory maternity pay in respect of such a week unless, and to the extent by which, the rate of statutory maternity pay exceeds the rate of maternity allowance[22] received by her in that week[23].

1 As to the meaning of 'statutory maternity pay' see PARA 401; and as to entitlement to statutory maternity pay see PARA 415 et seq.

2 Ie for the purposes of the Social Security Contributions and Benefits Act 1992 s 3 (meaning of 'earnings': see **WELFARE BENEFITS AND STATE PENSIONS** vol 104 (2014) PARA 382).

3 As to the meaning of 'employed earner' see the Social Security Contributions and Benefits Act 1992 s 2(1)(a), (3); and **WELFARE BENEFITS AND STATE PENSIONS** vol 104 (2014) PARA 381.

4 Social Security Contributions and Benefits Act 1992 s 4(1)(a)(ii).

5 See the Social Security Contributions and Benefits Act 1992 s 168, Sch 13 para 3(1). This provision is subject to Sch 13 para 3(2), (3) (see the text and notes 6–12): see Sch 13 para 3(1). Although 'contract of service' is defined for the purposes of statutory sick pay (see PARA 558 note 2), it is not so defined under the other statutory pay provisions (for which purposes see generally PARA 1 note 1).

6 As to the making of regulations under the Social Security Contributions and Benefits Act 1992 generally see PARA 407 note 3.

7 Social Security Contributions and Benefits Act 1992 Sch 13 para 3(3). At the date at which this volume states the law, no such regulations had been made but, by virtue of the Interpretation Act 1978 s 17(2)(b), the Statutory Maternity Pay (General) Regulations 1986, SI 1986/1960, have effect as if made under the Social Security Contributions and Benefits Act 1992 Sch 13. Accordingly, the payments which are for these purposes to be treated as contractual remuneration are sums payable under the contract of service (see the Statutory Maternity Pay (General) Regulations 1986, SI 1986/1960, reg 19(a); and see the Interpretation Act 1978 s 17(2)(a)):
   (1) by way of remuneration (Statutory Maternity Pay (General) Regulations 1986, SI 1986/1960, reg 19(a));
   (2) for incapacity for work due to sickness or injury (reg 19(b)); and
   (3) by reason of pregnancy or confinement (reg 19(c)).
   As to the meaning of 'confinement' see PARA 415 note 6.

8 As to the meaning of 'employer' for these purposes see PARA 414.

9 In the Social Security Contributions and Benefits Act 1992 Sch 13 para 3(2), 'week' means a period of seven days beginning with the day of the week on which the maternity pay period begins: see Sch 13 para 3(2A) (added by the Work and Families Act 2007 Sch 1 para 23).

10 As to the meaning of 'maternity pay period' see PARA 424.

11 Social Security Contributions and Benefits Act 1992 Sch 13 para 3(2)(a).

12 Social Security Contributions and Benefits Act 1992 Sch 13 para 3(2)(b).

13 For these purposes, 'prescribed' means specified in or determined in accordance with regulations: see the Social Security Contributions and Benefits Act 1992 s 171(1).

14 Ie for the purposes of the Social Security Contributions and Benefits Act 1992: see **WELFARE BENEFITS AND STATE PENSIONS** vol 104 (2014) PARA 1 et seq.

15 Social Security Contributions and Benefits Act 1992 Sch 13 para 1 (substituted by the Jobseekers Act 1995 Sch 2 para 37). As to incapacity benefit see **WELFARE BENEFITS AND STATE PENSIONS** vol 104 (2014) PARA 472 et seq. Regulations may provide that:
   (1) in prescribed circumstances a day which falls within the maternity pay period is to be treated as a day of incapacity for work for the purpose of determining entitlement to the higher rate of short-term incapacity benefit or to long-term incapacity benefit (Social Security Contributions and Benefits Act 1992 Sch 13 para 2(1) (Sch 13 para 2 substituted by the Social Security (Incapacity for Work) Act 1994 Sch 1 para 45(1), (3))); and
   (2) an amount equal to a woman's statutory maternity pay for a period is to be deducted from any such benefit in respect of the same period and a woman is to be entitled to such benefit only if there is a balance after the deduction and, if there is such a balance, at a weekly rate equal to it (Social Security Contributions and Benefits Act 1992 Sch 13 para 2(2) (as so substituted)).
   At the date at which this volume states the law, no such regulations had been made. Note, however, that the Statutory Maternity Pay (General) Regulations 1986, SI 1986/1960, reg 21A (made under the Social Security Contributions and Benefits Act 1992 Sch 13 para 2) has been revoked by SI 2002/2690. As from a day to be appointed under the Work and Families Act 2007

s 70(2), the Social Security Contributions and Benefits Act 1992 Sch 13 paras 1, 2 are repealed by the Work and Families Act 2007 s 67, Sch 8. However, at the date at which this volume states the law no such day had been appointed.

16 Statutory Maternity Pay (General) Regulations 1986, SI 1986/1960, reg 27. As to the power to make regulations relating to statutory maternity pay see PARA 402.

17 See the Statutory Maternity Pay (General) Regulations 1986, SI 1986/1960, reg 21B (reg 21B added by SI 1996/1335; and substituted by SI 2005/729).

18 Statutory Maternity Pay (General) Regulations 1986, SI 1986/1960, reg 21B(a) (as added and substituted: see note 17). Head (1) in the text refers to receipt of maternity allowance pursuant to the provisions of the Social Security Contributions and Benefits Act 1992 s 35 and s 35A (see WELFARE BENEFITS AND STATE PENSIONS vol 104 (2014) PARA 474): see the Statutory Maternity Pay (General) Regulations 1986, SI 1986/1960, reg 21B(a) (as so substituted).

19 Ie a pay increase referred to in the Statutory Maternity Pay (General) Regulations 1986, SI 1986/1960, reg 21(7): see PARA 429.

20 Ie under the Statutory Maternity Pay (General) Regulations 1986, SI 1986/1960, reg 20(4)(za): see PARA 430.

21 Statutory Maternity Pay (General) Regulations 1986, SI 1986/1960, reg 21B(b) (reg 21B as added and substituted (see note 17); reg 21B(b) amended by SI 2007/1154).

22 As to the rate of statutory maternity pay see PARA 428. As to the rate of maternity allowance see WELFARE BENEFITS AND STATE PENSIONS vol 104 (2014) PARA 474.

23 See the Statutory Maternity Pay (General) Regulations 1986, SI 1986/1960, reg 21B (as added and substituted: see note 17).

434. Payment to persons entitled to statutory maternity pay who are unable to act. Where in the case of any woman:

(1) statutory maternity pay[1] is payable to her or she is alleged to be entitled[2] to it[3];

(2) she is unable for the time being to act[4]; and

(3) no receiver has been appointed by the Court of Protection[5] with power to receive statutory maternity pay on her behalf[6],

the Commissioners for Revenue and Customs[7] may, on written application to them by a person who, if a natural person, is over the age of 18[8], appoint that person to exercise, on behalf of the woman, any right to which she may be entitled under the statutory maternity pay provisions that are set out in Part XII of the Social Security Contributions and Benefits Act 1992[9] and to deal on her behalf with any sums payable to her[10].

Anything required by Part XII of the Social Security Contributions and Benefits Act 1992[11] to be done by or to any woman who is unable to act may be done by or to the person so appointed to act on her behalf; and the receipt of the person so appointed is a good discharge to the woman's employer or former employer for any sum paid[12].

Where the Commissioners have made such an appointment[13]: (a) they may at any time in their absolute discretion revoke it[14]; (b) the person appointed may resign his office after having given one month's notice in writing to the Commissioners of his intention to do so[15]; and (c) the appointment terminates when the Commissioners are notified that a receiver under head (3) above has been appointed[16].

1 As to the meaning of 'statutory maternity pay' see PARA 401.

2 As to entitlement to statutory maternity pay see PARA 415 et seq.

3 Statutory Maternity Pay (General) Regulations 1986, SI 1986/1960, reg 31(1)(a).

4 Statutory Maternity Pay (General) Regulations 1986, SI 1986/1960, reg 31(1)(b).

5 As to the Court of Protection see MENTAL HEALTH AND CAPACITY vol 75 (2013) PARA 720 et seq.

6 Statutory Maternity Pay (General) Regulations 1986, SI 1986/1960, reg 31(1)(c)(i).

7 As to the Commissioners for Her Majesty's Revenue and Customs see INCOME TAXATION vol 58 (2014) PARAS 33–34.

8 A person attains a particular age expressed in years at the commencement of the relevant anniversary of the date of his birth: see the Family Law Reform Act 1969 s 9; and CHILDREN AND YOUNG PERSONS vol 9 (2012) PARA 2.
9 Ie the Social Security Contributions and Benefits Act 1992 Pt XII (ss 164–171).
10 Statutory Maternity Pay (General) Regulations 1986, SI 1986/1960, reg 31(1) (amended by the Social Security Contributions (Transfer of Functions, etc) Act 1999 Sch 2); and see the Interpretation Act 1978 s 17(2)(a).
11 Ie under the Social Security Contributions and Benefits Act 1992 Pt XII.
12 See the Statutory Maternity Pay (General) Regulations 1986, SI 1986/1960, reg 31(3); and see the Interpretation Act 1978 s 17(2)(a).
13 See the Statutory Maternity Pay (General) Regulations 1986, SI 1986/1960, reg 31(2) (amended by the Social Security Contributions (Transfer of Functions, etc) Act 1999 Sch 2).
14 Statutory Maternity Pay (General) Regulations 1986, SI 1986/1960, reg 31(2)(a).
15 Statutory Maternity Pay (General) Regulations 1986, SI 1986/1960, reg 31(2)(b) (amended by the Social Security Contributions (Transfer of Functions, etc) Act 1999 Sch 2).
16 Statutory Maternity Pay (General) Regulations 1986, SI 1986/1960, reg 31(2)(c) (amended by the Social Security Contributions (Transfer of Functions, etc) Act 1999 Sch 2).

G. INFORMATION AND RECORDS

435. Provision of information by the Secretary of State for purposes of statutory maternity pay. Where the Secretary of State[1] considers that it is reasonable for information held by him to be disclosed to a person liable to make payments of statutory maternity pay[2] for the purpose of enabling that person to determine[3]:

(1) whether a maternity pay period[4] exists in relation to a woman who is or has been an employee of his[5]; and

(2) if it does, the date of its commencement and the weeks[6] in it in respect of which he may be liable to pay statutory maternity pay[7],

he may disclose the information to that person[8].

1 As to the Secretary of State see PARA 5 note 21.
2 As to the meaning of 'statutory maternity pay' see PARA 401; and as to liability to make payments see PARA 401 et seq.
3 See the Social Security Administration Act 1992 s 131.
4 As to the meaning of 'maternity pay period' see PARA 424.
5 Social Security Administration Act 1992 s 131(a). As to the meaning of 'employee' for these purposes see PARA 406.
6 As to the meaning of 'week' for these purposes see PARA 402 note 5.
7 Social Security Administration Act 1992 s 131(b).
8 See the Social Security Administration Act 1992 s 131.

436. Power to make regulations in relation to records for purposes of statutory maternity pay. Regulations made with the concurrence of the Revenue and Customs[1]:

(1) may require employers[2] to maintain such records in connection with statutory maternity pay[3] as may be prescribed[4];

(2) may provide for: (a) any woman claiming to be entitled to statutory maternity pay[5]; or (b) any other person who is a party to proceedings[6] relating to statutory maternity pay[7], to furnish to the Secretary of State or the Revenue and Customs (as the regulations may require), within a prescribed period, any information required for the determination of any question arising in connection therewith[8]; and

(3) may require persons who have made payments of statutory maternity pay to furnish to the Secretary of State or the Revenue and Customs (as the regulations may require) such documents and information, at such time, as may be prescribed[9];

(4) may require employers to produce wages sheets and other documents and records to officers of the Revenue and Customs[10], within a prescribed period, for the purpose of enabling them to satisfy themselves that statutory maternity pay has been paid, and is being paid[11] to employees or former employees who are entitled to it[12].

Regulations may make provision requiring an employer in prescribed circumstances to furnish information in connection with the making, by a woman who is, or has been, an employee of that employer, of a claim for: (i) universal credit[13]; (ii) a maternity allowance[14]; (iii) an employment and support allowance[15]; (iv) short-term incapacity benefit[16]; or (v) a long-term incapacity benefit[17].

Such regulations must prescribe: (A) the kind of information to be furnished in accordance with the regulations[18]; (B) the person to whom information of the prescribed kind is to be furnished[19]; and (C) the manner in which, and period within which, it is to be furnished[20].

1 See the Social Security Administration Act 1992 s 132(3) (amended by the Social Security Contributions (Transfer of Functions, etc) Act 1999 Sch 1 para 27). As to the Commissioners for Her Majesty's Revenue and Customs see INCOME TAXATION vol 58 (2014) PARAS 33–34. As to the making of regulations under the Social Security Administration Act 1992 generally see WELFARE BENEFITS AND STATE PENSIONS vol 104 (2014) PARA 400. At the date at which this volume states the law, no such regulations had been made but, by virtue of the Interpretation Act 1978 s 17(2)(b), the Statutory Maternity Pay (General) Regulations 1986, SI 1986/1960, reg 25 (see PARA 438), reg 25A (see PARA 437 note 11) and reg 26 (see PARA 437) have effect as if made under the Social Security Administration Act 1992 s 132.
2 As to the meaning of 'employer' for these purposes see PARA 414.
3 As to the meaning of 'statutory maternity pay' see PARA 401.
4 Social Security Administration Act 1992 s 132(3)(a). 'Prescribed' means prescribed by regulations: see s 191 (definition amended by the Welfare Reform Act 2007 Sch 5 paras 2, 10). See note 1.
5 Social Security Administration Act 1992 s 132(3)(b)(i).
6 Ie arising under the Social Security Contributions and Benefits Act 1992 Pt XII (ss 164–171).
7 Social Security Administration Act 1992 s 132(3)(b)(ii).
8 See the Social Security Administration Act 1992 s 132(3)(b) (s 132(3)(b), (c) amended by the Social Security Contributions (Transfer of Functions, etc) Act 1999 Sch 1 para 27). See note 1.
9 Social Security Administration Act 1992 s 132(3)(c) (as amended: see note 8). See note 1.
10 As to the powers of inspectors appointed for the purposes of the Social Security Administration Act 1992 see WELFARE BENEFITS AND STATE PENSIONS vol 104 (2014) PARA 576 et seq.
11 Ie in accordance with regulations under the Social Security Administration Act 1992 s 5: see WELFARE BENEFITS AND STATE PENSIONS vol 104 (2014) PARA 526.
12 Social Security Administration Act 1992 s 132(4) (added by the National Insurance Contributions and Statutory Payments Act 2004 s 9(1), (3)). See note 1.
13 Social Security Administration Act 1992 s 132(1)(za) (added by the Welfare Reform Act 2012 s 31, Sch 2 paras 3, 21). As to universal credit see WELFARE BENEFITS AND STATE PENSIONS vol 104 (2014) PARA 124 et seq.
14 Social Security Administration Act 1992 s 132(1)(a). As to maternity allowance see WELFARE BENEFITS AND STATE PENSIONS vol 104 (2014) PARA 473 et seq.
15 Social Security Administration Act 1992 s 132(1)(aa) (added by the Welfare Reform Act 2007 s 28(1), Sch 3 para 10(1), (20)). As to employment and support allowance see WELFARE BENEFITS AND STATE PENSIONS vol 104 (2014) PARA 252 et seq.
16 Social Security Administration Act 1992 s 132(1)(b) (s 132(1)(b), (c) amended by the Social Security (Incapacity for Work) Act 1994 s 11(1), Sch 1 para 50). As from a day to be appointed under the Welfare Reform Act 2007 s 70(2), the Social Security Administration Act 1992 s 132(1)(b) is repealed by the Welfare Reform Act 2007 s 67, Sch 8. At the date at which this volume states the law, no such day had been appointed. As to short-term incapacity benefit see WELFARE BENEFITS AND STATE PENSIONS vol 104 (2014) PARA 472 et seq.
17 Social Security Administration Act 1992 s 132(1)(c) (as amended: see note 16). Head (v) in the text refers to a long-term incapacity benefit under the Social Security Contributions and Benefits Act 1992 s 30A, s 40 or s 41: see WELFARE BENEFITS AND STATE PENSIONS vol 104 (2014) PARA 472 et seq. As from a day to be appointed under the Welfare Reform Act 2007 s 70(2), the

that pay the Commissioners may use electronic communications: see the Statutory Payment Schemes (Electronic Communications) Regulations 2002, SI 2002/3047; and INCOME TAXATION.

440. Right of employers liable for statutory maternity pay to prescribed amount; recovery of amount due. An employer[1] who has made, or is liable to make, any payment of statutory maternity pay is entitled to recover[2]:

(1) an amount equal to 92 per cent of such payment[3]; or
(2) if he is a small employer[4], an amount equal to such payment, and an additional amount[5] to which he is entitled[6].

If an employer is entitled to recover such an amount[7] in respect of statutory maternity pay which he is required to pay to an employee or employees in any income tax month or income tax quarter[8], and the amount exceeds the aggregate of[9]:

(a) the total amount of tax which the employer is required to pay to the collector of taxes in respect of deductions from the emoluments of his employees[10] for that income tax month or income tax quarter[11];
(b) the total amount of deductions made by the employer[12] from the emoluments of his employees for that income tax month or income tax quarter[13];
(c) the total amount of contributions payments which the employer is required to pay[14] to the collector of taxes in respect of the emoluments of his employees, whether by means of deduction or otherwise, for that income tax month or income tax quarter[15];
(d) the total amount of payments which the employer is required to pay to the collector of taxes in respect of deductions made on account of tax from payments to sub-contractors[16] for that income tax month or income tax quarter[17]; and
(e) the statutory paternity pay[18], statutory adoption pay[19] and statutory maternity pay which the employer is required to pay to his employees in that income tax month or income tax quarter[20],

the employer may apply to the Commissioners for Revenue and Customs for funds ('advance funding') to pay that excess, or so much of it as remains outstanding, to the employee or employees[21]; and where the conditions described above[22] are satisfied, or where the employer considers that those conditions will be satisfied on the date of any subsequent payment of emoluments to one or more employees who are entitled to a payment of statutory maternity pay, the employer may apply to the Commissioners for advance funding on a form approved for that purpose by them[23]. Such an application by an employer must be for an amount not exceeding the amount of statutory maternity pay which the employer is entitled to recover[24] and which he is required to pay to an employee or employees for the income tax month or income tax quarter to which the payment of emoluments relates[25].

An employer who is entitled to recover an amount under head (1) or head (2) above may do so by making one or more deductions from the aggregate of the amounts specified in heads (a) to (e) above[26], except where and in so far as:

(i) those amounts relate to earnings paid before the beginning of the income tax month or income tax quarter in which the payment of statutory maternity pay was made[27];
(ii) those amounts are paid by him later than six years after the tax year in which the payment of statutory maternity pay was made[28];

(iii) the employer has received advance funding[29] from the Commissioners for Revenue and Customs[30]; or

(iv) the employer has made a request[31] in writing[32] that the amount which he is entitled to recover[33] be paid to him and he has not received notification by the Commissioners that such request is refused[34].

Where advance funding has been provided to an employer[35], the Commissioners may recover any part of it not used to pay statutory maternity pay (the 'overpayment')[36]. An officer of the Commissioners must decide to the best of his judgement the amount of the overpayment and give notice in writing of his decision to the employer[37]; and such a decision may be in respect of advance funding provided for one or more income tax months or income tax quarters in a tax year, either in respect of one or more classes of employees specified in a decision notice (where a notice does not name any individual employee), or in respect of one or more individual employees named in a decision notice[38].

1 For these purposes, 'employer' includes a person who was previously an employer of a woman to whom a payment of statutory maternity pay was made, whether or not that person remains her employer at the date any deduction from contributions payments is made by him in accordance with the Statutory Maternity Pay (Compensation of Employers) and Miscellaneous Amendment Regulations 1994, SI 1994/1882, reg 5 (see the text and notes 7–25) or, as the case may be, any payment is received by him in accordance with reg 6 (see the text and notes 26–34): see reg 1(4). 'Contributions payments' has the same meaning as in the Social Security Contributions and Benefits Act 1992 s 167(8) (see PARA 441 note 5): see the Statutory Maternity Pay (Compensation of Employers) and Miscellaneous Amendment Regulations 1994, SI 1994/1882, reg 1(4) (definition substituted by SI 2003/672). As to the meaning of 'statutory maternity pay' see PARA 401. As to the meaning of 'employer' and related expressions in relation to employment rights generally see PARA 2.

2 Ie in accordance with the Statutory Maternity Pay (Compensation of Employers) and Miscellaneous Amendment Regulations 1994, SI 1994/1882.

3 Statutory Maternity Pay (Compensation of Employers) and Miscellaneous Amendment Regulations 1994, SI 1994/1882, reg 4(a) (regs 4–6 substituted, regs 6A, 7A added, by SI 2003/672).

4 For these purposes, 'small employer' means an employer whose contributions payments for the qualifying tax year do not exceed £45,000: see the Statutory Maternity Pay (Compensation of Employers) and Miscellaneous Amendment Regulations 1994, SI 1994/1882, reg 2(1) (amended by SI 2004/698). 'Qualifying tax year' means the tax year preceding the tax year in which the qualifying day in question falls (see the Statutory Maternity Pay (Compensation of Employers) and Miscellaneous Amendment Regulations 1994, SI 1994/1882, reg 1(4)); 'tax year' means the period of 12 months beginning on 6 April in any year (see reg 1(4) (definition added by SI 2003/672)); and 'qualifying day' means the first day of the week immediately preceding the fourteenth week before the expected week of confinement in which a woman who is or has been an employee first satisfies the conditions of entitlement to statutory maternity pay for which a deduction from a contributions payment is made by her employer in respect of a payment of statutory maternity pay made by him (see the Statutory Maternity Pay (Compensation of Employers) and Miscellaneous Amendment Regulations 1994, SI 1994/1882, reg 1(4)). For these purposes, any reference to the employees of any employer includes, where the context permits, a reference to his former employees: reg 1(5) (substituted by SI 2003/672). As to the meaning of 'confinement' see PARA 415 note 6. As to the conditions of entitlement see PARA 415.

For these purposes, the amount of an employer's contributions payments is to be determined without regard to any deductions that may be made from them under any enactment or instrument: Statutory Maternity Pay (Compensation of Employers) and Miscellaneous Amendment Regulations 1994, SI 1994/1882, reg 2(2).

Where in the qualifying tax year an employer has made contributions payments in one or more, but fewer than 12, of the income tax months, the amount of his contributions payments for that tax year is to be estimated by adding together all of those payments, dividing the total amount by the number of those months in which he has made those payments and multiplying the resulting figure by 12: reg 2(3). For these purposes, 'income tax month' means the period beginning on the sixth day of any calendar month and ending on the fifth day of the following calendar month: see reg 1(4). Where in the qualifying tax year an employer has made no contributions payments, but does have such payments in one or more income tax months which fall both:

(1) in the tax year in which the qualifying day falls (reg 2(4)(a)); and
(2) before the qualifying day or, where there is more than one such day in that tax year, before the first of those days (reg 2(4)(b)),

then the amount of his contributions payments for the qualifying tax year is to be estimated in accordance with reg 2(3) but as if the amount of the contributions payments falling in those months had fallen instead in the corresponding tax months in the qualifying tax year (see reg 2(4)).

5 Ie under the Statutory Maternity Pay (Compensation of Employers) and Miscellaneous Amendment Regulations 1994, SI 1994/1882, reg 3. In respect of any payment of statutory maternity pay made in the tax year commencing 6 April 2011, or in any subsequent tax year, a small employer is entitled to recover an additional amount being an amount equal to 3.0% of the payment, that percentage being the total amount of secondary Class 1 contributions estimated by the Commissioners for Revenue and Customs as to be paid in respect of statutory maternity pay by all employers in that year, expressed as a percentage of the total amount of statutory maternity pay estimated by them to be paid by all employers in that year: reg 3 (amended by the Social Security Contributions (Transfer of Functions, etc) Act 1999 Sch 2; SI 1995/566; SI 2003/672; SI 2011/725). As to the Commissioners for Her Majesty's Revenue and Customs see INCOME TAXATION vol 58 (2014) PARAS 33–34.

6 Statutory Maternity Pay (Compensation of Employers) and Miscellaneous Amendment Regulations 1994, SI 1994/1882, reg 4(b) (as substituted: see note 3).

7 Ie determined in accordance with the Statutory Maternity Pay (Compensation of Employers) and Miscellaneous Amendment Regulations 1994, SI 1994/1882, reg 4: see the text and notes 1–6.

8 For these purposes, 'income tax quarter' means, in any tax year, the period beginning on 6 April and ending on 5 July, the period beginning on 6 July and ending on 5 October, the period beginning on 6 October and ending on 5 January, or the period beginning on 6 January and ending on 5 April: see the Statutory Maternity Pay (Compensation of Employers) and Miscellaneous Amendment Regulations 1994, SI 1994/1882, reg 1(4) (definition added by SI 2003/672).

9 See the Statutory Maternity Pay (Compensation of Employers) and Miscellaneous Amendment Regulations 1994, SI 1994/1882, reg 5(1) (as substituted: see note 3).

10 Ie in accordance with the Income Tax (Pay As You Earn) Regulations 2003, SI 2003/2682: see INCOME TAXATION vol 58 (2014) PARA 927 et seq.

11 Statutory Maternity Pay (Compensation of Employers) and Miscellaneous Amendment Regulations 1994, SI 1994/1882, reg 5(1)(a) (as substituted: see note 3); and see the Interpretation Act 1978 s 17(2)(a).

12 Ie in accordance with regulations made under the Teaching and Higher Education Act 1998 s 22(5): see EDUCATION vol 36 (2011) PARA 1249.

13 Statutory Maternity Pay (Compensation of Employers) and Miscellaneous Amendment Regulations 1994, SI 1994/1882, reg 5(1)(b) (as substituted: see note 3).

14 Ie in accordance with the Social Security (Contributions) Regulations 2001, SI 2001/1004: see WELFARE BENEFITS AND STATE PENSIONS vol 104 (2014) PARA 399 et seq.

15 Statutory Maternity Pay (Compensation of Employers) and Miscellaneous Amendment Regulations 1994, SI 1994/1882, reg 5(1)(c) (as substituted: see note 3).

16 Ie in accordance with the Income and Corporation Taxes Act 1988 s 559 (repealed).

17 Statutory Maternity Pay (Compensation of Employers) and Miscellaneous Amendment Regulations 1994, SI 1994/1882, reg 5(1)(d) (as substituted: see note 3).

18 For these purposes, 'statutory paternity pay' means any payment under the Social Security Contributions and Benefits Act 1992 ss 171ZA, 171ZB (see PARA 443 et seq): see the Statutory Maternity Pay (Compensation of Employers) and Miscellaneous Amendment Regulations 1994, SI 1994/1882, reg 1(4) (definition added by SI 2003/672).

19 For these purposes, 'statutory adoption pay' means any payment under the Social Security Contributions and Benefits Act 1992 s 171ZL (see PARA 488 et seq): see the Statutory Maternity Pay (Compensation of Employers) and Miscellaneous Amendment Regulations 1994, SI 1994/1882, reg 1(4) (definition added by SI 2003/672).

20 Statutory Maternity Pay (Compensation of Employers) and Miscellaneous Amendment Regulations 1994, SI 1994/1882, reg 5(1)(e) (as substituted: see note 3).

21 See the Statutory Maternity Pay (Compensation of Employers) and Miscellaneous Amendment Regulations 1994, SI 1994/1882, reg 5(1) (as substituted: see note 3).

22 Ie the conditions in the Statutory Maternity Pay (Compensation of Employers) and Miscellaneous Amendment Regulations 1994, SI 1994/1882, reg 5(1): see the text and notes 7–21.
23 Statutory Maternity Pay (Compensation of Employers) and Miscellaneous Amendment Regulations 1994, SI 1994/1882, reg 5(2) (as substituted: see note 3).
24 Ie under the Statutory Maternity Pay (Compensation of Employers) and Miscellaneous Amendment Regulations 1994, SI 1994/1882, reg 4: see the text and notes 1–6.
25 Statutory Maternity Pay (Compensation of Employers) and Miscellaneous Amendment Regulations 1994, SI 1994/1882, reg 5(3) (as substituted: see note 3).
26 See the Statutory Maternity Pay (Compensation of Employers) and Miscellaneous Amendment Regulations 1994, SI 1994/1882, reg 6 (as substituted: see note 3). Where an employer has made a deduction from a contributions payment under reg 6, the date on which it is to be treated as having been paid for the purposes of the Social Security Contributions and Benefits Act 1992 s 167(6) (see PARA 441) is (see the Statutory Maternity Pay (Compensation of Employers) and Miscellaneous Amendment Regulations 1994, SI 1994/1882, reg 7 (amended by SI 2003/672)):
   (1) in a case where the deduction did not extinguish the contributions payment, the date on which the remainder of the contributions payment or, as the case may be, the first date on which any part of the remainder of the contributions payment was paid (Statutory Maternity Pay (Compensation of Employers) and Miscellaneous Amendment Regulations 1994, SI 1994/1882, reg 7(a)); and
   (2) in a case where the deduction extinguished the contributions payment, the fourteenth day after the end of the income tax month during which there were paid the earnings in respect of which the contributions payment was payable (reg 7(b)).

   If, in an income tax month or an income tax quarter:
   (a) the total amount that the employer is entitled to deduct under reg 6 is less than the amount which the employer is entitled to recover under reg 4 (see the text and notes 1–6) (reg 6A(a) (as added: see note 3));
   (b) the Commissioners are satisfied that this is so (reg 6A(b) (as so added)); and
   (c) the employer has so requested in writing (reg 6A(c) (as so added)),

   the Commissioners must pay to the employer the sum that the employer is unable to deduct under reg 6 (see reg 6A (as so added)).
27 Statutory Maternity Pay (Compensation of Employers) and Miscellaneous Amendment Regulations 1994, SI 1994/1882, reg 6(a) (as substituted: see note 3).
28 Statutory Maternity Pay (Compensation of Employers) and Miscellaneous Amendment Regulations 1994, SI 1994/1882, reg 6(b) (as substituted: see note 3).
29 Ie in accordance with an application under the Statutory Maternity Pay (Compensation of Employers) and Miscellaneous Amendment Regulations 1994, SI 1994/1882, reg 5: see the text and notes 7–21.
30 Statutory Maternity Pay (Compensation of Employers) and Miscellaneous Amendment Regulations 1994, SI 1994/1882, reg 6(c) (as substituted: see note 3).
31 Ie under the Statutory Maternity Pay (Compensation of Employers) and Miscellaneous Amendment Regulations 1994, SI 1994/1882, reg 5: see the text and notes 7–21.
32 For these purposes, 'writing' includes writing delivered by means of electronic communications approved by directions issued by the Commissioners for Revenue and Customs pursuant to regulations made under the Finance Act 1999 s 132 (see **INCOME TAXATION** vol 59 (2014) PARA 2237): see the Statutory Maternity Pay (Compensation of Employers) and Miscellaneous Amendment Regulations 1994, SI 1994/1882, reg 1(4) (definition added by SI 2003/672).
33 Ie under the Statutory Maternity Pay (Compensation of Employers) and Miscellaneous Amendment Regulations 1994, SI 1994/1882, reg 4: see the text and notes 1–6.
34 Statutory Maternity Pay (Compensation of Employers) and Miscellaneous Amendment Regulations 1994, SI 1994/1882, reg 6(d) (as substituted: see note 3).
35 Ie in accordance with an application under the Statutory Maternity Pay (Compensation of Employers) and Miscellaneous Amendment Regulations 1994, SI 1994/1882, reg 5: see the text and notes 7–21.
36 Statutory Maternity Pay (Compensation of Employers) and Miscellaneous Amendment Regulations 1994, SI 1994/1882, reg 7A(1) (as added: see note 3).
37 Statutory Maternity Pay (Compensation of Employers) and Miscellaneous Amendment Regulations 1994, SI 1994/1882, reg 7A(2) (as added: see note 3). The Taxes Management Act 1970 Pt VI (ss 60–70A) (collection and recovery: see **INCOME TAXATION** vol 59 (2014) PARA 2304 et seq) applies with any necessary modifications to a decision under the Statutory Maternity Pay (Compensation of Employers) and Miscellaneous Amendment Regulations 1994, SI 1994/1882, reg 7A as if the amount specified were an assessment and as if the amount set out in the notice were income tax charged on the employer: reg 7A(4) (as so added). Where a

decision under reg 7A(2) relates to more than one employee, proceedings may be brought to recover the amount overpaid without distinguishing the sum to be repaid in respect of each employee and without specifying the employee in question (reg 7A(5) (as so added)); and a decision to recover an amount made in accordance with reg 7A gives rise to one cause of action or matter of complaint for the purpose of proceedings under the Taxes Management Act 1970 ss 65–66 (see INCOME TAXATION vol 59 (2014) PARAS 2310–2311) (Statutory Maternity Pay (Compensation of Employers) and Miscellaneous Amendment Regulations 1994, SI 1994/1882, reg 7A(6) (as so added)). However, nothing in reg 7A(5) prevents separate proceedings being brought for the recovery of any amount which the employer is liable to repay in respect of each employee to whom the decision relates: reg 7A(7) (as so added).

38 Statutory Maternity Pay (Compensation of Employers) and Miscellaneous Amendment Regulations 1994, SI 1994/1882, reg 7A(3) (as added: see note 3).

441. Treatment of amount deducted from employer's contributions payments for purposes of paying statutory maternity pay. Where, in accordance with any provision of regulations made[1] which make provision for the payment by employers[2] of statutory maternity pay[3] to be funded by the Commissioners for Revenue and Customs[4], an amount has been deducted from an employer's contributions payments[5], the amount deducted must be treated, except in such cases as may be prescribed, for the purposes of any provision made by or under any enactment in relation to primary or secondary Class 1 contributions[6]:

(1) as having been paid, on such date as may be determined in accordance with the regulations[7]; and

(2) as having been received by the Commissioners for Revenue and Customs[8],

towards discharging the employer's liability in respect of such contributions[9].

1 Ie regulations under the Social Security Contributions and Benefits Act 1992 s 167(1): see PARAS 439–440.

2 As to the meaning of 'employer' for these purposes see PARA 414.

3 As to the meaning of 'statutory maternity pay' see PARA 401.

4 As to the Commissioners for Her Majesty's Revenue and Customs see INCOME TAXATION vol 58 (2014) PARAS 33–34.

5 'Contributions payments', in relation to an employer, means any payments which the employer is required, by or under any enactment, to make in discharge of any liability in respect of primary or secondary Class 1 contributions: see the Social Security Contributions and Benefits Act 1992 s 167(8) (s 167 substituted by the Employment Act 2002 s 21(1)). As to primary and secondary Class 1 contributions see WELFARE BENEFITS AND STATE PENSIONS vol 104 (2014) PARA 385.

6 See the Social Security Contributions and Benefits Act 1992 s 167(6) (as substituted: see note 5). As to the date on which the deduction is treated for these purposes as having been paid see PARA 440 note 26.

7 Social Security Contributions and Benefits Act 1992 s 167(6)(a) (as substituted: see note 5).

8 Social Security Contributions and Benefits Act 1992 s 167(6)(b) (as substituted: see note 5).

9 See the Social Security Contributions and Benefits Act 1992 s 167(6) (as substituted: see note 5).

I. REPAYMENT OF CONTRACTUAL MATERNITY PAY

442. Refunds of contributions where contractual maternity pay becomes repayable. Where contractual maternity pay[1] becomes repayable after 31 March 1990[2], and:

(1) an application for refund of contributions paid in respect of that pay is made[3];

(2) the net amount of the refund which would otherwise be payable exceeds the amount of one-fifteenth of a standard rate[4] primary Class 1 contribution payable on earnings at the upper earnings limit in respect

of primary Class 1 contributions prescribed[5] for the last or only year in respect of which the contributions were paid[6],

the Commissioners for Revenue and Customs[7] must refund the whole of any primary or secondary Class 1 contributions paid in respect of that pay or, as the case may be, a prescribed part[8] of those contributions[9].

A person desiring to apply for the refund of any contribution must make the application in writing and within the period of six years from the end of the year in which that contribution was paid or, if the Commissioners are satisfied that the person making the application had good cause for not making it within that period, within such longer period as the Commissioners may allow[10]. No such application is, however, to be made unless: (a) where the application is by the employee, the contractual maternity pay has been repaid[11]; or (b) where the application is by the employer, he has been repaid the contractual maternity pay or can satisfy the Commissioners that he has taken all reasonable steps to recover it[12].

1 For these purposes, 'contractual maternity pay' means earnings payable under a contract of service by reason of pregnancy or confinement and repayable to the employer in the event of the employee failing to resume that employment after the birth or confinement: see the Social Security (Refunds) (Repayment of Contractual Maternity Pay) Regulations 1990, SI 1990/536, reg 2(4)(a). Although 'contract of service' is defined for the purposes of statutory sick pay (see PARA 558 note 2), it is not so defined under the other statutory pay provisions (for which purposes see generally PARA 1 note 1).

2 See the Social Security (Refunds) (Repayment of Contractual Maternity Pay) Regulations 1990, SI 1990/536, reg 2(1). 31 March 1990 is the date on which the Social Security (Refunds) (Repayment of Contractual Maternity Pay) Regulations 1990, SI 1990/536, came into force: see reg 1(1).

3 Social Security (Refunds) (Repayment of Contractual Maternity Pay) Regulations 1990, SI 1990/536, reg 2(1)(a). Head (1) in the text refers to an application for refund of contributions made in accordance with reg 2(3) (see the text and note 10) and is subject to reg 2(2) (see the text and notes 11–12): see reg 2(1)(a).

4 For these purposes, 'standard rate' means the appropriate percentage rate specified in the Social Security Contributions and Benefits Act 1992 s 8(2) (see **WELFARE BENEFITS AND STATE PENSIONS** vol 104 (2014) PARA 387): see the Social Security (Refunds) (Repayment of Contractual Maternity Pay) Regulations 1990, SI 1990/536, reg 2(4)(b); and see the Interpretation Act 1978 s 17(2)(a).

5 Ie in the Social Security (Contributions) Regulations 2001, SI 2001/1004, reg 10 (earnings limits and thresholds: see **WELFARE BENEFITS AND STATE PENSIONS** vol 104 (2014) PARA 384).

6 Social Security (Refunds) (Repayment of Contractual Maternity Pay) Regulations 1990, SI 1990/536, reg 2(1)(b); and see the Interpretation Act 1978 s 17(2)(a).

7 As to the Commissioners for Her Majesty's Revenue and Customs see **INCOME TAXATION** vol 58 (2014) PARAS 33–34.

8 Ie such part of those contributions as may be prescribed in the Social Security (Refunds) (Repayment of Contractual Maternity Pay) Regulations 1990, SI 1990/536, reg 3. Accordingly, where there has been paid an amount by way of any of the contributory benefits, as described in the Social Security Contributions and Benefits Act 1992 s 20(1) (see **WELFARE BENEFITS AND STATE PENSIONS** vol 104 (2014) PARA 409), which would not have been paid had any of the contributions in respect of which an application for their refund is duly made in accordance with the Social Security (Refunds) (Repayment of Contractual Maternity Pay) Regulations 1990, SI 1990/536, reg 2 not been paid in the first instance, the Commissioners must refund that part of the contributions remaining after the deduction of that amount paid by way of such benefits: reg 3 (amended by the Social Security Contributions (Transfer of Functions, etc) Act 1999 Sch 2; and SI 1990/2208); and see the Interpretation Act 1978 s 17(2)(a).

9 See the Social Security (Refunds) (Repayment of Contractual Maternity Pay) Regulations 1990, SI 1990/536, reg 2(1) (regs 2(1), (2)(b), (3) amended by the Social Security Contributions (Transfer of Functions, etc) Act 1999 Sch 2).

10 Social Security (Refunds) (Repayment of Contractual Maternity Pay) Regulations 1990, SI 1990/536, reg 2(3) (as amended: see note 9).

11 Social Security (Refunds) (Repayment of Contractual Maternity Pay) Regulations 1990, SI 1990/536, reg 2(2)(a).

12 Social Security (Refunds) (Repayment of Contractual Maternity Pay) Regulations 1990, SI 1990/536, reg 2(2)(b) (as amended: see note 9).

(iii) Statutory Paternity Pay

A. IN GENERAL

443. Liability of employer for payment of statutory paternity pay. Where a person satisfies the prescribed conditions[1], he is entitled[2], upon the birth or expected birth of a child or upon the placement for adoption of a child[3], to payments (known as 'statutory paternity pay')[4]. The liability to make such payments of statutory paternity pay is a liability of any person of whom the person entitled to such payments has been an employee[5] employed in accordance with the prescribed conditions[6].

Any agreement is void to the extent that it purports:

(1) to exclude, limit or otherwise modify any of the statutory paternity pay[7] provisions that are set out in Part XIIZA of the Social Security Contributions and Benefits Act 1992[8]; or

(2) to require an employee or former employee to contribute, whether directly or indirectly, towards any costs incurred by his employer[9] or former employer under those provisions[10],

but, for the avoidance of doubt, any agreement between an employer and an employee authorising any deductions from statutory paternity pay which the employer is liable to pay to the employee in respect of any period is not void by virtue of head (1) above if the employer[11]: (a) is authorised by that or another agreement to make the same deductions from any contractual remuneration which he is liable to pay in respect of the same period[12]; or (b) would be so authorised if he were liable to pay contractual remuneration in respect of that period[13].

1 Ie the conditions set out in the Social Security Contributions and Benefits Act 1992 s 171ZA(2) or s 171ZB(2): see PARA 457. For these purposes, 'prescribed' means prescribed by regulations: see s 171ZJ(1) (ss 171ZA, 171ZB, 171ZD, 171ZF, 171ZJ added by the Employment Act 2002 s 2).

2 Ie in accordance with the provisions of the Social Security Contributions and Benefits Act 1992 Pt XIIZA (ss 171ZA–171ZK) (statutory paternity pay).

3 As to the effect of the Social Security Contributions and Benefits Act 1992 s 171ZB in a case involving a child placed under the Children Act 1989 s 22C (local authority's duty to provide child is in its care with accommodation: see CHILDREN AND YOUNG PERSONS vol 10 (2012) PARA 858) by a local authority in England with a local authority foster parent who has been approved as a prospective adopter see PARA 457 note 8.

4 Social Security Contributions and Benefits Act 1992 s 171ZA(1) (s 171ZA as added (see note 1); s 171ZA(1) amended by the Work and Families Act 2006 Sch 1 para 12; and the Children and Families Act 2014 Sch 7 paras 6, 12(1), (2)); Social Security Contributions and Benefits Act 1992 s 171ZB(1) (s 171ZB as added (see note 1); s 171ZB(1) amended by the Work and Families Act 2006 Sch 1 para 13; and the Children and Families Act 2014 Sch 7 paras 6, 13(1), (2)). See also the Children and Families Act 2014 s 126. Statutory paternity pay under the Social Security Contributions and Benefits Act 1992 Pt XIIZA constitutes 'wages' for the purposes of the Employment Rights Act 1996 Pt II (ss 13–27) (protection of wages): see s 27(1); and PARA 254. Payments of statutory paternity pay under the Social Security Contributions and Benefits Act 1992 Pt XIIZA are charged to income tax under the Income Tax (Earnings and Pensions) Act 2003 Pts 2–7 (ss 3–554): see INCOME TAXATION vol 58 (2014) PARA 730 et seq.

5 Ie an employee as mentioned in the Social Security Contributions and Benefits Act 1992 s 171ZA(2)(b), (d) or s 171ZB(2)(b), (d): see PARA 457.

6 Social Security Contributions and Benefits Act 1992 s 171ZD(1) (s 171ZD as added (see note 1); s 171ZD(1) amended by the Work and Families Act 2006 Sch 1 para 15(1), (2); and the Children and Families Act 2014 Sch 7 paras 6, 15(1), (2)). As to the time limit for paying

statutory paternity pay see PARA 470. As to the liability of the Commissioners for Revenue and Customs for payments of statutory paternity pay see PARA 444.
7 Ie any of the provisions of the Social Security Contributions and Benefits Act 1992 Pt XIIZA (statutory paternity pay).
8 Social Security Contributions and Benefits Act 1992 s 171ZF(1)(a) (as added: see note 1).
9 As to the meaning of 'employer' for these purposes see PARA 456.
10 Social Security Contributions and Benefits Act 1992 s 171ZF(1)(b) (as added: see note 1).
11 See the Social Security Contributions and Benefits Act 1992 s 171ZF(2) (s 171ZF as added (see note 1); s 171ZF(2) amended by the Work and Families Act 2006 Sch 1 para 18; and the Children and Families Act 2014 Sch 7 paras 6, 19).
12 Social Security Contributions and Benefits Act 1992 s 171ZF(2)(a) (as added: see note 1).
13 Social Security Contributions and Benefits Act 1992 s 171ZF(2)(b) (as added: see note 1).

444. Liability of the Commissioners for Revenue and Customs for payment of statutory paternity pay. The Secretary of State[1] may, with the concurrence of the Commissioners for Revenue and Customs[2], by regulations[3] specify circumstances in which[4] liability to make payments of statutory paternity pay[5] is to be a liability of the Commissioners[6].

Accordingly, where:

(1) an officer of the Commissioners for Revenue and Customs has determined that an employer[7] is liable to make payments of statutory paternity pay to a person[8]; and
(2) the time for appealing against that determination has expired[9]; and
(3) no appeal against the determination has been lodged or leave to appeal against the determination is required and has been refused[10],

then for any week in respect of which the employer was liable to make payments of statutory paternity pay but did not do so, and for any subsequent weeks in the paternity pay period[11], the liability to make those payments is[12] that of the Commissioners for Revenue and Customs and not the employer[13].

Liability to make payments of statutory paternity pay is[14] a liability of the Commissioners and not the employer as from the week in which the employer first becomes insolvent[15] until the end of the paternity pay period[16].

1 As to the Secretary of State see PARA 5 note 21.
2 Ie with the concurrence of the Board. For these purposes, the 'Board' means the Commissioners for Revenue and Customs: see the Social Security Contributions and Benefits Act 1992 s 171ZJ(1) (ss 171ZD, 171ZJ added by the Employment Act 2002 s 2); the Employment Act 2002 s 16; and the Statutory Paternity Pay and Statutory Adoption Pay (General) Regulations 2002, SI 2002/2822, reg 2(1). As to the Commissioners for Her Majesty's Revenue and Customs see INCOME TAXATION vol 58 (2014) PARAS 33–34.
3 As to the making of regulations under the Social Security Contributions and Benefits Act 1992 generally see PARA 407 note 3. As to the regulations so made see note 6.
4 Ie notwithstanding the Social Security Contributions and Benefits Act 1992 s 171ZD: see also PARAS 443, 447.
5 As to the meaning of 'statutory paternity pay' see PARA 443.
6 See the Social Security Contributions and Benefits Act 1992 s 171ZD(3) (as added: see note 2). In exercise of the powers conferred by s 171ZD(3), and with the concurrence of the Commissioners for Revenue and Customs, the Secretary of State has made the Statutory Paternity Pay and Statutory Adoption Pay (General) Regulations 2002, SI 2002/2822 (see the text and notes 7–16), and the Statutory Paternity Pay (Adoption) and Statutory Adoption Pay (Adoptions from Overseas) (No 2) Regulations 2003, SI 2003/1194 (see PARA 485).
7 As to the meaning of 'employer' for these purposes see PARA 456.
8 Statutory Paternity Pay and Statutory Adoption Pay (General) Regulations 2002, SI 2002/2822, regs 31(1), 43(1)(a). See note 2.
9 Statutory Paternity Pay and Statutory Adoption Pay (General) Regulations 2002, SI 2002/2822, regs 31(1), 43(1)(b).
10 Statutory Paternity Pay and Statutory Adoption Pay (General) Regulations 2002, SI 2002/2822, regs 31(1), 43(1)(c).
11 As to the meaning of 'paternity pay period' see PARA 465.

12 Ie notwithstanding the Social Security Contributions and Benefits Act 1992 s 171ZD: see also PARAS 443, 447.

13 See the Statutory Paternity Pay and Statutory Adoption Pay (General) Regulations 2002, SI 2002/2822, regs 31(1), 43(1). As to the time limit for paying statutory paternity pay see PARA 471. In connection with the payment of statutory paternity pay or of any other sum in connection with that pay the Commissioners may use electronic communications: see the Statutory Payment Schemes (Electronic Communications) Regulations 2002, SI 2002/3047; and **INCOME TAXATION.**

14 Ie notwithstanding the Social Security Contributions and Benefits Act 1992 s 171ZD: see also PARAS 443, 447.

15 For these purposes, an employer is to be taken to be insolvent if, and only if, in England and Wales:

(1) he has been adjudged bankrupt or has made a composition or arrangement with his creditors (Statutory Paternity Pay and Statutory Adoption Pay (General) Regulations 2002, SI 2002/2822, regs 31(1), 43(3)(a)(i));

(2) he has died and his estate falls to be administered in accordance with an order made under the Insolvency Act 1986 s 421 (insolvent estates of deceased persons: see **BANKRUPTCY AND INDIVIDUAL INSOLVENCY** vol 5 (2013) PARA 830 et seq) (Statutory Paternity Pay and Statutory Adoption Pay (General) Regulations 2002, SI 2002/2822, regs 31(1), 43(3)(a)(ii)); or

(3) where an employer is a company (or a limited liability partnership), a winding-up order is made or a resolution for voluntary winding up is passed (or, in the case of a limited liability partnership, a determination for a voluntary winding up has been made) with respect to it, or it enters administration, or a receiver or manager of its undertaking is duly appointed, or possession is taken, by or on behalf of the holders of any debentures secured by a floating charge, of any property of the company or limited liability partnership comprised in or subject to the charge or a voluntary arrangement proposed for the purposes of the Insolvency Act 1986 Pt I (ss 1–7B) (company voluntary arrangements: see **COMPANY AND PARTNERSHIP INSOLVENCY** vol 16 (2011) PARA 83 et seq) is approved under Pt I (Statutory Paternity Pay and Statutory Adoption Pay (General) Regulations 2002, SI 2002/2822, regs 31(1), 43(3)(a)(iii) (amended by SI 2003/2096)).

As to the meanings of 'England' and 'Wales' see PARA 2 note 12. As to compositions or arrangements with creditors see **BANKRUPTCY AND INDIVIDUAL INSOLVENCY** vol 5 (2013) PARA 43 et seq; and as to bankruptcy generally see **BANKRUPTCY AND INDIVIDUAL INSOLVENCY** vol 5 (2013) PARA 129 et seq. As to winding-up orders see **COMPANY AND PARTNERSHIP INSOLVENCY** vol 16 (2011) PARA 386 et seq. As to voluntary winding-up see **COMPANY AND PARTNERSHIP INSOLVENCY** vol 17 (2011) PARA 898 et seq. As to administration orders see **COMPANY AND PARTNERSHIP INSOLVENCY** vol 16 (2011) PARA 159 et seq. As to the appointment of receivers and managers see **COMPANY AND PARTNERSHIP INSOLVENCY** vol 16 (2011) PARA 340 et seq. As to the taking of possession by or on behalf of the holders of debentures secured by a floating charge see **COMPANIES** vol 15 (2009) PARA 1333 et seq.

16 Statutory Paternity Pay and Statutory Adoption Pay (General) Regulations 2002, SI 2002/2822, regs 31(1), 43(2).

445. General power to make regulations in relation to statutory paternity pay. The Secretary of State[1] may by regulations[2]:

(1) provide that the conditions giving entitlement to statutory paternity pay[3] which relate to employment and earnings[4] have effect subject to prescribed[5] modifications in such cases as may be prescribed[6];

(2) provide that the notice requirements[7] are not to have effect, or are to have effect subject to prescribed modifications[8], in such cases as may be prescribed[9];

(3) impose requirements about evidence of entitlement[10];

(4) specify in what circumstances employment is to be treated[11] as continuous[12];

(5) provide that a person is to be treated[13] as being employed for a continuous period of at least 26 weeks[14], where:

(a) he has been employed by the same employer for at least 26 weeks under two or more separate contracts of service[15]; and

(b) those contracts were not continuous[16];

(6) provide for amounts earned by a person under separate contracts of service with the same employer to be aggregated[17];

(7) provide that:

(a) the amount of a person's earnings for any period[18]; or

(b) the amount of his earnings to be treated as comprised in any payment made to him or for his benefit[19],

is to be calculated or estimated[20] in such manner and on such basis as may be prescribed and that for that purpose payments of a particular class or description made or falling to be made to or by a person are, to such extent as may be prescribed, to be disregarded or, as the case may be, to be deducted from the amount of his earnings[21];

(8) make provision, upon the placement of a child for adoption, about elections for statutory paternity pay[22].

The Secretary of State may also by regulations specify circumstances in which there is to be no liability to pay statutory paternity pay in respect of a week[23].

1 As to the Secretary of State see PARA 5 note 21.

2 As to the making of regulations under the Social Security Contributions and Benefits Act 1992 generally see PARA 407 note 3.

3 As to the meaning of 'statutory paternity pay' see PARA 443.

4 Ie the Social Security Contributions and Benefits Act 1992 s 171ZA(2)(b), (c), (d) or s 171ZB(2)(b), (c), (d): see PARA 457.

5 For these purposes, 'prescribed' means prescribed by regulations: see the Social Security Contributions and Benefits Act 1992 s 171ZJ(1) (ss 171ZB, 171ZC, 171ZJ added by the Employment Act 2002 s 2).

6 Social Security Contributions and Benefits Act 1992 s 171ZC(3)(a) (as added: see note 5). In exercise of the powers conferred by s 171ZC(3)(a)–(d), (f), (g), the Secretary of State has made the Statutory Paternity Pay and Statutory Adoption Pay (General) Regulations 2002, SI 2002/2822 (see PARA 457) and the Statutory Paternity Pay (Adoption) and Statutory Adoption Pay (Adoptions from Overseas) (No 2) Regulations 2003, SI 2003/1194 (see PARA 485).

7 Ie under the Social Security Contributions and Benefits Act 1992 s 171ZC(1): see PARA 462.

8 For these purposes, 'modifications' includes additions, omissions and amendments; and related expressions are to be read accordingly: see the Social Security Contributions and Benefits Act 1992 s 171ZJ(1) (as added: see note 5).

9 Social Security Contributions and Benefits Act 1992 s 171ZC(3)(b) (as added: see note 5). As to the regulations made see note 6; and PARA 463.

10 Social Security Contributions and Benefits Act 1992 s 171ZC(3)(c) (as added: see note 5). As to the regulations made see note 6; and PARA 463.

11 Ie for the purposes of the Social Security Contributions and Benefits Act 1992 s 171ZA or s 171ZB (see PARAS 443, 457).

12 Social Security Contributions and Benefits Act 1992 s 171ZC(3)(d) (as added: see note 5). As to the regulations made see note 6; and PARAS 458–461.

13 Ie for the purposes of the Social Security Contributions and Benefits Act 1992 s 171ZA or s 171ZB (see PARAS 443, 457).

14 See the Social Security Contributions and Benefits Act 1992 s 171ZC(3)(e) (as added: see note 5). As to the regulations made see note 6; and PARA 458.

For these purposes, except in relation to s 171ZE (rate and period of pay: see PARA 446 note 4), 'week' means a period of seven days beginning with Sunday or such other period as may be prescribed in relation to any particular case or class of cases: see s 171ZJ(5) (s 171ZJ as added (see note 5); s 171ZJ(5) amended by the Work and Families Act 2006 Sch 1 para 20(1), (2); and the Children and Families Act 2014 Sch 7 paras 6, 21(1), (2)). Regulations under the Social Security Contributions and Benefits Act 1992 s 171ZJ(5) must be made with the concurrence of the Commissioners for Revenue and Customs: see s 171ZJ(1), (12) (as so added). At the date at which this volume states the law, no such regulations had been made. As to the Commissioners for Her Majesty's Revenue and Customs see INCOME TAXATION vol 58 (2014) PARAS 33–34; and see PARA 444 note 2.

15 Social Security Contributions and Benefits Act 1992 s 171ZC(3)(e)(i) (as added: see note 5). As to the meaning of 'employer' for these purposes see PARA 456. Although 'contract of service' is defined for the purposes of statutory sick pay (see PARA 558 note 2), it is not so defined under the other statutory pay provisions (for which purposes see generally PARA 1 note 1).

16 Social Security Contributions and Benefits Act 1992 s 171ZC(3)(e)(ii) (as added: see note 5).

17 Social Security Contributions and Benefits Act 1992 s 171ZC(3)(f) (as added: see note 5). Head (6) in the text refers to provision for amounts to be aggregated for the purposes of s 171ZA or s 171ZB (see PARAS 443, 457): see s 171ZC(3)(f) (as so added). As to the regulations made see note 6.

18 Social Security Contributions and Benefits Act 1992 s 171ZC(3)(g)(i) (as added: see note 5).

19 Social Security Contributions and Benefits Act 1992 s 171ZC(3)(g)(ii) (as added: see note 5).

20 Ie for the purposes of Social Security Contributions and Benefits Act 1992 s 171ZA or s 171ZB (see PARAS 443, 457).

21 Social Security Contributions and Benefits Act 1992 s 171ZC(3)(g) (as added: see note 5). As to the regulations made see note 6; and PARA 468.

22 Social Security Contributions and Benefits Act 1992 s 171ZB(5) (as added: see note 5). As to elections made for these purposes see s 171ZB(2)(e), (4); and PARA 457.

23 See the Social Security Contributions and Benefits Act 1992 s 171ZE(8); and PARA 446.

446. Circumstances in which liability to pay statutory paternity pay does not arise. The Secretary of State[1] may by regulations[2] specify circumstances in which there is to be no liability to pay statutory paternity pay[3] in respect of a statutory pay week[4]. Accordingly, there is no liability to pay statutory paternity pay in respect of any week[5]:

(1) during any part of which the person entitled to it is entitled[6] to statutory sick pay[7];

(2) following that in which the person claiming it has died[8]; or

(3) during any part of which the person entitled to it is detained in legal custody or sentenced to a term of imprisonment (except where the sentence is suspended), or which is a subsequent week within the same statutory paternity pay period[9].

Nor is a person liable to pay statutory paternity pay to another in respect of a statutory pay week during any part of which the other person works under a contract of service with him[10].

Statutory paternity pay is not payable to a person in respect of a statutory pay week:

(a) if it is not his purpose at the beginning of the week either to care for the child by reference to whom he is entitled[11] to statutory paternity pay, or to support the person by reference to whom he is entitled[12] to statutory paternity pay[13]; or

(b) if statutory shared parental pay[14] is payable to that person in respect of any part of that week or that person takes shared parental leave in any part of that week[15], or if statutory shared parental pay was payable to that person or that person has taken shared parental leave in respect of the child before that week[16]; or

(c) except in such cases as may be prescribed[17], during any part of a statutory pay week which he works for any employer[18] who is not liable to pay him statutory paternity pay[19].

Accordingly, pursuant to head (c) above, where there is more than one employer, statutory paternity pay[20] is payable to a person in respect of a statutory pay week during any part of which he works only for an employer[21]: (i) who is not liable to pay him statutory paternity pay (birth) or statutory paternity pay (adoption), as the case may be[22]; and (ii) for whom he has worked, in the case of statutory paternity pay (birth), in the week immediately preceding the fourteenth week before the expected week of the child's birth[23] or, in the case of statutory paternity pay (adoption), in the week in which the adopter is notified of being matched with the child[24].

1 As to the Secretary of State see PARA 5 note 21.
2 As to the making of regulations under the Social Security Contributions and Benefits Act 1992 generally see PARA 407 note 3.
3 As to the meaning of 'statutory paternity pay' see PARA 443. As to the persons liable to make payments of statutory paternity pay see PARA 443 et seq.
4 Social Security Contributions and Benefits Act 1992 s 171ZE(8) (ss 171ZE, 171ZJ added by the Employment Act 2002 s 2; the Social Security Contributions and Benefits Act 1992 s 171ZE(4), (7), (8), (11) amended by the Work and Families Act 2006 Sch 1 para 16(1), (2); and by the Children and Families Act 2014 Sch 7 para 16(1), (4), (6), (7), (9)). For this purpose, 'statutory pay week', in relation to a person entitled to statutory paternity pay, means a week chosen by him as a week in respect of which statutory paternity pay is to be payable; and 'week' means any period of seven days: see the Social Security Contributions and Benefits Act 1992 s 171ZE(11) (as so added and amended). In exercise of the powers conferred by s 171ZE(8), the Secretary of State has made the Statutory Paternity Pay and Statutory Adoption Pay (General) Regulations 2002, SI 2002/2822 (see the text and notes 5–9) and the Statutory Paternity Pay (Adoption) and Statutory Adoption Pay (Adoptions from Overseas) (No 2) Regulations 2003, SI 2003/1194 (see PARA 485).
5 See the Statutory Paternity Pay and Statutory Adoption Pay (General) Regulations 2002, SI 2002/2822, reg 18.
6 Ie under the Social Security Contributions and Benefits Act 1992 Pt XI (ss 151–163) (statutory sick pay): see PARA 558 et seq.
7 Statutory Paternity Pay and Statutory Adoption Pay (General) Regulations 2002, SI 2002/2822, reg 18(a).
8 Statutory Paternity Pay and Statutory Adoption Pay (General) Regulations 2002, SI 2002/2822, reg 18(b).
9 Statutory Paternity Pay and Statutory Adoption Pay (General) Regulations 2002, SI 2002/2822, reg 18(c). As to the meaning of 'paternity pay period' see PARA 465.
10 See the Social Security Contributions and Benefits Act 1992 s 171ZE(5) (s 171ZE as added (see note 4); s 171ZE(5) amended by the Work and Families Act 2006 Sch 1 paras 16(1), (2); and the Children and Families Act 2014 Sch 7 paras 6, 16(1), (5)). It is immaterial for these purposes whether the work referred to is work under a contract of service which existed immediately before the statutory pay week or a contract of service which did not so exist: Social Security Contributions and Benefits Act 1992 s 171ZE(6) (as so added). Although 'contract of service' is defined for the purposes of statutory sick pay (see PARA 558 note 2), it is not so defined under the other statutory pay provisions (for which purposes see generally PARA 1 note 1).
11 Ie where he satisfies the conditions as to relationship with a newborn child in the Social Security Contributions and Benefits Act 1992 s 171ZA(2)(a)(i) (see PARA 457) or with a child placed for adoption in s 171ZB(2)(a)(i) (see PARA 457).
12 Ie where he satisfies the conditions as to relationship with the child's mother in the Social Security Contributions and Benefits Act 1992 s 171ZA(2)(a)(ii) (see PARA 457) or with a person with whom a child is placed for adoption in s 171ZB(2)(a)(ii) (see PARA 457).
13 See the Social Security Contributions and Benefits Act 1992 s 171ZE(4) (as added and amended: see note 4).
14 As to shared parental pay see PARA 534 et seq.
15 Social Security Contributions and Benefits Act 1992 s 171ZE(3A)(a) (s 171ZE as added (see note 4); s 171ZE(3A) added by the Children and Families Act 2014 s 120(1), (5)).
16 Social Security Contributions and Benefits Act 1992 s 171ZE(3A)(b) (as added: see note 15).
17 For these purposes, 'prescribed' means prescribed by regulations: Social Security Contributions and Benefits Act 1992 s 171ZJ(1) (as added: see note 4). See note 19.
18 As to the meaning of 'employer' for these purposes see PARA 456.
19 See the Social Security Contributions and Benefits Act 1992 s 171ZE(7) (as added and amended: see note 4). In exercise of the powers conferred by s 171ZE(7), the Secretary of State has made the Statutory Paternity Pay and Statutory Adoption Pay (General) Regulations 2002, SI 2002/2822 (see the text and notes 20–24) and the Statutory Paternity Pay (Adoption) and Statutory Adoption Pay (Adoptions from Overseas) (No 2) Regulations 2003, SI 2003/1194 (see PARA 485).

20 Ie either statutory paternity pay (birth) (see the Statutory Paternity Pay and Statutory Adoption Pay (General) Regulations 2002, SI 2002/2822, reg 10) or statutory paternity pay (adoption) (see reg 16). For these purposes, 'statutory paternity pay (birth)' means statutory paternity pay payable in accordance with the provisions of the Social Security Contributions and Benefits Act 1992 Pt XIIZA (ss 171ZA–171ZK) (statutory paternity pay) where the conditions specified in s 171ZA(2) (see PARA 457) are satisfied; and 'statutory paternity pay (adoption)' means statutory paternity pay payable in accordance with the provisions of Pt XIIZA where the conditions specified in s 171ZB(2) (see PARA 457) are satisfied: see the Statutory Paternity Pay and Statutory Adoption Pay (General) Regulations 2002, SI 2002/2822, reg 2(1).

21 See the Statutory Paternity Pay and Statutory Adoption Pay (General) Regulations 2002, SI 2002/2822, regs 10, 16.

22 See the Statutory Paternity Pay and Statutory Adoption Pay (General) Regulations 2002, SI 2002/2822, regs 10(a), 16(a).

23 Statutory Paternity Pay and Statutory Adoption Pay (General) Regulations 2002, SI 2002/2822, reg 10(b). For these purposes, 'expected week', in relation to the birth of a child, means the week, beginning with midnight between Saturday and Sunday, in which it is expected that the child will be born: see reg 2(1).

24 Statutory Paternity Pay and Statutory Adoption Pay (General) Regulations 2002, SI 2002/2822, reg 16(b). For these purposes, a person is matched with a child for adoption when an adoption agency decides that that person would be a suitable adoptive parent for the child, either individually or jointly with another person (reg 2(2)(a)); and a person is notified of having been matched with a child on the date on which he receives notification of the adoption agency's decision under the Adoption Agencies Regulations 1983, SI 1983/1964, reg 11(2) (see **CHILDREN AND YOUNG PERSONS** vol 9 (2012) PARA 487) (Statutory Paternity Pay and Statutory Adoption Pay (General) Regulations 2002, SI 2002/2822, reg 2(2)(b)). 'Adoption agency' has the meaning given by the Adoption Act 1976 s 1(4) (repealed): see the Statutory Paternity Pay and Statutory Adoption Pay (General) Regulations 2002, SI 2002/2822, reg 2(1). As to adoption agencies within the meaning of the Adoption and Children Act 2002 s 2 see **CHILDREN AND YOUNG PERSONS** vol 9 (2012) PARAS 432–433.

447. Contract of service ended for the purpose of avoiding liability for statutory paternity pay. Regulations under the Social Security Contributions and Benefits Act 1992[1] must make provision as to a former employer's[2] liability to pay statutory paternity pay[3] to a person in any case where the former employer's contract of service[4] with him has been brought to an end by the former employer solely, or mainly, for the purpose of avoiding liability for statutory paternity pay[5].

Accordingly, a former employer is liable to make payments of statutory paternity pay to a former employee[6] in any case where the employee had been employed for a continuous period of at least eight weeks, and his contract of service was brought to an end by the former employer solely, or mainly, for the purpose of avoiding liability for statutory paternity pay[7]. In such a case: (1) the employee is treated as if he had been employed for a continuous period ending with the child's birth[8] or, as the case may be, the placement[9] of the child for adoption[10]; and (2) his normal weekly earnings are to be calculated by reference to his normal weekly earnings[11] for the period of eight weeks ending with the last day in respect of which he was paid under his former contract of service[12].

1 As to the making of regulations under the Social Security Contributions and Benefits Act 1992 generally see PARA 407 note 3.

2 As to the meaning of 'employer' for these purposes see PARA 456.

3 As to the meaning of 'statutory paternity pay' see PARA 443. See note 5.

4 Although 'contract of service' is defined for the purposes of statutory sick pay (see PARA 558 note 2), it is not so defined under the other statutory pay provisions (for which purposes see generally PARA 1 note 1).

5 Social Security Contributions and Benefits Act 1992 s 171ZD(2) (added by the Employment Act 2002 s 2; and amended by the Work and Families Act 2006 Sch 1 para 15(1), (3); and the Children and Families Act 2014 Sch 7 paras 6, 15(1), (3)). In exercise of the powers conferred by the Social Security Contributions and Benefits Act 1992 s 171ZD(2), the Secretary of State

has made the Statutory Paternity Pay and Statutory Adoption Pay (General) Regulations 2002, SI 2002/2822 (see the text and notes 6–12) and the Statutory Paternity Pay (Adoption) and Statutory Adoption Pay (Adoptions from Overseas) (No 2) Regulations 2003, SI 2003/1194 (see PARA 485).

6 As to the meaning of 'employee' for these purposes see PARA 448.

7 Statutory Paternity Pay and Statutory Adoption Pay (General) Regulations 2002, SI 2002/2822, reg 20(1). As to continuity of employment see PARA 458 et seq.

8 Ie where paternity pay is being claimed under the Social Security Contributions and Benefits Act 1992 s 171ZA (entitlement (birth): see PARA 443).

9 Ie where paternity pay is being claimed under the Social Security Contributions and Benefits Act 1992 s 171ZB (entitlement (adoption): see PARA 443).

10 Statutory Paternity Pay and Statutory Adoption Pay (General) Regulations 2002, SI 2002/2822, reg 20(2)(a).

11 As to the calculation of normal weekly earnings see PARA 468.

12 Statutory Paternity Pay and Statutory Adoption Pay (General) Regulations 2002, SI 2002/2822, reg 20(2)(b).

B. MEANING OF 'EMPLOYEE' AND 'EMPLOYER'

448. Meaning of 'employee' for purposes of statutory paternity pay; treatment of two or more contracts of service as one. For the purposes of the statutory paternity pay provisions that are set out in Part XIIZA of the Social Security Contributions and Benefits Act 1992[1], 'employee' means a person who is gainfully employed in Great Britain[2] either under a contract of service[3] or in an office (including elective office) with earnings (as defined)[4], but subject to regulations[5] which may provide for cases where any such person is not to be treated as an employee for those purposes[6], and for cases where a person who would not otherwise be an employee for those purposes is to be treated as an employee for those purposes[7].

Accordingly, in a case where, and in so far as, a person is treated as an employed earner[8], he is to be treated as an employee for the purposes of Part XIIZA of the Social Security Contributions and Benefits Act 1992; and, in a case where, and in so far as, such a person is treated otherwise than as an employed earner, he is not to be treated as an employee for those purposes[9].

Any person who is in employed earner's employment[10] under a contract of apprenticeship is to be treated[11] as an employee[12].

A person who is in employed earner's employment, but whose employer[13]:

(1) does not fulfil the prescribed conditions[14] as to residence or presence in Great Britain[15]; or

(2) is a person who, by reason of any international treaty to which the United Kingdom[16] is a party, or of any international convention binding the United Kingdom[17]: (a) is exempt from the provisions of the Social Security Contributions and Benefits Act 1992[18]; or (b) is a person against whom the provisions of that Act are not enforceable[19],

is not to be treated[20] as an employee[21].

Without prejudice to any other power to make regulations under Part XIIZA of the Social Security Contributions and Benefits Act 1992[22], regulations may specify cases in which two or more contracts of service in respect of which the same person is an employee are to be treated[23] as one[24]. Accordingly, where two or more contracts of service exist concurrently between one employer and one employee, they are to be treated[25] as one except where[26] the earnings from those contracts of service are not aggregated for the purposes of earnings-related contributions[27].

1 Ie in the Social Security Contributions and Benefits Act 1992 Pt XIIZA (ss 171ZA–171ZK) (statutory paternity pay). As to the meaning of 'statutory paternity pay' see PARA 443.
2 As to the meaning of 'Great Britain' for these purposes see PARA 407 note 7.
3 Although 'contract of service' is defined for the purposes of statutory sick pay (see PARA 558 note 2), it is not so defined under the other statutory pay provisions (for which purposes see generally PARA 1 note 1).
4 Social Security Contributions and Benefits Act 1992 s 171ZJ(2) (s 171ZJ added by the Employment Act 2002 s 2; and the Social Security Contributions and Benefits Act 1992 s 171ZJ(2) amended by the Income Tax (Earnings and Pensions) Act 2003 Sch 6 Pt 2 paras 169, 183; the National Insurance Contributions Act 2014 s 15(3), Sch 2 paras 1, 5; and SI 2006/1031). The reference in the text to earnings is to earnings within the meaning of the Social Security Contributions and Benefits Act 1992 Pts I–V (ss 1–110) (see ss 3, 4, 112, 122; and **WELFARE BENEFITS AND STATE PENSIONS** vol 104 (2014) PARAS 381, 382). As to the meaning of 'employee' and related expressions in relation to employment rights generally see PARA 2 et seq.
5 As to the making of regulations under the Social Security Contributions and Benefits Act 1992 generally see PARA 407 note 3.
6 Social Security Contributions and Benefits Act 1992 s 171ZJ(3)(a) (as added: see note 4). In exercise of the powers conferred by s 171ZJ(3), the Secretary of State has made the Statutory Paternity Pay and Statutory Adoption Pay (General) Regulations 2002, SI 2002/2822 (see the text and notes 8–19) and the Statutory Paternity Pay (Adoption) and Statutory Adoption Pay (Adoptions from Overseas) (No 2) Regulations 2003, SI 2003/1194 (see PARA 485).
7 Social Security Contributions and Benefits Act 1992 s 171ZJ(3)(b) (as added: see note 4). See note 6.
8 Ie by virtue of the Social Security (Categorisation of Earners) Regulations 1978, SI 1978/1689: see **WELFARE BENEFITS AND STATE PENSIONS** vol 104 (2014) PARA 381.
9 Statutory Paternity Pay and Statutory Adoption Pay (General) Regulations 2002, SI 2002/2822, regs 31(1), 32(1) (reg 32(1) amended by SI 2006/1031). The Statutory Paternity Pay and Statutory Adoption Pay (General) Regulations 2002, SI 2002/2822, reg 32(1) is subject to reg 32(1A): see reg 32(1) (as so amended). Accordingly, reg 32(1) has effect in relation to a person who:
   (1) is under the age of 16 (see regs 31(1), 32(1A)(a) (reg 32(1A) added by SI 2006/1031; and substituted by SI 2007/825)); and
   (2) would or, as the case may be, would not have been treated as an employed earner by virtue of the Social Security (Categorisation of Earners) Regulations 1978, SI 1978/1689 (see **WELFARE BENEFITS AND STATE PENSIONS** vol 104 (2014) PARA 381) had he been over that age (Statutory Paternity Pay and Statutory Adoption Pay (General) Regulations 2002, SI 2002/2822, regs 31(1), 32(1A)(b) (reg 32(1A) as so added and substituted)),

   as it has effect in relation to a person who is or, as the case may be, is not so treated (see regs 31(1), 32(1A) (reg 32(1A) as so added and substituted)). A person who would not be treated under reg 32 as an employee for the purposes of the Social Security Contributions and Benefits Act 1992 Pt XIIZA (statutory paternity pay) if his employment were in Great Britain is not to be treated as an employee under the Statutory Paternity Pay and Statutory Adoption Pay (Persons Abroad and Mariners) Regulations 2002, SI 2002/2821: see reg 2 (amended by SI 2010/151).
10 Ie within the meaning of the Social Security Contributions and Benefits Act 1992: see **WELFARE BENEFITS AND STATE PENSIONS** vol 104 (2014) PARA 176.
11 Ie for the purposes of the Social Security Contributions and Benefits Act 1992 Pt XIIZA (statutory paternity pay).
12 Statutory Paternity Pay and Statutory Adoption Pay (General) Regulations 2002, SI 2002/2822, regs 31(1), 32(2). As to the position of apprentices and youth trainees at common law see PARAS 112, 128–129, 636, 747–754. As to the statutory law on apprenticeships see **EDUCATION** vol 35 (2011) PARA 682 et seq.
13 See the Statutory Paternity Pay and Statutory Adoption Pay (General) Regulations 2002, SI 2002/2822, regs 31(1), 32(3).
14 Ie the conditions prescribed in the Social Security (Contributions) Regulations 2001, SI 2001/1004, reg 145(1) (conditions as to residence or presence in Great Britain: see **WELFARE BENEFITS AND STATE PENSIONS** vol 104 (2014) PARA 406).
15 Statutory Paternity Pay and Statutory Adoption Pay (General) Regulations 2002, SI 2002/2822, regs 31(1), 32(3)(a).
16 As to the meaning of 'United Kingdom' for these purposes see PARA 407 note 7.

17 Statutory Paternity Pay and Statutory Adoption Pay (General) Regulations 2002, SI 2002/2822, regs 31(1), 32(3)(b).
18 Statutory Paternity Pay and Statutory Adoption Pay (General) Regulations 2002, SI 2002/2822, regs 31(1), 32(3)(b)(i).
19 Statutory Paternity Pay and Statutory Adoption Pay (General) Regulations 2002, SI 2002/2822, regs 31(1), 32(3)(b)(ii).
20 Ie for the purposes of the Social Security Contributions and Benefits Act 1992 Pt XIIZA (statutory paternity pay).
21 See the Statutory Paternity Pay and Statutory Adoption Pay (General) Regulations 2002, SI 2002/2822, regs 31(1), 32(3).
22 Ie under the Social Security Contributions and Benefits Act 1992 Pt XIIZA (statutory paternity pay).
23 Ie for the purposes of the Social Security Contributions and Benefits Act 1992 Pt XIIZA (statutory paternity pay) or such provisions of Pt XIIZA as may be prescribed.
24 Social Security Contributions and Benefits Act 1992 s 171ZJ(4)(b) (as added: see note 4). Regulations under s 171ZJ(4) must be made with the concurrence of the Commissioners for Revenue and Customs: see s 171ZJ(1), (12) (as so added). As to the Commissioners for Her Majesty's Revenue and Customs see INCOME TAXATION vol 58 (2014) PARAS 33–34; and see PARA 444 note 2. In exercise of the powers conferred by s 171ZJ(4), the Secretary of State has, with the concurrence of the Commissioners for Revenue and Customs, made the Statutory Paternity Pay and Statutory Adoption Pay (General) Regulations 2002, SI 2002/2822 (see the text and notes 25–27) and the Statutory Paternity Pay (Adoption) and Statutory Adoption Pay (Adoptions from Overseas) (No 2) Regulations 2003, SI 2003/1194 (see PARA 485).
25 Ie for the purposes of the Social Security Contributions and Benefits Act 1992 Pt XIIZA (statutory paternity pay).
26 Ie by virtue of the Social Security (Contributions) Regulations 2001, SI 2001/1004, reg 14 (aggregation of earnings paid in respect of separate employed earner's employments under the same employer: see WELFARE BENEFITS AND STATE PENSIONS vol 104 (2014) PARA 382).
27 Statutory Paternity Pay and Statutory Adoption Pay (General) Regulations 2002, SI 2002/2822, regs 31(1), 38(3).

449. Modification of statutory provisions relating to statutory paternity pay to accommodate special classes of person. The Secretary of State[1] may, with the concurrence of the Treasury[2], make regulations[3] modifying any of the statutory paternity pay provisions that are set out in Part XIIZA of the Social Security Contributions and Benefits Act 1992[4], in such manner as he thinks proper, in its application to any person who is, has been or is to be[5]:

(1) employed on board any ship, vessel, hovercraft or aircraft[6];
(2) outside Great Britain[7] at any prescribed[8] time or in any prescribed circumstances[9]; or
(3) in prescribed employment in connection with continental shelf operations[10].

Such regulations may, in particular, provide:

(a) for any provision of Part XIIZA of the Social Security Contributions and Benefits Act 1992[11] to apply to any such person, notwithstanding that it would not otherwise apply[12];
(b) for any such provision not to apply to any such person, notwithstanding that it would otherwise apply[13];
(c) for excepting any such person from the application of any such provision where he neither is domiciled[14] nor has a place of residence in any part of Great Britain[15];
(d) for the taking of evidence, for the purposes of the determination of any question arising under any such provision, in a country or territory outside Great Britain, by a British consular official or such other person as may be determined in accordance with the regulations[16].

The Secretary of State may also make regulations modifying the provisions relating to statutory paternity pay in relation to other cases which involve adoption[17].

1 As to the Secretary of State see PARA 5 note 21.
2 As to the Treasury see CONSTITUTIONAL AND ADMINISTRATIVE LAW vol 20 (2014) PARAS 262–265.
3 As to the making of regulations under the Social Security Contributions and Benefits Act 1992 see PARA 407 note 3; and as to the Secretary of State's general power to make regulations relating to statutory paternity pay see PARA 445.
4 Ie any provision of the Social Security Contributions and Benefits Act 1992 Pt XIIZA (ss 171ZA–171ZK) (statutory paternity pay). As to the meaning of 'statutory paternity pay' see PARA 443.
5 See the Social Security Contributions and Benefits Act 1992 s 171ZI(1) (ss 171ZI, 171ZJ added by the Employment Act 2002 s 2).
6 Social Security Contributions and Benefits Act 1992 s 171ZI(1)(a) (as added: see note 5).
7 As to the meaning of 'Great Britain' for these purposes see PARA 407 note 7.
8 For these purposes, 'prescribed' means prescribed by regulations: see the Social Security Contributions and Benefits Act 1992 s 171ZJ(1) (as added: see note 5).
9 Social Security Contributions and Benefits Act 1992 s 171ZI(1)(b) (as added: see note 5).
10 Social Security Contributions and Benefits Act 1992 s 171ZI(1)(c) (as added: see note 5). 'Continental shelf operations' means any activities which, if the Petroleum Act 1998 s 11(8)(a), (d) (application of civil law to certain offshore activities) were omitted, would nevertheless fall within s 11(2) (see ENERGY AND CLIMATE CHANGE vol 44 (2011) PARA 1080): see the Social Security Contributions and Benefits Act 1992 s 120(2) (amended by the Petroleum Act 1998 Sch 4 para 30); definition applied by the Social Security Contributions and Benefits Act 1992 s 171ZI(1)(c) (as so added). In exercise of the powers conferred under head (3) in the text, the Secretary of State has, with the concurrence of the Treasury, made the Statutory Paternity Pay and Statutory Adoption Pay (Persons Abroad and Mariners) Regulations 2002, SI 2002/2821 (see PARA 450 et seq), and the Ordinary Statutory Paternity Pay (Adoption), Additional Statutory Paternity Pay (Adoption) and Statutory Adoption Pay (Adoptions from Overseas) (Persons Abroad and Mariners) Regulations 2010, SI 2010/150 (see PARA 487).
11 Ie any provision of the Social Security Contributions and Benefits Act 1992 Pt XIIZA (statutory paternity pay).
12 Social Security Contributions and Benefits Act 1992 s 171ZI(2)(a) (as added: see note 5).
13 Social Security Contributions and Benefits Act 1992 s 171ZI(2)(b) (as added: see note 5).
14 As to domicile see CONFLICT OF LAWS vol 19 (2011) PARA 336 et seq.
15 Social Security Contributions and Benefits Act 1992 s 171ZI(2)(c) (as added: see note 5).
16 Social Security Contributions and Benefits Act 1992 s 171ZI(2)(d) (as added: see note 5).
17 See the Social Security Contributions and Benefits Act 1992 s 171ZK; and PARA 484.

450. Time for compliance with provisions relating to statutory paternity pay; employee outside the United Kingdom. Where:

(1) a person is outside the United Kingdom[1];
(2) the statutory paternity pay provisions that are set out in Part XIIZA of the Social Security Contributions and Benefits Act 1992[2] (or regulations made thereunder) require any act to be done forthwith or on the happening of a certain event or within a specified time[3]; and
(3) because the person is outside the United Kingdom, he or his employer[4] cannot comply with the requirement[5],

the person or the employer, as the case may be, is deemed to have complied with it if the act is performed as soon as reasonably practicable[6].

1 Statutory Paternity Pay and Statutory Adoption Pay (Persons Abroad and Mariners) Regulations 2002, SI 2002/2821, reg 7(a). As to the meaning of 'United Kingdom' for these purposes see PARA 407 note 7.
2 Ie the Social Security Contributions and Benefits Act 1992 Pt XIIZA (ss 171ZA–171ZK) (statutory paternity pay). As to the meaning of 'statutory paternity pay' see PARA 443.
3 Statutory Paternity Pay and Statutory Adoption Pay (Persons Abroad and Mariners) Regulations 2002, SI 2002/2821, reg 7(b).

4 As to the meaning of 'employer' for these purposes see PARA 456.
5 Statutory Paternity Pay and Statutory Adoption Pay (Persons Abroad and Mariners) Regulations 2002, SI 2002/2821, reg 7(c).
6 See the Statutory Paternity Pay and Statutory Adoption Pay (Persons Abroad and Mariners) Regulations 2002, SI 2002/2821, reg 7.

451. Treatment of persons in other member states or absent from Great Britain for purposes of statutory paternity pay. A person who is:

(1) gainfully employed in an EEA state[1] other than the United Kingdom[2] in such circumstances that, if his employment were in Great Britain[3], he would be an employee[4] for the purposes of the statutory paternity pay provisions that are set out in Part XIIZA of the Social Security Contributions and Benefits Act 1992[5] or a person treated[6] as such an employee[7]; and
(2) subject[8] to the legislation of the United Kingdom[9],

is to be treated[10] as an employee for those purposes notwithstanding that he is not employed in Great Britain[11].

Where a person, while absent from Great Britain for any purpose, is gainfully employed by an employer who is liable to pay in respect of his employment secondary Class 1 contributions[12], he is to be treated[13] as an employee[14].

1 For these purposes, 'EEA state' means a state which is a contracting party to the Agreement on the European Economic Area (Oporto, 2 May 1992; OJ L1, 3.1.94, p 3; Cm 2073) as adjusted by the Protocol (Brussels, 17 March 1993; OJ L1, 3.1.94, p 571; Cm 2183): see the Statutory Paternity Pay and Statutory Adoption Pay (Persons Abroad and Mariners) Regulations 2002, SI 2002/2821, reg 1(2).
2 As to the meaning of 'United Kingdom' for these purposes see PARA 407 note 7.
3 As to the meaning of 'Great Britain' for these purposes see PARA 407 note 7.
4 As to the meaning of 'employee' for these purposes see PARA 448.
5 Ie for the purposes of the Social Security Contributions and Benefits Act 1992 Pt XIIZA (ss 171ZA–171ZK) (statutory paternity pay). As to the meaning of 'statutory paternity pay' see PARA 443.
6 Ie under the Statutory Paternity Pay and Statutory Adoption Pay (General) Regulations 2002, SI 2002/2822, reg 32: see PARA 448.
7 Statutory Paternity Pay and Statutory Adoption Pay (Persons Abroad and Mariners) Regulations 2002, SI 2002/2821, reg 3(a).
8 Ie under Council Regulation (EC) 1408/71 (OJ L149, 5.7.71, p 2) on the application of social security schemes to employed persons and their families moving within the Community (repealed: see now Council Regulation (EC) 883/2004 of 29 April 2004 (OJ L166, 30.4.2004, p 1) on the coordination of social security systems; and WELFARE BENEFITS AND STATE PENSIONS vol 104 (2014) PARA 600 et seq).
9 Statutory Paternity Pay and Statutory Adoption Pay (Persons Abroad and Mariners) Regulations 2002, SI 2002/2821, reg 3(b).
10 Ie for the purposes of the Social Security Contributions and Benefits Act 1992 Pt XIIZA (statutory paternity pay).
11 See the Statutory Paternity Pay and Statutory Adoption Pay (Persons Abroad and Mariners) Regulations 2002, SI 2002/2821, reg 3.
12 Ie under the Social Security Contributions and Benefits Act 1992 s 6 (see WELFARE BENEFITS AND STATE PENSIONS vol 104 (2014) PARA 385) or the Social Security (Contributions) Regulations 2001, SI 2001/1004, reg 146 (payment of contributions for periods abroad: see WELFARE BENEFITS AND STATE PENSIONS vol 104 (2014) PARA 380).
13 Ie for the purposes of the Social Security Contributions and Benefits Act 1992 Pt XIIZA (statutory paternity pay), but subject to the Statutory Paternity Pay and Statutory Adoption Pay (Persons Abroad and Mariners) Regulations 2002, SI 2002/2821, reg 8(3) (see PARA 452).
14 Statutory Paternity Pay and Statutory Adoption Pay (Persons Abroad and Mariners) Regulations 2002, SI 2002/2821, reg 4.

452. Treatment of mariners for purposes of statutory paternity pay. A mariner[1] engaged in employment on board a home-trade ship[2] with an employer[3] who has a place of business within the United Kingdom is to be treated as an employee[4] for the purposes of the statutory paternity pay provisions that are set out in Part XIIZA of the Social Security Contributions and Benefits Act 1992[5], notwithstanding that he may not be employed in Great Britain[6]. However, a mariner who is engaged in employment:

(1) on a foreign-going ship[7]; or
(2) on a home-trade ship with an employer who does not have a place of business within the United Kingdom[8],

is not to be so treated as an employee, notwithstanding that he may have been employed in Great Britain[9].

1 For these purposes, 'mariner' means a person who is or has been in employment under a contract of service either as a master or member of the crew of any ship or vessel, or in any other capacity on board any ship or vessel where: (1) the employment in that other capacity is for the purposes of that ship or vessel or her crew or any passengers or cargo or mails carried by the ship or vessel; and (2) the contract is entered into in the United Kingdom with a view to its performance, in whole or in part, while the ship or vessel is on her voyage, but does not include a person in so far as her employment is as a serving member of the forces: see the Statutory Paternity Pay and Statutory Adoption Pay (Persons Abroad and Mariners) Regulations 2002, SI 2002/2821, reg 1(2). The expressions 'ship' and 'ship or vessel', except in reg 8(3) (see the text and notes 7–9), include hovercraft: see reg 1(4) (added by SI 2010/151). As to the meaning of 'United Kingdom' for these purposes see PARA 407 note 7. Although 'contract of service' is defined for the purposes of statutory sick pay (see PARA 558 note 2), it is not so defined under the other statutory pay provisions (for which purposes see generally PARA 1 note 1).

2 For these purposes, 'home-trade ship' includes: (1) every ship or vessel employed in trading or going within the following limits, ie the United Kingdom (including for this purpose the Republic of Ireland), the Channel Islands, the Isle of Man, and the continent of Europe between the river Elbe and Brest inclusive; (2) every fishing vessel not proceeding beyond the following limits: on the South, Latitude 48° 30' N; on the West, Longitude 12° W; on the North, Latitude 61° N: see the Statutory Paternity Pay and Statutory Adoption Pay (Persons Abroad and Mariners) Regulations 2002, SI 2002/2821, reg 1(2) (definition added by SI 2010/151).

3 As to the meaning of 'employer' for these purposes see PARA 456.

4 As to the meaning of 'employee' for these purposes see PARA 448.

5 Ie for the purposes of the Social Security Contributions and Benefits Act 1992 Pt XIIZA (ss 171ZA–171ZK) (statutory paternity pay). As to the meaning of 'statutory paternity pay' see PARA 443.

6 Statutory Paternity Pay and Statutory Adoption Pay (Persons Abroad and Mariners) Regulations 2002, SI 2002/2821, reg 8(2). As to the meaning of 'Great Britain' for these purposes see PARA 407 note 7.

7 Statutory Paternity Pay and Statutory Adoption Pay (Persons Abroad and Mariners) Regulations 2002, SI 2002/2821, reg 8(3)(a). For these purposes, 'foreign-going ship' means any ship or vessel which is not a home-trade ship: see reg 1(2) (definition added by SI 2010/151).

8 Statutory Paternity Pay and Statutory Adoption Pay (Persons Abroad and Mariners) Regulations 2002, SI 2002/2821, reg 8(3)(b).

9 See the Statutory Paternity Pay and Statutory Adoption Pay (Persons Abroad and Mariners) Regulations 2002, SI 2002/2821, reg 8(3).

453. Treatment of persons employed in operations on the continental shelf for purposes of statutory paternity pay. A person in prescribed employment[1] is to be treated as an employee[2] for the purposes of the statutory paternity pay provisions that are set out in Part XIIZA of the Social Security Contributions and Benefits Act 1992[3], notwithstanding that he may not be employed in Great Britain[4].

1 For these purposes, 'prescribed employment' means any employment (whether under a contract of service or not) in a designated area in connection with continental shelf operations (as defined in the Social Security Contributions and Benefits Act 1992 s 120(2) (see PARA 449 note 10)); and 'designated area' means any area which may from time to time be designated by Order in Council under the Continental Shelf Act 1964 (see s 1(7); and ENERGY AND CLIMATE CHANGE vol 44 (2011) PARAS 1033, 1040; INTERNATIONAL RELATIONS LAW vol 61 (2010) PARA 172) as

an area within which the rights of the United Kingdom with respect to the sea bed and subsoil and their natural resources may be exercised: see the Statutory Paternity Pay and Statutory Adoption Pay (Persons Abroad and Mariners) Regulations 2002, SI 2002/2821, reg 9(1). As to the meaning of 'United Kingdom' for these purposes see PARA 407 note 7. Although 'contract of service' is defined for the purposes of statutory sick pay (see PARA 558 note 2), it is not so defined under the other statutory pay provisions (for which purposes see generally PARA 1 note 1).

2 As to the meaning of 'employee' for these purposes see PARA 448.

3 Ie for the purposes of the Social Security Contributions and Benefits Act 1992 Pt XIIZA (ss 171ZA–171ZK) (statutory paternity pay). As to the meaning of 'statutory paternity pay' see PARA 443.

4 Statutory Paternity Pay and Statutory Adoption Pay (Persons Abroad and Mariners) Regulations 2002, SI 2002/2821, reg 9(2). As to the meaning of 'Great Britain' for these purposes see PARA 407 note 7.

454. Crown employment for purposes of statutory paternity pay. The statutory paternity pay provisions that are set out in Part XIIZA of the Social Security Contributions and Benefits Act 1992[1] apply in relation to persons employed by or under the Crown as they apply in relation to persons employed otherwise than by or under the Crown[2].

1 Ie the provisions of the Social Security Contributions and Benefits Act 1992 Pt XIIZA (ss 171ZA–171ZK) (statutory paternity pay). As to the meaning of 'statutory paternity pay' see PARA 443.

2 Social Security Contributions and Benefits Act 1992 s 171ZH (added by the Employment Act 2002 s 2).

455. Treatment of National Health Service employees for purposes of statutory paternity pay. Where, in consequence of the establishment of one or more National Health Service trusts[1], a person's contract of employment is treated by a scheme[2] as divided so as to constitute two or more contracts, or where an order[3] provides that a person's contract of employment is so divided, regulations[4] may make provision enabling the person to elect for all of those contracts to be treated as one contract for the purposes of the statutory paternity pay provisions that are set out in Part XIIZA of the Social Security Contributions and Benefits Act 1992[5], or such of those provisions as may be prescribed[6]. Any such regulations may prescribe[7]:

(1) the conditions that must be satisfied if a person is to be entitled to make such an election[8];

(2) the manner in which, and the time within which, such an election is to be made[9];

(3) the persons to whom, and the manner in which, notice of such an election is to be given[10];

(4) the information which a person who makes such an election is to provide, and the persons to whom, and the time within which, he is to provide it[11];

(5) the time for which such an election is to have effect[12];

(6) which one of the person's employers[13] under the two or more contracts is to be regarded for the purposes of statutory paternity pay as his employer under the one contract[14].

The powers so conferred are without prejudice to any other power[15] to make regulations[16].

Accordingly, where, in consequence of the establishment of one or more National Health Service trusts[17], a person's contract of employment is treated by a scheme[18] as divided so as to constitute two or more contracts, he may elect for

The conditions prescribed under s 171ZA(2)(a) are those prescribed in the Paternity and Adoption Leave Regulations 2002, SI 2002/2788, reg 4(2)(b), (c): Statutory Paternity Pay and Statutory Adoption Pay (General) Regulations 2002, SI 2002/2822, reg 4. Accordingly, the conditions are that the person:

(1) is either: (a) the father of the child (Paternity and Adoption Leave Regulations 2002, SI 2002/2788, reg 4(2)(b)(i)); or (b) married to, the civil partner or the partner of the child's mother, but not the child's father (reg 4(2)(b)(ii) (reg 4(2)(b)(ii), (c)(ii) amended by SI 2005/2114));

(2) has, or expects to have: (a) if he is the child's father, responsibility for the upbringing of the child (Paternity and Adoption Leave Regulations 2002, SI 2002/2788, reg 4(2)(c)(i)); or (b) if he is the mother's husband, civil partner or partner but not the child's father, the main responsibility, apart from any responsibility of the mother, for the upbringing of the child (reg 4(2)(c)(ii) (as so amended)).

An employee is to be treated as having satisfied the condition in reg 4(2)(b)(ii) (see head (1)(b) above) if he would have satisfied it but for the fact that the child's mother has died (reg 4(4)); and an employee is to be treated as having satisfied the condition in reg 4(2)(c) (see head (2) above) if he would have satisfied it but for the fact that the child was stillborn after 24 weeks of pregnancy or has died (reg 4(5)). As to the meaning of 'child' see PARA 370 note 2; and as to the meaning of 'partner' for these purposes see PARA 370 note 7.

Marriage of same sex couples is lawful in the law of England and Wales, and such marriages have the same effect as marriages of opposite sex couples: see the Marriage (Same Sex Couples) Act 2013 s 1(1), 11(1); and **MATRIMONIAL AND CIVIL PARTNERSHIP LAW** vol 72 (2009) PARA 1 et seq.

6 Social Security Contributions and Benefits Act 1992 s 171ZA(2)(a)(ii) (as added: see note 1). See note 5.

7 Ie under the Social Security Contributions and Benefits Act 1992 s 171ZB(1): see PARA 443. A person's entitlement to statutory paternity pay under s 171ZB is not affected by the placement for adoption of more than one child as part of the same arrangement: s 171ZB(6) (s 171ZB as added (see note 1); s 171ZB(6) amended by the Work and Families Act 2006 Sch 1 para 13; and the Children and Families Act 2014 Sch 7 paras 6, 13(1), (4)). See also note 8.

8 Social Security Contributions and Benefits Act 1992 s 171ZB(2)(a)(i) (as added: see note 1). As to the meaning of 'United Kingdom' for these purposes see PARA 407 note 7. As to the law relating to child adoption see **CHILDREN AND YOUNG PERSONS** vol 9 (2012) PARA 360 et seq.

The conditions prescribed under s 171ZB(2)(a) are that a person:

(1) is married to, the civil partner or the partner of a child's adopter (or in a case where there are two adopters, married to, the civil partner or the partner of the other adopter) (Statutory Paternity Pay and Statutory Adoption Pay (General) Regulations 2002, SI 2002/2822, reg 11(1)(a) (amended by SI 2005/2114)); and

(2) has, or expects to have, the main responsibility (apart from the responsibility of the child's adopter, or in a case where there two adopters, together with the other adopter) for the upbringing of the child (Statutory Paternity Pay and Statutory Adoption Pay (General) Regulations 2002, SI 2002/2822, reg 11(1)(b)).

For these purposes, 'partner' means a person (whether of a different sex or the same sex) who lives with the adopter and the child in an enduring family relationship but is not the adopter's parent, grandparent, sister, brother, aunt or uncle: see reg 11(2), (2A) (reg 11(2), (3) amended, reg 11(2A) added, by SI 2004/488). The references to relationships are references to relationships of the full blood or half blood, or, in the case of an adopted person, such of those relationships as would exist but for the adoption, and include the relationship of a child with his adoptive or former adoptive parents but do not include any other adoptive relationships: Statutory Paternity Pay and Statutory Adoption Pay (General) Regulations 2002, SI 2002/2822, reg 11(3) (as so amended). For these purposes, 'adopter', in relation to a child, means a person who has been matched with the child for adoption (see reg 2(1)); and a person is matched with a child for adoption when an adoption agency decides that that person would be a suitable adoptive parent for the child, either individually or jointly with another person (reg 2(2)(a)).

The Social Security Contributions and Benefits Act 1992 s 171ZB has effect in a case involving a child placed under the Children Act 1989 s 22C (local authority's duty to provide child is in its care with accommodation: see **CHILDREN AND YOUNG PERSONS** vol 10 (2012) PARA 858) by a local authority in England with a local authority foster parent who has been approved as a prospective adopter with the following modifications (see the Social Security Contributions and Benefits Act 1992 s 171ZB(8) (s 171ZB as so added; s 171ZB(8), (9) added by the Children and Families Act 2014 s 121(3))):

(1) the references in the Social Security Contributions and Benefits Act 1992 s 171ZB(2) to a child being placed for adoption under the law of any part of the United Kingdom are

to be treated as references to a child being placed under the Children Act 1989 s 22C in that manner (Social Security Contributions and Benefits Act 1992 s 171ZB(8)(a) (as so added));

(2) the reference in s 171ZB(3) (see note 13) to the week in which the adopter is notified of being matched with the child for the purposes of adoption is to be treated as a reference to the week in which the prospective adopter is notified that the child is to be, or is expected to be, placed with the prospective adopter under the Children Act 1989 s 22C (Social Security Contributions and Benefits Act 1992 s 171ZB(8)(b) (as so added));

(3) the reference in s 171ZB(6) (note 7) to placement for adoption is to be treated as a reference to placement under the Children Act 1989 s 22C (Social Security Contributions and Benefits Act 1992 s 171ZB(8)(c) (as so added));

(4) the definition in s 171ZB(7) (see note 13) is to be treated as if it were a definition of 'prospective adopter' (s 171ZB(8)(d) (as so added)).

Where, by virtue of s 171ZB(8), a person becomes entitled to statutory paternity pay in connection with the placement of a child under the Children Act 1989 s 22C, the person may not become entitled to payments of statutory paternity pay in connection with the placement of the child for adoption: Social Security Contributions and Benefits Act 1992 s 171ZB(9) (as so added). For these purposes, 'local authority' has the same meaning as in the Children Act 1989 (see s 105(1); and CHILDREN AND YOUNG PERSONS vol 9 (2012) PARA 155); and 'local authority foster parent' has the same meaning as in the Children Act 1989 (see s 22C(12); and CHILDREN AND YOUNG PERSONS vol 10 (2012) PARA 845): see the Social Security Contributions and Benefits Act 1992 s 171ZJ(1) (s 171ZJ as added (see note 1); definitions added by the Children and Families Act 2014 s 121(7)(a)). As to the meaning of 'England' see PARA 2 note 12. Where statutory paternity pay is payable to a person by virtue of the Social Security Contributions and Benefits Act 1992 s 171ZB(8), then s 171ZE(3)(b), (10) (paternity pay period: see PARA 465 note 4) has effect with modifications: see s 171ZE(12); and PARA 465 note 4.

Marriage of same sex couples is lawful in the law of England and Wales, and such marriages have the same effect as marriages of opposite sex couples: see the Marriage (Same Sex Couples) Act 2013 s 1(1), 11(1); and MATRIMONIAL AND CIVIL PARTNERSHIP LAW vol 72 (2009) PARA 1 et seq.

9 Social Security Contributions and Benefits Act 1992 s 171ZB(2)(a)(ii) (as added: see note 1). See note 8.

10 As to the meaning of 'employed earner' see the Social Security Contributions and Benefits Act 1992 s 2(1)(a), (3); and WELFARE BENEFITS AND STATE PENSIONS vol 104 (2014) PARA 381.

11 As to the meaning of 'employer' for these purposes see PARA 456.

12 As to the meaning of 'week' for these purposes see PARA 445 note 14.

13 Social Security Contributions and Benefits Act 1992 s 171ZA(2)(b) (as added: see note 1); s 171ZB(2)(b) (as added: see note 1). The references in s 171ZA(2) to the relevant week are references to the week immediately preceding the fourteenth week before the expected week of the child's birth (s 171ZA(3) (as so added)); and the references in s 171ZB(2) to the relevant week are references to the week in which the adopter is notified of being matched with the child for the purposes of adoption (s 171ZB(3) (as so added)). For these purposes, 'adopter', in relation to a person who satisfies the condition under s 171ZB(2)(a)(ii) (see the text and note 9), means the person by reference to whom he satisfies that condition: see s 171ZB(7) (as so added). See note 8.

14 As from a day to be appointed under the Welfare Reform Act 2012 s 150(3), the Social Security Contributions and Benefits Act 1992 ss 171ZA(2)(ba), 171ZB(2)(ba) are added by the Welfare Reform Act 2012 s 63(1), (4)(a), (5)(a). However, at the date at which this volume states the law, no such day had been appointed.

15 Social Security Contributions and Benefits Act 1992 s 171ZA(2)(ba) (s 171ZA as added (see note 1); s 171ZA(ba) prospectively added (see note 14)); s 171ZB(2)(ba) (s 171ZB as added (see note 1); s 171ZB(ba) prospectively added (see note 14)).

As from a day to be appointed under the Welfare Reform Act 2012 s 150(3), the Social Security Contributions and Benefits Act 1992 ss 171ZA(3A), 171ZB(3A) are added allowing for regulations to provide for circumstances in which s 171ZA(2)(ba) (not yet in force) or s 171ZB(2)(ba) (not yet in force), as, the case may be, does not apply: see ss 171ZA(3A), 171ZB(3A) (prospectively added by the Welfare Reform Act 2012 s 63(1), (4)(b), (5)(b)). However, at the date at which this volume states the law, no such day had been appointed.

16 As to the meaning of 'normal weekly earnings' see PARA 468.

17 Ie under the Social Security Contributions and Benefits Act 1992 s 5(1)(a) (earnings limits and thresholds for Class 1 contributions: see WELFARE BENEFITS AND STATE PENSIONS vol 104 (2014) PARA 384).

18 Social Security Contributions and Benefits Act 1992 s 171ZA(2)(c) (as added: see note 1); s 171ZB(2)(c) (as added: see note 1).
19 Social Security Contributions and Benefits Act 1992 s 171ZA(2)(d) (as added: see note 1); s 171ZB(2)(d) (as added: see note 1). As to employed earner's employment within the meaning of the Social Security Contributions and Benefits Act 1992 see WELFARE BENEFITS AND STATE PENSIONS vol 104 (2014) PARA 176.
20 Social Security Contributions and Benefits Act 1992 s 171ZB(2)(e) (as added: see note 1). A person may not elect to receive statutory paternity pay if he has elected in accordance with s 171ZL (see PARA 503) to receive statutory adoption pay: s 171ZB(4) (s 171ZB as so added; s 171ZB(4) amended by the Work and Families Act 2006 Sch 1 para 13; and the Children and Families Act 2014 Sch 7 paras 6, 13(1), (3)).
21 Ie the conditions specified in the Social Security Contributions and Benefits Act 1992 s 171ZA(2)(b)–(d) (see heads (2) to (5) in the text): see the Statutory Paternity Pay and Statutory Adoption Pay (General) Regulations 2002, SI 2002/2822, reg 5.
22 See the Statutory Paternity Pay and Statutory Adoption Pay (General) Regulations 2002, SI 2002/2822, reg 5. The modifications specified are that the conditions set out in heads (2) to (5) in the text are substituted by the following conditions (see reg 5), namely that:
   (1) the person would, but for the date on which the birth occurred, have been in employed earner's employment with an employer for a continuous period of at least 26 weeks ending with the week immediately preceding the fourteenth week before the expected week of the child's birth (reg 5(a)); and
   (2) his normal weekly earnings for the period of eight weeks ending with the week immediately preceding the week in which the child is born are not less than the lower earnings limit in force under the Social Security Contributions and Benefits Act 1992 s 5(1)(a) (earnings limits and thresholds for Class 1 contributions: see WELFARE BENEFITS AND STATE PENSIONS vol 104 (2014) PARA 384) immediately before the commencement of the week in which the child is born (Statutory Paternity Pay and Statutory Adoption Pay (General) Regulations 2002, SI 2002/2822, reg 5(b)).

   As to the meaning of 'expected week', in relation to the birth of a child, for these purposes see PARA 446 note 23.
23 Ie under the Statutory Paternity Pay and Statutory Adoption Pay (Persons Abroad and Mariners) Regulations 2002, SI 2002/2821, reg 3: see PARA 451.
24 See the Statutory Paternity Pay and Statutory Adoption Pay (Persons Abroad and Mariners) Regulations 2002, SI 2002/2821, reg 5(1), (2) (reg 5 substituted by SI 2010/151).
25 As to the meaning of 'Great Britain' for these purposes see PARA 407 note 7.
26 For these purposes, 'week' means a period of seven days beginning with Sunday: see the Statutory Paternity Pay and Statutory Adoption Pay (Persons Abroad and Mariners) Regulations 2002, SI 2002/2821, reg 1(2).
27 Statutory Paternity Pay and Statutory Adoption Pay (Persons Abroad and Mariners) Regulations 2002, SI 2002/2821, reg 5(1)(a) (as substituted: see note 24).
28 Statutory Paternity Pay and Statutory Adoption Pay (Persons Abroad and Mariners) Regulations 2002, SI 2002/2821, reg 5(2)(a) (as substituted: see note 24). For these purposes, a person is matched with a child for adoption when an adoption agency decides that that person would be a suitable adoptive parent for the child; and a person is notified of having been matched with a child on the date on which the person receives notification of the agency's decision, under the Adoption Agencies Regulations 2005, SI 2005/389, reg 33(3)(a) (see CHILDREN AND YOUNG PERSONS vol 9 (2012) PARA 482), or under the Adoption Agencies (Wales) Regulations 2005, SI 2005/1313, reg 28(3) (see CHILDREN AND YOUNG PERSONS vol 9 (2012) PARA 478): see the Statutory Paternity Pay and Statutory Adoption Pay (Persons Abroad and Mariners) Regulations 2002, SI 2002/2821, reg 1(3) (substituted by SI 2010/151).
29 See the Statutory Paternity Pay and Statutory Adoption Pay (Persons Abroad and Mariners) Regulations 2002, SI 2002/2821, reg 5(1)(b), (2)(b) (as substituted: see note 24). As to the meaning of 'EEA state' for these purposes see PARA 451 note 1.
30 Ie for the purposes of the Social Security Contributions and Benefits Act 1992 s 171ZA (entitlement (birth): see also PARA 443) or s 171ZB (entitlement (adoption): see also PARA 443), as the case may be.
31 See the Statutory Paternity Pay and Statutory Adoption Pay (Persons Abroad and Mariners) Regulations 2002, SI 2002/2821, regs 1(2), 5(1), (2) (as substituted: see note 24).

458. Continuous employment; in general. Where in any week[1] a person is, for the whole or part of the week[2]:

(1) incapable of work in consequence of sickness or injury[3]; or

(2) absent from work on account of a temporary cessation of work[4];
(3) absent from work in circumstances such that, by arrangement or custom, he is regarded as continuing in the employment of his employer for all purposes or for any purpose[5],

and he returns to work for his employer after the incapacity for or absence from work, that week is to be treated for the purpose of the provisions relating to statutory paternity pay[6] as part of a continuous period of employment with that employer, notwithstanding that no contract of service exists with that employer in respect of that week[7].

Where a person:

(a) is an employee in an employed earner's[8] employment in which the custom is for the employer[9]:
  (i) to offer work for a fixed period of not more than 26 consecutive weeks[10];
  (ii) to offer work for such period on two or more occasions in a year for periods which do not overlap[11]; and
  (iii) to offer the work available to those persons who had worked for him during the last or a recent such period[12]; but
(b) is absent from work because of incapacity arising from some specific disease or bodily or mental disablement[13],

then in his case the provisions governing continuous employment[14] apply subject to modification[15].

1 As to the meaning of 'week' for these purposes see PARA 445 note 14.
2 See the Statutory Paternity Pay and Statutory Adoption Pay (General) Regulations 2002, SI 2002/2822, regs 31(1), 33(1). Regulation 33(1) is subject to regs 31(1), 33(2)–(3) (see the text and notes 3, 8–15): see regs 31(1), 33(1).
3 Statutory Paternity Pay and Statutory Adoption Pay (General) Regulations 2002, SI 2002/2822, regs 31(1), 33(1)(a). Incapacity for work which lasts for more than 26 consecutive weeks does not count for the purposes of head (1) in the text, however: regs 31(1), 33(2).
4 Statutory Paternity Pay and Statutory Adoption Pay (General) Regulations 2002, SI 2002/2822, regs 31(1), 33(1)(b).
5 Statutory Paternity Pay and Statutory Adoption Pay (General) Regulations 2002, SI 2002/2822, regs 31(1), 33(1)(c).
6 Ie for the purposes of the Social Security Contributions and Benefits Act 1992 s 171ZA (entitlement (birth): see PARA 443) or s 171ZB (entitlement (adoption): see PARA 443), as the case may be.
7 See the Statutory Paternity Pay and Statutory Adoption Pay (General) Regulations 2002, SI 2002/2822, regs 31(1), 33(1). Although 'contract of service' is defined for the purposes of statutory sick pay (see PARA 558 note 2), it is not so defined under the other statutory pay provisions (for which purposes see generally PARA 1 note 1).
8 As to the meaning of 'employed earner' see the Social Security Contributions and Benefits Act 1992 s 2(1)(a), (3); and **WELFARE BENEFITS AND STATE PENSIONS** vol 104 (2014) PARA 381.
9 See the Statutory Paternity Pay and Statutory Adoption Pay (General) Regulations 2002, SI 2002/2822, regs 31(1), 33(3)(a).
10 Statutory Paternity Pay and Statutory Adoption Pay (General) Regulations 2002, SI 2002/2822, regs 31(1), 33(3)(a)(i).
11 Statutory Paternity Pay and Statutory Adoption Pay (General) Regulations 2002, SI 2002/2822, regs 31(1), 33(3)(a)(ii).
12 Statutory Paternity Pay and Statutory Adoption Pay (General) Regulations 2002, SI 2002/2822, regs 31(1), 33(3)(a)(iii).
13 Statutory Paternity Pay and Statutory Adoption Pay (General) Regulations 2002, SI 2002/2822, regs 31(1), 33(3)(b).
14 Ie the Statutory Paternity Pay and Statutory Adoption Pay (General) Regulations 2002, SI 2002/2822, regs 31(1), 33(1): see the text and notes 1–7.

(i) the date on which the child is placed with the adopter[17] or, where the person is at work on that day, the following day[18];

(ii) the date falling such number of days after the date on which the child is placed with the adopter as the person may specify[19];

(iii) a predetermined date, specified by the person, which is later than the date on which the child is expected to be placed with the adopter[20].

A person may choose for statutory paternity pay (birth) or statutory paternity pay (adoption) (as the case may be) to be paid in respect of a period of a week[21].

1 As to the meaning of 'statutory paternity pay' see PARA 443.

2 See the Social Security Contributions and Benefits Act 1992 s 171ZE(2) (s 171ZE added by the Employment Act 2002 s 2; the Social Security Contributions and Benefits Act 1992 s 171ZE(2) amended by the Work and Families Act 2006 Sch 1 para 16(1), (2); and the Children and Families Act 2014 s 123(1), (3)(a), Sch 7 paras 6, 16(1), (3)(a)).

3 As to the meaning of 'week' for these purposes see PARA 445 note 14.

4 Social Security Contributions and Benefits Act 1992 s 171ZE(2)(a) (s 171ZE as added (see note 2); s 171ZE(2)(a), (b) substituted by the Children and Families Act 2014 s 123(1), (3)(a)). For these purposes, the qualifying period is determined in accordance with regulations, which must secure that it is a period of at least 56 days beginning:

(1) in the case of a person to whom the conditions in the Social Security Contributions and Benefits Act 1992 s 171ZA(2) (see PARA 457) apply, with the date of the child's birth (s 171ZE(3)(a) (as so added)); and

(2) in the case of a person to whom the conditions in s 171ZB(2) (see PARA 457) apply, with the date of the child's placement for adoption (s 171ZE(3)(b) (as so added)).

Where more than one child is born as a result of the same pregnancy, the reference in head (1) above to the date of the child's birth must be read as a reference to the date of birth of the first child born as a result of the pregnancy (s 171ZE(9) (as so added)); and where more than one child is placed for adoption as part of the same arrangement, the reference in head (2) above to the date of the child's placement must be read as a reference to the date of placement of the first child to be placed as part of the arrangement (s 171ZE(10) (as so added)). Where statutory paternity pay is payable to a person by virtue of s 171ZB(8) (see PARA 457 note 8), s 171ZE has effect as if: (a) the references in s 171ZE(3)(b) (see head (2) above), and in s 171ZE(10), to placement for adoption were references to placement under the Children Act 1989 s 22C (local authority's duty to provide child is in its care with accommodation: see **CHILDREN AND YOUNG PERSONS** vol 10 (2012) PARA 858) (Social Security Contributions and Benefits Act 1992 s 171ZE(12)(a) (s 171ZE(12) added by the Children and Families Act 2014 s 121(4)); and (b) the references in the Social Security Contributions and Benefits Act 1992 s 171ZE(10) to being placed for adoption were references to being placed under the Children Act 1989 s 22C (Social Security Contributions and Benefits Act 1992 s 171ZE(12)(b) (as so added)).

Accordingly, the qualifying period for the purposes of s 171ZE(2) (statutory paternity pay (birth)) is a period which begins on the date of the child's birth and ends (see the Statutory Paternity Pay and Statutory Adoption Pay (General) Regulations 2002, SI 2002/2822, reg 8):

(a)except in the case referred to in head (þ) below, 56 days after that date (reg 8(a));

(b)in a case where the child is born before the first day of the expected week of its birth, 56 days after that day (reg 8(b)).

The qualifying period for the purposes of the Social Security Contributions and Benefits Act 1992 s 171ZE(2) (statutory paternity pay (adoption)) is a period of 56 days beginning with the date of the child's placement for adoption: reg 14.

5 Social Security Contributions and Benefits Act 1992 s 171ZE(2)(b) (s 171ZE as added (see note 2); s 171ZE(2)(b) as substituted (see note 4)). Provision under head (2) in the text is to secure that the prescribed number of weeks is not less than two: s 171ZE(2A) (s 171ZE as so added; s 171ZE(2A) added by the Children and Families Act 2014 s 123(1), (3)(b)). A statutory instrument containing, whether alone or with other provisions, regulations made by virtue of the Social Security Contributions and Benefits Act 1992 s 171ZE(2)(b), must not be made unless a draft of the instrument has been laid before Parliament and been approved by a resolution of each House: see s 176(1)(a) (amended by the Social Security (Incapacity for Work) Act 1994 Sch 1 para 37, Sch 2; the Welfare Reform and Pensions Act 1999 Sch 8 Pt II paras 20, 25; the Employment Act 2002 Sch 7 paras 2, 7; the National Insurance Contributions Act 2006 ss 1(2)(a), 3(2); the Work and Families Act 2006 Sch 1 para 22; the Welfare Reform Act 2007 ss 31(2), 67, Sch 8; the National Insurance Contributions Act 2014 ss 9(1), (5), 13(1), (3), 25,

Sch 15 paras 1, 11; the Pensions Act 2014 s 25, Sch 15 Pt 1 paras 1, 11; the Children and Families Act 2014 ss 119(2), 123(1), (4), Sch 7 para 22; and SI 1995/512). See note 6.

6 See the Social Security Contributions and Benefits Act 1992 s 171ZE(2) (as added and amended: see note 2). As to the making of regulations under the Social Security Contributions and Benefits Act 1992 generally see PARA 407 note 3. See also note 5. In exercise of the powers conferred by s 171ZE(2)(a), (b)(i), (3) (s 171ZE(2)(a), (b) as originally enacted), the Secretary of State has made the Statutory Paternity Pay and Statutory Adoption Pay (General) Regulations 2002, SI 2002/2822 (see the text and notes 8–21) and the Statutory Paternity Pay (Adoption) and Statutory Adoption Pay (Adoptions from Overseas) (No 2) Regulations 2003, SI 2003/1194 (see PARA 485).

7 Social Security Contributions and Benefits Act 1992 s 171ZE(2B) (s 171ZE as added (see note 2); s 171ZE(2B) added by the Children and Families Act 2014 s 123(1), (3)(c)).

8 As to the meaning of 'statutory paternity pay (birth)' for these purposes see PARA 446 note 20.

9 Ie subject to the Statutory Paternity Pay and Statutory Adoption Pay (General) Regulations 2002, SI 2002/2822, reg 8: see note 4.

10 See the Statutory Paternity Pay and Statutory Adoption Pay (General) Regulations 2002, SI 2002/2822, reg 6(1). A choice made in accordance with reg 6(1) is not irrevocable, but where a person subsequently makes a different choice in relation to the beginning of the statutory pay period, the Social Security Contributions and Benefits Act 1992 s 171ZC(1) (see PARA 462) applies to it: Statutory Paternity Pay and Statutory Adoption Pay (General) Regulations 2002, SI 2002/2822, reg 6(4). See also notes 11–13.

11 Statutory Paternity Pay and Statutory Adoption Pay (General) Regulations 2002, SI 2002/2822, reg 6(1)(a). Where the choice made by a person in accordance with reg 6(1), and notified in accordance with the Social Security Contributions and Benefits Act 1992 s 171ZC(1) (see PARA 462), is that mentioned in head (a) or head (b) in the text, the person must give further notice to the person liable to pay him statutory paternity pay, as soon as is reasonably practicable after the child's birth, of the date the child was born: Statutory Paternity Pay and Statutory Adoption Pay (General) Regulations 2002, SI 2002/2822, reg 7(1). The date may be any date chosen in accordance with reg 6(1): see reg 7(3). For these purposes, a notice given in writing contained in an envelope which is properly addressed and sent by prepaid post is deemed to be given on the date on which it is posted: see regs 31(1), 47.

12 Statutory Paternity Pay and Statutory Adoption Pay (General) Regulations 2002, SI 2002/2822, reg 6(1)(b). See note 11.

13 Statutory Paternity Pay and Statutory Adoption Pay (General) Regulations 2002, SI 2002/2822, reg 6(1)(c). As to the meaning of 'expected week', in relation to the birth of a child, see PARA 446 note 23. Where the choice made by a person in accordance with reg 6(1), and notified in accordance with the Social Security Contributions and Benefits Act 1992 s 171ZC(1) (see PARA 462), is that specified in head (c) in the text, and the date of the child's birth is later than the date so specified, the person must, if he wishes to claim statutory paternity pay (birth), give notice to the person liable to pay it, as soon as is reasonably practicable, that the period in respect of which statutory paternity pay is to be paid is to begin on a date different from that originally chosen by him: reg 7(2). The date may be any date chosen in accordance with reg 6(1): see reg 7(3). See note 11.

14 As to the meaning of 'statutory paternity pay (adoption)' for these purposes see PARA 446 note 20.

15 Ie subject to the Statutory Paternity Pay and Statutory Adoption Pay (General) Regulations 2002, SI 2002/2822, reg 14: see note 4.

16 See the Statutory Paternity Pay and Statutory Adoption Pay (General) Regulations 2002, SI 2002/2822, reg 12(1). A choice made in accordance with reg 12(1) is not irrevocable, but where a person subsequently makes a different choice in relation to the beginning of the statutory pay period, the Social Security Contributions and Benefits Act 1992 s 171ZC(1) (see PARA 462) applies to it: Statutory Paternity Pay and Statutory Adoption Pay (General) Regulations 2002, SI 2002/2822, reg 12(4). See also notes 18–20.

17 As to the meaning of 'adopter' see PARA 457 note 8.

18 Statutory Paternity Pay and Statutory Adoption Pay (General) Regulations 2002, SI 2002/2822, reg 12(1)(a). Where the choice made by a person in accordance with reg 12(1), and notified in accordance with the Social Security Contributions and Benefits Act 1992 s 171ZC(1) (see PARA 462), is that mentioned in head (i) or head (ii) in the text, the person must give further notice to the person liable to pay him statutory paternity pay, as soon as is reasonably practicable, of the date on which the placement occurred: Statutory Paternity Pay and Statutory Adoption Pay (General) Regulations 2002, SI 2002/2822, reg 13(1). The date may be any date chosen in accordance with reg 12(1): see reg 13(3).

19 Statutory Paternity Pay and Statutory Adoption Pay (General) Regulations 2002, SI 2002/2822, reg 12(1)(b). See note 18.

20 Statutory Paternity Pay and Statutory Adoption Pay (General) Regulations 2002, SI 2002/2822, reg 12(1)(c). Where the choice made by a person in accordance with reg 12(1), and notified in accordance with the Social Security Contributions and Benefits Act 1992 s 171ZC(1) (see PARA 462), is that mentioned in head (iii) in the text, and the child is placed for adoption later than the date so specified, the person must, if he wishes to claim statutory paternity pay (adoption), give notice to the person liable to pay it, as soon as is reasonably practicable, that the period in respect of which statutory paternity pay is to be paid is to begin on a date different from that originally chosen by him: reg 13(2). The date may be any date chosen in accordance with reg 12(1): see reg 13(3). See note 18.

21 See the Statutory Paternity Pay and Statutory Adoption Pay (General) Regulations 2002, SI 2002/2822, regs 6(3), 12(3).

466. Work during a paternity pay period. Where, in a case where statutory paternity pay[1] is being paid to a person who works during the paternity pay period[2] for an employer[3] who is not liable to pay him statutory paternity pay[4] and for whom he did not work, in the case of statutory paternity pay (birth)[5], in the week immediately preceding the fourteenth week before the expected week of the child's birth[6] or, as the case may be, in the case of statutory paternity pay (adoption)[7], in which he is notified of being matched with the child[8], there is no liability to pay statutory paternity pay in respect of any remaining part of the paternity pay period[9]. In such a case, the person must notify the person liable to pay statutory paternity pay within seven days of the first day during which he works during the paternity pay period[10]; and such notification must be in writing if the person who has been liable to pay statutory paternity pay so requests[11].

1 As to the meaning of 'statutory paternity pay' see PARA 443.

2 As to the meaning of 'paternity pay period' see PARA 465.

3 As to the meaning of 'employer' for these purposes see PARA 456.

4 As to liability to make payments of statutory paternity pay see PARA 443 et seq.

5 As to the meaning of 'statutory paternity pay (birth)' see PARA 446 note 20.

6 Ie the employer does not falls within the Statutory Paternity Pay and Statutory Adoption Pay (General) Regulations 2002, SI 2002/2822, reg 10(b): see PARA 446.

7 As to the meaning of 'statutory paternity pay (adoption)' see PARA 446 note 20.

8 Ie the employer does not fall within the Statutory Paternity Pay and Statutory Adoption Pay (General) Regulations 2002, SI 2002/2822, reg 16(b): see PARA 446. As to the date on which a person receives notification of having been matched with a child see PARA 446 note 24.

9 Statutory Paternity Pay and Statutory Adoption Pay (General) Regulations 2002, SI 2002/2822, reg 17(1).

10 Statutory Paternity Pay and Statutory Adoption Pay (General) Regulations 2002, SI 2002/2822, reg 17(2).

11 Statutory Paternity Pay and Statutory Adoption Pay (General) Regulations 2002, SI 2002/2822, reg 17(3).

F. PAYMENT OF PATERNITY PAY

467. Rates of payment for statutory paternity pay. Statutory paternity pay[1] is payable at such fixed or earnings-related weekly rate as may be prescribed by regulations, which may prescribe different kinds of rate for different cases[2]. Accordingly, at the date at which this volume states the law, the weekly rate of payment of statutory paternity pay is set as the smaller of the following two amounts[3]:

(1) £138.18[4];

(2) 90 per cent of the normal weekly earnings of the person claiming statutory paternity pay[5].

Where two or more employers are treated as one[6], liability for statutory paternity pay must be apportioned between them in such proportions as they may agree or, in default of agreement, in the proportions which the person's earnings from each employment bear to the amount of the aggregated earnings[7].

Payment of statutory paternity pay may be made in a like manner to payments of remuneration but must not include payments in kind or by way of the provision of board or lodgings or of services or other facilities[14].

1 As to the meaning of 'statutory paternity pay' see PARA 443. See note 2.

2 Social Security Contributions and Benefits Act 1992 s 171ZE(1) (s 171ZE added by the Employment Act 2002 s 2; the Social Security Contributions and Benefits Act 1992 s 171ZE(1) amended by the Work and Families Act 2006 Sch 1 para 16(1), (2); and the Children and Families Act 2014 Sch 7 paras 6, 16(1), (2)). A statutory instrument containing, whether alone or with other provisions, regulations made by virtue of the Social Security Contributions and Benefits Act 1992 s 171ZE(1), must not be made unless a draft of the instrument has been laid before Parliament and been approved by a resolution of each House: see s 176(1)(a) (as amended: see PARA 465 note 5). As to the making of regulations under the Social Security Contributions and Benefits Act 1992 generally see PARA 407 note 3. In exercise of the powers conferred by s 171ZE(1), the Secretary of State has made the Statutory Paternity Pay and Statutory Adoption Pay (Weekly Rates) Regulations 2002, SI 2002/2818 (see the text and notes 3–8).

3 See the Statutory Paternity Pay and Statutory Adoption Pay (Weekly Rates) Regulations 2002, SI 2002/2818, reg 2 (reg 2 substituted by SI 2004/925).

Where for any purpose of the Social Security Contributions and Benefits Act 1992 Pt XIIZA (ss 171ZA–171ZK) (statutory paternity pay), or of regulations, it is necessary to calculate the daily rate of statutory paternity pay, the amount payable by way of statutory paternity pay for any day must be taken as one seventh of the weekly rate: s 171ZE(10A) (s 171ZE as added (see note 2); s 171ZE(10A) added by the Work and Families Act 2006 Sch 1 para 16(3); and amended by the Children and Families Act 2014 Sch 7 paras 6, 16(1), (8)). Where any payment of statutory paternity pay is made on the basis of a calculation at:

(1) the weekly rate specified in head (2) in the text (Statutory Paternity Pay and Statutory Adoption Pay (Weekly Rates) Regulations 2002, SI 2002/2818, reg 4(a)(i) (reg 4 substituted by SI 2006/2236)); or

(2) the daily rate of one-seventh of the weekly rate specified in head (1) or head (2) in the text (Statutory Paternity Pay and Statutory Adoption Pay (Weekly Rates) Regulations 2002, SI 2002/2818, reg 4(a)(ii) (as so substituted)),

and where that amount includes a fraction of a penny, the payment must be rounded up to the next whole number of pence (see reg 4 (as so substituted)).

4 Statutory Paternity Pay and Statutory Adoption Pay (Weekly Rates) Regulations 2002, SI 2002/2818, reg 2(a) (reg 2 as substituted (see note 3); reg 2(a) amended by SI 2014/147). See note 3.

5 Statutory Paternity Pay and Statutory Adoption Pay (Weekly Rates) Regulations 2002, SI 2002/2818, reg 2(b) (as substituted: see note 3). Head (2) in the text refers to 90% of the normal weekly earnings of the person claiming statutory paternity pay, determined in accordance with the Statutory Paternity Pay and Statutory Adoption Pay (General) Regulations 2002, SI 2002/2822, regs 31(1), 39–40 (see PARAS 468–469): see the Statutory Paternity Pay and Statutory Adoption Pay (Weekly Rates) Regulations 2002, SI 2002/2818, reg 2(b) (as so substituted). See also note 3.

6 Ie under the provisions of the Statutory Paternity Pay and Statutory Adoption Pay (General) Regulations 2002, SI 2002/2822, regs 31(1), 38(1): see PARA 456.

7 Statutory Paternity Pay and Statutory Adoption Pay (General) Regulations 2002, SI 2002/2822, regs 31(1), 38(2).

8 Statutory Paternity Pay and Statutory Adoption Pay (General) Regulations 2002, SI 2002/2822, regs 31(1), 41.

468. Calculation of normal weekly earnings for the purposes of statutory paternity pay. For the purposes of the statutory paternity pay[1] provisions that are set out in Part XIIZA of the Social Security Contributions and Benefits Act 1992[2], a person's normal weekly earnings[3] are to be taken to be the average weekly earnings which in the relevant period[4] have been paid to him or paid for his benefit under the contract of service with the employer[5] in question[6]. However, in such cases as may be prescribed[7], a person's normal weekly earnings are to be calculated in accordance with regulations[8].

Accordingly, in a case where a person has normal pay days at intervals of or approximating to one or more calendar months, including intervals of or approximating to a year, his normal weekly earnings must be calculated by dividing his earnings in the relevant period by the number of calendar months in that period (or, if it is not a whole number, the nearest whole number), multiplying the result by 12 and dividing by 52[9]. In cases where a person does not have normal pay days at intervals of or approximating to one or more calendar month[10], and where the relevant period is not an exact number of weeks, the person's normal weekly earnings must be calculated by dividing his earnings in the relevant period by the number of days in the relevant period and multiplying the result by seven[11]. In any case where a person receives a back-dated pay increase which includes a sum in respect of a relevant period, normal weekly earnings must be calculated as if such a sum was paid in that relevant period, even though received after that period[12].

1 As to the meaning of 'statutory paternity pay' see PARA 443.

2 Ie for the purposes of the Social Security Contributions and Benefits Act 1992 Pt XIIZA (ss 171ZA–171ZK) (statutory paternity pay).

3 For these purposes, 'earnings' has the meaning given to it by regulations (see PARA 469): see the Social Security Contributions and Benefits Act 1992 s 171ZJ(7) (s 171ZJ added by the Employment Act 2002 s 2). Regulations under the Social Security Contributions and Benefits Act 1992 s 171ZJ(7) must be made with the concurrence of the Commissioners for Revenue and Customs: see s 171ZJ(1), (12) (as so added). As to the making of regulations under the Social Security Contributions and Benefits Act 1992 generally see PARA 407 note 3. As to the Commissioners for Her Majesty's Revenue and Customs see **INCOME TAXATION** vol 58 (2014) PARAS 33–34; and see PARA 444 note 2. In exercise of the powers conferred by s 171ZJ(7), (8), the Secretary of State has made the Statutory Paternity Pay and Statutory Adoption Pay (General) Regulations 2002, SI 2002/2822 (see the text and notes 4, 9–12; and PARA 469) and the Statutory Paternity Pay (Adoption) and Statutory Adoption Pay (Adoptions from Overseas) (No 2) Regulations 2003, SI 2003/1194 (see PARA 485).

4 For these purposes, 'relevant period' has the meaning given to it by regulations: see the Social Security Contributions and Benefits Act 1992 s 171ZJ(7) (as added: see note 3). As to the regulations so made see note 3. Accordingly, the relevant period for the purposes of s 171ZJ(6) is the period between:

(1) the last normal pay day to fall before the appropriate date (Statutory Paternity Pay and Statutory Adoption Pay (General) Regulations 2002, SI 2002/2822, regs 31(1), 40(1), (3)(a)); and

(2) the last normal pay day to fall at least eight weeks earlier than the normal pay day mentioned in head (1) above (regs 31(1), 40(1), (3)(b)),

including the normal pay day mentioned in head (1) above, but excluding that first mentioned in head (2) above (see regs 31(1), 40(1), (3)). For these purposes, 'appropriate date' means:

(a) in relation to statutory paternity pay (birth), the first day of the fourteenth week before the expected week of the child's birth or the first day in the week in which the child is born, whichever is the earlier (regs 31(1), 40(1), (2)(b));

(b) in relation to statutory paternity pay (adoption), the first day of the week after the week in which the adopter is notified of being matched with the child for the purposes of adoption (regs 31(1), 40(1), (2)(b)).

'Normal pay day' means a day on which the terms of a person's contract of service require him to be paid, or the practice in his employment is for him to be paid, if any payment is due to him: regs 31(1), 40(1), (2). In a case where a person has no identifiable normal pay day, regs 31(1), 40(3) have effect as if the words 'day of payment' were substituted for the words 'normal pay day' in each place where they occur: see regs 31(1), 40(1), (4). 'Day of payment' means a day on which the person was paid: see regs 31(1), 40(1), (2). As to the meanings of 'statutory paternity pay (birth)' and 'statutory paternity pay (adoption)' see PARA 446 note 20; as to the meaning of 'adopter' see PARA 457 note 8. Although 'contract of service' is defined for the purposes of statutory sick pay (see PARA 558 note 2), it is not so defined under the other statutory pay provisions (for which purposes see generally PARA 1 note 1).

5 As to the meaning of 'employer' for these purposes see PARA 456.

6 Social Security Contributions and Benefits Act 1992 s 171ZJ(6) (as added: see note 3).

7 For these purposes, 'prescribed' means prescribed by regulations: see the Social Security Contributions and Benefits Act 1992 s 171ZJ(1) (as added: see note 3). Regulations under s 171ZJ(8) must be made with the concurrence of the Commissioners for Revenue and Customs: see s 171ZJ(1), (12) (as so added). As to the regulations so made see note 3.

8 Social Security Contributions and Benefits Act 1992 s 171ZJ(8) (as added: see note 3). As to the regulations so made see note 3.

9 Statutory Paternity Pay and Statutory Adoption Pay (General) Regulations 2002, SI 2002/2822, regs 31(1), 40(1), (5).

10 Ie in cases where the Statutory Paternity Pay and Statutory Adoption Pay (General) Regulations 2002, SI 2002/2822, regs 31(1), 40(5) do not apply: see the text and note 9.

11 Statutory Paternity Pay and Statutory Adoption Pay (General) Regulations 2002, SI 2002/2822, regs 31(1), 40(1), (6).

12 Statutory Paternity Pay and Statutory Adoption Pay (General) Regulations 2002, SI 2002/2822, regs 31(1), 40(1), (7).

469. Meaning of 'earnings' for the purposes of statutory paternity pay. The expression 'earnings'[1] refers to gross earnings and includes any remuneration or profit derived from a person's employment, except any payment or amount which is[2]:

(1) excluded from the computation of a person's earnings[3] (or would have been so excluded had he not been under the age of 16)[4];

(2) a chargeable emolument[5], except where, as a consequence of such a chargeable emolument being excluded from earnings, a person would not be entitled to statutory paternity pay (or where such a payment or amount would have been so excluded and in consequence he would not have been entitled to statutory paternity pay had he not been under the age of 16)[6].

For the avoidance of doubt, the expression 'earnings'[7] also includes[8]:

(a) any amount retrospectively treated[9] as earnings by regulations made by virtue of the Social Security Contributions and Benefits Act 1992[10];

(b) any sum payable in respect of arrears of pay in pursuance of an order[11] for reinstatement or re-engagement[12];

(c) any sum payable by way of pay in pursuance of an order[13] for the continuation of a contract of employment[14];

(d) any sum payable by way of remuneration in pursuance[15] of a protective award[16];

(e) any sum payable[17] by way of statutory sick pay[18];

(f) any sum payable by way of statutory maternity pay[19];

(g) any sum payable by way of statutory paternity pay[20]; and

(h) any sum payable by way of statutory adoption pay[21].

1 Ie for the purposes of the Social Security Contributions and Benefits Act 1992 s 171ZJ(6) (normal weekly earnings for the purposes of statutory paternity pay): see PARA 468.

2 See the Statutory Paternity Pay and Statutory Adoption Pay (General) Regulations 2002, SI 2002/2822, regs 31(1), 39(1), (2).

3 Ie under the Social Security (Contributions) Regulations 2001, SI 2001/1004, regs 25, 27, 123 or Sch 3 (payments to be disregarded and payments to directors to be disregarded: see WELFARE BENEFITS AND STATE PENSIONS vol 104 (2014) PARA 382).

4 Statutory Paternity Pay and Statutory Adoption Pay (General) Regulations 2002, SI 2002/2822, regs 31(1), 39(1), (2)(a) (reg 39(2)(a), (b) amended by SI 2006/1031).

5 Ie under the Social Security Contributions and Benefits Act 1992 s 10A (class 1B contributions: see WELFARE BENEFITS AND STATE PENSIONS vol 104 (2014) PARA 392).

(2) for the production of wages sheets and other documents and records to officers of the Commissioners for Revenue and Customs for the purpose of enabling them to satisfy themselves that statutory paternity pay has been paid, and is being paid, in accordance with the regulations, to employees[6] who are entitled to it[7];

(3) for requiring employers to provide information to employees, in their itemised pay statements or otherwise[8];

(4) for requiring employers to make returns to the Commissioners containing such particulars with respect to payments of statutory paternity pay as the regulations may provide[9].

Where a person fails to keep records in accordance with such regulations, he is liable to a penalty[10]; and where a person fails to produce any document or record, provide any information or make any return, in accordance with such regulations[11], he is liable[12] to: (a) a penalty[13]; and (b) if the failure continues after a penalty is imposed under head (a) above, a further penalty or penalties[14] for each day on which the failure continues after the day on which the penalty was imposed[15].

None of the above penalties is to be imposed[16] at any time after the failure concerned has been remedied[17], except in relation to the imposition of a penalty under head (a) above[18].

Where, in the case of any employee, an employer refuses or repeatedly fails to make payments of statutory paternity pay in accordance with regulations made under heads (1) to (4) above, the employer is liable to a penalty[19].

Where a person fraudulently or negligently makes any incorrect statement or declaration in connection with establishing entitlement to statutory paternity pay[20], he is liable to a penalty[21].

Where an employer fraudulently or negligently:

(i) makes incorrect payments of statutory paternity pay[22]; or

(ii) produces any incorrect document or record, provides any incorrect information or makes any incorrect return, of a kind mentioned in regulations under heads (1) to (4) above[23],

he is liable to a penalty[24].

The general provisions as to procedure and appeals[25] have effect in relation to any of the penalties[26] described above[27].

1 As to the Secretary of State see PARA 5 note 21.

2 Regulations under the Employment Act 2002 s 8(1) must be made with the concurrence of the Commissioners for Revenue and Customs: see s 8(3). Any power of the Secretary of State to make orders or regulations under the Employment Act 2002 includes power to make different provision for different cases or circumstances, and to make such incidental, supplementary, consequential or transitional provision as the Secretary of State thinks fit: see s 51(1). Any power of the Secretary of State to make orders or regulations under the Employment Act 2002 is exercisable by statutory instrument (s 51(2)); but no order may be so made unless a draft of the order has been laid before and approved by resolution of each House of Parliament (s 51(3)). A statutory instrument containing regulations is subject to annulment in pursuance of a resolution of either House of Parliament: s 51(5). As to the Commissioners for Her Majesty's Revenue and Customs see INCOME TAXATION vol 58 (2014) PARAS 33–34; and see PARA 444 note 2. In exercise of the powers so conferred, the Secretary of State has, with the concurrence of the Commissioners for Revenue and Customs, made the Statutory Paternity Pay and Statutory Adoption Pay (Administration) Regulations 2002, SI 2002/2820 (see PARAS 475, 476); and the Statutory Paternity Pay (Adoption) and Statutory Adoption Pay (Adoption from Overseas) (Administration) Regulations 2003, SI 2003/1192 (see PARA 486).

3 For these purposes, 'employer' has the same meaning as in the Social Security Contributions and Benefits Act 1992 Pt XIIZA (ss 171ZA–171ZK) (statutory paternity pay: see PARA 456): see the Employment Act 2002 s 16.

4 See the Employment Act 2002 s 8(1) (amended by the Work and Families Act 2006 Sch 1 para 51; and the Children and Families Act 2014 Sch 7 paras 50, 52(1), (2)(a)). As to the meaning of 'statutory paternity pay' see PARA 443.
5 Employment Act 2002 s 8(2)(a) (amended by the Work and Families Act 2006 Sch 1 para 51; and the Children and Families Act 2014 Sch 7 paras 50, 52(1), (3)(a)).
6 For these purposes, 'employee' has the same meaning as in the Social Security Contributions and Benefits Act 1992 Pt XIIZA (see PARA 448): see the Employment Act 2002 s 16.
7 Employment Act 2002 s 8(2)(b) (amended by the Work and Families Act 2006 Sch 1 para 51; and the Children and Families Act 2014 Sch 7 paras 50, 52(1), (3)(b)).
8 Employment Act 2002 s 8(2)(c).
9 Employment Act 2002 s 8(2)(d) (amended by the Work and Families Act 2006 Sch 1 para 51; and the Children and Families Act 2014 Sch 7 paras 50, 52(1), (3)(c)).
10 Employment Act 2002 s 11(3). The penalty must not exceed £3,000: see s 11(3). The Taxes Management Act 1970 s 118(2) (extra time for compliance etc: see INCOME TAXATION vol 59 (2014) PARA 2136) applies for the purposes of the Employment Act 2002 s 11(1) (see the text and notes 11–12), s 11(3) and s 11(6) (see the text and note 19) as it applies for the purposes of the Taxes Management Act 1970: Employment Act 2002 s 11(7).
11 Employment Act 2002 s 11(1)(a). See note 10.
12 See the Employment Act 2002 s 11(1). See note 10.
13 Employment Act 2002 s 11(2)(a). The penalty must not exceed £300: see s 11(2)(a).
14 Ie not exceeding £60: see the Employment Act 2002 s 11(2)(b).
15 Employment Act 2002 s 11(2)(b). Any day for which a penalty under head (b) in the text has already been imposed is excluded for those purposes: see s 11(2)(b).
16 Ie under the Employment Act 2002 s 11(2) (see the text and notes 13–15) or s 11(3) (see the text and note 10).
17 Employment Act 2002 s 11(4).
18 Employment Act 2002 s 11(5).
19 Employment Act 2002 s 11(6) (amended by the Work and Families Act 2006 Sch 1 para 53; and the Children and Families Act 2014 Sch 7 paras 50, 54). The penalty must not exceed £3,000: see the Employment Act 2002 s 11(6) (as so amended). See note 10.
20 Employment Act 2002 s 12(1)(a) (amended by the Work and Families Act 2006 Sch 1 para 54(1), (2); and the Children and Families Act 2014 Sch 7 paras 50, 55(1), (2)(a)).
21 Employment Act 2002 s 12(1). The penalty must not exceed £300: see s 12(1).
22 Employment Act 2002 s 12(3) (s 12(3), (5) amended by the Work and Families Act 2006 Sch 1 para 54(1), (2), (4); and the Children and Families Act 2014 Sch 7 paras 50, 55(1), (4), (6)).
23 Employment Act 2002 s 12(5)(a).
24 Employment Act 2002 s 12(3), (5) (as amended: see note 22). The penalty must not exceed £300: see s 12(3), (5) (as so amended).
25 See the Employment Act 2002 ss 11(8), 12(6), Sch 1; and PARA 479.
26 Ie imposed under either the Employment Act 2002 s 11 or s 12: see the text and notes 10–24.
27 See the Employment Act 2002 ss 11(8), 12(6).

475. Records of statutory paternity payments to be maintained by employers. Every employer[1] must maintain for three years after the end of a tax year[2] in which he made payments of statutory paternity pay[3] to any employee[4] of his a record[5] of:

(1) if the employee's paternity pay period began in that year[6]: (a) the date on which that period began[7]; and (b) the evidence of entitlement to statutory paternity pay provided by the employee[8];
(2) the weeks in that tax year in which statutory paternity pay was paid to the employee and the amount paid in each week[9]; and
(3) any week in that tax year which was within his paternity pay period but for which no payment of statutory paternity pay was made to him and the reason no payment was made[10].

1 As to the meaning of 'employer' for these purposes see PARA 456.
2 For these purposes, 'tax year' means the 12 months beginning with 6 April in any year: see the Statutory Paternity Pay and Statutory Adoption Pay (Administration) Regulations 2002, SI 2002/2820, reg 2(1).
3 As to the meaning of 'statutory paternity pay' see PARA 464 note 3.

4 As to the meaning of 'employee' for these purposes see PARA 448.
5 See the Statutory Paternity Pay and Statutory Adoption Pay (Administration) Regulations 2002, SI 2002/2820, reg 9.
6 See the Statutory Paternity Pay and Statutory Adoption Pay (Administration) Regulations 2002, SI 2002/2820, reg 9(a). For these purposes, 'paternity pay period' means the period determined in accordance with the Social Security Contributions and Benefits Act 1992 s 171ZE(2) (see PARA 465), as the period in respect of which statutory paternity pay is payable to a person: see the Statutory Paternity Pay and Statutory Adoption Pay (Administration) Regulations 2002, SI 2002/2820, reg 2(1).
7 Statutory Paternity Pay and Statutory Adoption Pay (Administration) Regulations 2002, SI 2002/2820, reg 9(a)(i).
8 Statutory Paternity Pay and Statutory Adoption Pay (Administration) Regulations 2002, SI 2002/2820, reg 9(a)(ii). Head (b) in the text refers to evidence provided by the employee pursuant to regulations made under the Social Security Contributions and Benefits Act 1992 s 171ZC(3)(c): see PARA 445.
9 Statutory Paternity Pay and Statutory Adoption Pay (Administration) Regulations 2002, SI 2002/2820, reg 9(b).
10 Statutory Paternity Pay and Statutory Adoption Pay (Administration) Regulations 2002, SI 2002/2820, reg 9(c).

476. Inspection of employers' records regarding statutory paternity pay. Every employer[1], whenever called upon to do so by any authorised officer of the Commissioners for Revenue and Customs[2], must produce to that officer for inspection, at such time as that officer may reasonably require, at the prescribed place[3], the following documents and records[4]:

(1) all wages sheets, deductions working sheets, records kept[5] and other documents and records whatsoever relating to the calculation or payment of statutory paternity pay[6] to his employees in respect of the years specified by such officer[7]; or
(2) such of those wages sheets, deductions working sheets, or other documents and records as may be specified by the authorised officer[8].

The authorised officer may:

(a) take copies of, or make extracts from, any document or record so produced to him for inspection[9]; and
(b) remove any document or record so produced if it appears to him to be necessary to do so, at a reasonable time and for a reasonable period[10].

Where any document or record is removed in accordance with head (b) above, the authorised officer must provide a receipt for the document or record so removed, and a copy of the document or record, free of charge, within seven days, to the person by whom it was produced or caused to be produced where the document or record is reasonably required for the proper conduct of a business[11].

Where records are maintained by computer, the person required to make them available for inspection must provide the authorised officer with all facilities necessary for obtaining information from them[12].

1 As to the meaning of 'employer' for these purposes see PARA 456.
2 As to the Commissioners for Her Majesty's Revenue and Customs see INCOME TAXATION vol 58 (2014) PARAS 33–34; and see PARA 444 note 2.
3 See the Statutory Paternity Pay and Statutory Adoption Pay (Administration) Regulations 2002, SI 2002/2820, reg 10(1). For these purposes, the 'prescribed place' means:
   (1) such place in Great Britain as the employer and the authorised officer may agree upon (reg 10(3)(a)); or
   (2) in default of such agreement, the place in Great Britain at which the documents and records referred to in head (1) above are normally kept (reg 10(3)(b)); or
   (3) in default of such agreement, and if there is no such place as is referred to in head (2) above, the employer's principal place of business in Great Britain (reg 10(3)(c)).

As to the meaning of 'Great Britain' for these purposes see PARA 407 note 7.

4 See the Statutory Paternity Pay and Statutory Adoption Pay (Administration) Regulations 2002, SI 2002/2820, reg 10(1), (2).

5 Ie in accordance with the Statutory Paternity Pay and Statutory Adoption Pay (Administration) Regulations 2002, SI 2002/2820, reg 9: see PARA 475.

6 As to the meaning of 'statutory paternity pay' see PARA 464 note 3.

7 Statutory Paternity Pay and Statutory Adoption Pay (Administration) Regulations 2002, SI 2002/2820, reg 10(2)(a).

8 Statutory Paternity Pay and Statutory Adoption Pay (Administration) Regulations 2002, SI 2002/2820, reg 10(2)(b).

9 Statutory Paternity Pay and Statutory Adoption Pay (Administration) Regulations 2002, SI 2002/2820, reg 10(4)(a).

10 Statutory Paternity Pay and Statutory Adoption Pay (Administration) Regulations 2002, SI 2002/2820, reg 10(4)(b). Where a lien is claimed on a document produced in accordance with reg 10(1) (see the text and notes 1–4), the removal of the document in accordance with reg 10(4)(b) is not to be regarded as breaking the lien: reg 10(6).

11 See the Statutory Paternity Pay and Statutory Adoption Pay (Administration) Regulations 2002, SI 2002/2820, reg 10(5).

12 Statutory Paternity Pay and Statutory Adoption Pay (Administration) Regulations 2002, SI 2002/2820, reg 10(7).

477. Power to make regulations regarding the production of information or documents relating to statutory paternity pay; penalties. The Secretary of State[1] may by regulations[2] make provision enabling an officer of the Commissioners for Revenue and Customs, authorised by them for these purposes, to require persons of a description specified in the regulations to provide, or produce for inspection, within such period as the regulations may require, such information or documents as the officer may reasonably require for the purpose of ascertaining whether statutory paternity pay[3] is or was payable to or in respect of any person[4]. The descriptions of person which may be specified by such regulations include, in particular[5]:

(1) any person claiming to be entitled to statutory paternity pay[6];
(2) any person who is, or has been, the spouse or partner of such a person as is mentioned in head (1) above[7];
(3) any person who is, or has been, an employer[8] of such a person as is mentioned in head (1) above[9];
(4) any person carrying on an agency or other business for the introduction or supply to persons requiring them of persons available to do work or to perform services[10]; and
(5) any person who is a servant or agent of any such person as is specified in heads (1) to (4) above[11].

Where a person fails to provide any information or document, in accordance with such regulations[12], he is liable[13] to: (a) a penalty[14]; and (b) if the failure continues after a penalty is imposed under head (a) above, a further penalty or penalties[15] for each day on which the failure continues after the day on which the penalty was imposed[16].

Neither of the above penalties is to be imposed[17] at any time after the failure concerned has been remedied[18].

Where a person fraudulently or negligently provides any incorrect information or document of a kind mentioned in the regulations[19], so far as relating to statutory paternity pay[20], he is liable to a penalty[21].

The general provisions as to procedure and appeals[22] have effect in relation to any of the penalties[23] described above[24].

1 As to the Secretary of State see PARA 5 note 21.

2 Regulations under the Employment Act 2002 s 10(1) must be made with the concurrence of the Commissioners for Revenue and Customs: see s 10(3). As to the Commissioners for Her Majesty's Revenue and Customs see INCOME TAXATION vol 58 (2014) PARAS 33–34; and see PARA 444 note 2. As to the power to make regulations under the Employment Act 2002 see s 51; and PARA 474 note 2. In exercise of the powers so conferred, the Secretary of State has, with the concurrence of the Commissioners for Revenue and Customs, made the Statutory Paternity Pay and Statutory Adoption Pay (Administration) Regulations 2002, SI 2002/2820 (see PARA 478), and the Statutory Paternity Pay (Adoption) and Statutory Adoption Pay (Adoption from Overseas) (Administration) Regulations 2003, SI 2003/1192 (see PARA 486).
3 As to the meaning of 'statutory paternity pay' see PARA 443.
4 Employment Act 2002 s 10(1) (amended by the Work and Families Act 2006 Sch 1 para 52; and the Children and Families Act 2014 Sch 7 paras 50, 53(1), (2)(a)).
5 See the Employment Act 2002 s 10(2).
6 Employment Act 2002 s 10(2)(a) (amended by the Work and Families Act 2006 Sch 1 para 52; and the Children and Families Act 2014 Sch 7 paras 50, 53(1), (3)(a)). As to entitlement to statutory paternity pay see PARA 443 et seq.
7 Employment Act 2002 s 10(2)(b).
8 As to the meaning of 'employer' for these purposes see PARA 474 note 3.
9 Employment Act 2002 s 10(2)(c).
10 Employment Act 2002 s 10(2)(d).
11 Employment Act 2002 s 10(2)(e).
12 See the Employment Act 2002 s 11(1)(b).
13 See the Employment Act 2002 s 11(1). The Taxes Management Act 1970 s 118(2) (extra time for compliance etc: see INCOME TAXATION vol 59 (2014) PARA 2136) applies for the purposes of the Employment Act 2002 s 11(1) as it applies for the purposes of the Taxes Management Act 1970: Employment Act 2002 s 11(7).
14 Employment Act 2002 s 11(2)(a). The penalty must not exceed £300: see s 11(2)(a).
15 Ie not exceeding £60: see the Employment Act 2002 s 11(2)(b).
16 Employment Act 2002 s 11(2)(b). Any day for which a penalty under head (b) in the text has already been imposed is excluded for those purposes: see s 11(2)(b).
17 Ie under the Employment Act 2002 s 11(2): see heads (a), (b) in the text.
18 Employment Act 2002 s 11(4).
19 Ie in regulations under the Employment Act 2002 s 10(1): see the text and notes 1–4.
20 Employment Act 2002 s 12(1)(b) (amended by the Work and Families Act 2006 Sch 1 para 54(1), (2); and the Children and Families Act 2014 Sch 7 paras 50, 55(1), (2)(b)).
21 Employment Act 2002 s 12(1). The penalty must not exceed £300: see s 12(1).
22 Ie contained in the Employment Act 2002 ss 11(8), 12(6), Sch 1: see PARA 479.
23 Ie imposed under either the Employment Act 2002 s 11 or s 12: see the text and notes 12–21.
24 See the Employment Act 2002 ss 11(8), 12(6).

478. Provision of information in connection with determination of questions relating to statutory paternity pay. Any person[1]:

(1) claiming to be entitled to statutory paternity pay[2];
(2) who is, or has been, the spouse, civil partner or partner of such a person as is specified in head (1) above[3];
(3) who is, or has been, an employer[4] of such a person as is specified in head (1) above[5];
(4) carrying on an agency or other business for the introduction or supply to persons requiring them of persons available to do work or to perform services[6]; and
(5) who is a servant or agent of any such person as is specified in heads (1) to (4) above[7],

must, where information or documents are reasonably required from him to ascertain whether statutory paternity pay is or was payable[8], furnish that information or those documents within 30 days of receiving a notification from an officer of the Commissioners for Revenue and Customs[9] requesting such information or documents[10].

1 Ie any person specified in the Statutory Paternity Pay and Statutory Adoption Pay (Administration) Regulations 2002, SI 2002/2820, reg 14(2) (see heads (1) to (5) in the text): see reg 14(1).
2 Statutory Paternity Pay and Statutory Adoption Pay (Administration) Regulations 2002, SI 2002/2820, reg 14(2)(a). As to the meaning of 'statutory paternity pay' see PARA 464 note 3.
3 Statutory Paternity Pay and Statutory Adoption Pay (Administration) Regulations 2002, SI 2002/2820, reg 14(2)(b) (amended by SI 2005/2114).
4 As to the meaning of 'employer' for these purposes see PARA 456.
5 Statutory Paternity Pay and Statutory Adoption Pay (Administration) Regulations 2002, SI 2002/2820, reg 14(2)(c).
6 Statutory Paternity Pay and Statutory Adoption Pay (Administration) Regulations 2002, SI 2002/2820, reg 14(2)(d).
7 Statutory Paternity Pay and Statutory Adoption Pay (Administration) Regulations 2002, SI 2002/2820, reg 14(2)(e).
8 As to the right to apply for the determination of any issue arising as to, or in connection with, entitlement to statutory paternity pay see PARA 595.
9 As to the Commissioners for Her Majesty's Revenue and Customs see INCOME TAXATION vol 58 (2014) PARAS 33–34; and see PARA 444 note 2.
10 See the Statutory Paternity Pay and Statutory Adoption Pay (Administration) Regulations 2002, SI 2002/2820, reg 14(1). As to the time for compliance where an employee is outside the United Kingdom see PARA 450. Electronic communications may be used for the delivery of information to or by the Commissioners, the delivery of which is required or authorised in connection with the payment of statutory paternity pay or of any other sum in connection with that pay: see the Statutory Payment Schemes (Electronic Communications) Regulations 2002, SI 2002/3047; and INCOME TAXATION.

479. Penalties for failure to comply with regulations or for fraud or negligence in providing information or making payments relating to statutory paternity pay: procedure and appeals. An officer of the Commissioners for Revenue and Customs[1] authorised by the Commissioners for the purpose may make a determination[2] imposing a penalty[3] under the provisions regarding a failure to comply with regulations relating to statutory paternity pay[4], or relating to fraud or negligence in providing information or making payments[5], and setting it at such amount as, in his opinion, is correct or appropriate[6]. Notice of such a determination of a penalty must be served on the person liable to the penalty and must state the date on which it is issued and the time within which an appeal against the determination may be made[7]. After such notice of a determination has been served the determination must not be altered except on appeal[8]; but if it is discovered by an officer of the Commissioners for Revenue and Customs authorised by them for these purposes that the amount of a penalty so determined is or has become insufficient, the officer may make a determination in a further amount so that the penalty is set at the amount which, in his opinion, is correct or appropriate[9]. A penalty determined in this way is due and payable at the end of the period of 30 days beginning with the date of the issue of the notice of determination[10]; and the provisions of the Taxes Management Act 1970 relating to collection and recovery[11] apply in relation to a penalty so determined as if it were tax charged in an assessment and due and payable[12].

An appeal may be brought against a penalty so determined[13]; and the provisions of the Taxes Management Act 1970 relating to appeals[14] have effect in relation to an appeal against such a determination as they have effect in relation to an appeal against an assessment to tax except that references to the tribunal are taken to be references to the First-tier Tribunal[15]. On such an appeal, the First-tier Tribunal has powers to confirm, vary or set aside the determination of the penalty[16]; and, in addition to any right of appeal on a point of law[17], the person liable to the penalty may appeal to the Upper Tribunal against the amount of the penalty which had been so determined on appeal[18], but not against any decision which was made in connection with the determination of the amount of the penalty[19].

Where, in the opinion of the Commissioners for Revenue and Customs, the liability of any person to a penalty for a failure to comply with regulations[20], or for fraud or negligence in providing information or making payments[21], arises by reason of the fraud of that or any other person, proceedings for the penalty may be instituted before the High Court[22], in the name of the Attorney General[23]. Any proceedings so instituted are deemed to be civil proceedings[24] by the Crown[25]. If in such proceedings the court does not find that fraud is proved but considers that the person concerned is nevertheless liable to a penalty, the court may determine a penalty notwithstanding that, but for the opinion of the Commissioners for Revenue and Customs as to fraud, the penalty would not have been a matter for the court[26].

The Commissioners for Revenue and Customs may in their discretion mitigate any penalty for failure to comply with regulations[27], or for fraud or negligence in providing information or making payments[28], or they may stay or compound any proceedings for a penalty, and they may also, after judgment, further mitigate or entirely remit the penalty[29].

A penalty under the provisions regarding a failure to comply with regulations[30], or relating to fraud or negligence in providing information or making payments[31], may be determined by an officer of the Commissioners for Revenue and Customs, or proceedings for the penalty may be commenced before the tribunal[32] or the court[33], at any time within six years after the date on which the penalty was incurred or began to be incurred[34].

1 As to the Commissioners for Her Majesty's Revenue and Customs see INCOME TAXATION vol 58 (2014) PARAS 33–34; and see PARA 444 note 2.

2 Ie except where penalty proceedings have been instituted before a court under the Employment Act 2002 ss 11(8), 12(6), Sch 1 para 5: see the text and notes 20–26.

3 Ie except where such a penalty has been imposed as is mentioned in the Employment Act 2002 s 11(2)(a) (ie a penalty of £300 imposed on a person who fails to produce any document or record, provide any information or make any return in accordance with regulations made under s 8 (see PARA 474) or who fails to provide any information or document in accordance with regulations made under s 10 (see PARA 477): see PARAS 474, 477): Sch 1 para 1(2). An officer of the Commissioners for Revenue and Customs authorised by them for these purposes may commence proceedings for any penalty to which Sch 1 para 1(1) does not apply by virtue of Sch 1 para 1(2), however: Sch 1 para 4(1). The person liable to the penalty is a party to the proceedings: Sch 1 para 4(2) (Sch 1 para 4(2), (4) substituted, Sch 1 para 4(4A) added, by SI 2009/56). The Taxes Management Act 1970 Pt VI (ss 60–70A) (collection and recovery: see INCOME TAXATION vol 59 (2014) PARA 2304 et seq) applies in relation to a penalty determined in proceedings under the Employment Act 2002 Sch 1 para 4 as if it were tax charged in an assessment and due and payable: Sch 1 para 4(3). In addition to any right of appeal on a point of law under the Tribunals, Courts and Enforcement Act 2007 s 11(2) (see COURTS AND TRIBUNALS vol 24 (2010) PARA 928), the person liable to the penalty may appeal to the Upper Tribunal against the determination of a penalty in proceedings under the Employment Act 2002 Sch 1 para 4(1), but not against any decision which falls under the Tribunals, Courts and Enforcement Act 2007 s 11(5)(d), (e) (see COURTS AND TRIBUNALS vol 24 (2010) PARA 928) and was made in connection with the determination of the amount of the penalty: Employment Act 2002 Sch 1 para 4(4) (as so substituted). The Tribunals, Courts and Enforcement Act 2007 s 11(3), (4) (see COURTS AND TRIBUNALS vol 24 (2010) PARA 928) applies to the right of appeal under the Employment Act 2002 Sch 1 para 4(4) as it applies to the right of appeal under the Tribunals, Courts and Enforcement Act 2007 s 11(2): Employment Act 2002 Sch 1 para 4(4A) (as so added). On any such appeal, the Upper Tribunal may (see Sch 1 para 4(5) (amended by SI 2009/56)):

(1) if it appears that no penalty has been incurred, set the determination aside (Employment Act 2002 Sch 1 para 4(5)(a));

(2) if the amount determined appears to be appropriate, confirm the determination (Sch 1 para 4(5)(b));

(3) if the amount determined appears to be excessive, reduce it to such other amount (including nil) as the Upper Tribunal considers appropriate (Sch 1 para 4(5)(c) (amended by SI 2009/56));
(4) if the amount determined appears to be insufficient, increase it to such amount not exceeding the permitted maximum as the Upper Tribunal considers appropriate (Employment Act 2002 Sch 1 para 4(5)(d) (amended by SI 2009/56)).

As to the First-tier Tribunal and the Upper Tribunal see COURTS AND TRIBUNALS vol 24 (2010) PARA 874 et seq.

4 Ie under the Employment Act 2002 s 11: see PARAS 474, 477. As to the meaning of 'statutory paternity pay' see PARA 443.
5 Ie under the Employment Act 2002 s 12: see PARAS 474, 477.
6 See the Employment Act 2002 Sch 1 para 1(1). As to the determination of claims generally see WELFARE BENEFITS AND STATE PENSIONS vol 104 (2014) PARA 575 et seq.
7 Employment Act 2002 Sch 1 para 1(3).
8 Employment Act 2002 Sch 1 para 1(4).
9 Employment Act 2002 Sch 1 para 1(5).
10 Employment Act 2002 Sch 1 para 2(1). A penalty under s 11 (see note 4) or s 12 (see note 5) carries interest at the rate applicable under the Finance Act 1989 s 178 (see INCOME TAXATION vol 59 (2014) PARA 2303) from the date on which it becomes due and payable until payment: Employment Act 2002 Sch 1 para 8(2).
11 Ie the Taxes Management Act 1970 Pt VI (ss 60–70A) (collection and recovery: see INCOME TAXATION vol 59 (2014) PARA 2304 et seq).
12 Employment Act 2002 Sch 1 para 2(2).
13 Employment Act 2002 Sch 1 para 3(1).
14 Ie the Taxes Management Act 1970 Pt V (ss 46D–57) (appeals and other proceedings: see INCOME TAXATION vol 59 (2014) PARA 2244 et seq), except s 50(6)–(8).
15 Employment Act 2002 Sch 1 para 3(2) (amended by SI 2009/56).
16 Ie, on an appeal by virtue of the Employment Act 2002 Sch 1 para 3(2) (see the text and notes 14–15) against the determination of a penalty under Sch 1 para 1 (see the text and notes 1–9), the First-tier Tribunal may (see Sch 1 para 3(3) (amended by SI 2009/56)):
(1) if it appears that no penalty has been incurred, set the determination aside (Employment Act 2002 Sch 1 para 3(3)(a) (Sch 1 para 3(3)(a)–(d) amended by SI 2009/56));
(2) if the amount determined appears to be appropriate, confirm the determination (Employment Act 2002 Sch 1 para 3(3)(b) (as so amended));
(3) if the amount determined appears to be excessive, reduce it to such other amount (including nil) as the First-tier Tribunal considers appropriate (Sch 1 para 3(3)(c) (as so amended));
(4) if the amount determined appears to be insufficient, increase it to such amount not exceeding the permitted maximum as the First-tier Tribunal considers appropriate (Sch 1 para 3(3)(d) (as so amended)).
17 Ie under the Tribunals, Courts and Enforcement Act 2007 s 11(2): see COURTS AND TRIBUNALS vol 24 (2010) PARA 928.
18 Ie under the Employment Act 2002 Sch 1 para 3.
19 Employment Act 2002 Sch 1 para 3(4) (Sch 1 para 3(4) substituted, Sch 1 para 3(4A), (4B) added, by SI 2009/56). The reference in the text is to any decision which falls under the Tribunals, Courts and Enforcement Act 2007 s 11(5)(d), (e) (see COURTS AND TRIBUNALS vol 24 (2010) PARA 928): see the Employment Act 2002 Sch 1 para 3(4) (as so substituted). The Tribunals, Courts and Enforcement Act 2007 s 11(3), (4) (see COURTS AND TRIBUNALS vol 24 (2010) PARA 928) applies to the right of appeal under the Employment Act 2002 Sch 1 para 3(4) as it applies to the right of appeal under the Tribunals, Courts and Enforcement Act 2007 s 11(2) (see COURTS AND TRIBUNALS vol 24 (2010) PARA 928): Employment Act 2002 Sch 1 para 3(4A) (as so added). On an appeal under Sch 1 para 3, the Upper Tribunal has the like jurisdiction as is conferred on the First-tier Tribunal by virtue of Sch 1 para 3 (see the text and notes 13–15): Sch 1 para 3(4B) (as so added).
20 See note 4.
21 See note 5.
22 See the Employment Act 2002 Sch 1 para 5(1).
23 See the Employment Act 2002 Sch 1 para 5(2)(a). However, this provision does not prevent proceedings under Sch 1 para 4 being instituted under the Crown Proceedings Act 1947 (see CROWN PROCEEDINGS AND CROWN PRACTICE vol 12(1) (Reissue) PARA 102 et seq) by and in the name of the Commissioners for Revenue and Customs as an authorised department for the

purposes of that Act: Employment Act 2002 Sch 1 para 5(3). As to the Attorney General see CONSTITUTIONAL AND ADMINISTRATIVE LAW vol 20 (2014) PARA 273 et seq.
24 Ie within the meaning of the Crown Proceedings Act 1947 Pt II (ss 13–23) (jurisdiction and procedure: see CROWN PROCEEDINGS AND CROWN PRACTICE vol 12(1) (Reissue) PARA 116).
25 Employment Act 2002 Sch 1 para 5(4).
26 Employment Act 2002 Sch 1 para 5(5).
27 See note 4.
28 See note 5.
29 Employment Act 2002 Sch 1 para 6.
30 See note 4.
31 See note 5.
32 Ie before the First-tier Tribunal: see the Employment Act 2002 Sch 1 para 4; and note 3.
33 See the Employment Act 2002 Sch 1 para 5; and the text and notes 20–26.
34 Employment Act 2002 Sch 1 para 7 (amended by SI 2009/56).

480. Supply and use of information. Information which is held for the purposes of functions relating to statutory paternity pay[1] by the Commissioners for Revenue and Customs[2], or by a person providing services to the Commissioners in connection with the provision of those services[3], may be supplied to the Secretary of State[4], or to a person providing services to the Secretary of State[5], for use for the purposes of functions relating to social security[6], child support[7], or war pensions[8].

Information which is held for the purposes of functions relating to statutory paternity pay by the Secretary of State[9], or by a person providing services to the Secretary of State[10] in connection with the provision of those services[11], may be supplied to the Commissioners, or to a person providing services to the Commissioners, for use for the purposes of functions relating to statutory paternity pay[12].

Information which is held by the Commissioners, or by a person providing services to the Commissioners in connection with the provision of those services, for the purposes of[13]:

(1) the functions of the Commissioners in relation to statutory paternity pay[14];
(2) their functions in relation to statutory adoption pay[15]; and
(3) their functions in relation to statutory shared parental pay[16]; and
(4) their functions in relation to tax[17], contributions[18], statutory sick pay[19], statutory maternity pay[20] or tax credits[21], or functions[22] relating to the certification of pension schemes[23],

may be used for the purposes of, or for any purposes connected with, the exercise of any functions specified in any other of heads (1) to (4) above, and may be supplied to any person providing services to the Commissioners for those purposes[24].

1 As to statutory paternity pay see PARA 443 et seq.
2 As to the Commissioners for Her Majesty's Revenue and Customs see INCOME TAXATION vol 58 (2014) PARAS 33–34; and see PARA 444 note 2.
3 See the Employment Act 2002 s 13(1) (amended by the Work and Families Act 2006 Sch 1 para 55; and the Children and Families Act 2014 Sch 7 paras 50, 56(a)).
4 Or, in Northern Ireland, the Department for Social Development or the Department for Employment and Learning. As to the Secretary of State see PARA 5 note 21.
5 See note 4.
6 See WELFARE BENEFITS AND STATE PENSIONS vol 104 (2014) PARA 2 et seq.
7 See CHILDREN AND YOUNG PERSONS vol 9 (2012) PARA 573 et seq.
8 See the Employment Act 2002 s 13(2) (amended by SI 2008/2656; SI 2012/2007). As to war pensions see ARMED FORCES vol 3 (2011) PARA 718 et seq.
9 See note 4.
10 See note 4.

11 See the Employment Act 2002 s 14(1) (amended by the Work and Families Act 2006 Sch 1 para 56; and the Children and Families Act 2014 Sch 7 paras 50, 57(1), (2)(a)).
12 See the Employment Act 2002 s 14(2) (amended by the Work and Families Act 2006 Sch 1 para 56; and the Children and Families Act 2014 Sch 7 paras 50, 57(1), (3)(a)).
13 See the Employment Act 2002 s 15(1). The text refers to information so held for the purposes of any functions specified in s 15(2) (see heads (1) to (4) in the text): see s 15(1).
14 Employment Act 2002 s 15(2)(a) (amended by the Work and Families Act 2006 Sch 1 para 57(a); and the Children and Families Act 2014 Sch 7 paras 50, 58(a)).
15 Employment Act 2002 s 15(2)(b) (amended by the Children and Families Act 2014 Sch 7 paras 50, 58(c)). As to statutory adoption pay see PARA 488 et seq.
16 Employment Act 2002 s 15(2)(ba) (added by the Children and Families Act 2014 Sch 7 paras 50, 58(d)). As to statutory shared parental pay see PARA 534 et seq.
17 See INCOME TAXATION vol 58 (2014) PARAS 33–34.
18 For these purposes, 'contributions' means contributions under the Social Security Contributions and Benefits Act 1992 Pt 1 (ss 1–19A) (see WELFARE BENEFITS AND STATE PENSIONS vol 104 (2014) PARA 384 et seq) or the Social Security Contributions and Benefits (Northern Ireland) Act 1992 Pt 1: see the Employment Act 2002 s 15(3).
19 As to statutory sick pay see PARA 558 et seq.
20 As to statutory maternity pay see PARA 401 et seq.
21 See WELFARE BENEFITS AND STATE PENSIONS vol 104 (2014) PARA 335 et seq.
22 Ie under the Pension Schemes Act 1993 Pt III (ss 7–68) (see PERSONAL AND OCCUPATIONAL PENSIONS vol 80 (2013) PARA 395 et seq) or, in Northern Ireland, the Pension Schemes (Northern Ireland) Act 1993 Pt III.
23 Employment Act 2002 s 15(2)(c).
24 See the Employment Act 2002 s 15(1).

H. RECOVERY OF AMOUNTS PAID

481. Power to make provision for funding of employers' liabilities for statutory paternity pay. The Secretary of State[1] must by regulations[2] make provision for the payment by employers[3] of statutory paternity pay[4] to be funded by the Commissioners for Revenue and Customs[5] to such extent as the regulations may specify[6]. Such regulations:

(1) must make provision for a person who has made a payment of statutory paternity pay to be entitled, except in such circumstances as the regulations may provide, to recover an amount equal to the sum of[7]:
  (a) the aggregate of such of those payments as qualify for small employers' relief[8]; and
  (b) an amount equal to 92 per cent of the aggregate of such of those payments as do not so qualify[9]; and
(2) must include provision for a person who has made a payment of statutory paternity pay qualifying for small employers' relief to be entitled, except in such circumstances as the regulations may provide, to recover an additional amount equal to the amount to which the person would have been entitled[10] had the payment been a payment of statutory maternity pay[11]; and
(3) may, in particular, make provision:
  (a) for funding in advance as well as in arrear[12];
  (b) for funding, or the recovery of amounts due under provision made by virtue of head (2) above, by means of deductions from such amounts for which employers are accountable to the Commissioners as the regulations may provide, or otherwise[13];
  (c) for the recovery by the Commissioners of any sums overpaid to employers under such regulations[14].

Where an employer fraudulently or negligently receives incorrect payments in pursuance of such regulations, he is liable to a penalty[15].

9 Employment Act 2002 s 7(5)(b).
10 See the Employment Act 2002 s 7(5). As to the date on which the deduction is treated as having been paid see PARA 482 note 28.

I. ADOPTIONS FROM OVERSEAS

484. Application of statutory paternity pay provisions to adoption cases. The Secretary of State[1] may by regulations[2] provide for the statutory provisions relating to statutory paternity pay[3] to have effect in relation to cases which involve adoption, but not the placement of a child for adoption under the law of any part of the United Kingdom[4], with such modifications[5] as the regulations may prescribe[6]. Accordingly, the statutory provisions generally apply in relation to adoptions from overseas[7] regarding:

(1) entitlement to statutory paternity pay[8];
(2) the liability to make such payments[9];
(3) the rate and period of such payments[10];
(4) the restrictions on contracting out[11];
(5) the relationship of statutory paternity pay to contractual remuneration[12];
(6) Crown employment[13]; and
(7) provision for special classes of person[14].

However, under head (1) above, the conditions the fulfilment of which is necessary to entitlement to statutory paternity pay[15] are modified[16], in relation to an adoption from overseas[17] so that a person is entitled to statutory paternity pay in the case of adoptions from overseas if:

(a) he satisfies prescribed conditions:
 (i) as to relationship with a child who is adopted from overseas; and
 (ii) as to relationship with an adopter[18] of the child[19];
(b) he has been in employed earner's employment[20] with an employer[21] for a continuous period of at least 26 weeks[22];
(c) his normal weekly earnings[23] for the period of eight weeks ending with the relevant week are not less than the lower earnings limit in force[24] at the end of the relevant week[25];
(d) he has been in employed earner's employment with the employer by reference to whom the condition in head (b) above is satisfied for a continuous period beginning with the end of the relevant week[26] and ending with the day on which the child enters Great Britain[27]; and
(e) where he is an adopter of the child, he has elected to receive statutory paternity pay[28].

In relation to head (3) above, the rule which determines the start date for the statutory paternity pay period[29] is modified[30] in relation to the start date[31], so that regulations must secure that the qualifying period[32] is a period of at least 56 days beginning[33] with the date of the child's entry into Great Britain[34].

1 As to the Secretary of State see PARA 5 note 21.
2 As to the making of regulations under the Social Security Contributions and Benefits Act 1992 generally see PARA 407 note 3.
3 Ie the provisions of the Social Security Contributions and Benefits Act 1992 Pt XIIZA (ss 171ZA–171ZK) (statutory paternity pay): see PARA 443 et seq. As to the meaning of 'statutory paternity pay' see PARA 443.
4 As to the meaning of 'United Kingdom' see PARA 407 note 7. As to the law relating to child adoption see CHILDREN AND YOUNG PERSONS vol 9 (2012) PARA 360 et seq.
5 As to the meaning of 'modifications' see PARA 445 note 8.

6 Social Security Contributions and Benefits Act 1992 s 171ZK(1) (ss 171ZB, 171ZE, 171ZJ, 171ZK added by the Employment Act 2002 s 2; the Social Security Contributions and Benefits Act 1992 s 171ZK(1) numbered as such, s 171ZK(2) added, by the Children and Families Act 2014 s 122(5)(b), (c)). The Secretary of State may by regulations also provide for the Social Security Contributions and Benefits Act 1992 Pt XIIZA (statutory paternity pay) to have effect in relation to cases which involve an employee who has applied, or intends to apply, with another person for a parental order under the Human Fertilisation and Embryology Act 2008 s 54 (parental orders: see **CHILDREN AND YOUNG PERSONS** vol 9 (2012) PARA 129) and a child who is, or will be, the subject of the order, with such modifications as the regulations may prescribe: Social Security Contributions and Benefits Act 1992 s 171ZK(2) (as so added). For these purposes, 'prescribed' means prescribed by regulations: see s 171ZJ(1) (as so added). In exercise of these powers, the Secretary of State has made the Social Security Contributions and Benefits Act 1992 (Application of Parts 12ZA and 12ZB to Adoptions from Overseas) Regulations 2003, SI 2003/499, and the Statutory Paternity Pay and Statutory Adoption Pay (Amendment) Regulations 2004, SI 2004/488.

7 For these purposes, 'adoption from overseas' means the adoption of a child who enters Great Britain from outside the United Kingdom in connection with or for the purposes of adoption which does not involve the placement of the child for adoption under the law of any part of the United Kingdom: see the Social Security Contributions and Benefits Act 1992 (Application of Parts 12ZA and 12ZB to Adoptions from Overseas) Regulations 2003, SI 2003/499, reg 1(2). As to the meaning of 'Great Britain' for these purposes see PARA 407 note 7.

8 Ie the Social Security Contributions and Benefits Act 1992 ss 171ZA–171ZC (see PARAS 443, 445, 462): see the Social Security Contributions and Benefits Act 1992 (Application of Parts 12ZA and 12ZB to Adoptions from Overseas) Regulations 2003, SI 2003/499, reg 2. See also the text and notes 15–28.

9 Ie the Social Security Contributions and Benefits Act 1992 s 171ZD (see PARAS 443–447): see the Social Security Contributions and Benefits Act 1992 (Application of Parts 12ZA and 12ZB to Adoptions from Overseas) Regulations 2003, SI 2003/499, reg 2.

10 Ie the Social Security Contributions and Benefits Act 1992 s 171ZE (see PARAS 446, 465, 467): see the Social Security Contributions and Benefits Act 1992 (Application of Parts 12ZA and 12ZB to Adoptions from Overseas) Regulations 2003, SI 2003/499, reg 2. See also the text and notes 29–34.

11 Ie the Social Security Contributions and Benefits Act 1992 s 171ZF (see PARA 443): see the Social Security Contributions and Benefits Act 1992 (Application of Parts 12ZA and 12ZB to Adoptions from Overseas) Regulations 2003, SI 2003/499, reg 2.

12 Ie the Social Security Contributions and Benefits Act 1992 s 171ZG (see PARA 472): see the Social Security Contributions and Benefits Act 1992 (Application of Parts 12ZA and 12ZB to Adoptions from Overseas) Regulations 2003, SI 2003/499, reg 2.

13 Ie the Social Security Contributions and Benefits Act 1992 s 171ZH (see PARA 454): see the Social Security Contributions and Benefits Act 1992 (Application of Parts 12ZA and 12ZB to Adoptions from Overseas) Regulations 2003, SI 2003/499, reg 2.

14 Ie the Social Security Contributions and Benefits Act 1992 s 171ZI (see PARA 449): see the Social Security Contributions and Benefits Act 1992 (Application of Parts 12ZA and 12ZB to Adoptions from Overseas) Regulations 2003, SI 2003/499, reg 2.

15 Ie the Social Security Contributions and Benefits Act 1992 s 171ZB(2), (3), (6), (7) (see PARA 457) as mentioned in s 171ZB(1) (entitlement: adoption): see PARA 443.

16 Ie the provisions of the Social Security Contributions and Benefits Act 1992 s 171ZB(2), (3), (6), (7) are modified and associated definitions are added to s 171ZJ(1) as specified in the Social Security Contributions and Benefits Act 1992 (Application of Parts 12ZA and 12ZB to Adoptions from Overseas) Regulations 2003, SI 2003/499, reg 2, Sch 1.

17 Social Security Contributions and Benefits Act 1992 (Application of Parts 12ZA and 12ZB to Adoptions from Overseas) Regulations 2003, SI 2003/499, reg 2 (amended by SI 2010/153).

18 For these purposes, 'adopter', in relation to a child, means a person by whom the child has been or is to be adopted: see the Social Security Contributions and Benefits Act 1992 s 171ZJ(1) (s 171ZJ as added (see note 6); definition added by the Social Security Contributions and Benefits Act 1992 (Application of Parts 12ZA and 12ZB to Adoptions from Overseas) Regulations 2003, SI 2003/499, Sch 1). Accordingly, the definition of 'adopter' given in the Social Security Contributions and Benefits Act 1992 s 171ZB(7) (see PARA 457 note 13) is omitted for these purposes: see the Social Security Contributions and Benefits Act 1992 (Application of Parts 12ZA and 12ZB to Adoptions from Overseas) Regulations 2003, SI 2003/499, Sch 1.

19 Social Security Contributions and Benefits Act 1992 s 171ZB(2)(a) (s 171ZB as added (see note 6); s 171ZB(2)(a) modified by the Social Security Contributions and Benefits Act 1992

8 Ie the Statutory Paternity Pay and Statutory Adoption Pay (General) Regulations 2002, SI 2002/2822, reg 17 (see PARA 466): see the Statutory Paternity Pay (Adoption) and Statutory Adoption Pay (Adoptions from Overseas) (No 2) Regulation 2003, SI 2003/1194, reg 3(1), (3).
9 Ie the Statutory Paternity Pay and Statutory Adoption Pay (General) Regulations 2002, SI 2002/2822, reg 18 (see PARA 446): see the Statutory Paternity Pay (Adoption) and Statutory Adoption Pay (Adoptions from Overseas) (No 2) Regulation 2003, SI 2003/1194, reg 3(1), (3).
10 Ie the Statutory Paternity Pay and Statutory Adoption Pay (General) Regulations 2002, SI 2002/2822, reg 19 (see PARA 472 note 11): see the Statutory Paternity Pay (Adoption) and Statutory Adoption Pay (Adoptions from Overseas) (No 2) Regulation 2003, SI 2003/1194, reg 3(1), (3).
11 Ie the Statutory Paternity Pay and Statutory Adoption Pay (General) Regulations 2002, SI 2002/2822, regs 31(1), 32 (see PARA 448): see the Statutory Paternity Pay (Adoption) and Statutory Adoption Pay (Adoptions from Overseas) (No 2) Regulation 2003, SI 2003/1194, reg 3(1), (3).
12 Ie the Statutory Paternity Pay and Statutory Adoption Pay (General) Regulations 2002, SI 2002/2822, regs 31(1), 33–37 (see PARAS 458–461): see the Statutory Paternity Pay (Adoption) and Statutory Adoption Pay (Adoptions from Overseas) (No 2) Regulation 2003, SI 2003/1194, reg 3(1), (3). As to continuous employment see PARA 458 et seq.
13 Ie the Statutory Paternity Pay and Statutory Adoption Pay (General) Regulations 2002, SI 2002/2822, regs 31(1), 38 (see PARAS 448, 456, 467): see the Statutory Paternity Pay (Adoption) and Statutory Adoption Pay (Adoptions from Overseas) (No 2) Regulation 2003, SI 2003/1194, reg 3(1), (3).
14 Ie the Statutory Paternity Pay and Statutory Adoption Pay (General) Regulations 2002, SI 2002/2822, regs 31(1), 39 (see PARA 469): see the Statutory Paternity Pay (Adoption) and Statutory Adoption Pay (Adoptions from Overseas) (No 2) Regulation 2003, SI 2003/1194, reg 3(1), (3).
15 Ie the Statutory Paternity Pay and Statutory Adoption Pay (General) Regulations 2002, SI 2002/2822, regs 31(1), 41 (see PARA 444) and regs 31(1), 42 (see PARA 470): see the Statutory Paternity Pay (Adoption) and Statutory Adoption Pay (Adoptions from Overseas) (No 2) Regulation 2003, SI 2003/1194, reg 3(1), (3).
16 Ie the Statutory Paternity Pay and Statutory Adoption Pay (General) Regulations 2002, SI 2002/2822, regs 31(1), 43 (see PARA 444): see the Statutory Paternity Pay (Adoption) and Statutory Adoption Pay (Adoptions from Overseas) (No 2) Regulation 2003, SI 2003/1194, reg 3(1), (3). As to the Commissioners for Her Majesty's Revenue and Customs see **INCOME TAXATION** vol 58 (2014) PARAS 33–34; and see PARA 444 note 2.
17 Ie the Statutory Paternity Pay and Statutory Adoption Pay (General) Regulations 2002, SI 2002/2822, regs 31(1), 45 (see PARA 471): see the Statutory Paternity Pay (Adoption) and Statutory Adoption Pay (Adoptions from Overseas) (No 2) Regulation 2003, SI 2003/1194, reg 3(1), (3).
18 Ie the Statutory Paternity Pay and Statutory Adoption Pay (General) Regulations 2002, SI 2002/2822, regs 31(1), 46 (see PARA 473): see the Statutory Paternity Pay (Adoption) and Statutory Adoption Pay (Adoptions from Overseas) (No 2) Regulation 2003, SI 2003/1194, reg 3(1), (3).
19 Ie the Statutory Paternity Pay and Statutory Adoption Pay (General) Regulations 2002, SI 2002/2822, regs 31(1), 47 (see PARA 511 note 19): see the Statutory Paternity Pay (Adoption) and Statutory Adoption Pay (Adoptions from Overseas) (No 2) Regulation 2003, SI 2003/1194, reg 3(1), (3).
20 Ie the Statutory Paternity Pay and Statutory Adoption Pay (General) Regulations 2002, SI 2002/2822, regs 31(1), 40: see PARA 468.
21 For these purposes, in the Statutory Paternity Pay and Statutory Adoption Pay (General) Regulations 2002, SI 2002/2822, regs 31(1), 40, 'appropriate date' (see PARA 468 note 4) means the first day of the week after the week in which official notification is sent to the adopter or the week in which the person satisfies the condition in the Social Security Contributions and Benefits Act 1992 s 171ZB(2)(b) (as modified: see note 5) (ie 26 weeks' continuous employment: see PARA 484), whichever is the later: Statutory Paternity Pay and Statutory Adoption Pay (General) Regulations 2002, SI 2002/2822, regs 31(1), 40(2)(b) (modified by the Statutory Paternity Pay (Adoption) and Statutory Adoption Pay (Adoptions from Overseas) (No 2) Regulation 2003, SI 2003/1194, reg 3(4)). For these purposes, 'adopter', in relation to a child, means a person by whom the child has been or is to be adopted: reg 2(1). 'Official notification' means written notification, issued by or on behalf of the relevant domestic authority, that it is prepared to issue a certificate to the overseas authority concerned with the adoption of the child, or has issued a certificate and sent it to that authority, confirming, in either case, that the adopter is eligible to adopt and has been assessed and approved as being a

suitable adoptive parent; and 'relevant domestic authority' means: (1) in the case of an adopter to whom the Intercountry Adoption (Hague Convention) Regulations 2003, SI 2003/118 (see now the Adoptions with a Foreign Element Regulations 2005, SI 2005/392) apply (see CHILDREN AND YOUNG PERSONS vol 9 (2012) PARAS 521, 528 et seq) and who is habitually resident in Wales, the National Assembly for Wales; and (2) in any other case, the Secretary of State: see the Statutory Paternity Pay (Adoption) and Statutory Adoption Pay (Adoptions from Overseas) (No 2) Regulation 2003, SI 2003/1194, reg 2(1). As to the meaning of 'Wales' see PARA 2 note 12. As to the National Assembly for Wales see CONSTITUTIONAL AND ADMINISTRATIVE LAW vol 20 (2014) PARA 351 et seq. As to the Secretary of State see PARA 5 note 21. As to habitual residence see CONFLICT OF LAWS vol 19 (2011) PARA 360 et seq.

22 Ie the Statutory Paternity Pay and Statutory Adoption Pay (General) Regulations 2002, SI 2002/2822, reg 11: see PARA 457 note 8. The conditions prescribed are that a person: (1) is married to, the civil partner or the partner of a child's adopter (or in a case where there are two adopters, married to or the partner of the other adopter); and (2) has, or expects to have, the main responsibility (apart from the responsibility of the child's adopter or, in a case where there are two adopters, together with the other adopter) for the upbringing of the child: Statutory Paternity Pay (Adoption) and Statutory Adoption Pay (Adoptions from Overseas) (No 2) Regulation 2003, SI 2003/1194, reg 5(1) (amended by SI 2005/2114). For these purposes, 'partner' means a person (whether of a different sex or the same sex) who lives with the adopter and the child in an enduring family relationship but is not the adopter's parent, grandparent, sister, brother, aunt or uncle: see the Statutory Paternity Pay (Adoption) and Statutory Adoption Pay (Adoptions from Overseas) (No 2) Regulation 2003, SI 2003/1194, reg 5(2), (3). References to relationships: (a) are references to relationships of the full blood or half blood or, in the case of an adopted person, such of those relationships as would exist but for the adoption; and (b) include the relationship of a child with his adoptive or former adoptive parents but do not include any other adoptive relationships: see reg 5(4).

Marriage of same sex couples is lawful in the law of England and Wales, and such marriages have the same effect as marriages of opposite sex couples: see the Marriage (Same Sex Couples) Act 2013 s 1(1), 11(1); and MATRIMONIAL AND CIVIL PARTNERSHIP LAW vol 72 (2009) PARA 1 et seq.

23 Ie the Statutory Paternity Pay and Statutory Adoption Pay (General) Regulations 2002, SI 2002/2822, reg 12: see PARA 465.

24 Ie subject to notice under the Social Security Contributions and Benefits Act 1992 s 171ZC(1) (as applied: see note 5) (see PARA 484) and the Statutory Paternity Pay (Adoption) and Statutory Adoption Pay (Adoptions from Overseas) (No 2) Regulation 2003, SI 2003/1194, reg 8 (see the text and notes 28–29).

25 As to the statutory paternity pay period which applies otherwise, i e under the law of any part of the United Kingdom, see PARA 465.

26 See the Statutory Paternity Pay (Adoption) and Statutory Adoption Pay (Adoptions from Overseas) (No 2) Regulation 2003, SI 2003/1194, reg 6(1). A choice made in accordance with reg 6(1) is not irrevocable, but where a person subsequently makes a different choice in relation to the beginning of the statutory pay period, the Social Security Contributions and Benefits Act 1992 s 171ZC(1) (as applied: see note 5) (see PARA 484) applies to it: Statutory Paternity Pay (Adoption) and Statutory Adoption Pay (Adoptions from Overseas) (No 2) Regulation 2003, SI 2003/1194, reg 6(4).

27 Statutory Adoption Pay (Adoptions from Overseas) (No 2) Regulation 2003, SI 2003/1194, reg 6(3).

28 Ie for the purposes of the Social Security Contributions and Benefits Act 1992 s 171ZE(2) (as applied: see note 5) (see PARA 484): see the Statutory Paternity Pay and Statutory Adoption Pay (General) Regulations 2002, SI 2002/2822, reg 14; and PARA 465 note 4.

29 Statutory Paternity Pay (Adoption) and Statutory Adoption Pay (Adoptions from Overseas) (No 2) Regulation 2003, SI 2003/1194, reg 8.

30 Ie the Statutory Paternity Pay and Statutory Adoption Pay (General) Regulations 2002, SI 2002/2822, reg 13: see PARA 465.

31 Ie under the Social Security Contributions and Benefits Act 1992 s 171ZC(1) (as applied: see note 5) (see PARA 484).

32 See the Statutory Paternity Pay (Adoption) and Statutory Adoption Pay (Adoptions from Overseas) (No 2) Regulation 2003, SI 2003/1194, reg 7(1).

33 Statutory Adoption Pay (Adoptions from Overseas) (No 2) Regulation 2003, SI 2003/1194, reg 7(2). That date may be any date chosen in accordance with reg 6(1) (see the text and notes 23–26): reg 7(3).

34 Statutory Adoption Pay (Adoptions from Overseas) (No 2) Regulation 2003, SI 2003/1194, reg 7(4).

35 Ie the Statutory Paternity Pay and Statutory Adoption Pay (General) Regulations 2002, SI 2002/2822, reg 15: see PARA 463.
36 See the Statutory Paternity Pay (Adoption) and Statutory Adoption Pay (Adoptions from Overseas) (No 2) Regulation 2003, SI 2003/1194, reg 9(1).
37 Ie the conditions prescribed in the Social Security Contributions and Benefits Act 1992 s 171ZB(2)(a) (as modified: see note 5) (see PARA 484).
38 Ie by virtue of the provisions of the Social Security Contributions and Benefits Act 1992 s 171ZE(4) (as applied: see note 5) (see PARA 484).
39 Statutory Paternity Pay (Adoption) and Statutory Adoption Pay (Adoptions from Overseas) (No 2) Regulation 2003, SI 2003/1194, reg 9(2)(a).
40 Statutory Paternity Pay (Adoption) and Statutory Adoption Pay (Adoptions from Overseas) (No 2) Regulation 2003, SI 2003/1194, reg 9(2)(b). Statutory adoption pay is payable under the Social Security Contributions and Benefits Act 1992 Pt XIIZB (statutory adoption pay: see PARA 488 et seq).
41 Statutory Paternity Pay (Adoption) and Statutory Adoption Pay (Adoptions from Overseas) (No 2) Regulation 2003, SI 2003/1194, reg 9(2)(c).
42 See the Statutory Paternity Pay (Adoption) and Statutory Adoption Pay (Adoptions from Overseas) (No 2) Regulation 2003, SI 2003/1194, reg 9(3).
43 Statutory Paternity Pay (Adoption) and Statutory Adoption Pay (Adoptions from Overseas) (No 2) Regulation 2003, SI 2003/1194, reg 9(4).
44 Ie the Statutory Paternity Pay and Statutory Adoption Pay (General) Regulations 2002, SI 2002/2822, reg 16: see PARA 446. As to the meaning of 'employer' for these purposes see PARA 456.
45 As to the meaning of 'statutory pay week' see PARA 446 note 4.
46 Statutory Paternity Pay (Adoption) and Statutory Adoption Pay (Adoptions from Overseas) (No 2) Regulation 2003, SI 2003/1194, reg 10(a).
47 Statutory Paternity Pay (Adoption) and Statutory Adoption Pay (Adoptions from Overseas) (No 2) Regulation 2003, SI 2003/1194, reg 10(b).
48 Ie the Statutory Paternity Pay and Statutory Adoption Pay (General) Regulations 2002, SI 2002/2822, reg 20: see PARA 447.
49 Although 'contract of service' is defined for the purposes of statutory sick pay (see PARA 558 note 2), it is not so defined under the other statutory pay provisions (for which purposes see generally PARA 1 note 1).
50 Statutory Paternity Pay (Adoption) and Statutory Adoption Pay (Adoptions from Overseas) (No 2) Regulation 2003, SI 2003/1194, reg 11(1).
51 See the Statutory Paternity Pay (Adoption) and Statutory Adoption Pay (Adoptions from Overseas) (No 2) Regulation 2003, SI 2003/1194, reg 11(2).

486. Application of statutory paternity pay regulations regarding payments made by the Commissioners for Revenue and Customs to adoptions from overseas. Regulations made under the statutory provisions relating to statutory paternity pay[1], as they have effect with modifications[2] in relation to adoptions from overseas[3], apply statutory paternity pay regulations which provide for payments of statutory paternity pay to be made by the Commissioners for Revenue and Customs[4] to such adoptions with such modifications as are required[5].

Accordingly, the regulations which provide for payments of statutory paternity pay to be made by the Commissioners also apply to adoptions from overseas[6] without modification in relation to:

(1) the funding by the Commissioners of employers' liabilities to make payments of statutory paternity pay[7];
(2) the requirement for employers to maintain records relevant to such payments and to provide such records upon request[8];
(3) the determination by officers of the Commissioners of issues relating to a person's entitlement to such payments[9];
(4) the requirement placed on employers, employment agencies, persons claiming statutory paternity pay and others to furnish information or documents to an officer of the Commissioners on request[10].

However, the regulation which requires that an employer who has been given evidence of an employee's entitlement to statutory paternity pay, but decides that he has no liability to make payments, must furnish the employee with details of the decision and the reasons for it[11], is modified[12].

1 Ie the Social Security Contributions and Benefits Act 1992 Pt XIIZA (ss 171ZA–171ZK): see PARA 443 et seq. As to the meaning of 'statutory paternity pay' see PARA 443. As to the making of regulations under the Social Security Contributions and Benefits Act 1992 generally see PARA 407 note 3.
2 See PARA 484. As to the meaning of 'modifications' see PARA 445 note 8.
3 As to the meaning of 'adoption from overseas' see PARA 484 note 7.
4 Ie the Statutory Paternity Pay and Statutory Adoption Pay (Administration) Regulations 2002, SI 2002/2820: see PARA 464 et seq.
5 See the Statutory Paternity Pay (Adoption) and Statutory Adoption Pay (Adoptions from Overseas) (Administration) Regulations 2003, SI 2003/1192, reg 3(1). References to provisions of the Social Security Contributions and Benefits Act 1992 Pt XIIZA (statutory paternity pay: see PARA 443 et seq) and Pt XIIZB (ss 171ZL–171ZT) (statutory adoption pay: see PARA 488 et seq) in the Statutory Paternity Pay and Statutory Adoption Pay (Administration) Regulations 2002, SI 2002/2820 (as modified) (see the text and notes 6–12) are to be construed as references to the Social Security Contributions and Benefits Act 1992 Pt XIIZA or Pt XIIZB as modified by the Social Security Contributions and Benefits Act 1992 (Application of Parts 12ZA and 12ZB to Adoptions from Overseas) Regulations 2003, SI 2003/499 (see PARA 484): Statutory Paternity Pay and Statutory Adoption Pay (Administration) Regulations 2002, SI 2002/2820, reg 2(3) (added by the Statutory Paternity Pay (Adoption) and Statutory Adoption Pay (Adoptions from Overseas) (Administration) Regulations 2003, SI 2003/1192, reg 2(3)).
6 For these purposes, 'adoption from overseas' means the adoption of a child who enters Great Britain from outside the United Kingdom in connection with or for the purposes of adoption which does not involve the placement of the child for adoption under the law of any part of the United Kingdom: see the Statutory Paternity Pay (Adoption) and Statutory Adoption Pay (Adoptions from Overseas) (Administration) Regulations 2003, SI 2003/1192, reg 2. As to the meanings of 'Great Britain' and 'United Kingdom' see PARA 407 note 7. As to the law relating to child adoption see **CHILDREN AND YOUNG PERSONS** vol 9 (2012) PARA 360 et seq.
7 Ie the Statutory Paternity Pay and Statutory Adoption Pay (Administration) Regulations 2002, SI 2002/2820, regs 3–8 (see PARA 482): see the Statutory Paternity Pay (Adoption) and Statutory Adoption Pay (Adoptions from Overseas) (Administration) Regulations 2003, SI 2003/1192, reg 3(1).
8 Ie the Statutory Paternity Pay and Statutory Adoption Pay (Administration) Regulations 2002, SI 2002/2820, regs 9–10 (see PARAS 475–476): see the Statutory Paternity Pay (Adoption) and Statutory Adoption Pay (Adoptions from Overseas) (Administration) Regulations 2003, SI 2003/1192, reg 3(1).
9 Ie the Statutory Paternity Pay and Statutory Adoption Pay (Administration) Regulations 2002, SI 2002/2820, regs 12–13 (see PARA 595): see the Statutory Paternity Pay (Adoption) and Statutory Adoption Pay (Adoptions from Overseas) (Administration) Regulations 2003, SI 2003/1192, reg 3(1).
10 Ie the Statutory Paternity Pay and Statutory Adoption Pay (Administration) Regulations 2002, SI 2002/2820, reg 14 (see PARA 478): see the Statutory Paternity Pay (Adoption) and Statutory Adoption Pay (Adoptions from Overseas) (Administration) Regulations 2003, SI 2003/1192, reg 3(1).
11 Ie the Statutory Paternity Pay and Statutory Adoption Pay (Administration) Regulations 2002, SI 2002/2820, reg 11: see PARA 464.
12 The modifications take account of the fact that there is no matching of a child with an adopter in the case of adoptions from overseas. Accordingly, the Statutory Paternity Pay and Statutory Adoption Pay (Administration) Regulations 2002, SI 2002/2820, reg 11(4), which defines what is meant by an adopter being notified of having been matched with a child (see PARA 464 note 12), is omitted (Statutory Paternity Pay (Adoption) and Statutory Adoption Pay (Adoptions from Overseas) (Administration) Regulations 2003, SI 2003/1192, reg 3(5)); and the Statutory Paternity Pay and Statutory Adoption Pay (Administration) Regulations 2002, SI 2002/2820, reg 11(3)(b)(ii) (see PARA 464) provides that, in the case of entitlement to statutory paternity pay under the Social Security Contributions and Benefits Act 1992 s 171ZB(1) (see PARA 443), the time within which an employer is required to give a decision that he has no liability to make payments is the date on which the employee's evidence was provided, or, where not all of the

evidence referred to in the Statutory Paternity Pay and Statutory Adoption Pay (Administration) Regulations 2002, SI 2002/2820, reg 11(1) was provided on one date, the date on which the last of the evidence was provided (reg 11(3)(b)(ii) (modified by the Statutory Paternity Pay (Adoption) and Statutory Adoption Pay (Adoptions from Overseas) (Administration) Regulations 2003, SI 2003/1192, reg 3(4))).

487. Application of statutory paternity pay regulations regarding persons abroad and mariners to adoptions from overseas. Regulations made under the statutory provisions relating to statutory paternity pay[1], as they have effect with modifications[2] in relation to adoptions from overseas[3], apply the statutory paternity pay regulations which provide for persons abroad, persons who work as mariners and persons who work on the continental shelf to be treated as employees, and for employment in a member state to be treated as employed earner's employment, for the purposes of statutory paternity pay[4], to such adoptions with such modifications as are required[5].

Accordingly, those regulations apply in relation to adoptions from overseas[6], but with one modification, in relation to the entitlement to statutory paternity pay (adoption)[7].

1 Ie the Social Security Contributions and Benefits Act 1992 Pt XIIZA (ss 171ZA–171ZK): see PARA 443 et seq. As to the meaning of 'statutory paternity pay' see PARA 443. As to the making of regulations under the Social Security Contributions and Benefits Act 1992 generally see PARA 407 note 3.
2 See PARA 484. As to the meaning of 'modifications' see PARA 445 note 8.
3 As to the meaning of 'adoption from overseas' for these purposes see PARA 484 note 7.
4 Ie the Statutory Paternity Pay and Statutory Adoption Pay (Persons Abroad and Mariners) Regulations 2002, SI 2002/2821: see PARA 450 et seq. As to employed earner's employment within the meaning of the Social Security Contributions and Benefits Act 1992 see **WELFARE BENEFITS AND STATE PENSIONS** vol 104 (2014) PARA 176.
5 Ordinary Statutory Paternity Pay (Adoption), Additional Statutory Paternity Pay (Adoption) and Statutory Adoption Pay (Adoptions from Overseas) (Persons Abroad and Mariners) Regulations 2010, SI 2010/150, reg 4(1). References to the provisions of the Social Security Contributions and Benefits Act 1992 Pt XIIZA (statutory paternity pay: see PARA 443 et seq) and Pt XIIZB (ss 171ZL–171ZT) (statutory adoption pay: see PARA 488 et seq) in the Statutory Paternity Pay and Statutory Adoption Pay (Persons Abroad and Mariners) Regulations 2002, SI 2002/2821 (as modified) are to be construed as references to the Social Security Contributions and Benefits Act 1992 Pt XIIZA or Pt XIIZB as modified by the Social Security Contributions and Benefits Act 1992 (Application of Parts 12ZA and 12ZB to Adoptions from Overseas) Regulations 2003, SI 2003/499 (see PARA 484): Statutory Paternity Pay and Statutory Adoption Pay (Persons Abroad and Mariners) Regulations 2002, SI 2002/2821, reg 1(3) (substituted by the Ordinary Statutory Paternity Pay (Adoption), Additional Statutory Paternity Pay (Adoption) and Statutory Adoption Pay (Adoptions from Overseas) (Persons Abroad and Mariners) Regulations 2010, SI 2010/150, reg 4(3)).
6 For these purposes, 'adoption from overseas' means the adoption of a child who enters Great Britain from outside the United Kingdom in connection with or for the purposes of adoption which does not involve the placement of the child for adoption under the law of any part of the United Kingdom: see the Ordinary Statutory Paternity Pay (Adoption), Additional Statutory Paternity Pay (Adoption) and Statutory Adoption Pay (Adoptions from Overseas) (Persons Abroad and Mariners) Regulations 2010, SI 2010/150, reg 2. As to the meanings of 'Great Britain' and 'United Kingdom' see PARA 407 note 7. As to the law relating to child adoption see **CHILDREN AND YOUNG PERSONS** vol 9 (2012) PARA 360 et seq.
7 See the Ordinary Statutory Paternity Pay (Adoption), Additional Statutory Paternity Pay (Adoption) and Statutory Adoption Pay (Adoptions from Overseas) (Persons Abroad and Mariners) Regulations 2010, SI 2010/150, reg 4(1), (4). The modification, which takes account of the fact that there is no matching of a child with an adopter in the case of adoptions from overseas, requires that a person who is an employee or treated as an employee under the Statutory Paternity Pay and Statutory Adoption Pay (Persons Abroad and Mariners) Regulations 2002, SI 2002/2821, reg 3 (see PARA 451) and who, in the week in which the person receives an official notification or completes 26 weeks' continuous employment with his employer, whichever is the later: (1) was in employed earner's employment with an employer in

Great Britain; and (2) had in any week within the period of 26 weeks immediately preceding that week been employed by the same employer in another EEA state, must be treated for the purposes of the Social Security Contributions and Benefits Act 1992 s 171ZB (entitlement to statutory paternity pay (adoption): see PARA 443) as having been employed in employed earner's employment in those weeks in which he was so employed in the other EEA state: Statutory Paternity Pay and Statutory Adoption Pay (Persons Abroad and Mariners) Regulations 2002, SI 2002/2821, reg 5(2) (substituted by SI 2010/151; and modified by the Ordinary Statutory Paternity Pay (Adoption), Additional Statutory Paternity Pay (Adoption) and Statutory Adoption Pay (Adoptions from Overseas) (Persons Abroad and Mariners) Regulations 2010, SI 2010/150, reg 4(4)). For these purposes, 'adopter', in relation to a child adopted from overseas, means either a person by whom the child has been or is to be adopted, or (in a case where the child has been or is to be adopted by two people jointly) whichever of them has elected to take adoption leave under the Employment Rights Act 1996 s 75A or s 75B (power to make regulations in relation to ordinary and additional adoption leave: see PARA 377) in respect of the child: see the Statutory Paternity Pay and Statutory Adoption Pay (Persons Abroad and Mariners) Regulations 2002, SI 2002/2821, reg 1(2) (definition substituted by the Ordinary Statutory Paternity Pay (Adoption), Additional Statutory Paternity Pay (Adoption) and Statutory Adoption Pay (Adoptions from Overseas) (Persons Abroad and Mariners) Regulations 2010, SI 2010/150, reg 4(2)(b)). 'Official notification' means written notification, issued by or on behalf of the relevant domestic authority, that it is prepared to issue a certificate to the overseas authority concerned with the adoption of the child, or has issued a certificate and sent it to that authority, confirming, in either case, that the adopter is eligible to adopt and has been assessed and approved as being a suitable adoptive parent; and 'relevant domestic authority' means: (a) in the case of an adopter to whom the Intercountry Adoption (Hague Convention) Regulations 2003, SI 2003/118 (see now the Adoptions with a Foreign Element Regulations 2005, SI 2005/392) apply (see CHILDREN AND YOUNG PERSONS vol 9 (2012) PARAS 521, 528 et seq) and who is habitually resident in Wales, the National Assembly for Wales; and (b) in any other case, the Secretary of State: Statutory Paternity Pay and Statutory Adoption Pay (Persons Abroad and Mariners) Regulations 2002, SI 2002/2821, reg 1(2) (definitions added by the Ordinary Statutory Paternity Pay (Adoption), Additional Statutory Paternity Pay (Adoption) and Statutory Adoption Pay (Adoptions from Overseas) (Persons Abroad and Mariners) Regulations 2010, SI 2010/150, reg 4(2)(c), (d)). As to the meaning of 'Wales' see PARA 2 note 12. As to the National Assembly for Wales see CONSTITUTIONAL AND ADMINISTRATIVE LAW vol 20 (2014) PARA 351 et seq. As to the Secretary of State see PARA 5 note 21. As to habitual residence see CONFLICT OF LAWS vol 19 (2011) PARA 360 et seq.

(iv) Statutory Adoption Pay

A. IN GENERAL

488. Liability of employer for payment of statutory adoption pay. Where a person who is or has been an employee[1] satisfies the prescribed conditions[2], he is entitled[3] to payments (known as 'statutory adoption pay')[4]. The liability to make payments of statutory adoption pay is a liability of any person of whom the person entitled to such payments has been an employee[5] employed in accordance with the prescribed conditions[6].

Any agreement is void to the extent that it purports:

(1) to exclude, limit or otherwise modify any of the statutory adoption pay provisions[7] that are set out in Part XIIZB of the Social Security Contributions and Benefits Act 1992[8]; or

(2) to require an employee or former employee to contribute, whether directly or indirectly, towards any costs incurred by his employer[9] or former employer under those provisions[10],

but, for the avoidance of doubt, any agreement between an employer and an employee authorising any deductions from statutory adoption pay which the employer is liable to pay to the employee in respect of any period is not void by virtue of head (1) above if the employer: (a) is authorised by that or another agreement to make the same deductions from any contractual remuneration which he is liable to pay in respect of the same period[11]; or (b) would be so authorised if he were liable to pay contractual remuneration in respect of that period[12].

1 As to the meaning of 'employee' for these purposes see PARA 494.
2 Ie the conditions set out in the Social Security Contributions and Benefits Act 1992 s 171ZL(2): see PARA 503. For these purposes, 'prescribed' means prescribed by regulations: see s 171ZS(1) (ss 171ZL, 171ZM, 171ZO, 171ZS added by the Employment Act 2002 s 4).
3 Ie in accordance with the provisions of the Social Security Contributions and Benefits Act 1992 Pt XIIZB (ss 171ZL–171ZT) (statutory adoption pay): see also PARA 503 et seq.
4 Social Security Contributions and Benefits Act 1992 s 171ZL(1) (as added: see note 2). Statutory adoption pay under the Social Security Contributions and Benefits Act 1992 Pt XIIZB constitutes 'wages' for the purposes of the Employment Rights Act 1996 Pt II (ss 13–27) (protection of wages): see s 27(1); and PARA 254. Payments of statutory adoption pay under the Social Security Contributions and Benefits Act 1992 Pt XIIZB are charged to income tax under the Income Tax (Earnings and Pensions) Act 2003 Pts 2–7 (ss 3–554): see INCOME TAXATION vol 58 (2014) PARA 730 et seq. As to the effect of the Social Security Contributions and Benefits Act 1992 s 171ZL in a case involving a child placed under the Children Act 1989 s 22C (local authority's duty to provide child is in its care with accommodation: see CHILDREN AND YOUNG PERSONS vol 10 (2012) PARA 858) by a local authority in England with a local authority foster parent who has been approved as a prospective adopter see PARA 503 note 3.
5 Ie as mentioned in the Social Security Contributions and Benefits Act 1992 s 171ZL(2)(b): see PARA 503.
6 Social Security Contributions and Benefits Act 1992 s 171ZM(1) (as added: see note 2). As to the time limit for paying statutory adoption pay see PARA 516. As to the liability of the Commissioners for Revenue and Customs for payments of statutory adoption pay see PARA 489.
7 Ie any provision of the Social Security Contributions and Benefits Act 1992 Pt XIIZB (statutory adoption pay: see also PARA 489 et seq).
8 Social Security Contributions and Benefits Act 1992 s 171ZO(1)(a) (as added: see note 2).
9 As to the meaning of 'employer' for these purposes see PARA 502.
10 Social Security Contributions and Benefits Act 1992 s 171ZO(1)(b) (as added: see note 2).
11 Social Security Contributions and Benefits Act 1992 s 171ZO(2)(a) (as added: see note 2).
12 Social Security Contributions and Benefits Act 1992 s 171ZO(2)(b) (as added: see note 2).

489. Liability of the Commissioners for Revenue and Customs for payment of statutory adoption pay. The Secretary of State[1] may, with the concurrence of the Commissioners for Revenue and Customs[2], by regulations[3] specify circumstances in which[4] liability to make payments of statutory adoption pay[5] is to be a liability of the Commissioners[6].

Accordingly, where:

(1) an officer of the Commissioners for Revenue and Customs has determined that an employer[7] is liable to make payments of statutory adoption pay to a person[8]; and
(2) the time for appealing against that determination has expired[9]; and
(3) no appeal against the determination has been lodged or leave to appeal against the determination is required and has been refused[10],

then for any week in respect of which the employer was liable to make payments of statutory adoption pay but did not do so, and for any subsequent weeks in the adoption pay period[11], the liability to make those payments is[12] that of the Commissioners and not the employer[13].

Liability to make payments of statutory adoption pay is[14] a liability of the Commissioners and not the employer as from the week in which the employer first becomes insolvent[15] until the end of the adoption pay period[16].

1 As to the Secretary of State see PARA 5 note 21.
2 Ie with the concurrence of the Board. For these purposes, the 'Board' means the Commissioners for Revenue and Customs: see the Social Security Contributions and Benefits Act 1992 s 171ZS(1) (ss 171ZM, 171ZS added by the Employment Act 2002 s 4); the Employment

Act 2002 s 16; and the Statutory Paternity Pay and Statutory Adoption Pay (General) Regulations 2002, SI 2002/2822, reg 2(1). As to the Commissioners for Her Majesty's Revenue and Customs see INCOME TAXATION vol 58 (2014) PARAS 33–34.

3 As to the making of regulations under the Social Security Contributions and Benefits Act 1992 see PARA 407 note 3.
4 Ie notwithstanding the Social Security Contributions and Benefits Act 1992 s 171ZM: see PARAS 488, 493.
5 As to the meaning of 'statutory adoption pay' see PARA 488.
6 Social Security Contributions and Benefits Act 1992 s 171ZM(3) (as added: see note 2). In exercise of the powers conferred by s 171ZM(3), the Secretary of State has made the Statutory Paternity Pay and Statutory Adoption Pay (General) Regulations 2002, SI 2002/2822 (see the text and notes 7–16) and the Statutory Paternity Pay (Adoption) and Statutory Adoption Pay (Adoptions from Overseas) (No 2) Regulations 2003, SI 2003/1194 (see PARA 531).
7 As to the meaning of 'employer' for these purposes see PARA 502.
8 Statutory Paternity Pay and Statutory Adoption Pay (General) Regulations 2002, SI 2002/2822, regs 31(1), 43(1)(a). See note 2.
9 Statutory Paternity Pay and Statutory Adoption Pay (General) Regulations 2002, SI 2002/2822, regs 31(1), 43(1)(b).
10 Statutory Paternity Pay and Statutory Adoption Pay (General) Regulations 2002, SI 2002/2822, regs 31(1), 43(1)(c).
11 As to the meaning of 'adoption pay period' see PARA 511.
12 Ie notwithstanding the Social Security Contributions and Benefits Act 1992 s 171ZM: see PARAS 488, 493.
13 See the Statutory Paternity Pay and Statutory Adoption Pay (General) Regulations 2002, SI 2002/2822, regs 31(1), 43(1). As to the time limit for paying statutory adoption pay see PARA 517. In connection with the payment of statutory adoption pay or of any other sum in connection with that pay the Commissioners may use electronic communications: see the Statutory Payment Schemes (Electronic Communications) Regulations 2002, SI 2002/3047; and INCOME TAXATION.
14 Ie notwithstanding the Social Security Contributions and Benefits Act 1992 s 171ZM: see PARAS 488, 493.
15 For these purposes, an employer is to be taken to be insolvent if, and only if, in England and Wales:
    (1) he has been adjudged bankrupt or has made a composition or arrangement with his creditors (Statutory Paternity Pay and Statutory Adoption Pay (General) Regulations 2002, SI 2002/2822, regs 31(1), 43(3)(a)(i));
    (2) he has died and his estate falls to be administered in accordance with an order under the Insolvency Act 1986 s 421 (insolvent estates of deceased persons: see BANKRUPTCY AND INDIVIDUAL INSOLVENCY vol 5 (2013) PARA 830 et seq) (Statutory Paternity Pay and Statutory Adoption Pay (General) Regulations 2002, SI 2002/2822, regs 31(1), 43(3)(a)(ii)); or
    (3) where an employer is a company or a limited liability partnership, a winding-up order is made or a resolution for voluntary winding up is passed (or, in the case of a limited liability partnership, a determination for a voluntary winding up has been made) with respect to it or it enters administration, or a receiver or manager of its undertaking is duly appointed, or possession is taken, by or on behalf of the holders of any debentures secured by a floating charge, of any property of the company or limited liability partnership comprised in or subject to the charge or a voluntary arrangement proposed for the purposes of the Insolvency Act 1986 Pt I (ss 1–7B) (company voluntary arrangements: see COMPANY AND PARTNERSHIP INSOLVENCY vol 16 (2011) PARA 83 et seq) is approved under Pt I (Statutory Paternity Pay and Statutory Adoption Pay (General) Regulations 2002, SI 2002/2822, regs 31(1), 43(3)(a)(iii) (amended by SI 2003/2096)).

As to the meanings of 'England' and 'Wales' see PARA 2 note 12. As to compositions or arrangements with creditors see BANKRUPTCY AND INDIVIDUAL INSOLVENCY vol 5 (2013) PARA 43 et seq; and as to bankruptcy generally see BANKRUPTCY AND INDIVIDUAL INSOLVENCY vol 5 (2013) PARA 129 et seq. As to winding-up orders see COMPANY AND PARTNERSHIP INSOLVENCY vol 16 (2011) PARA 386 et seq. As to voluntary winding-up see COMPANY AND PARTNERSHIP INSOLVENCY vol 17 (2011) PARA 898 et seq. As to administration orders see COMPANY AND PARTNERSHIP INSOLVENCY vol 16 (2011) PARA 159 et seq. As to the appointment of receivers and managers see COMPANY AND PARTNERSHIP INSOLVENCY vol 16 (2011) PARA 340 et seq. As to the taking of possession by or on behalf of the holders of debentures secured by a floating charge see COMPANIES vol 15 (2009) PARA 1333 et seq.

16 Statutory Paternity Pay and Statutory Adoption Pay (General) Regulations 2002, SI 2002/2822, regs 31(1), 43(2).

490. General power to make regulations in relation to statutory adoption pay. The Secretary of State[1] may by regulations[2]:

(1) provide that the conditions giving entitlement to statutory adoption pay[3] which relate to employment and earnings[4] have effect subject to prescribed[5] modifications in such cases as may be prescribed[6];

(2) provide that the notice requirements[7] are not to have effect, or are to have effect subject to prescribed modifications[8], in such cases as may be prescribed[9];

(3) impose requirements about evidence of entitlement[10];

(4) specify in what circumstances employment is to be treated[11] as continuous[12];

(5) provide that a person is to be treated[13] as being employed for a continuous period of at least 26 weeks[14], where:

  (a) he has been employed by the same employer for at least 26 weeks under two or more separate contracts of service[15]; and

  (b) those contracts were not continuous[16];

(6) provide for amounts earned by a person under separate contracts of service with the same employer to be aggregated[17];

(7) provide that:

  (a) the amount of a person's earnings for any period[18]; or

  (b) the amount of his earnings to be treated as comprised in any payment made to him or for his benefit[19],

is to be calculated or estimated[20] in such manner and on such basis as may be prescribed and that for that purpose payments of a particular class or description made or falling to be made to or by a person are, to such extent as may be prescribed, to be disregarded or, as the case may be, to be deducted from the amount of his earnings[21];

(8) make provision about elections for statutory adoption pay[22].

The Secretary of State may also by regulations specify circumstances in which there is to be no liability to pay statutory adoption pay in respect of a week[23].

1 As to the Secretary of State see PARA 5 note 21.
2 As to the making of regulations under the Social Security Contributions and Benefits Act 1992 generally see PARA 407 note 3.
3 As to the meaning of 'statutory adoption pay' see PARA 488.
4 Ie the Social Security Contributions and Benefits Act 1992 s 171ZL(2)(b)–(d): see PARA 503.
5 For these purposes, 'prescribed' means prescribed by regulations: see the Social Security Contributions and Benefits Act 1992 s 171ZS(1) (ss 171ZL, 171ZS added by the Employment Act 2002 s 4).
6 Social Security Contributions and Benefits Act 1992 s 171ZL(8)(a) (as added: see note 5).

As from a day to be appointed under the Welfare Reform Act 2012 s 150(3), the Social Security Contributions and Benefits Act 1992 s 171ZL(8)(za) is added allowing for regulations to provide for circumstances in which s 171ZL(2)(ba) (not yet in force) (entitlement to be in qualifying employment: see PARA 503) does not apply: see s 171ZL(8)(za) (prospectively added by the Welfare Reform Act 2012 s 63(1), (8)(c)). However, at the date at which this volume states the law, no such day had been appointed.

7 Ie under the Social Security Contributions and Benefits Act 1992 s 171ZL(6): see PARA 508.
8 For these purposes, 'modifications' includes additions, omissions and amendments; and related expressions are to be read accordingly: see the Social Security Contributions and Benefits Act 1992 s 171ZS(1) (as added: see note 5).
9 Social Security Contributions and Benefits Act 1992 s 171ZL(8)(b) (as added: see note 5). In exercise of the powers conferred by s 171ZL(8)(b)–(d), (f), (g), the Secretary of State has made the Statutory Paternity Pay and Statutory Adoption Pay (General) Regulations 2002,

SI 2002/2822 (see PARA 488 et seq) and the Statutory Paternity Pay (Adoption) and Statutory Adoption Pay (Adoptions from Overseas) (No 2) Regulations 2003, SI 2003/1194 (see PARA 531).

10 Social Security Contributions and Benefits Act 1992 s 171ZL(8)(c) (as added: see note 5). As to the regulations made see note 9; and PARA 509. Regulations under s 171ZT(2) may modify s 171ZL(8)(c) so as to enable regulations to impose requirements to make statutory declarations as to eligibility to apply for a parental order under the Human Fertilisation and Embryology Act 2008 s 54 (parental orders: see **CHILDREN AND YOUNG PERSONS** vol 9 (2012) PARA 129), and as to intention to apply for such an order: see the Social Security Contributions and Benefits Act 1992 s 171ZT(3); and PARA 530 note 6.

11 Ie for the purposes of the Social Security Contributions and Benefits Act 1992 s 171ZL.

12 Social Security Contributions and Benefits Act 1992 s 171ZL(8)(d) (as added: see note 5). As to the regulations made see note 9; and PARA 504.

13 Ie for the purposes of the Social Security Contributions and Benefits Act 1992 s 171ZL.

14 See the Social Security Contributions and Benefits Act 1992 s 171ZL(8)(e) (as added: see note 5). As to the regulations made see note 9; and PARA 504.

For these purposes, except in relation to s 171ZN (rate and period of pay: see PARA 491 note 4) and s 171ZP (relationship with benefits and other payments: see PARA 518 note 4), 'week' means a period of seven days beginning with Sunday or such other period as may be prescribed in relation to any particular case or class of cases: see the Social Security Contributions and Benefits Act 1992 s 171ZS(5) (as added: see note 5). Regulations under s 171ZS(5) must be made with the concurrence of the Commissioners for Revenue and Customs: see s 171ZS(1), (12) (as so added). At the date at which this volume states the law, no such regulations had been made. As to the Commissioners for Her Majesty's Revenue and Customs see **INCOME TAXATION** vol 58 (2014) PARAS 33–34; and see PARA 489 note 2.

15 Social Security Contributions and Benefits Act 1992 s 171ZL(8)(e)(i) (as added: see note 5). As to the meaning of 'employer' for these purposes see PARA 502.

16 Social Security Contributions and Benefits Act 1992 s 171ZL(8)(e)(ii) (as added: see note 5).

17 Social Security Contributions and Benefits Act 1992 s 171ZL(8)(f) (as added: see note 5). Head (6) in the text refers to provision for amounts to be aggregated for the purposes of s 171ZL: see s 171ZL(8)(f) (as so added). As to the regulations made see note 9.

18 Social Security Contributions and Benefits Act 1992 s 171ZL(8)(g)(i) (as added: see note 5).

19 Social Security Contributions and Benefits Act 1992 s 171ZL(8)(g)(ii) (as added: see note 5).

20 Ie for the purposes of the Social Security Contributions and Benefits Act 1992 s 171ZL.

21 Social Security Contributions and Benefits Act 1992 s 171ZL(8)(g) (as added: see note 5). As to the regulations made see note 9; and PARA 514.

22 Social Security Contributions and Benefits Act 1992 s 171ZL(8)(h) (as added: see note 5).

23 See the Social Security Contributions and Benefits Act 1992 s 171ZN(6); and PARA 491.

491. Circumstances in which liability to pay statutory adoption pay does not arise. The Secretary of State[1] may by regulations[2] specify circumstances in which there is to be no liability to pay statutory adoption pay[3] in respect of a week[4]. Accordingly, no liability to make payments of statutory adoption pay to a person arises in respect of any week:

(1) during any part of which the person entitled to it is entitled[5] to statutory sick pay[6];
(2) following that in which the person claiming it has died[7]; or
(3) during any part of which the person entitled to it is detained in legal custody[8], where that person is:
    (a) released subsequently without charge[9];
    (b) subsequently found not guilty of any offence and is released[10]; or
    (c) convicted of an offence but does not receive a custodial sentence[11],

    or where that person is sentenced to a term of imprisonment (except where the sentence is suspended)[12].

Where there is liability to pay statutory adoption pay in respect of a period which is subsequent to the last week falling within head (3) above, or where there is liability to pay statutory adoption pay during a period of detention in legal custody by virtue of the provisions of heads (3)(a) to (3)(c) above, the liability is[13] that of the Commissioners for Revenue and Customs[14] and not the employer[15].

Except in such cases as may be prescribed[16]:

(i) a person is not liable to pay statutory adoption pay to another in respect of any week[17] during any part of which the other person works under a contract of service with him[18]; and

(ii) statutory adoption pay is not payable to a person in respect of any week[19] during any part of which he works for any employer[20] who is not liable to pay him statutory adoption pay[21].

Accordingly, pursuant to head (ii) above, where there is more than one employer, statutory adoption pay is payable to a person in respect of a week during any part of which he works only for an employer who is not liable to pay him statutory adoption pay[22], and for whom he has worked in the week in which he is notified of being matched with the child[23].

1 As to the Secretary of State see PARA 5 note 21.

2 As to the making of regulations under the Social Security Contributions and Benefits Act 1992 see PARA 407 note 3.

3 As to the meaning of 'statutory adoption pay' see PARA 488. As to the persons liable to make payments of statutory adoption pay see PARA 488 et seq.

4 Social Security Contributions and Benefits Act 1992 s 171ZN(6) (ss 171ZN, 171ZS added by the Employment Act 2002 s 4). For this purpose, 'week' means a period of seven days beginning with the day of the week on which the adoption pay period begins: see the Social Security Contributions and Benefits Act 1992 s 171ZN(8) (as so added). As to the meaning of 'adoption pay period' see PARA 511. In exercise of the powers conferred by s 171ZN(6), the Secretary of State has made the Statutory Paternity Pay and Statutory Adoption Pay (General) Regulations 2002, SI 2002/2822 (see the text and notes 5–15) and the Statutory Paternity Pay (Adoption) and Statutory Adoption Pay (Adoptions from Overseas) (No 2) Regulations 2003, SI 2003/1194 (see PARA 531).

5 Ie under the Social Security Contributions and Benefits Act 1992 Pt XI (ss 151–163) (statutory sick pay): see PARA 558 et seq.

6 Statutory Paternity Pay and Statutory Adoption Pay (General) Regulations 2002, SI 2002/2822, reg 27(1)(a).

7 Statutory Paternity Pay and Statutory Adoption Pay (General) Regulations 2002, SI 2002/2822, reg 27(1)(b).

8 See the Statutory Paternity Pay and Statutory Adoption Pay (General) Regulations 2002, SI 2002/2822, reg 27(1)(c), (2).

9 Statutory Paternity Pay and Statutory Adoption Pay (General) Regulations 2002, SI 2002/2822, reg 27(2)(a).

10 Statutory Paternity Pay and Statutory Adoption Pay (General) Regulations 2002, SI 2002/2822, reg 27(2)(b).

11 Statutory Paternity Pay and Statutory Adoption Pay (General) Regulations 2002, SI 2002/2822, reg 27(2)(c).

12 See the Statutory Paternity Pay and Statutory Adoption Pay (General) Regulations 2002, SI 2002/2822, reg 27(1)(c).

13 Ie notwithstanding the Social Security Contributions and Benefits Act 1992 s 171ZM: see PARAS 488, 493.

14 As to the Commissioners for Her Majesty's Revenue and Customs see INCOME TAXATION vol 58 (2014) PARAS 33–34; and see PARA 489 note 2.

15 See the Statutory Paternity Pay and Statutory Adoption Pay (General) Regulations 2002, SI 2002/2822, regs 31(2), 44. As to payment by the Commissioners for Revenue and Customs see further PARA 517.

16 For these purposes, 'prescribed' means prescribed by regulations: see the Social Security Contributions and Benefits Act 1992 s 171ZS(1) (as added: see note 4).

17 For this purpose, 'week' means a period of seven days beginning with the day of the week on which the adoption pay period begins: see the Social Security Contributions and Benefits Act 1992 s 171ZN(8) (as added: see note 4).

18 Social Security Contributions and Benefits Act 1992 s 171ZN(3) (s 171ZN as added (see note 4); s 171ZN(3) amended by the Work and Families Act 2006 Sch 1 para 21(1), (2)). It is

immaterial for these purposes whether the work referred to is work under a contract of service which existed immediately before the adoption pay period or a contract of service which did not so exist: Social Security Contributions and Benefits Act 1992 s 171ZN(4) (as so added). Although 'contract of service' is defined for the purposes of statutory sick pay (see PARA 558 note 2), it is not so defined under the other statutory pay provisions (for which purposes see generally PARA 1 note 1). As to limited working during the adoption pay period see PARA 492.

19 See note 17.

20 As to the meaning of 'employer' for these purposes see PARA 502.

21 Social Security Contributions and Benefits Act 1992 s 171ZN(5) (as added: see note 4). In exercise of the powers conferred by s 171ZN(5), the Secretary of State has made the Statutory Paternity Pay and Statutory Adoption Pay (General) Regulations 2002, SI 2002/2822 (see the text and notes 22–23) and the Statutory Paternity Pay (Adoption) and Statutory Adoption Pay (Adoptions from Overseas) (No 2) Regulations 2003, SI 2003/1194 (see PARA 531).

22 See the Statutory Paternity Pay and Statutory Adoption Pay (General) Regulations 2002, SI 2002/2822, reg 25(a).

23 See the Statutory Paternity Pay and Statutory Adoption Pay (General) Regulations 2002, SI 2002/2822, reg 25(b). As to the date on which a person receives notification of having been matched with a child see PARA 446 note 24.

492. Working during adoption pay period. Where an employee[1] does any work under a contract of service[2] with his employer[3] on any day for not more than ten such days during his adoption pay period[4], whether consecutive or not, statutory adoption pay[5] continues to be payable to the employee by the employer[6].

1 As to the meaning of 'employee' for these purposes see PARA 494.

2 Although 'contract of service' is defined for the purposes of statutory sick pay (see PARA 558 note 2), it is not so defined under the other statutory pay provisions (for which purposes see generally PARA 1 note 1).

3 As to the meaning of 'employer' for these purposes see PARA 502.

4 As to the meaning of 'adoption pay period' see PARA 511.

5 As to the meaning of 'statutory adoption pay' see PARA 488.

6 Statutory Paternity Pay and Statutory Adoption Pay (General) Regulations 2002, SI 2002/2822, reg 27A (added by SI 2006/2236).

493. Contract of service ended for the purpose of avoiding liability for statutory adoption pay. Regulations under the Social Security Contributions and Benefits Act 1992[1] must make provision as to a former employer's[2] liability to pay statutory adoption pay[3] to a person in any case where the former employer's contract of service[4] with him has been brought to an end by the former employer solely, or mainly, for the purpose of avoiding liability for statutory adoption pay[5].

Accordingly, a former employer is liable to make payments of statutory adoption pay to a former employee[6] in any case where the employee had been employed for a continuous period of at least eight weeks and his contract of service was brought to an end by the former employer solely, or mainly, for the purpose of avoiding liability for statutory adoption pay[7]. In such a case: (1) the employee is treated as if he had been employed for a continuous period ending with the week in which he was notified of having been matched with a child for adoption[8]; and (2) his normal weekly earnings are to be calculated by reference to his normal weekly earnings[9] for the period of eight weeks ending with the last day in respect of which he was paid under his former contract of service[10].

1 As to the making of regulations under the Social Security Contributions and Benefits Act 1992 see PARA 407 note 3.

2 As to the meaning of 'employer' for these purposes see PARA 502.

3 As to the meaning of 'statutory adoption pay' see PARA 488.

4 Although 'contract of service' is defined for the purposes of statutory sick pay (see PARA 558 note 2), it is not so defined under the other statutory pay provisions (for which purposes see generally PARA 1 note 1).
5 Social Security Contributions and Benefits Act 1992 s 171ZM(2) (added by the Employment Act 2002 s 4). In exercise of the powers conferred by the Social Security Contributions and Benefits Act 1992 s 171ZM(2), the Secretary of State has made the Statutory Paternity Pay and Statutory Adoption Pay (General) Regulations 2002, SI 2002/2822 (see the text and notes 6–10) and the Statutory Paternity Pay (Adoption) and Statutory Adoption Pay (Adoptions from Overseas) (No 2) Regulations 2003, SI 2003/1194 (see PARA 531).
6 As to the meaning of 'employee' for these purposes see PARA 494.
7 Statutory Paternity Pay and Statutory Adoption Pay (General) Regulations 2002, SI 2002/2822, reg 30(1). As to continuity of employment see PARA 504 et seq.
8 Statutory Paternity Pay and Statutory Adoption Pay (General) Regulations 2002, SI 2002/2822, reg 30(2)(a). As to the date on which a person is notified of having been matched with a child see PARA 446 note 24.
9 As to the calculation of normal weekly earnings see PARA 514.
10 Statutory Paternity Pay and Statutory Adoption Pay (General) Regulations 2002, SI 2002/2822, reg 30(2)(b).

B. MEANING OF 'EMPLOYEE' AND 'EMPLOYER'

494. Meaning of 'employee'; treatment of two or more contracts of service as one. For the purposes of the statutory adoption pay provisions that are set out in Part XIIZB of the Social Security Contributions and Benefits Act 1992[1], 'employee' means a person who is gainfully employed in Great Britain[2] either under a contract of service[3] or in an office (including elective office) with earnings (as defined)[4], but subject to regulations[5] which may provide for cases where any such person is not to be treated as an employee for those purposes[6], and for cases where a person who would not otherwise be an employee for those purposes is to be treated as an employee for those purposes[7].

Accordingly, in a case where, and in so far as, a person over the age of 16 is treated as an employed earner[8], he is to be treated as an employee for the purposes of Part XIIZB of the Social Security Contributions and Benefits Act 1992; and, in a case where, and in so far as, such a person is treated otherwise than as an employed earner, he is not to be treated as an employee for those purposes[9].

Any person who is in employed earner's employment[10] under a contract of apprenticeship is to be treated[11] as an employee[12].

A person who is in employed earner's employment but whose employer[13]:

(1) does not fulfil the prescribed conditions[14] as to residence or presence in Great Britain[15]; or
(2) is a person who, by reason of any international treaty to which the United Kingdom[16] is a party or of any international convention binding the United Kingdom[17]: (a) is exempt from the provisions of the Social Security Contributions and Benefits Act 1992[18]; or (b) is a person against whom the provisions of that Act are not enforceable[19],

is not to be treated[20] as an employee[21].

Without prejudice to any other power to make regulations under Part XIIZB of the Social Security Contributions and Benefits Act 1992[22], regulations may specify cases in which two or more contracts of service in respect of which the same person is an employee are to be treated[23] as one[24]. Accordingly, where two or more contracts of service exist concurrently between one employer and one employee, they are to be treated[25] as one except where[26] the earnings from those contracts of service are not aggregated for the purposes of earnings-related contributions[27].

1 Ie in the Social Security Contributions and Benefits Act 1992 Pt XIIZB (ss 171ZL–171ZT) (statutory adoption pay: see also PARAS 488 et seq, 495 et seq).

2 As to the meaning of 'Great Britain' for these purposes see PARA 407 note 7.

3 Although 'contract of service' is defined for the purposes of statutory sick pay (see PARA 558 note 2), it is not so defined under the other statutory pay provisions (for which purposes see generally PARA 1 note 1).

4 Social Security Contributions and Benefits Act 1992 s 171ZS(2) (s 171ZS added by the Employment Act 2002 s 4; the Social Security Contributions and Benefits Act 1992 s 171ZS(2) amended by the Income Tax (Earnings and Pensions) Act 2003 Sch 6 Pt 2 paras 169, 184; the National Insurance Contributions Act 2014 s 15(3), Sch 2 paras 1, 6; and SI 2006/1031). The reference in the text to earnings is to earnings within the meaning of the Social Security Contributions and Benefits Act 1992 Pts I–V (ss 1–110) (see ss 3, 4, 112, 122; and **WELFARE BENEFITS AND STATE PENSIONS** vol 104 (2014) PARAS 381, 382). As to the meaning of 'employee' and related expressions in relation to employment rights generally see PARA 2 et seq.

5 As to the making of regulations under the Social Security Contributions and Benefits Act 1992 see PARA 407 note 3.

6 Social Security Contributions and Benefits Act 1992 s 171ZS(3)(a) (as added: see note 4). In exercise of the powers conferred by s 171ZS(3), the Secretary of State has made the Statutory Paternity Pay and Statutory Adoption Pay (General) Regulations 2002, SI 2002/2822 (see the text and notes 8–19) and the Statutory Paternity Pay (Adoption) and Statutory Adoption Pay (Adoptions from Overseas) (No 2) Regulations 2003, SI 2003/1194 (see PARA 531).

7 Social Security Contributions and Benefits Act 1992 s 171ZS(3)(b) (as added: see note 4). See note 6.

8 Ie by virtue of the Social Security (Categorisation of Earners) Regulations 1978, SI 1978/1689: see **WELFARE BENEFITS AND STATE PENSIONS** vol 104 (2014) PARA 381.

9 Statutory Paternity Pay and Statutory Adoption Pay (General) Regulations 2002, SI 2002/2822, regs 31(1), 32(1) (reg 32(1) amended by SI 2006/1031). The Statutory Paternity Pay and Statutory Adoption Pay (General) Regulations 2002, SI 2002/2822, reg 32(1) is subject to reg 32(1A): see reg 32(1) (as so amended). Accordingly, reg 32(1) has effect in relation to a person who:

(1) is under the age of 16 (see regs 31(1), 32(1A)(a) (reg 32(1A) added by SI 2006/1031; and substituted by SI 2007/825)); and

(2) would or, as the case may be, would not have been treated as an employed earner by virtue of the Social Security (Categorisation of Earners) Regulations 1978, SI 1978/1689 (see **WELFARE BENEFITS AND STATE PENSIONS** vol 104 (2014) PARA 381) had he been over that age (Statutory Paternity Pay and Statutory Adoption Pay (General) Regulations 2002, SI 2002/2822, regs 31(1), 32(1A)(b) (reg 32(1A) as so added and substituted)),

as it has effect in relation to a person who is or, as the case may be, is not so treated (see regs 31(1), 32(1A) (reg 32(1A) as so added and substituted)). A person who would not be treated under reg 32 as an employee for the purposes of the Social Security Contributions and Benefits Act 1992 Pt XIIZB (statutory adoption pay: see also PARAS 488 et seq, 495 et seq) if his employment were in Great Britain is not to be treated as an employee under the Statutory Paternity Pay and Statutory Adoption Pay (Persons Abroad and Mariners) Regulations 2002, SI 2002/2821: see reg 2 (amended by SI 2010/151).

10 Ie within the meaning of the Social Security Contributions and Benefits Act 1992: see **WELFARE BENEFITS AND STATE PENSIONS** vol 104 (2014) PARA 176.

11 Ie for the purposes of the Social Security Contributions and Benefits Act 1992 Pt XIIZB (statutory adoption pay: see also PARAS 488 et seq, 495 et seq).

12 Statutory Paternity Pay and Statutory Adoption Pay (General) Regulations 2002, SI 2002/2822, regs 31(1), 32(2). As to the position of apprentices and youth trainees at common law see PARAS 112, 128–129, 636, 747–754. As to the statutory law on apprenticeships see **EDUCATION** vol 35 (2011) PARA 682 et seq.

13 See the Statutory Paternity Pay and Statutory Adoption Pay (General) Regulations 2002, SI 2002/2822, regs 31(1), 32(3).

14 Ie the conditions prescribed in the Social Security (Contributions) Regulations 2001, SI 2001/1004, reg 145(1) (conditions as to residence or presence in Great Britain: see **WELFARE BENEFITS AND STATE PENSIONS** vol 104 (2014) PARA 406).

15 Statutory Paternity Pay and Statutory Adoption Pay (General) Regulations 2002, SI 2002/2822, regs 31(1), 32(3)(a).

16 As to the meaning of 'United Kingdom' for these purposes see PARA 407 note 7.

17 Statutory Paternity Pay and Statutory Adoption Pay (General) Regulations 2002, SI 2002/2822, regs 31(1), 32(3)(b).

18 Statutory Paternity Pay and Statutory Adoption Pay (General) Regulations 2002, SI 2002/2822, regs 31(1), 32(3)(b)(i).
19 Statutory Paternity Pay and Statutory Adoption Pay (General) Regulations 2002, SI 2002/2822, regs 31(1), 32(3)(b)(ii).
20 Ie for the purposes of the Social Security Contributions and Benefits Act 1992 Pt XIIZB (statutory adoption pay: see also PARAS 488 et seq, 495 et seq).
21 See the Statutory Paternity Pay and Statutory Adoption Pay (General) Regulations 2002, SI 2002/2822, regs 31(1), 32(3).
22 Ie under the Social Security Contributions and Benefits Act 1992 Pt XIIZB (statutory adoption pay: see also PARAS 488 et seq, 495 et seq).
23 Ie for the purposes of the Social Security Contributions and Benefits Act 1992 Pt XIIZB (statutory adoption pay: see also PARAS 488 et seq, 495 et seq) or such provisions of Pt XIIZB as may be prescribed.
24 Social Security Contributions and Benefits Act 1992 s 171ZS(4)(b) (as added: see note 4). Regulations under s 171ZS(4) must be made with the concurrence of the Commissioners for Revenue and Customs: s 171ZS(1), (12) (as so added). As to the Commissioners for Her Majesty's Revenue and Customs see **INCOME TAXATION** vol 58 (2014) PARAS 33–34; and see PARA 489 note 2. In exercise of the powers conferred by s 171ZS(4), the Secretary of State has, with the concurrence of the Commissioners, made the Statutory Paternity Pay and Statutory Adoption Pay (General) Regulations 2002, SI 2002/2822 (see the text and notes 25–27) and the Statutory Paternity Pay (Adoption) and Statutory Adoption Pay (Adoptions from Overseas) (No 2) Regulations 2003, SI 2003/1194 (see PARA 531).
25 Ie for the purposes of the Social Security Contributions and Benefits Act 1992 Pt XIIZB (statutory adoption pay: see also PARAS 488 et seq, 495 et seq).
26 Ie by virtue of the Social Security (Contributions) Regulations 2001, SI 2001/1004, reg 14 (aggregation of earnings paid in respect of separate employed earner's employments under the same employer: see **WELFARE BENEFITS AND STATE PENSIONS** vol 104 (2014) PARA 382).
27 Statutory Paternity Pay and Statutory Adoption Pay (General) Regulations 2002, SI 2002/2822, regs 31(1), 38(3).

495. Modification of statutory provisions relating to statutory adoption pay to accommodate special classes of person. The Secretary of State[1] may, with the concurrence of the Treasury[2], make regulations[3] modifying any of the statutory adoption pay provisions that are set out in Part XIIZB of the Social Security Contributions and Benefits Act 1992[4], in such manner as he thinks proper, in their application to any person who is, has been or is to be[5]:

(1) employed on board any ship, vessel, hovercraft or aircraft[6];
(2) outside Great Britain[7] at any prescribed[8] time or in any prescribed circumstances[9]; or
(3) in prescribed employment in connection with continental shelf operations[10].

Such regulations may, in particular, provide:

(a) for any provision of Part XIIZB of the Social Security Contributions and Benefits Act 1992[11] to apply to any such person, notwithstanding that it would not otherwise apply[12];
(b) for any such provision not to apply to any such person, notwithstanding that it would otherwise apply[13];
(c) for excepting any such person from the application of any such provision where he neither is domiciled[14] nor has a place of residence in any part of Great Britain[15];
(d) for the taking of evidence, for the purposes of the determination of any question arising under any such provision, in a country or territory outside Great Britain, by a British consular official or such other person as may be determined in accordance with the regulations[16].

The Secretary of State may also make regulations modifying the provisions relating to statutory adoption pay in relation to other cases which involve adoption[17].

1 As to the Secretary of State see PARA 5 note 21.
2 As to the Treasury see CONSTITUTIONAL AND ADMINISTRATIVE LAW vol 20 (2014) PARAS 262–265.
3 As to the making of regulations under the Social Security Contributions and Benefits Act 1992 see PARA 407 note 3; and as to the Secretary of State's general power to make regulations relating to statutory adoption pay see PARA 490.
4 Ie any provision of the Social Security Contributions and Benefits Act 1992 Pt XIIZB (ss 171ZL–171ZT) (statutory adoption pay: see also PARAS 488 et seq, 500 et seq). As to the meaning of 'statutory adoption pay' see PARA 488.
5 See the Social Security Contributions and Benefits Act 1992 s 171ZR(1) (ss 171ZR, 171ZS added by the Employment Act 2002 s 4).
6 Social Security Contributions and Benefits Act 1992 s 171ZR(1)(a) (as added: see note 5).
7 As to the meaning of 'Great Britain' for these purposes see PARA 407 note 7.
8 For these purposes, 'prescribed' means prescribed by regulations: see the Social Security Contributions and Benefits Act 1992 s 171ZS(1) (as added: see note 5).
9 Social Security Contributions and Benefits Act 1992 s 171ZR(1)(b) (as added: see note 5).
10 Social Security Contributions and Benefits Act 1992 s 171ZR(1)(c) (as added: see note 5). 'Continental shelf operations' means any activities which, if the Petroleum Act 1998 s 11(8)(a), (d) (application of civil law to certain offshore activities) were omitted, would nevertheless fall within s 11(2) (see ENERGY AND CLIMATE CHANGE vol 44 (2011) PARA 1080): see the Social Security Contributions and Benefits Act 1992 s 120(2) (amended by the Petroleum Act 1998 Sch 4 para 30); definition applied by the Social Security Contributions and Benefits Act 1992 s 171ZR(1)(c) (as so added). In exercise of the powers conferred under head (3) in the text, the Secretary of State has, with the concurrence of the Treasury, made the Statutory Paternity Pay and Statutory Adoption Pay (Persons Abroad and Mariners) Regulations 2002, SI 2002/2821 (see PARA 496 et seq), and the Ordinary Statutory Paternity Pay (Adoption), Additional Statutory Paternity Pay (Adoption) and Statutory Adoption Pay (Adoptions from Overseas) (Persons Abroad and Mariners) Regulations 2010, SI 2010/150 (see PARA 533).
11 Ie any provision of the Social Security Contributions and Benefits Act 1992 Pt XIIZB (statutory adoption pay: see also PARAS 488 et seq, 495 et seq).
12 Social Security Contributions and Benefits Act 1992 s 171ZR(2)(a) (as added: see note 5).
13 Social Security Contributions and Benefits Act 1992 s 171ZR(2)(b) (as added: see note 5).
14 As to domicile see CONFLICT OF LAWS vol 19 (2011) PARA 336 et seq.
15 Social Security Contributions and Benefits Act 1992 s 171ZR(2)(c) (as added: see note 5).
16 Social Security Contributions and Benefits Act 1992 s 171ZR(2)(d) (as added: see note 5).
17 See the Social Security Contributions and Benefits Act 1992 s 171ZT; and PARA 530.

496. Time for compliance with provisions relating to statutory adoption pay; employee outside the United Kingdom. Where:

(1) a person is outside the United Kingdom[1];
(2) the statutory adoption pay provisions that are set out in Part XIIZB of the Social Security Contributions and Benefits Act 1992[2] (or regulations made thereunder) require any act to be done forthwith or on the happening of a certain event or within a specified time[3]; and
(3) because the person is outside the United Kingdom, he or his employer[4] cannot comply with the requirement[5],

the person or the employer, as the case may be, is deemed to have complied with it if the act is performed as soon as reasonably practicable[6].

1 Statutory Paternity Pay and Statutory Adoption Pay (Persons Abroad and Mariners) Regulations 2002, SI 2002/2821, reg 7(a). As to the meaning of 'United Kingdom' for these purposes see PARA 407 note 7.
2 Ie the Social Security Contributions and Benefits Act 1992 Pt XIIZB (ss 171ZL–171ZT) (statutory adoption pay: see also PARAS 488 et seq, 500 et seq). As to the meaning of 'statutory adoption pay' see PARA 488.
3 Statutory Paternity Pay and Statutory Adoption Pay (Persons Abroad and Mariners) Regulations 2002, SI 2002/2821, reg 7(b).
4 As to the meaning of 'employer' for these purposes see PARA 502.
5 Statutory Paternity Pay and Statutory Adoption Pay (Persons Abroad and Mariners) Regulations 2002, SI 2002/2821, reg 7(c).

6 See the Statutory Paternity Pay and Statutory Adoption Pay (Persons Abroad and Mariners) Regulations 2002, SI 2002/2821, reg 7.

497. Persons in other member states or absent from Great Britain for purposes of statutory adoption pay. A person who is:

(1) gainfully employed in an EEA state[1] other than the United Kingdom[2] in such circumstances that, if his employment were in Great Britain[3], he would be an employee[4] for the purposes of the statutory adoption pay provisions that are set out in Part XIIZB of the Social Security Contributions and Benefits Act 1992[5] or a person treated[6] as such an employee[7]; and

(2) subject[8] to the legislation of the United Kingdom[9],

is to be treated[10] as an employee for those purposes notwithstanding that he is not employed in Great Britain[11].

Where a person, while absent from Great Britain for any purpose, is gainfully employed by an employer who is liable to pay in respect of his employment secondary Class 1 contributions[12], he is to be treated[13] as an employee[14].

1 For these purposes, 'EEA state' means a state which is a contracting party to the Agreement on the European Economic Area (Oporto, 2 May 1992; OJ L1, 3.1.94, p 3; Cm 2073) as adjusted by the Protocol (Brussels, 17 March 1993; OJ L1, 3.1.94, p 571; Cm 2183): see the Statutory Paternity Pay and Statutory Adoption Pay (Persons Abroad and Mariners) Regulations 2002, SI 2002/2821, reg 1(2).
2 As to the meaning of 'United Kingdom' for these purposes see PARA 407 note 7.
3 As to the meaning of 'Great Britain' for these purposes see PARA 407 note 7.
4 As to the meaning of 'employee' for these purposes see PARA 494.
5 Ie for the purposes of the Social Security Contributions and Benefits Act 1992 Pt XIIZB (ss 171ZL–171ZT) (statutory adoption pay: see also PARAS 488 et seq, 500 et seq). As to the meaning of 'statutory adoption pay' see PARA 488.
6 Ie under the Statutory Paternity Pay and Statutory Adoption Pay (General) Regulations 2002, SI 2002/2822, regs 31(1), 32: see PARA 494.
7 Statutory Paternity Pay and Statutory Adoption Pay (Persons Abroad and Mariners) Regulations 2002, SI 2002/2821, reg 3(a).
8 Ie under Council Regulation (EC) 1408/71 (OJ L149, 5.7.71, p 2) on the application of social security schemes to employed persons and their families moving within the Community (repealed: see now Council Regulation (EC) 883/2004 of 29 April 2004 (OJ L166, 30.4.2004, p 1) on the coordination of social security systems; and **WELFARE BENEFITS AND STATE PENSIONS** vol 104 (2014) PARA 600 et seq).
9 Statutory Paternity Pay and Statutory Adoption Pay (Persons Abroad and Mariners) Regulations 2002, SI 2002/2821, reg 3(b).
10 Ie for the purposes of the Social Security Contributions and Benefits Act 1992 Pt XIIZB (statutory adoption pay: see also PARAS 488 et seq, 500 et seq).
11 See the Statutory Paternity Pay and Statutory Adoption Pay (Persons Abroad and Mariners) Regulations 2002, SI 2002/2821, reg 3.
12 Ie under the Social Security Contributions and Benefits Act 1992 s 6 (see **WELFARE BENEFITS AND STATE PENSIONS** vol 104 (2014) PARA 385) or the Social Security (Contributions) Regulations 2001, SI 2001/1004, reg 146 (payment of contributions for periods abroad: see **WELFARE BENEFITS AND STATE PENSIONS** vol 104 (2014) PARA 380).
13 Ie for the purposes of the Social Security Contributions and Benefits Act 1992 Pt XIIZB (statutory adoption pay: see also PARAS 488 et seq, 500 et seq), but subject to the Statutory Paternity Pay and Statutory Adoption Pay (Persons Abroad and Mariners) Regulations 2002, SI 2002/2821, reg 8(3) (see PARA 498).
14 Statutory Paternity Pay and Statutory Adoption Pay (Persons Abroad and Mariners) Regulations 2002, SI 2002/2821, reg 4.

498. Treatment of mariners for purposes of statutory adoption pay. A mariner[1] engaged in employment on board a home-trade ship[2] with an employer[3] who has a place of business within the United Kingdom[4] is to be treated as an employee[5] for the purposes of the statutory adoption pay provisions that are set out in Part XIIZB of the Social Security Contributions and Benefits Act 1992[6], notwithstanding that he may not be employed in Great Britain[7]. However, a mariner who is engaged in employment:

(1) on a foreign-going ship[8]; or
(2) on a home-trade ship with an employer who does not have a place of business within the United Kingdom[9],

is not to be so treated as an employee, notwithstanding that he may have been employed in Great Britain[10].

1 As to the meaning of 'mariner' for these purposes see PARA 452 note 1.
2 As to the meaning of 'home-trade ship' see PARA 452 note 2.
3 As to the meaning of 'employer' for these purposes see PARA 502.
4 As to the meaning of 'United Kingdom' for these purposes see PARA 407 note 7.
5 As to the meaning of 'employee' for these purposes see PARA 494.
6 Ie for the purposes of the Social Security Contributions and Benefits Act 1992 Pt XIIZB (ss 171ZL–171ZT) (statutory adoption pay: see also PARAS 488 et seq, 500 et seq). As to the meaning of 'statutory adoption pay' see PARA 488.
7 Statutory Paternity Pay and Statutory Adoption Pay (Persons Abroad and Mariners) Regulations 2002, SI 2002/2821, reg 8(2). As to the meaning of 'Great Britain' for these purposes see PARA 407 note 7.
8 Statutory Paternity Pay and Statutory Adoption Pay (Persons Abroad and Mariners) Regulations 2002, SI 2002/2821, reg 8(3)(a). As to the meaning of 'foreign-going ship' see PARA 452 note 7.
9 Statutory Paternity Pay and Statutory Adoption Pay (Persons Abroad and Mariners) Regulations 2002, SI 2002/2821, reg 8(3)(b).
10 See the Statutory Paternity Pay and Statutory Adoption Pay (Persons Abroad and Mariners) Regulations 2002, SI 2002/2821, reg 8(3).

499. Treatment of persons employed in operations on the continental shelf for purposes of statutory adoption pay. A person in prescribed employment[1] is to be treated as an employee[2] for the purposes of the statutory adoption pay provisions that are set out in Part XIIZB of the Social Security Contributions and Benefits Act 1992[3], notwithstanding that he may not be employed in Great Britain[4].

1 As to the meaning of 'prescribed employment' for these purposes see PARA 453 note 1.
2 As to the meaning of 'employee' for these purposes see PARA 448.
3 Ie for the purposes of the Social Security Contributions and Benefits Act 1992 Pt XIIZB (ss 171ZL–171ZT) (statutory adoption pay: see also PARAS 488 et seq, 500 et seq). As to the meaning of 'statutory adoption pay' see PARA 488.
4 Statutory Paternity Pay and Statutory Adoption Pay (Persons Abroad and Mariners) Regulations 2002, SI 2002/2821, reg 9(2). As to the meaning of 'Great Britain' for these purposes see PARA 407 note 7.

500. Crown employment for purposes of statutory adoption pay. The statutory adoption pay provisions that are set out in Part XIIZB of the Social Security Contributions and Benefits Act 1992[1] apply in relation to persons employed by or under the Crown as they apply in relation to persons employed otherwise than by or under the Crown[2].

1 Ie the Social Security Contributions and Benefits Act 1992 Pt XIIZB (ss 171ZL–171ZT) (statutory adoption pay: see also PARAS 488 et seq, 501 et seq). As to the meaning of 'statutory adoption pay' see PARA 488.
2 Social Security Contributions and Benefits Act 1992 s 171ZQ (added by the Employment Act 2002 s 4).

501. Treatment of National Health Service employees for purposes of statutory adoption pay. Where, in consequence of the establishment of one or more National Health Service trusts[1], a person's contract of employment is treated by a scheme[2] as divided so as to constitute two or more contracts, or where an order[3] provides that a person's contract of employment is so divided, regulations[4] may make provision enabling the person to elect for all of those contracts to be treated as one contract for the purposes of the statutory adoption pay provisions that are set out in Part XIIZB of the Social Security Contributions and Benefits Act 1992[5] or such of those provisions as may be prescribed[6]. Any such regulations may prescribe[7]:

(1) the conditions that must be satisfied if a person is to be entitled to make such an election[8];
(2) the manner in which, and the time within which, such an election is to be made[9];
(3) the persons to whom, and the manner in which, notice of such an election is to be given[10];
(4) the information which a person who makes such an election is to provide, and the persons to whom, and the time within which, he is to provide it[11];
(5) the time for which such an election is to have effect[12];
(6) which one of the person's employers[13] under the two or more contracts is to be regarded for the purposes of statutory adoption pay as his employer under the one contract[14],

and the powers so conferred are without prejudice to any other power[15] to make regulations[16].

Where, in consequence of the establishment of one or more National Health Service trusts[17], a person's contract of employment is treated by a scheme[18] as divided so as to constitute two or more contracts, he may elect for all those contracts to be treated as one contract for the purposes of the statutory adoption pay provisions[19] that are set out in Part XIIZB of the Social Security Contributions and Benefits Act 1992[20]. A person who makes such an election must:

(a) give written notification of that election to each of his employers under the two or more contracts of service at least 28 days before the beginning of the statutory adoption pay period[21] or, if in the particular circumstances that is not practicable, as soon as is reasonably practicable[22];
(b) within 28 days of giving notification of that election or, if in the particular circumstances that is not practicable, as soon as is reasonably practicable thereafter, provide each of his employers under the two or more contracts of service with the following information[23]:
    (i) the name and address of each of those employers[24]; and
    (ii) the date his employment with each of those employers commenced[25]; and
    (iii) details of his normal weekly earnings[26] during the relevant period[27] from each employer[28].

An election so made lapses at the end of the adoption pay period[29].

1 Ie under the National Health Service Act 2006 or the National Health Service (Wales) Act 2006: see HEALTH SERVICES vol 54 (2008) PARA 155 et seq.

2 See note 1.

3 Ie an order under the National Health Service Act 2006 Sch 3 para 26(1) (repealed): see HEALTH SERVICES vol 54 (2008) PARA 125.

4 As to the making of regulations under the Social Security Contributions and Benefits Act 1992 generally see PARA 407 note 3.

5 Ie for the purposes of the Social Security Contributions and Benefits Act 1992 Pt XIIZB (ss 171ZL–171ZT) (statutory adoption pay: see also PARAS 488 et seq, 502 et seq). As to the meaning of 'statutory adoption pay' see PARA 488.

6 See the Social Security Contributions and Benefits Act 1992 s 171ZS(9) (s 171ZS added by the Employment Act 2002 s 2; the Social Security Contributions and Benefits Act 1992 s 171ZS(9) amended by the National Health Service (Consequential Provisions) Act 2006 Sch 1 paras 142, 150). For these purposes, 'prescribed' means prescribed by regulations: see the Social Security Contributions and Benefits Act 1992 s 171ZS(1) (as so added). Regulations under s 171ZS(9) must be made with the concurrence of the Commissioners for Revenue and Customs: see s 171ZS(1), (12) (as so added). In exercise of the powers conferred by virtue of s 171ZS(9), the Secretary of State has, with the concurrence of the Commissioners for Revenue and Customs, made the Statutory Paternity Pay and Statutory Adoption Pay (National Health Service Employees) Regulations 2002, SI 2002/2819; and the text and notes 17–29. As to the Commissioners for Her Majesty's Revenue and Customs see **INCOME TAXATION** vol 58 (2014) PARAS 33–34; and see PARA 489 note 2.

As from a day to be appointed under the Health and Social Care Act 2012 s 306(4), the reference to 'the National Health Service Act 2006' in the Social Security Contributions and Benefits Act 1992 s 171ZS(9) is repealed: see s 171ZS(9) (as so added and amended; prospectively further amended by the Health and Social Care Act 2012 s 179(6), Sch 14 Pt 2 paras 58, 62). However, at the date at which this volume states the law, no such day had been appointed.

7 See the Social Security Contributions and Benefits Act 1992 s 171ZS(10) (as added: see note 6). Regulations under s 171ZS(10) must be made with the concurrence of the Commissioners for Revenue and Customs: see s 171ZS(1), (12) (as so added). In exercise of the powers conferred by virtue of s 171ZS(10), the Secretary of State has, with the concurrence of the Commissioners for Revenue and Customs, made the Statutory Paternity Pay and Statutory Adoption Pay (National Health Service Employees) Regulations 2002, SI 2002/2819; and the text and notes 17–29.

8 Social Security Contributions and Benefits Act 1992 s 171ZS(10)(a) (as added: see note 6).

9 Social Security Contributions and Benefits Act 1992 s 171ZS(10)(b) (as added: see note 6).

10 Social Security Contributions and Benefits Act 1992 s 171ZS(10)(c) (as added: see note 6).

11 Social Security Contributions and Benefits Act 1992 s 171ZS(10)(d) (as added: see note 6).

12 Social Security Contributions and Benefits Act 1992 s 171ZS(10)(e) (as added: see note 6).

13 As to the meaning of 'employer' for these purposes see PARA 456.

14 Social Security Contributions and Benefits Act 1992 s 171ZS(10)(f) (as added: see note 6).

15 Ie under the Social Security Contributions and Benefits Act 1992 Pt XIIZB (statutory adoption pay: see also PARAS 488 et seq, 502 et seq).

16 Social Security Contributions and Benefits Act 1992 s 171ZS(11) (as added: see note 6).

17 See note 1. For these purposes, 'NHS trust' is to be construed to include a reference to an NHS foundation trust within the meaning of the Health and Social Care (Community Health and Standards) Act 2003 s 1(1) (see **HEALTH SERVICES** vol 54 (2008) PARA 75 et seq) where the application for authorisation to become an NHS foundation trust was made by an NHS trust: see the Statutory Paternity Pay and Statutory Adoption Pay (National Health Service Employees) Regulations 2002, SI 2002/2819, reg 1(2) (definition added by SI 2004/696).

18 See note 1.

19 Ie for the purposes of the Social Security Contributions and Benefits Act 1992 Pt XIIZB (statutory adoption pay: see also PARAS 488 et seq, 502 et seq).

20 Statutory Paternity Pay and Statutory Adoption Pay (National Health Service Employees) Regulations 2002, SI 2002/2819, reg 2 (amended by SI 2013/235); and see the Interpretation Act 1978 s 17(2)(a). As to the employer to be regarded for the purposes of statutory adoption pay as the employer under the one contract where two or more contracts of service are so treated as one see the Statutory Paternity Pay and Statutory Adoption Pay (National Health Service Employees) Regulations 2002, SI 2002/2819, reg 5 (amended by SI 2013/235); and see the Interpretation Act 1978 s 17(2)(a). Although 'contract of service' is defined for the purposes of statutory sick pay (see PARA 558 note 2), it is not so defined under the other statutory pay provisions (for which purposes see generally PARA 1 note 1).

21 For these purposes, 'statutory adoption pay period' means the period prescribed under the Social Security Contributions and Benefits Act 1992 s 171ZN(2) (see PARA 511) as the period in respect of which statutory adoption pay is payable to a person: see the Statutory Paternity Pay and Statutory Adoption Pay (National Health Service Employees) Regulations 2002, SI 2002/2819, reg 1(2).

22 Statutory Paternity Pay and Statutory Adoption Pay (National Health Service Employees) Regulations 2002, SI 2002/2819, reg 3.

(iii) to offer the work available to those persons who had worked for him during the last or a recent such period[15]; but

(b) is absent from work because of incapacity arising from some specific disease or bodily or mental disablement[16],

then in his case the provisions governing continuous employment[17] apply subject to modification[18].

1 As to the meaning of 'week' for these purposes see PARA 490 note 14.
2 See the Statutory Paternity Pay and Statutory Adoption Pay (General) Regulations 2002, SI 2002/2822, regs 31(1), 33(1). Regulation 33(1) is subject to regs 31(1), 33(2)–(4) (see the text and notes 3, 8–18): see regs 31(1), 33(1).
3 Statutory Paternity Pay and Statutory Adoption Pay (General) Regulations 2002, SI 2002/2822, regs 31(1), 33(1)(a). Incapacity for work which lasts for more than 26 consecutive weeks does not count for the purposes of head (1) in the text, however: regs 31(1), 33(2).
4 Statutory Paternity Pay and Statutory Adoption Pay (General) Regulations 2002, SI 2002/2822, regs 31(1), 33(1)(b).
5 Statutory Paternity Pay and Statutory Adoption Pay (General) Regulations 2002, SI 2002/2822, regs 31(1), 33(1)(c).
6 Ie for the purposes of the Social Security Contributions and Benefits Act 1992 s 171ZL (see PARA 488 et seq). As to the meaning of 'statutory adoption pay' see PARA 488.
7 See the Statutory Paternity Pay and Statutory Adoption Pay (General) Regulations 2002, SI 2002/2822, regs 31(1), 33(1). Although 'contract of service' is defined for the purposes of statutory sick pay (see PARA 558 note 2), it is not so defined under the other statutory pay provisions (for which purposes see generally PARA 1 note 1).
8 Ie within the meaning of the Social Security Contributions and Benefits Act 1992 s 171ZL(3) (entitlement to statutory pay: see PARA 503 notes 7, 9, 12).
9 Ie for the purposes of the Social Security Contributions and Benefits Act 1992 s 171ZL (see PARA 488 et seq).
10 Statutory Paternity Pay and Statutory Adoption Pay (General) Regulations 2002, SI 2002/2822, regs 31(1), 33(4).
11 As to the meaning of 'employed earner' see the Social Security Contributions and Benefits Act 1992 s 2(1)(a), (3); and WELFARE BENEFITS AND STATE PENSIONS vol 104 (2014) PARA 381.
12 See the Statutory Paternity Pay and Statutory Adoption Pay (General) Regulations 2002, SI 2002/2822, regs 31(1), 33(3)(a).
13 Statutory Paternity Pay and Statutory Adoption Pay (General) Regulations 2002, SI 2002/2822, regs 31(1), 33(3)(a)(i).
14 Statutory Paternity Pay and Statutory Adoption Pay (General) Regulations 2002, SI 2002/2822, regs 31(1), 33(3)(a)(ii).
15 Statutory Paternity Pay and Statutory Adoption Pay (General) Regulations 2002, SI 2002/2822, regs 31(1), 33(3)(a)(iii).
16 Statutory Paternity Pay and Statutory Adoption Pay (General) Regulations 2002, SI 2002/2822, regs 31(1), 33(3)(b).
17 Ie the Statutory Paternity Pay and Statutory Adoption Pay (General) Regulations 2002, SI 2002/2822, regs 31(1), 33: see also the text and notes 1–16.
18 See the Statutory Paternity Pay and Statutory Adoption Pay (General) Regulations 2002, SI 2002/2822, regs 31(1), 33(3). The modifications specified are that: (1) the provisions of regs 31(1), 33(1) (see the text and notes 1–7) apply as if the words 'and returns to work for his employer after the incapacity for or absence from work' were omitted; and (2) the provisions of regs 31(1), 33(4) (see the text and notes 8–10) do not apply: see regs 31(1), 33(3).

505. Continuous employment and unfair dismissal for purposes of statutory adoption pay. A person in relation to whose dismissal an action is commenced which consists of:

(1) the presentation by him of a complaint of unfair dismissal[1]; or

(2) his making a claim in accordance with a dismissal procedures agreement[2] designated by an order[3]; or

(3) any action taken by a conciliation officer under the Employment Tribunals Act 1996[4]; or

(4) a decision arising out of the use of a statutory dispute resolution procedure[5] in a case where[6] such a procedure applies[7],

has the continuity of his employment preserved[8] if, in consequence of such an action, he is reinstated or re-engaged by his employer[9] or by a successor[10] or associated employer[11] of that employer; and any week which falls within the interval beginning with the effective date of termination and ending with the date of reinstatement or re-engagement, as the case may be, counts in the computation of his period of continuous employment[12].

1 Statutory Paternity Pay and Statutory Adoption Pay (General) Regulations 2002, SI 2002/2822, regs 31(1), 34(1)(a). Head (1) in the text refers to a complaint under the Employment Rights Act 1996 s 111(1): see PARA 804.
2 For these purposes, 'dismissals procedure agreement' has the same meaning as in the Employment Rights Act 1996 s 235(1) (see PARA 150 note 9): see the Statutory Paternity Pay and Statutory Adoption Pay (General) Regulations 2002, SI 2002/2822, regs 31(1), 34(3).
3 Statutory Paternity Pay and Statutory Adoption Pay (General) Regulations 2002, SI 2002/2822, regs 31(1), 34(1)(b) (34(1)(b) amended, 34(1)(d) added, by SI 2005/358). Head (2) in the text refers to an agreement designated by an order under the Employment Rights Act 1996 s 110: see PARAS 759–760.
4 Statutory Paternity Pay and Statutory Adoption Pay (General) Regulations 2002, SI 2002/2822, regs 31(1), 34(1)(c) (34(1)(c) amended by SI 2014/386). Head (3) in the text refers to action taken by a conciliation officer under any of the Employment Tribunals Act 1996 ss 18A–18C (requirement to contact ACAS before instituting proceedings: see PARAS 152, 153).
5 Ie contained in the Employment Act 2002 Sch 2 (repealed).
6 Ie in accordance with the Employment (Dispute Resolution) Regulations 2004, SI 2004/752 (revoked).
7 Statutory Paternity Pay and Statutory Adoption Pay (General) Regulations 2002, SI 2002/2822, regs 31(1), 34(1)(d) (34(1)(d) as added: see note 3).
8 Ie for the purposes of the Social Security Contributions and Benefits Act 1992 Pt XIIZB (ss 171ZL–171ZT) (statutory adoption pay: see also PARAS 488 et seq, 508 et seq).
9 As to the meaning of 'employer' for these purposes see PARA 502.
10 For these purposes, 'successor' has the same meaning as in the Employment Rights Act 1996 s 235(1) (see PARA 133 note 10): see the Statutory Paternity Pay and Statutory Adoption Pay (General) Regulations 2002, SI 2002/2822, regs 31(1), 34(3).
11 For these purposes, 'associated employer' is to be construed in accordance with the Employment Rights Act 1996 s 231 (see PARA 3): see the Statutory Paternity Pay and Statutory Adoption Pay (General) Regulations 2002, SI 2002/2822, regs 31(1), 34(3).
12 Statutory Paternity Pay and Statutory Adoption Pay (General) Regulations 2002, SI 2002/2822, regs 31(1), 34(2).

506. Continuous employment and stoppages of work for purposes of statutory adoption pay. Where for any week[1] or part of a week a person does no work because there is a stoppage of work due to a trade dispute[2] at his place of employment, the continuity of his employment is to be treated[3] as continuing throughout the stoppage; but no such week counts[4] in the computation of his period of employment[5].

1 As to the meaning of 'week' for these purposes see PARA 490 note 14.
2 Ie a trade dispute within the meaning of the Jobseekers Act 1995 s 35(1): see WELFARE BENEFITS AND STATE PENSIONS vol 104 (2014) PARA 438.
3 Ie subject to the Statutory Paternity Pay and Statutory Adoption Pay (General) Regulations 2002, SI 2002/2822, regs 31(1), 35(2): see note 5.
4 Ie subject to the Statutory Paternity Pay and Statutory Adoption Pay (General) Regulations 2002, SI 2002/2822, regs 31(1), 35(3): see note 5.
5 Statutory Paternity Pay and Statutory Adoption Pay (General) Regulations 2002, SI 2002/2822, regs 31(1), 35(1). Where during the stoppage of work a person is dismissed from his employment, the continuity of his employment is not to be treated, in accordance with regs 31(1), 35(1), as continuing beyond the commencement of the day he stopped work: regs 31(1), 35(2). The provisions of regs 31(1), 35(1), to the extent that they provide that a week in which the stoppage of work occurred does not count in the computation of a period of

employment, and regs 31(1), 35(2) do not apply to a person who proves that at no time did he have a direct interest in the trade dispute in question: regs 31(1), 35(3).

507. Change of employer for purposes of statutory adoption pay; reinstatement after service with armed forces etc. A person's employment is to be treated, notwithstanding a change of employer[1], as continuous employment with the second employer where[2]:

(1) the employer's trade or business or an undertaking, whether or not it is an undertaking established by or under an Act of Parliament, is transferred from one person to another[3];

(2) by or under an Act of Parliament, whether public or local and whenever passed, a contract of employment between any body corporate and the person is modified and some other body corporate is substituted as his employer[4];

(3) on the death of his employer, the person is taken into employment of the personal representatives or trustees of the deceased[5];

(4) the person is employed by partners, personal representatives or trustees and there is a change in the partners, or, as the case may be, personal representatives or trustees[6];

(5) the person is taken into the employment of an employer who is, at the time he entered his employment, an associated employer[7] of his previous employer[8];

(6) on the termination of his employment with an employer he is taken into the employment of another employer and those employers are the governors of a school maintained by a local authority and that authority[9].

If a person who is entitled to apply to his former employer under the Reserve Forces (Safeguard of Employment) Act 1985[10] enters the employment of that employer within the statutory six-month period[11], his previous period of employment with that employer (or, if there was more than one such period, the last of those periods) and the period of employment beginning in that six-month period are to be treated as continuous[12].

1 As to the meaning of 'employer' for these purposes see PARA 502.

2 See the Statutory Paternity Pay and Statutory Adoption Pay (General) Regulations 2002, SI 2002/2822, regs 31(1), 36.

3 Statutory Paternity Pay and Statutory Adoption Pay (General) Regulations 2002, SI 2002/2822, regs 31(1), 36(a).

4 Statutory Paternity Pay and Statutory Adoption Pay (General) Regulations 2002, SI 2002/2822, regs 31(1), 36(b).

5 Statutory Paternity Pay and Statutory Adoption Pay (General) Regulations 2002, SI 2002/2822, regs 31(1), 36(c).

6 Statutory Paternity Pay and Statutory Adoption Pay (General) Regulations 2002, SI 2002/2822, regs 31(1), 36(d).

7 For these purposes, 'associated employer' is to be construed in accordance with the Employment Rights Act 1996 s 231 (see PARA 3): see the Statutory Paternity Pay and Statutory Adoption Pay (General) Regulations 2002, SI 2002/2822, regs 31(1), 36(e).

8 Statutory Paternity Pay and Statutory Adoption Pay (General) Regulations 2002, SI 2002/2822, regs 31(1), 36(e).

9 Statutory Paternity Pay and Statutory Adoption Pay (General) Regulations 2002, SI 2002/2822, regs 31(1), 36(f) (reg 36(f) amended by SI 2010/1172). As to a local authority referred to for the purposes of head (6) in the text see the Education Act 1996 s 579(1); and EDUCATION vol 35 (2011) PARA 24.

10 As to the right to reinstatement under the Reserve Forces (Safeguard of Employment) Act 1985 see ARMED FORCES vol 3 (2011) PARA 370.

11 Ie the six-month period mentioned in the Reserve Forces (Safeguard of Employment) Act 1985 s 1(4)(b). A former employer's obligation under s 1 is discharged if after giving reasonable notice to the applicant he makes appropriate employment available to him at that first opportunity, except that:
 (1) an opportunity for taking the applicant into his former employer's employment is not to be deemed for the purposes of s 1(3), (4) (see **ARMED FORCES** vol 3 (2011) PARA 370) to have arisen if the former employer makes employment available to the applicant, but the applicant has, or reasonably believes that he has, reasonable cause for not taking it, and if the facts on which the applicant relies as constituting the reasonable cause are notified in writing to the former employer by him or by some person acting with his authority as soon as may be after he has been notified by the former employer that the employment is being made available to him (see s 1(4)(a)); and
 (2) in no case is the former employer to be under any obligation under s 1 to take the applicant into his employment after six months have elapsed from the end of the applicant's whole-time service (see s 1(4)(b)).

12 Statutory Paternity Pay and Statutory Adoption Pay (General) Regulations 2002, SI 2002/2822, regs 31(1), 37.

D. NOTICE OF ABSENCE; EVIDENCE OF ENTITLEMENT TO ADOPTION PAY

508. Notice of absence from work required for payment of statutory adoption pay. A person is entitled to payments of statutory adoption pay[1] only if:
 (1) he gives the person who will be liable to pay it notice of the date from which he expects the liability to pay him statutory adoption pay to begin[2]; and
 (2) the notice is given at least 28 days before that date or, if that is not reasonably practicable, as soon as is reasonably practicable[3].

The notice must be in writing[4] if the person who is liable to pay the statutory adoption pay so requests[5].

1 As to the meaning of 'statutory adoption pay' see PARA 488.

2 Social Security Contributions and Benefits Act 1992 s 171ZL(6)(a) (s 171ZL added by the Employment Act 2002 s 4). Where a person gives notice under the Social Security Contributions and Benefits Act 1992 s 171ZL(6) he must at the same time give notice of the date on which the child is expected to be placed for adoption: Statutory Paternity Pay and Statutory Adoption Pay (General) Regulations 2002, SI 2002/2822, reg 23(1). Where the choice of adoption pay period is made in accordance with reg 21(1) (see PARA 511) and notified in accordance with the Social Security Contributions and Benefits Act 1992 s 171ZL(6), the person must give further notice to the person liable to pay him statutory adoption pay as soon as is reasonably practicable of the date the child is placed for adoption: see the Statutory Paternity Pay and Statutory Adoption Pay (General) Regulations 2002, SI 2002/2822, reg 23(2); and PARA 511 note 17.

3 Social Security Contributions and Benefits Act 1992 s 171ZL(6)(b) (as added: see note 2). As to the time for compliance where an employee is outside the United Kingdom see PARA 496.

4 As to the meaning of 'writing' see PARA 2 note 8.

5 Social Security Contributions and Benefits Act 1992 s 171ZL(7) (as added: see note 2).

509. Employee's evidence of entitlement to statutory adoption pay. Regulations made under the Social Security Administration Act 1992[1] may provide for information and evidence to be furnished in connection with the payment of statutory adoption pay[2]; and regulations made under the Social Security Contributions and Benefits Act 1992 may impose requirements about evidence of entitlement to such pay[3].

Accordingly, a person must provide evidence of his entitlement to statutory adoption pay by providing to the person who is liable to pay it[4]:
 (1) a declaration that he has elected to receive statutory adoption pay and not statutory paternity pay (adoption)[5]; and
 (2) the following information, in the form of one or more documents provided to him by an adoption agency[6] containing the information[7]:

(a) the name and address of the adoption agency and of the person claiming payment of statutory adoption pay[8];

(b) the date on which the child is expected to be placed for adoption or, where the child has already been placed for adoption, the date of placement[9]; and

(c) the date on which the person claiming payment of statutory adoption pay was informed by the adoption agency that the child would be placed for adoption with him[10].

The information and declaration must be provided to the person liable to pay statutory adoption pay at least 28 days before the date chosen[11] as the beginning of the adoption pay period[12], or, if that is not reasonably practicable, as soon as is reasonably practicable thereafter[13].

1 As to the making of regulations under the Social Security Administration Act 1992 generally see WELFARE BENEFITS AND STATE PENSIONS vol 104 (2014) PARA 400.

2 See the Social Security Administration Act 1992 s 5(1)(i), (5) (s 5(5) amended by the Employment Act 2002 s 53, Sch 7 paras 8, 11; the Work and Families Act 2006 Sch 1 para 24; and the Children and Families Act 2014 Sch 7 paras 23, 24(a)). In exercise of the powers conferred by the Social Security Administration Act 1992 s 5(1)(i), the Secretary of State has made the Statutory Paternity Pay and Statutory Adoption Pay (General) Regulations 2002, SI 2002/2822 (see the text and notes 3–13) and the Statutory Paternity Pay (Adoption) and Statutory Adoption Pay (Adoptions from Overseas) (No 2) Regulations 2003, SI 2003/1194 (see PARA 531). As to the effect of the Social Security Administration Act 1992 s 5 generally see WELFARE BENEFITS AND STATE PENSIONS vol 104 (2014) PARA 526.

3 As to the general power to make regulations under the Social Security Contributions and Benefits Act 1992 with regard to statutory adoption pay see PARA 490. As to the meaning of 'statutory adoption pay' see PARA 488.

4 See the Statutory Paternity Pay and Statutory Adoption Pay (General) Regulations 2002, SI 2002/2822, reg 24(1).

5 Statutory Paternity Pay and Statutory Adoption Pay (General) Regulations 2002, SI 2002/2822, reg 24(1)(b). As to the meaning of 'statutory paternity pay (adoption)' see PARA 446 note 20.

6 As to the meaning of 'adoption agency' see PARA 446 note 24.

7 See the Statutory Paternity Pay and Statutory Adoption Pay (General) Regulations 2002, SI 2002/2822, reg 24(1)(a), (2).

8 Statutory Paternity Pay and Statutory Adoption Pay (General) Regulations 2002, SI 2002/2822, reg 24(2)(a).

9 Statutory Paternity Pay and Statutory Adoption Pay (General) Regulations 2002, SI 2002/2822, reg 24(2)(b).

10 Statutory Paternity Pay and Statutory Adoption Pay (General) Regulations 2002, SI 2002/2822, reg 24(2)(c). As to the date on which a person receives notification of having been matched with a child see PARA 446 note 24.

11 Ie in accordance with the Statutory Paternity Pay and Statutory Adoption Pay (General) Regulations 2002, SI 2002/2822, reg 21(1): see PARA 511.

12 As to the adoption pay period see PARA 511.

13 Statutory Paternity Pay and Statutory Adoption Pay (General) Regulations 2002, SI 2002/2822, reg 24(3).

510. Provision of information by employer given evidence of entitlement to statutory adoption pay. Where an employer[1] who has been given[2] evidence of entitlement to statutory adoption pay[3] by a person who is or has been an employee[4] decides that he has no liability to make payments of statutory adoption pay to the employee[5], the employer must furnish the employee with details of the decision and the reasons for it[6].

Where an employer who has been given such evidence of entitlement to statutory adoption pay has made one or more payments of statutory adoption pay to the employee but decides, before the end of the adoption pay period[7], that he has no liability to make further payments to the employee because he has been detained in legal custody or sentenced to a term of imprisonment which was not suspended[8], the employer must furnish the employee with:

(1) details of his decision and the reasons for it[9]; and

(2) details of the last week in respect of which a liability to pay statutory adoption pay arose and the total number of weeks within the adoption pay period in which such a liability arose[10].

The employer must: (a) return to the employee any evidence so provided by him[11]; and (b) where he decides that he has no liability to make payments of statutory adoption pay[12], comply with the requirements to furnish the employee with the required information[13] within 28 days of the end of the seven-day period that starts on the date on which the adopter is notified of having been matched with the child[14]; (c) where he decides that he has no liability to make further payments of statutory adoption pay on account of the employee's detention in legal custody or sentencing to a term of imprisonment[15], comply with the requirements to furnish the employee with information[16] within seven days of being notified of the employee's detention or sentence[17].

1 As to the meaning of 'employer' for these purposes see PARA 502.

2 Ie pursuant to regulations made under the Social Security Contributions and Benefits Act 1992 s 171ZL(8)(c): see PARA 490.

3 As to the evidence specified see PARA 509. For these purposes, 'statutory adoption pay' means any payment under the Social Security Contributions and Benefits Act 1992 s 171ZL (see PARA 488): see the Statutory Paternity Pay and Statutory Adoption Pay (Administration) Regulations 2002, SI 2002/2820, reg 2(1).

4 As to the meaning of 'employee' for these purposes see PARA 494. Any reference in the Statutory Paternity Pay and Statutory Adoption Pay (Administration) Regulations 2002, SI 2002/2820, to the employees of an employer includes former employees of his: reg 2(2).

5 As to liability to make payments of statutory adoption pay see PARA 488 et seq.

6 Statutory Paternity Pay and Statutory Adoption Pay (Administration) Regulations 2002, SI 2002/2820, reg 11(1).

7 For these purposes, 'adoption pay period' means the period prescribed under the Social Security Contributions and Benefits Act 1992 s 171ZN(2) (see PARA 511) in respect of which statutory adoption pay is payable to a person: see the Statutory Paternity Pay and Statutory Adoption Pay (Administration) Regulations 2002, SI 2002/2820, reg 2(1).

8 See the Statutory Paternity Pay and Statutory Adoption Pay (Administration) Regulations 2002, SI 2002/2820, reg 11(2). As to circumstances in which liability to pay statutory adoption pay does not arise see PARA 491.

9 Statutory Paternity Pay and Statutory Adoption Pay (Administration) Regulations 2002, SI 2002/2820, reg 11(2)(a).

10 Statutory Paternity Pay and Statutory Adoption Pay (Administration) Regulations 2002, SI 2002/2820, reg 11(2)(b).

11 Statutory Paternity Pay and Statutory Adoption Pay (Administration) Regulations 2002, SI 2002/2820, reg 11(3)(a). Head (a) in the text refers to evidence provided by the employee under reg 11(1) (see the text and notes 1–6) or reg 11(2) (see the text and notes 7–10).

12 Ie under the Statutory Paternity Pay and Statutory Adoption Pay (Administration) Regulations 2002, SI 2002/2820, reg 11(1) (see the text and notes 1–6).

13 Ie the information required under the Statutory Paternity Pay and Statutory Adoption Pay (Administration) Regulations 2002, SI 2002/2820, reg 11(1) (see the text and notes 1–6).

14 Statutory Paternity Pay and Statutory Adoption Pay (Administration) Regulations 2002, SI 2002/2820, reg 11(3)(b)(ii). As to when an adopter is notified of having been matched with a child for these purposes, and as to the meaning of 'adopter', see PARA 464 note 12.

15 Ie under the Statutory Paternity Pay and Statutory Adoption Pay (Administration) Regulations 2002, SI 2002/2820, reg 11(2) (see the text and notes 7–10).

16 Ie required under the Statutory Paternity Pay and Statutory Adoption Pay (Administration) Regulations 2002, SI 2002/2820, reg 11(2) (see the text and notes 7–10).

17 Statutory Paternity Pay and Statutory Adoption Pay (Administration) Regulations 2002, SI 2002/2820, reg 11(3)(c).

E. THE ADOPTION PAY PERIOD

511. The adoption pay period. Statutory adoption pay[1] is payable[2] in respect of each week[3] during a prescribed[4] period (the 'adoption pay period') of a duration not exceeding 52 weeks[5], although regulations may provide for:

(1) the duration of the adoption pay period as it applies to a person to be reduced, subject to prescribed restrictions and conditions[6]; and

(2) a reduction in the duration of the adoption pay period as it applies to a person to be revoked, or to be treated as revoked, subject to prescribed restrictions and conditions[7].

Accordingly, the duration of any adoption pay period so prescribed is a continuous period of 39 weeks[8]. However, where:

(a) after a child has been placed for adoption, either the child dies[9], or the child is returned to the adoption agency[10]; or

(b) the adoption pay period has begun prior to the date the child has been placed for adoption, but the placement does not take place[11],

the adoption pay period must terminate as specified in the regulations[12], namely eight weeks after the end of the week[13]:

(i) in a case falling within head (a) above, during which the child dies[14], or during which the child is returned to the adoption agency[15];

(ii) in a case falling within head (b) above, during which the person with whom the child was to be placed for adoption is notified that the placement will not be made[16].

A person entitled to statutory adoption pay may choose the adoption pay period to begin:

(A) on the date on which the child is placed with him for adoption (or, where he is at work on that day, on the following day)[17];

(B) on a predetermined date, specified by him, which is no more than 14 days before the date on which the child is expected to be placed with him and no later than that date[18].

Where the choice made is that mentioned in head (B) above, the adoption pay period begins, unless the employer agrees to the adoption pay period beginning earlier, no earlier than 28 days after the required statutory notice[19] has been given[20].

Where the employment of a person who satisfies the conditions of entitlement to statutory adoption pay terminates for whatever reason (including dismissal) before the adoption pay period so chosen[21] has begun, the period begins 14 days before the expected date of placement or, where the termination occurs on, or within 14 days before, the expected date of placement, on the day immediately following the last day of his employment[22]. In such a case, the requirements for statutory notice[23] do not apply[24].

1 As to the meaning of 'statutory adoption pay' see PARA 488.

2 Ie subject to the provisions of the Social Security Contributions and Benefits Act 1992 Pt XIIZB (ss 171ZL–171ZT) (statutory adoption pay: see also PARAS 488 et seq, 513 et seq).

3 For this purpose, 'week' means any period of seven days: see the Social Security Contributions and Benefits Act 1992 s 171ZN(7) (ss 171ZN, 171ZS added by the Employment Act 2002 s 4).

4 For these purposes, 'prescribed' means prescribed by regulations: Social Security Contributions and Benefits Act 1992 s 171ZS(1) (as added: see note 3). As to the making of regulations under the Social Security Contributions and Benefits Act 1992 see PARA 407 note 3. As to regulations so made see note 5.

5 Social Security Contributions and Benefits Act 1992 s 171ZN(2) (s 171ZN as added (see note 3); s 171ZN(2) amended by the Work and Families Act 2006 s 2). For the purposes of the Social Security Contributions and Benefits Act 1992 Pt XIIZB (statutory adoption pay: see also

PARAS 488 et seq, 513 et seq), 'adoption pay period' has the meaning given by s 171ZN(2): see s 171ZS(1) (as added: see note 3). In exercise of the powers conferred by s 171ZN(2), the Secretary of State has made the Statutory Paternity Pay and Statutory Adoption Pay (General) Regulations 2002, SI 2002/2822 (see the text and notes 8–24) and the Statutory Paternity Pay (Adoption) and Statutory Adoption Pay (Adoptions from Overseas) (No 2) Regulations 2003, SI 2003/1194 (see PARA 531).

6 Social Security Contributions and Benefits Act 1992 s 171ZN(2A) (s 171ZN as added (see note 3); s 171ZN(2A)–(2D) added by the Children and Families Act 2014 s 120(1), (6)). Regulations under the Social Security Contributions and Benefits Act 1992 s 171ZN(2A) are to secure that the reduced period ends at a time:
   (1) after a prescribed part of the adoption pay period has expired (s 171ZN(2B)(a) (as so added)); and
   (2) when at least a prescribed part of the adoption pay period remains unexpired (s 171ZN(2B)(b) (as so added))).

   Regulations under s 171ZN(2A) may, in particular, prescribe restrictions and conditions relating to:
   (a) the end of entitlement for the person mentioned in head (1) in the text ('A') to adoption leave (s 171ZN(2C)(a) (as so added));
   (b) the doing of work by A (s 171ZN(2C)(b) (as so added));
   (c) the taking of prescribed steps by A or another person as regards leave under the Employment Rights Act 1996 s 75G (shared parental leave on adoption : see PARA 399) in respect of the child (Social Security Contributions and Benefits Act 1992 s 171ZN(2C)(c) (as so added));
   (d) the taking of prescribed steps by A or another person as regards statutory shared parental pay in respect of the child (s 171ZN(2C)(d) (as so added)).

   At the date at which this volume states the law, no such regulations had been made. As to statutory shared parental pay see PARA 534 et seq.

7 Social Security Contributions and Benefits Act 1992 s 171ZN(2D) (as added: see note 6). At the date at which this volume states the law, no such regulations had been made.

8 Statutory Paternity Pay and Statutory Adoption Pay (General) Regulations 2002, SI 2002/2822, reg 21(5) (amended by SI 2006/2236). This provision is subject to the Statutory Paternity Pay and Statutory Adoption Pay (General) Regulations 2002, SI 2002/2822, reg 22 (see the text and notes 9–16): see reg 21(5) (as so amended).

9 Statutory Paternity Pay and Statutory Adoption Pay (General) Regulations 2002, SI 2002/2822, reg 22(1)(a)(i).

10 Statutory Paternity Pay and Statutory Adoption Pay (General) Regulations 2002, SI 2002/2822, reg 22(1)(a)(ii); and see the Interpretation Act 1978 s 17(2)(a). The reference to the text is to a child returned to the adoption agency under the Adoption Act 1976 s 30(3) (repealed) (see now the Adoption and Children Act 2002 s 35; and **CHILDREN AND YOUNG PERSONS** vol 9 (2012) PARA 388). As to the meaning of 'adoption agency' see PARA 446 note 24.

11 Statutory Paternity Pay and Statutory Adoption Pay (General) Regulations 2002, SI 2002/2822, reg 22(1)(b).

12 See the Statutory Paternity Pay and Statutory Adoption Pay (General) Regulations 2002, SI 2002/2822, reg 22(1). The text refers to an adoption pay period which must terminate in accordance with the provisions of reg 22(2) (see the text and notes 13–16): see reg 22(1).

13 See the Statutory Paternity Pay and Statutory Adoption Pay (General) Regulations 2002, SI 2002/2822, reg 22(2). For these purposes, 'week' means a period of seven days beginning with Sunday: see reg 22(4).

14 Statutory Paternity Pay and Statutory Adoption Pay (General) Regulations 2002, SI 2002/2822, reg 22(3)(a). The provision made by reg 22(3)(a) applies in a case falling within reg 22(1)(a)(i) (see the text and note 9).

15 Statutory Paternity Pay and Statutory Adoption Pay (General) Regulations 2002, SI 2002/2822, reg 22(3)(b). The provision made by reg 22(3)(b) applies in a case falling within reg 22(1)(a)(ii) (see the text and note 10).

16 Statutory Paternity Pay and Statutory Adoption Pay (General) Regulations 2002, SI 2002/2822, reg 22(3)(c). The provision made by reg 22(3)(c) applies in a case falling within reg 22(1)(b) (see the text and note 11).

17 Statutory Paternity Pay and Statutory Adoption Pay (General) Regulations 2002, SI 2002/2822, reg 21(1)(a). A choice made under reg 21(1) is not irrevocable, but where a person subsequently makes a different choice, the Social Security Contributions and Benefits Act 1992 s 171ZL(6) (notice of absence from work: see PARA 508) applies to it: see the Statutory Paternity Pay and Statutory Adoption Pay (General) Regulations 2002, SI 2002/2822, reg 21(6). Where the choice made in accordance with reg 21(1), and notified in accordance with the Social Security

(a) any amount retrospectively treated[9] as earnings by regulations made by virtue of the Social Security Contributions and Benefits Act 1992[10];
(b) any sum payable in respect of arrears of pay in pursuance of an order[11] for reinstatement or re-engagement[12];
(c) any sum payable by way of pay in pursuance of an order[13] for the continuation of a contract of employment[14];
(d) any sum payable by way of remuneration in pursuance[15] of a protective award[16];
(e) any sum payable[17] by way of statutory sick pay[18];
(f) any sum payable by way of statutory maternity pay[19];
(g) any sum payable by way of statutory paternity pay[20]; and
(h) any sum payable by way of statutory adoption pay[21].

1 Ie for the purposes of the Social Security Contributions and Benefits Act 1992 1992 s 171ZS(6) (normal weekly earnings for the purposes of statutory adoption pay): see PARA 514.
2 See the Statutory Paternity Pay and Statutory Adoption Pay (General) Regulations 2002, SI 2002/2822, regs 31(1), 39(1), (2).
3 Ie under the Social Security (Contributions) Regulations 2001, SI 2001/1004, regs 25, 27, 123 or Sch 3 (payments to be disregarded and payments to directors to be disregarded: see **WELFARE BENEFITS AND STATE PENSIONS** vol 104 (2014) PARA 382).
4 Statutory Paternity Pay and Statutory Adoption Pay (General) Regulations 2002, SI 2002/2822, regs 31(1), 39(1), (2)(a) (reg 39(2)(a), (b) amended by SI 2006/1031).
5 Ie under the Social Security Contributions and Benefits Act 1992 s 10A (class 1B contributions: see **WELFARE BENEFITS AND STATE PENSIONS** vol 104 (2014) PARA 392).
6 Statutory Paternity Pay and Statutory Adoption Pay (General) Regulations 2002, SI 2002/2822, regs 31(1), 39(1), (2)(b) (reg 39(2)(b) as amended: see note 4). As to statutory adoption pay see PARA 488 et seq.
7 See note 1.
8 See the Statutory Paternity Pay and Statutory Adoption Pay (General) Regulations 2002, SI 2002/2822, regs 31(1), 39(1), (3).
9 Ie by regulations made by virtue of the Social Security Contributions and Benefits Act 1992 s 4B(2): see **WELFARE BENEFITS AND STATE PENSIONS** vol 104 (2014) PARA 383.
10 Statutory Paternity Pay and Statutory Adoption Pay (General) Regulations 2002, SI 2002/2822, regs 31(1), 39(1), (3)(za) (reg 39(3)(za) added by SI 2007/1154).
11 Ie under the Employment Rights Act 1996: see PARA 811.
12 Statutory Paternity Pay and Statutory Adoption Pay (General) Regulations 2002, SI 2002/2822, regs 31(1), 39(1), (3)(a).
13 Ie under the Employment Rights Act 1996: see PARA 807.
14 Statutory Paternity Pay and Statutory Adoption Pay (General) Regulations 2002, SI 2002/2822, regs 31(1), 39(1), (3)(b).
15 Ie under the Trade Union and Labour Relations (Consolidation) Act 1992 s 189: see PARA 1189.
16 Statutory Paternity Pay and Statutory Adoption Pay (General) Regulations 2002, SI 2002/2822, regs 31(1), 39(1), (3)(c).
17 Ie including sums payable in accordance with regulations under the Social Security Contributions and Benefits Act 1992 s 151(6): see PARA 559.
18 Statutory Paternity Pay and Statutory Adoption Pay (General) Regulations 2002, SI 2002/2822, regs 31(1), 39(1), (3)(d). As to statutory sick pay see PARA 558 et seq.
19 Statutory Paternity Pay and Statutory Adoption Pay (General) Regulations 2002, SI 2002/2822, regs 31(1), 39(1), (3)(e). As to statutory maternity pay see PARA 401 et seq.
20 Statutory Paternity Pay and Statutory Adoption Pay (General) Regulations 2002, SI 2002/2822, regs 31(1), 39(1), (3)(f). As to statutory paternity pay see PARA 443 et seq.
21 Statutory Paternity Pay and Statutory Adoption Pay (General) Regulations 2002, SI 2002/2822, regs 31(1), 39(1), (3)(g).

516. Time limit for paying statutory adoption pay; payment by employer. In any case where:
(1) a decision has been made by an officer of the Commissioners for Revenue and Customs[1] as a result of which a person is entitled to an amount of statutory adoption pay[2]; and

(2) the time for bringing an appeal against the decision has expired[3], and either: (a) no such appeal has been brought[4]; or (b) such an appeal has been brought and has been finally disposed of[5],

that amount of statutory adoption pay must be paid within the time specified[6] as follows[7].

The employer[8] or former employer must pay the amount not later than the first pay day[9] after[10]:

(i) where an appeal has been brought, the day on which the employer or former employer receives notification that the appeal has been finally disposed of[11];

(ii) where leave to appeal has been refused and there remains no further opportunity to apply for leave, the day on which the employer or former employer receives notification of the refusal[12]; and

(iii) in any other case, the day on which the time for bringing an appeal expires[13].

However, where it is impracticable, in view of the employer's or former employer's methods of accounting for and paying remuneration, for the requirement of such payment to be met by that pay day, it must be met not later than the next following pay day[14].

1 Ie under the Social Security Contributions (Transfer of Functions, etc) Act 1999 s 8(1): see WELFARE BENEFITS AND STATE PENSIONS vol 104 (2014) PARA 574. As to the Commissioners for Her Majesty's Revenue and Customs see INCOME TAXATION vol 58 (2014) PARAS 33–34; and see PARA 489 note 2.

2 Statutory Paternity Pay and Statutory Adoption Pay (General) Regulations 2002, SI 2002/2822, regs 31(1), 42(2)(a). As to the meaning of 'statutory adoption pay' see PARA 488.

3 See the Statutory Paternity Pay and Statutory Adoption Pay (General) Regulations 2002, SI 2002/2822, regs 31(1), 42(2)(b). As to the right to apply for the determination of any issue arising as to, or in connection with, entitlement to statutory adoption pay see PARA 595.

4 Statutory Paternity Pay and Statutory Adoption Pay (General) Regulations 2002, SI 2002/2822, regs 31(1), 42(2)(b)(i).

5 Statutory Paternity Pay and Statutory Adoption Pay (General) Regulations 2002, SI 2002/2822, regs 31(1), 42(2)(b)(ii).

6 Ie the time specified in the Statutory Paternity Pay and Statutory Adoption Pay (General) Regulations 2002, SI 2002/2822, regs 31(1), 42(3) (see the text and notes 8–13).

7 See the Statutory Paternity Pay and Statutory Adoption Pay (General) Regulations 2002, SI 2002/2822, regs 31(1), 42(2).

8 As to the meaning of 'employer' for these purposes see PARA 502.

9 For these purposes, 'pay day' means a day on which it has been agreed, or it is the normal practice between an employer or former employer and a person who is or was an employee of his, that payments by way of remuneration are to be made, or, where there is no such agreement or normal practice, the last day of a calendar month: see the Statutory Paternity Pay and Statutory Adoption Pay (General) Regulations 2002, SI 2002/2822, regs 31(1), 42(1). As to the meaning of 'employee' for these purposes see PARA 494.

10 See the Statutory Paternity Pay and Statutory Adoption Pay (General) Regulations 2002, SI 2002/2822, regs 31(1), 42(3). This provision is subject to reg 42(4), (5) (see the text and note 14): see reg 42(3).

11 Statutory Paternity Pay and Statutory Adoption Pay (General) Regulations 2002, SI 2002/2822, regs 31(1), 42(3)(a).

12 Statutory Paternity Pay and Statutory Adoption Pay (General) Regulations 2002, SI 2002/2822, regs 31(1), 42(3)(b).

13 Statutory Paternity Pay and Statutory Adoption Pay (General) Regulations 2002, SI 2002/2822, regs 31(1), 42(3)(c).

14 Statutory Paternity Pay and Statutory Adoption Pay (General) Regulations 2002, SI 2002/2822, regs 31(1), 42(4). Where the employer or former employer would not have remunerated the person for his work in the week in question as early as the pay day specified in regs 31(1), 42(3) (see the text and notes 8–13) or, if they apply, regs 31(1), 42(4), the requirement of payment

must be met on the first day on which the person would have been remunerated for his work in that week: regs 31(1), 42(5). As to the time for compliance where an employee is outside the United Kingdom see PARA 496.

517. Time limit for paying statutory adoption pay; payment by the Commissioners for Revenue and Customs. Where the Commissioners for Revenue and Customs[1] become liable[2] to make payments of statutory adoption pay[3] to a person, the first payment must be made as soon as reasonably practicable after they become so liable, and payments thereafter must be made at weekly intervals, by means of an instrument of payment or by such other means as appears to the Commissioners to be appropriate in the circumstances of any particular case[4].

1 As to the Commissioners for Her Majesty's Revenue and Customs see INCOME TAXATION vol 58 (2014) PARAS 33–34; and see PARA 489 note 2.
2 Ie in accordance with the Statutory Paternity Pay and Statutory Adoption Pay (General) Regulations 2002, SI 2002/2822, regs 31(1), 43 (see PARA 489) or regs 31(2), 44 (see PARA 491).
3 As to the meaning of 'statutory adoption pay' see PARA 488.
4 Statutory Paternity Pay and Statutory Adoption Pay (General) Regulations 2002, SI 2002/2822, regs 31(1), 45.

518. Payments treated as remuneration for purposes of statutory adoption pay; relationship with other payments. Any sum paid to, or for the benefit of, a person in satisfaction, whether in whole or in part, of any entitlement of his to statutory adoption pay[1] is to be treated[2] as remuneration derived from employed earner's[3] employment[4].

Any entitlement to statutory adoption pay does not affect any right of a person in relation to remuneration under any contract of service ('contractual remuneration')[5]; any contractual remuneration paid to a person by an employer[7] of his in respect of a week[8] in the adoption pay period goes towards discharging any liability of that employer to pay statutory adoption pay to him in respect of that week[9]; and any statutory adoption pay paid by an employer to a person who is an employee of his in respect of a week in the adoption pay period goes towards discharging any liability of that employer to pay contractual remuneration to him in respect of that week[10]. Regulations may make provision as to payments which are, and those which are not, to be treated as contractual remuneration for these purposes[6].

1 As to the meaning of 'statutory adoption pay' see PARA 488; and as to entitlement to statutory adoption pay see PARA 503 et seq.
2 Ie for the purposes of the Social Security Contributions and Benefits Act 1992 s 3 (meaning of 'earnings': see WELFARE BENEFITS AND STATE PENSIONS vol 104 (2014) PARA 382).
3 As to the meaning of 'employed earner' see the Social Security Contributions and Benefits Act 1992 s 2(1)(a), (3); and WELFARE BENEFITS AND STATE PENSIONS vol 104 (2014) PARA 381.
4 Social Security Contributions and Benefits Act 1992 s 4(1)(a)(v) (added by the Work and Families Act 2006 Sch 1 para 4; and amended by the Children and Families Act 2014 Sch 7 para 8(c)).

Until a day to be appointed under the Welfare Reform Act 2007 s 70(2), any day which falls within the adoption pay period is not to be treated as a day of incapacity for work for the purpose of determining, for the purposes of the Social Security Contributions and Benefits Act 1992, whether it forms part of a period of interruption of incapacity for work for the purposes of incapacity benefit, except as may be prescribed: s 171ZP(1) (ss 171ZP, 171ZS added by the Employment Act 2002 s 4; the Social Security Contributions and Benefits Act 1992 s 171ZP(1)–(3) prospectively repealed by the Welfare Reform Act 2007 Sch 8). For these purposes, 'prescribed' means prescribed by regulations: see s 171ZS(1) (as so added). At the date at which this volume states the law, no such day had been appointed. Until such a day is appointed, regulations may provide:

(1) that in prescribed circumstances a day which falls within the adoption pay period is to

be treated as a day of incapacity for work for the purpose of determining entitlement to the higher rate of short-term incapacity benefit or to long-term incapacity benefit (Social Security Contributions and Benefits Act 1992 s 171ZP(2) (s 171ZP as so added; s 171ZP(2) prospectively repealed)); and

(2) that an amount equal to a person's statutory adoption pay for a period is to be deducted from any such benefit in respect of the same period and a person is to be entitled to such benefit only if there is a balance after the deduction and, if there is such a balance, at a weekly rate equal to it (s 171ZP(3) (s 171ZP as so added; s 171ZP(3) prospectively repealed)).

In exercise of the powers so conferred, the Secretary of State has made the Social Security, Statutory Maternity Pay and Statutory Sick Pay (Miscellaneous Amendments) Regulations 2002, SI 2002/2690, which (in reg 10) adds the Social Security (Incapacity Benefit) Regulations 1994, SI 1994/2946, regs 7A, 7B: see WELFARE BENEFITS AND STATE PENSIONS vol 104 (2014) PARA 472 et seq. As to the making of regulations under the Social Security Contributions and Benefits Act 1992 see PARA 407 note 3. As to the meaning of 'adoption pay period' see PARA 511.

5 Social Security Contributions and Benefits Act 1992 s 171ZP(4) (as added: see note 4). This provision is subject to s 171ZP(5), (6) (see the text and notes 6–10): see s 171ZP(4) (as so added). Although 'contract of service' is defined for the purposes of statutory sick pay (see PARA 558 note 2), it is not so defined under the other statutory pay provisions (for which purposes see generally PARA 1 note 1).

6 As to the meaning of 'employer' for these purposes see PARA 502.

7 For this purpose, 'week' means a period of seven days beginning with the day of the week on which the adoption pay period begins: see the Social Security Contributions and Benefits Act 1992 s 171ZP(7) (as added: see note 4).

8 Social Security Contributions and Benefits Act 1992 s 171ZP(5)(a) (as added: see note 4). See note 5.

9 Social Security Contributions and Benefits Act 1992 s 171ZP(5)(b) (as added: see note 4).See note 5.

10 Social Security Contributions and Benefits Act 1992 s 171ZP(6) (as added: see note 4). See note 5. In exercise of the powers conferred by s 171ZP(6), the Secretary of State has made the Statutory Paternity Pay and Statutory Adoption Pay (General) Regulations 2002, SI 2002/2822 and the Statutory Paternity Pay (Adoption) and Statutory Adoption Pay (Adoptions from Overseas) (No 2) Regulations 2003, SI 2003/1194 (see PARA 531). Accordingly, for the purposes of the Social Security Contributions and Benefits Act 1992 s 171ZP(4) (see the text and note 5) and s 171ZP(5) (see the text and notes 6–9), the payments which are to be treated as contractual remuneration are sums payable under a contract of service (see the Statutory Paternity Pay and Statutory Adoption Pay (General) Regulations 2002, SI 2002/2822, reg 28): (1) by way of remuneration (reg 28(a)); (2) for incapacity for work due to sickness or injury (reg 28(b)); and (3) by reason of the adoption of a child (reg 28(c)).

519. Payment to persons entitled to statutory adoption pay who are unable to act. Where in the case of any person:

(1) statutory adoption pay[1] is payable to him or he is alleged to be entitled[2] to it[3];

(2) he is unable for the time being to act[4]; and

(3) no receiver has been appointed by the Court of Protection[5] with power to receive statutory adoption pay on his behalf[6],

the Commissioners for Revenue and Customs[7] may, upon written application to them by a person who, if a natural person, is over the age of 18[8], appoint that person to exercise, on behalf of the person unable to act, any right to which he may be entitled under the provisions relating to statutory adoption pay[9] and to deal on his behalf with any sums payable to him[10].

Anything required[11] to be done by or to any person who is unable to act may be done by or to the person so appointed to act on his behalf; and the receipt of the person so appointed is a good discharge to the person's employer or former employer for any sum paid[12].

Where the Commissioners have made such an appointment[13]: (a) they may at any time in their absolute discretion revoke it[14]; (b) the person appointed may

inspection, within such period as the regulations may require, such information or documents as the officer may reasonably require for the purpose of ascertaining whether statutory adoption pay[3] is or was payable to or in respect of any person[4]. The descriptions of person which may be specified by such regulations include, in particular[5]:

(1) any person claiming to be entitled to statutory adoption pay[6];
(2) any person who is, or has been, the spouse or partner of such a person as is mentioned in head (1) above[7];
(3) any person who is, or has been, an employer[8] of such a person as is mentioned in head (1) above[9];
(4) any person carrying on an agency or other business for the introduction or supply to persons requiring them of persons available to do work or to perform services[10]; and
(5) any person who is a servant or agent of any such person as is specified in heads (1) to (4) above[11].

Where a person fails to provide any information or document, in accordance with such regulations[12], he is liable[13] to: (a) a penalty[14]; and (b) if the failure continues after a penalty is imposed under head (a) above, a further penalty or penalties[15] for each day on which the failure continues after the day on which the penalty was imposed[16].

Neither of the above penalties is to be imposed[17] at any time after the failure concerned has been remedied[18].

Where a person fraudulently or negligently provides any incorrect information or document of a kind mentioned in the regulations[19], so far as relating to statutory adoption pay[20], he is liable to a penalty[21].

The general provisions as to procedure and appeals[22] have effect in relation to any of the penalties[23] described above[24].

1 As to the Secretary of State see PARA 5 note 21.
2 Regulations under the Employment Act 2002 s 10(1) must be made with the concurrence of the Commissioners for Revenue and Customs: see s 10(3). As to the Commissioners for Her Majesty's Revenue and Customs see **INCOME TAXATION** vol 58 (2014) PARAS 33–34; and PARA 489 note 2. As to the power to make regulations under the Employment Act 2002 see s 51; and PARA 474 note 2. In exercise of the powers so conferred, the Secretary of State has, with the concurrence of the Commissioners for Revenue and Customs, made the Statutory Paternity Pay and Statutory Adoption Pay (Administration) Regulations 2002, SI 2002/2820 (see PARA 524), and the Statutory Paternity Pay (Adoption) and Statutory Adoption Pay (Adoption from Overseas) (Administration) Regulations 2003, SI 2003/1192 (see PARA 532).
3 As to statutory adoption pay see PARA 488 et seq.
4 Employment Act 2002 s 10(1) (amended by the Work and Families Act 2006 Sch 1 para 52; and the Children and Families Act 2014 Sch 7 paras 50, 53(1), (2)(a)).
5 See the Employment Act 2002 s 10(2).
6 Employment Act 2002 s 10(2)(a) (amended by the Work and Families Act 2006 Sch 1 para 52; and the Children and Families Act 2014 Sch 7 paras 50, 53(1), (3)(a)). As to entitlement to statutory adoption pay see PARA 488 et seq.
7 Employment Act 2002 s 10(2)(b).
8 As to the meaning of 'employer' for these purposes see PARA 520 note 3.
9 Employment Act 2002 s 10(2)(c).
10 Employment Act 2002 s 10(2)(d).
11 Employment Act 2002 s 10(2)(e).
12 See the Employment Act 2002 s 11(1)(b).
13 See the Employment Act 2002 s 11(1). The Taxes Management Act 1970 s 118(2) (extra time for compliance etc: see **INCOME TAXATION** vol 59 (2014) PARA 2136) applies for the purposes of the Employment Act 2002 s 11(1) as it applies for the purposes of the Taxes Management Act 1970: Employment Act 2002 s 11(7).
14 Employment Act 2002 s 11(2)(a). The penalty must not exceed £300: see s 11(2)(a).
15 Ie not exceeding £60: see the Employment Act 2002 s 11(2)(b).

16 Employment Act 2002 s 11(2)(b). Any day for which a penalty under head (b) in the text has already been imposed is excluded for those purposes: see s 11(2)(b).
17 Ie under the Employment Act 2002 s 11(2): see heads (a), (b) in the text.
18 Employment Act 2002 s 11(4).
19 Ie in regulations under the Employment Act 2002 s 10(1): see the text and notes 1–4.
20 Employment Act 2002 s 12(2)(b) (amended by the Work and Families Act 2006 Sch 1 para 54(1), (3); and the Children and Families Act 2014 Sch 7 paras 50, 55(1), (3)(b)).
21 Employment Act 2002 s 12(2). The penalty must not exceed £3000: see s 12(2).
22 Ie contained in the Employment Act 2002 ss 11(8), 12(6), Sch 1: see PARA 479.
23 Ie imposed under either the Employment Act 2002 s 11 or s 12: see the text and notes 12–21.
24 See the Employment Act 2002 ss 11(8), 12(6).

524. Provision of information in connection with determination of questions relating to statutory adoption pay. Any person[1]:

(1) claiming to be entitled to statutory adoption pay[2];
(2) who is, or has been, the spouse, civil partner or partner of such a person as is specified in head (1) above[3];
(3) who is, or has been, an employer[4] of such a person as is specified in head (1) above[5];
(4) carrying on an agency or other business for the introduction or supply to persons requiring them of persons available to do work or to perform services[6]; and
(5) who is a servant or agent of any such person as is specified in heads (1) to (4) above[7],

must, where information or documents are reasonably required from him to ascertain whether statutory adoption pay is or was payable[8], furnish that information or those documents within 30 days of receiving a notification from an officer of the Commissioners for Revenue and Customs[9] requesting such information or documents[10].

1 Ie any person specified in the Statutory Paternity Pay and Statutory Adoption Pay (Administration) Regulations 2002, SI 2002/2820, reg 14(2) (see heads (1) to (5) in the text): see reg 14(1).
2 Statutory Paternity Pay and Statutory Adoption Pay (Administration) Regulations 2002, SI 2002/2820, reg 14(2)(a). As to the meaning of 'statutory adoption pay' see PARA 510 note 3. As to entitlement to statutory adoption pay see PARA 488 et seq.
3 Statutory Paternity Pay and Statutory Adoption Pay (Administration) Regulations 2002, SI 2002/2820, reg 14(2)(b) (amended by SI 2005/2114).
4 As to the meaning of 'employer' for these purposes see PARA 502.
5 Statutory Paternity Pay and Statutory Adoption Pay (Administration) Regulations 2002, SI 2002/2820, reg 14(2)(c).
6 Statutory Paternity Pay and Statutory Adoption Pay (Administration) Regulations 2002, SI 2002/2820, reg 14(2)(d).
7 Statutory Paternity Pay and Statutory Adoption Pay (Administration) Regulations 2002, SI 2002/2820, reg 14(2)(e).
8 As to the right to apply for the determination of any issue arising as to, or in connection with, entitlement to statutory paternity pay see PARA 595.
9 As to the Commissioners for Her Majesty's Revenue and Customs see INCOME TAXATION vol 58 (2014) PARAS 33–34; and see PARA 489 note 2.
10 See the Statutory Paternity Pay and Statutory Adoption Pay (Administration) Regulations 2002, SI 2002/2820, reg 14(1). As to the time for compliance where an employee is outside the United Kingdom see PARA 496. Electronic communications may be used for the delivery of information to or by the Commissioners, the delivery of which is required or authorised in connection with the payment of statutory adoption pay or of any other sum in connection with that pay: see the Statutory Payment Schemes (Electronic Communications) Regulations 2002, SI 2002/3047; and INCOME TAXATION.

525. Penalties for failure to comply with regulations or for fraud or negligence in providing information or making payments relating to statutory adoption pay: procedure and appeals. An officer of the Commissioners for Revenue and Customs[1] authorised by the Commissioners for the purpose may make a determination[2] imposing a penalty[3] for failure to comply with regulations relating to statutory adoption pay[4] or for fraud or negligence in providing information or making payments[5], and may set it at such amount as, in his opinion, is correct or appropriate[6]. Notice of such a determination of a penalty must be served on the person liable to the penalty and must state the date on which it is issued and the time within which an appeal against the determination may be made[7]. After such notice of a determination has been served the determination must not be altered except on appeal[8]; or if it is discovered by an officer of the Commissioners for Revenue and Customs authorised by them for these purposes that the amount of a penalty so determined is or has become insufficient, the officer may make a determination in a further amount so that the penalty is set at the amount which, in his opinion, is correct or appropriate[9]. A penalty determined in this way is due and payable at the end of the period of 30 days beginning with the date of the issue of the notice of determination[10]; and the provisions of the Taxes Management Act 1970 relating to collection and recovery[11] apply in relation to a penalty so determined as if it were tax charged in an assessment and due and payable[12].

An appeal may be brought against a penalty so determined[13]; and the provisions of the Taxes Management Act 1970 relating to appeals[14] have effect in relation to an appeal against such a determination as they have effect in relation to an appeal against an assessment to tax except that references to the tribunal are taken to be references to the First-tier Tribunal[15]. On such an appeal, the First-tier Tribunal has powers to confirm, vary or set aside the determination of the penalty[16]; and, in addition to any right of appeal on a point of law[17], the person liable to the penalty may appeal to the Upper Tribunal against the amount of the penalty which had been so determined on appeal[18], but not against any decision which was made in connection with the determination of the amount of the penalty[19].

Where, in the opinion of the Commissioners for Revenue and Customs, the liability of any person to a penalty for failure to comply with regulations[20] or for fraud or negligence in providing information or making payments[21] arises by reason of the fraud of that or any other person, proceedings for the penalty may be instituted before the High Court[22], in the name of the Attorney General[23]. Any proceedings so instituted are deemed to be civil proceedings[24] by the Crown[25]. If in such proceedings the court does not find that fraud is proved but considers that the person concerned is nevertheless liable to a penalty, the court may determine a penalty notwithstanding that, but for the opinion of the Commissioners for Revenue and Customs as to fraud, the penalty would not have been a matter for the court[26].

The Commissioners for Revenue and Customs may in their discretion mitigate any penalty for failure to comply with regulations[27] or for fraud or negligence in providing information or making payments[28], or may stay or compound any proceedings for a penalty, and they may also, after judgment, further mitigate or entirely remit the penalty[29].

A penalty for failure to comply with regulations[30] or for fraud or negligence in providing information or making payments[31] may be determined by an officer of the Commissioners for Revenue and Customs, or proceedings for the penalty may be commenced before the tribunal[32] or the court[33], at any time within six years after the date on which the penalty was incurred or began to be incurred[34].

1 As to the Commissioners for Her Majesty's Revenue and Customs see INCOME TAXATION vol 58 (2014) PARAS 33–34; and see PARA 489 note 2.

2 Ie except where penalty proceedings have been instituted before a court under the Employment Act 2002 ss 11(8), 12(6), Sch 1 para 5: see the text and notes 20–26.

3 Ie except where such a penalty has been imposed as is mentioned in the Employment Act 2002 s 11(2)(a) (ie a penalty of £300 imposed on a person who fails to produce any document or record, provide any information or make any return in accordance with regulations made under s 8 (see PARA 520) or who fails to provide any information or document in accordance with regulations made under s 10 (see PARA 523): see PARAS 520, 523): Sch 1 para 1(2). An officer of the Commissioners for Revenue and Customs authorised by them for these purposes may commence proceedings for any penalty to which Sch 1 para 1(1) does not apply by virtue of Sch 1 para 1(2), however: Sch 1 para 4(1). The person liable to the penalty is a party to the proceedings: Sch 1 para 4(2) (Sch 1 para 4(2), (4) substituted, Sch 1 para 4(4A) added, by SI 2009/56). The Taxes Management Act 1970 Pt VI (ss 60–70A) (collection and recovery: see INCOME TAXATION vol 59 (2014) PARA 2304 et seq) applies in relation to a penalty determined in proceedings under the Employment Act 2002 Sch 1 para 4 as if it were tax charged in an assessment and due and payable: Sch 1 para 4(3). In addition to any right of appeal on a point of law under the Tribunals, Courts and Enforcement Act 2007 s 11(2) (see COURTS AND TRIBUNALS vol 24 (2010) PARA 928), the person liable to the penalty may appeal to the Upper Tribunal against the determination of a penalty in proceedings under the Employment Act 2002 Sch 1 para 4(1), but not against any decision which falls under the Tribunals, Courts and Enforcement Act 2007 s 11(5)(d), (e) (see COURTS AND TRIBUNALS vol 24 (2010) PARA 928) and was made in connection with the determination of the amount of the penalty: Employment Act 2002 Sch 1 para 4(4) (as so substituted). The Tribunals, Courts and Enforcement Act 2007 s 11(3), (4) (see COURTS AND TRIBUNALS vol 24 (2010) PARA 928) applies to the right of appeal under the Employment Act 2002 Sch 1 para 4(4) as it applies to the right of appeal under the Tribunals, Courts and Enforcement Act 2007 s 11(2): Employment Act 2002 Sch 1 para 4(4A) (as so added). On any such appeal, the Upper Tribunal may (see Sch 1 para 4(5) (amended by SI 2009/56)):

(1) if it appears that no penalty has been incurred, set the determination aside (Employment Act 2002 Sch 1 para 4(5)(a));
(2) if the amount determined appears to be appropriate, confirm the determination (Sch 1 para 4(5)(b));
(3) if the amount determined appears to be excessive, reduce it to such other amount (including nil) as the Upper Tribunal considers appropriate (Sch 1 para 4(5)(c) (amended by SI 2009/56));
(4) if the amount determined appears to be insufficient, increase it to such amount not exceeding the permitted maximum as the Upper Tribunal considers appropriate (Employment Act 2002 Sch 1 para 4(5)(d) (amended by SI 2009/56)).

As to the First-tier Tribunal and the Upper Tribunal see COURTS AND TRIBUNALS vol 24 (2010) PARA 874 et seq.

4 See the Employment Act 2002 s 11: see PARAS 520, 523. As to statutory adoption pay see PARA 488 et seq.

5 See the Employment Act 2002 s 12: see PARAS 520, 523.

6 See the Employment Act 2002 Sch 1 para 1(1). As to the determination of claims generally see WELFARE BENEFITS AND STATE PENSIONS vol 104 (2014) PARA 575 et seq.

7 Employment Act 2002 Sch 1 para 1(3).

8 Employment Act 2002 Sch 1 para 1(4).

9 Employment Act 2002 Sch 1 para 1(5).

10 Employment Act 2002 Sch 1 para 2(1). A penalty under s 11 (see note 4) or s 12 (see note 5) carries interest at the rate applicable under the Finance Act 1989 s 178 (see INCOME TAXATION vol 59 (2014) PARA 2303) from the date on which it becomes due and payable until payment: Employment Act 2002 Sch 1 para 8(2).

11 Ie the Taxes Management Act 1970 Pt VI (ss 60–70A) (collection and recovery: see INCOME TAXATION vol 59 (2014) PARA 2304 et seq).

12 Employment Act 2002 Sch 1 para 2(2).

13 Employment Act 2002 Sch 1 para 3(1).

14 Ie the Taxes Management Act 1970 Pt V (ss 46D–57) (appeals and other proceedings: see INCOME TAXATION vol 59 (2014) PARA 2244 et seq), except s 50(6)–(8).

15 Employment Act 2002 Sch 1 para 3(2) (amended by SI 2009/56).
16 Ie, on an appeal by virtue of the Employment Act 2002 Sch 1 para 3(2) (see the text and notes 14–15) against the determination of a penalty under Sch 1 para 1 (see the text and notes 1–9), the First-tier Tribunal may (see Sch 1 para 3(3) (amended by SI 2009/56)):
(1) if it appears that no penalty has been incurred, set the determination aside (Employment Act 2002 Sch 1 para 3(3)(a) (Sch 1 para 3(3)(a)–(d) amended by SI 2009/56));
(2) if the amount determined appears to be appropriate, confirm the determination (Employment Act 2002 Sch 1 para 3(3)(b) (as so amended));
(3) if the amount determined appears to be excessive, reduce it to such other amount (including nil) as the First-tier Tribunal considers appropriate (Sch 1 para 3(3)(c) (as so amended));
(4) if the amount determined appears to be insufficient, increase it to such amount not exceeding the permitted maximum as the First-tier Tribunal considers appropriate (Sch 1 para 3(3)(d) (as so amended)).
17 Ie under the Tribunals, Courts and Enforcement Act 2007 s 11(2): see COURTS AND TRIBUNALS vol 24 (2010) PARA 928.
18 Ie under the Employment Act 2002 Sch 1 para 3.
19 Employment Act 2002 Sch 1 para 3(4) (Sch 1 para 3(4) substituted, Sch 1 para 3(4A), (4B) added, by SI 2009/56). The reference in the text is to any decision which falls under the Tribunals, Courts and Enforcement Act 2007 s 11(5)(d), (e) (see COURTS AND TRIBUNALS vol 24 (2010) PARA 928): see the Employment Act 2002 Sch 1 para 3(4) (as so substituted). The Tribunals, Courts and Enforcement Act 2007 s 11(3), (4) (see COURTS AND TRIBUNALS vol 24 (2010) PARA 928) applies to the right of appeal under the Employment Act 2002 Sch 1 para 3(4) as it applies to the right of appeal under the Tribunals, Courts and Enforcement Act 2007 s 11(2) (see COURTS AND TRIBUNALS vol 24 (2010) PARA 928): Employment Act 2002 Sch 1 para 3(4A) (as so added). On an appeal under Sch 1 para 3, the Upper Tribunal has the like jurisdiction as is conferred on the First-tier Tribunal by virtue of Sch 1 para 3 (see the text and notes 13–16): Sch 1 para 3(4B) (as so added).
20 See note 4.
21 See note 5.
22 See the Employment Act 2002 Sch 1 para 5(1).
23 See the Employment Act 2002 Sch 1 para 5(2)(a). However, this provision does not prevent proceedings under Sch 1 para 4 being instituted under the Crown Proceedings Act 1947 (see CROWN PROCEEDINGS AND CROWN PRACTICE vol 12(1) (Reissue) PARA 102 et seq) by and in the name of the Commissioners for Revenue and Customs as an authorised department for the purposes of that Act: Employment Act 2002 Sch 1 para 5(3). As to the Attorney General see CONSTITUTIONAL AND ADMINISTRATIVE LAW vol 20 (2014) PARA 273 et seq.
24 Ie within the meaning of the Crown Proceedings Act 1947 Pt II (ss 13–23) (jurisdiction and procedure: see CROWN PROCEEDINGS AND CROWN PRACTICE vol 12(1) (Reissue) PARA 116).
25 Employment Act 2002 Sch 1 para 5(4).
26 Employment Act 2002 Sch 1 para 5(5).
27 See note 4.
28 See note 5.
29 Employment Act 2002 Sch 1 para 6.
30 See note 4.
31 See note 5.
32 Ie before the First-tier Tribunal: see the Employment Act 2002 Sch 1 para 4; and note 3.
33 See the Employment Act 2002 Sch 1 para 5; and the text and notes 20–26.
34 Employment Act 2002 Sch 1 para 7 (amended by SI 2009/56).

526. Supply and use of information. Information which is held for the purposes of functions relating to statutory adoption pay[1] by the Commissioners for Revenue and Customs[2], or by a person providing services to the Commissioners in connection with the provision of those services[3], may be supplied to the Secretary of State[4], or to a person providing services to the Secretary of State[5], for use for the purposes of functions relating to social security[6], child support[7] or war pensions[8].

Information which is held for the purposes of functions relating to statutory adoption pay by the Secretary of State[9], or by a person providing services to the

Secretary of State[10] in connection with the provision of those services[11], may be supplied to the Commissioners, or to a person providing services to the Commissioners, for use for the purposes of functions relating to statutory adoption pay[12].

Information which is held by the Commissioners, or by a person providing services to the Commissioners in connection with the provision of those services, for the purposes of[13]:

(1) the functions of the Commissioners in relation to statutory paternity pay[14];
(2) their functions in relation to statutory adoption pay[15]; and
(3) their functions in relation to statutory shared parental pay[16]; and
(4) their functions in relation to tax[17], contributions[18], statutory sick pay[19], statutory maternity pay[20] or tax credits[21], or functions[22] relating to the certification of pension schemes[23],

may be used for the purposes of, or for any purposes connected with, the exercise of any functions specified in any other of heads (1) to (4) above, and may be supplied to any person providing services to the Commissioners for those purposes[24].

1 As to statutory adoption pay see PARA 488 et seq.
2 As to the Commissioners for Her Majesty's Revenue and Customs see INCOME TAXATION vol 58 (2014) PARAS 33–34; and see PARA 489 note 2.
3 See the Employment Act 2002 s 13(1) (amended by the Work and Families Act 2006 Sch 1 para 55; and the Children and Families Act 2014 Sch 7 paras 50, 56(a)).
4 Or, in Northern Ireland, the Department for Social Development or the Department for Employment and Learning. As to the Secretary of State see PARA 5 note 21.
5 See note 4.
6 See WELFARE BENEFITS AND STATE PENSIONS vol 104 (2014) PARA 2 et seq.
7 See CHILDREN AND YOUNG PERSONS vol 9 (2012) PARA 573 et seq.
8 See the Employment Act 2002 s 13(2) (amended by SI 2008/2656; SI 2012/2007). As to war pensions see ARMED FORCES vol 3 (2011) PARA 718 et seq.
9 See note 4.
10 See note 4.
11 See the Employment Act 2002 s 14(1) (amended by the Work and Families Act 2006 Sch 1 para 56; and the Children and Families Act 2014 Sch 7 paras 50, 57(1), (2)(a)).
12 See the Employment Act 2002 s 14(2) (amended by the Work and Families Act 2006 Sch 1 para 56; and the Children and Families Act 2014 Sch 7 paras 50, 57(1), (3)(a)).
13 See the Employment Act 2002 s 15(1). The text refers to information so held for the purposes of any functions specified in s 15(2) (see heads (1) to (4) in the text): see s 15(1).
14 Employment Act 2002 s 15(2)(a) (amended by the Work and Families Act 2006 Sch 1 para 57(a); and the Children and Families Act 2014 Sch 7 paras 50, 58(a)). As to statutory paternity pay see PARA 443 et seq.
15 Employment Act 2002 s 15(2)(b) (amended by the Children and Families Act 2014 Sch 7 paras 50, 58(c)).
16 Employment Act 2002 s 15(2)(ba) (added by the Children and Families Act 2014 Sch 7 paras 50, 58(d)). As to statutory shared parental pay see PARA 534 et seq.
17 See INCOME TAXATION vol 58 (2014) PARAS 33–34.
18 For these purposes, 'contributions' means contributions under the Social Security Contributions and Benefits Act 1992 Pt 1 (ss 1–19A) (see WELFARE BENEFITS AND STATE PENSIONS vol 104 (2014) PARA 384 et seq) or the Social Security Contributions and Benefits (Northern Ireland) Act 1992 Pt 1: see the Employment Act 2002 s 15(3).
19 As to statutory sick pay see PARA 558 et seq.
20 As to statutory maternity pay see PARA 401 et seq.
21 See WELFARE BENEFITS AND STATE PENSIONS vol 104 (2014) PARA 335 et seq.
22 Ie under the Pension Schemes Act 1993 Pt III (ss 7–68) (see PERSONAL AND OCCUPATIONAL PENSIONS vol 80 (2013) PARA 395 et seq) or, in Northern Ireland, the Pension Schemes (Northern Ireland) Act 1993 Pt III.
23 Employment Act 2002 s 15(2)(c).
24 See the Employment Act 2002 s 15(1).

H. RECOVERY OF AMOUNTS PAID

527. Power to make provision for funding of employers' liabilities for statutory adoption pay. The Secretary of State[1] must by regulations[2] make provision for the payment by employers[3] of statutory adoption pay[4] to be funded by the Commissioners for Revenue and Customs[5] to such extent as the regulations may specify[6]. Such regulations:

(1) must make provision for a person who has made a payment of statutory adoption pay to be entitled, except in such circumstances as the regulations may provide, to recover an amount equal to the sum of[7]:
  (a) the aggregate of such of those payments as qualify for small employers' relief[8]; and
  (b) an amount equal to 92 per cent of the aggregate of such of those payments as do not so qualify[9]; and

(2) must include provision for a person who has made a payment of statutory adoption pay qualifying for small employers' relief to be entitled, except in such circumstances as the regulations may provide, to recover an additional amount equal to the amount to which the person would have been entitled[10] had the payment been a payment of statutory maternity pay[11]; and

(3) may, in particular, make provision:
  (a) for funding in advance as well as in arrear[12];
  (b) for funding, or the recovery of amounts due under provision made by virtue of head (2) above, by means of deductions from such amounts for which employers are accountable to the Commissioners as the regulations may provide, or otherwise[13];
  (c) for the recovery by the Commissioners of any sums overpaid to employers under such regulations[14].

Where an employer fraudulently or negligently receives incorrect payments in pursuance of such regulations, he is liable to a penalty[15].

1 As to the Secretary of State see PARA 5 note 21.
2 Regulations under the Employment Act 2002 s 7(1) must be made with the concurrence of the Commissioners for Revenue and Customs: see s 7(6). As to the Commissioners for Her Majesty's Revenue and Customs see **INCOME TAXATION** vol 58 (2014) PARAS 33–34; and see PARA 489 note 2. As to the power to make regulations under the Employment Act 2002 see s 51; and PARA 474 note 2. In exercise of the powers so conferred, the Secretary of State has, with the concurrence of the Commissioners for Revenue and Customs, made the Statutory Paternity Pay and Statutory Adoption Pay (Administration) Regulations 2002, SI 2002/2820 (see PARA 528), and the Statutory Paternity Pay (Adoption) and Statutory Adoption Pay (Adoption from Overseas) (Administration) Regulations 2003, SI 2003/1192 (see PARA 532).
3 As to the meaning of 'employer' for these purposes see PARA 502.
4 As to statutory adoption pay see PARA 488 et seq.
5 See note 2.
6 Employment Act 2002 s 7(1) (amended by the Work and Families Act 2006 Sch 1 para 50(1), (2); and the Children and Families Act 2014 Sch 7 paras 50, 51(1), (2)(a)).
7 See the Employment Act 2002 s 7(2)(a) (amended by the Work and Families Act 2006 Sch 1 para 50(1), (3); and the Children and Families Act 2014 Sch 7 paras 50, 51(1), (3)(a)).
8 Employment Act 2002 s 7(2)(a)(i). For these purposes, a payment of statutory adoption pay qualifies for small employers' relief if it would have so qualified were it a payment of statutory maternity pay, treating the period for which the payment of statutory adoption pay is made as the maternity pay period: see s 7(3) (amended by the Work and Families Act 2006 Sch 1 para 50(1), (4); and the Children and Families Act 2014 Sch 7 paras 50, 51(1), (4)(c)). As to the meaning of 'maternity pay period' see PARA 424.
9 Employment Act 2002 s 7(2)(a)(ii).
10 Ie under the Social Security Contributions and Benefits Act 1992 s 167(2)(b) (corresponding provision for statutory maternity pay: see PARA 439).

11 Employment Act 2002 s 7(2)(b) (amended by the Work and Families Act 2006 Sch 1 para 50(1), (3); and the Children and Families Act 2014 Sch 7 paras 50, 51(1), (3)(b)).
12 Employment Act 2002 s 7(4)(a).
13 Employment Act 2002 s 7(4)(b). The Commissioners may use electronic communications in connection with the recovery of statutory adoption pay or of any other sum in connection with that pay: see the Statutory Payment Schemes (Electronic Communications) Regulations 2002, SI 2002/3047; and INCOME TAXATION.
14 Employment Act 2002 s 7(4)(c).
15 Employment Act 2002 s 12(5) (amended by the Work and Families Act 2006 Sch 1 para 54(1), (4); and the Children and Families Act 2014 Sch 7 paras 50, 55(1), (6)). The penalty must not exceed £3000: see the Employment Act 2002 s 12(5) (as so amended).

528. Funding of employers' liabilities to make payments of statutory adoption pay; recovery of amount due. An employer[1] who has made any payment of statutory adoption pay[2] is entitled:

(1) to an amount equal to 92 per cent of such payment[3]; or
(2) if the payment qualifies for small employer's relief[4], to an amount equal to such payment, and to an additional payment equal to the amount to which he would have been entitled[5] had the payment been a payment of statutory maternity pay[6].

The employer is entitled in either case under head (1) or head (2) above to apply for advance funding in respect of such payment[7], or to deduct it[8] from amounts otherwise payable by him[9].

If an employer is entitled to such a funding payment[10] in respect of statutory adoption pay which he is required to pay to an employee[11] or employees in any income tax month[12] or income tax quarter[13], and the amount exceeds the aggregate of:

(a) the total amount of tax which the employer is required to pay to the collector of taxes in respect of deductions from the emoluments of his employees[14] for that income tax month or income tax quarter;
(b) the total amount of the deductions made by the employer[15] from the emoluments of his employees for the same income tax month or income tax quarter;
(c) the total amount of contributions payments which the employer is required to pay[16] to the collector of taxes in respect of the emoluments of his employees, whether by means of deduction or otherwise, for that income tax month or income tax quarter; and
(d) the total amount of payments which the employer is required to pay to the collector of taxes in respect of deductions made on account of tax from payments to sub-contractors[17] for that income tax month or income tax quarter,

the employer may apply to the Commissioners for Revenue and Customs for funds to pay the statutory adoption pay, or so much of it as remains outstanding, to the employee or employees[18]; and where this condition[19] is satisfied, or where the employer considers that the condition will be satisfied on the date of any subsequent payment of emoluments to one or more employees who are entitled to a payment of statutory adoption pay, the employer may apply to the Commissioners for funding in a form approved for that purpose by them[20]. Such an application by an employer must be for an amount up to, but not exceeding, the amount of the payment to which the employer is entitled[21] in respect of statutory adoption pay which he is required to pay to an employee or employees for the income tax month or income tax quarter to which the payment of emoluments relates[22].

An employer who is entitled to such a funding payment[23] may recover it by making one or more deductions from the aggregate of the amounts specified in heads (a) to (d) above, except where and in so far as:

(i) those amounts relate to earnings paid before the beginning of the income tax month or income tax quarter in which the payment of statutory adoption pay was made;

(ii) those amounts are paid by him later than six years after the end of the tax year in which the payment of statutory adoption pay was made;

(iii) the employer has received payment[24] from the Commissioners for Revenue and Customs; or

(iv) the employer has made a request[25] in writing[26] that the payment to which he is entitled[27] be paid to him and he has not received notification by the Commissioners that such request is refused[28].

Where funds have been provided to an employer[29] in respect of one or more employees and it appears to an officer of the Commissioners that the employer has not used the whole or part of those funds to pay statutory adoption pay[30], such an officer must decide to the best of his judgement the amount of funds so provided and not used to pay statutory adoption pay and must serve notice in writing of his decision on the employer[31]. Such a decision may cover funds so provided for any one income tax month or income tax quarter, or more than one income tax month or income tax quarter, in a tax year, and in respect of a class or classes of employees specified in the decision notice, without naming the individual employees, or in respect of one or more employees named in the decision notice[32].

1 As to the meaning of 'employer' for these purposes see PARA 502.
2 As to the meaning of 'statutory adoption pay' for these purposes see PARA 510 note 3.
3 Statutory Paternity Pay and Statutory Adoption Pay (Administration) Regulations 2002, SI 2002/2820, reg 3(1)(a).
4 Ie by virtue of the Employment Act 2002 s 7(3): see PARA 527 note 8.
5 Ie under the Social Security Contributions and Benefits Act 1992 s 167(2)(b) (corresponding provision for statutory maternity pay: see PARA 439).
6 Statutory Paternity Pay and Statutory Adoption Pay (Administration) Regulations 2002, SI 2002/2820, reg 3(1)(b). As to statutory maternity pay see PARA 401 et seq.
7 Ie in accordance with the Statutory Paternity Pay and Statutory Adoption Pay (Administration) Regulations 2002, SI 2002/2820, reg 4: see the text and notes 10–22.
8 Ie in accordance with the Statutory Paternity Pay and Statutory Adoption Pay (Administration) Regulations 2002, SI 2002/2820, reg 5: see the text and notes 23–28.
9 Statutory Paternity Pay and Statutory Adoption Pay (Administration) Regulations 2002, SI 2002/2820, reg 3(2).
10 Ie determined in accordance with the Statutory Paternity Pay and Statutory Adoption Pay (Administration) Regulations 2002, SI 2002/2820, reg 3: see the text and notes 1–9.
11 As to the meaning of 'employee' for these purposes see PARA 494.
12 As to the meaning of 'income tax month' for these purposes see PARA 482 note 12.
13 As to the meaning of 'income tax quarter' for these purposes see PARA 482 note 13.
14 Ie in accordance with the Income Tax (Pay As You Earn) Regulations 2003, SI 2003/2682: see INCOME TAXATION vol 58 (2014) PARA 927 et seq.
15 Ie in accordance with regulations made under the Teaching and Higher Education Act 1998 s 22(5): see EDUCATION vol 36 (2011) PARA 1249.
16 Ie in accordance with the Social Security (Contributions) Regulations 2001, SI 2001/1004: see WELFARE BENEFITS AND STATE PENSIONS vol 104 (2014) PARA 399 et seq.
17 Ie in accordance with the Income and Corporation Taxes Act 1988 s 559 (repealed).
18 See the Statutory Paternity Pay and Statutory Adoption Pay (Administration) Regulations 2002, SI 2002/2820, reg 4(1); and see the Interpretation Act 1978 s 17(2)(a). As to the Commissioners for Her Majesty's Revenue and Customs see INCOME TAXATION vol 58 (2014) PARAS 33–34.
19 Ie in the Statutory Paternity Pay and Statutory Adoption Pay (Administration) Regulations 2002, SI 2002/2820, reg 4(1): see the text and notes 10–18.

20 See the Statutory Paternity Pay and Statutory Adoption Pay (Administration) Regulations 2002, SI 2002/2820, reg 4(2).
21 Ie under the Statutory Paternity Pay and Statutory Adoption Pay (Administration) Regulations 2002, SI 2002/2820, reg 3: see the text and notes 1–9.
22 Statutory Paternity Pay and Statutory Adoption Pay (Administration) Regulations 2002, SI 2002/2820, reg 4(3).
23 Ie determined in accordance with the Statutory Paternity Pay and Statutory Adoption Pay (Administration) Regulations 2002, SI 2002/2820, reg 3: see the text and notes 1–9.
24 Ie under the Statutory Paternity Pay and Statutory Adoption Pay (Administration) Regulations 2002, SI 2002/2820, reg 4: see the text and notes 10–22.
25 See note 24.
26 As to the meaning of 'writing' see PARA 482 note 26.
27 Ie under the Statutory Paternity Pay and Statutory Adoption Pay (Administration) Regulations 2002, SI 2002/2820, reg 3: see the text and notes 1–9.
28 See the Statutory Paternity Pay and Statutory Adoption Pay (Administration) Regulations 2002, SI 2002/2820, reg 5. Where an employer has made a deduction from a contributions payment under reg 5, the date on which it is to be treated as having been paid for the purposes of the Employment Act 2002 s 7(5) (see PARA 529) is:
   (1) in a case where the deduction did not extinguish the contributions payment, the date on which the remainder of the contributions payment or, as the case may be, the first date on which any part of the remainder of the contributions payment was paid (Statutory Paternity Pay and Statutory Adoption Pay (Administration) Regulations 2002, SI 2002/2820, reg 7(a)); and
   (2) in a case where the deduction extinguished the contributions payment, the fourteenth day after the end of the income tax month or income tax quarter during which there were paid the earnings in respect of which the contributions payment was payable (reg 7(b)).

   For these purposes, 'contributions payments' has the same meaning as in the Employment Act 2002 s 7 (see PARA 483 note 5): see the Statutory Paternity Pay and Statutory Adoption Pay (Administration) Regulations 2002, SI 2002/2820, reg 2(1).

   If the total amount which an employer is or would otherwise be entitled to deduct under reg 5 is less than the payment to which the employer is entitled in accordance with reg 3 in an income tax month or income tax quarter, and the Commissioners are satisfied that this is so, then provided that the employer has in writing requested them to do so, the Commissioners must pay to the employer such amount as the employer was unable to deduct: reg 6.
29 Ie pursuant to the Statutory Paternity Pay and Statutory Adoption Pay (Administration) Regulations 2002, SI 2002/2820, reg 4: see the text and notes 10–22.
30 See the Statutory Paternity Pay and Statutory Adoption Pay (Administration) Regulations 2002, SI 2002/2820, reg 8(1).
31 See the Statutory Paternity Pay and Statutory Adoption Pay (Administration) Regulations 2002, SI 2002/2820, reg 8(2).
32 See the Statutory Paternity Pay and Statutory Adoption Pay (Administration) Regulations 2002, SI 2002/2820, reg 8(3). The Taxes Management Act 1970 Pt VI (ss 60–70A) (collection and recovery: see **INCOME TAXATION** vol 59 (2014) PARA 2304 et seq) applies with any necessary modifications to a decision under the Statutory Paternity Pay and Statutory Adoption Pay (Administration) Regulations 2002, SI 2002/2820, reg 8 as if it were an assessment and as if the amount of funds determined were income tax charged on the employer: reg 8(4). Where an amount of funds determined under reg 8 relates to more than one employee, proceedings may be brought for the recovery of that amount without distinguishing the amounts making up that sum which the employer is liable to repay in respect of each employee and without specifying the employee in question, and the amount determined under reg 8 is one cause of action or one matter of complaint for the purposes of proceedings under the Taxes Management Act 1970 ss 65–67 (see **INCOME TAXATION** vol 59 (2014) PARAS 2310–2311): Statutory Paternity Pay and Statutory Adoption Pay (Administration) Regulations 2002, SI 2002/2820, reg 8(5). However, nothing in reg 8(5) prevents the bringing of separate proceedings for the recovery of any amount which the employer is liable to repay in respect of each employee: reg 8(6).

529. Treatment of amount deducted from contributions. Where, in accordance with any provision of regulations[1] which make provision for the payment by employers[2] of statutory adoption pay[3] to be funded by the Commissioners for Revenue and Customs[4], an amount has been deducted from an employer's contributions payments[5], the amount so deducted must be treated, except in such cases as the Secretary of State[6] may by regulations provide, for the purposes of any provision made by or under any enactment in relation to primary or secondary Class 1 contributions[7]:

(1) as having been paid on such date as may be determined in accordance with the regulations[8]; and

(2) as having been received by the Commissioners for Revenue and Customs[9],

towards discharging the employer's liability in respect of such contributions[10].

1 Ie regulations made under the Employment Act 2002 s 7(1): see PARA 527.
2 As to the meaning of 'employer' for these purposes see PARA 502.
3 As to statutory adoption pay see PARA 488 et seq.
4 As to the Commissioners for Her Majesty's Revenue and Customs see **INCOME TAXATION** vol 58 (2014) PARAS 33–34; and PARA 489 note 2.
5 As to the meaning of 'contributions payments' see PARA 483 note 5.
6 As to the Secretary of State see PARA 5 note 21.
7 See the Employment Act 2002 s 7(5). As to primary and secondary Class 1 contributions see **WELFARE BENEFITS AND STATE PENSIONS** vol 104 (2014) PARA 385.
8 Employment Act 2002 s 7(5)(a).
9 Employment Act 2002 s 7(5)(b).
10 See the Employment Act 2002 s 7(5). As to the date on which the deduction is treated as having been paid see PARA 528 note 28.

I. ADOPTIONS FROM OVERSEAS

530. Application of statutory adoption pay provisions to adoption cases. The Secretary of State[1] may by regulations[2] provide for the statutory provisions relating to statutory adoption pay[3] to have effect in relation to cases which involve adoption, but not the placement of a child for adoption under the law of any part of the United Kingdom[4], with such modifications[5] as the regulations may prescribe[6]. Accordingly, the statutory provisions generally apply in relation to adoptions from overseas[7] regarding:

(1) entitlement to statutory adoption pay[8];
(2) the liability to make payments of statutory adoption pay[9];
(3) the rate and period of such payments[10];
(4) the restrictions on contracting out[11];
(5) the relationship of statutory adoption pay with benefits and other payments[12];
(6) Crown employment[13]; and
(7) provision for special classes of person[14].

However, under head (1) above, the conditions whose fulfilment are necessary for entitlement to statutory adoption pay[15] are modified[16] so that a person is entitled to statutory adoption pay in relation to an adoption from overseas if:

(a) he is a person who is, or is expected to be, an adopter[17] of a child from overseas[18];
(b) he has been in employed earner's[19] employment with an employer[20] for a continuous period of at least 26 weeks[21];
(c) he has ceased to work for the employer[22];
(d) his normal weekly earnings[23] for the period of eight weeks ending with the relevant week[24] are not less than the lower earnings limit in force[25] at the end of the relevant week[26]; and
(e) he has elected to receive statutory adoption pay[27].

1 As to the Secretary of State see PARA 5 note 21.

2 As to the making of regulations under the Social Security Contributions and Benefits Act 1992 see PARA 407 note 3.
3 Ie the provisions of the Social Security Contributions and Benefits Act 1992 Pt XIIZB (ss 171ZL–171ZT) (statutory adoption pay: see PARA 488 et seq). As to the meaning of 'statutory adoption pay' see PARA 488.
4 As to the meaning of 'United Kingdom' see PARA 407 note 7. As to the law relating to child adoption see **CHILDREN AND YOUNG PERSONS** vol 9 (2012) PARA 360 et seq.
5 As to the meaning of 'modifications' see PARA 490 note 8.
6 Social Security Contributions and Benefits Act 1992 s 171ZT(1) (ss 171ZL, 171ZS, 171ZT added by the Employment Act 2002 s 4; the Social Security Contributions and Benefits Act 1992 s 171ZT(1) numbered as such, s 171ZT(2), (3) added, by the Children and Families Act 2014 s 122(6)(b), (c)). The Secretary of State may by regulations also provide for the Social Security Contributions and Benefits Act 1992 Pt XIIZB (statutory adoption pay: see PARA 488 et seq) to have effect in relation to cases which involve an person who has applied, or intends to apply, with another person for a parental order under the Human Fertilisation and Embryology Act 2008 s 54 (parental orders: see **CHILDREN AND YOUNG PERSONS** vol 9 (2012) PARA 129) and a child who is, or will be, the subject of the order, with such modifications as the regulations may prescribe: Social Security Contributions and Benefits Act 1992 s 171ZT(2) (as so added). Regulations under s 171ZT(2) may modify s 171ZL(8)(c) (see PARA 490) so as to enable regulations to impose requirements to make statutory declarations as to eligibility to apply for a parental order, and as to intention to apply for such an order: s 171ZT(3) (as so added). For these purposes, 'prescribed' means prescribed by regulations: see s 171ZS(1) (as so added). In exercise of the powers conferred by s 171ZT, the Secretary of State has made the Social Security Contributions and Benefits Act 1992 (Application of Parts 12ZA and 12ZB to Adoptions from Overseas) Regulations 2003, SI 2003/499, and the Statutory Paternity Pay and Statutory Adoption Pay (Amendment) Regulations 2004, SI 2004/488 (see the text and notes 7–17).
7 As to the meaning of 'adoption from overseas' see PARA 484 note 7.
8 Ie the general provisions of the Social Security Contributions and Benefits Act 1992 s 171ZL (see PARA 503; but see also the text and notes 18–27): see the Social Security Contributions and Benefits Act 1992 (Application of Parts 12ZA and 12ZB to Adoptions from Overseas) Regulations 2003, SI 2003/499, reg 3.
9 Ie the Social Security Contributions and Benefits Act 1992 s 171ZM (see PARAS 488–489, 493): see the Social Security Contributions and Benefits Act 1992 (Application of Parts 12ZA and 12ZB to Adoptions from Overseas) Regulations 2003, SI 2003/499, reg 3.
10 Ie the Social Security Contributions and Benefits Act 1992 s 171ZN (see PARAS 491, 511, 513): see the Social Security Contributions and Benefits Act 1992 (Application of Parts 12ZA and 12ZB to Adoptions from Overseas) Regulations 2003, SI 2003/499, reg 3.
11 Ie the Social Security Contributions and Benefits Act 1992 s 171ZO (see PARA 488): see the Social Security Contributions and Benefits Act 1992 (Application of Parts 12ZA and 12ZB to Adoptions from Overseas) Regulations 2003, SI 2003/499, reg 3.
12 Ie the Social Security Contributions and Benefits Act 1992 s 171ZP (see PARA 518 note 4): see the Social Security Contributions and Benefits Act 1992 (Application of Parts 12ZA and 12ZB to Adoptions from Overseas) Regulations 2003, SI 2003/499, reg 3.
13 Ie the Social Security Contributions and Benefits Act 1992 s 171ZQ (see PARA 500): see the Social Security Contributions and Benefits Act 1992 (Application of Parts 12ZA and 12ZB to Adoptions from Overseas) Regulations 2003, SI 2003/499, reg 3.
14 Ie the Social Security Contributions and Benefits Act 1992 s 171ZR (see PARA 495): see the Social Security Contributions and Benefits Act 1992 (Application of Parts 12ZA and 12ZB to Adoptions from Overseas) Regulations 2003, SI 2003/499, reg 3.
15 Ie the conditions mentioned in the Social Security Contributions and Benefits Act 1992 s 171ZL(2)–(5) (see PARA 503) are modified and associated definitions are added to s 171ZS(1) as specified in the Social Security Contributions and Benefits Act 1992 (Application of Parts 12ZA and 12ZB to Adoptions from Overseas) Regulations 2003, SI 2003/499, reg 3, Sch 2.
16 Social Security Contributions and Benefits Act 1992 (Application of Parts 12ZA and 12ZB to Adoptions from Overseas) Regulations 2003, SI 2003/499, reg 3.
17 For these purposes, 'adopter', in relation to a child, means a person by whom the child has been or is to be adopted: see the Social Security Contributions and Benefits Act 1992 s 171ZS(1) (s 171ZS as added (see note 6); definition added by the Social Security Contributions and Benefits Act 1992 (Application of Parts 12ZA and 12ZB to Adoptions from Overseas) Regulations 2003, SI 2003/499, Sch 2).
18 Social Security Contributions and Benefits Act 1992 s 171ZL(2)(a) (s 171ZL as added (see note 6); s 171ZL(2)(a) modified by the Social Security Contributions and Benefits Act 1992

(Application of Parts 12ZA and 12ZB to Adoptions from Overseas) Regulations 2003, SI 2003/499, Sch 2). A person's entitlement to statutory adoption pay is not affected by the adoption, or expected adoption, from overseas of more than one child as part of the same arrangement: Social Security Contributions and Benefits Act 1992 s 171ZL(5) (s 171ZL as so added; s 171ZL(5) modified by the Social Security Contributions and Benefits Act 1992 (Application of Parts 12ZA and 12ZB to Adoptions from Overseas) Regulations 2003, SI 2003/499, Sch 2). For these purposes, 'adoption from overseas' means the adoption of a child who enters Great Britain from outside the United Kingdom in connection with or for the purposes of adoption which does not involve the placement of the child for adoption under the law of any part of the United Kingdom; and the references to a child adopted from overseas must be construed accordingly: see the Social Security Contributions and Benefits Act 1992 s 171ZS(1) (s 171ZS as added (see note 6); definition added by the Social Security Contributions and Benefits Act 1992 (Application of Parts 12ZA and 12ZB to Adoptions from Overseas) Regulations 2003, SI 2003/499, Sch 2).

19 As to the meaning of 'employed earner' see the Social Security Contributions and Benefits Act 1992 s 2(1)(a), (3); and WELFARE BENEFITS AND STATE PENSIONS vol 104 (2014) PARA 381.

20 As to the meaning of 'employer' for these purposes see PARA 502.

21 Social Security Contributions and Benefits Act 1992 s 171ZL(2)(b) (s 171ZL as added (see note 6); s 171ZL(2)(b) modified by the Social Security Contributions and Benefits Act 1992 (Application of Parts 12ZA and 12ZB to Adoptions from Overseas) Regulations 2003, SI 2003/499, Sch 2 (amended by SI 2004/488)). As to the meaning of 'week' for these purposes see PARA 490 note 14.

22 Social Security Contributions and Benefits Act 1992 s 171ZL(2)(c) (as added: see note 6).

23 As to the meaning of 'normal weekly earnings' see PARA 514.

24 The reference in the Social Security Contributions and Benefits Act 1992 s 171ZL(2)(d) to the relevant week is a reference to either the week in which official notification is sent to the adopter, or the week at the end of which the person satisfies the condition in s 171ZL(2)(b) (see head (b) in the text), whichever is the later: s 171ZL(3) (s 171ZL as added (see note 6); s 171ZL(3) substituted by the Social Security Contributions and Benefits Act 1992 (Application of Parts 12ZA and 12ZB to Adoptions from Overseas) Regulations 2003, SI 2003/499, Sch 2 (amended by SI 2004/488)). For these purposes, 'official notification' means written notification, issued by or on behalf of the relevant domestic authority, that it is prepared to issue a certificate to the overseas authority concerned with the adoption of the child, or has issued a certificate and sent it to that authority, confirming, in either case, that the adopter is eligible to adopt and has been assessed and approved as being a suitable adoptive parent; and 'relevant domestic authority' means: (1) in the case of an adopter to whom the Intercountry Adoption (Hague Convention) Regulations 2003, SI 2003/118 (see now the Adoptions with a Foreign Element Regulations 2005, SI 2005/392) apply (see CHILDREN AND YOUNG PERSONS vol 9 (2012) PARAS 521, 528 et seq) and who is habitually resident in Wales, the National Assembly for Wales; and (2) in any other case, the Secretary of State: see the Social Security Contributions and Benefits Act 1992 s 171ZS(1) (s 171ZS as added (see note 6); definition added by the Social Security Contributions and Benefits Act 1992 (Application of Parts 12ZA and 12ZB to Adoptions from Overseas) Regulations 2003, SI 2003/499, Sch 2). As to the meaning of 'Wales' see PARA 2 note 12. As to the National Assembly for Wales see CONSTITUTIONAL AND ADMINISTRATIVE LAW vol 20 (2014) PARA 351 et seq. As to habitual residence see CONFLICT OF LAWS vol 19 (2011) PARA 360 et seq.

25 Ie under the Social Security Contributions and Benefits Act 1992 s 5(1)(a) (earnings limits and thresholds for Class 1 contributions: see WELFARE BENEFITS AND STATE PENSIONS vol 104 (2014) PARA 384).

26 Social Security Contributions and Benefits Act 1992 s 171ZL(2)(d) (as added: see note 6).

27 Social Security Contributions and Benefits Act 1992 s 171ZL(2)(e) (as added: see note 6). A person may not elect to receive statutory adoption pay if: (1) he has elected in accordance with s 171ZB (see PARA 484) to receive statutory paternity pay; or (2) where the child is, or is expected to be, adopted by him as a member of a married couple or civil partnership and his spouse or civil partner is a person to whom the conditions in s 171ZL(2) (see heads (a) to (e) in the text) apply, his spouse or civil partner has elected to receive statutory adoption pay: see s 171ZL(4) (s 171ZL as so added; s 171ZL(4) amended by the Civil Partnership Act 2004 Sch 24 para 50; and modified by the Social Security Contributions and Benefits Act 1992 (Application of Parts 12ZA and 12ZB to Adoptions from Overseas) Regulations 2003, SI 2003/499, Sch 2).

Marriage of same sex couples is lawful in the law of England and Wales, and such marriages have the same effect as marriages of opposite sex couples: see the Marriage (Same Sex Couples) Act 2013 s 1(1), 11(1); and MATRIMONIAL AND CIVIL PARTNERSHIP LAW vol 72 (2009) PARA 1 et seq.

531. Application of general statutory adoption pay regulations in relation to adoptions from overseas. Regulations made under the statutory provisions relating to statutory adoption pay[1], as they have effect with modifications[2] in relation to adoptions from overseas[3], apply the general statutory adoption pay regulations[4] to such adoptions with such modifications as are required[5].

Accordingly, the general statutory adoption pay regulations apply to adoptions from overseas[6] without modification in relation to the following matters:

(1) work during an adoption pay period[7];
(2) cases where there is no liability to pay statutory adoption pay[8];
(3) the circumstances in which payments of statutory adoption pay are to be treated as contractual remuneration[9];
(4) the conditions under which persons are and are not to be treated as employees in connection with statutory adoption pay[10];
(5) what is to be treated as continuous employment[11];
(6) cases where two or more employers or two or more contracts of service are to be treated as one[12];
(7) the definition of 'earnings'[13];
(8) how payment of statutory adoption pay is to be made and the time of payment[14];
(9) conditions under which the Commissioners for Revenue and Customs pay statutory adoption pay[15];
(10) liability of the Commissioners for Revenue and Customs to pay statutory adoption pay in cases of legal custody or imprisonment[16];
(11) how the Commissioners make payments of statutory adoption pay and the time of payment[17];
(12) the appointment by the Commissioners of a person to act on behalf of a person unable to act[18];
(13) the rule which determines when a notice properly sent by post is treated as having been given[19].

However, the provisions which set out how normal weekly earnings are to be calculated[20] are modified in relation to the appropriate date[21].

The regulations which govern the adoption pay period[22] are substituted so that a person entitled to statutory adoption pay in respect of an adoption from overseas may choose the statutory adoption pay period[23] to begin either on the date on which the child enters Great Britain (or the following day where the person is at work on that day)[24], or on the predetermined date, specified by him, which is no later than 28 days after the date on which the child enters Great Britain[25]. The duration of any adoption pay period is[26] a continuous period of 26 weeks[27]. Where, after a child enters Great Britain, the child either dies, or ceases to live with the adopter, the adoption pay period terminates eight weeks after the end of the specified[28] week[29].

The regulations which specify the additional notice requirements for statutory adoption pay[30] are substituted so that where a person gives notice of absence from work[31] in relation to adoptions from overseas he must give further notice of the following matters to the person liable to pay him statutory adoption pay:

(a) the date on which official notification was received, within 28 days of

provide for payments of statutory adoption pay to be made by the Commissioners for Revenue and Customs[4] in relation to such adoptions with such modifications as are required[5].

Accordingly, the regulations which provide for payments of statutory adoption pay to be made by the Commissioners for Revenue and Customs also apply to adoptions from overseas[6] without modification in relation to:

(1) the funding by the Commissioners of employers' liabilities to make payments of statutory adoption pay[7];

(2) the requirement for employers to maintain records relevant to such payments and to provide such records upon request[8];

(3) the determination by officers of the Commissioners of issues relating to a person's entitlement to such payments[9];

(4) the requirement placed on employers, employment agencies, persons claiming statutory adoption pay and others to furnish information or documents to an officer of the Commissioners on request[10].

However, the regulation which requires that an employer who has been given evidence of an employee's entitlement to statutory adoption pay, but decides that he has no liability to make payments, must furnish the employee with details of the decision, and the reasons for it[11], is modified[12].

1 Ie under the Social Security Contributions and Benefits Act 1992 Pt XIIZB (ss 171ZL–171ZT) (statutory adoption pay: see PARA 488 et seq). As to the meaning of 'statutory adoption pay' see PARA 488. As to the making of regulations under the Social Security Contributions and Benefits Act 1992 generally see PARA 407 note 3.

2 See PARA 530. As to the meaning of 'modifications' see PARA 490 note 8.

3 As to the meaning of 'adoption from overseas' for these purposes see PARA 530 note 18.

4 Ie the Statutory Paternity Pay and Statutory Adoption Pay (Administration) Regulations 2002, SI 2002/2820: see PARA 464 et seq.

5 See the Statutory Paternity Pay (Adoption) and Statutory Adoption Pay (Adoptions from Overseas) (Administration) Regulations 2003, SI 2003/1192, reg 3(1). References to provisions of the Social Security Contributions and Benefits Act 1992 Pt XIIZA (ss 171ZA–171ZK) (statutory paternity pay: see PARA 443 et seq) and Pt XIIZB (statutory adoption pay: see PARA 488 et seq) in the Statutory Paternity Pay and Statutory Adoption Pay (Administration) Regulations 2002, SI 2002/2820 (as modified) (see the text and notes 6–12) are to be construed as references to the Social Security Contributions and Benefits Act 1992 Pt XIIZA or Pt XIIZB as modified by the Social Security Contributions and Benefits Act 1992 (Application of Parts 12ZA and 12ZB to Adoptions from Overseas) Regulations 2003, SI 2003/499 (see PARA 530): Statutory Paternity Pay and Statutory Adoption Pay (Administration) Regulations 2002, SI 2002/2820, reg 2(3) (added by the Statutory Paternity Pay (Adoption) and Statutory Adoption Pay (Adoptions from Overseas) (Administration) Regulations 2003, SI 2003/1192, reg 2(3)).

6 For these purposes, 'adoption from overseas' means the adoption of a child who enters Great Britain from outside the United Kingdom in connection with or for the purposes of adoption which does not involve the placement of the child for adoption under the law of any part of the United Kingdom: Statutory Paternity Pay (Adoption) and Statutory Adoption Pay (Adoptions from Overseas) (Administration) Regulations 2003, SI 2003/1192, reg 2. As to the meanings of 'Great Britain' and 'United Kingdom' see PARA 407 note 7. As to the law relating to child adoption see **CHILDREN AND YOUNG PERSONS** vol 9 (2012) PARA 360 et seq.

7 Ie the Statutory Paternity Pay and Statutory Adoption Pay (Administration) Regulations 2002, SI 2002/2820, regs 3–8 (see PARA 482): see the Statutory Paternity Pay (Adoption) and Statutory Adoption Pay (Adoptions from Overseas) (Administration) Regulations 2003, SI 2003/1192, reg 3(1).

8 Ie the Statutory Paternity Pay and Statutory Adoption Pay (Administration) Regulations 2002, SI 2002/2820, regs 9, 10 (see PARAS 475–476): see the Statutory Paternity Pay (Adoption) and Statutory Adoption Pay (Adoptions from Overseas) (Administration) Regulations 2003, SI 2003/1192, reg 3(1).

9 Ie the Statutory Paternity Pay and Statutory Adoption Pay (Administration) Regulations 2002, SI 2002/2820, regs 12–13 (see PARA 595): see the Statutory Paternity Pay (Adoption) and Statutory Adoption Pay (Adoptions from Overseas) (Administration) Regulations 2003, SI 2003/1192, reg 3(1).

10 Ie the Statutory Paternity Pay and Statutory Adoption Pay (Administration) Regulations 2002, SI 2002/2820, reg 14 (see PARA 478): see the Statutory Paternity Pay (Adoption) and Statutory Adoption Pay (Adoptions from Overseas) (Administration) Regulations 2003, SI 2003/1192, reg 3(1).

11 Ie the Statutory Paternity Pay and Statutory Adoption Pay (Administration) Regulations 2002, SI 2002/2820, reg 11: see PARA 464.

12 The modifications take account of the fact that there is no matching of a child with an adopter in the case of adoptions from overseas. Accordingly, the Statutory Paternity Pay and Statutory Adoption Pay (Administration) Regulations 2002, SI 2002/2820, reg 11(4), which defines what is meant by an adopter being notified of having been matched with a child (see PARA 464 note 12), is omitted (Statutory Paternity Pay (Adoption) and Statutory Adoption Pay (Adoptions from Overseas) (Administration) Regulations 2003, SI 2003/1192, reg 3(5)); and the Statutory Paternity Pay and Statutory Adoption Pay (Administration) Regulations 2002, SI 2002/2820, reg 11(3)(b)(ii) (see PARA 464) provides that, in the case of entitlement to statutory adoption pay under the Social Security Contributions and Benefits Act 1992 s 171ZL(1) (as applied: see note 5) (see PARA 530), an employer is required to give a decision that he has no liability to make payments within 28 days of the date on which the employee's evidence was provided, or, where not all of the evidence referred to in the Statutory Paternity Pay and Statutory Adoption Pay (Administration) Regulations 2002, SI 2002/2820, reg 11(1) (see PARA 464) was provided on one date, the date on which the last of the evidence was provided (reg 11(3)(b)(ii) (modified by the Statutory Paternity Pay (Adoption) and Statutory Adoption Pay (Adoptions from Overseas) (Administration) Regulations 2003, SI 2003/1192, reg 3(4))).

533. Application of statutory adoption pay regulations regarding persons abroad and mariners in relation to adoptions from overseas. Regulations made under the statutory provisions relating to statutory adoption pay[1], as they have effect with modifications[2] in relation to adoptions from overseas[3], apply the statutory adoption pay regulations which provide for persons abroad, persons who work as mariners and persons who work on the continental shelf to be treated as employees, and for employment in a member state to be treated as employed earner's employment, for the purposes of statutory adoption pay[4], to such adoptions with such modifications as are required[5].

Accordingly, those regulations apply in relation to adoptions from overseas[6], but with one modification in relation to the entitlement to statutory adoption pay[7].

1 Ie under the Social Security Contributions and Benefits Act 1992 Pt XIIZB (ss 171ZL–171ZT) (statutory adoption pay: see PARA 488 et seq). As to the meaning of 'statutory adoption pay' see PARA 488. As to the making of regulations under the Social Security Contributions and Benefits Act 1992 generally see PARA 407 note 3.

2 See PARA 530. As to the meaning of 'modifications' see PARA 490 note 8.

3 As to the meaning of 'adoption from overseas' for these purposes see PARA 530 note 18.

4 Ie the Statutory Paternity Pay and Statutory Adoption Pay (Persons Abroad and Mariners) Regulations 2002, SI 2002/2821: see PARA 450 et seq. As to employed earner's employment within the meaning of the Social Security Contributions and Benefits Act 1992 see WELFARE BENEFITS AND STATE PENSIONS vol 104 (2014) PARA 176.

5 Ordinary Statutory Paternity Pay (Adoption), Additional Statutory Paternity Pay (Adoption) and Statutory Adoption Pay (Adoptions from Overseas) (Persons Abroad and Mariners) Regulations 2010, SI 2010/150, reg 4(1). References to the provisions of the Social Security Contributions and Benefits Act 1992 Pt XIIZA (ss 171ZA–171ZK) (statutory paternity pay: see PARA 443 et seq) and Pt XIIZB (statutory adoption pay: see PARA 488 et seq) in the Statutory Paternity Pay and Statutory Adoption Pay (Persons Abroad and Mariners) Regulations 2002, SI 2002/2821 (as modified) are to be construed as references to the Social Security Contributions and Benefits Act 1992 Pt XIIZA or Pt XIIZB as modified by the Social Security Contributions and Benefits Act 1992 (Application of Parts 12ZA and 12ZB to Adoptions from Overseas) Regulations 2003, SI 2003/499 (see PARA 484): Statutory Paternity Pay and Statutory Adoption

Pay (Persons Abroad and Mariners) Regulations 2002, SI 2002/2821, reg 1(3) (substituted by the Ordinary Statutory Paternity Pay (Adoption), Additional Statutory Paternity Pay (Adoption) and Statutory Adoption Pay (Adoptions from Overseas) (Persons Abroad and Mariners) Regulations 2010, SI 2010/150, reg 4(3)).

6 As to the meaning of 'adoption from overseas' for these purposes see PARA 487 note 6.

7 See the Ordinary Statutory Paternity Pay (Adoption), Additional Statutory Paternity Pay (Adoption) and Statutory Adoption Pay (Adoptions from Overseas) (Persons Abroad and Mariners) Regulations 2010, SI 2010/150, reg 4(1), (5). The modification, which takes account of the fact that there is no matching of a child with an adopter in the case of adoptions from overseas, requires that a person who is an employee or treated as an employee under the Statutory Paternity Pay and Statutory Adoption Pay (Persons Abroad and Mariners) Regulations 2002, SI 2002/2821, reg 3 (as applied) (see PARA 451) and who, in the week in which the person receives an official notification or completes 26 weeks' continuous employment with the person's employer, whichever is the later: (1) was in employed earner's employment with an employer in Great Britain; and (2) had in any week within the period of 26 weeks immediately preceding that week been employed by the same employer in another EEA state, must be treated for the purposes of the Social Security Contributions and Benefits Act 1992 s 171ZL (as modified: see note 5) (entitlement to statutory adoption pay: see PARA 530) as having been employed in employed earner's employment in those weeks in which the person was so employed in the other EEA state: Statutory Paternity Pay and Statutory Adoption Pay (Persons Abroad and Mariners) Regulations 2002, SI 2002/2821, reg 6 (modified by the Ordinary Statutory Paternity Pay (Adoption), Additional Statutory Paternity Pay (Adoption) and Statutory Adoption Pay (Adoptions from Overseas) (Persons Abroad and Mariners) Regulations 2010, SI 2010/150, reg 4(5)). As to the meaning of 'official notification' for these purposes see PARA 487 note 7.

(v) Statutory Shared Parental Pay on Birth or Adoption

A. IN GENERAL

534. Liability of employer for payment of statutory shared parental pay. Regulations made under the Social Security Contributions and Benefits Act 1992[1] may provide that where a person:

(1) who is the mother of a child ('the claimant mother')[2]; or

(2) who together with another person who is the mother of a child[3]; or

(3) with whom a child is, or is expected to be, placed for adoption under the law of any part of the United Kingdom[4]; or

(4) who together with another person with whom a child is, or is expected to be, placed for adoption under the law of any part of the United Kingdom[5];

satisfies the prescribed conditions[6], then the person mentioned in any of heads (1) to (4) above is entitled[7] to payments (known as 'statutory shared parental pay')[8]. The liability to make such payments of statutory shared parental pay is a liability of any person of whom the person entitled to such payments has been an employee[9] employed in accordance with the prescribed conditions[10].

Any agreement is void to the extent that it purports:

(a) to exclude, limit or otherwise modify any of the statutory shared parental pay provisions[11] that are set out in Part XIIZC of the Social Security Contributions and Benefits Act 1992[12]; or

(b) to require a person to contribute, whether directly or indirectly, towards any costs incurred by that person's employer[13] or former employer under those provisions[14],

but, for the avoidance of doubt, any agreement between an employer and an employee authorising deductions from statutory shared parental pay which the employer is liable to pay to the employee in respect of any period is not void by virtue of head (a) above if the employer[15]: (i) is authorised by that or another agreement to make the same deductions from any contractual remuneration which he is liable to pay in respect of the same period[16]; or (ii) would be so authorised if he were liable to pay contractual remuneration in respect of that period[17].

1 As to the making of regulations under the Social Security Contributions and Benefits Act 1992 generally see PARA 407 note 3.
2 See the Social Security Contributions and Benefits Act 1992 s 171ZU(1) (ss 171ZU, 171ZV, 171ZX, 171ZZ, 171ZZ4 added by the Children and Families Act 2014 s 119(1)).
3 See the Social Security Contributions and Benefits Act 1992 s 171ZU(3) (as added: see note 2).
4 See the Social Security Contributions and Benefits Act 1992 s 171ZV(1) (as added: see note 2). As to the meaning of 'United Kingdom' see PARA 407 note 7. As to the law relating to child adoption see CHILDREN AND YOUNG PERSONS vol 9 (2012) PARA 360 et seq.
5 See the Social Security Contributions and Benefits Act 1992 s 171ZV(3) (as added: see note 2).
6 Ie the conditions set out:
   (1) in relation to head (1) in the text, in the Social Security Contributions and Benefits Act 1992 s 171ZU(2) (see PARA 544) (see s 171ZU(1) (as added: see note 2));
   (2) in relation to head (2) in the text, in s 171ZU(4) (see PARA 545) (see s 171ZU(3) (as so added));
   (3) in relation to head (3) in the text, in s 171ZV(2) (see PARA 544) (see s 171ZV(1) (as so added));
   (4) in relation to head (4) in the text, in s 171ZV(4) (see PARA 545) (see s 171ZV(3) (as so added)).

   For these purposes, 'prescribed' means prescribed by regulations: see s 171ZZ4(1) (as added: see note 2).
7 Ie in accordance with the provisions of the Social Security Contributions and Benefits Act 1992 Pt XIIZC (ss 171ZU–171ZZ5) (statutory shared parental pay: see also PARA 535 et seq).
8 See the Social Security Contributions and Benefits Act 1992 ss 171ZU(1), (3), 171ZV(1), (3) (ss 171ZU, 171ZV as added: see note 2). A statutory instrument containing, whether alone or with other provisions, regulations made by virtue of any of ss 171ZU–171ZY, must not be made unless a draft of the instrument has been laid before Parliament and been approved by a resolution of each House: see s 176(1)(a) (as amended: see PARA 465 note 5). At the date at which this volume states the law, no such regulations had been made.

   Statutory shared parental pay under the Social Security Contributions and Benefits Act 1992 Pt XIIZC constitutes 'wages' for the purposes of the Employment Rights Act 1996 Pt II (ss 13–27) (protection of wages): see s 27(1); and PARA 254. Payments of statutory shared parental pay under the Social Security Contributions and Benefits Act 1992 Pt XIIZC are charged to income tax under the Income Tax (Earnings and Pensions) Act 2003 Pts 2–7 (ss 3–554): see INCOME TAXATION vol 58 (2014) PARA 730 et seq.
9 Ie an employee as mentioned in the Social Security Contributions and Benefits Act 1992 s 171ZU(2)(c), (d) or s 171ZV(2)(c), (d): see PARA 544. As to the meaning of 'employee' for these purposes see PARA 539.
10 Social Security Contributions and Benefits Act 1992 s 171ZX(1) (as added: see note 2). As to the liability of the Commissioners for Revenue and Customs for payments of statutory shared parental pay see PARA 535.
11 Ie any of the provisions of the Social Security Contributions and Benefits Act 1992 Pt XIIZC (statutory shared parental pay: see also PARA 535 et seq).
12 Social Security Contributions and Benefits Act 1992 s 171ZZ(1)(a) (as added: see note 2).
13 As to the meaning of 'employer' for these purposes see PARA 543.
14 Social Security Contributions and Benefits Act 1992 s 171ZZ(1)(b) (as added: see note 2).
15 See the Social Security Contributions and Benefits Act 1992 s 171ZZ(2) (as added: see note 2).
16 Social Security Contributions and Benefits Act 1992 s 171ZZ(2)(a) (as added: see note 2).
17 Social Security Contributions and Benefits Act 1992 s 171ZZ(2)(b) (as added: see note 2).

535. Liability of the Commissioners for Revenue and Customs for payment of statutory shared parental pay. The Secretary of State[1] may, with the concurrence of the Commissioners for Revenue and Customs[2], by regulations[3] specify circumstances in which[4] liability to make payments of statutory shared parental pay[5] is to be a liability of the Commissioners[6].

1 As to the Secretary of State see PARA 5 note 21.

2 As to the Commissioners for Her Majesty's Revenue and Customs see INCOME TAXATION vol 58 (2014) PARAS 33–34.
3 As to the making of regulations under the Social Security Contributions and Benefits Act 1992 generally see PARA 407 note 3; and see PARA 534 note 8.
4 Ie notwithstanding the Social Security Contributions and Benefits Act 1992 s 171ZX: see also PARAS 534, 538.
5 As to the meaning of 'statutory shared parental pay' see PARA 534.
6 See the Social Security Contributions and Benefits Act 1992 s 171ZX(3) (s 171ZX added by the Children and Families Act 2014 s 119(1)). At the date at which this volume states the law, no such regulations had been made.

536. General power to make regulations in relation to statutory shared parental pay. Regulations made under the Social Security Contributions and Benefits Act 1992[1] may:

(1) provide that conditions giving entitlement to statutory shared parental pay[2] have effect subject to prescribed[3] modifications[4], in such cases as may be prescribed[5];
(2) impose requirements about evidence of entitlement and procedures to be followed[6];
(3) specify in what circumstances employment is to be treated[7] as continuous[8];
(4) provide that a person is to be treated[9] as being employed for a continuous period of at least the prescribed period[10], where:
 (a) he has been employed by the same employer for at least the prescribed period under two or more separate contracts of service[11]; and
 (b) those contracts were not continuous[12];
(5) provide for amounts earned by a person under separate contracts of service with the same employer to be aggregated[13];
(6) provide that:
 (a) the amount of a person's earnings for any period[14]; or
 (b) the amount of his earnings to be treated as comprised in any payment made to him or for his benefit[15],

 is to be calculated or estimated[16] in such manner and on such basis as may be prescribed and that for that purpose payments of a particular class or description made or falling to be made to or by a person are, to such extent as may be prescribed, to be disregarded or, as the case may be, to be deducted from the amount of his earnings[17].

The Secretary of State may also by regulations specify circumstances in which there is to be no liability to pay statutory shared parental pay in respect of a week[18].

1 As to the making of regulations under the Social Security Contributions and Benefits Act 1992 generally see PARA 407 note 3; and see PARA 534 note 8.
2 Ie the Social Security Contributions and Benefits Act 1992 ss 171ZU(2)(a)–(o), 171ZV(2)(a)–(o) (see PARA 544), ss 171ZU(4)(a)–(p), 171ZV(4)(a)–(p) (see PARA 545), ss 171ZU(13)(a), (b), 171ZV(13)(a), (b) (see PARA 547 note 32), and ss 171ZU(15)(a)–(c), 171ZV(15)(a)–(c) (see PARA 547 note 33). As to the meaning of 'statutory shared parental pay' see PARA 534.
3 For these purposes, 'prescribed' means prescribed by regulations: see the Social Security Contributions and Benefits Act 1992 s 171ZZ4(1) (ss 171ZW, 171ZZ4 added by the Children and Families Act 2014 s 119(1)).
4 For these purposes, 'modifications' includes additions, omissions and amendments; and related expressions are to be read accordingly: see the Social Security Contributions and Benefits Act 1992 s 171ZZ4(1) (as added: see note 3).
5 Social Security Contributions and Benefits Act 1992 s 171ZW(1)(a) (as added: see note 3). At the date at which this volume states the law, no such regulations had been made.

6 Social Security Contributions and Benefits Act 1992 s 171ZW(1)(b) (as added: see note 3). The persons upon whom requirements may be imposed by virtue of s 171ZW(1)(b) include:
   (1) a person who, in connection with another person's claim to be paid statutory shared parental pay, is required to satisfy conditions prescribed under ss 171ZU(2)(b), 171ZV(2)(b) (see PARA 544), or ss 171ZU(4)(c), 171ZV(4)(c) (see PARA 545) (s 171ZW(2)(a) (as so added));
   (2) an employer or former employer of such a person (s 171ZW(2)(b) (as so added)).

Where s 171ZW(1)(b) has effect in relation to such cases as are described in s 171ZZ5(2) (power to apply Pt XIIZC: see PARA 557), regulations under s 171ZW(1)(b) may impose requirements to make statutory declarations as to eligibility to apply for a parental order under the Human Fertilisation and Embryology Act 2008 s 54 (parental orders: see **CHILDREN AND YOUNG PERSONS** vol 9 (2012) PARA 129), and as to intention to apply for such an order: see the Social Security Contributions and Benefits Act 1992 s 171ZZ5(3); and PARA 557. As to the meaning of 'employer' for these purposes see PARA 543.

7 Ie for the purposes of the Social Security Contributions and Benefits Act 1992 s 171ZU or s 171ZV (see PARAS 544, 545).
8 Social Security Contributions and Benefits Act 1992 s 171ZW(1)(c) (as added: see note 3).
9 Ie for the purposes of the Social Security Contributions and Benefits Act 1992 s 171ZU or s 171ZV (see PARAS 544, 545).
10 See the Social Security Contributions and Benefits Act 1992 s 171ZW(1)(d) (as added: see note 3). For this purpose, the 'prescribed period' means the period of the length prescribed by regulations under ss 171ZU(2)(c), 171ZV(2)(c) (see PARA 544), or ss 171ZU(4)(d), 171ZV(4)(d) (see PARA 545), as the case may be: s 171ZW(3) (as so added).
11 Social Security Contributions and Benefits Act 1992 s 171ZW(1)(d)(i) (as added: see note 3). Although 'contract of service' is defined for the purposes of statutory sick pay (see PARA 558 note 2), it is not so defined under the other statutory pay provisions (for which purposes see generally PARA 1 note 1).
12 Social Security Contributions and Benefits Act 1992 s 171ZW(1)(d)(ii) (as added: see note 3).
13 Social Security Contributions and Benefits Act 1992 s 171ZW(1)(e) (as added: see note 3). Head (5) in the text refers to provision for amounts to be aggregated for the purposes of s 171ZU or s 171ZV (see PARAS 544, 545).
14 Social Security Contributions and Benefits Act 1992 s 171ZW(1)(f)(i) (as added: see note 3).
15 Social Security Contributions and Benefits Act 1992 s 171ZW(1)(f)(ii) (as added: see note 3).
16 Ie for the purposes of Social Security Contributions and Benefits Act 1992 s 171ZU or s 171ZV (see PARAS 544, 545).
17 Social Security Contributions and Benefits Act 1992 s 171ZW(1)(f) (as added: see note 3).
18 See the Social Security Contributions and Benefits Act 1992 s 171ZY(5); and PARA 537.

537. Circumstances in which liability to pay statutory shared parental pay does not arise. The Secretary of State[1] may by regulations[2] specify circumstances in which there is to be no liability to pay statutory shared parental pay[3] in respect of a week falling within a relevant period[4]. Except in such cases as may be prescribed[5], statutory shared parental pay is not payable to a person in respect of a week falling within a relevant period:
   (1) if it is not his intention at the beginning of the week to care for the child by reference to whom he is entitled[6] to statutory shared parental pay[7]; or
   (2) during any part of which he works for any employer[8].

1 As to the Secretary of State see PARA 5 note 21.
2 As to the making of regulations under the Social Security Contributions and Benefits Act 1992 generally see PARA 407 note 3; and see PARA 534 note 8.
3 As to the meaning of 'statutory shared parental pay' see PARA 534. As to the persons liable to make payments of statutory shared parental pay see PARAS 534 et seq, 538 et seq.
4 Social Security Contributions and Benefits Act 1992 s 171ZY(5) (ss 171ZY, 171ZZ4 added by the Children and Families Act 2014 s 119(1)). For this purpose, a week falls within a relevant period if it falls within a period specified in a notice under:
   (1) the Social Security Contributions and Benefits Act 1992 s 171ZU(2)(j) (see PARA 544), s 171ZU(4)(k) (see PARA 545), s 171ZU(13)(a) (see PARA 547 note 32) (s 171ZY(7)(a) (as so added)); or

STATE PENSIONS vol 104 (2014) PARA 385), or but for the employee being under the age of 16. As to the meaning of 'earnings' see PARA 549 note 3.

6 See the Social Security Contributions and Benefits Act 1992 s 171ZZ4(1) (s 171ZZ4 added by the Children and Families Act 2014 s 119(1)). As to the meaning of 'employer' and related expressions in relation to employment rights generally see PARA 2 et seq. As to secondary Class 1 contributions see **WELFARE BENEFITS AND STATE PENSIONS** vol 104 (2014) PARA 385.

7 Ie under the Social Security Contributions and Benefits Act 1992 Pt XIIZC (statutory shared parental pay: see also PARAS 534 et seq, 544 et seq). As to the making of regulations under the Social Security Contributions and Benefits Act 1992 generally see PARA 407 note 3.

8 Ie for the purposes of the Social Security Contributions and Benefits Act 1992 Pt XIIZC (statutory shared parental pay: see also PARAS 534 et seq, 544 et seq) or such provisions of Pt XIIZC as may be prescribed.

9 Social Security Contributions and Benefits Act 1992 s 171ZZ4(4)(a) (as added: see note 6). Regulations under s 171ZZ4(4) must be made with the concurrence of the Commissioners for Revenue and Customs: see s 171ZZ4(1), (12) (as so added). As to the Commissioners for Her Majesty's Revenue and Customs see **INCOME TAXATION** vol 58 (2014) PARAS 33–34. At the date at which this volume states the law, no such regulations had been made.

C. CONDITIONS FOR ENTITLEMENT TO SHARED PARENTAL PAY

544. Conditions for entitlement to statutory shared parental pay: claim by claimant mother or prospective adopter. The conditions governing entitlement to statutory shared parental pay[1] that have to be satisfied in relation to either a claimant mother[2], or a person ('claimant A') with whom a child is, or is expected to be, placed for adoption[3], are:

(1) that prescribed conditions[4] are satisfied: (a) by the claimant mother and another person ('P')[5]; or (b) by claimant A and another person ('X')[6], as to caring or intending to care for the child[7];

(2) that person 'P' or person 'X' (as the case may be):
  - (a) satisfies prescribed conditions: (i) as to employment or self-employment[8]; (ii) as to having earnings of a prescribed amount for a prescribed period[9]; and (ii) as to relationship with the child, on the one hand, or with the claimant mother or claimant A (as the case may be), on the other[10];
  - (b) consents to the extent of the claimant mother's intended claim (if person 'P'), or consents to the extent of claimant A's intended claim (if person 'X'), for statutory shared parental pay[11];

(3) that the claimant mother or claimant A (as the case may be):
  - (a) has been in employed earner's employment with an employer[12] for a continuous period of at least the prescribed length ending with a prescribed week[13];
  - (b) was entitled to be in that employment at the end of the prescribed week mentioned in head (3)(a) above[14];
  - (c) had normal weekly earnings[15] for a prescribed period ending with a prescribed week not less than the lower earnings limit in force[16] at the end of that week[17];
  - (d) if regulations so provide, continues in employed earner's employment (whether or not with the employer by reference to whom the condition mentioned in head (3)(a) above is satisfied) until a prescribed time[18];
  - (e) became entitled to statutory maternity pay by reference to the birth of the child (if the claimant mother)[19], or became entitled to statutory adoption pay by reference to the placement for adoption of the child (if claimant A)[20];

(f) satisfies prescribed conditions as to the reduction of the duration of the maternity pay period (if the claimant mother)[21], or as to the reduction of the duration of the adoption pay period (if claimant A)[22];

(g) has given the person who will be liable to pay statutory shared parental pay to him or to her (as the case may be) notice of: (i) the number of weeks in respect of which he or she (as the case may be) would be entitled to claim statutory shared parental pay in respect of the child if the entitlement were fully exercised[23]; (ii) the number of weeks in respect of which he or she (as the case may be) intends to claim statutory shared parental pay[24]; and (iii) the number of weeks in respect of which person 'P' or person 'X' (as the case may be) intends to claim statutory shared parental pay[25];

(h) has given the person who will be liable to pay statutory shared parental pay to him or to her (as the case may be) notice of the period or periods during which he or she (as the case may be) intends to claim statutory shared parental pay in respect of the child[26];

(i) intends to care for the child during each week in respect of which statutory shared parental pay is paid to him or to her (as the case may be)[27];

(j) is absent from work during each week in respect of which statutory shared parental pay is paid to him or to her (as the case may be)[28];

(k) is absent from work[29] during each such week on shared parental leave[30]; and

(4) that a notice under head (3)(g) or head (3)(h) above: (a) is given by such time as may be prescribed[31]; and (b) satisfies prescribed conditions as to form and content[32].

1 Ie in accordance with the provisions of the Social Security Contributions and Benefits Act 1992 Pt XIIZC (ss 171ZU–171ZZ5) (statutory shared parental pay: see also PARAS 534 et seq, 545 et seq). As to the meaning of 'statutory shared parental pay' see PARA 534.

2 Ie the conditions mentioned in the Social Security Contributions and Benefits Act 1992 s 171ZU(1) (see PARA 534): see s 171ZU(2) (ss 171ZU, 171ZV, 171ZZ4 added by the Children and Families Act 2014 s 119(1)). A person's entitlement to statutory shared parental pay under the Social Security Contributions and Benefits Act 1992 s 171ZU is not affected by the birth of more than one child as a result of the same pregnancy: s 171ZU(16) (as so added). As to the meaning of 'claimant mother' for these purposes see PARA 534.

3 Ie the conditions mentioned in the Social Security Contributions and Benefits Act 1992 s 171ZV(1) (see PARA 534): see s 171ZV(2) (as added: see note 2). The text refers to a person with whom a child is, or is expected to be, placed for adoption under the law of any part of the United Kingdom: see s 171ZV(2) (as so added). A person's entitlement to statutory shared parental pay under s 171ZV is not affected by the placement for adoption of more than one child as part of the same arrangement: s 171ZV(16) (as so added). As to the meaning of 'United Kingdom' for these purposes see PARA 407 note 7. As to the law relating to child adoption see **CHILDREN AND YOUNG PERSONS** vol 9 (2012) PARA 360 et seq.

Regulations must provide for entitlement to statutory shared parental pay in respect of a child placed, or expected to be placed, under the Children Act 1989 s 22C (local authority's duty to provide child is in its care with accommodation: see **CHILDREN AND YOUNG PERSONS** vol 10 (2012) PARA 858) by a local authority in England with a local authority foster parent who has been approved as a prospective adopter: Social Security Contributions and Benefits Act 1992 s 171ZV(17) (as so added). In relation to any regulations made by virtue of s 171ZV(17), s 171ZV has effect as if:

(1) references to a child being placed for adoption under the law of any part of the United

Kingdom were references to a child being placed under the Children Act 1989 s 22C with a local authority foster parent who has been approved as a prospective adopter (Social Security Contributions and Benefits Act 1992 s 171ZV(18)(a) (as so added));

(2) references to placement for adoption were references to placement under the Children Act 1989 s 22C with such a person (Social Security Contributions and Benefits Act 1992 s 171ZV(18)(b) (as so added)).

For these purposes, 'local authority' has the same meaning as in the Children Act 1989 (see s 105(1); and CHILDREN AND YOUNG PERSONS vol 9 (2012) PARA 155); and 'local authority foster parent' has the same meaning as in the Children Act 1989 (see s 22C(12); and CHILDREN AND YOUNG PERSONS vol 10 (2012) PARA 845): see the Social Security Contributions and Benefits Act 1992 s 171ZZ4(1) (as added: see note 2). As to the meaning of 'England' see PARA 2 note 12. As to the making of regulations under the Social Security Contributions and Benefits Act 1992 generally see PARA 407 note 3; and see PARA 534 note 8. At the date at which this volume states the law, no such regulations had been made.

4 For these purposes, 'prescribed' means prescribed by regulations: see the Social Security Contributions and Benefits Act 1992 s 171ZZ4(1) (as added: see note 2).

5 See the Social Security Contributions and Benefits Act 1992 s 171ZU(2)(a) (as added: see note 2).

6 See the Social Security Contributions and Benefits Act 1992 s 171ZV(2)(a) (as added: see note 2).

7 See the Social Security Contributions and Benefits Act 1992 ss 171ZU(2)(a), 171ZV(2)(a) (as added: see note 2).

8 See the Social Security Contributions and Benefits Act 1992 ss 171ZU(2)(b)(i), 171ZV(2)(b)(i) (as added: see note 2).

9 See the Social Security Contributions and Benefits Act 1992 ss 171ZU(2)(b)(ii), 171ZV(2)(b)(ii) (as added: see note 2). As to the meaning of 'earnings' see PARA 549 note 3.

10 See the Social Security Contributions and Benefits Act 1992 ss 171ZU(2)(b)(iii), 171ZV(2)(b)(iii) (as added: see note 2).

11 See the Social Security Contributions and Benefits Act 1992 ss 171ZU(2)(l), 171ZV(2)(l) (as added: see note 2).

12 As to the meaning of 'employer' for these purposes see PARA 543. As to the meaning of 'employed earner' see the Social Security Contributions and Benefits Act 1992 s 2(1)(a), (3); and WELFARE BENEFITS AND STATE PENSIONS vol 104 (2014) PARA 381. As to employed earner's employment within the meaning of the Social Security Contributions and Benefits Act 1992 see WELFARE BENEFITS AND STATE PENSIONS vol 104 (2014) PARA 176.

13 See the Social Security Contributions and Benefits Act 1992 ss 171ZU(2)(c), 171ZV(2)(c) (as added: see note 2). For the purposes of Pt XIIZC (statutory shared parental pay: see also PARAS 534 et seq, 545 et seq), except where otherwise provided, 'week' means a period of seven days beginning with Sunday or such other period as may be prescribed in relation to any particular case or class of cases: s 171ZZ4(5) (as added: see note 2). Regulations under s 171ZZ4(5) must be made with the concurrence of the Commissioners for Revenue and Customs: see s 171ZZ4(1), (12) (as so added). As to the Commissioners for Her Majesty's Revenue and Customs see INCOME TAXATION vol 58 (2014) PARAS 33–34. At the date at which this volume states the law, no such regulations had been made.

14 See the Social Security Contributions and Benefits Act 1992 ss 171ZU(2)(d), 171ZV(2)(d) (as added: see note 2).

15 As to the meaning of 'normal weekly earnings' see PARA 549.

16 Ie under the Social Security Contributions and Benefits Act 1992 s 5(1)(a) (earnings limits and thresholds for Class 1 contributions: see WELFARE BENEFITS AND STATE PENSIONS vol 104 (2014) PARA 384).

17 See the Social Security Contributions and Benefits Act 1992 ss 171ZU(2)(e), 171ZV(2)(e) (as added: see note 2).

18 See the Social Security Contributions and Benefits Act 1992 ss 171ZU(2)(f), 171ZV(2)(f) (as added: see note 2).

19 See the Social Security Contributions and Benefits Act 1992 s 171ZU(2)(g) (as added: see note 2). As to statutory maternity pay see PARA 401 et seq.

20 See the Social Security Contributions and Benefits Act 1992 s 171ZV(2)(g) (as added: see note 2). As to statutory adoption pay see PARA 488 et seq.

21 See the Social Security Contributions and Benefits Act 1992 s 171ZU(2)(h) (as added: see note 2). For these purposes, 'maternity pay period' has the meaning given by s 165(1) (see PARA 424): see s 171ZZ4(1) (as added: see note 2).

22 See the Social Security Contributions and Benefits Act 1992 s 171ZV(2)(h) (as added: see note 2). For these purposes, 'adoption pay period' has the meaning given by s 171ZN(2) (see PARA 511) see s 171ZZ4(1) (as added: see note 2).
23 See the Social Security Contributions and Benefits Act 1992 ss 171ZU(2)(i)(i), 171ZV(2)(i)(i) (as added: see note 2). For these purposes, any intention of P or of X (as the case may be) to claim statutory shared parental pay in respect of the child is disregarded: see ss 171ZU(2)(i)(i), 171ZV(2)(i)(i) (as so added).
24 See the Social Security Contributions and Benefits Act 1992 ss 171ZU(2)(i)(ii), 171ZV(2)(i)(ii) (as added: see note 2).
25 See the Social Security Contributions and Benefits Act 1992 ss 171ZU(2)(i)(iii), 171ZV(2)(i)(iii) (as added: see note 2).
26 See the Social Security Contributions and Benefits Act 1992 ss 171ZU(2)(j), 171ZV(2)(j) (as added: see note 2).
27 See the Social Security Contributions and Benefits Act 1992 ss 171ZU(2)(m), 171ZV(2)(m) (as added: see note 2).
28 See the Social Security Contributions and Benefits Act 1992 ss 171ZU(2)(n), 171ZV(2)(n) (as added: see note 2).
29 Ie where the claimant mother or claimant A (as the case may be) is an employee within the meaning of the Employment Rights Act 1996 (see PARA 2)
30 See the Social Security Contributions and Benefits Act 1992 ss 171ZU(2)(o), 171ZV(2)(o) (as added: see note 2).
31 See the Social Security Contributions and Benefits Act 1992 ss 171ZU(2)(k)(i), 171ZV(2)(k)(i) (as added: see note 2).
32 See the Social Security Contributions and Benefits Act 1992 ss 171ZU(2)(k)(ii), 171ZV(2)(k)(ii) (as added: see note 2).

545. Conditions for entitlement to statutory shared parental pay: joint claim involving mother of a child or prospective adopter and another person. The conditions governing entitlement to statutory shared parental pay[1] that have to be satisfied in relation to a claim involving two people, one of whom is either the mother of a child (person 'M')[2], or a person ('Y') with whom a child is, or is expected to be, placed for adoption[3], are:

(1) that prescribed conditions[4] are satisfied: (a) by a claimant ('the claimant') and person 'M'[5]; or (b) by a claimant ('claimant B') and person 'Y'[6], as to caring or intending to care for the child[7];
(2) that person 'M' or person 'Y' (as the case may be):
  (a) satisfies prescribed conditions: (i) as to employment or self-employment[8]; and (ii) as to having earnings of a prescribed amount for a prescribed period[9];
  (b) became entitled to a maternity allowance[10], or to statutory maternity pay[11], by reference to the birth of the child (if person 'M')[12], or became entitled to statutory adoption pay[13] by reference to the placement for adoption of the child (if person 'Y')[14];
  (c) satisfies prescribed conditions as to the reduction of the duration of the maternity allowance period[15], or of the maternity pay period (if person 'M')[16], or as to the reduction of the duration of the adoption pay period (if person 'Y')[17];
  (d) consents to the extent of the claimant's intended claim (if person 'M'), or to the extent of claimant B's intended claim (if person 'Y'), for statutory shared parental pay[18];
(3) that the claimant or claimant B (as the case may be):
  (a) satisfies prescribed conditions: (i) as to relationship with the child[19]; or (ii) as to relationship with person 'M' or person 'Y' (as the case may be)[20];

5 Social Security Contributions and Benefits Act 1992 s 171ZY(2) (ss 171ZU, 171ZV, 171ZY added by the Children and Families Act 2014 s 119(1)). The text refers to regulations under the Social Security Contributions and Benefits Act 1992 s 171ZU(5) or s 171ZV(5) (see the text and notes 6–31). As to the making of regulations under the Social Security Contributions and Benefits Act 1992 generally see PARA 407 note 3; and see PARA 534 note 8. At the date at which this volume states the law, no such regulations had been made.
6 See the Social Security Contributions and Benefits Act 1992 ss 171ZU(5), 171ZV(5) (as added: see note 5).
7 Social Security Contributions and Benefits Act 1992 ss 171ZU(5)(a), 171ZV(5)(a) (as added: see note 5).
8 Social Security Contributions and Benefits Act 1992 ss 171ZU(5)(b), 171ZV(5)(b) (as added: see note 5).
9 See the Social Security Contributions and Benefits Act 1992 s 171ZU(6) (as added: see note 5). As to the meaning of 'maternity pay period' see PARA 544 note 21.
10 See the Social Security Contributions and Benefits Act 1992 s 171ZV(6) (as added: see note 5). As to the meaning of 'adoption pay period' see PARA 544 note 22.
11 See the Social Security Contributions and Benefits Act 1992 ss 171ZU(6), 171ZV(6) (as added: see note 5).
12 Ie for the purposes of the Social Security Contributions and Benefits Act 1992 s 171ZU: see s 171ZU(6)(a) (as added: see note 5).
13 Ie under the Social Security Contributions and Benefits Act 1992 s 171ZU(4)(i)(i) (see PARA 545): see s 171ZU(6)(a) (as added: see note 5). As to the meaning of 'maternity allowance period' see PARA 545 note 15.
14 Ie under the Social Security Contributions and Benefits Act 1992 s 171ZU(2)(h) (see PARA 544), or s 171ZU(4)(i)(ii) (see PARA 545): see s 171ZU(6)(a) (as added: see note 5).
15 Social Security Contributions and Benefits Act 1992 s 171ZU(6)(a) (as added: see note 5).
16 For this purpose, 'relevant week' means:
(1) where maternity allowance is payable to a mother, a week or part of a week falling before the time at which the mother takes action that is treated by regulations as constituting, for the purposes of the Social Security Contributions and Benefits Act 1992 s 171ZU, her return to work (s 171ZU(7)(a) (as added: see note 5));
(2) where statutory maternity pay is payable to a mother, a week falling before the week in which the mother takes action that is so treated (s 171ZU(7)(b) (as so added)).
In relation to maternity allowance, 'week' has the meaning given by s 122(1) (see **WELFARE BENEFITS AND STATE PENSIONS** vol 104 (2014) PARA 381) or, in relation to statutory maternity pay, the meaning given by s 165(8) (see PARA 424 note 3): see s 171ZU(7) (as so added).
17 Social Security Contributions and Benefits Act 1992 s 171ZU(6)(a)(i) (as added: see note 5). As to statutory maternity pay see PARA 401 et seq. As to maternity allowance see **WELFARE BENEFITS AND STATE PENSIONS** vol 104 (2014) PARA 473 et seq.
18 Ie for the purposes of the Social Security Contributions and Benefits Act 1992 s 171ZV: see s 171ZV(6)(a) (as added: see note 5).
19 Ie under the Social Security Contributions and Benefits Act 1992 s 171ZV(2)(h) (see PARA 544), or s 171ZV(4)(i) (see PARA 545): see s 171ZV(6)(a) (as added: see note 5).
20 Social Security Contributions and Benefits Act 1992 s 171ZV(6)(a) (as added: see note 5).
21 For this purpose, 'relevant week' means a week falling before the week in which a person takes action that is treated by regulations as constituting, for the purposes of the Social Security Contributions and Benefits Act 1992 s 171ZV, the person's return to work, and, for these purposes, 'week' has the meaning given by s 171ZN(8) (adoption pay period: see PARA 491 notes 4, 17): see s 171ZV(7) (as so added).
22 Social Security Contributions and Benefits Act 1992 s 171ZV(6)(a)(i) (as added: see note 5). As to statutory adoption pay see PARA 488 et seq.
23 Social Security Contributions and Benefits Act 1992 ss 171ZU(6)(a)(ii), 171ZV(6)(a)(ii) (as added: see note 5).
24 Ie, in relation to the maternity allowance period, by virtue of the Social Security Contributions and Benefits Act 1992 s 35(3A) (see **WELFARE BENEFITS AND STATE PENSIONS** vol 104 (2014) PARA 473), or, as the case may be, in relation to the maternity pay period, by virtue of s 165(3A) (see PARA 424 note 8): see s 171ZU(6)(b) (as added: see note 5). In determining the number of weeks for the purposes of s 171ZU(6)(b), 'week' has the same meaning as in s 171ZU(7) (see note 16), and a part of a week is to be treated as a week:: see s 171ZU(8) (as so added).
25 Social Security Contributions and Benefits Act 1992 s 171ZU(6)(b) (as added: see note 5).
26 Ie by virtue of the Social Security Contributions and Benefits Act 1992 s 171ZN(2A) (adoption pay period: see PARA 511): see s 171ZV(6)(b) (as added: see note 5). In determining the number

of weeks for the purposes of s 171ZV(6)(b), 'week' has the same meaning as in s 171ZV(7) (see note 21), and a part of a week is to be treated as a week: see s 171ZV(8) (as so added).
27 Social Security Contributions and Benefits Act 1992 s 171ZV(6)(b) (as added: see note 5).
28 Social Security Contributions and Benefits Act 1992 ss 171ZU(9), 171ZV(9) (as added: see note 5).
29 Social Security Contributions and Benefits Act 1992 ss 171ZU(10), 171ZV(10) (as added: see note 5).
30 Social Security Contributions and Benefits Act 1992 s 171ZU(11) (as added: see note 5).
31 Social Security Contributions and Benefits Act 1992 s 171ZV(11) (as added: see note 5).
32 Ie in relation to a person who is entitled under the Social Security Contributions and Benefits Act 1992 ss 171ZU(1), 171ZV(1) or ss 171ZU(3), 171ZV(3), as the case may be (see PARA 534): see ss 171ZU(12), 171ZV(12) (as added: see note 5). The conditions that person 'V' must satisfy are those in s 171ZU(13) or s 171ZV(13), accordingly: see ss 171ZU(12), 171ZV(12) (as so added). The conditions are:
   (1) that person 'V' has given the person who will be liable to pay statutory shared parental pay to person 'V' notice of an intention to vary the period or periods during which person 'V' intends to claim statutory shared parental pay (ss 171ZU(13)(a), 171ZV(13)(a) (as so added));
   (2) that a notice under head (1) above is given by such time as may be prescribed, and satisfies prescribed conditions as to form and content (ss 171ZU(13)(b), 171ZV(13)(b) (as so added)).
33 Social Security Contributions and Benefits Act 1992 ss 171ZU(12), 171ZV(12) (as added: see note 5). This provision is subject to person 'V' complying with s 171ZU(14) or s 171ZV(14), as the case may be, where relevant: see ss 171ZU(12), 171ZV(12) (as so added). Accordingly, regulations may provide that, where the conditions in s 171ZU(15) or in s 171ZV(15), as the case may be, are satisfied in relation to person 'V', person 'V' may vary the number of weeks in respect of which he or she intends to claim statutory shared parental pay: ss 171ZU(14), 171ZV(14) (as so added). The conditions are:
   (1) that person 'V' has given the person who is liable to pay statutory shared parental pay to person 'V' notice of (see ss 171ZU(15)(a), 171ZV(15)(a) (as so added)):
      (a) the extent to which person 'V' has exercised an entitlement to statutory shared parental pay in respect of the child (ss 171ZU(15)(a)(i), 171ZV(15)(a)(i) (as so added));
      (b) the extent to which person 'V' intends to claim statutory shared parental pay in respect of the child (ss 171ZU(15)(a)(ii), 171ZV(15)(a)(ii) (as so added));
      (c) the extent to which another person has exercised an entitlement to statutory shared parental pay in respect of the child (ss 171ZU(15)(a)(iii), 171ZV(15)(a)(iii) (as so added)); and
      (d) the extent to which another person intends to claim statutory shared parental pay in respect of the child (ss 171ZU(15)(a)(iv), 171ZV(15)(a)(iv) (as so added));
   (2) that a notice under head (1) above is given by such time as may be prescribed, and satisfies prescribed conditions as to form and content (ss 171ZU(15)(b), 171ZV(15)(b) (as so added));
   (3) that the person consents to that variation who is, in relation to person 'V': (a) where statutory shared parental pay is payable on birth, either person 'P' (see PARA 544) or, as the case may be, person 'M' (see PARA 545) (see s 171ZU(15)(c) (as so added)); or (b) where statutory shared parental pay is payable on adoption, either person 'X' (see PARA 544) or, as the case may be, person 'Y' (see PARA 545) (see s 171ZV(15)(c) (as so added)); or

F. PAYMENT OF SHARED PARENTAL PAY

548. Rates of payment for statutory shared parental pay. Statutory shared parental pay[1] is payable at such fixed or earnings-related weekly rate as may be prescribed by regulations[2], which may prescribe different kinds of rate for different cases[3].

1 As to the meaning of 'statutory shared parental pay' see PARA 534.
2 As to the making of regulations under the Social Security Contributions and Benefits Act 1992 generally see PARA 407 note 3; and see PARA 534 note 8. At the date at which this volume states the law, no such regulations had been made.

3 Social Security Contributions and Benefits Act 1992 s 171ZY(1) (s 171ZY added by the Children and Families Act 2014 s 119(1)). Where for any purpose of the Social Security Contributions and Benefits Act 1992 Pt XIIZC (ss 171ZU–171ZZ5) (statutory shared parental pay: see also PARAS 534 et seq, 549 et seq), or of regulations, it is necessary to calculate the daily rate of statutory shared parental pay, the amount payable by way of statutory shared parental pay for any day must be taken as one seventh of the weekly rate: s 171ZY(6A) (as so added).

549. Calculation of normal weekly earnings for the purposes of statutory shared parental pay. For the purposes of the statutory shared parental pay[1] provisions that are set out in Part XIIZC of the Social Security Contributions and Benefits Act 1992[2], a person's normal weekly earnings[3] are to be taken to be the average weekly earnings which in the relevant period[4] have been paid to the person or paid for the person's benefit under the contract of service[5] with the employer in question[6]. However, in such cases as may be prescribed[7], a person's normal weekly earnings are to be calculated in accordance with regulations[8].

1 As to the meaning of 'statutory shared parental pay' see PARA 534.
2 Ie for the purposes of the Social Security Contributions and Benefits Act 1992 Pt XIIZC (ss 171ZU–171ZZ5) (statutory shared parental pay: see also PARAS 534 et seq, 550, 557).
3 For these purposes, 'earnings' has the meaning given to it by regulations: see the Social Security Contributions and Benefits Act 1992 s 171ZZ4(7) (s 171ZZ4 added by the Children and Families Act 2014 s 119(1)). Regulations under the Social Security Contributions and Benefits Act 1992 s 171ZZ4(7) must be made with the concurrence of the Commissioners for Revenue and Customs: see s 171ZZ4(1), (12) (as so added). As to the Commissioners for Her Majesty's Revenue and Customs see INCOME TAXATION vol 58 (2014) PARAS 33–34. As to the making of regulations under the Social Security Contributions and Benefits Act 1992 generally see PARA 407 note 3; and see PARA 534 note 8. At the date at which this volume states the law, no such regulations had been made.
4 For these purposes, 'relevant period' has the meaning given to it by regulations: see the Social Security Contributions and Benefits Act 1992 s 171ZZ4(7) (as added: see note 3).
5 Although 'contract of service' is defined for the purposes of statutory sick pay (see PARA 558 note 2), it is not so defined under the other statutory pay provisions (for which purposes see generally PARA 1 note 1).
6 Social Security Contributions and Benefits Act 1992 s 171ZZ4(6) (as added: see note 3). Regulations under s 171ZZ4(6) must be made with the concurrence of the Commissioners for Revenue and Customs: see s 171ZZ4(1), (12) (as so added). As to the meaning of 'employer' for these purposes see PARA 543.
7 For these purposes, 'prescribed' means prescribed by regulations: see the Social Security Contributions and Benefits Act 1992 s 171ZZ4(1) (as added: see note 3).
8 Social Security Contributions and Benefits Act 1992 s 171ZZ4(8) (as added: see note 3). Regulations under s 171ZZ4(8) must be made with the concurrence of the Commissioners for Revenue and Customs: see s 171ZZ4(1), (12) (as so added).

550. Payments treated as remuneration for purposes of statutory shared parental pay; relationship with other payments. Any sum paid to, or for the benefit of, a person in satisfaction, whether in whole or in part, of any entitlement of his to statutory shared parental pay[1] is to be treated[2] as remuneration derived from employed earner's[3] employment[4].

Any entitlement to statutory shared parental pay does not affect any right of a person in relation to remuneration under any contract of service ('contractual remuneration')[5]; any contractual remuneration paid to a person by an employer[6] of his in respect of any period goes towards discharging any liability of that employer to pay statutory shared parental pay to him in respect of that period[7]; and any statutory shared parental pay paid by an employer to a person who is an employee of his in respect of any period goes towards discharging any liability of that employer to pay contractual remuneration to him in respect of that period[8]. Regulations[9] may make provision as to payments which are, and those which are not, to be treated as contractual remuneration for these purposes[10].

1 As to the meaning of 'statutory shared parental pay' see PARA 534; and as to entitlement to statutory shared parental pay see PARAS 534 et seq, 557.
2 Ie for the purposes of the Social Security Contributions and Benefits Act 1992 s 3 (meaning of 'earnings': see **WELFARE BENEFITS AND STATE PENSIONS** vol 104 (2014) PARA 382).
3 As to the meaning of 'employed earner' see the Social Security Contributions and Benefits Act 1992 s 2(1)(a), (3); and **WELFARE BENEFITS AND STATE PENSIONS** vol 104 (2014) PARA 381.
4 Social Security Contributions and Benefits Act 1992 s 4(1)(a)(vi) (added by the Children and Families Act 2014 Sch 7 para 8(c)).
5 Social Security Contributions and Benefits Act 1992 s 171ZZ1(1) (s 171ZZ1 added by the Children and Families Act 2014 s 119(1)). Although 'contract of service' is defined for the purposes of statutory sick pay (see PARA 558 note 2), it is not so defined under the other statutory pay provisions (for which purposes see generally PARA 1 note 1).
6 As to the meaning of 'employer' for these purposes see PARA 543.
7 Social Security Contributions and Benefits Act 1992 s 171ZZ1(2)(a) (as added: see note 5). As to the shared parental pay period see PARA 547.
8 Social Security Contributions and Benefits Act 1992 s 171ZZ1(2)(b) (as added: see note 5).
9 As to the making of regulations under the Social Security Contributions and Benefits Act 1992 generally see PARA 407 note 3; and see PARA 534 note 8.
10 Social Security Contributions and Benefits Act 1992 s 171ZZ1(3) (as added: see note 5). At the date at which this volume states the law, no such regulations had been made.

G. RECORDS AND INFORMATION

551. Power to make regulations about records and information relating to payment of statutory shared parental pay; penalties. The Secretary of State[1] may make regulations[2] with respect to the payment by employers[3] of statutory shared parental pay[4], including provision:

(1) about the records to be kept by employers in relation to statutory shared parental pay, including the length of time for which they are to be retained[5];
(2) for the production of wages sheets and other documents and records to officers of the Commissioners for Revenue and Customs for the purpose of enabling them to satisfy themselves that statutory shared parental pay has been paid, and is being paid, in accordance with the regulations, to employees[6] who are entitled to it[7];
(3) for requiring employers to provide information to employees, in their itemised pay statements or otherwise[8];
(4) for requiring employers to make returns to the Commissioners containing such particulars with respect to payments of statutory shared parental pay as the regulations may provide[9].

Where a person fails to keep records in accordance with such regulations, he is liable to a penalty[10]; and where a person fails to produce any document or record, provide any information or make any return, in accordance with such regulations[11], he is liable[12] to: (a) a penalty[13]; and (b) if the failure continues after a penalty is imposed under head (a) above, a further penalty or penalties[14] for each day on which the failure continues after the day on which the penalty was imposed[15].

None of the above penalties is to be imposed[16] at any time after the failure concerned has been remedied[17], except in relation to the imposition of a penalty under head (a) above[18].

Where, in the case of any employee, an employer refuses or repeatedly fails to make payments of statutory shared parental pay in accordance with regulations made under heads (1) to (4) above, the employer is liable to a penalty[19].

Where a person fraudulently or negligently makes any incorrect statement or declaration in connection with establishing entitlement to statutory shared parental pay[20], he is liable to a penalty[21].

Where an employer fraudulently or negligently:

(i) makes incorrect payments of statutory shared parental pay[22]; or

(ii) produces any incorrect document or record, provides any incorrect information or makes any incorrect return, of a kind mentioned in regulations under heads (1) to (4) above[23],

he is liable to a penalty[24].

The general provisions as to procedure and appeals[25] have effect in relation to any of the penalties[26] described above[27].

1 As to the Secretary of State see PARA 5 note 21.
2 Regulations under the Employment Act 2002 s 8(1) must be made with the concurrence of the Board: see s 8(3). For these purposes, the 'Board' means the Commissioners for Revenue and Customs: see the Employment Act 2002 s 16. As to the Commissioners for Her Majesty's Revenue and Customs see INCOME TAXATION vol 58 (2014) PARAS 33–34. As to the power to make regulations under the Employment Act 2002 see s 51; and PARA 474 note 2. At the date at which this volume states the law, no such regulations had been made.
3 As to the meaning of 'employer' for these purposes see PARA 543.
4 See the Employment Act 2002 s 8(1) (amended by the Work and Families Act 2006 Sch 1 para 51; and the Children and Families Act 2014 Sch 7 paras 50, 52(1), (2)(b)). As to the meaning of 'statutory shared parental pay' see PARA 534.
5 Employment Act 2002 s 8(2)(a) (amended by the Work and Families Act 2006 Sch 1 para 51; and the Children and Families Act 2014 Sch 7 paras 50, 52(1), (3)(a)).
6 As to the meaning of 'employee' for these purposes see PARA 539.
7 Employment Act 2002 s 8(2)(b) (amended by the Work and Families Act 2006 Sch 1 para 51; and the Children and Families Act 2014 Sch 7 paras 50, 52(1), (3)(b)).
8 Employment Act 2002 s 8(2)(c).
9 Employment Act 2002 s 8(2)(d) (amended by the Work and Families Act 2006 Sch 1 para 51; and the Children and Families Act 2014 Sch 7 paras 50, 52(1), (3)(c)).
10 Employment Act 2002 s 11(3). The penalty must not exceed £3,000: see s 11(3). The Taxes Management Act 1970 s 118(2) (extra time for compliance etc: see INCOME TAXATION vol 59 (2014) PARA 2136) applies for the purposes of the Employment Act 2002 s 11(1) (see the text and notes 11–12), s 11(3) and s 11(6) (see the text and note 19) as it applies for the purposes of the Taxes Management Act 1970: Employment Act 2002 s 11(7).
11 Employment Act 2002 s 11(1)(a). See note 10.
12 See the Employment Act 2002 s 11(1). See note 10.
13 Employment Act 2002 s 11(2)(a). The penalty must not exceed £300: see s 11(2)(a).
14 Ie not exceeding £60: see the Employment Act 2002 s 11(2)(b).
15 Employment Act 2002 s 11(2)(b). Any day for which a penalty under head (b) in the text has already been imposed is excluded for those purposes: see s 11(2)(b).
16 Ie under the Employment Act 2002 s 11(2) (see the text and notes 13–15) or s 11(3) (see the text and note 10).
17 Employment Act 2002 s 11(4).
18 Employment Act 2002 s 11(5).
19 Employment Act 2002 s 11(6) (amended by the Work and Families Act 2006 Sch 1 para 53; and the Children and Families Act 2014 Sch 7 paras 50, 54). The penalty must not exceed £3,000: see the Employment Act 2002 s 11(6) (as so amended). See note 10.
20 Employment Act 2002 s 12(2)(a) (amended by the Work and Families Act 2006 Sch 1 para 54(1), (2); and the Children and Families Act 2014 Sch 7 paras 50, 55(1), (3)(a)).
21 Employment Act 2002 s 12(2). The penalty must not exceed £3000: see s 12(2).
22 Employment Act 2002 s 12(4) (s 12(4), (5) amended by the Work and Families Act 2006 Sch 1 para 54(1), (3), (4); and the Children and Families Act 2014 Sch 7 paras 50, 55(1), (5), (6)).
23 Employment Act 2002 s 12(5)(a).
24 Employment Act 2002 s 12(4), (5) (as amended: see note 22). The penalty must not exceed £3000: see s 12(3), (5) (as so amended).
25 See the Employment Act 2002 ss 11(8), 12(6), Sch 1; and PARA 553.
26 Ie imposed under either the Employment Act 2002 s 11 or s 12: see the text and notes 10–24.
27 See the Employment Act 2002 ss 11(8), 12(6).

552. Power to make regulations regarding the production of information or documents relating to statutory shared parental pay; penalties. The Secretary of State[1] may by regulations[2] make provision enabling an officer of the Commissioners for Revenue and Customs, authorised by them for these purposes, to require persons of a description specified in the regulations to provide, or produce for inspection, within such period as the regulations may require, such information or documents as the officer may reasonably require for the purpose of ascertaining whether statutory shared parental pay[3] is or was payable to or in respect of any person[4]. The descriptions of person which may be specified by such regulations include, in particular[5]:

(1) any person claiming to be entitled to statutory shared parental pay[6];

(2) any person who is, or has been, the spouse or partner of such a person as is mentioned in head (1) above[7];

(3) any person who is, or has been, an employer[8] of such a person as is mentioned in head (1) above[9];

(4) any person carrying on an agency or other business for the introduction or supply to persons requiring them of persons available to do work or to perform services[10]; and

(5) any person who is a servant or agent of any such person as is specified in heads (1) to (4) above[11].

Where a person fails to provide any information or document, in accordance with such regulations[12], he is liable[13] to: (a) a penalty[14]; and (b) if the failure continues after a penalty is imposed under head (a) above, a further penalty or penalties[15] for each day on which the failure continues after the day on which the penalty was imposed[16].

Neither of the above penalties is to be imposed[17] at any time after the failure concerned has been remedied[18].

Where a person fraudulently or negligently provides any incorrect information or document of a kind mentioned in the regulations[19], so far as relating to statutory shared parental pay[20], he is liable to a penalty[21].

The general provisions as to procedure and appeals[22] have effect in relation to any of the penalties[23] described above[24].

1 As to the Secretary of State see PARA 5 note 21.

2 Regulations under the Employment Act 2002 s 10(1) must be made with the concurrence of the Commissioners for Revenue and Customs: see s 10(3). As to the Commissioners for Her Majesty's Revenue and Customs see **INCOME TAXATION** vol 58 (2014) PARAS 33–34; and see PARA 551 note 2. As to the power to make regulations under the Employment Act 2002 see s 51; and PARA 474 note 2. At the date at which this volume states the law, no such regulations had been made.

3 As to the meaning of 'statutory shared parental pay' see PARA 534.

4 Employment Act 2002 s 10(1) (amended by the Work and Families Act 2006 Sch 1 para 52; and the Children and Families Act 2014 Sch 7 paras 50, 53(1), (2)(b)).

5 See the Employment Act 2002 s 10(2).

6 Employment Act 2002 s 10(2)(a) (amended by the Work and Families Act 2006 Sch 1 para 52; and the Children and Families Act 2014 Sch 7 paras 50, 53(1), (3)(a)). As to entitlement to statutory shared parental pay see PARA 534 et seq.

7 Employment Act 2002 s 10(2)(b).

8 As to the meaning of 'employer' for these purposes see PARA 543.

9 Employment Act 2002 s 10(2)(c).

10 Employment Act 2002 s 10(2)(d).

11 Employment Act 2002 s 10(2)(e).

12 See the Employment Act 2002 s 11(1)(b).

13 See the Employment Act 2002 s 11(1). The Taxes Management Act 1970 s 118(2) (extra time for compliance etc: see INCOME TAXATION vol 59 (2014) PARA 2136) applies for the purposes of the Employment Act 2002 s 11(1) as it applies for the purposes of the Taxes Management Act 1970: Employment Act 2002 s 11(7).
14 Employment Act 2002 s 11(2)(a). The penalty must not exceed £300: see s 11(2)(a).
15 Ie not exceeding £60: see the Employment Act 2002 s 11(2)(b).
16 Employment Act 2002 s 11(2)(b). Any day for which a penalty under head (b) in the text has already been imposed is excluded for those purposes: see s 11(2)(b).
17 Ie under the Employment Act 2002 s 11(2): see heads (a), (b) in the text.
18 Employment Act 2002 s 11(4).
19 Ie in regulations under the Employment Act 2002 s 10(1): see the text and notes 1–4.
20 Employment Act 2002 s 12(2)(b) (amended by the Work and Families Act 2006 Sch 1 para 54(1), (3); and the Children and Families Act 2014 Sch 7 paras 50, 55(1), (3)(b)).
21 Employment Act 2002 s 12(2). The penalty must not exceed £3000: see s 12(2).
22 Ie contained in the Employment Act 2002 ss 11(8), 12(6), Sch 1: see PARA 553.
23 Ie imposed under either the Employment Act 2002 s 11 or s 12: see the text and notes 12–21.
24 See the Employment Act 2002 ss 11(8), 12(6).

553. Penalties for failure to comply with regulations or for fraud or negligence in providing information or making payments relating to statutory shared parental pay: procedure and appeals. An officer of the Commissioners for Revenue and Customs[1] authorised by the Commissioners for the purpose may make a determination[2] imposing a penalty[3] under the provisions regarding a failure to comply with regulations[4], or relating to fraud or negligence in providing information or making payments[5], and setting it at such amount as, in his opinion, is correct or appropriate[6]. Notice of such a determination of a penalty must be served on the person liable to the penalty and must state the date on which it is issued and the time within which an appeal against the determination may be made[7]. After such notice of a determination has been served the determination must not be altered except on appeal[8]; but if it is discovered by an officer of the Commissioners for Revenue and Customs authorised by them for these purposes that the amount of a penalty so determined is or has become insufficient, the officer may make a determination in a further amount so that the penalty is set at the amount which, in his opinion, is correct or appropriate[9]. A penalty determined in this way is due and payable at the end of the period of 30 days beginning with the date of the issue of the notice of determination[10]; and the provisions of the Taxes Management Act 1970 relating to collection and recovery[11] apply in relation to a penalty so determined as if it were tax charged in an assessment and due and payable[12].

An appeal may be brought against a penalty so determined[13]; and the provisions of the Taxes Management Act 1970 relating to appeals[14] have effect in relation to an appeal against such a determination as they have effect in relation to an appeal against an assessment to tax except that references to the tribunal are taken to be references to the First-tier Tribunal[15]. On such an appeal, the First-tier Tribunal has powers to confirm, vary or set aside the determination of the penalty[16]; and, in addition to any right of appeal on a point of law[17], the person liable to the penalty may appeal to the Upper Tribunal against the amount of the penalty which had been so determined on appeal[18], but not against any decision which was made in connection with the determination of the amount of the penalty[19].

Where, in the opinion of the Commissioners for Revenue and Customs, the liability of any person to a penalty for a failure to comply with regulations[20], or for fraud or negligence in providing information or making payments[21], arises by reason of the fraud of that or any other person, proceedings for the penalty may be instituted before the High Court[22], in the name of the Attorney General[23]. Any proceedings so instituted are deemed to be civil proceedings[24] by the Crown[25]. If in such proceedings the court does not find that fraud is proved but considers that the person concerned is nevertheless liable to a penalty, the court may determine a penalty notwithstanding that, but for the opinion of the Commissioners for Revenue and Customs as to fraud, the penalty would not have been a matter for the court[26].

The Commissioners for Revenue and Customs may in their discretion mitigate any penalty for failure to comply with regulations[27], or for fraud or negligence in providing information or making payments[28], or they may stay or compound any proceedings for a penalty, and they may also, after judgment, further mitigate or entirely remit the penalty[29].

A penalty under the provisions regarding a failure to comply with regulations[30], or relating to fraud or negligence in providing information or making payments[31], may be determined by an officer of the Commissioners for Revenue and Customs, or proceedings for the penalty may be commenced before the tribunal[32] or the court[33], at any time within six years after the date on which the penalty was incurred or began to be incurred[34].

1 As to the Commissioners for Her Majesty's Revenue and Customs see INCOME TAXATION vol 58 (2014) PARAS 33–34; and see PARA 551 note 2.

2 Ie except where penalty proceedings have been instituted before a court under the Employment Act 2002 ss 11(8), 12(6), Sch 1 para 5: see the text and notes 20–26.

3 Ie except where such a penalty has been imposed as is mentioned in the Employment Act 2002 s 11(2)(a) (ie a penalty of £300 imposed on a person who fails to produce any document or record, provide any information or make any return in accordance with regulations made under s 8 (see PARA 551) or who fails to provide any information or document in accordance with regulations made under s 10 (see PARA 552): see PARAS 551, 552): Sch 1 para 1(2). An officer of the Commissioners for Revenue and Customs authorised by them for these purposes may commence proceedings for any penalty to which Sch 1 para 1(1) does not apply by virtue of Sch 1 para 1(2), however: Sch 1 para 4(1). The person liable to the penalty is a party to the proceedings: Sch 1 para 4(2) (Sch 1 para 4(2), (4) substituted, Sch 1 para 4(4A) added, by SI 2009/56). The Taxes Management Act 1970 Pt VI (ss 60–70A) (collection and recovery: see INCOME TAXATION vol 59 (2014) PARA 2304 et seq) applies in relation to a penalty determined in proceedings under the Employment Act 2002 Sch 1 para 4 as if it were tax charged in an assessment and due and payable: Sch 1 para 4(3). In addition to any right of appeal on a point of law under the Tribunals, Courts and Enforcement Act 2007 s 11(2) (see COURTS AND TRIBUNALS vol 24 (2010) PARA 928), the person liable to the penalty may appeal to the Upper Tribunal against the determination of a penalty in proceedings under the Employment Act 2002 Sch 1 para 4(1), but not against any decision which falls under the Tribunals, Courts and Enforcement Act 2007 s 11(5)(d), (e) (see COURTS AND TRIBUNALS vol 24 (2010) PARA 928) and was made in connection with the determination of the amount of the penalty: Employment Act 2002 Sch 1 para 4(4) (as so substituted). The Tribunals, Courts and Enforcement Act 2007 s 11(3), (4) (see COURTS AND TRIBUNALS vol 24 (2010) PARA 928) applies to the right of appeal under the Employment Act 2002 Sch 1 para 4(4) as it applies to the right of appeal under the Tribunals, Courts and Enforcement Act 2007 s 11(2): Employment Act 2002 Sch 1 para 4(4A) (as so added). On any such appeal, the Upper Tribunal may (see Sch 1 para 4(5) (amended by SI 2009/56)):

(1) if it appears that no penalty has been incurred, set the determination aside (Employment Act 2002 Sch 1 para 4(5)(a));
(2) if the amount determined appears to be appropriate, confirm the determination (Sch 1 para 4(5)(b));
(3) if the amount determined appears to be excessive, reduce it to such other amount (including nil) as the Upper Tribunal considers appropriate (Sch 1 para 4(5)(c) (amended by SI 2009/56));
(4) if the amount determined appears to be insufficient, increase it to such amount not exceeding the permitted maximum as the Upper Tribunal considers appropriate (Employment Act 2002 Sch 1 para 4(5)(d) (amended by SI 2009/56)).

As to the First-tier Tribunal and the Upper Tribunal see COURTS AND TRIBUNALS vol 24 (2010) PARA 874 et seq.
4 Ie under the Employment Act 2002 s 11: see PARAS 551, 552.
5 Ie under the Employment Act 2002 s 12: see PARAS 551, 552.
6 See the Employment Act 2002 Sch 1 para 1(1). As to the determination of claims generally see WELFARE BENEFITS AND STATE PENSIONS vol 104 (2014) PARA 575 et seq.
7 Employment Act 2002 Sch 1 para 1(3).
8 Employment Act 2002 Sch 1 para 1(4).
9 Employment Act 2002 Sch 1 para 1(5).
10 Employment Act 2002 Sch 1 para 2(1). A penalty under s 11 (see note 4) or s 12 (see note 5) carries interest at the rate applicable under the Finance Act 1989 s 178 (see INCOME TAXATION vol 59 (2014) PARA 2303) from the date on which it becomes due and payable until payment: Employment Act 2002 Sch 1 para 8(2).
11 Ie the Taxes Management Act 1970 Pt VI (ss 60–70A) (collection and recovery: see INCOME TAXATION vol 59 (2014) PARA 2304 et seq).
12 Employment Act 2002 Sch 1 para 2(2).
13 Employment Act 2002 Sch 1 para 3(1).
14 Ie the Taxes Management Act 1970 Pt V (ss 46D–57) (appeals and other proceedings: see INCOME TAXATION vol 59 (2014) PARA 2244 et seq), except s 50(6)–(8).
15 Employment Act 2002 Sch 1 para 3(2) (amended by SI 2009/56).
16 Ie, on an appeal by virtue of the Employment Act 2002 Sch 1 para 3(2) (see the text and notes 14–15) against the determination of a penalty under Sch 1 para 1 (see the text and notes 1–9), the First-tier Tribunal may (see Sch 1 para 3(3) (amended by SI 2009/56)):
    (1) if it appears that no penalty has been incurred, set the determination aside (Employment Act 2002 Sch 1 para 3(3)(a) (Sch 1 para 3(3)(a)–(d) amended by SI 2009/56));
    (2) if the amount determined appears to be appropriate, confirm the determination (Employment Act 2002 Sch 1 para 3(3)(b) (as so amended));
    (3) if the amount determined appears to be excessive, reduce it to such other amount (including nil) as the First-tier Tribunal considers appropriate (Sch 1 para 3(3)(c) (as so amended));
    (4) if the amount determined appears to be insufficient, increase it to such amount not exceeding the permitted maximum as the First-tier Tribunal considers appropriate (Sch 1 para 3(3)(d) (as so amended)).
17 Ie under the Tribunals, Courts and Enforcement Act 2007 s 11(2): see COURTS AND TRIBUNALS vol 24 (2010) PARA 928.
18 Ie under the Employment Act 2002 Sch 1 para 3.
19 Employment Act 2002 Sch 1 para 3(4) (Sch 1 para 3(4) substituted, Sch 1 para 3(4A), (4B) added, by SI 2009/56). The reference in the text is to any decision which falls under the Tribunals, Courts and Enforcement Act 2007 s 11(5)(d), (e) (see COURTS AND TRIBUNALS vol 24 (2010) PARA 928): see the Employment Act 2002 Sch 1 para 3(4) (as so substituted). The Tribunals, Courts and Enforcement Act 2007 s 11(3), (4) (see COURTS AND TRIBUNALS vol 24 (2010) PARA 928) applies to the right of appeal under the Employment Act 2002 Sch 1 para 3(4) as it applies to the right of appeal under the Tribunals, Courts and Enforcement Act 2007 s 11(2) (see COURTS AND TRIBUNALS vol 24 (2010) PARA 928): Employment Act 2002 Sch 1 para 3(4A) (as so added). On an appeal under Sch 1 para 3, the Upper Tribunal has the like jurisdiction as is conferred on the First-tier Tribunal by virtue of Sch 1 para 3 (see the text and notes 13–16): Sch 1 para 3(4B) (as so added).
20 See note 4.
21 See note 5.
22 See the Employment Act 2002 Sch 1 para 5(1).
23 See the Employment Act 2002 Sch 1 para 5(2)(a). However, this provision does not prevent proceedings under Sch 1 para 4 being instituted under the Crown Proceedings Act 1947 (see CROWN PROCEEDINGS AND CROWN PRACTICE vol 12(1) (Reissue) PARA 102 et seq) by and in the name of the Commissioners for Revenue and Customs as an authorised department for the purposes of that Act: Employment Act 2002 Sch 1 para 5(3). As to the Attorney General see CONSTITUTIONAL AND ADMINISTRATIVE LAW vol 20 (2014) PARA 273 et seq.
24 Ie within the meaning of the Crown Proceedings Act 1947 Pt II (ss 13–23) (jurisdiction and procedure: see CROWN PROCEEDINGS AND CROWN PRACTICE vol 12(1) (Reissue) PARA 116).
25 Employment Act 2002 Sch 1 para 5(4).
26 Employment Act 2002 Sch 1 para 5(5).
27 See note 4.
28 See note 5.

29 Employment Act 2002 Sch 1 para 6.
30 See note 4.
31 See note 5.
32 Ie before the First-tier Tribunal: see the Employment Act 2002 Sch 1 para 4; and note 3.
33 See the Employment Act 2002 Sch 1 para 5; and the text and notes 20–26.
34 Employment Act 2002 Sch 1 para 7 (amended by SI 2009/56).

554. Supply and use of information. Information which is held for the purposes of functions relating to statutory shared parental pay[1] by the Commissioners for Revenue and Customs[2], or by a person providing services to the Commissioners in connection with the provision of those services[3], may be supplied to the Secretary of State[4], or to a person providing services to the Secretary of State[5], for use for the purposes of functions relating to social security[6], child support[7], or war pensions[8].

Information which is held for the purposes of functions relating to statutory shared parental pay by the Secretary of State[9], or by a person providing services to the Secretary of State[10] in connection with the provision of those services[11], may be supplied to the Commissioners, or to a person providing services to the Commissioners, for use for the purposes of functions relating to statutory shared parental pay[12].

Information which is held by the Commissioners, or by a person providing services to the Commissioners in connection with the provision of those services, for the purposes of[13]:

(1) the functions of the Commissioners in relation to statutory paternity pay[14];
(2) their functions in relation to statutory adoption pay[15]; and
(3) their functions in relation to statutory shared parental pay[16]; and
(4) their functions in relation to tax[17], contributions[18], statutory sick pay[19], statutory maternity pay[20] or tax credits[21], or functions[22] relating to the certification of pension schemes[23],

may be used for the purposes of, or for any purposes connected with, the exercise of any functions specified in any other of heads (1) to (4) above, and may be supplied to any person providing services to the Commissioners for those purposes[24].

1 As to statutory shared parental pay see PARA 534 et seq.
2 As to the Commissioners for Her Majesty's Revenue and Customs see **INCOME TAXATION** vol 58 (2014) PARAS 33–34; and see PARA 551 note 2.
3 See the Employment Act 2002 s 13(1) (amended by the Work and Families Act 2006 Sch 1 para 55; and the Children and Families Act 2014 Sch 7 paras 50, 56(b)).
4 Or, in Northern Ireland, the Department for Social Development or the Department for Employment and Learning. As to the Secretary of State see PARA 5 note 21.
5 See note 4.
6 See **WELFARE BENEFITS AND STATE PENSIONS** vol 104 (2014) PARA 2 et seq.
7 See **CHILDREN AND YOUNG PERSONS** vol 9 (2012) PARA 573 et seq.
8 See the Employment Act 2002 s 13(2) (amended by SI 2008/2656; SI 2012/2007). As to war pensions see **ARMED FORCES** vol 3 (2011) PARA 718 et seq.
9 See note 4.
10 See note 4.
11 See the Employment Act 2002 s 14(1) (amended by the Work and Families Act 2006 Sch 1 para 56; and the Children and Families Act 2014 Sch 7 paras 50, 57(1), (2)(b)).
12 See the Employment Act 2002 s 14(2) (amended by the Work and Families Act 2006 Sch 1 para 56; and the Children and Families Act 2014 Sch 7 paras 50, 57(1), (3)(b)).
13 See the Employment Act 2002 s 15(1). The text refers to information so held for the purposes of any functions specified in s 15(2) (see heads (1) to (4) in the text): see s 15(1).

14 Employment Act 2002 s 15(2)(a) (amended by the Work and Families Act 2006 Sch 1 para 57(a); and the Children and Families Act 2014 Sch 7 paras 50, 58(a)). As to statutory paternity pay see PARA 443 et seq.
15 Employment Act 2002 s 15(2)(b) (amended by the Children and Families Act 2014 Sch 7 paras 50, 58(c)). As to statutory adoption pay see PARA 488 et seq.
16 Employment Act 2002 s 15(2)(ba) (added by the Children and Families Act 2014 Sch 7 paras 50, 58(d)).
17 See INCOME TAXATION vol 58 (2014) PARAS 33–34.
18 For these purposes, 'contributions' means contributions under the Social Security Contributions and Benefits Act 1992 Pt 1 (ss 1–19A) (see WELFARE BENEFITS AND STATE PENSIONS vol 104 (2014) PARA 384 et seq) or the Social Security Contributions and Benefits (Northern Ireland) Act 1992 Pt 1: see the Employment Act 2002 s 15(3).
19 As to statutory sick pay see PARA 558 et seq.
20 As to statutory maternity pay see PARA 401 et seq.
21 See WELFARE BENEFITS AND STATE PENSIONS vol 104 (2014) PARA 335 et seq.
22 Ie under the Pension Schemes Act 1993 Pt III (ss 7–68) (see PERSONAL AND OCCUPATIONAL PENSIONS vol 80 (2013) PARA 395 et seq) or, in Northern Ireland, the Pension Schemes (Northern Ireland) Act 1993 Pt III.
23 Employment Act 2002 s 15(2)(c).
24 See the Employment Act 2002 s 15(1).

H. RECOVERY OF AMOUNTS PAID

555. Power to make provision for funding of employers' liabilities for statutory shared parental pay. The Secretary of State[1] must by regulations[2] make provision for the payment by employers[3] of statutory shared parental pay[4] to be funded by the Commissioners for Revenue and Customs[5] to such extent as the regulations may specify[6]. Such regulations:

(1) must make provision for a person who has made a payment of statutory shared parental pay to be entitled, except in such circumstances as the regulations may provide, to recover an amount equal to the sum of[7]:
  (a) the aggregate of such of those payments as qualify for small employers' relief[8]; and
  (b) an amount equal to 92 per cent of the aggregate of such of those payments as do not so qualify[9]; and
(2) must include provision for a person who has made a payment of statutory shared parental pay qualifying for small employers' relief to be entitled, except in such circumstances as the regulations may provide, to recover an additional amount equal to the amount to which the person would have been entitled[10] had the payment been a payment of statutory maternity pay[11]; and
(3) may, in particular, make provision:
  (a) for funding in advance as well as in arrear[12];
  (b) for funding, or the recovery of amounts due under provision made by virtue of head (2) above, by means of deductions from such amounts for which employers are accountable to the Commissioners as the regulations may provide, or otherwise[13];
  (c) for the recovery by the Commissioners of any sums overpaid to employers under such regulations[14].

Where an employer fraudulently or negligently receives incorrect payments in pursuance of such regulations, he is liable to a penalty[15].

1 As to the Secretary of State see PARA 5 note 21.
2 Regulations under the Employment Act 2002 s 7(1) must be made with the concurrence of the Commissioners for Revenue and Customs: see s 7(6). As to the Commissioners for Her Majesty's Revenue and Customs see INCOME TAXATION vol 58 (2014) PARAS 33–34; and see

PARA 551 note 2. As to the power to make regulations under the Employment Act 2002 see s 51; and PARA 474 note 2. At the date at which this volume states the law, no such regulations had been made.

3 As to the meaning of 'employer' for these purposes see PARA 543.

4 As to the meaning of 'statutory shared parental pay' see PARA 534.

5 See note 2.

6 Employment Act 2002 s 7(1) (amended by the Work and Families Act 2006 Sch 1 para 50(1), (2); and the Children and Families Act 2014 Sch 7 paras 50, 51(1), (2)(b)).

7 See the Employment Act 2002 s 7(2)(a) (amended by the Work and Families Act 2006 Sch 1 para 50(1), (3); and the Children and Families Act 2014 Sch 7 paras 50, 51(1), (3)(a)).

8 Employment Act 2002 s 7(2)(a)(i). For these purposes, a payment of statutory shared parental pay qualifies for small employers' relief if it would have so qualified were it a payment of statutory maternity pay, treating the period for which the payment of statutory shared parental pay is made as the maternity pay period : see s 7(3) (amended by the Work and Families Act 2006 Sch 1 para 50(1), (4); and the Children and Families Act 2014 Sch 7 paras 50, 51(1), (4)(b), (c)). As to the meaning of 'maternity pay period' see PARA 424. As to statutory shared parental pay see PARA 534 et seq.

9 Employment Act 2002 s 7(2)(a)(ii).

10 Ie under the Social Security Contributions and Benefits Act 1992 s 167(2)(b) (corresponding provision for statutory maternity pay: see PARA 439).

11 Employment Act 2002 s 7(2)(b) (amended by the Work and Families Act 2006 Sch 1 para 50(1), (3); and the Children and Families Act 2014 Sch 7 paras 50, 51(1), (3)(b)).

12 Employment Act 2002 s 7(4)(a).

13 Employment Act 2002 s 7(4)(b). The Commissioners may use electronic communications in connection with the recovery of statutory paternity pay or of any other sum in connection with that pay: see the Statutory Payment Schemes (Electronic Communications) Regulations 2002, SI 2002/3047; and INCOME TAXATION.

14 Employment Act 2002 s 7(4)(c).

15 Employment Act 2002 s 12(5) (amended by the Work and Families Act 2006 Sch 1 para 54(1), (4); and the Children and Families Act 2014 Sch 7 paras 50, 55(1), (6)). The penalty must not exceed £3000: see the Employment Act 2002 s 12(5) (as so amended).

556. Treatment of amount deducted from contributions. Where, in accordance with any provision of regulations[1] which make provision for the payment by employers[2] of statutory shared parental pay[3] to be funded by the Commissioners for Revenue and Customs[4], an amount has been deducted from an employer's contributions payments[5], the amount so deducted must be treated, except in such cases as the Secretary of State[6] may by regulations provide, for the purposes of any provision made by or under any enactment in relation to primary or secondary Class 1 contributions[7]:

(1) as having been paid, on such date as may be determined in accordance with the regulations[8]; and

(2) as having been received by the Commissioners for Revenue and Customs[9],

towards discharging the employer's liability in respect of such contributions[10].

1 Ie regulations made under the Employment Act 2002 s 7(1): see PARA 555.

2 As to the meaning of 'employer' for these purposes see PARA 543.

3 As to the meaning of 'statutory shared parental pay' see PARA 534.

4 As to the Commissioners for Her Majesty's Revenue and Customs see INCOME TAXATION vol 58 (2014) PARAS 33–34; and see PARA 551 note 2.

5 For these purposes, 'contributions payments', in relation to an employer, means any payments which the employer is required, by or under any enactment, to make in discharge of any liability in respect of primary or secondary Class 1 contributions: Employment Act 2002 s 7(7). As to primary and secondary Class 1 contributions see WELFARE BENEFITS AND STATE PENSIONS vol 104 (2014) PARA 385.

6 As to the Secretary of State see PARA 5 note 21.

7 See the Employment Act 2002 s 7(5).

8 Employment Act 2002 s 7(5)(a).

9 Employment Act 2002 s 7(5)(b).

10 See the Employment Act 2002 s 7(5). As to the date on which the deduction is treated as having been paid see PARA 482 note 28.

I. ADOPTIONS FROM OVERSEAS

557. Application of statutory shared parental pay provisions to adoption cases. The Secretary of State[1] may by regulations[2] provide for the statutory provisions relating to statutory shared parental pay[3] to have effect in relation to cases which involve adoption, but not the placement of a child for adoption under the law of any part of the United Kingdom[4], with such modifications[5] as the regulations may prescribe[6].

1 As to the Secretary of State see PARA 5 note 21.
2 As to the making of regulations under the Social Security Contributions and Benefits Act 1992 generally see PARA 407 note 3; and see PARA 534 note 8.
3 Ie the provisions of the Social Security Contributions and Benefits Act 1992 Pt XIIZC (ss 171ZU–171ZZ5) (statutory shared parental pay: see also PARA 534 et seq). As to the meaning of 'statutory shared parental pay' see PARA 534.
4 As to the meaning of 'United Kingdom' see PARA 407 note 7. As to the law relating to child adoption see **CHILDREN AND YOUNG PERSONS** vol 9 (2012) PARA 360 et seq.
5 As to the meaning of 'modifications' see PARA 536 note 4.
6 Social Security Contributions and Benefits Act 1992 s 171ZZ5(1) (ss 171ZZ4, 171ZZ5 added by the Children and Families Act 2014 s 119(1)). The Secretary of State may by regulations also provide for the Social Security Contributions and Benefits Act 1992 Pt XIIZC (statutory shared parental pay: see also PARA 534 et seq) to have effect in relation to cases which involve a person who has applied, or intends to apply, with another person for a parental order under the Human Fertilisation and Embryology Act 2008 s 54 (parental orders: see **CHILDREN AND YOUNG PERSONS** vol 9 (2012) PARA 129) and a child who is, or will be, the subject of the order, with such modifications as the regulations may prescribe: Social Security Contributions and Benefits Act 1992 s 171ZZ5(2) (as so added). For these purposes, 'prescribed' means prescribed by regulations: see s 171ZZ4(1) (as so added). Where s 171ZW(1)(b) (evidence as to entitlement and procedures: see PARA 536) has effect in relation to such cases as are described in s 171ZZ5(2), regulations under s 171ZW(1)(b) may impose requirements to make statutory declarations as to eligibility to apply for a parental order, and as to intention to apply for such an order: see s 171ZZ5(3) (as so added). At the date at which this volume states the law, no such regulations had been made.

(12) STATUTORY SICK PAY

(i) In general

558. Liability of employer for payment of statutory sick pay. Where an employee[1] has a day of incapacity for work in relation to his contract of service with an employer[2], that employer is liable, if the prescribed conditions[3] are satisfied, to make to him a payment (known as 'statutory sick pay') in respect of that day[4]. For the purposes of the statutory sick pay provisions that are set out in Part XI of the Social Security Contributions and Benefits Act 1992[5], a 'day of incapacity for work', in relation to a contract of service, means a day on which the employee concerned is, or is deemed in accordance with regulations to be, incapable by reason of some specific disease or bodily or mental disablement of doing work which he can reasonably be expected to do under that contract[6].

Any agreement is void to the extent that it purports:

(1) to exclude, limit or otherwise modify any of the provisions of Part XI of the Social Security Contributions and Benefits Act 1992[7]; or
(2) to require an employee to contribute, whether directly or indirectly, towards any costs incurred by his employer under those provisions[8],

but, for the avoidance of doubt, any agreement between an employer and an employee authorising any deductions from statutory sick pay which the employer is liable to pay the employee in respect of any period is not void by reason only of head (1) above if the employer: (a) is authorised by that or another agreement to make the same deductions from any contractual remuneration which he is liable to pay in respect of the same period[9]; or (b) would be so authorised if he were liable to pay contractual remuneration in respect of that period[10].

1 As to the meaning of 'employee' for these purposes see PARA 562.

2 For the purposes of the Social Security Contributions and Benefits Act 1992 Pt XI (ss 151–163) (statutory sick pay: see also PARA 559 et seq), 'contract of service', except in the first limb of the definition of 'employee' (see PARA 562) includes any arrangement providing for the terms of appointment of an employee: see s 163(1). As to the meaning of 'employer' for these purposes see PARA 571. As to the meaning of 'contract of service' generally see PARA 1 note 1.

Many contracts of employment also provide for contractual sick pay, which normally operates by 'topping up' statutory sick pay to a set figure. Such terms are not affected by the statutory sick pay scheme and must be included in an employee's written particulars of terms of employment: see PARA 119. As to the position of apprentices and youth trainees at common law see PARAS 112, 128–129, 636, 747–754. As to the statutory law on apprenticeships see EDUCATION vol 35 (2011) PARA 682 et seq.

3 Ie the conditions set out in the Social Security Contributions and Benefits Act 1992 ss 152–154, Sch 11: see PARAS 561, 572–575.

4 Social Security Contributions and Benefits Act 1992 s 151(1). Regulations may provide for periods of work which begin on one day and finish on the following day to be treated for the purposes of Pt XI (statutory sick pay: see also PARA 559 et seq) as falling solely within one or other of those days: s 163(7). As to the making of regulations under the Social Security Contributions and Benefits Act 1992 see PARA 407 note 3. At the date at which this volume states the law, no such regulations had been made.

Statutory sick pay under the Social Security Contributions and Benefits Act 1992 Pt XI constitutes 'wages' for the purposes of the Employment Rights Act 1996 Pt II (ss 13–27) (protection of wages): see s 27(1); and PARA 254. Payments of statutory sick pay under the Social Security Contributions and Benefits Act 1992 Pt XI are charged to income tax under the Income Tax (Earnings and Pensions) Act 2003 Pts 2–7 (ss 3–554): see INCOME TAXATION vol 58 (2014) PARA 730 et seq.

As to the liability of the Commissioners for Revenue and Customs for payment of statutory sick pay see PARA 559; and as to the time limit for paying statutory sick pay see PARA 584.

5 Ie for the purposes of the Social Security Contributions and Benefits Act 1992 Pt XI (statutory sick pay: see also PARA 559 et seq).

6 Social Security Contributions and Benefits Act 1992 s 151(4) (amended by the Social Security (Incapacity for Work) Act 1994 Sch 1 para 34). As to the persons deemed incapable of work see PARA 560.

7 Social Security Contributions and Benefits Act 1992 s 151(2)(a).

8 Social Security Contributions and Benefits Act 1992 s 151(2)(b).

9 Social Security Contributions and Benefits Act 1992 s 151(3)(a).

10 Social Security Contributions and Benefits Act 1992 s 151(3)(b).

559. Liability of the Commissioners for Revenue and Customs for payment of statutory sick pay. Circumstances may be prescribed[1] in which the liability to make payments of statutory sick pay[2] is to be[3] a liability of the Commissioners for Revenue and Customs[4].

Accordingly, where:

(1) an adjudicating authority[5] has determined that an employer is liable to make payments of statutory sick pay to an employee[6]; and

(2) the time for appealing against that determination has expired[7]; and

(3) no appeal against the determination has been lodged or leave to appeal against the determination is required and has been refused[8],

then for any day of incapacity for work in respect of which it was determined that the employer was liable to make those payments, and for any further days of incapacity for work which fall within the same spell of incapacity for work[9] and in respect of which the employer was liable to make payments of statutory sick pay to that employee, the liability to make payments of statutory sick pay in respect of those days is[10], to the extent that payment has not been made by the employer, that of the Commissioners and not the employer[11].

Any liability to make a payment of statutory sick pay[12] in respect of a day of incapacity for work in relation to an employee's contract of service[13] with his employer is[14] that of the Commissioners and not that of the employer where the employer is insolvent[15] on that day[16].

1 For these purposes, 'prescribed' means prescribed by regulations: see the Social Security Contributions and Benefits Act 1992 s 163(1). Regulations under s 151(6) must be made with the concurrence of the Commissioners for Revenue and Customs: s 151(7) (s 151(6) amended, s 151(7) added, by the Social Security Contributions (Transfer of Functions, etc) Act 1999 Sch 1 para 9). As to the making of regulations under the Social Security Contributions and Benefits Act 1992 see PARA 407 note 3. As to the Commissioners for Her Majesty's Revenue and Customs see **INCOME TAXATION** vol 58 (2014) PARAS 33–34.

2 As to the meaning of 'statutory sick pay' see PARA 558.

3 Ie notwithstanding the provisions of the Social Security Contributions and Benefits Act 1992 s 151(1)–(5): see PARAS 558, 571.

4 Social Security Contributions and Benefits Act 1992 s 151(6) (as amended: see note 1). At the date at which this volume states the law, no such regulations had been made but, by virtue of the Interpretation Act 1978 s 17(2)(b), the Statutory Sick Pay (General) Regulations 1982, SI 1982/894 (see the text and notes 5–16) have effect as if so made.

5 For these purposes, 'adjudicating authority' means, as the case may be, the chief or any other adjudication officer, the First-tier Tribunal or the Upper Tribunal: Statutory Sick Pay (General) Regulations 1982, SI 1982/894, reg 9A(3) (regs 9A, 9B added by SI 1987/372; the Statutory Sick Pay (General) Regulations 1982, SI 1982/894, reg 9A(3) amended by SI 2008/2683). As to adjudication officers see **WELFARE BENEFITS AND STATE PENSIONS** vol 104 (2014) PARA 575; and as to the First-tier Tribunal and the Upper Tribunal see **COURTS AND TRIBUNALS** vol 24 (2010) PARA 874 et seq.

6 Statutory Sick Pay (General) Regulations 1982, SI 1982/894, reg 9A(1)(a) (as added: see note 5). As to the meaning of 'employee' for these purposes see PARA 562; and as to the meaning of 'employer' for these purposes see PARA 571.

7 Statutory Sick Pay (General) Regulations 1982, SI 1982/894, reg 9A(1)(b) (as added: see note 5).

8 Statutory Sick Pay (General) Regulations 1982, SI 1982/894, reg 9A(1)(c) (as added: see note 5).

9 For these purposes, a spell of incapacity for work consists of consecutive days of incapacity for work with no day of the week disregarded: see the Statutory Sick Pay (General) Regulations 1982, SI 1982/894, reg 9A(2) (as added: see note 5). As to the meaning of 'day of incapacity for work' see PARA 558.

The provision made by reg 9A does not, however, apply to any liability of an employer to make a payment of statutory sick pay where the day of incapacity for work in respect of which the liability arose falls within a period of entitlement which commenced before 6 April 1987: reg 9A(4) (as so added). As to the meaning of 'period of entitlement' see PARA 573 note 4.

10 Ie notwithstanding the provisions of the Social Security Contributions and Benefits Act 1992 s 151 (see also PARAS 558, 571) and subject to the Statutory Sick Pay (General) Regulations 1982, SI 1982/894, reg 9A(4) (see note 9).

11 See the Statutory Sick Pay (General) Regulations 1982, SI 1982/894, reg 9A(1) (reg 9A as added (see note 5); regs 9A(1), 9B(1) amended by the Social Security Contributions (Transfer of Functions, etc) Act 1999 Sch 2); and see the Interpretation Act 1978 s 17(2)(a). As to the time limit for statutory sick pay paid by the Commissioners see PARA 585.

12 Ie any liability arising under the Social Security Contributions and Benefits Act 1992 Pt XI (ss 151–163) (statutory sick pay: see also PARAS 558, 561 et seq).

13 As to the meaning of 'contract of service' for these purposes see PARA 558 note 2.

14 Ie notwithstanding the provisions of the Social Security Contributions and Benefits Act 1992 s 151 (see also PARAS 558, 571) and subject to the Statutory Sick Pay (General) Regulations 1982, SI 1982/894, reg 9B(3) (see note 16).

15 For these purposes, an employer is to be taken to be insolvent if, and only if, in England and Wales:

(1) he has been adjudged bankrupt or has made a composition or arrangement with his creditors (Statutory Sick Pay (General) Regulations 1982, SI 1982/894, reg 9B(2)(a)(i) (as added: see note 5));
(2) he has died and his estate falls to be administered in accordance with an order under the Insolvency Act 1986 s 421 (insolvent estates of deceased persons: see BANKRUPTCY AND INDIVIDUAL INSOLVENCY vol 5 (2013) PARA 830 et seq) (Statutory Sick Pay (General) Regulations 1982, SI 1982/894, reg 9B(2)(a)(ii) (as so added)); or
(3) where an employer is a company, a winding-up order is made or a resolution for voluntary winding up is passed with respect to it or it enters administration, or a receiver or manager of its undertaking is duly appointed, or possession is taken, by or on behalf of the holders of any debentures secured by a floating charge, of any property of the company comprised in or subject to the charge or a voluntary arrangement proposed for the purposes of the Insolvency Act 1986 Pt I (ss 1–7B) (company voluntary arrangements: see COMPANY AND PARTNERSHIP INSOLVENCY vol 16 (2011) PARA 83 et seq) is approved under Pt I (Statutory Sick Pay (General) Regulations 1982, SI 1982/894, reg 9B(2)(a)(iii) (reg 9B as so added; reg 9B(2)(a)(iii) amended by SI 2003/2096)).

As to the meanings of 'England' and 'Wales' see PARA 2 note 12. As to compositions or arrangements with creditors see BANKRUPTCY AND INDIVIDUAL INSOLVENCY vol 5 (2013) PARA 43 et seq; and as to bankruptcy generally see BANKRUPTCY AND INDIVIDUAL INSOLVENCY vol 5 (2013) PARA 129 et seq. As to winding-up orders see COMPANY AND PARTNERSHIP INSOLVENCY vol 16 (2011) PARA 386 et seq. As to voluntary winding-up see COMPANY AND PARTNERSHIP INSOLVENCY vol 17 (2011) PARA 898 et seq. As to administration orders see COMPANY AND PARTNERSHIP INSOLVENCY vol 16 (2011) PARA 159 et seq. As to the appointment of receivers and managers see COMPANY AND PARTNERSHIP INSOLVENCY vol 16 (2011) PARA 340 et seq. As to the taking of possession by or on behalf of the holders of debentures secured by a floating charge see COMPANIES vol 15 (2009) PARA 1333 et seq.

16 Statutory Sick Pay (General) Regulations 1982, SI 1982/894, reg 9B(1) (reg 9B as added (see note 5); reg 9B(1) as amended (see note 11)); and see the Interpretation Act 1978 s 17(2)(a). The Statutory Sick Pay (General) Regulations 1982, SI 1982/894, reg 9B does not, however, apply where the employer became insolvent before 6 April 1987: reg 9B(3) (as so added).

560. Persons deemed incapable of work. A person who is not incapable of work which he can reasonably be expected to do under a particular contract of service[1] may be deemed to be incapable of work of such a kind by reason of some specific disease or bodily or mental disablement for any day on which[2]:

(1) he is under medical care in respect of such a disease or disablement[3]; it is stated by a registered medical practitioner[4] that for precautionary or convalescent reasons consequential on such disease or disablement he should abstain from work, or from work of such a kind[5]; and he does not work under that contract of service[6]; or
(2) he is excluded or abstains from work, or from work of such a kind, pursuant to a request or notice in writing lawfully made under an enactment[7]; or otherwise prevented from working pursuant to an enactment[8], by reason of it being known or reasonably suspected that he is infected or contaminated by, or has been in contact with a case of, a relevant infection or contamination[9].

A person who at the commencement of any day is, or thereafter on that day becomes, incapable of work of such a kind by reason of some specific disease or bodily or mental disablement[10], and:

(a) on that day, under that contract of service, does no work, or no work except during a shift which ends on that day having begun on the previous day[11]; and
(b) does no work under that contract of service during a shift which begins on that day and ends on the next[12],

is deemed to be incapable of work of such a kind by reason of that disease or bodily or mental disablement throughout that day[13].

Act 1978 s 17(2)(b), the Statutory Sick Pay (Mariners, Airmen and Persons Abroad) Regulations 1982, SI 1982/1349 (see PARAS 562, 564 et seq) have effect as if so made.
11 Social Security Contributions and Benefits Act 1992 s 162(2)(a).
12 Social Security Contributions and Benefits Act 1992 s 162(2)(b).
13 As to domicile see CONFLICT OF LAWS vol 19 (2011) PARA 336 et seq.
14 Social Security Contributions and Benefits Act 1992 s 162(2)(c).
15 Social Security Contributions and Benefits Act 1992 s 162(2)(d).

564. Time for compliance with provisions relating to statutory sick pay; employee outside the United Kingdom. Where:

(1) an employee[1] is outside the United Kingdom[2];
(2) any act is required[3] to be done forthwith or on the happening of a certain event or within a specified time[4]; and
(3) because the employee is outside the United Kingdom, he or his employer[5] cannot comply with the requirement[6],

the employee or the employer, as the case may be, is deemed to have complied with it if he performs the act as soon as reasonably practicable[7].

1 As to the meaning of 'employee' for these purposes see PARA 562.
2 Statutory Sick Pay (Mariners, Airmen and Persons Abroad) Regulations 1982, SI 1982/1349, reg 14(a). As to the meaning of 'United Kingdom' for these purposes see PARA 407 note 7.
3 Ie by the Social Security Contributions and Benefits Act 1992 Pt XI (ss 151–163) (statutory sick pay: see also PARAS 558 et seq, 569 et seq) or by regulations made thereunder.
4 Statutory Sick Pay (Mariners, Airmen and Persons Abroad) Regulations 1982, SI 1982/1349, reg 14(b); and see the Interpretation Act 1978 s 17(2)(a).
5 As to the meaning of 'employer' for these purposes see PARA 571.
6 Statutory Sick Pay (Mariners, Airmen and Persons Abroad) Regulations 1982, SI 1982/1349, reg 14(c).
7 See the Statutory Sick Pay (Mariners, Airmen and Persons Abroad) Regulations 1982, SI 1982/1349, reg 14.

565. Treatment of persons in other member states or absent from Great Britain for purposes of statutory sick pay. A person who is:

(1) gainfully employed in a member state other than the United Kingdom[1] in such circumstances that, if his employment were in Great Britain[2], he would be an employee[3] for the purposes of the statutory sick pay provisions that are set out in Part XI of the Social Security Contributions and Benefits Act 1992[4], or a person treated[5] as such an employee[6]; and
(2) subject[7] to the legislation of the United Kingdom[8],

is to be treated[9] as an employee for those purposes, notwithstanding that he is not employed in Great Britain[10].

Where a person, while absent from Great Britain for any purpose, is gainfully employed by an employer[11] who is liable to pay in respect of him secondary Class 1 contributions[12], he is to be treated[13] as an employee[14].

1 As to the meaning of 'United Kingdom' for these purposes see PARA 407 note 7.
2 As to the meaning of 'Great Britain' for these purposes see PARA 407 note 7.
3 As to the meaning of 'employee' for these purposes see PARA 562.
4 Ie for the purposes of the Social Security Contributions and Benefits Act 1992 Pt XI (ss 151–163) (statutory sick pay: see also PARAS 558 et seq, 569 et seq).
5 Ie under the Statutory Sick Pay (General) Regulations 1982, SI 1982/894, reg 16: see PARA 562.
6 Statutory Sick Pay (Mariners, Airmen and Persons Abroad) Regulations 1982, SI 1982/1349, reg 5(a); and see the Interpretation Act 1978 s 17(2)(a).
7 Ie under Council Regulation (EC) 1408/71 (OJ L149, 5.7.71, p 2) on the application of social security schemes to employed persons and their families moving within the Community

(repealed: see now Council Regulation (EC) 883/2004 of 29 April 2004 (OJ L166, 30.4.2004, p 1) on the coordination of social security systems; and WELFARE BENEFITS AND STATE PENSIONS vol 104 (2014) PARA 600 et seq).

8 Statutory Sick Pay (Mariners, Airmen and Persons Abroad) Regulations 1982, SI 1982/1349, reg 5(b); and see the Interpretation Act 1978 s 17(2)(a).

9 Ie for the purposes of the Social Security Contributions and Benefits Act 1992 Pt XI (statutory sick pay: see also PARAS 558 et seq, 569 et seq), but subject to the Statutory Sick Pay (Mariners, Airmen and Persons Abroad) Regulations 1982, SI 1982/1349, reg 6(2) (see PARA 566), reg 7(2) (see PARA 567) and reg 9 (see PARA 562 note 9).

10 Statutory Sick Pay (Mariners, Airmen and Persons Abroad) Regulations 1982, SI 1982/1349, reg 5; and see the Interpretation Act 1978 s 17(2)(a).

11 As to the meaning of 'employer' for these purposes see PARA 571.

12 Ie under the Social Security Contributions and Benefits Act 1992 s 6 (see WELFARE BENEFITS AND STATE PENSIONS vol 104 (2014) PARA 385) or the Social Security (Contributions) Regulations 2001, SI 2001/1004, reg 146 (payment of contributions for periods abroad: see WELFARE BENEFITS AND STATE PENSIONS vol 104 (2014) PARA 380).

13 Ie for the purposes of the Social Security Contributions and Benefits Act 1992 Pt XI (statutory sick pay: see also PARAS 558 et seq, 569 et seq) but subject to the Statutory Sick Pay (Mariners, Airmen and Persons Abroad) Regulations 1982, SI 1982/1349, reg 5 (see the text and notes 1–10), reg 6(2) (see PARA 566), reg 7(2) (see PARA 567) and reg 9 (see PARA 562 note 9).

14 Statutory Sick Pay (Mariners, Airmen and Persons Abroad) Regulations 1982, SI 1982/1349, reg 5A (added by SI 1996/777); and see the Interpretation Act 1978 s 17(2)(a).

566. Treatment of mariners for purposes of statutory sick pay. Where a mariner[1]:

(1) is employed as such[2], and:
   (a) the employment is on board a British ship[3]; or
   (b) the employment is on board a ship and the contract in respect of the employment is entered into in the United Kingdom with a view to its performance (in whole or in part) while the ship or vessel is on her voyage[4]; and
   (c) in a case to which head (1)(b) above applies, the person by whom the mariner's earnings are paid or, in the case of employment as a master or member of the crew of a ship or vessel, either that person or the owner of the ship or vessel (or the managing owner[5] if there is more than one owner) has a place of business in Great Britain[6]; or

(2) is employed as a master, member of the crew or radio officer[7] on board any ship or vessel, not being a mariner to whom head (1) above applies[8]; and:
   (a) in the case of the employment being as a radio officer, if the contract under which the employment is performed is entered into in the United Kingdom, the employer[9] or person paying the radio officer his earnings for that employment has a place of business in Great Britain[10]; or
   (b) in the case of the employment being as a master, member of the crew or radio officer, if the contract is not entered into in the United Kingdom, the employer or the person paying the earnings has his principal place of business in Great Britain[11],

then he is to be treated[12] as an employee for the purposes of the statutory sick pay provisions that are set out in Part XI of the Social Security Contributions and Benefits Act 1992[13], notwithstanding that he may not be employed in Great Britain[14].

However, a mariner who:

(i) is in employment (including any period of leave, other than leave for the purpose of study, accruing from the employment) as a master or member of the crew of a ship[15], where:

(A) the employment is on a foreign-going ship[16]; or

(B) the employment is partly on a foreign-going ship and partly otherwise than on such a ship, and it is a requirement of the contract of service which relates to that employment that any payment of earnings in respect of that employment is to be made during the employment on the foreign-going ship[17]; or

(ii) has been in such employment as is mentioned in head (i) above where[18]:

(A) not more than 13 weeks have elapsed since he was last in such employment[19];

(B) he continues to be employed by the employer by whom he was employed when he was last in such employment[20]; and

(C) he is not employed, by that employer or any other, on terms which are inconsistent with his being able to resume such employment as is mentioned in head (i) above after not more than 13 weeks have elapsed since he was last in such employment[21],

is not to be treated as an employee for those purposes, notwithstanding that he may be employed in Great Britain[22].

1 For these purposes, 'mariner' means a person who is or has been in employment under a contract of service either as a master or member of the crew of any ship or vessel, or in any other capacity on board any ship or vessel where: (1) the employment in that other capacity is for the purposes of that ship or vessel or her crew or any passengers or cargo or mails carried thereby; and (2) the contract is entered into in the United Kingdom with a view to its performance, in whole or in part, while the ship or vessel is on her voyage, but does not include a person in so far as her employment is as a serving member of the forces: see the Social Security (Contributions) Regulations 2001, SI 2001/1004, reg 115; definition applied by the Statutory Sick Pay (Mariners, Airmen and Persons Abroad) Regulations 1982, SI 1982/1349, reg 2; and see the Interpretation Act 1978 s 17(2)(a). The expressions 'ship' and 'ship or vessel', except in the Statutory Sick Pay (Mariners, Airmen and Persons Abroad) Regulations 1982, SI 1982/1349, reg 6(2) (see the text and notes 15–22), include hovercraft: see reg 2. As to the meaning of 'contract of service' for these purposes see PARA 558 note 2. As to the meaning of 'United Kingdom' for these purposes see PARA 407 note 7.

2 See the Statutory Sick Pay (Mariners, Airmen and Persons Abroad) Regulations 1982, SI 1982/1349, reg 6(1)(a).

3 Statutory Sick Pay (Mariners, Airmen and Persons Abroad) Regulations 1982, SI 1982/1349, reg 6(1)(a)(i). For these purposes, 'British ship' means: (1) any ship or vessel belonging to Her Majesty; or (2) any ship or vessel whose port of registry is a port in Great Britain; or (3) a hovercraft which is registered in the United Kingdom: see the Social Security (Contributions) Regulations 2001, SI 2001/1004, reg 115; definition applied by the Statutory Sick Pay (Mariners, Airmen and Persons Abroad) Regulations 1982, SI 1982/1349, reg 2; and see the Interpretation Act 1978 s 17(2)(a). As to the meaning of 'Great Britain' for these purposes see PARA 407 note 7.

4 Statutory Sick Pay (Mariners, Airmen and Persons Abroad) Regulations 1982, SI 1982/1349, reg 6(1)(a)(ii).

5 For these purposes, 'managing owner' means that owner of any ship or vessel who, where there is more than one such owner, is responsible for the control and management of that ship or vessel; 'owner', in relation to any ship or vessel, means the person to whom the ship or vessel belongs and who, subject to the right of control of the captain or master of the ship or vessel (the 'master's rights'), is entitled to control of that ship or vessel; and references to the owner of a ship or vessel are to be construed, in relation to a ship or vessel which has been demised, as referring to the person who for the time being is entitled as charterer to possession and, subject as aforesaid, control of the ship or vessel by virtue of the demise or any sub-demise: see the Social Security (Contributions) Regulations 2001, SI 2001/1004, reg 115; definition applied by the Statutory Sick Pay (Mariners, Airmen and Persons Abroad) Regulations 1982, SI 1982/1349, reg 2; and see the Interpretation Act 1978 s 17(2)(a).

6 Statutory Sick Pay (Mariners, Airmen and Persons Abroad) Regulations 1982, SI 1982/1349, reg 6(1)(a)(iii).

7 For these purposes, 'radio officer' means a mariner employed in connection with the radio apparatus of any ship or vessel and holding a certificate of competence in radio telephony granted by the Secretary of State or by an authority empowered in that behalf by the legislature of some part of the Commonwealth or of the Republic of Ireland and recognised by the Secretary of State as equivalent to the like certificate granted by him: see the Social Security (Contributions) Regulations 2001, SI 2001/1004, reg 115; definition applied by the Statutory Sick Pay (Mariners, Airmen and Persons Abroad) Regulations 1982, SI 1982/1349, reg 2; and see the Interpretation Act 1978 s 17(2)(a). As to the Secretary of State see PARA 5 note 21.
8 See the Statutory Sick Pay (Mariners, Airmen and Persons Abroad) Regulations 1982, SI 1982/1349, reg 6(1)(b).
9 As to the meaning of 'employer' for these purposes see PARA 571.
10 Statutory Sick Pay (Mariners, Airmen and Persons Abroad) Regulations 1982, SI 1982/1349, reg 6(1)(b)(i).
11 Statutory Sick Pay (Mariners, Airmen and Persons Abroad) Regulations 1982, SI 1982/1349, reg 6(1)(b)(ii).
12 Ie subject to the Statutory Sick Pay (Mariners, Airmen and Persons Abroad) Regulations 1982, SI 1982/1349, reg 9: see PARA 562 note 9.
13 Ie the Social Security Contributions and Benefits Act 1992 Pt XI (ss 151–163) (statutory sick pay: see also PARAS 558 et seq, 569 et seq). As to the meaning of 'employee' for these purposes see PARA 562.
14 See the Statutory Sick Pay (Mariners, Airmen and Persons Abroad) Regulations 1982, SI 1982/1349, reg 6(1); and see the Interpretation Act 1978 s 17(2)(a). The Statutory Sick Pay (Mariners, Airmen and Persons Abroad) Regulations 1982, SI 1982/1349, reg 6(1) does not apply to a mariner to whom reg 6(2) (see the text and notes 15–22) applies: see reg 6(1).
15 See the Statutory Sick Pay (Mariners, Airmen and Persons Abroad) Regulations 1982, SI 1982/1349, reg 6(2)(a).
16 Statutory Sick Pay (Mariners, Airmen and Persons Abroad) Regulations 1982, SI 1982/1349, reg 6(2)(a)(i). For these purposes, 'foreign-going ship' means any ship or vessel which is not a home-trade ship: see the Social Security (Contributions) Regulations 2001, SI 2001/1004, reg 115; definition applied by the Statutory Sick Pay (Mariners, Airmen and Persons Abroad) Regulations 1982, SI 1982/1349, reg 2; and see the Interpretation Act 1978 s 17(2)(a).
17 Statutory Sick Pay (Mariners, Airmen and Persons Abroad) Regulations 1982, SI 1982/1349, reg 6(2)(a)(ii).
18 See the Statutory Sick Pay (Mariners, Airmen and Persons Abroad) Regulations 1982, SI 1982/1349, reg 6(2)(b).
19 Statutory Sick Pay (Mariners, Airmen and Persons Abroad) Regulations 1982, SI 1982/1349, reg 6(2)(b)(i).
20 Statutory Sick Pay (Mariners, Airmen and Persons Abroad) Regulations 1982, SI 1982/1349, reg 6(2)(b)(ii).
21 Statutory Sick Pay (Mariners, Airmen and Persons Abroad) Regulations 1982, SI 1982/1349, reg 6(2)(b)(iii).
22 See the Statutory Sick Pay (Mariners, Airmen and Persons Abroad) Regulations 1982, SI 1982/1349, reg 6(2); and see the Interpretation Act 1978 s 17(2)(a).

567. Treatment of airmen for purposes of statutory sick pay. Where an airman[1] is employed as such on board any aircraft, and the employer[2] of that airman or the person paying the airman his earnings in respect of the employment (whether or not the person making the payment is acting as agent for the employer) or the person under whose directions the terms of the airman's employment and the amount of the earnings to be paid in respect thereof are determined has[3]:

(1) in the case of the aircraft being a British aircraft[4], a place of business in Great Britain[5]; or

(2) in any other case, his principal place of business in Great Britain[6],

the airman is to be treated[7] as an employee for the purposes of the statutory sick pay provisions that are set out in Part XI of the Social Security Contributions and Benefits Act 1992[8], notwithstanding that he may not be employed in Great Britain[9].

3 As to the meaning of 'contract of service' for these purposes see PARA 558 note 2.
4 Ie under the Social Security Contributions and Benefits Act 1992 s 6: see WELFARE BENEFITS AND STATE PENSIONS vol 104 (2014) PARA 385.
5 Ie but for the condition in the Social Security Contributions and Benefits Act 1992 s 6(1)(b) (exclusion of liability where earnings are below lower earnings limit: see WELFARE BENEFITS AND STATE PENSIONS vol 104 (2014) PARA 385), or but for the employee being under the age of 16.
6 As to secondary Class 1 contributions see WELFARE BENEFITS AND STATE PENSIONS vol 104 (2014) PARA 385.
7 See the Social Security Contributions and Benefits Act 1992 s 163(1) (definition substituted by SI 2006/1031). As to the meaning of 'earnings' see PARA 582 note 3. As to the meaning of 'employer' and related expressions in relation to employment rights generally see PARA 2 et seq.
8 Ie except in such cases as may be prescribed and subject to the Social Security Contributions and Benefits Act 1992 Pt XI (statutory sick pay: see also PARAS 558 et seq, 572 et seq). For these purposes, 'prescribed' means prescribed by regulations: see s 163(1). At the date at which this volume states the law, no such regulations had been made.
9 Social Security Contributions and Benefits Act 1992 s 151(5).
10 Ie under the Social Security Contributions and Benefits Act 1992 Pt XI (statutory sick pay: see also PARAS 558 et seq, 572 et seq).
11 Ie for the purposes of the Social Security Contributions and Benefits Act 1992 Pt XI (statutory sick pay: see also PARAS 558 et seq, 572 et seq), or of such provisions of Pt XI as may be prescribed.
12 Social Security Contributions and Benefits Act 1992 s 163(5)(a). At the date at which this volume states the law, no such regulations had been made but, by virtue of the Interpretation Act 1978 s 17(2)(b), the Statutory Sick Pay (General) Regulations 1982, SI 1982/894 (see the text and notes 13–14) have effect as if so made.
13 Ie under the Social Security (Contributions) Regulations 2001, SI 2001/1004, reg 15 (aggregation of earnings paid in respect of different employed earner's employments by different persons and apportionment of contribution liability: see WELFARE BENEFITS AND STATE PENSIONS vol 104 (2014) PARA 382).
14 Statutory Sick Pay (General) Regulations 1982, SI 1982/894, reg 20(1); and see the Interpretation Act 1978 s 17(2)(a).

(iii) Qualifying Conditions for receipt of Statutory Sick Pay

572. First condition for receipt of statutory sick pay: period of incapacity for work. The first condition for receipt of statutory sick pay[1] is that the day in question forms part of a period of incapacity for work[2]; and any two periods of incapacity for work which are separated by a period of not more than eight weeks are to be treated as a single period of incapacity for work[3].

A day may be a day of incapacity for work in relation to a contract of service, and so form part of a period of incapacity for work[4], notwithstanding that: (1) it falls before the making of the contract or after the contract expires or is brought to an end[5]; or (2) it is not a day on which the employee[6] concerned would be required by that contract to be available for work[7].

1 As to the meaning of 'statutory sick pay' see PARA 558. As to the need to satisfy prescribed conditions for entitlement see PARA 558.
2 Social Security Contributions and Benefits Act 1992 s 152(1). For the purposes of Pt XI (ss 151–163) (statutory sick pay: see also PARAS 558 et seq, 573 et seq), 'period of incapacity for work' means any period of four or more consecutive days, each of which is a day of incapacity for work in relation to the contract of service in question: see ss 152(2), 163(1). As to the meaning of 'day of incapacity for work' see PARA 558; and as to the meaning of 'contract of service' for these purposes see PARA 558 note 2.
No day of the week is to be disregarded in calculating any period of consecutive days for the purposes of s 152: see s 152(5). For the purposes of Pt XI, 'week' means any period of seven days: see s 163(1); but see also note 3.
3 Social Security Contributions and Benefits Act 1992 s 152(3). The Secretary of State may by regulations direct that a larger number of weeks specified in the regulations is to be substituted for the number of weeks for the time being specified in s 152(3): see s 152(4). As to the Secretary

of State see PARA 5 note 21. As to the making of regulations under the Social Security Contributions and Benefits Act 1992 see PARA 407 note 3.

4 See the Social Security Contributions and Benefits Act 1992 s 152(6).

5 Social Security Contributions and Benefits Act 1992 s 152(6)(a).

6 As to the meaning of 'employee' for these purposes see PARA 562.

7 Social Security Contributions and Benefits Act 1992 s 152(6)(b).

573. Second condition for receipt of statutory sick pay: period of entitlement. The second condition for receipt of statutory sick pay[1] is that the day in question falls within a period which is, as between the employee[2] and his employer[3], a period of entitlement[4].

For these purposes, a period of entitlement, as between an employee and his employer, is a period beginning with the commencement of a period of incapacity for work[5] and ending with whichever of the following first occurs[6]:

(1) the termination of that period of incapacity for work[7];

(2) the day on which the employee reaches, as against the employer concerned, his maximum entitlement[8] to statutory sick pay[9];

(3) the day on which the employee's contract of service[10] with the employer concerned expires or is brought to an end[11];

(4) in the case of an employee who is, or has been, pregnant, the day immediately preceding the beginning of the disqualifying period[12].

A period of entitlement as between an employee and an employer of his may also be, or form part of, a period of entitlement as between him and another employer of his[13].

In a case where the employee's contract of service first takes effect on a day which falls within a period of incapacity for work, the period of entitlement begins with that day[14]; and, in a case where the employee's contract of service first takes effect between two periods of incapacity for work which are treated[15] as one, the period of entitlement begins with the first day of the second of those periods[16].

1 As to the meaning of 'statutory sick pay' see PARA 558. As to the need to satisfy prescribed conditions for entitlement see PARA 558.

2 As to the meaning of 'employee' for these purposes see PARA 562.

3 As to the meaning of 'employer' for these purposes see PARA 571.

4 Social Security Contributions and Benefits Act 1992 s 153(1). For the purposes of Pt XI (ss 151–163) (statutory sick pay: see also PARAS 558 et seq, 574 et seq), 'period of entitlement' has the meaning given by s 153 (see also the text and notes 5–13): see s 163(1).

5 The Social Security Contributions and Benefits Act 1992 s 153(3), Sch 11 (see PARA 574) has effect for the purpose of specifying circumstances in which a period of entitlement does not arise in relation to a particular period of incapacity for work: s 153(3). As to the meaning of 'period of incapacity for work' see PARA 572 note 2.

6 See the Social Security Contributions and Benefits Act 1992 s 153(2). Regulations may provide, in relation to prescribed cases, for a period of entitlement to end otherwise than in accordance with s 153(2): s 153(6). 'Prescribed' means prescribed by regulations: see s 163(1). As to the making of regulations under the Social Security Contributions and Benefits Act 1992 see PARA 407 note 3.

7 Social Security Contributions and Benefits Act 1992 s 153(2)(a). See note 6.

8 Ie determined in accordance with the Social Security Contributions and Benefits Act 1992 s 155: see PARAS 578–579. The Secretary of State may by regulations:

(1) specify circumstances in which, for the purpose of determining whether an employee's maximum entitlement to statutory sick pay has been reached in a period of entitlement as between him and an employer of his, days falling within a previous period of entitlement as between the employee and any person who is or has in the past been an employer of his are to be counted (s 153(5)(a)); and

(2) direct that in prescribed circumstances an employer must provide a person who is about to leave his employment, or who has been employed by him in the past, with a

statement in the prescribed form containing such information as may be prescribed in relation to any entitlement of the employee to statutory sick pay (s 153(5)(b)).

For these purposes, 'prescribed' means prescribed by regulations: s 163(1). As to the Secretary of State see PARA 5 note 21. At the date at which this volume states the law, no such regulations had been made but, by virtue of the Interpretation Act 1978 s 17(2)(b), the Statutory Sick Pay (General) Regulations 1982, SI 1982/894 (see PARA 575) have effect as if so made.

9 Social Security Contributions and Benefits Act 1992 s 153(2)(b). See note 6.

10 As to the meaning of 'contract of service' for these purposes see PARA 558 note 2.

11 Social Security Contributions and Benefits Act 1992 s 153(2)(c). See note 6.

12 Social Security Contributions and Benefits Act 1992 s 153(2)(d). Head (4) in the text does not, however, apply in relation to an employee who has been pregnant, if her pregnancy terminated before the beginning of the disqualifying period, otherwise than by confinement: s 153(11). For these purposes, 'confinement' is to be construed in accordance with s 171(1) (see PARA 415 note 6); and 'disqualifying period' means: (1) in relation to a woman entitled to statutory maternity pay, the maternity pay period; and (2) in relation to a woman entitled to maternity allowance, the maternity allowance period: see s 153(12). 'Maternity allowance period' has the meaning assigned to it by s 35(2) (see **WELFARE BENEFITS AND STATE PENSIONS** vol 104 (2014) PARA 474); and 'maternity pay period' has the meaning assigned to it by s 165(1) (see PARA 424): see s 153(12). See note 6.

13 Social Security Contributions and Benefits Act 1992 s 153(4).

14 Social Security Contributions and Benefits Act 1992 s 153(7). In any case where, otherwise than by virtue of s 6(1)(b) (exclusion of liability where earnings are below the lower earnings limit: see **WELFARE BENEFITS AND STATE PENSIONS** vol 104 (2014) PARA 385), an employee's earnings under a contract of service in respect of the day on which the contract takes effect do not attract a liability to pay secondary Class 1 contributions, the provisions of s 153(7), (8) (see also the text and notes 15–16) have effect as if for any reference to the contract first taking effect there were substituted a reference to the first day in respect of which the employee's earnings attract such a liability: s 153(9). As to secondary Class 1 contributions see **WELFARE BENEFITS AND STATE PENSIONS** vol 104 (2014) PARA 385.

15 Ie by virtue of the Social Security Contributions and Benefits Act 1992 s 152(3): see PARA 572.

16 Social Security Contributions and Benefits Act 1992 s 153(8). See note 14.

574. Circumstances in which periods of entitlement to statutory sick pay do not arise. A period of entitlement for receipt of statutory sick pay[1] does not arise in relation to a particular period of incapacity for work[2] in any of the specified circumstances[3] or in such other circumstances as may be prescribed[4].

The specified circumstances are that:

(1) at the relevant date[5] the employee's[6] normal weekly earnings[7] are less than the lower earnings limit[8] then in force[9];

(2) until a day to be appointed[10], in the period of 57 days ending immediately before the relevant date the employee has at least one day on which he was entitled to incapacity benefit, or would have been had he satisfied the contribution conditions[11];

(3) in the period of 85 days ending immediately before the relevant date the employee had at least one day on which he was entitled to an employment and support allowance (or would have been so entitled had he satisfied the relevant requirements in the Welfare Reform Act 2007)[12];

(4) the employee has done no work for his employer[13] under his contract of service[14];

(5) on the relevant date there is a stoppage of work due to a trade dispute at the employer's place of employment[15];

(6) the employee is, or has been, pregnant and the relevant date falls within the disqualifying period[16];

(7) as from a day to be appointed[17], the employee is not entitled to be in his employment on the relevant date[18].

1 As to the meaning of 'statutory sick pay' see PARA 558. As to the meaning of 'period of entitlement' see PARA 573.
2 As to the meaning of 'period of incapacity for work' see PARA 572 note 2.
3 Ie the circumstances set out in the Social Security Contributions and Benefits Act 1992 s 153(3), Sch 11 para 2: see the text and notes 5–18.
4 Social Security Contributions and Benefits Act 1992 Sch 11 para 1. For these purposes, 'prescribed' means prescribed by regulations: s 163(1). Regulations under Sch 11 para 1 must be made with the concurrence of the Treasury: Sch 11 para 1A (added by the Social Security Contributions (Transfer of Functions, etc) Act 1999 Sch 1 para 20). As to the making of regulations under the Social Security Contributions and Benefits Act 1992 see PARA 407 note 3. As to the Treasury see CONSTITUTIONAL AND ADMINISTRATIVE LAW vol 20 (2014) PARAS 262–265.
5 For these purposes, 'relevant date' means the date on which a period of entitlement would begin in accordance with the Social Security Contributions and Benefits Act 1992 s 153 (see PARA 573) if Sch 11 did not prevent it from arising: see Sch 11 para 3.
6 As to the meaning of 'employee' for these purposes see PARA 562.
7 As to the calculation of normal weekly earnings for these purposes see PARA 582. On their ordinary meaning, the words 'normal weekly earnings' in the Social Security Contributions and Benefits Act 1992 Sch 11 para 2(c) had to mean the actual entitlement under the contract of service: *Seaton v Revenue and Customs Comrs* [2011] UKUT 297 (TCC), [2011] All ER (D) 87 (Oct).
8 Ie under the Social Security Contributions and Benefits Act 1992 s 5(1)(a) (earnings limits and thresholds for Class 1 contributions: see WELFARE BENEFITS AND STATE PENSIONS vol 104 (2014) PARA 384).
9 Social Security Contributions and Benefits Act 1992 Sch 11 para 2(c). An employer's failure to pay an employee is not a circumstance that falls within the exception provided by Sch 11 para 2(c): *Seaton v Revenue and Customs Comrs* [2011] UKUT 297 (TCC), [2011] All ER (D) 87 (Oct).
10 As from a day to be appointed under the Welfare Reform Act 2007 s 70(2), the Social Security Contributions and Benefits Act 1992 Sch 11 para 2(d)(i) (see head (2) in the text) is repealed by the Welfare Reform Act 2007 s 67, Sch 8. However, at the date at which this volume states the law, no such day had been appointed.
11 Social Security Contributions and Benefits Act 1992 Sch 11 para 2(d)(i) (Sch 11 para 2(d) substituted by the Social Security (Incapacity for Work) Act 1994 Sch 1 para 43(2), Sch 2; and amended by the Social Security Act 1998 Sch 8; and the Welfare Reform and Pensions Act 1999 Sch 13 Pt IV). See note 10. The conditions referred to in the text are those mentioned in the Social Security Contributions and Benefits Act 1992 s 30A(2)(a): see WELFARE BENEFITS AND STATE PENSIONS vol 104 (2014) PARA 472. Head (2) in the text does not apply if, at the relevant date, the employee is over pensionable age and is not entitled to incapacity benefit: Social Security Contributions and Benefits Act 1992 Sch 11 para 5A(1) (Sch 11 para 5A added by SI 2007/825). Head (2) in the text also ceases to apply if, at any time after the relevant date, the employee is over pensionable age and is not entitled to incapacity benefit: Social Security Contributions and Benefits Act 1992 Sch 11 para 5A(2) (as so added). For these purposes, 'pensionable age' has the meaning given by the rules in the Pensions Act 1995 Sch 4 para 1 (see WELFARE BENEFITS AND STATE PENSIONS vol 104 (2014) PARA 488): see the Social Security Contributions and Benefits Act 1992 Sch 11 para 5A(3) (as so added). As to incapacity benefit see WELFARE BENEFITS AND STATE PENSIONS vol 104 (2014) PARA 472 et seq.
12 Social Security Contributions and Benefits Act 1992 Sch 11 para 2(dd) (added by SI 2008/1554). The requirements referred to are those contained in the Welfare Reform Act 2007 s 1(2): see WELFARE BENEFITS AND STATE PENSIONS vol 104 (2014) PARA 252.
13 As to the meaning of 'employer' for these purposes see PARA 571.
14 Social Security Contributions and Benefits Act 1992 Sch 11 para 2(f). For these purposes, if an employee enters into a contract of service which is to take effect not more than eight weeks after the date on which a previous contract of service entered into by him with the same employer ceased to have effect, the two contracts are to be treated as one: Sch 11 para 6. As to the meaning of 'contract of service' for these purposes see PARA 558 note 2; and as to the meaning of 'week' for these purposes see PARA 572 note 2.
15 Social Security Contributions and Benefits Act 1992 Sch 11 para 2(g) (amended by the Jobseekers Act 1995 Sch 3). The Social Security Contributions and Benefits Act 1992 Sch 11 para 2(g) does not, however, apply in the case of an employee who proves that at no time on or before the relevant date did he have a direct interest in the trade dispute in question: Sch 11 para 7.

16 Social Security Contributions and Benefits Act 1992 Sch 11 para 2(h). For these purposes, 'disqualifying period' has the meaning given by s 153(12) (see PARA 573 note 12): see Sch 11 para 2(h). Schedule 11 para 2(h) does not, however, apply in relation to an employee who has been pregnant if her pregnancy terminated, before the beginning of the disqualifying period, otherwise than by 'confinement' (within the meaning of s 171(1): see PARA 415 note 6): Sch 11 para 8.
17 As from a day to be appointed under the Welfare Reform Act 2012 s 150(3), the Social Security Contributions and Benefits Act 1992 Sch 11 paras 2(i), 9 are added by the Welfare Reform Act 2012 s 63(1), (10). However, at the date at which this volume states the law, no such day had been appointed.
18 Social Security Contributions and Benefits Act 1992 Sch 11 para 2(i) (prospectively added: see note 17). Head (7) in the text does not apply in prescribed circumstances: Sch 11 para 9 (prospectively added).

575. Third condition for receipt of statutory sick pay: qualifying days. The third condition for receipt of statutory sick pay[1] is that the day in question is a qualifying day[2]. For these purposes, the days which are to be qualifying days as between an employee[3] and an employer[4] of his (that is to say, those days of the week[5] on which he is required by his contract of service[6] with that employer to be available for work or which are chosen to reflect the terms of that contract) are such day, or days, as may, subject to regulations[7], be agreed between the employee and his employer or, failing such agreement, as may be determined in accordance with regulations[8].

In any case where qualifying days are determined by agreement between an employee and his employer there must be, in each week, beginning with Sunday, at least one qualifying day[9]. A day which is a qualifying day as between an employee and an employer of his may also be a qualifying day as between him and another employer of his[10].

Accordingly, where an employee and an employer of his have not agreed which day or days in any week[11] are or were qualifying days, or where in any week the only day or days are or were specified days[12], the qualifying day or days in that week is or are[13]:

(1) the day or days on which it is agreed between the employer and the employee that the employee is or was required to work, if not incapable, for that employer; or, if it is so agreed that there is or was no such day[14];
(2) the Wednesday; or, if there is no such agreement between the employer and employee as mentioned in head (1) above[15];
(3) every day, except that or those, if any, on which it is agreed between the employer and the employee that none of that employer's employees is or was required to work, any agreement that all days are or were such days being ignored[16].

No effect is to be given to any agreement between an employee and his employer to treat as qualifying days[17]: (a) any day where the day is identified, whether expressly or otherwise, by reference to that or another day being a day of incapacity for work[18] in relation to the employee's contract of service with an employer[19]; (b) any day identified, whether expressly or otherwise, by reference to a period of entitlement[20] or to a period of incapacity for work[21].

1 As to the meaning of 'statutory sick pay' see PARA 558. As to the need to satisfy prescribed conditions for entitlement see PARA 558.
2 Social Security Contributions and Benefits Act 1992 s 154(1). For the purposes of Pt XI (ss 151–163) (statutory sick pay: see also PARAS 558 et seq, 576 et seq), 'qualifying day' has the meaning given by s 154 (see also the text and notes 3–10): see s 163(1).
3 As to the meaning of 'employee' for these purposes see PARA 562.
4 As to the meaning of 'employer' for these purposes see PARA 571.
5 As to the meaning of 'week' for these purposes see PARA 572 note 2.

6 As to the meaning of 'contract of service' for these purposes see PARA 558 note 2.
7 As to the making of regulations under the Social Security Contributions and Benefits Act 1992 see PARA 407 note 3.
8 Social Security Contributions and Benefits Act 1992 s 154(2). At the date at which this volume states the law, no such regulations had been made but, by virtue of the Interpretation Act 1978 s 17(2)(b), the Statutory Sick Pay (General) Regulations 1982, SI 1982/894 (see the text and notes 11–21), have effect as if so made.
9 Social Security Contributions and Benefits Act 1992 s 154(3).
10 Social Security Contributions and Benefits Act 1992 s 154(4).
11 For these purposes, 'week' means a period of seven consecutive days beginning with Sunday: see the Statutory Sick Pay (General) Regulations 1982, SI 1982/894, reg 5(1).
12 Ie the only day or days are or were such as are referred to in the Statutory Sick Pay (General) Regulations 1982, SI 1982/894, reg 5(3): see the text and notes 17–21.
13 See the Statutory Sick Pay (General) Regulations 1982, SI 1982/894, reg 5(2) (reg 5(2) amended, reg 5(3) added, by SI 1985/126).
14 Statutory Sick Pay (General) Regulations 1982, SI 1982/894, reg 5(2)(a).
15 Statutory Sick Pay (General) Regulations 1982, SI 1982/894, reg 5(2)(b).
16 Statutory Sick Pay (General) Regulations 1982, SI 1982/894, reg 5(2)(c).
17 See the Statutory Sick Pay (General) Regulations 1982, SI 1982/894, reg 5(3) (as added: see note 13).
18 As to the meaning of 'day of incapacity for work' see PARA 558.
19 Statutory Sick Pay (General) Regulations 1982, SI 1982/894, reg 5(3)(a) (as added: see note 13).
20 As to the meaning of 'period of entitlement' see PARA 573 note 4.
21 Statutory Sick Pay (General) Regulations 1982, SI 1982/894, reg 5(3)(b) (as added: see note 13). As to the meaning of 'period of incapacity for work' see PARA 572 note 2.

(iv) Notification of Incapacity for Work for purposes of Statutory Sick Pay

576. Required notification of incapacity for work for purposes of statutory sick pay. Regulations[1] must prescribe the manner in which, and the time within which, notice of any day of incapacity for work[2] is to be given by or on behalf of an employee[3] to his employer[4].

Notice of any day of incapacity for work must be given[5] by or on behalf of an employee to his employer[6]:

(1) in a case where the employer has decided on a time limit (not being one which requires the notice to be given earlier than the first qualifying day[7] in the period of incapacity for work[8] or by a specified time during that qualifying day which includes that day of incapacity for work), and taken reasonable steps to make it known to the employee, within that time limit[9]; and
(2) in any other case, on or before the seventh day after that day of incapacity for work[10].

Notice of any day of incapacity for work must be given by or on behalf of an employee to his employer[11]:

(a) in a case where the employer has decided on a manner in which it is to be given (not being a manner which imposes a prescribed requirement[12]) and taken reasonable steps to make it known to the employee, in that manner[13]; and
(b) in any other case, in any manner, provided that, unless otherwise agreed between the employer and employee, it must be given in writing[14].

An employer who would otherwise be liable to pay an amount of statutory sick pay[15] to an employee in respect of a qualifying day (the 'day in question') is entitled to withhold payment of that amount if[16]: (i) the day in question is one in respect of which he has not been duly[17] notified[18]; or (ii) he has not been so notified in respect of any of the first three qualifying days in a period of entitlement (a 'waiting day') and the day in question is the first qualifying day in that period of entitlement in respect of which the employer is not entitled[19] to withhold payment[20].

1 As to the making of regulations under the Social Security Contributions and Benefits Act 1992 see PARA 407 note 3.
2 As to the meaning of 'day of incapacity for work' see PARA 558.
3 As to the meaning of 'employee' for these purposes see PARA 562.
4 Social Security Contributions and Benefits Act 1992 s 156(1). As to the meaning of 'employer' for these purposes see PARA 571. At the date at which this volume states the law, no such regulations had been made but, by virtue of the Interpretation Act 1978 s 17(2)(b), the Statutory Sick Pay (General) Regulations 1982, SI 1982/894 (see the text and notes 5–14), have effect as if so made. As to the time for compliance where an employee is outside the United Kingdom see PARA 564.
5 Ie subject to the Statutory Sick Pay (General) Regulations 1982, SI 1982/894, reg 7(2): see note 9. A notice contained in a letter which is properly addressed and sent by prepaid post is deemed to have been given on the day on which it was posted: reg 7(3).
6 See the Statutory Sick Pay (General) Regulations 1982, SI 1982/894, reg 7(1).
7 As to the meaning of 'qualifying day' see PARA 575 note 2.
8 As to the meaning of 'period of incapacity for work' see PARA 572 note 2.
9 Statutory Sick Pay (General) Regulations 1982, SI 1982/894, reg 7(1)(a) (amended by SI 1984/385). Notice of any day of incapacity for work may, however, be given one month later than as provided by the Statutory Sick Pay (General) Regulations 1982, SI 1982/894, reg 7(1) where there is good cause for giving it later or if in the particular circumstances that is not practicable, as soon as is reasonably practicable thereafter; but it must in any event be given on or before the ninety-first day after that day: reg 7(2) (amended by SI 1996/777).
10 Statutory Sick Pay (General) Regulations 1982, SI 1982/894, reg 7(1)(b). See note 9.
11 See the Statutory Sick Pay (General) Regulations 1982, SI 1982/894, reg 7(4).
12 The requirements prescribed as mentioned in head (a) in the text are that notice must be given:
 (1) personally (Statutory Sick Pay (General) Regulations 1982, SI 1982/894, reg 7(5)(a));
 (2) in the form of medical evidence (reg 7(5)(b));
 (3) more than once in every seven days during a period of entitlement (reg 7(5)(c));
 (4) on a document supplied by the employer (reg 7(5)(d)); or
 (5) on a printed form (reg 7(5)(e)).
 As to the provision of medical evidence see PARA 577.
13 Statutory Sick Pay (General) Regulations 1982, SI 1982/894, reg 7(4)(a).
14 Statutory Sick Pay (General) Regulations 1982, SI 1982/894, reg 7(4)(b).
15 As to the meaning of 'statutory sick pay' see PARA 558.
16 See the Social Security Contributions and Benefits Act 1992 s 156(2).
17 Ie in accordance with regulations under the Social Security Contributions and Benefits Act 1992 s 156(1): see the text and notes 1–4.
18 Social Security Contributions and Benefits Act 1992 s 156(2)(a).
19 Ie by virtue of the Social Security Contributions and Benefits Act 1992 s 156(2)(a) (see head (i) in the text) or in respect of an earlier waiting day by virtue of s 156(2)(b) (see head (ii) in the text).
20 Social Security Contributions and Benefits Act 1992 s 156(2)(b). Where an employer so withholds any amount of statutory sick pay: (1) the period of entitlement in question is not affected (s 156(3)(a)); and (2) for the purposes of calculating his maximum entitlement in accordance with s 155 (see PARAS 578–579), the employee is not to be taken to have become entitled to the amount so withheld (s 156(3)(b)).

577. Medical evidence required for purposes of statutory sick pay. Any employee[1] who claims to be entitled to statutory sick pay[2] from his employer[3] must, if so required by his employer, provide such information as may reasonably be required for the purpose of determining the duration of the period of entitlement[4] in question or whether a period of entitlement exists as between them[5]. The Secretary of State[6] may by regulations made with the concurrence of the Revenue and Customs[7] direct[8]:

(1) that medical information so required is to be provided, in such cases as may be prescribed[9], in a prescribed form[10];

(2) that an employee is not to be so required to provide medical information in respect of such days as may be prescribed in a period of incapacity for work[11].

Accordingly, medical information so required relating to incapacity for work must be provided[12], either:

(a) in the form of a statement given by a doctor in accordance with the prescribed rules[13]; or

(b) by such other means as may be sufficient in the circumstances of any particular case[14].

An employee is not, however, to be so required to provide medical evidence in respect of the first seven days in any spell of incapacity for work[15].

Where a doctor issues a statement to a patient[16], it must be in the prescribed form[17], and it must be signed by that doctor[18]. In any other case[19], the doctor's statement must be either in the prescribed form[20], or in a form to like effect, and it must be signed by the doctor attending the patient[21]. Every doctor's statement must be completed in ink or other indelible substance, and it must contain the following particulars[22]:

(i) the patient's name[23];

(ii) the date of the assessment (whether by consultation or consideration of a report as the case may be) on which the doctor's statement is based[24];

(iii) the condition[25] in respect of which the doctor advises the patient they are not fit for work[26];

(iv) a statement, where the doctor considers it appropriate, that the patient may be fit for work[27];

(v) a statement that the doctor will or, as the case may be will not, need to assess the patient's fitness for work again[28];

(vi) the date on which the doctor's statement is given[29];

(vii) the address of the doctor[30],

and it must bear, opposite the words 'Doctor's signature', the signature in ink of the doctor making the statement[31].

A doctor's statement must be based on an assessment made by that doctor[32]. The condition in respect of which the doctor is advising the patient is not fit for work or, as the case may be, which has caused the patient's absence from work, must be specified as precisely as the doctor's knowledge of the patient's condition at the time of the assessment permits[33]. A doctor's statement may be given on a date after the date of the assessment on which it is based, but no further doctor's statement is to be furnished in respect of that assessment other than a doctor's statement by way of replacement of an original which has been lost (in which case it must be clearly marked 'duplicate')[34].

Where a doctor considers that a patient may be fit for work, the doctor must state the reasons for that advice and, where this is considered appropriate, the arrangements which the patient might make, with their employer's agreement, to return to work[35]. Where, in the doctor's opinion, the patient will become fit for work on a day not later than 14 days after the date of the assessment on which the doctor's statement is based, the doctor's statement must specify that day[36].

The doctor's statement must specify the minimum period for which, in the doctor's opinion, the patient will not be fit for work or, as the case may be, for which they may be fit for work[37]. The period specified must begin on the date of the assessment on which the doctor's statement is based and is not to exceed three months unless the patient has, on the advice of a doctor, refrained from work for at least six months immediately preceding that date[38]. However, where:

(A) the patient has been advised by a doctor that they are not fit for work and, in consequence, has refrained from work for at least six months immediately preceding the date of the assessment on which the doctor's statement is based[39]; and

(B) in the doctor's opinion, the patient will not be fit for work for the foreseeable future[40],

instead of specifying a period, the doctor may, having regard to the circumstances of the particular case, enter the words 'an indefinite period' on the prescribed form[41].

1 As to the meaning of 'employee' for these purposes see PARA 562.
2 As to the meaning of 'statutory sick pay' see PARA 558.
3 As to the meaning of 'employer' for these purposes see PARA 571.
4 As to the meaning of 'period of entitlement' see PARA 573 note 4.
5 Social Security Administration Act 1992 s 14(1).
6 As to the Secretary of State see PARA 5 note 21.
7 As to the making of regulations under the Social Security Administration Act 1992 generally see **WELFARE BENEFITS AND STATE PENSIONS** vol 104 (2014) PARA 400. As to the Commissioners for Her Majesty's Revenue and Customs see **INCOME TAXATION** vol 58 (2014) PARAS 33–34.
8 See the Social Security Administration Act 1992 s 14(2) (amended by the Social Security Contributions (Transfer of Functions, etc) Act 1999 Sch 3 para 42). At the date at which this volume states the law, no such regulations had been made but, by virtue of the Interpretation Act 1978 s 17(2)(b), the Statutory Sick Pay (Medical Evidence) Regulations 1985, SI 1985/1604 (see the text and notes 12–41) have effect as if so made.
9 For these purposes, 'prescribe' means prescribe by regulations and 'prescribed' must be construed accordingly: see the Social Security Administration Act 1992 s 191(1) (definition amended by the Welfare Reform Act 2007 Sch 5 paras 2, 10).
10 Social Security Administration Act 1992 s 14(2)(a). See note 8. As to the time for compliance where an employee is outside the United Kingdom see PARA 564.
11 Social Security Administration Act 1992 s 14(2)(b). See note 8. As to the meaning of 'period of incapacity for work' see PARA 572 note 2.
12 See the Statutory Sick Pay (Medical Evidence) Regulations 1985, SI 1985/1604, reg 2(1) (reg 2(1) substituted, reg 2(2) amended, by SI 2010/137).
13 Statutory Sick Pay (Medical Evidence) Regulations 1985, SI 1985/1604, reg 2(1)(a) (as substituted: see note 12). Head (a) in the text refers to a statement given by a doctor in accordance with the rules set out in Sch 1 Pt I: see the text and notes 16–41.
14 Statutory Sick Pay (Medical Evidence) Regulations 1985, SI 1985/1604, reg 2(1)(b) (as substituted: see note 12).
15 Statutory Sick Pay (Medical Evidence) Regulations 1985, SI 1985/1604, reg 2(2) (as amended: see note 12). For these purposes, 'spell of incapacity' means a continuous period of incapacity for work which is immediately preceded by a day on which the claimant either worked or was not incapable of work: see reg 2(2) (as so amended).
16 Ie where a doctor issues a statement to a patient in accordance with an obligation arising under a contract, agreement or arrangement under the National Health Service Act 2006 Pt 4 (ss 83–98A) (medical services: see **HEALTH SERVICES** vol 54 (2008) PARA 241 et seq) or the National Health Service (Wales) Act 2006 Pt 4 (ss 41–55) (medical services: see **HEALTH SERVICES** vol 54 (2008) PARAS 74, 241 et seq): see the Statutory Sick Pay (Medical Evidence) Regulations 1985, SI 1985/1604, Sch 1 Pt I r 2 (Sch 1 substituted by SI 2010/137). For these purposes, 'doctor' means a registered medical practitioner, not being the patient; and 'patient' means the person in respect of whom a statement is given in accordance with the rules contained in the Statutory Sick Pay (Medical Evidence) Regulations 1985, SI 1985/1604, Sch 1 Pt I (rr 1–13): see Sch 1 Pt I r 1 (as so substituted). As to the meaning of 'registered medical practitioner' see **MEDICAL PROFESSIONS** vol 74 (2011) PARA 176.
17 Ie the doctor's statement must be in a form set out at the Statutory Sick Pay (Medical Evidence) Regulations 1985, SI 1985/1604, Sch 1 Pt II (Form of Doctor's Statement).
18 Statutory Sick Pay (Medical Evidence) Regulations 1985, SI 1985/1604, Sch 1 Pt I r 2 (as substituted: see note 16). In relation to a statement given in accordance with the Statutory Sick Pay (Medical Evidence) Regulations 1985, SI 1985/1604, 'signature' means the name by which the person giving that statement is usually known (any name other than the surname being either in full or otherwise indicated) written by that person in his own handwriting; and 'signed' is to be construed accordingly: reg 1(2).

19 Ie where a doctor issues a statement in any case other than in accordance with the Statutory Sick Pay (Medical Evidence) Regulations 1985, SI 1985/1604, Sch 1 Pt I r 2 (see the text and notes 16–18),
20 See note 17.
21 Statutory Sick Pay (Medical Evidence) Regulations 1985, SI 1985/1604, Sch 1 Pt I r 3 (as substituted: see note 16).
22 See the Statutory Sick Pay (Medical Evidence) Regulations 1985, SI 1985/1604, Sch 1 Pt I r 5 (as substituted: see note 16).
23 Statutory Sick Pay (Medical Evidence) Regulations 1985, SI 1985/1604, Sch 1 Pt I r 5(a) (as substituted: see note 16).
24 Statutory Sick Pay (Medical Evidence) Regulations 1985, SI 1985/1604, Sch 1 Pt I r 5(b) (as substituted: see note 16). For these purposes, 'assessment' means either a consultation between a patient and a doctor which takes place in person or by telephone or a consideration by a doctor of a written report by another doctor or other health care professional: see Sch 1 Pt I r 1 (as so substituted). 'Other health care professional' means a person (other than a registered medical practitioner and not being the patient) who is a registered nurse, a registered midwife, an occupational therapist or physiotherapist registered with a regulatory body established by an Order in Council under the Health Act 1999 s 60 (see MEDICAL PROFESSIONS vol 74 (2011) PARA 3), or a member of any profession regulated by a body mentioned in the National Health Service Reform and Health Care Professions Act 2002 s 25(3) (see MEDICAL PROFESSIONS vol 74 (2011) PARA 48): see the Statutory Sick Pay (Medical Evidence) Regulations 1985, SI 1985/1604, Sch 1 Pt I r 1 (as so substituted). As to registered nurses and registered midwifes see MEDICAL PROFESSIONS vol 74 (2011) PARA 691 et seq.
25 For these purposes, 'condition' means a specific disease or bodily or mental disability: see the Statutory Sick Pay (Medical Evidence) Regulations 1985, SI 1985/1604, Sch 1 Pt I r 1 (as substituted: see note 16).
26 Statutory Sick Pay (Medical Evidence) Regulations 1985, SI 1985/1604, Sch 1 Pt I r 5(c) (as substituted: see note 16).
27 Statutory Sick Pay (Medical Evidence) Regulations 1985, SI 1985/1604, Sch 1 Pt I r 5(d) (as substituted: see note 16).
28 Statutory Sick Pay (Medical Evidence) Regulations 1985, SI 1985/1604, Sch 1 Pt I r 5(e) (as substituted: see note 16).
29 Statutory Sick Pay (Medical Evidence) Regulations 1985, SI 1985/1604, Sch 1 Pt I r 5(f) (as substituted: see note 16).
30 Statutory Sick Pay (Medical Evidence) Regulations 1985, SI 1985/1604, Sch 1 Pt I r 5(g) (as substituted: see note 16).
31 See the Statutory Sick Pay (Medical Evidence) Regulations 1985, SI 1985/1604, Sch 1 Pt I r 5 (as substituted: see note 16).
32 Statutory Sick Pay (Medical Evidence) Regulations 1985, SI 1985/1604, Sch 1 Pt I r 4 (as substituted: see note 16).
33 Statutory Sick Pay (Medical Evidence) Regulations 1985, SI 1985/1604, Sch 1 Pt I r 6 (as substituted: see note 16). This provision is subject to Sch 1 Pt I r 8: see Sch 1 Pt I r 6 (as so substituted). Accordingly, the condition may be specified less precisely where, in the doctor's opinion, disclosure of the precise condition would be prejudicial to the patient's well-being, or to the patient's position with their employer: Sch 1 Pt I r 8 (as so substituted).
34 Statutory Sick Pay (Medical Evidence) Regulations 1985, SI 1985/1604, Sch 1 Pt I r 9 (as substituted: see note 16).
35 Statutory Sick Pay (Medical Evidence) Regulations 1985, SI 1985/1604, Sch 1 Pt I r 7 (as substituted: see note 16).
36 Statutory Sick Pay (Medical Evidence) Regulations 1985, SI 1985/1604, Sch 1 Pt I r 10 (as substituted: see note 16).
37 Statutory Sick Pay (Medical Evidence) Regulations 1985, SI 1985/1604, Sch 1 Pt I r 11 (as substituted: see note 16). This provision is subject to Sch 1 Pt I rr 12, 13 (see the text and notes 38–41): see Sch 1 Pt I r 11 (as so substituted).
38 Statutory Sick Pay (Medical Evidence) Regulations 1985, SI 1985/1604, Sch 1 Pt I r 12 (as substituted: see note 16).
39 Statutory Sick Pay (Medical Evidence) Regulations 1985, SI 1985/1604, Sch 1 Pt I r 13(a) (as substituted: see note 16).
40 Statutory Sick Pay (Medical Evidence) Regulations 1985, SI 1985/1604, Sch 1 Pt I r 13(b) (as substituted: see note 16).
41 See the Statutory Sick Pay (Medical Evidence) Regulations 1985, SI 1985/1604, Sch 1 Pt I r 13 (as substituted: see note 16). The text refers to the words 'an indefinite period' being entered on

the form set out at Sch 1 Pt II (Form of Doctor's Statement) (see note 17), after the words 'This will be the case for': see Sch 1 Pt I r 13 (as so substituted).

(v) Limitations on Entitlement etc to Statutory Sick Pay

578. Limitation on entitlement to statutory sick pay. Statutory sick pay[1] is not payable for the first three qualifying days[2] in any period of entitlement[3].

An employee[4] is not entitled, as against any one employer[5], to an aggregate amount of statutory sick pay in respect of any one period of entitlement which exceeds his maximum entitlement[6]. The maximum entitlement as against any one employer is reached on the day on which the amount to which the employee has become entitled by way of statutory sick pay during the period of entitlement in question first reaches or passes the entitlement limit[7].

Where a contract of service[8] (the 'current contract') was preceded by a contract of service entered into between the same employer and employee (the 'previous contract') and the interval between the date on which the previous contract ceased to have effect and that on which the current contract came into force was not more than eight weeks, then, for the purposes of establishing the employee's maximum entitlement to statutory sick pay[9], the statutory sick pay provisions that are set out in Part XI of the Social Security Contributions and Benefits Act 1992[10] do not have effect as if the employer were a different employer in relation to each of those contracts of service[11]. However, where a contract of service (the 'current contract') was preceded by two or more contracts of service entered into between the same employer and employee (the 'previous contracts'), and the previous contracts:

(1) existed concurrently for at least part of their length[12]; and
(2) the interval between the dates on which each of the previous contracts ceased to have effect and that on which the current contract came into force was not more than eight weeks[13],

then, for the purposes of establishing the employee's maximum entitlement to statutory sick pay[14], the provisions relating to statutory sick pay[15] do not have effect as if the employer were a different employer in relation to the current contract and whichever of the previous contracts was the contract by virtue of which the employer had become liable to pay the greatest proportion of statutory sick pay in respect of any tax year or period of entitlement[16].

1 As to the meaning of 'statutory sick pay' see PARA 558.
2 As to the meaning of 'qualifying day' see PARA 575 note 2.
3 Social Security Contributions and Benefits Act 1992 s 155(1). As to the meaning of 'period of entitlement' see PARA 573 note 4.
4 As to the meaning of 'employee' for these purposes see PARA 562.
5 As to the meaning of 'employer' for these purposes see PARA 571.
6 Social Security Contributions and Benefits Act 1992 s 155(2).
7 Social Security Contributions and Benefits Act 1992 s 155(3). As to the calculation of the entitlement limit see PARA 579.
8 As to the meaning of 'contract of service' for these purposes see PARA 558 note 2.
9 Ie within the meaning of the Social Security Contributions and Benefits Act 1992 s 155: see the text and notes 1–7.
10 Ie the Social Security Contributions and Benefits Act 1992 Pt XI (ss 151–163) (statutory sick pay: see also PARAS 558 et seq, 579 et seq).
11 Statutory Sick Pay (General) Regulations 1982, SI 1982/894, reg 20(3) (reg 20(3) amended, reg 20(4), (5) added, by SI 1983/376); and see the Interpretation Act 1978 s 17(2)(a).
12 Statutory Sick Pay (General) Regulations 1982, SI 1982/894, reg 20(4)(a) (as added: see note 11).
13 Statutory Sick Pay (General) Regulations 1982, SI 1982/894, reg 20(4)(b) (as added: see note 11).

14 See note 9.
15 See note 10.
16 See the Statutory Sick Pay (General) Regulations 1982, SI 1982/894, reg 20(4) (as added: see note 11); and see the Interpretation Act 1978 s 17(2)(a). If, in any case to which the Statutory Sick Pay (General) Regulations 1982, SI 1982/894, reg 20(4) applies, the same proportion of the employer's liability for statutory sick pay becomes due under each of the previous contracts, then, for the purpose of establishing the employee's maximum entitlement within the meaning of the Social Security Contributions and Benefits Act 1992 s 155 (see the text and notes 1–7), the provisions of Pt XI (statutory sick pay: see also PARAS 558 et seq, 579 et seq) have effect in relation to only one of the previous contracts: Statutory Sick Pay (General) Regulations 1982, SI 1982/894, reg 20(5) (as so added); and see the Interpretation Act 1978 s 17(2)(a).

579. Calculation of entitlement limit to statutory sick pay. The entitlement limit to statutory sick pay[1] is an amount equal to 28 times the applicable weekly rate[2]. However, regulations[3] may make provision for calculating the entitlement limit in any case where an employee's[4] entitlement to statutory sick pay is calculated by reference to different weekly rates in the same period of entitlement[5]. Accordingly, where an employee's entitlement to statutory sick pay is calculated by reference to different weekly rates in the same period of entitlement, the entitlement limit must be calculated in the prescribed manner[6]. For the purpose of determining whether an employee has reached his maximum entitlement[7] to statutory sick pay in respect of a period of entitlement, there must be calculated[8]:

(1) the amount of statutory sick pay to which the employee became entitled during the part of the period of entitlement[9] before the change in the weekly rate[10];
(2) the number by which the weekly rate, before the change, must be multiplied in order to produce the amount mentioned in head (1) above[11];
(3) the amount of statutory sick pay to which the employee has so far become entitled during the part of the period of entitlement after the change in the weekly rate[12]; and
(4) the number by which the weekly rate, after the change, must be multiplied in order to produce the amount mentioned in head (3) above[13];
(5) the sum of the amounts mentioned in heads (1) and (3) above[14]; and
(6) the sum of the numbers mentioned in heads (2) and (4) above[15].

When the sum mentioned in head (6) above reaches 28, the sum mentioned in head (5) above reaches the entitlement limit[16].

1 As to the meaning of 'statutory sick pay' see PARA 558.
2 Social Security Contributions and Benefits Act 1992 s 155(4) (amended by the Social Security (Incapacity for Work) Act 1994 s 8(4)). The weekly rate mentioned in the text is applicable in accordance with the Social Security Contributions and Benefits Act 1992 s 157: see PARA 581.
3 As to the making of regulations under the Social Security Contributions and Benefits Act 1992 see PARA 407 note 3.
4 As to the meaning of 'employee' for these purposes see PARA 562.
5 Social Security Contributions and Benefits Act 1992 s 155(5). At the date at which this volume states the law, no such regulations had been made but, by virtue of the Interpretation Act 1978 s 17(2)(b), the Statutory Sick Pay (General) Regulations 1982, SI 1982/894 (see the text and notes 6–16) have effect as if so made.
6 Statutory Sick Pay (General) Regulations 1982, SI 1982/894, reg 6(1) (reg 6(1), (3) amended by SI 1986/477). The text refers to the manner described in the Statutory Sick Pay (General) Regulations 1982, SI 1982/894, reg 6(2), (3): see the text and notes 7–16.
7 As to the maximum entitlement see PARA 578.
8 See the Statutory Sick Pay (General) Regulations 1982, SI 1982/894, reg 6(2).
9 As to the meaning of 'period of entitlement' see PARA 573 note 4.

10 Statutory Sick Pay (General) Regulations 1982, SI 1982/894, reg 6(2)(a).
11 Statutory Sick Pay (General) Regulations 1982, SI 1982/894, reg 6(2)(b). Where a number referred to in reg 6(2)(b) is not a whole number of thousandths, it must be rounded up to the next thousandth: see reg 6(1) (amended by SI 1984/385).
12 Statutory Sick Pay (General) Regulations 1982, SI 1982/894, reg 6(2)(c).
13 Statutory Sick Pay (General) Regulations 1982, SI 1982/894, reg 6(2)(d). Where a number referred to in reg 6(2)(d) is not a whole number of thousandths, it must be rounded up to the next thousandth: see reg 6(1) (as amended: see note 11).
14 Statutory Sick Pay (General) Regulations 1982, SI 1982/894, reg 6(2)(e).
15 Statutory Sick Pay (General) Regulations 1982, SI 1982/894, reg 6(2)(f).
16 Statutory Sick Pay (General) Regulations 1982, SI 1982/894, reg 6(3) (as amended: see note 6).

580. Where a period of entitlement to statutory sick pay ends or does not arise. In a case where:

(1) a mariner[1];
(2) an airman[2]; or
(3) a continental shelf employee[3]; or
(4) a person who is an employee or is treated as an employee for these purposes[4],

is incapable of work during a period of entitlement[5] to statutory sick pay[6] while absent from Great Britain[7], his entitlement to statutory sick pay ceases only if he fails to satisfy the conditions of entitlement[8], notwithstanding that his employer[9] ceases, during the period of entitlement, to be liable to pay[10], in respect of him, secondary Class 1 contributions[11].

In a case where an employee is detained in legal custody or sentenced to a term of imprisonment (except where the sentence is suspended) on a day which, in relation to him, falls within a period of entitlement, that period ends with that day[12]. A period of entitlement does not arise in relation to a period of incapacity for work[13] where at any time on the first day of that period of incapacity for work the employee in question is in legal custody or sentenced to or undergoing a term of imprisonment (except where the sentence is suspended)[14].

Where a period of entitlement is current as between an employee and her employer[15], and the employee:

(a) is pregnant or has been confined[16]; and
(b) is incapable of work wholly or partly because of pregnancy or confinement on any day which falls on or after the beginning of the fourth week before the expected week of confinement[17]; and
(c) is not by virtue of that pregnancy or confinement entitled[18] to statutory maternity pay or to maternity allowance[19],

the period of entitlement ends on that day, or, if earlier, on the day the employee was confined[20].

Where an employee:

(i) is pregnant or has been confined[21]; and
(ii) is incapable of work wholly or partly because of pregnancy or confinement on any day which falls on or after the beginning of the fourth week before the expected week of confinement[22]; and
(iii) is not by virtue of that pregnancy or confinement entitled[23] to statutory maternity pay or to maternity allowance[24],

a period of entitlement as between the employee and her employer does not arise in relation to a period of incapacity for work where the first day in that period falls within 18 weeks of the beginning of the week containing the day referred to in head (ii) above or, if earlier, of the week in which the employee was confined[25].

A period of entitlement in respect of an employee who was entitled to incapacity benefit[26], maternity allowance or severe disablement allowance[27] does not arise in relation to any day within a period of incapacity for work beginning with the first day on which the exclusion from statutory sick pay on the basis of entitlement to incapacity benefit[28] ceases to have effect, where the employee is a person to whom the welfare to work beneficiaries provisions[29] apply[30].

A period of entitlement in respect of an employee who was entitled to employment and support allowance[31] does not arise in relation to any day within a period of limited capability for work beginning with the first day on which the exclusion from statutory sick pay on the basis of entitlement to such an allowance[32] ceases to have effect where the employee in question is a person to whom the work and training beneficiaries provisions[33] apply[34].

A period of entitlement as between an employee and employer ends after three years if it has not otherwise ended[35] in accordance with the Social Security Contributions and Benefits Act 1992[36].

1 Ie within the meaning of the Statutory Sick Pay (Mariners, Airmen and Persons Abroad) Regulations 1982, SI 1982/1349, reg 6(1): see PARA 566.
2 Ie within the meaning of the Statutory Sick Pay (Mariners, Airmen and Persons Abroad) Regulations 1982, SI 1982/1349, reg 7: see PARA 567.
3 Ie a person employed in operations on the continental shelf within the meaning of the Statutory Sick Pay (Mariners, Airmen and Persons Abroad) Regulations 1982, SI 1982/1349, reg 8: see PARA 568.
4 Ie under the Statutory Sick Pay (Mariners, Airmen and Persons Abroad) Regulations 1982, SI 1982/1349, reg 5 (see PARA 565) or reg 5A (see PARA 565). As to the meaning of 'employee' for these purposes see PARA 562.
5 As to the meaning of 'period of entitlement' see PARA 573 note 4.
6 As to the meaning of 'statutory sick pay' see PARA 558.
7 As to the meaning of 'Great Britain' for these purposes see PARA 407 note 7.
8 Ie the Social Security Contributions and Benefits Act 1992 Pt XI (ss 151–163) (statutory sick pay: see also PARAS 558 et seq, 581 et seq). As to the conditions of entitlement see PARA 572 et seq.
9 As to the meaning of 'employer' for these purposes see PARA 571.
10 Ie under the Social Security Contributions and Benefits Act 1992 s 6 (see **WELFARE BENEFITS AND STATE PENSIONS** vol 104 (2014) PARA 385) or the Social Security (Contributions) Regulations 2001, SI 2001/1004, reg 146 (payment of contributions for periods abroad: see **WELFARE BENEFITS AND STATE PENSIONS** vol 104 (2014) PARA 380).
11 Statutory Sick Pay (Mariners, Airmen and Persons Abroad) Regulations 1982, SI 1982/1349, reg 10 (substituted by SI 1996/777); and see the Interpretation Act 1978 s 17(2)(a).
12 Statutory Sick Pay (General) Regulations 1982, SI 1982/894, reg 3(1).
13 As to the meaning of 'period of incapacity for work' see PARA 572 note 2.
14 Statutory Sick Pay (General) Regulations 1982, SI 1982/894, reg 3(2).
15 See the Statutory Sick Pay (General) Regulations 1982, SI 1982/894, reg 3(4) (reg 3(4), (5) added by SI 1987/868; and substituted by SI 1994/1367).
16 Statutory Sick Pay (General) Regulations 1982, SI 1982/894, reg 3(4)(a) (as added and substituted: see note 15). For these purposes, 'confinement' and 'confined' have the same meaning as in the Social Security Contributions and Benefits Act 1992 s 171(1) (see PARA 415 note 6): see the Statutory Sick Pay (General) Regulations 1982, SI 1982/894, reg 3(6) (added by SI 1987/868; and amended by SI 1994/1367).
17 Statutory Sick Pay (General) Regulations 1982, SI 1982/894, reg 3(4)(b) (reg 3(4) as added and substituted (see note 15); reg 3(4)(b) amended by SI 2002/2690).
18 Ie under the Social Security Contributions and Benefits Act 1992 Pt XII (ss 164–171) (statutory maternity pay: see PARA 401 et seq) or under s 35 (maternity allowance: see **WELFARE BENEFITS AND STATE PENSIONS** vol 104 (2014) PARA 474).
19 Statutory Sick Pay (General) Regulations 1982, SI 1982/894, reg 3(4)(c) (as added and substituted: see note 15).
20 See the Statutory Sick Pay (General) Regulations 1982, SI 1982/894, reg 3(4) (as added and substituted: see note 15).
21 Statutory Sick Pay (General) Regulations 1982, SI 1982/894, reg 3(5)(a) (as added and substituted: see note 15).

22 Statutory Sick Pay (General) Regulations 1982, SI 1982/894, reg 3(5)(b) (reg 3(5) as added and substituted (see note 15); reg 3(5)(b) amended by SI 2002/2690).
23 Ie under the Social Security Contributions and Benefits Act 1992 Pt XII (statutory maternity pay: see PARA 401 et seq) or under s 35 (maternity allowance: see **WELFARE BENEFITS AND STATE PENSIONS** vol 104 (2014) PARA 474).
24 Statutory Sick Pay (General) Regulations 1982, SI 1982/894, reg 3(5)(c) (as added and substituted: see note 15).
25 See the Statutory Sick Pay (General) Regulations 1982, SI 1982/894, reg 3(5) (as added and substituted: see note 15).
26 As to incapacity benefit see **WELFARE BENEFITS AND STATE PENSIONS** vol 104 (2014) PARA 472 et seq.
27 As to severe disablement allowance see **WELFARE BENEFITS AND STATE PENSIONS** vol 104 (2014) PARA 121 et seq.
28 Ie the Social Security Contributions and Benefits Act 1992 Sch 11 para 2(d): see PARA 574.
29 Ie the Social Security (Incapacity for Work) (General) Regulations 1995, SI 1995/311, reg 13A: see **WELFARE BENEFITS AND STATE PENSIONS** vol 104 (2014) PARA 515.
30 Statutory Sick Pay (General) Regulations 1982, SI 1982/894, reg 3(2A) (reg 3(2A) added by SI 1998/2231). The Statutory Sick Pay (General) Regulations 1982, SI 1982/894, reg 3(2A) does not apply, in the case of an employee who was entitled to incapacity benefit, where the Social Security Contributions and Benefits Act 1992 Sch 11 para 2(d)(i) (see PARA 574) ceases to have effect by virtue of Sch 11 para 5A (see PARA 574 note 11): Statutory Sick Pay (General) Regulations 1982, SI 1982/894, reg 3(2B) (added by SI 2007/825).
31 As to employment and support allowance see **WELFARE BENEFITS AND STATE PENSIONS** vol 104 (2014) PARA 252.
32 Ie the Social Security Contributions and Benefits Act 1992 Sch 11 para 2(dd): see PARA 574.
33 Ie the Employment and Support Allowance Regulations 2008, SI 2008/794, reg 148: see **WELFARE BENEFITS AND STATE PENSIONS** vol 104 (2014) PARA 443.
34 Statutory Sick Pay (General) Regulations 1982, SI 1982/894, reg 3(2C) (added by SI 2008/1554).
35 Ie if it has not otherwise ended in accordance with the Social Security Contributions and Benefits Act 1992 s 153(2) (see PARA 573) or with regulations, other than the Statutory Sick Pay (General) Regulations 1982, SI 1982/894, reg 3(3), made under the Social Security Contributions and Benefits Act 1992 s 153(6) (see PARA 573 note 6).
36 Statutory Sick Pay (General) Regulations 1982, SI 1982/894, reg 3(3) (added by SI 1986/477; and amended by SI 1994/1367).

(vi) Payment

581. Rates of payment for statutory sick pay. Statutory sick pay[1] is payable by an employer[2] at a weekly rate[3].

The amount of statutory sick pay payable by any one employer in respect of any day is the weekly rate applicable on that day divided by the number of days which are, in the week[4] (beginning with Sunday) in which that day falls, qualifying days[5] as between that employer and the employee[6] concerned[7].

Where two or more employers are treated as one[8], liability for the statutory sick pay payable by them to the employee must be apportioned between them in such proportions as they may agree or, in default of agreement, in the proportions which the employee's earnings[9] from each employment bear to the amount of the aggregated earnings[10].

Statutory sick pay may not be paid in kind or by way of the provision of board or lodging or of services or other facilities[11].

1 As to the meaning of 'statutory sick pay' see PARA 558.
2 As to the meaning of 'employer' for these purposes see PARA 571.
3 Social Security Contributions and Benefits Act 1992 s 157(1) (amended by SI 2014/147). At the date at which this volume states the law, the weekly rate is £87.55: see the Social Security Contributions and Benefits Act 1992 s 157(1) (as so amended). The Secretary of State may by order:

(1) amend s 157(1) so as to substitute different provisions as to the weekly rate or rates of statutory sick pay (s 157(2)(a) (substituted by the Social Security (Incapacity for Work) Act 1994 s 8(1), (3))); and
(2) make such consequential amendments of any provision contained in the Social Security Contributions and Benefits Act 1992 Pt XI (ss 151–163) (statutory sick pay: see also PARAS 558 et seq, 582 et seq) as appear to him to be required (s 157(2)(b)).

A statutory instrument containing, whether alone or with other provisions, an order made by virtue of s 157(2), must not be made unless a draft of the instrument has been laid before Parliament and been approved by a resolution of each House: see s 176(1)(c) (amended by the Statutory Sick Pay Act 1994 s 3(2); the Social Security (Incapacity for Work) Act 1994 s 11, Sch 1 para 37, Sch 2; the Welfare Reform and Pensions Act 1999 s 70, Sch 8 Pt VI paras 30, 32; the Pensions Act 2007 s 12(4), Sch 1 Pt 7 para 35(a); the Welfare Reform Act 2007 s 31(2)(b); the National Insurance Contributions Act 2008 s 4(2), Sch 2; and SI 1995/512). As to the making of orders and regulations under the Social Security Contributions and Benefits Act 1992 generally see PARA 407 note 3. As to the Secretary of State see PARA 5 note 21.

4 As to the meaning of 'week' for these purposes see PARA 572 note 2.
5 As to the meaning of 'qualifying day' see PARA 575 note 2.
6 As to the meaning of 'employee' for these purposes see PARA 562.
7 Social Security Contributions and Benefits Act 1992 s 157(3).
Where any payment of statutory sick pay is made and the statutory sick pay due for the period for which the payment purports to be made includes a fraction of a penny, the payment must be rounded up to the next whole number of pence: Statutory Sick Pay (General) Regulations 1982, SI 1982/894, reg 11.
8 Ie under the Statutory Sick Pay (General) Regulations 1982, SI 1982/894, reg 20(1): see PARA 571.
9 As to the meaning of 'earnings' for these purposes see PARA 583.
10 Statutory Sick Pay (General) Regulations 1982, SI 1982/894, reg 20(2).
11 Statutory Sick Pay (General) Regulations 1982, SI 1982/894, reg 8.

582. Calculation of normal weekly earnings for purposes of statutory sick pay. For the purposes of the statutory sick pay provisions that are set out in Part XI of the Social Security Contributions and Benefits Act 1992[1], an employee's[2] normal weekly earnings[3] must be taken to be the average weekly earnings which in the relevant period[4] have been paid to him or paid for his benefit under his contract of service with the employer in question[5]. However, in such cases as may be prescribed[6], an employee's normal weekly earnings are to be calculated in accordance with regulations[7]. Accordingly, in a case where an employee has normal pay days at intervals of, or approximating to, one or more calendar months, including intervals of, or approximating to, a year, his normal weekly earnings are to be calculated by dividing his earnings in the relevant period by the number of calendar months in that period or, if it is not a whole number, the nearest whole number, multiplying the result by 12 and dividing by 52[8]. In a case where a person does not have normal pay days in this way[9], and where the relevant period is not an exact number of weeks, the employee's normal weekly earnings are to be calculated by dividing his earnings in the relevant period by the number of days in the relevant period and multiplying the result by seven[10].

1 Ie in the Social Security Contributions and Benefits Act 1992 Pt XI (ss 151–163) (statutory sick pay: see also PARAS 558 et seq, 586 et seq). As to the meaning of 'statutory sick pay' see PARA 558.
2 As to the meaning of 'employee' for these purposes see PARA 562.
3 For these purposes, 'earnings' has the meaning given to it by regulations: see the Social Security Contributions and Benefits Act 1992 s 163(3). As to the making of regulations under the Social Security Contributions and Benefits Act 1992 see PARA 407 note 3. At the date at which this volume states the law, no such regulations had been made but, by virtue of the Interpretation Act 1978 s 17(2)(b), the Statutory Sick Pay (General) Regulations 1982, SI 1982/894 (see PARA 583) have effect as if so made.

4 For these purposes, 'relevant period' has the meaning given to it by regulations (see note 3): see the Social Security Contributions and Benefits Act 1992 s 163(3). Accordingly, the relevant period for these purposes is the period between: (1) the last normal pay day to fall before the critical date; and (2) the last normal pay day to fall at least eight weeks earlier than the normal pay day mentioned in head (1) above, including the normal pay day mentioned in head (1) above, but excluding that first mentioned in head (2) above: see the Statutory Sick Pay (General) Regulations 1982, SI 1982/894, reg 19(1), (3); and see the Interpretation Act 1978 s 17(2)(a). 'Critical date' means the first day of the period of entitlement in relation to which a person's normal weekly earnings fall to be determined or, in a case to which the Social Security Contributions and Benefits Act 1992 Sch 11 para 2(c) (see PARA 574) applies, the relevant date within the meaning of Sch 11 (see PARA 574 note 5); and 'normal pay day' means a day on which the terms of an employee's contract of service require him to be paid, or the practice in his employment is for him to be paid, if any payment is due to him: see the Statutory Sick Pay (General) Regulations 1982, SI 1982/894, reg 19(1), (2); and see the Interpretation Act 1978 s 17(2)(a). As to the meaning of 'contract of service' for these purposes see PARA 558 note 2.

In a case, however, where an employee has no identifiable normal pay day, the Statutory Sick Pay (General) Regulations 1982, SI 1982/894, reg 19(3) has effect as if the words 'day of payment' were substituted for the words 'normal pay day' in each place where they occur: see reg 19(1), (4); and see the Interpretation Act 1978 s 17(2)(a). For these purposes, 'day of payment' means a day on which the employee was paid: see the Statutory Sick Pay (General) Regulations 1982, SI 1982/894, reg 19(1), (2); and see the Interpretation Act 1978 s 17(2)(a). In a case where the normal pay day mentioned in head (1) above exists but that first mentioned in head (2) above does not yet exist, the employee's normal weekly earnings are to be calculated as if the period for which all the earnings under his contract of service received by him before the critical date represented payment were the relevant period: see the Statutory Sick Pay (General) Regulations 1982, SI 1982/894, reg 19(1), (7); and see the Interpretation Act 1978 s 17(2)(a). In a case where neither of the normal pay days mentioned in the Statutory Sick Pay (General) Regulations 1982, SI 1982/894, reg 19(3) yet exists, the employee's normal weekly earnings are the remuneration to which he is entitled, in accordance with the terms of his contract of service, for, as the case may be: (a) a week's work; or (b) a number of calendar months' work, divided by that number of months, multiplied by 12 and divided by 52: see reg 19(1), (8); and see the Interpretation Act 1978 s 17(2)(a).

5 Social Security Contributions and Benefits Act 1992 s 163(2). As to the meaning of 'employer' for these purposes see PARA 571.

6 For these purposes, 'prescribed' means prescribed by regulations (see note 3): see the Social Security Contributions and Benefits Act 1992 s 163(1).

7 Social Security Contributions and Benefits Act 1992 s 163(4).

8 Statutory Sick Pay (General) Regulations 1982, SI 1982/894, reg 19(1), (5); and see the Interpretation Act 1978 s 17(2)(a).

9 Ie where the Statutory Sick Pay (General) Regulations 1982, SI 1982/894, reg 19(5) does not apply: see the text and note 8.

10 Statutory Sick Pay (General) Regulations 1982, SI 1982/894, reg 19(1), (6); and see the Interpretation Act 1978 s 17(2)(a).

583. Meaning of 'earnings' for purposes of statutory sick pay. For the purposes of calculating normal weekly earnings in relation to statutory sick pay[1], the expression 'earnings' refers to gross earnings and includes any remuneration or profit derived from a person's employment, except any payment or amount which is[2]:

(1) excluded or disregarded in the calculation of a person's earnings[3] (or would have been so excluded had he not been under the age of 16)[4];

(2) a chargeable emolument[5], except where, in consequence of such a chargeable emolument being excluded from earnings, a person would not be entitled to statutory sick pay (or where such payment or amount would have been so excluded and in consequence he would not have been entitled to statutory sick pay had he not been under the age of 16)[6].

For these purposes[7], the expression 'earnings' also includes[8]:

(a) any amount retrospectively treated[9] as earnings by regulations made by virtue of the Social Security Contributions and Benefits Act 1992[10];
(b) any sum payable by way of maternity pay or payable by the Commissioners for Revenue and Customs[11] in respect of maternity pay[12];
(c) any sum which is payable by the Secretary of State[13] in respect of arrears of pay and which is[14] to go towards discharging a liability to pay maternity pay[15];
(d) any sum payable in respect of arrears of pay in pursuance of an order[16] for reinstatement or re-engagement[17];
(e) any sum payable by way of pay in pursuance of an order[18] for the continuation of a contract of employment[19];
(f) any sum payable[20] by way of remuneration in pursuance of a protective award[21];
(g) any sum payable[22] to an employee under the Temporary Short-time Working Compensation Scheme[23];
(h) any sum paid in satisfaction of any entitlement to statutory sick pay[24];
(i) any sum payable[25] by way of statutory maternity pay[26];
(j) any sum payable[27] by way of statutory paternity pay[28]; and
(k) any sum payable[29] by way of statutory adoption pay[30].

1 Ie for the purposes of the Social Security Contributions and Benefits Act 1992 s 163(2): see PARA 582. As to the meaning of 'statutory sick pay' see PARA 558.
2 See the Statutory Sick Pay (General) Regulations 1982, SI 1982/894, reg 17(2) (substituted by SI 1999/567).
3 Ie under the Social Security (Contributions) Regulations 2001, SI 2001/1004, regs 25, 27, 123 or Sch 3 (payments to be disregarded and payments to directors to be disregarded: see WELFARE BENEFITS AND STATE PENSIONS vol 104 (2014) PARA 382).
4 Statutory Sick Pay (General) Regulations 1982, SI 1982/894, reg 17(2)(a) (reg 17(2) as substituted (see note 2); reg 17(2)(a) amended by SI 2006/1031; SI 2007/1154).
5 Ie under the Social Security Contributions and Benefits Act 1992 s 10A (class 1B contributions: see WELFARE BENEFITS AND STATE PENSIONS vol 104 (2014) PARA 392).
6 Statutory Sick Pay (General) Regulations 1982, SI 1982/894, reg 17(2)(b) (reg 17(2) as substituted (see note 2); reg 17(2)(b) amended by SI 2006/1031).
7 See note 1.
8 See the Statutory Sick Pay (General) Regulations 1982, SI 1982/894, reg 17(3) (amended by SI 2002/2690).
9 Ie by regulations made by virtue of the Social Security Contributions and Benefits Act 1992 s 4B(2): see WELFARE BENEFITS AND STATE PENSIONS vol 104 (2014) PARA 383.
10 Statutory Sick Pay (General) Regulations 1982, SI 1982/894, reg 17(3)(za) (added by SI 2007/1154).
11 Ie in pursuance of the Social Security Contributions and Benefits Act 1992 Pt XII (ss 164–171): see PARA 403. As to the Commissioners for Her Majesty's Revenue and Customs see INCOME TAXATION vol 58 (2014) PARAS 33–34.
12 Statutory Sick Pay (General) Regulations 1982, SI 1982/894, reg 17(3)(a); and see the Interpretation Act 1978 s 17(2)(a).
13 Ie by virtue of the Employment Rights Act 1996 s 184(1)(a): see PARA 628. As to the Secretary of State see PARA 5 note 21.
14 Ie by virtue of the Employment Rights Act 1996 s 82(1) (repealed).
15 Statutory Sick Pay (General) Regulations 1982, SI 1982/894, reg 17(3)(b); and see the Interpretation Act 1978 s 17(2)(a).
16 Ie an order for reinstatement or re-engagement under the Employment Rights Act 1996: see PARA 811.
17 Statutory Sick Pay (General) Regulations 1982, SI 1982/894, reg 17(3)(c); and see the Interpretation Act 1978 s 17(2)(a).
18 Ie under the Employment Rights Act 1996: see PARA 807.
19 Statutory Sick Pay (General) Regulations 1982, SI 1982/894, reg 17(3)(d); and see the Interpretation Act 1978 s 17(2)(a).

20 Ie under the Trade Union and Labour Relations (Consolidation) Act 1992 s 189: see PARA 1189.
21 Statutory Sick Pay (General) Regulations 1982, SI 1982/894, reg 17(3)(e); and see the Interpretation Act 1978 s 17(2)(a).
22 Ie under the scheme administered under powers conferred by the Employment Subsidies Act 1978 (repealed).
23 Statutory Sick Pay (General) Regulations 1982, SI 1982/894, reg 17(3)(f).
24 Statutory Sick Pay (General) Regulations 1982, SI 1982/894, reg 17(3)(g). As to payments of statutory sick pay see PARA 581 et seq.
25 Ie under the Social Security Contributions and Benefits Act 1992 Pt XII (see PARA 401 et seq), including sums payable in accordance with regulations under s 164(9)(b): see PARA 402.
26 Statutory Sick Pay (General) Regulations 1982, SI 1982/894, reg 17(3)(h) (added by SI 1987/868); and see the Interpretation Act 1978 s 17(2)(a). As to statutory maternity pay see PARA 401 et seq.
27 Ie including any sums payable in accordance with regulations under the Social Security Contributions and Benefits Act 1992 s 171ZD(3): see PARA 444.
28 Statutory Sick Pay (General) Regulations 1982, SI 1982/894, reg 17(3)(i) (reg 17(3)(i), (j) added by SI 2002/2690). As to statutory paternity pay see PARA 443 et seq.
29 Ie including any sums payable in accordance with regulations under the Social Security Contributions and Benefits Act 1992 s 171ZM(3): see PARA 489.
30 Statutory Sick Pay (General) Regulations 1982, SI 1982/894, reg 17(3)(j) (as added: see note 28). As to statutory adoption pay see PARA 488 et seq.

584. Time limits for paying statutory sick pay; payment by employer. In any case where:

(1) a decision has been made by an adjudication officer[1], Social Security Appeal Tribunal[2] or commissioner[3] in proceedings[4] that an employee[5] is entitled to an amount of statutory sick pay[6]; and
(2) the time for bringing an appeal[7] against the decision has expired[8], and either: (a) no such appeal has been brought[9]; or (b) such an appeal has been brought and has been finally disposed of[10],

that amount of statutory sick pay must be paid within the time specified[11] as follows[12].

The employer[13] is required to pay the amount not later than the first pay day[14] after[15]:

(i) where an appeal has been brought, the day on which the employer receives notification that it has been finally disposed of[16];
(ii) where leave to appeal has been refused and there remains no further opportunity to apply for leave, the day on which the employer receives notification of the refusal[17]; and
(iii) in any other case, the day on which the time for bringing an appeal expires[18].

Where it is impracticable, in view of the employer's methods of accounting for and paying remuneration, for the requirement of payment to be met by that pay day, it must be met not later than the next following pay day[19].

1 As to adjudication officers see WELFARE BENEFITS AND STATE PENSIONS vol 104 (2014) PARA 575.
2 As to Social Security Appeal Tribunals see WELFARE BENEFITS AND STATE PENSIONS vol 104 (2014) PARA 575.
3 As to social security commissioners see WELFARE BENEFITS AND STATE PENSIONS vol 104 (2014) PARA 559.
4 Ie under the Social Security Contributions and Benefits Act 1992 Pt XII (ss 164–171): see PARA 595.
5 As to the meaning of 'employee' for these purposes see PARA 562.
6 Statutory Sick Pay (General) Regulations 1982, SI 1982/894, reg 9(2)(a) (amended by virtue of the Health and Social Services and Social Security Adjudications Act 1983 Sch 8 Pt I para 1(1), (3)(a)); and see the Interpretation Act 1978 s 17(2)(a). As to the meaning of 'statutory sick pay' see PARA 558.

7 As to the right to apply for the determination of any issue arising as to, or in connection with, entitlement to statutory sick pay see PARA 595.
8 See the Statutory Sick Pay (General) Regulations 1982, SI 1982/894, reg 9(2)(b).
9 See the Statutory Sick Pay (General) Regulations 1982, SI 1982/894, reg 9(2)(b)(i).
10 See the Statutory Sick Pay (General) Regulations 1982, SI 1982/894, reg 9(2)(b)(ii).
11 Ie the time specified in the Statutory Sick Pay (General) Regulations 1982, SI 1982/894, reg 9(3) (see the text and notes 13–18).
12 See the Statutory Sick Pay (General) Regulations 1982, SI 1982/894, reg 9(2).
13 As to the meaning of 'employer' for these purposes see PARA 571.
14 For these purposes, 'pay day' means a day on which it has been agreed, or it is the normal practice, between an employer and an employee of his, that payments by way of remuneration are to be made, or, where there is no such agreement or normal practice, the last day of a calendar month: Statutory Sick Pay (General) Regulations 1982, SI 1982/894, reg 9(1).
15 See the Statutory Sick Pay (General) Regulations 1982, SI 1982/894, reg 9(3). This provision is subject to reg 9(4), (5) (see the text and note 19): see reg 9(3).
16 Statutory Sick Pay (General) Regulations 1982, SI 1982/894, reg 9(3)(a).
17 Statutory Sick Pay (General) Regulations 1982, SI 1982/894, reg 9(3)(b).
18 Statutory Sick Pay (General) Regulations 1982, SI 1982/894, reg 9(3)(c).
19 Statutory Sick Pay (General) Regulations 1982, SI 1982/894, reg 9(4). However, where the employer would not have remunerated the employee for his work on the day of incapacity for work in question (if it had not been a day of incapacity for work) as early as the pay day specified in reg 9(3) (see the text and notes 13–18), or, if it applies, reg 9(4), the requirement of payment must be met on the first day on which the employee would have been remunerated for his work on that day: reg 9(5). As to the time for compliance where an employee is outside the United Kingdom see PARA 564. As to the penalties imposed for a failure to produce any document or record or to provide any information and for the fraudulent or negligent production or provision of any document or record or information and for any incorrect statement or declaration fraudulently or negligently made in connection with establishing entitlement to statutory sick pay see the Social Security Administration Act 1992 ss 113A–113B; and WELFARE BENEFITS AND STATE PENSIONS vol 104 (2014) PARAS 582, 583.

585. Time limits for paying statutory sick pay; payment by the Commissioners for Revenue and Customs. Where the Commissioners for Revenue and Customs[1] become liable[2] to make payments of statutory sick pay[3] to a person, the first payment must be made as soon as reasonably practicable after they become so liable; and payments thereafter must be made at weekly intervals, by means of an instrument of payment, instrument for benefit payment, or by such other means as appears to the Commissioners to be appropriate in the circumstances of the particular case[4].

1 As to the Commissioners for Her Majesty's Revenue and Customs see INCOME TAXATION vol 58 (2014) PARAS 33–34.
2 Ie in accordance with the Statutory Sick Pay (General) Regulations 1982, SI 1982/894, reg 9A or reg 9B: see PARA 559.
3 As to the meaning of 'statutory sick pay' see PARA 558.
4 Statutory Sick Pay (General) Regulations 1982, SI 1982/894, reg 9C (added by SI 1987/372; amended by the Social Security Contributions (Transfer of Functions, etc) Act 1999 Sch 2; and by SI 1996/672).

586. Payments treated as remuneration for purposes of statutory sick pay; relationship with other payments. Any sum paid to, or for the benefit of, a person in satisfaction, whether in whole or in part, of any entitlement of that person to statutory sick pay[1] is to be treated[2] as remuneration derived from an employed earner's[3] employment[4].

Any entitlement to statutory sick pay does not affect any right of an employee[5] in relation to remuneration under any contract of service[6] ('contractual remuneration')[7]; any contractual remuneration paid to an employee by an employer[8] in respect of a day of incapacity for work[9] goes towards discharging any liability of that employer to pay statutory sick pay to that

(2) where a period of entitlement has come to an end but the period of incapacity for work which was running immediately before the period of entitlement came to an end continues (s 130(3)(b)); and
(3) where a period of entitlement has not come to an end but, on the assumption that: (a) the period of incapacity for work in question continues to run for a prescribed period (s 130(3)(c)(i)); and (b) there is no material change in circumstances (s 130(3)(c)(ii)), the period of entitlement will have ended on or before the end of the prescribed period (s 130(3)(c)).

As to the meaning of 'period of incapacity for work' see PARA 572 note 2. For the purposes of head (3)(a) above, the prescribed period is 14 days: Statutory Sick Pay (General) Regulations 1982, SI 1982/894, reg 15(5); and see the Interpretation Act 1978 s 17(2)(a).

15 Social Security Administration Act 1992 s 130(1)(za) (added by the Welfare Reform Act 2012 s 31, Sch 2 paras 3, 20). As to universal credit see WELFARE BENEFITS AND STATE PENSIONS vol 104 (2014) PARA 124 et seq.

16 Social Security Administration Act 1992 s 130(1)(a) (s 130(1)(a), (c) substituted by the Social Security (Incapacity for Work) Act 1994 s 11(1), Sch 1 para 49). As to short-term incapacity benefit see WELFARE BENEFITS AND STATE PENSIONS vol 104 (2014) PARA 472 et seq. As from a day to be appointed under the Welfare Reform Act 2007 s 70(2), the Social Security Administration Act 1992 s 130(1)(a) is repealed by the Welfare Reform Act 2007 s 67, Sch 8. At the date at which this volume states the law, no such day had been appointed.

17 Social Security Administration Act 1992 s 130(1)(b). As to maternity allowance see WELFARE BENEFITS AND STATE PENSIONS vol 104 (2014) PARA 473 et seq.

18 Social Security Administration Act 1992 s 130(1)(c) (as substituted: see note 16). As to long-term incapacity benefit see WELFARE BENEFITS AND STATE PENSIONS vol 104 (2014) PARA 472 et seq. As from a day to be appointed under the Welfare Reform Act 2007 s 70(2), the Social Security Administration Act 1992 s 130(1)(c) is repealed by the Welfare Reform Act 2007 s 67, Sch 8. At the date at which this volume states the law, no such day had been appointed.

19 Social Security Administration Act 1992 s 130(1)(d) (amended by the Welfare Reform and Pensions Act 1999 Sch 13 Pt IV). As to industrial injuries benefit see WELFARE BENEFITS AND STATE PENSIONS vol 104 (2014) PARA 214 et seq.

20 Social Security Administration Act 1992 s 130(1)(f) (added by the Welfare Reform Act 2007 s 28(1), Sch 3 para 10(1), (19)). As to employment and support allowance see WELFARE BENEFITS AND STATE PENSIONS vol 104 (2014) PARA 252 et seq.

21 Social Security Administration Act 1992 s 130(2)(a).

22 Social Security Administration Act 1992 s 130(2)(b).

23 Social Security Administration Act 1992 s 130(2)(c).

590. Records to be maintained by employers relating to the payment of statutory sick pay. An authorised officer of the Commissioners for Revenue and Customs[1] may by notice[2] require an employer[3] to produce to him at the place of keeping[4] such records[5] as are in the employer's possession or power and as, in the officer's reasonable opinion, contain, or may contain, information relevant to satisfy him that statutory sick pay[6] has been paid and is being paid[7] to employees[8] or former employees who are entitled to it[9].

1 As to the powers of inspectors appointed for the purposes of the Social Security Administration Act 1992 see WELFARE BENEFITS AND STATE PENSIONS vol 104 (2014) PARA 576 et seq.

2 Such a notice must be in writing and the employer must produce the records referred to within 30 days after the date of such a notice: Statutory Sick Pay (General) Regulations 1982, SI 1982/894, reg 13A(2) (reg 13A added by SI 2005/989).

3 As to the meaning of 'employer' for these purposes see PARA 571.

4 For these purposes, 'place of keeping' means such place in Great Britain that an employer and an authorised officer may agree upon, or, in the absence of such agreement: (1) any place in Great Britain where records referred to in the Statutory Sick Pay (General) Regulations 1982, SI 1982/894, reg 13A(1) are normally kept; or (2) if there is no such place, the employer's principal place of business in Great Britain: see reg 13A(5) (as added: see note 2). As to the meaning of 'Great Britain' see PARA 2 note 12.

5 For these purposes, references to records means:
(1) any wage sheet or deductions working sheet (Statutory Sick Pay (General) Regulations 1982, SI 1982/894, reg 13A(4)(a) (as added: see note 2)); or

(2) any other document which relates to the calculation or payment of statutory sick pay to his employees or former employees (reg 13A(4)(b) (as so added)),

whether kept in written form, electronically, or otherwise (see reg 13A(4) (as so added)).

6 As to the meaning of 'statutory sick pay' see PARA 558.

7 Ie in accordance with the Statutory Sick Pay (General) Regulations 1982, SI 1982/894 (see PARA 559 et seq).

8 As to the meaning of 'employee' for these purposes see PARA 562.

9 Statutory Sick Pay (General) Regulations 1982, SI 1982/894, reg 13A(1) (as added: see note 2). The production of records in pursuance of reg 13A is without prejudice to any lien which a third party may have in respect of those records: reg 13A(3) (as so added). As to the penalties imposed for a failure to produce any document or record or to provide any information and for the fraudulent or negligent production or provision of any document or record or information and for any incorrect statement or declaration fraudulently or negligently made in connection with establishing entitlement to statutory sick pay see the Social Security Administration Act 1992 ss 113A–113B; and WELFARE BENEFITS AND STATE PENSIONS vol 104 (2014) PARAS 582, 583.

591. Provision of information in connection with determination of questions relating to statutory sick pay. Any person claiming to be entitled to statutory sick pay[1], or any other person who is a party to proceedings arising under the statutory sick pay provisions that are set out in Part XI of the Social Security Contributions and Benefits Act 1992[2], must, if he receives notification from the Commissioners for Revenue and Customs[3] that any information is required from him for the determination of any question arising in connection therewith, furnish that information to the Commissioners within ten days of receiving that notification[4].

1 As to the meaning of 'statutory sick pay' see PARA 558.

2 Ie under the Social Security Contributions and Benefits Act 1992 Pt XI (ss 151–163) (statutory sick pay: see also PARAS 558 et seq, 593).

3 As to the Commissioners for Her Majesty's Revenue and Customs see INCOME TAXATION vol 58 (2014) PARAS 33–34.

4 Statutory Sick Pay (General) Regulations 1982, SI 1982/894, reg 14 (amended by the Social Security Contributions (Transfer of Functions, etc) Act 1999 s 1(2), Sch 2); and see the Interpretation Act 1978 s 17(2)(a). As to the right to apply for the determination of any issue arising as to, or in connection with, entitlement to statutory sick pay see PARA 595. As to the penalties imposed for a failure to produce any document or record or to provide any information and for the fraudulent or negligent production or provision of any document or record or information and for any incorrect statement or declaration fraudulently or negligently made in connection with establishing entitlement to statutory sick pay see the Social Security Administration Act 1992 ss 113A–113B; and WELFARE BENEFITS AND STATE PENSIONS vol 104 (2014) PARAS 582, 583.

592. Provision of information relating to statutory sick pay by employers to employees. In a case where information is to be furnished by employers[1] in connection with an employee's claim for certain benefits or allowances[2], the employer must furnish to his employee, in writing on a form approved by the Secretary of State[3] for the purpose (or in a form in which it can be processed by equipment operating automatically in response to instructions given for that purpose), specified[4] information within the specified[5] time[6].

In a case where no period of entitlement[7] arises[8] in relation to a period of incapacity for work[9], the specified information is a statement of all the reasons why[10] a period of entitlement does not arise[11]; and it must be furnished not more than seven days after the day on which the employer is notified by or on behalf of the employee of the employee's incapacity for work on the fourth day of the period of incapacity for work[12].

In a case where the period of entitlement ends but the period of incapacity for work continues[13]:

(1) the specified information is a statement informing the employee of: (a) the reason why the period of entitlement ended[14]; (b) the date of the last day in respect of which the employer is or was liable to make a payment of statutory sick pay[15] to him[16]; and
(2) the statement must be furnished not more than seven days after the day on which the period of entitlement ended, or, if earlier, on the day on which it is already required[17] to be furnished[18].

In a case where the period of entitlement is expected to end before the period of incapacity for work ends[19]:

(i) the specified information is a statement informing the employee of: (A) the reason why the period of entitlement is expected to end[20]; (B) the date of the last day in respect of which the employer is or was expected to be liable to make a payment of statutory sick pay to him[21]; and
(ii) the statement must be furnished[22]: (A) in a case where the period of entitlement is expected to end where the employee is entitled to maximum statutory sick pay[23], on or before the forty-second day before the period of entitlement is expected to end[24]; or (B) in any other case, on or before the seventh day before the period of entitlement is expected to end[25].

1 As to the meaning of 'employer' for these purposes see PARA 571.
2 Ie in a case which falls within the Social Security Administration Act 1992 s 130(3)(a), (b) or (c): see PARA 589 note 14. As to the meaning of 'employee' for these purposes see PARA 562.
3 As to the Secretary of State see PARA 5 note 21.
4 Ie the information specified in the Statutory Sick Pay (General) Regulations 1982, SI 1982/894, reg 15(2) (see the text and notes 7–12), reg 15(3) (see heads (1), (2) in the text) or reg 15(4) (see heads (i), (ii) in the text).
5 Ie within the time specified in the Statutory Sick Pay (General) Regulations 1982, SI 1982/894, reg 15(2) (see the text and notes 7–12), reg 15(3) (see heads (1), (2) in the text) or reg 15(4) (see heads (i), (ii) in the text).
6 Statutory Sick Pay (General) Regulations 1982, SI 1982/894, reg 15(1) (amended by SI 1995/829; SI 1996/777); and see the Interpretation Act 1978 s 17(2)(a). Where, for these purposes, in the particular circumstances of a case, it is not practicable for the employer to furnish the information within the specified time under the Statutory Sick Pay (General) Regulations 1982, SI 1982/894, reg 15(2) (see the text and notes 7–12), reg 15(3) (see heads (1), (2) in the text), reg 15(4)(b)(ii) (see head (ii)(B) in the text) or reg 15(5) (see PARA 589 note 14), he must, not later than the first pay day (within the meaning of reg 9(1): see PARA 584 note 14) immediately following the relevant specified time, furnish the information to his employee: reg 15(1A) (added by SI 1996/777). As to the penalties imposed for a failure to produce any document or record or to provide any information and for the fraudulent or negligent production or provision of any document or record or information and for any incorrect statement or declaration fraudulently or negligently made in connection with establishing entitlement to statutory sick pay see the Social Security Administration Act 1992 ss 113A–113B; and **WELFARE BENEFITS AND STATE PENSIONS** vol 104 (2014) PARAS 582, 583.
7 As to the meaning of 'period of entitlement' see PARA 573 note 4.
8 Ie in a case falling within the Social Security Administration Act 1992 s 130(3)(a): see PARA 589 note 14.
9 See the Statutory Sick Pay (General) Regulations 1982, SI 1982/894, reg 15(2); and see the Interpretation Act 1978 s 17(2)(a). As to the meaning of 'period of incapacity for work' see PARA 572 note 2.
10 Ie under the provisions of the Social Security Contributions and Benefits Act 1992 Sch 11 para 1 (see PARA 574) and regulations made thereunder.
11 Statutory Sick Pay (General) Regulations 1982, SI 1982/894, reg 15(2)(a); and see the Interpretation Act 1978 s 17(2)(a).
12 Statutory Sick Pay (General) Regulations 1982, SI 1982/894, reg 15(2)(b).
13 See the Statutory Sick Pay (General) Regulations 1982, SI 1982/894, reg 15(3); and see the Interpretation Act 1978 s 17(2)(a). The case referred to in the text is one which falls within the Social Security Administration Act 1992 s 130(3)(b): see PARA 589 note 14.

14 Statutory Sick Pay (General) Regulations 1982, SI 1982/894, reg 15(3)(a)(i) (reg 15(3)(a) substituted by SI 1986/477; and further substituted by SI 2008/1735).
15 As to the meaning of 'statutory sick pay' see PARA 558.
16 Statutory Sick Pay (General) Regulations 1982, SI 1982/894, reg 15(3)(a)(ii) (as substituted: see note 14).
17 Ie under the Statutory Sick Pay (General) Regulations 1982, SI 1982/894, reg 15(4): see heads (i), (ii) in the text.
18 Statutory Sick Pay (General) Regulations 1982, SI 1982/894, reg 15(3)(b) (substituted by SI 1986/477).
19 See the Statutory Sick Pay (General) Regulations 1982, SI 1982/894, reg 15(4); and see the Interpretation Act 1978 s 17(2)(a). The case referred to in the text is a one which falls within the Social Security Administration Act 1992 s 130(3)(c): see PARA 589 note 14.
20 Statutory Sick Pay (General) Regulations 1982, SI 1982/894, reg 15(4)(a)(i) (reg 15(4)(a) substituted by SI 1986/477; and further substituted by SI 2008/1735).
21 Statutory Sick Pay (General) Regulations 1982, SI 1982/894, reg 15(4)(a)(ii) (as substituted: see note 20).
22 Statutory Sick Pay (General) Regulations 1982, SI 1982/894, reg 15(4)(b) (substituted by SI 1986/477; and amended by SI 1996/777).
23 Ie in accordance with the Social Security Contributions and Benefits Act 1992 s 153(2)(b): see PARA 573.
24 Statutory Sick Pay (General) Regulations 1982, SI 1982/894, reg 15(4)(b)(i) (as substituted: see note 22); and see the Interpretation Act 1978 s 17(2)(a).
25 Statutory Sick Pay (General) Regulations 1982, SI 1982/894, reg 15(4)(b)(ii) (as substituted: see note 22).

(viii) Recovery of Amounts paid by way of Statutory Sick Pay

593. Recovery by employers of amounts paid by way of statutory sick pay; power to make regulations. The Secretary of State[1] may by order provide for the recovery by employers[2], in accordance with the order, of the amount, if any, by which their payments of, or liability incurred for, statutory sick pay[3] in any period exceeds the specified[4] percentage of the amount of their liability for contributions payments[5] in respect of the corresponding period[6]. Such an order may include provision[7]:

(1) as to the periods by reference to which the calculation referred to above is to be made[8];
(2) for amounts which would otherwise be recoverable but which do not exceed the specified minimum for recovery not to be recoverable[9];
(3) for the rounding up or down of any fraction of a pound which would otherwise result from a calculation made in accordance with the order[10]; and
(4) for any deduction from contributions payments made in accordance with the order to be disregarded for such purposes as may be specified[11].

1 As to the Secretary of State see PARA 5 note 21.
2 As to the meaning of 'employer' for these purposes see PARA 571.
3 As to the meaning of 'statutory sick pay' see PARA 558. As to an employer's liability for statutory sick pay see PARA 558 et seq. As to payments of statutory sick pay see PARA 581 et seq.
4 For these purposes, 'specified' means specified in or determined in accordance with an order under the Social Security Contributions and Benefits Act 1992 s 159A(1): see s 159A(3) (s 159A added by the Statutory Sick Pay Act 1994 s 3(1)).
5 For these purposes, 'contributions payments' means payments which a person is required by or under any enactment to make in discharge of any liability of his as an employer in respect of primary or secondary Class 1 contributions: see the Social Security Contributions and Benefits Act 1992 s 159A(3) (as added: see note 4). As to primary and secondary Class 1 contributions see WELFARE BENEFITS AND STATE PENSIONS vol 104 (2014) PARA 385.
6 Social Security Contributions and Benefits Act 1992 s 159A(1) (as added: see note 4). As to the making of orders under the Social Security Contributions and Benefits Act 1992 see PARA 407

note 3. A statutory instrument containing, whether alone or with other provisions, an order made by virtue of s 159A(1), must not be made unless a draft of the instrument has been laid before Parliament and been approved by a resolution of each House: see s 176(1)(c) (as amended: see PARA 581 note 3). The Secretary of State may by regulations make transitional and consequential provisions in relation to such an order: s 159A(4) (as so added). As to the regulations that have been so made see the Statutory Sick Pay Percentage Threshold (Revocations, Transitional and Saving Provisions) (Great Britain and Northern Ireland) Order 2014, SI 2014/897, revoking the Statutory Sick Pay Percentage Threshold Order 1995, SI 1995/512 (which came into force on 6 April 1995: see reg 1), and making transitional provision (see PARA 594). By virtue of the Interpretation Act 1978 s 17(2)(b), the Statutory Maternity Pay (General) Regulations 1986, SI 1986/1960, also have effect as if so made. Accordingly, for the purposes of the Social Security Contributions and Benefits Act 1992 s 159A, and of any order made under s 159A, where an employer has made two or more elections under the Income Tax (Pay As You Earn) Regulations 2003, SI 2003/2682, regs 98, 99 (see INCOME TAXATION vol 58 (2014) PARA 928) to be treated as a different employer in respect of each of the groups of employees specified in the election, the different employers covered by each of those elections are to be treated as one employer: Statutory Sick Pay (General) Regulations 1982, SI 1982/894, reg 21A(1), (2) (reg 21A added by SI 1995/513); and see the Interpretation Act 1978 s 17(2)(a).

7 See the Social Security Contributions and Benefits Act 1992 s 159A(2) (as added: see note 4).
8 Social Security Contributions and Benefits Act 1992 s 159A(2)(a) (as added: see note 4).
9 Social Security Contributions and Benefits Act 1992 s 159A(2)(b) (as added: see note 4).
10 Social Security Contributions and Benefits Act 1992 s 159A(2)(c) (as added: see note 4).
11 Social Security Contributions and Benefits Act 1992 s 159A(2)(d) (as added: see note 4).

594. Payments of statutory sick pay deducted from contributions. The following provisions continue to have effect for a period of two years beginning with 6 April 2014, for the purposes of entitling an employer[1] to recover an amount of statutory sick pay[2] (whether paid before, on or after 6 April 2014) is respect of any day of incapacity for work[3] falling before 6 April 2014[4].

An employer is entitled[5] to recover the amount, if any, by which the payments of statutory sick pay made by him in any income tax month exceed 13 per cent of the amount of his liability for contributions payments[6] in respect of that income tax month[7].

An employer may recover any amount so determined in respect of any income tax month by making one or more deductions[8] from his contributions payments for that or any following income tax month within six years from the end of the tax year in which he became entitled to recover that amount[9].

If the amount which an employer is or would otherwise be entitled so to deduct exceeds the amount of his contributions payments in respect of earnings paid in an income tax month, and the Commissioners for Revenue and Customs are satisfied that that is so, then, provided that the employer has requested them in writing to do so, there must be repaid to the employer by or on behalf of the Commissioners such amount as the employer was unable to deduct[10]. If an employer is not liable for any contributions payments in an income tax month but would otherwise be entitled so to deduct an amount, and the Commissioners are satisfied that that is so, then, provided that the employer has in writing requested them to do so, that amount must be repaid to the employer by or on behalf of the Commissioners[11].

These transitional provisions apart, statute now provides that there is no reimbursement of statutory sick pay for the employer at all, regardless of how much has been paid out.

1 As to the meaning of 'employer' for these purposes see PARA 571; and see PARA 593 note 6.
2 As to the meaning of 'statutory sick pay' see PARA 558. As to an employer's liability for statutory sick pay see PARA 558 et seq, As to payments of statutory sick pay see PARA 581 et seq.
3 As to the meaning of 'day of incapacity for work' see PARA 558.

4 See the Statutory Sick Pay Percentage Threshold (Revocations, Transitional and Saving Provisions) (Great Britain and Northern Ireland) Order 2014, SI 2014/897, art 3. The Statutory Sick Pay Percentage Threshold Order 1995, SI 1995/512 (see the text and notes 5–11), is revoked by the Statutory Sick Pay Percentage Threshold (Revocations, Transitional and Saving Provisions) (Great Britain and Northern Ireland) Order 2014, SI 2014/897, art 2, with effect from 6 April 2014, but subject to the transitional and saving provisions set out in art 3.

5 For the purposes of calculating the amount an employer is entitled so to recover, there must be excluded any payment of statutory sick pay which is not made:
  (1) in the income tax month in which he received notice, in accordance with the Statutory Sick Pay (General) Regulations 1982, SI 1982/894, reg 7 (see PARA 576), of the day or days of incapacity for work to which the payment related (Statutory Sick Pay Percentage Threshold Order 1995, SI 1995/512, art 2(2)(a));
  (2) in a case where it would have been impracticable to make the payment in that income tax month in view of the employer's methods of accounting for and paying remuneration, in the following income tax month (art 2(2)(b)); or
  (3) in a case where a decision had been made by an adjudication officer, social security appeal tribunal or commissioner that the employee was entitled to that payment, within the time limits set out in reg 9 (see PARA 584) (Statutory Sick Pay Percentage Threshold Order 1995, SI 1995/512, art 2(2)(c)).

'Income tax month' means, unless the context otherwise requires, the period beginning on the sixth day of any calendar month and ending on the fifth day of the following calendar month: see art 1(2). As to the adjudication of claims for benefit and questions arising from such claims see WELFARE BENEFITS AND STATE PENSIONS vol 104 (2014) PARA 575 et seq. As to social security commissioners see WELFARE BENEFITS AND STATE PENSIONS vol 104 (2014) PARA 575.

6 As to the meaning of 'contributions payments' see PARA 593 note 5.

7 Statutory Sick Pay Percentage Threshold Order 1995, SI 1995/512, art 2(1).

8 Any such deduction is to be disregarded for the purposes of determining whether an employer has discharged any liability of his in respect of Class 1 contributions: Statutory Sick Pay Percentage Threshold Order 1995, SI 1995/512, art 3(2). As to Class 1 contributions see WELFARE BENEFITS AND STATE PENSIONS vol 104 (2014) PARA 385.

9 Statutory Sick Pay Percentage Threshold Order 1995, SI 1995/512, art 3(1). However, art 3(1) does not apply where, and in so far as:
  (1) the amount has been repaid to him by or on behalf of the Commissioners for Revenue and Customs under art 4 (see the text and notes 10–11) (art 3(1)(a)); or
  (2) the employer has made a request in writing under art 4 that the amount be repaid to him and he has not received notification by or on behalf of the Commissioners that the request is refused (art 3(1)(b)).

As to the Commissioners for Her Majesty's Revenue and Customs see INCOME TAXATION vol 58 (2014) PARAS 33–34.

10 Statutory Sick Pay Percentage Threshold Order 1995, SI 1995/512, art 4(1) (art 4(1), (2) amended by the Social Security Contributions (Transfer of Functions, etc) Act 1999 Sch 2).

11 Statutory Sick Pay Percentage Threshold Order 1995, SI 1995/512, art 4(2) (as amended: see note 10).

(13) DETERMINATION OF ISSUES ARISING FROM STATUTORY PAY PROVISIONS

595. Issues arising from statutory maternity, paternity and adoption pay and statutory sick pay to be determined by Commissioners. An application for the determination of any issue arising as to, or in connection with, entitlement to:
  (1) statutory sick pay[1]; or
  (2) statutory maternity pay[2]; or
  (3) statutory paternity pay[3]; or
  (4) statutory adoption pay[4],

may be submitted to an officer of the Commissioners for Revenue and Customs[5] by the employee[6] concerned[7]. An application made under head (1) or head (2) above may be submitted alternatively by the Secretary of State[8].

Such an issue is to be decided by the officer only on the basis of such an application or on his own initiative[9].

An application for the determination of any such issue must be made in a form approved for the purpose by the Commissioners[10]. Where such an application is submitted by the employee, it must:

(a) be delivered or sent to an office of the Commissioners within six months of the earliest day in respect of which entitlement under head (1) or head (2) above is in issue[11], or be made to an officer of the Commissioners within six months of the earliest day in respect of which entitlement under head (3) or head (4) above is in issue[12];

(b) state the period in respect of which entitlement under any of heads (1) to (4) above is in issue[13]; and

(c) state the grounds, if any, on which the applicant's employer[14] has denied liability under any of heads (1) to (4) above in respect of the period specified in the application[15].

1 As to statutory sick pay see PARA 558 et seq.
2 As to statutory maternity pay see PARA 401 et seq.
3 As to statutory paternity pay see PARA 443 et seq.
4 As to statutory adoption pay see PARA 488 et seq.
5 In the Statutory Paternity Pay and Statutory Adoption Pay (Administration) Regulations 2002, SI 2002/2820, references are to the 'Board', which is defined to mean the Commissioners for Revenue and Customs: see reg 2(1). As to the Commissioners for Her Majesty's Revenue and Customs see **INCOME TAXATION** vol 58 (2014) PARAS 33–34.
6 For these purposes, 'employee' has the meaning given (in relation to statutory sick pay) by the Social Security Contributions and Benefits Act 1992 s 163(1) (see PARA 562), or (in relation to statutory maternity pay) by s 171(1) (see PARA 406): see the Statutory Sick Pay and Statutory Maternity Pay (Decisions) Regulations 1999, SI 1999/776, reg 1(2). As to the meaning of 'employee' in relation to statutory paternity pay see PARA 448; and as to the meaning of 'employee' in relation to statutory adoption pay see PARA 494.
7 Statutory Sick Pay and Statutory Maternity Pay (Decisions) Regulations 1999, SI 1999/776, reg 2(1); Statutory Paternity Pay and Statutory Adoption Pay (Administration) Regulations 2002, SI 2002/2820, reg 12(1). Statute has clearly provided for the officers of the Board of Inland Revenue and, on appeal, the Commissioners of Inland Revenue (now Revenue and Customs) to have exclusive jurisdiction to determine entitlement to sick pay so an employment tribunal has jurisdiction only where entitlement to statutory sick pay is not disputed: *Taylor Gordon & Co Ltd (t/a Plan Personnel) v Timmons* [2004] IRLR 180, EAT.
8 See the Statutory Sick Pay and Statutory Maternity Pay (Decisions) Regulations 1999, SI 1999/776, reg 2(1). As to the Secretary of State see PARA 5 note 21.
9 Statutory Sick Pay and Statutory Maternity Pay (Decisions) Regulations 1999, SI 1999/776, reg 2(2); Statutory Paternity Pay and Statutory Adoption Pay (Administration) Regulations 2002, SI 2002/2820, reg 12(2).
10 Statutory Sick Pay and Statutory Maternity Pay (Decisions) Regulations 1999, SI 1999/776, reg 3(1); Statutory Paternity Pay and Statutory Adoption Pay (Administration) Regulations 2002, SI 2002/2820, reg 13(1). If the application is being made in connection with entitlement to statutory maternity pay or statutory sick pay, it may be made in such other manner, being in writing, as an officer of the Commissioners may accept as sufficient in the circumstances: see the Statutory Sick Pay and Statutory Maternity Pay (Decisions) Regulations 1999, SI 1999/776, reg 3(1).
11 Statutory Sick Pay and Statutory Maternity Pay (Decisions) Regulations 1999, SI 1999/776, reg 3(2)(a).
12 Statutory Paternity Pay and Statutory Adoption Pay (Administration) Regulations 2002, SI 2002/2820, reg 13(2)(a).
13 Statutory Sick Pay and Statutory Maternity Pay (Decisions) Regulations 1999, SI 1999/776, reg 3(2)(b); Statutory Paternity Pay and Statutory Adoption Pay (Administration) Regulations 2002, SI 2002/2820, reg 13(2)(b).
14 For these purposes, 'employer' has the meaning given (in relation to statutory sick pay) by the Social Security Contributions and Benefits Act 1992 s 163(1) (see PARA 571), or (in relation to statutory maternity pay) by s 171(1) (see PARA 414): see the Statutory Sick Pay and Statutory Maternity Pay (Decisions) Regulations 1999, SI 1999/776, reg 1(2). As to the meaning of 'employer' in relation to statutory paternity pay see PARA 456; and as to the meaning of 'employer' in relation to statutory adoption pay see PARA 502.

15 Statutory Sick Pay and Statutory Maternity Pay (Decisions) Regulations 1999, SI 1999/776, reg 3(2)(c); Statutory Paternity Pay and Statutory Adoption Pay (Administration) Regulations 2002, SI 2002/2820, reg 13(2)(c).

(14) SUSPENSION FROM WORK OR END OF SUPPLY ON MEDICAL OR MATERNITY GROUNDS

(i) Employee Suspended from Work on Medical Grounds

596. Right to remuneration of employee suspended on medical grounds. An employee[1] who is suspended from work by his employer[2] on medical grounds[3] is entitled[4] to be paid remuneration by his employer while he is so suspended for a period not exceeding 26 weeks[5]. For these purposes[6], an employee is suspended from work on medical grounds if he is suspended from work in consequence of[7]:

(1) a requirement imposed by or under a specified provision of an enactment or of an instrument made under an enactment[8]; or

(2) a recommendation in a provision of a code of practice issued or approved under the Health and Safety at Work etc Act 1974[9].

An employee is not, however, entitled to such remuneration unless he has been continuously employed for a period of not less than one month ending with the day before that on which the suspension begins[10].

1 As to the meaning of 'employee' see PARA 2.

2 As to the meaning of 'employer' see PARA 2.

3 For the purposes of the Employment Rights Act 1996 Pt VII (ss 64–70A) (suspension from work: see also PARA 597 et seq), an employee is to be regarded as suspended from work on medical grounds only if, and for so long as, he:

(1) continues to be employed by his employer (s 64(5)(a)); but

(2) is not provided with work or does not perform the work he normally performed before the suspension (s 64(5)(b)).

As to the dismissal of a temporary replacement taken on to replace the employee during suspension from work on medical grounds see PARA 801.

4 Ie subject to the Employment Rights Act 1996 s 65: see the text and note 10; and PARA 597.

5 Employment Rights Act 1996 s 64(1). As to the calculation of remuneration see PARA 604. As to the right of complaint to an employment tribunal see PARA 606.

6 Ie for the purposes of the Employment Rights Act 1996 Pt VII (suspension from work: see also PARA 597 et seq).

7 See the Employment Rights Act 1996 s 64(2). If an employee is dismissed by reason of any such requirement or recommendation as is referred to in s 64(2) (see heads (1), (2) in the text), then s 108(1) (see PARA 758) has effect in relation to that dismissal as if for the words 'two years' there were substituted the words 'one month': see s 108(2); and PARA 758.

8 Employment Rights Act 1996 s 64(2)(a). The provision in question must be for the time being specified in s 64(3): see s 64(2). The provisions so specified are:

(1) the Control of Lead at Work Regulations 2002, SI 2002/2676, reg 10 (medical surveillance: see HEALTH AND SAFETY AT WORK vol 53 (2014) PARA 606) (Employment Rights Act 1996 ss 64(3)(a), 241, Sch 2 para 2(1));

(2) the Ionising Radiations Regulations 1999, SI 1999/3232, reg 24 (medical surveillance: see HEALTH AND SAFETY AT WORK vol 53 (2014) PARA 613) (Employment Rights Act 1996 s 64(3)(b) (amended by SI 1999/3232)); and

(3) the Control of Substances Hazardous to Health Regulations 2002, SI 2002/2677, reg 11 (health surveillance: see HEALTH AND SAFETY AT WORK vol 53 (2014) PARA 587) (Employment Rights Act 1996 ss 64(3)(c), 241, Sch 2 para 2(1)).

The Secretary of State may by order add provisions to, or remove provisions from, the list of provisions in s 64(3): s 64(4). At the date at which this volume states the law, no such order had been made. As to the Secretary of State see PARA 5 note 21. As to the making of orders under the Employment Rights Act 1996 generally see PARA 162.

9 Employment Rights Act 1996 s 64(2)(b). Head (2) in the text refers to a code of practice issued or approved under the Health and Safety at Work etc Act 1974 s 16: see HEALTH AND SAFETY AT WORK vol 52 (2014) PARA 390.

10 Employment Rights Act 1996 s 65(1). As to continuity of employment see PARAS 130 et seq, 861 et seq. As to the modification of s 65(1) in relation to National Health Service employees see PARA 326 note 13.

597. Exclusions from the right to remuneration on suspension on medical grounds. An employee[1] is not entitled to remuneration on suspension on medical grounds[2] in respect of any period:

(1) during which he is incapable of work by reason of disease or bodily or mental disablement[3]; or

(2) if his employer[4] has offered to provide him with suitable alternative work, whether or not it is work which the employee is under his contract, or was under the contract in force before the suspension, employed to perform, and the employee has unreasonably refused to perform that work[5]; or

(3) if he does not comply with reasonable requirements imposed by his employer with a view to ensuring that his services are available[6].

1 As to the meaning of 'employee' see PARA 2.
2 Ie under the Employment Rights Act 1996 s 64: see PARA 596.
3 Employment Rights Act 1996 s 65(3).
4 As to the meaning of 'employer' see PARA 2.
5 Employment Rights Act 1996 s 65(4)(a).
6 Employment Rights Act 1996 s 65(4)(b).

(ii) Employee's Work or Agency Worker's Supply ended on Maternity Grounds

A. EMPLOYEE SUSPENDED ON MATERNITY GROUNDS

598. Right to remuneration of employee suspended on maternity grounds. An employee[1] who is suspended from work on maternity grounds[2] is entitled[3] to be paid remuneration by her employer[4] while she is so suspended[5]. For these purposes[6], an employee is suspended from work on maternity grounds, if, in consequence of any relevant requirement[7] or relevant recommendation[8], she is suspended from work by her employer on the ground that: (1) she is pregnant; (2) she has recently given birth; or (3) she is breastfeeding a child[9].

1 As to the meaning of 'employee' see PARA 2.
2 For the purposes of the Employment Rights Act 1996 Pt VII (ss 64–70A) (suspension from work: see also PARAS 596, 597, 599 et seq), an employee is to be regarded as suspended from work on maternity grounds only if, and for so long as, she:
   (1) continues to be employed by her employer (s 66(3)(a)); but
   (2) is not provided with work or, disregarding alternative work for the purposes of s 67 (see PARA 600), does not perform the work she normally performed before the suspension (s 66(3)(b)).

   As to the dismissal of a temporary replacement taken on to replace the employee during suspension from work on maternity grounds see PARA 801. As to the meaning of 'suspended' (and also in regard to appropriate risk assessment) see *Stevenson v Skinner & Co* [2008] All ER (D) 28 (May), EAT. As to the modification of the Employment Rights Act 1996 ss 66, 68 in relation to governing bodies of schools having a right to a delegated budget, acting in the exercise of their employment powers, see EDUCATION vol 35 (2011) PARA 355 et seq.
3 Ie subject to the Employment Rights Act 1996 s 68(2): see PARA 599.
4 As to the meaning of 'employer' see PARA 2.
5 Employment Rights Act 1996 s 68(1). As to the calculation of remuneration see PARA 604. As to the right of complaint to an employment tribunal see PARA 606.
6 Ie for the purposes of the Employment Rights Act 1996 Pt VII (suspension from work: see also PARAS 596, 597, 599 et seq).
7 For these purposes, 'relevant requirement' means a requirement imposed by or under a specified provision of an enactment or an instrument made under an enactment; and 'specified provision'

means a provision for the time being specified in an order made by the Secretary of State under the Employment Rights Act 1996 s 66(2): see s 66(2). As to the Secretary of State see PARA 5 note 21. As to the making of orders under the Employment Rights Act 1996 generally see PARA 162. In exercise of the power so conferred, the Secretary of State has made the Suspension from Work on Maternity Grounds (Merchant Shipping and Fishing Vessels) Order 1998, SI 1998/587, art 2 (specifying the Merchant Shipping and Fishing Vessels (Health and Safety at Work) Regulations 1997, SI 1997/2962, regs 8(3), 9(2) (new or expectant mothers: see **SHIPPING AND MARITIME LAW** vol 94 (2008) PARA 623) for the purposes of the Employment Rights Act 1996 s 66(2)). See also, by virtue of the Employment Rights Act 1996 s 241, Sch 2 para 2(1) (see PARA 162), the Suspension from Work (On Maternity Grounds) Order 1994, SI 1994/2930, art 2 (specifying what are now the Management of Health and Safety at Work Regulations 1999, SI 1999/3242, regs 16(3), 17 (new or expectant mothers: see **HEALTH AND SAFETY AT WORK** vol 52 (2014) PARA 395) for the purposes of the Employment Rights Act 1996 s 66(2)).

8 For these purposes, 'relevant recommendation' means a recommendation in a specified provision of a code of practice issued or approved under the Health and Safety at Work etc Act 1974 s 16 (see **HEALTH AND SAFETY AT WORK** vol 52 (2014) PARA 390): see the Employment Rights Act 1996 s 66(2).

9 Employment Rights Act 1996 s 66(1).

599. Exclusion from right to remuneration for employee suspended on maternity grounds. An employee[1] is not entitled to remuneration on suspension from work on maternity grounds[2] in respect of any period if: (1) her employer has offered to provide her during the period with work which is suitable alternative work[3] for her[4]; and (2) she has unreasonably refused to perform that work[5].

1 As to the meaning of 'employee' see PARA 2.

2 Ie under the Employment Rights Act 1996 s 68: see PARA 598. As to the modification of ss 67, 68 in relation to governing bodies of schools having a right to a delegated budget, acting in the exercise of their employment powers, see **EDUCATION** vol 35 (2011) PARA 355 et seq.

3 Ie for the purposes of the Employment Rights Act 1996 s 67: see PARA 600.

4 Employment Rights Act 1996 s 68(2)(a).

5 Employment Rights Act 1996 s 68(2)(b).

600. Right to offer of alternative work before employee suspended on maternity grounds. Where an employer[1] has available suitable alternative work for an employee[2], the employee has a right to be offered to be provided with the alternative work before being suspended from work on maternity grounds[3]. For alternative work to be suitable for an employee for these purposes: (1) the work must be of a kind which is both suitable in relation to her and appropriate for her to do in the circumstances[4]; and (2) the terms and conditions applicable to her for performing the work, if they differ from the corresponding terms and conditions applicable to her for performing the work she normally performs under her contract of employment[5], must not be substantially less favourable to her than those corresponding terms and conditions[6].

1 As to the meaning of 'employer' see PARA 2.

2 As to the meaning of 'employee' see PARA 2.

3 Employment Rights Act 1996 s 67(1). As to the meaning of 'suspension from work on maternity grounds' see PARA 598. As to the modification of s 67 in relation to governing bodies of schools having a right to a delegated budget, acting in the exercise of their employment powers, see **EDUCATION** vol 35 (2011) PARA 355 et seq.

4 Employment Rights Act 1996 s 67(2)(a). See also note 3.

5 As to the meaning of 'contract of employment' see PARA 2.

6 Employment Rights Act 1996 s 67(2)(b). See also note 3. In *British Airways (European Operations at Gatwick) Ltd v Moore* [2000] ICR 678, [2000] IRLR 296, EAT, the transfer of pregnant flight staff to ground work was held not to be on terms 'not less favourable' because the employees no longer received their flying allowances (which contained an element of profit, in addition to reimbursement of expenses).

B. SUPPLY OF AGENCY WORKER ENDED ON MATERNITY GROUNDS

601. Right to remuneration of agency worker whose supply was ended on maternity grounds. Where the supply of an agency worker[1] to a hirer is ended on maternity grounds, that agency worker is entitled[2] to be paid remuneration by the temporary work agency[3]. For these purposes[4], the supply of an agency worker to a hirer is ended on maternity grounds, if, in consequence of action taken pursuant to a listed provision[5], her supply to the hirer is ended on the ground that: (1) she is pregnant; (2) she has recently given birth; or (3) she is breastfeeding a child[6].

1 As to the meaning of 'agency worker' see PARA 97; definition in the Agency Workers Regulations 2010, SI 2010/93, reg 3, applied by the Employment Rights Act 1996 s 68D(4) (ss 68A, 68C, 68D added by SI 2010/93). The Employment Rights Act 1996 ss 68A–68C do not apply where ss 66–68 (employees suspended on maternity grounds: see PARAS 598–600) apply: s 68D(3) (as so added). Without prejudice to any other duties of the hirer or temporary work agency under any enactment or rule of law, ss 68A–68C do not apply where the agency worker either has not completed the qualifying period, or is no longer entitled to the rights conferred by the Agency Workers Regulations 2010, SI 2010/93, reg 5 (see PARA 98), pursuant to reg 8(a), (b) (see PARA 99): see the Employment Rights Act 1996 s 68D(1) (as so added). As to the meaning of 'hirer' see PARA 97 note 3; definition in the Agency Workers Regulations 2010, SI 2010/93, reg 2, applied by the Employment Rights Act 1996 s 68D(4) (as so added). As to the meaning of 'qualifying period' see PARA 99; definition in the Agency Workers Regulations 2010, SI 2010/93, reg 7, applied by the Employment Rights Act 1996 s 68D(4) (as so added). As to the meaning of 'temporary work agency' see PARA 97; definition in the Agency Workers Regulations 2010, SI 2010/93, reg 4, applied by the Employment Rights Act 1996 s 68D(4) (as so added).

2 Ie subject to the Employment Rights Act 1996 s 68C(2): see PARA 602.

3 Employment Rights Act 1996 s 68C(1) (as added: see note 1). Nothing in ss 68A–68C imposes a duty, however, on the hirer or temporary work agency beyond the original intended duration, or likely duration, of the assignment (whichever is the longer): s 68D(2) (as so added). Nor does anything in s 68C impose a duty on the temporary work agency to pay remuneration beyond the original intended duration, or likely duration, whichever is the longer, of the assignment which ended when the supply of the agency worker to the hirer was ended on maternity grounds: s 68C(3) (as so added). As to the meaning of 'assignment' see PARA 99 note 4; definition in the Agency Workers Regulations 2010, SI 2010/93, reg 2, applied by the Employment Rights Act 1996 s 68D(4) (as so added). As to the calculation of remuneration see PARA 605. As to the right of complaint to an employment tribunal see PARA 607.

4 Ie for the purposes of the Employment Rights Act 1996 Pt VII (ss 64–70A) (suspension from work: see also PARAS 596 et seq, 602 et seq).

5 Ie a provision listed in the Employment Rights Act 1996 s 68A(2): see s 68A(1) (as added: see note 1). The provisions so specified are:

(1) the Merchant Shipping and Fishing Vessels (Health and Safety at Work) Regulations 1997, SI 1997/2962, regs 8(3), 9(2) (new or expectant mothers: see SHIPPING AND MARITIME LAW vol 94 (2008) PARA 623) (Employment Rights Act 1996 s 68A(2)(a) (as so added));

(2) the Management of Health and Safety at Work Regulations 1999, SI 1999/3242, regs 16A(2), 17A (new or expectant mothers (agency workers: see HEALTH AND SAFETY AT WORK vol 52 (2014) PARA 395) (Employment Rights Act 1996 s 68A(2)(b) (as so added)); and

(3) the Conduct of Employment Agencies and Employment Businesses Regulations 2003, SI 2003/3319, reg 20 (protection of work-seeker and hirer: see TRADE AND INDUSTRY vol 97 (2010) PARA 884) (Employment Rights Act 1996 s 68A(2)(c) (as so added)).

6 Employment Rights Act 1996 s 68A(1) (as added: see note 1).

602. Exclusion from the right to remuneration of agency worker whose supply was ended on maternity grounds. An agency worker[1] whose supply to a hirer has been ended on maternity grounds[2] is not entitled to remuneration[3] in respect of any period[4] if: (1) the temporary work agency has[5]: (a) offered to propose the agency worker to a hirer that has alternative work available which is suitable alternative work[6] for her[7]; or (b) proposed the agency worker to a hirer that has such suitable alternative work available, and that hirer has agreed to the supply of that agency worker[8]; and (2) she has unreasonably refused that offer or to perform that work[9].

1 As to the meaning of 'agency worker' for these purposes see PARA 601 note 1. The Employment Rights Act 1996 ss 68A–68C do not apply where ss 66–68 (employees suspended on maternity grounds: see PARAS 598–600) apply: s 68D(3) (ss 68C, 68D added by SI 2010/93). Without prejudice to any other duties of the hirer or temporary work agency under any enactment or rule of law the Employment Rights Act 1996 ss 68A–68C do not apply where the agency worker either has not completed the qualifying period, or is no longer entitled to the rights conferred by the Agency Workers Regulations 2010, SI 2010/93, reg 5 (see PARA 98), pursuant to reg 8(a), (b) (see PARA 99): see the Employment Rights Act 1996 s 68D(1) (as so added). As to the meanings of 'hirer' and 'temporary work agency' for these purposes see PARA 601 note 1.
2 As to when the supply of an agency worker is ended on maternity grounds see PARA 601.
3 Ie under the Employment Rights Act 1996 s 68C: see PARA 601.
4 Nothing in the Employment Rights Act 1996 ss 68A–68C imposes a duty, however, on the hirer or temporary work agency beyond the original intended duration, or likely duration, of the assignment (whichever is the longer): s 68D(2) (as added: see note 1). Nor does anything in s 68C impose a duty on the temporary work agency to pay remuneration beyond the original intended duration, or likely duration, whichever is the longer, of the assignment which ended when the supply of the agency worker to the hirer was ended on maternity grounds: s 68C(3) (as so added). As to the meaning of 'assignment' for these purposes see PARA 601 note 1.
5 See the Employment Rights Act 1996 s 68C(2)(a) (as added: see note 1).
6 Ie for the purposes of the Employment Rights Act 1996 s 68B: see PARA 603.
7 Employment Rights Act 1996 s 68C(2)(a)(i) (as added: see note 1).
8 Employment Rights Act 1996 s 68C(2)(a)(ii) (as added: see note 1).
9 Employment Rights Act 1996 s 68C(2)(b) (as added: see note 1).

603. Right to offer of alternative work for agency worker whose supply was ended on maternity grounds. Where the supply of an agency worker[1] to a hirer has been ended on maternity grounds[2] and the temporary work agency has available suitable alternative work, the agency worker has a right to be offered to be proposed for such alternative work[3]. For alternative work to be suitable for an agency worker for these purposes:

(1) the work must be of a kind which is both suitable in relation to her and appropriate for her to do in the circumstances[4]; and
(2) the terms and conditions applicable to her whilst performing the work, if they differ from the corresponding terms and conditions which would have applied to her but for the fact that the supply of the agency worker to the hirer was ended on maternity grounds, must not be substantially less favourable to her than those corresponding terms and conditions[5].

The right to be offered to be proposed for such alternative work[6] does not apply, however: (a) where the agency worker has confirmed in writing that she no longer requires the work-finding services of the temporary work agency[7]; or (b) beyond the original intended duration, or likely duration, whichever is the longer, of the assignment which ended when the supply of the agency worker to the hirer was ended on maternity grounds[8].

1 As to the meaning of 'agency worker' for these purposes see PARA 601 note 1. The Employment Rights Act 1996 ss 68A–68C do not apply where ss 66–68 (employees suspended on maternity grounds: see PARAS 598–600) apply: s 68D(3) (ss 68B, 68D added by SI 2010/93). Without prejudice to any other duties of the hirer or temporary work agency under any enactment or rule of law the Employment Rights Act 1996 ss 68A–68C do not apply where the agency worker either has not completed the qualifying period, or is no longer entitled to the rights conferred by the Agency Workers Regulations 2010, SI 2010/93, reg 5 (see PARA 98), pursuant to reg 8(a), (b) (see PARA 99): see the Employment Rights Act 1996 s 68D(1) (as so added). As to the meanings of 'hirer' and 'temporary work agency' for these purposes see PARA 601 note 1.
2 As to when the supply of an agency worker is ended on maternity grounds see PARA 601.

3 Employment Rights Act 1996 s 68B(1) (as added: see note 1). Nothing in ss 68A–68C imposes a duty, however, on the hirer or temporary work agency beyond the original intended duration, or likely duration, of the assignment (whichever is the longer): s 68D(2) (as so added).
4 Employment Rights Act 1996 s 68B(2)(a) (as added: see note 1).
5 Employment Rights Act 1996 s 68B(2)(b) (as added: see note 1).
6 Ie the provision made by the Employment Rights Act 1996 s 68B(1) (see the text and notes 1–3).
7 Employment Rights Act 1996 s 68B(3)(a) (as added: see note 1).
8 Employment Rights Act 1996 s 68B(3)(b) (as added: see note 1).

(iii) Calculation of Remuneration where Employee's Work or Agency Worker's Supply ended on Medical or Maternity Grounds

A. EMPLOYEE SUSPENDED ON MEDICAL OR MATERNITY GROUNDS

604. Calculation of remuneration for employee suspended from work on medical or maternity grounds. The amount of remuneration payable[1] by an employer[2] to an employee[3] suspended from work by his or her employer on either medical[4] or on maternity grounds[5] is a week's pay[6] in respect of each week[7] of the period of suspension[8]; and if, in any week, remuneration is payable in respect of only part of that week, the amount of a week's pay is to be reduced proportionately[9].

Any such right to remuneration[10] does not affect any right of an employee in relation to remuneration under the employee's contract of employment ('contractual remuneration')[11]. Any contractual remuneration paid by an employer to an employee in respect of any period goes towards discharging the employer's liability[12], in respect of that period[13]; and, conversely, any payment of remuneration in discharge of an employer's liability[14] in respect of any period goes towards discharging any obligation of the employer to pay contractual remuneration in respect of that period[15].

1 Ie under the Employment Rights Act 1996 s 64 (employee suspended on medical grounds: see PARA 596) or, as the case may be, s 68 (employee suspended on maternity grounds: see PARA 598).
2 As to the meaning of 'employer' see PARA 2.
3 As to the meaning of 'employee' see PARA 2.
4 As to the meaning of 'suspension from work on medical grounds' see PARA 596.
5 As to the meaning of 'suspension from work on maternity grounds' see PARA 598.
6 As to the calculation of a week's pay see PARA 143 et seq; and as to the calculation date for these purposes see the Employment Rights Act 1996 s 225(5); and PARA 146. There is no statutory limit on the amount of a week's pay for these purposes.
7 As to the meaning of 'week' see PARA 126 note 13.
8 See the Employment Rights Act 1996 s 69(1). The period referred to in the text is the period of suspension referred to in s 64 (see PARA 596) or, as the case may be, s 68 (see PARA 598).
9 See the Employment Rights Act 1996 s 69(1).
10 See note 1.
11 Employment Rights Act 1996 s 69(2). As to the meaning of 'contract of employment' see PARA 2.
12 See note 1.
13 See the Employment Rights Act 1996 s 69(3).
14 See note 1.
15 See the Employment Rights Act 1996 s 69(3).

B. SUPPLY OF AGENCY WORKER ENDED ON MATERNITY GROUNDS

605. Calculation of remuneration for agency worker whose supply was ended on maternity grounds. The amount of remuneration payable[1] by a temporary work agency[2] to an agency worker[3] whose supply to a hirer[4] has been ended on maternity grounds[5] is a week's pay[6] in respect of each week[7] for which remuneration is payable[8]; and if, in any week, remuneration is payable in respect of only part of that week the amount of a week's pay is to be reduced proportionately[9].

Any such right to remuneration[10] does not affect any right of the agency worker in relation to remuneration under the contract with the temporary work agency ('contractual remuneration')[11]. Any contractual remuneration paid by the temporary work agency to an agency worker in respect of any period goes towards discharging the temporary work agency's liability[12] in respect of that period[13]; and, conversely, any payment of remuneration in discharge of a temporary work agency's liability[14] in respect of any period goes towards discharging any obligation of the temporary work agency to pay contractual remuneration in respect of that period[15].

1 Ie under the Employment Rights Act 1996 s 68C (see PARA 601).
2 Expressions used in the Employment Rights Act 1996 s 69A have the same meaning as in ss 68A–68C (see s 68D; and PARAS 601–603): see s 69A(5) (s 69A added by SI 2010/93). Accordingly, as to the meaning of 'temporary work agency' see PARA 97; definition in the Agency Workers Regulations 2010, SI 2010/93, reg 4, applied by the Employment Rights Act 1996 s 69A(5) (as so added).
3 As to the meaning of 'agency worker' see PARA 97; definition in the Agency Workers Regulations 2010, SI 2010/93, reg 3, applied by the Employment Rights Act 1996 s 69A(5) (as added: see note 2).
4 As to the meaning of 'hirer' see PARA 97 note 3; definition in the Agency Workers Regulations 2010, SI 2010/93, reg 2, applied by the Employment Rights Act 1996 s 69A(5) (as added: see note 2).
5 As to when the supply of an agency worker is ended on maternity grounds see PARA 601.
6 For these purposes, a week's pay is the weekly amount that would have been payable to the agency worker for performing the work, according to the terms of the contract with the temporary work agency, but for the fact that the supply of the agency worker to the hirer was ended on maternity grounds: Employment Rights Act 1996 s 69A(4) (as added: see note 2).
7 As to the meaning of 'week' see PARA 126 note 13.
8 See the Employment Rights Act 1996 s 69A(1) (as added: see note 2). The text refers to remuneration payable in accordance with s 68C (see PARA 601).
9 See the Employment Rights Act 1996 s 69A(1) (as added: see note 2).
10 See note 1.
11 See the Employment Rights Act 1996 s 69A(2) (as added: see note 2).
12 See note 1.
13 See the Employment Rights Act 1996 s 69A(3) (as added: see note 2).
14 See note 1.
15 See the Employment Rights Act 1996 s 69A(3) (as added: see note 2).

(iv) Complaint to Employment Tribunal: Employee's Work or Agency Worker's Supply ended on Medical or Maternity Grounds

A. EMPLOYEE SUSPENDED ON MEDICAL OR MATERNITY GROUNDS

606. Complaint to employment tribunal of employee suspended from work on medical or maternity grounds. An employee[1] may present a complaint to an employment tribunal[2] that his or her employer[3] has failed to pay the whole or any part of remuneration to which the employee is entitled[4] following suspension from work on either medical[5] or maternity grounds[6]. An employment tribunal must not consider such a complaint relating to remuneration in respect of any day unless it is presented[7]:

(1) before the end of the period of three months beginning with that day[8]; or
(2) within such further period as the tribunal considers reasonable in a case

where it is satisfied that it was not reasonably practicable for the complaint to be presented within the period of three months[9].

Where an employment tribunal finds such a complaint well-founded, the tribunal must order the employer to pay the employee the amount of remuneration which it finds is due to him or her[10].

An employee may also present a complaint to an employment tribunal that her employer has failed[11] to offer to provide her with alternative work[12]. An employment tribunal must not consider such a complaint unless it is presented[13]:

(a) before the end of the period of three months beginning with the first day of the suspension[14]; or

(b) within such further period as the tribunal considers reasonable in a case where it is satisfied that it was not reasonably practicable for the complaint to be presented within that period of three months[15].

Where an employment tribunal finds such a complaint well-founded, the tribunal may make an award of compensation to be paid by the employer to the employee[16], the amount of such compensation to be such as the tribunal considers just and equitable in all the circumstances having regard to: (i) the infringement of the employee's right to be offered alternative work[17] by the failure on the part of the employer to which the complaint relates[18]; and (ii) any loss sustained by the employee which is attributable to that failure[19].

1 As to the meaning of 'employee' see PARA 2.

2 As to employment tribunals see PARA 1399 et seq; and as to the procedure on a complaint made to an employment tribunal see PARA 1453 et seq.

3 As to the meaning of 'employer' see PARA 2.

4 Ie under the Employment Rights Act 1996 s 64 (employee suspended on medical grounds: see PARA 596) or, as the case may be, s 68 (employee suspended on maternity grounds: see PARA 598). The remedy of an employee for infringement of any right conferred by s 64 or, as the case may be, s 68 is by way of complaint to an employment tribunal and not otherwise: see s 205(1); and PARA 1406.

5 As to the meaning of 'suspension from work on medical grounds' see PARA 596.

6 Employment Rights Act 1996 s 70(1) (s 70(1)–(6) amended by the Employment Rights (Dispute Resolution) Act 1998 s 1(2)(a)). As to the meaning of 'suspension from work on maternity grounds' see PARA 598.

There is a requirement for early ACAS conciliation to be tried in order to promote a settlement before tribunal proceedings are instituted on a complaint under the Employment Rights Act 1996 s 70: see the Employment Tribunals Act 1996 s 18(1)(b); and PARA 152 note 1. As to the constitution and powers of ACAS see PARA 1213 et seq. As to the modification of the Employment Rights Act 1996 s 70 in relation to governing bodies of schools having a right to a delegated budget, acting in the exercise of their employment powers, see EDUCATION vol 35 (2011) PARA 355 et seq.

7 See the Employment Rights Act 1996 s 70(2) (as amended: see note 6).

8 Employment Rights Act 1996 s 70(2)(a). For the purposes of s 70(2)(a), s 207A(3) (extension because mediation in certain European cross-border disputes starts before the time limit expires: see PARA 1454) and s 207B (extension of time limits to facilitate conciliation before institution of proceedings: see PARA 1455) apply: see s 70(8) (added by SI 2011/1133; and amended by the Enterprise and Regulatory Reform Act 2013 s 8, Sch 2 paras 15, 29). As to time limits generally see PARA 1453.

9 Employment Rights Act 1996 s 70(2)(b).

10 Employment Rights Act 1996 s 70(3) (as amended: see note 6).

11 Ie in contravention of the Employment Rights Act 1996 s 67: see PARA 600.

12 Employment Rights Act 1996 s 70(4) (as amended: see note 6).

13 See the Employment Rights Act 1996 s 70(5) (as amended: see note 6).

14 Employment Rights Act 1996 s 70(5)(a). For the purposes of s 70(5)(a), s 207A(3) (extension because mediation in certain European cross-border disputes starts before the time limit expires: see PARA 1454) and s 207B (extension of time limits to facilitate conciliation before institution of proceedings: see PARA 1455) apply: see s 70(8) (as added and amended: see note 8).

15 Employment Rights Act 1996 s 70(5)(b).

16 See the Employment Rights Act 1996 s 70(6) (as amended: see note 6).
17 Ie under the Employment Rights Act 1996 s 67: see PARA 600.
18 Employment Rights Act 1996 s 70(7)(a).
19 Employment Rights Act 1996 s 70(7)(b).

B. SUPPLY OF AGENCY WORKER ENDED ON MATERNITY GROUNDS

607. Complaint to employment tribunal by agency worker whose supply was ended on maternity grounds. An agency worker[1] may present a complaint to an employment tribunal[2] that the temporary work agency[3] has failed to pay the whole or any part of remuneration to which the agency worker is entitled[4] when her supply to a hirer[5] has been ended on maternity grounds[6]. An employment tribunal must not consider such a complaint relating to remuneration in respect of any day unless it is presented[7]:

(1) before the end of the period of three months beginning with the day on which the supply of the agency worker to a hirer was ended on maternity grounds[8]; or
(2) within such further period as the tribunal considers reasonable in a case where it is satisfied that it was not reasonably practicable for the complaint to be presented within that period of three months[9].

Where an employment tribunal finds such a complaint well-founded, the tribunal must order the temporary work agency to pay the agency worker the amount of remuneration which it finds is due to her[10].

An agency worker may also present a complaint to an employment tribunal that the temporary work agency has failed[11] to offer to propose the agency worker to a hirer that has suitable alternative work available[12]. An employment tribunal must not consider such a complaint unless it is presented[13]:

(a) before the end of the period of three months beginning with the day on which the supply of the agency worker to a hirer was ended on maternity grounds[14]; or
(b) within such further period as the tribunal considers reasonable in a case where it is satisfied that it was not reasonably practicable for the complaint to be presented within that period of three months[15].

Where an employment tribunal finds such a complaint well-founded, the tribunal must order the temporary work agency to pay the agency worker the amount of compensation which it finds is due to her[16], the amount of such compensation to be such as the tribunal considers just and equitable in all the circumstances having regard to: (i) the infringement of the agency worker's right to be offered alternative work[17] by the failure on the part of the temporary work agency to which the complaint relates[18]; and (ii) any loss sustained by the agency worker which is attributable to that failure[19].

1 Expressions used in the Employment Rights Act 1996 s 70A have the same meaning as in ss 68A–68C (see s 68D; and PARAS 601–603): see s 70A(8) (s 70A added by SI 2010/93). Accordingly, as to the meaning of 'agency worker' see PARA 97; definition in the Agency Workers Regulations 2010, SI 2010/93, reg 3, applied by the Employment Rights Act 1996 s 70A(8) (as so added).
2 As to employment tribunals see PARA 1399 et seq; and as to the procedure on a complaint made to an employment tribunal see PARA 1453 et seq.
3 As to the meaning of 'temporary work agency' see PARA 97; definition in the Agency Workers Regulations 2010, SI 2010/93, reg 4, applied by the Employment Rights Act 1996 s 70A(8) (as added: see note 1).
4 Ie under the Employment Rights Act 1996 s 68C (see PARA 601). The remedy of an employee for infringement of any right conferred by s 68C (see PARA 601) is by way of complaint to an employment tribunal and not otherwise: see s 205(1); and PARA 1406.

5 As to the meaning of 'hirer' see PARA 97 note 3; definition in the Agency Workers Regulations 2010, SI 2010/93, reg 2, applied by the Employment Rights Act 1996 s 70A(8) (as added: see note 1).
6 Employment Rights Act 1996 s 70A(1) (as added: see note 1). As to when the supply of an agency worker is ended on maternity grounds see PARA 601.
There is a requirement for early ACAS conciliation to be tried in order to promote a settlement before tribunal proceedings are instituted on a complaint under s 70A: see the Employment Tribunals Act 1996 s 18(1)(b); and PARA 152 note 1. As to the constitution and powers of ACAS see PARA 1213 et seq.
7 See the Employment Rights Act 1996 s 70A(2) (as added: see note 1).
8 Employment Rights Act 1996 s 70A(2)(a) (as added: see note 1). For the purposes of s 70A(2)(a), s 207A(3) (extension because mediation in certain European cross-border disputes starts before the time limit expires: see PARA 1454) and s 207B (extension of time limits to facilitate conciliation before institution of proceedings: see PARA 1455) apply: see s 70A(7A) (s 70A as so added; s 70A(7A) added by the Enterprise and Regulatory Reform Act 2013 s 8, Sch 2 paras 15, 30). As to time limits generally see PARA 1453.
9 Employment Rights Act 1996 s 70A(2)(b) (as added: see note 1).
10 Employment Rights Act 1996 s 70A(3) (as added: see note 1).
11 Ie in contravention of the Employment Rights Act 1996 s 68B (see PARA 603).
12 Employment Rights Act 1996 s 70A(4) (as added: see note 1).
13 See the Employment Rights Act 1996 s 70A(5) (as added: see note 1).
14 Employment Rights Act 1996 s 70A(5)(a) (as added: see note 1). For the purposes of s 70A(5)(a), s 207A(3) (extension because mediation in certain European cross-border disputes starts before the time limit expires: see PARA 1454) and s 207B (extension of time limits to facilitate conciliation before institution of proceedings: see PARA 1455) apply: see s 70A(7A) (as added: see note 8).
15 Employment Rights Act 1996 s 70A(5)(b) (as added: see note 1).
16 See the Employment Rights Act 1996 s 70A(6) (as added: see note 1).
17 Ie under the Employment Rights Act 1996 s 68B (see PARA 603).
18 Employment Rights Act 1996 s 70A(7)(a) (as added: see note 1).
19 Employment Rights Act 1996 s 70A(7)(b) (as added: see note 1).

(15) PROTECTION FROM DISCRIMINATION IN EMPLOYMENT; SHELTERED EMPLOYMENT

A. GENERAL PROVISION MADE UNDER THE EQUALITY ACT 2010

608. Law of discrimination under the Equality Act 2010. The Equality Act 2010, which brings together previously-disparate elements of statutory law that dealt with discrimination[1] under a system that relies upon the key concepts of 'protected characteristics' and 'prohibited conduct', is dealt with elsewhere in the work, including the application of that Act as it relates specifically to employment[2].

1 Eg the Equal Pay Act 1970, the Sex Discrimination Act 1975, the Race Relations Act 1976, the Disability Discrimination Act 1995, the Employment Equality (Religion and Belief) Regulations 2003, SI 2003/1660, the Employment Equality (Sexual Orientation) Regulations 2003, SI 2003/1661, and the Employment Equality (Age) Regulations 2006, SI 2006/1031: see DISCRIMINATION vol 33 (2013) PARA 1 et seq.
2 See PARA 51. As to specific provision that is made for employment tribunals to order equal pay audits see PARA 609. As to employment, discrimination and victimisation generally see DISCRIMINATION vol 33 (2013) PARA 110 et seq.

609. Equal pay audits. Regulations under the Equality Act 2010[1] may make provision requiring an employment tribunal[2] to order the respondent to carry out an equal pay audit in any case where the tribunal finds that there has been an equal pay breach[3]. An equal pay audit is an audit designed to identify action to be taken to avoid equal pay breaches occurring or continuing[4].

The regulations may make further provision about equal pay audits[5], including provision about:

(1) the content of an audit[6];
(2) the powers and duties of a tribunal for deciding whether its order has been complied with[7];
(3) any circumstances in which an audit may be required to be published or may be disclosed to any person[8].

The regulations must provide for an equal pay audit not to be ordered where the tribunal considers that[9]:

(a) an audit completed by the respondent in the previous three years meets requirements prescribed for this purpose[10];
(b) it is clear without an audit whether any action is required to avoid equal pay breaches occurring or continuing[11];
(c) the breach the tribunal has found gives no reason to think that there may be other breaches[12]; or
(d) the disadvantages of an equal pay audit would outweigh its benefits[13].

The regulations may provide for an employment tribunal to have power, where a person fails to comply with an order to carry out an equal pay audit, to order that person to pay a penalty to the Secretary of State[14] of not more than an amount specified in the regulations[15]; and the regulations may provide for that power to be exercisable in prescribed circumstances[16], and more than once (if the failure to comply continues)[17].

1 As to the making of subordinate legislation under the Equality Act 2010 see ss 207–210; and DISCRIMINATION vol 33 (2013) PARA 4.

2 As to employment tribunals see PARA 1399 et seq; and as to the procedure on a complaint made to an employment tribunal see PARA 1453 et seq.

3 Equality Act 2010 s 139A(1) (s 139A added by the Enterprise and Regulatory Reform Act 2013 s 98(1), (2)). For these purposes, an equal pay breach is:

(1) a breach of an equality clause (Equality Act 2010 s 139A(2)(a) (as so added)); or
(2) a contravention in relation to pay of s 39(2) (see DISCRIMINATION vol 33 (2013) PARA 111), 49(6) (see DISCRIMINATION vol 33 (2013) PARA 119) or 50(6) (see DISCRIMINATION vol 33 (2013) PARA 120), so far as relating to sex discrimination (s 139A(2)(b) (as so added)).

Before making regulations under s 139A, a Minister of the Crown must consult any other Minister of the Crown with responsibility for employment tribunals: s 139A(12) (as so added). The first regulations under s 139A must specify an exemption period during which the requirement to order an equal pay audit does not apply in the case of a business that had fewer than 10 employees immediately before a specified time, or was begun as a new business in a specified period: see s 139A(10) (as so added). For these purposes, 'specified' means specified in the regulations, and the number of employees a business had or the time when a business was begun as a new business is to be determined in accordance with the regulations: see s 139A(11) (as so added). As to equality clauses defined for the purposes of the Equality Act 2010 see DISCRIMINATION vol 33 (2013) PARA 111. As to equality of terms and equal pay generally see DISCRIMINATION vol 33 (2013) PARA 130 et seq.

In exercise of the powers conferred by ss 139A and 207(1), (4), the Secretary of State has made the Equality Act 2010 (Equal Pay Audits) Regulations 2014, SI 2014/2559, which came into force on 1 October 2014 (see reg 1), and which:

(a) require a tribunal to order the respondent to carry out an audit unless one of the exceptions in reg 3 or reg 4 applies (see head (b) below) (see reg 2);
(b) set out exceptions to the requirement to order the respondent to carry out an audit (see reg 3), and exempt new businesses and micro-businesses from the requirement to carry out an audit during the exemption period (see reg 4, Schedule);
(c) make provision in relation to the content of the tribunal's order under reg 2 (see head (a) above) and requires the order to specify the persons about whom information should be included in the audit, the period of time to which the audit must relate and the time by which an audit must be received by the tribunal (see reg 5);
(d) require an audit to include information relating to the pay of men and women in

respect of whom the respondent could be liable for an equal pay breach under the Equality Act 2010 ('relevant gender pay information'), to explain the content of the audit, and set out an action plan for avoiding equal pay breaches occurring or continuing (see the Equality Act 2010 (Equal Pay Audits) Regulations 2014, SI 2014/2559, reg 6);

(e) set out the powers of the tribunal to determine, on the papers, whether an audit received by the tribunal by the date set out in its order complies with that part of its order relating to the content of the audit (see reg 7);

(f) set out the procedure applicable where the tribunal is not satisfied that an audit complies with that part of its order relating to the content of the audit, or where no audit has been received (see reg 8);

(g) set out the manner in and time by which the respondent must publish the audit and send evidence of publication to the tribunal, subject to an exception where publication would be likely to result in a breach of a legal obligation and where the tribunal agrees (see reg 9);

(h) set out the procedure applicable to the tribunal when determining whether the respondent has complied with its order in so far as it relates to the requirement to publish the order (see reg 10); and

(i) provide that a tribunal may order the respondent to pay a penalty to the Secretary of State where the respondent fails to comply with an order made under reg 2 (see head (a) above) or reg 8 (see head (f) above), the amount of any individual penalty not exceeding £5,000 (see reg 11).

4 Equality Act 2010 s 139A(3) (as added: see note 3).
5 See the Equality Act 2010 s 139A(4) (as added: see note 3).
6 Equality Act 2010 s 139A(4)(a) (as added: see note 3).
7 Equality Act 2010 s 139A(4)(b) (as added: see note 3).
8 Equality Act 2010 s 139A(4)(c) (as added: see note 3).
9 See the Equality Act 2010 s 139A(5) (as added: see note 3).
10 Equality Act 2010 s 139A(5)(a) (as added: see note 3).
11 Equality Act 2010 s 139A(5)(b) (as added: see note 3).
12 Equality Act 2010 s 139A(5)(c) (as added: see note 3).
13 Equality Act 2010 s 139A(5)(d) (as added: see note 3).
14 As to the Secretary of State for these purposes see DISCRIMINATION vol 33 (2013) PARA 4.
15 See the Equality Act 2010 s 139A(6) (as added: see note 3). The first regulations made by virtue of s 139A(6) must not specify an amount of more than £5,000: s 139A(8) (as so added). Sums received by the Secretary of State under the regulations must be paid into the Consolidated Fund: s 139A(9) (as so added). As to the Consolidated Fund see CONSTITUTIONAL AND ADMINISTRATIVE LAW vol 20 (2014) PARA 480 et seq; PARLIAMENT vol 78 (2010) PARAS 1028–1031.
16 Equality Act 2010 s 139A(7)(a) (as added: see note 3).
17 Equality Act 2010 s 139A(7)(b) (as added: see note 3).

B. SPECIFIC PROVISION MADE FOR SHELTERED EMPLOYMENT

610. Provision of sheltered employment for seriously disabled persons. Facilities may be provided[1] for enabling disabled persons[2] who, by reason of the nature or severity of their disability[3], are unlikely, either at any time or until after the lapse of a prolonged period, to be able otherwise to obtain employment, or to undertake work on their own account[4], to obtain employment or to undertake such work under special conditions, and for the training of such persons for the employment or work in question[5].

The nature of the facilities to be so provided are such as the Secretary of State[6] may determine; and the Secretary of State may, with the approval of the Treasury[7], make arrangements for the provision thereof by any company, association or body which appears to the Secretary of State to be able and willing to provide the requisite facilities in an efficient and proper manner[8].

The Secretary of State, or with his authorisation any such company, association or body so providing facilities, may defray or contribute towards expenses incurred by persons for whom facilities are so provided in travelling to and from the place where they are employed or work or where training is provided, and may make payments to or in respect of such persons, up to such amounts as the Secretary of State may, with the approval of the Treasury, determine and in such manner as he may determine[9].

Payments may be made by the Secretary of State:

(1) in respect of the expenses of the formation and incorporation of any such company[10];

(2) to any such company, association or body in respect of expenses incurred by it in providing such facilities, or of other specified expenses incurred[11] by it[12]; and

(3) to any local authority in respect of expenses incurred by it under any enactment conferring powers on it in that behalf in providing under arrangements made between the Secretary of State and the authority facilities approved by him[13], in defraying or contributing towards expenses incurred by persons for whom such facilities are so provided in travelling[14], or in making payments to or in respect of such persons[15],

up to such amounts as the Secretary of State may, with the approval of the Treasury, determine[16].

The Secretary of State must so exercise his discretion in selecting persons for facilities[17] at any time while it appears to him that they cannot for the time being be provided for all persons in need of them, as to secure that, so far as consistent with the efficient exercise of his powers, preference is given to persons who have served whole-time in the armed forces of the Crown or in the merchant navy or the mercantile marine and whose disability is due to that service[18].

1 Ie as specified in the Disabled Persons (Employment) Act 1944 s 15.

2 For these purposes, a person is a disabled person if he is a disabled person for the purposes of the Equality Act 2010 (see DISCRIMINATION vol 33 (2013) PARA 50 et seq): see the Disabled Persons (Employment) Act 1944 s 15(5A) (added by the Disability Discrimination Act 1995 s 61(1), (5); and amended by the Equality Act 2010 s 211(1), Sch 26 para 1 (added by SI 2010/2279)).

3 For these purposes, 'disability' has the same meaning as in the Equality Act 2010 (see DISCRIMINATION vol 33 (2013) PARA 50 et seq): see the Disabled Persons (Employment) Act 1944 s 15(5A) (as added and amended: see note 2).

4 Ie whether because employment or such work would not be available to them or because they would be unlikely to be able to compete therein on terms comparable as respects earnings and security with those enjoyed by persons engaged therein who do not have a disability: see the Disabled Persons (Employment) Act 1944 s 15(1) (amended by the Disability Discrimination Act 1995 s 61(1), (2)).

5 Disabled Persons (Employment) Act 1944 s 15(1) (as amended: see note 4).

6 As to the Secretary of State for these purposes see DISCRIMINATION vol 33 (2013) PARA 4.

7 As to the Treasury see CONSTITUTIONAL AND ADMINISTRATIVE LAW vol 20 (2014) PARAS 262–265.

8 Disabled Persons (Employment) Act 1944 s 15(2) (amended by the Disability Discrimination Act 1995 s 61(1), (3)). The only kind of company which the Secretary of State himself may form in exercising his powers under the Disabled Persons (Employment) Act 1944 s 15 is a company which is:

(1) required by its constitution to apply its profits, if any, or other income in promoting its objects (s 15(2A)(a) (s 15(2A) added by the Disability Discrimination Act 1995 s 61(1), (4))); and

(2) prohibited by its constitution from paying any dividend to its members (s 15(2A)(b) (as so added)).

The objects of any company to be so formed may include all such objects as appear to the Secretary of State to be requisite for enabling it to act effectively for these purposes; and any such company must be constituted so as to enable all or any of its operations to be controlled by the Secretary of State or persons acting on his behalf as may appear to the Secretary of State to be requisite: s 15(3).

9 Disabled Persons (Employment) Act 1944 s 15(4).

These provisions do not apply where the detriment in question amounts to dismissal[9].

1 As to the meaning of 'employee' see PARA 2.
2 There is no statutory definition of the term 'detriment': see PARA 614 note 2. See also note 7.
3 As to the meaning of 'act' for these purposes see PARA 614 note 3.
4 As to the meaning of 'employer' see PARA 2.
5 See the Employment Rights Act 1996 s 43M(1) (s 43M added by the Employment Relations Act 2004 s 40(1)). As to the right to make a complaint to an employment tribunal see PARA 625; and as to remedies see PARA 626.
6 Ie under the Juries Act 1974 (see **JURIES** vol 61 (2010) PARA 812 et seq) or the Coroners and Justice Act 2009 Pt 1 (ss 1–50) (see **CORONERS** vol 24 (2010) PARA 138 et seq).
7 Employment Rights Act 1996 s 43M(1)(a) (s 43M as added (see note 5); s 43M(1)(a) amended by the Coroners and Justice Act 2009 s 177(1), Sch 21 para 36(1), (2)).
For the purposes of the Employment Rights Act 1996 s 43M, an employee is not to be regarded as having been subjected to a detriment by a failure to pay remuneration in respect of a relevant period unless under his contract of employment he is entitled to be paid that remuneration: s 43M(3) (as so added). A 'relevant period' means any period during which the employee is absent from work because of his attendance at any place in pursuance of being summoned as mentioned in s 43M(1)(a): see s 43M(4) (as so added). As to the meaning of 'contract of employment' see PARA 2. In addition, the right conferred by s 43M does not apply to a share fisherman (see s 199(2); and PARA 167) or to a police officer (see s 200(1); and PARA 168), and may also be lost for some other reason than statutory exclusion, in particular because the contract of employment is illegal (see PARA 18) or has terminated for some reason other than dismissal (see PARA 725 et seq).
8 Employment Rights Act 1996 s 43M(1)(b) (as added: see note 5).
9 See the Employment Rights Act 1996 s 43M(2) (as added: see note 5). For these purposes, 'dismissal' has the meaning given in Pt X (ss 94–134A) (unfair dismissal: see PARA 757 et seq): see s 43M(2) (as so added). As to the provisions governing dismissal for jury service see PARA 785.

614. Detriment arising from health and safety cases. An employee[1] has the right not to be subjected to any detriment[2] by any act[3], or any deliberate failure to act, by his employer[4] on the ground that:

(1) having been designated by the employer to carry out activities in connection with preventing or reducing risks to health and safety at work, the employee carried out, or proposed to carry out, any such activities[5];
(2) being a representative of workers[6] on matters of health and safety at work or member of a safety committee:
 (a) in accordance with arrangements established under or by virtue of any enactment; or
 (b) by reason of being acknowledged as such by the employer,
 the employee performed, or proposed to perform, any functions as such a representative or a member of such a committee[7];
(3) the employee took part, or proposed to take part, in consultation with the employer on matters of health and safety[8] or in an election of representatives of employee safety[9], whether as a candidate or otherwise[10];
(4) being an employee at a place where:
 (a) there was no such representative or safety committee; or
 (b) there was such a representative or safety committee but it was not reasonably practicable for the employee to raise the matter by those means,
 he brought to his employer's attention, by reasonable means, circumstances connected with his work which he reasonably believed were harmful or potentially harmful to health or safety[11];

(5) in circumstances of danger[12] which the employee reasonably believed to be serious and imminent and which he could not reasonably have been expected to avert, he left, or proposed to leave, or, while the danger persisted, refused to return to his place of work or any dangerous part of his place of work[13]; or

(6) in circumstances of danger which the employee reasonably believed to be serious and imminent, he took, or proposed to take, appropriate steps[14] to protect himself or other persons[15] from the danger[16].

These provisions do not apply where the detriment in question amounts to dismissal[17].

The provisions are extended to the police by providing that for these purposes[18] the holding, otherwise than under a contract of employment[19], of the office of constable or an appointment as police cadet is to be treated as employment[20] by the relevant officer[21] under a contract of employment[22].

1 As to the meaning of 'employee' see PARA 2.

2 There is no statutory definition of the term 'detriment'. Cf the similar provisions of the Trade Union and Labour Relations (Consolidation) Act 1992 s 146 (as originally enacted) (see PARA 612 note 5) under which an employee had the right not to 'have action short of dismissal taken against him as an individual' by his employer on grounds related to union membership or activities, which was held to cover disciplinary measures (*British Airways Board v Clark and Havill* [1982] IRLR 238, EAT) and refusal of promotion (*Gallacher v Department of Transport* [1994] ICR 967, [1994] IRLR 231, CA).

3 For these purposes, except in so far as the context otherwise requires, 'act' and 'action' each includes omission; and references to doing an act or taking action are to be construed accordingly: see the Employment Rights Act 1996 s 235(1).

4 As to the meaning of 'employer' see PARA 2.

5 Employment Rights Act 1996 s 44(1)(a). As to the right to make a complaint to an employment tribunal see PARA 625; and as to remedies see PARA 626.

6 Ie a representative under the Safety Representatives and Safety Committees Regulations 1977, SI 1977/500: see PARA 1073 et seq; and **HEALTH AND SAFETY AT WORK** vol 52 (2014) PARA 414. As to the scope of the representative's authority see *Shillito v Van Leer (UK) Ltd* [1997] IRLR 495, EAT.

7 Employment Rights Act 1996 s 44(1)(b).

8 Ie pursuant to the Health and Safety (Consultation with Employees) Regulations 1996, SI 1996/1513: see PARAS 1203–1204; and **HEALTH AND SAFETY AT WORK** vol 52 (2014) PARA 415. The Health and Safety (Consultation with Employees) Regulations 1996, SI 1996/1513, supplement the Safety Representatives and Safety Committees Regulations 1977, SI 1977/500 (see note 6) by putting in place a system for direct election of employee safety representatives where there is no recognised trade union, in order to achieve coverage of all employees as required by Council Directive (EC) 89/391 (OJ L183, 29.6.89, p 1): see PARA 1203; and **HEALTH AND SAFETY AT WORK** vol 52 (2014) PARA 311.

9 Ie within the meaning of the Health and Safety (Consultation with Employees) Regulations 1996, SI 1996/1513: see **HEALTH AND SAFETY AT WORK** vol 52 (2014) PARA 415.

10 Employment Rights Act 1996 s 44(1)(ba) (added by SI 1996/1513).

11 Employment Rights Act 1996 s 44(1)(c). The Employment Rights Act 1996 s 44(1)(c) does not apply where the employee has been unable to demonstrate any detriment through health and safety disclosures, other than a factor which had been an ingredient in the decision to dismiss: *Breslin v Sherlock Jenkins Boswell* [2004] All ER (D) 54 (Nov), EAT (ample evidence to support conclusion that employee was dismissed due to concerns about standard of work).

12 'Danger' is to be construed broadly and is not confined to physical danger from machinery: *Harvest Press Ltd v McCaffrey* [1999] IRLR 778, EAT (immediate threats of violence from fellow employee covered; decided under the Employment Rights Act 1996 s 100: see PARA 786).

13 Employment Rights Act 1996 s 44(1)(d).

14 For the purposes of head (6) in the text, whether steps which an employee took, or proposed to take, were appropriate is to be judged by reference to all the circumstances including, in particular, his knowledge and the facilities and advice available to him at the time: Employment Rights Act 1996 s 44(2).

or appeal in relation to study or training, or the employee's right, at his request, at such a meeting[12] to be accompanied or to accompany another employee[13].

As from a day to be appointed[14], an employee in England also has the right not to be subjected to any detriment by any act, or any deliberate failure to act, by his employer done on the ground that, being a person entitled to be permitted to participate in education or training[15], the employee exercised, or proposed to exercise, that right[16]. These provisions do not apply where the detriment in question amounts to dismissal[17].

1 As to the meaning of 'employee' see PARA 2.
2 There is no statutory definition of the term 'detriment': see PARA 614 note 2.
3 As to the meaning of 'act' for these purposes see PARA 614 note 3.
4 As to the meaning of 'employer' see PARA 2.
5 Ie within the meaning of the Employment Rights Act 1996 s 63A(3): see PARA 331.
6 Ie under the Employment Rights Act 1996 s 63A(1) or s 63A(3): see PARA 331. As to the meaning of 'Wales' see PARA 2 note 12.
7 Ie under the Employment Rights Act 1996 s 63B(1): see PARA 331.
8 Employment Rights Act 1996 s 47A(1) (s 47A added by the Teaching and Higher Education Act 1998 Sch 3 para 10). As to the right to make a complaint to an employment tribunal see PARA 625; and as to remedies see PARA 626.
9 See the Employment Rights Act 1996 s 47A(2) (as added (see note 8); and amended by the Employment Relations Act 1999 ss 18(1), (2), 44, Sch 9). For these purposes, 'dismissal' has the meaning given in the Employment Rights Act 1996 Pt X (ss 94–134A) (unfair dismissal: see PARA 757 et seq): see s 47A(2) (as so added and amended).
10 As to the meaning of 'England' see PARA 2 note 12.
11 Ie the right under the Employee Study and Training (Procedural Requirements) Regulations 2010, SI 2010/155, reg 16(2) (see PARA 328) or reg 16(5) (see PARA 328): see reg 18(1).
12 Ie at a meeting held under the Employee Study and Training (Procedural Requirements) Regulations 2010, SI 2010/155, reg 4(1) (see PARA 328) or reg 10(1) (see PARA 329): see reg 18(1).
13 Employee Study and Training (Procedural Requirements) Regulations 2010, SI 2010/155, reg 18(1).
14 The Employment Rights Act 1996 s 47AA is added by the Education and Skills Act 2008 s 37 as from a day to be appointed under s 173(4). At the date at which this volume states the law, no such day had been appointed.
15 Ie by the Education and Skills Act 2008 s 27 (not yet in force) (see PARA 649) or s 28 (not yet in force) (see PARA 650).
16 Employment Rights Act 1996 s 47AA(1) (prospectively added: see note 14).
17 See the Employment Rights Act 1996 s 47AA(2) (prospectively added: see note 14). For these purposes, 'dismissal' has the meaning given in Pt X (ss 94–134A) (unfair dismissal: see PARA 757 et seq): see s 47AA(2) (prospectively added).

619. Detriment arising from protected disclosures. A worker[1] has the right not to be subjected to any detriment[2] by any act[3], or any deliberate failure to act, by his employer[4] done on the ground that the worker has made a protected disclosure[5].

A worker also has the right not to be subjected to any detriment by any act, or any deliberate failure to act, done[6]:

(1) by an individual co-worker of his employer in the course of that co-worker's employment[7]; or

(2) by an agent of his employer acting with the employer's authority[8],

on the ground that the worker has made a protected disclosure[9]. A person acting under head (1) or head (2) above is not liable in this way[10] for doing something that subjects the worker to detriment if the co-worker or agent concerned does that thing in reliance on a statement by the employer that doing it does not contravene the Employment Rights Act 1996[11], and if it is reasonable for that co-worker or agent to rely on the statement[12].

These provisions do not apply where: (a) the worker is an employee[13]; and (b) the detriment in question amounts to dismissal[14].

1 For these purposes, and for the purposes of the Employment Rights Act 1996 s 48 (see PARA 625) and s 49 (see PARA 626), so far as relating to s 47B, 'worker' has the extended meaning given by s 43K (see PARA 69 note 3): see s 47B(3) (s 47B added by the Public Interest Disclosure Act 1998 ss 2, 18(2)). See *BP plc v Elstone* [2011] 1 All ER 718, [2010] ICR 879, EAT (there is no reason to suppose that there is an implied restriction of the expressions 'worker' and 'employer' in the Employment Rights Act 1996 s 43A (see PARA 69) and s 43B (see PARA 70) to that which was work under the same contract and for the same employer as that referred to in s 47B); and see note 2.

2 There is no statutory definition of the term 'detriment': see PARA 614 note 2. For these purposes, 'detriment' can include acts committed after the termination of employment: *Woodward v Abbey National plc* [2006] EWCA Civ 822, [2006] 4 All ER 1209, [2006] ICR 1436. The courts are obliged therefore to take a purposive approach to the statutory provisions, so as to advance the protection of whistle-blowers from later retribution by an employer, and the protection a worker enjoys under the Employment Rights Act 1996 s 47B includes protection against a detriment suffered by the actions of his employer in respect of a protected disclosure which had been made at a time when he had neither been a worker for nor an employee of that employer (eg where the disclosure which inspired the hostile act by his current employer might be related to any earlier time at which the current worker was then of worker status, whoever was his employer): *BP plc v Elstone* [2011] 1 All ER 718, [2010] ICR 879, EAT.

3 As to the meaning of 'act' for these purposes see PARA 614 note 3.

4 For these purposes, and for the purposes of the Employment Rights Act 1996 s 48 (see PARA 625) and s 49 (see PARA 626), so far as relating to s 47B, 'employer' has the extended meaning given by s 43K (see PARA 69 note 5): see s 47B(3) (as added: see note 1). See also *BP plc v Elstone* [2011] 1 All ER 718, [2010] ICR 879, EAT; and notes 1, 2.

5 Employment Rights Act 1996 s 47B(1) (as added: see note 1). As to the meaning of 'protected disclosure' see PARA 69. As to the right to make a complaint to an employment tribunal see PARA 625; and as to remedies see PARA 626. See also *Flynn v Warrior Square Recoveries Ltd* [2012] All ER (D) 351 (Oct), EAT; and PARA 625 note 16.

In order to establish liability under the Employment Rights Act 1996 s 47B, it must be shown that the protected disclosure has influenced the act or omission complained of; it is not sufficient to show that the act or omission simply relates to the disclosure: *Harrow London Borough Council v Knight* [2003] IRLR 140, EAT (chief executive's failure to respond to the employee's letters was related to the protected disclosure but there had been no examination of the factors influencing the chief executive's failure to respond). See also *Meteorological Office v Edgar* [2002] ICR 149, EAT (disclosure pre-dating the coming into force of the Public Interest Disclosure Act 1998 s 43B (see PARA 70) but with the facts giving rise to the respondent's cause of action not pre-dating the coming into force of s 47B; the statutory tort was not completed until the appellant performed an act of victimisation by subjecting him to a detriment, as a result of his having earlier made a protected disclosure).

As a matter of statutory construction, the Employment Rights Act 1996 s 47B does not prohibit the drawing of a distinction between the making of protected disclosures and the manner or way in which an employee goes about the process of dealing with protected disclosures: *Evans v Bolton School* [2006] EWCA Civ 1653, [2007] ICR 641 sub nom *Bolton School v Evans* [2007] IRLR 140 (worker hacked into computer system to demonstrate that it failed to comply with data protection legislation: conduct was not part of the disclosure because acts taken consequent to the disclosure are not part of it); applied in *Panayiotou v Chief Constable of Hampshire Police* [2014] IRLR 500, EAT (the question is whether the factors relied upon by the employer can properly be treated as separable from the making of protected disclosures and if so, whether those factors were, in fact, the reasons why the employer acted as he did; it had been permissible for the tribunal in this case to treat the particular features of the case, and the consequences of the complaints that had been made, as separable from the fact that the claimant had made protected disclosures).

6 See the Employment Rights Act 1996 s 47B(1A) (s 47B as added (see note 1); s 47B(1A)–(1E) added by the Enterprise and Regulatory Reform Act 2013 s 19(1)). Where a worker is subjected to detriment by anything done as mentioned in the Employment Rights Act 1996 s 47B(1A), that thing is treated as also done by the worker's employer: s 47B(1B) (as so added). For these purposes, it is immaterial whether the thing is done with the knowledge or approval of the worker's employer: s 47B(1C) (as so added). As to case law on vicarious liability and victimisation that pre-dated this statutory provision see *Pinnington v Swansea City and County Council* [2005] EWCA Civ 135, [2005] ICR 685; *Fecitt v NHS Manchester* [2011] EWCA Civ

621. Detriment arising from exercise of tax credit rights. An employee[1] has the right not to be subjected to any detriment[2] by any act[3], or any deliberate failure to act, by his employer[4], done on the ground that:

(1) any action was taken, or was proposed to be taken, by or on behalf of the employee with a view to enforcing, or otherwise securing the benefit of, a right conferred[5] on the employee[6];

(2) a penalty was imposed on the employer, or proceedings for a penalty were brought against him[7] as a result of action taken by or on behalf of the employee for the purpose of enforcing, or otherwise securing the benefit of, such a right[8]; or

(3) the employee is entitled, or will or may be entitled, to working tax credit[9].

These provisions do not apply to an employee if the detriment in question amounts to dismissal[10].

1 The provisions of the Employment Rights Act 1996 s 47D(1), (2) (see heads (1)–(3) in the text) apply to a person who is not an employee within the meaning of the Employment Rights Act 1996 (see PARA 2) but who is an employee within the meaning of the Tax Credits Act 2002 s 25 (see WELFARE BENEFITS AND STATE PENSIONS vol 104 (2014) PARA 358), with references to his employer in the Employment Rights Act 1996 s 47D(1), (2), and s 48(2), (4) (see PARA 625) and s 49(1) (see PARA 626), being construed in accordance with the Tax Credits Act 2002 s 25: Employment Rights Act 1996 s 47D(3) (s 47D added by Tax Credits Act 2002 Sch 1 para 1(1), (2)).

2 There is no statutory definition of the term 'detriment': see PARA 614 note 2.

3 As to the meaning of 'act' for these purposes see PARA 614 note 3.

4 As to the meaning of 'employer' see PARA 2.

5 Ie by regulations under the Tax Credits Act 2002 s 25: see WELFARE BENEFITS AND STATE PENSIONS vol 104 (2014) PARA 358.

6 Employment Rights Act 1996 s 47D(1)(a) (as added: see note 1). For the purposes of s 47D(1)(a) and s 47D(1)(b) (see head (2) in the text), it is immaterial: (1) whether or not the worker has the right; or (2) whether or not the right has been infringed, but for s 47D(1)(a), (b) to apply, the claim to the right and (if applicable) the claim that it has been infringed must be made in good faith: see s 47D(2) (as so added).

7 Ie under the Tax Credits Act 2002: see WELFARE BENEFITS AND STATE PENSIONS vol 104 (2014) PARA 335 et seq.

8 Employment Rights Act 1996 s 47D(1)(b) (as added: see note 1). See also note 6.

9 Employment Rights Act 1996 s 47D(1)(c) (as added: see note 1). As to working tax credit see WELFARE BENEFITS AND STATE PENSIONS vol 104 (2014) PARA 335 et seq.

10 See the Employment Rights Act 1996 s 47D(4) (as added: see note 1). For these purposes, 'dismissal' has the meaning given in Pt X (ss 94–134A) (unfair dismissal: see PARA 757 et seq): see s 47D(4) (as so added). As to the provisions governing dismissal in relation to tax credit rights see PARA 795.

622. Detriment arising from flexible working cases. An employee[1] has the right not to be subjected to any detriment[2] by any act[3], or any deliberate failure to act, by his employer[4] done on the ground that the employee[5]:

(1) made, or proposed to make, an application[6] for a change in his terms and conditions to allow for flexible working[7];

(2) brought proceedings[8] against the employer alleging that the employer has failed to comply with his statutory duties in relation to such an application or that a decision by his employer to reject the application was based on incorrect facts[9]; or

(3) alleged the existence of any circumstance which would constitute a ground for bringing such proceedings[10].

These provisions do not apply where the detriment in question amounts to dismissal[11].

1 As to the meaning of 'employee' see PARA 2.
2 There is no statutory definition of the term 'detriment': see PARA 614 note 2.
3 As to the meaning of 'act' for these purposes see PARA 614 note 3.
4 As to the meaning of 'employer' see PARA 2.
5 See the Employment Rights Act 1996 s 47E(1) (s 47E added by the Employment Act 2002 s 47(1), (3)).
6 Ie under the Employment Rights Act 1996 s 80F: see PARA 108.
7 Employment Rights Act 1996 s 47E(1)(a) (as added: see note 5).
8 Ie under the Employment Rights Act 1996 s 80H: see PARA 111.
9 Employment Rights Act 1996 s 47E(1)(c) (as added: see note 5).
10 Employment Rights Act 1996 s 47E(1)(d) (as added: see note 5).
11 See the Employment Rights Act 1996 s 47E(2) (as added: see note 5). For these purposes, 'dismissal' has the meaning given in Pt X (ss 94–134A) (unfair dismissal: see PARA 757 et seq): see s 47E(2) (as so added). As to the provisions governing dismissal in relation to flexible working see PARA 796.

623. Detriment arising from study and training application cases. An employee[1] has the right not to be subjected to any detriment[2] by any act[3], or any deliberate failure to act, by his employer[4] done on the ground that the employee[5]:

(1) made, or proposed to make, an application[6] pursuant to his right to request study or training[7];
(2) exercised, or proposed to exercise, a right conferred on him[8] in relation to such an application[9];
(3) brought proceedings[10] against the employer alleging that the employer has failed to comply with his statutory duties in relation to such an application or that a decision by his employer to reject the application was based on incorrect facts[11]; or
(4) alleged the existence of any circumstance which would constitute a ground for bringing such proceedings[12].

These provisions do not apply where the detriment in question amounts to dismissal[13].

1 As to the meaning of 'employee' see PARA 2.
2 There is no statutory definition of the term 'detriment': see PARA 614 note 2.
3 As to the meaning of 'act' for these purposes see PARA 614 note 3.
4 As to the meaning of 'employer' see PARA 2. At the date at which this volume states the law, small employers are excluded from this provision: see note 5.
5 See the Employment Rights Act 1996 s 47F(1) (s 47F added by the Apprenticeships, Skills, Children and Learning Act 2009 s 40(1), (3)).

At the date at which this volume states the law, the Apprenticeships, Skills, Children and Learning Act 2009 s 40 has come into force for all purposes except in relation to small employers and their employees: see the Apprenticeships, Skills, Children and Learning Act 2009 (Commencement No 2 and Transitional and Saving Provisions) Order 2010, SI 2010/303, art 4, Sch 3. As to the meaning of 'small employer' for these purposes see PARA 328 note 1.
6 Ie under the Employment Rights Act 1996 s 63D: see PARA 328.
7 Employment Rights Act 1996 s 47F(1)(a) (as added: see note 5).
8 Ie under the Employment Rights Act 1996 s 63F: see PARA 328.
9 Employment Rights Act 1996 s 47F(1)(b) (as added: see note 5).
10 Ie under the Employment Rights Act 1996 s 63I: see PARA 330.
11 Employment Rights Act 1996 s 47F(1)(c) (as added: see note 5).
12 Employment Rights Act 1996 s 47F(1)(d) (as added: see note 5).
13 See the Employment Rights Act 1996 s 47F(2) (as added: see note 5). For these purposes, 'dismissal' has the meaning given in Pt X (ss 94–134A) (unfair dismissal: see PARA 757 et seq): see s 47F(2) (as so added). As to the provisions governing dismissal in relation to flexible working see PARA 796.

624. Detriment arising from refusal to accept offer to become an employee shareholder. An employee[1] has the right not to be subjected to a detriment[2] by any act[3], or any deliberate failure to act, by his employer[4] done on the ground that the employee refused to accept an offer by the employer for the employee to become an employee shareholder[5].

This provision does not apply where the detriment in question amounts to dismissal[6].

1 As to the meaning of 'employee' see PARA 2.
2 There is no statutory definition of the term 'detriment': see PARA 614 note 2.
3 As to the meaning of 'act' for these purposes see PARA 614 note 3.
4 As to the meaning of 'employer' see PARA 2.
5 Employment Rights Act 1996 s 47G(1) (s 47G added by the Growth and Infrastructure Act 2013 s 31(2)). The text refers to an employee shareholder within the meaning of the Employment Rights Act 1996 s 205A (see PARA 154): see s 47G(1) (as so added).
6 See the Employment Rights Act 1996 s 47G(2) (as added: see note 5). For these purposes, 'dismissal' has the meaning given in Pt X (ss 94–134A) (unfair dismissal: see PARA 757 et seq): see s 47G(2) (as so added). As to the provisions governing dismissal in relation to flexible working see PARA 796.

(ii) Enforcement of Right Not to be Subjected to Detriment

625. Complaint to employment tribunal: employee, worker or agency worker subjected to detriment. A complaint that an employee[1] has been subjected to a detriment in contravention of the statutory provisions relating to[2]:

(1) jury service[3];
(2) health and safety[4];
(3) Sunday working for shop and betting workers[5];
(4) trustees of occupational pension schemes[6];
(5) employee representatives[7];
(6) time off for study or training[8];
(7) leave for family and domestic reasons[9];
(8) flexible working[10];
(9) applications for employee study and training[11]; or
(10) employee shareholder status[12],

may be presented by that employee to an employment tribunal[13]. Additionally:

(a) a worker[14] may present a complaint to an employment tribunal that he has been subjected to a detriment in contravention of the statutory provisions relating to working time[15], and those relating to protected disclosures[16]; and
(b) a person may present a complaint to an employment tribunal that he has been subjected to a detriment in contravention of the statutory provisions relating to tax credits[17].

On such a complaint[18], it is for the employer[19] to show the ground on which any act[20], or deliberate failure to act, was done[21].

An employment tribunal must not consider such a complaint, however, unless it is presented[22]:

(i) before the end of the period of three months beginning with the date of the act or failure to act to which the complaint relates or, where the act or failure is part of a series of similar acts or failures, the last of them[23]; or
(ii) within such further period as the tribunal considers reasonable in a case

where it is satisfied that it was not reasonably practicable for the complaint to be presented before the end of that period of three months[24].

An agency worker[25] may present a complaint to an employment tribunal that he has been subjected to a detriment in contravention of the statutory provisions relating to time off (both paid and unpaid)[26] by the temporary work agency[27] or the hirer[28]; and, on such a complaint, it is for the temporary work agency or (as the case may be) the hirer to show the ground on which any act, or deliberate failure to act, was done[29].

1 As to the meaning of 'employee' see PARA 2.

2 See the Employment Rights Act 1996 s 48(1) (amended by the Teaching and Higher Education Act 1998 Sch 3 para 11(a); the Employment Rights (Dispute Resolution) Act 1998 s 1(2)(a); the Employment Relations Act 1999 Sch 4 Pt III paras 5, 9; the Employment Act 2002 Sch 7 paras 24, 27; the Employment Relations Act 2004 ss 40(2), 41(3); the Apprenticeships, Skills, Children and Learning Act 2009 Sch 1 paras 1, 2; the Growth and Infrastructure Act 2013 s 31(3); and the Children and Families Act 2014 s 129(2)(a)).

The Employment Rights Act 1996 s 48 also applies in relation to contraventions of the Employee Study and Training (Procedural Requirements) Regulations 2010, SI 2010/155, reg 18(1) (see PARA 618) as it applies in relation to contraventions of certain sections of that Act: Employee Study and Training (Procedural Requirements) Regulations 2010, SI 2010/155, reg 18(2).

3 Ie the Employment Rights Act 1996 s 43M: see PARA 613.

4 Ie the Employment Rights Act 1996 s 44: see PARA 614. As to the application of s 48, so far as relating to s 44, see PARA 614.

5 Ie the Employment Rights Act 1996 s 45: see PARA 615.

6 Ie the Employment Rights Act 1996 s 46: see PARA 617.

7 Ie the Employment Rights Act 1996 s 47: see PARA 1208.

8 Ie the Employment Rights Act 1996 s 47A: see PARA 618. See *Tait v Redcar and Cleveland Borough Council* [2008] All ER (D) 17 (Apr), EAT.

9 Ie the Employment Rights Act 1996 s 47C(1): see PARA 620.

10 Ie the Employment Rights Act 1996 s 47E: see PARA 622.

11 Ie the Employment Rights Act 1996 s 47F: see PARA 623.

12 Ie the Employment Rights Act 1996 s 47G: see PARA 624.

13 See the Employment Rights Act 1996 s 48(1) (as amended: see note 2). As to remedies see PARA 626. As to employment tribunals see PARA 1399 et seq; and as to the procedure on a complaint made to an employment tribunal see PARA 1453 et seq.

14 As to the meaning of 'worker' for these purposes see PARA 619 note 1.

15 Employment Rights Act 1996 s 48(1ZA) (added by SI 1998/1833). The working time regulations are those contained in the Employment Rights Act 1996 s 45A (see PARA 616): see s 48(1ZA) (as so added).

16 Employment Rights Act 1996 s 48(1A) (added by the Public Interest Disclosure Act 1998 ss 3, 18(2)). The statutory provisions relating to protected disclosures are those contained in the Employment Rights Act 1996 s 47B (see PARA 619): see s 48(1A) (as so added). See also *Flynn v Warrior Square Recoveries Ltd* [2012] All ER (D) 351 (Oct), EAT (if a tribunal is properly to address questions of time limits under the Employment Rights Act 1996 s 48 (see the text and notes 22–24), the tribunal must identify the act, or deliberate failure to act, and this requires the cause and effect of the words of s 47B to be carefully distinguished: the deliberate failure to act, had to be a cause of the detriment; the act, or the failure to act, had to be done on the ground specified by the employer; the detriment, however, is coincidental, or consequent upon, the act, or deliberate failure to act).

17 Employment Rights Act 1996 s 48(1B) (added by the Tax Credits Act 2003 Sch 1 para 1(1), (3)). The statutory provisions relating to tax credits are those contained in the Employment Rights Act 1996 s 47D (see PARA 621): see s 48(1B) (as so added).

18 Ie a complaint under the Employment Rights Act 1996 s 48(1), (1ZA), (1A), (1B): see the text and notes 1–17.

19 As to the meaning of 'employer' for these purposes see PARA 619 note 4. For these purposes, and for the purposes of the Employment Rights Act 1996 s 49 (see PARA 626), any reference to the employer includes: (1) where a person complains that he has been subjected to a detriment in contravention of s 47A (see PARA 618), the principal (within the meaning of s 63A(3): see PARA 331); and (2) in the case of proceedings against a worker or agent under the Employment

Rights Act 1996 s 47B(1A) (see PARA 619), the worker or agent: see s 48(5) (added by the Teaching and Higher Education Act 1998 Sch 3 para 11(b); and amended by the Enterprise and Regulatory Reform Act 2013 s 19(2)).

20 As to the meaning of 'act' for these purposes see PARA 614 note 3.

21 Employment Rights Act 1996 s 48(2) (amended by the Children and Families Act 2014 s 129(2)(c)). As to the application of the Employment Rights Act 1996 s 48(2), (3), (4) (see also the text and notes 22–24) to complaints under the National Minimum Wage Act 1998 s 24 see PARA 249 note 14.

22 See the Employment Rights Act 1996 s 48(3) (amended by the Employment Rights (Dispute Resolution) Act 1998 s 1(2)(a)). See also note 21.

23 Employment Rights Act 1996 s 48(3)(a). For these purposes, where an act extends over a period, the 'date of the act' means the last day of that period (Employment Rights Act 1996 s 48(4)(a)); and a deliberate failure to act is to be treated as done when it was decided on (s 48(4)(b)). In the absence of evidence establishing the contrary, an employer is to be taken to decide on a failure to act when he does an act inconsistent with doing the failed act or, if he has done no such inconsistent act, when the period expires within which he might reasonably have been expected to do the failed act if it was to be done: see s 48(4). See *Arthur v London Eastern Railway Ltd (t/a One Stansted Express)* [2006] EWCA Civ 1358, [2007] ICR 193, [2007] IRLR 58 (as to what was required to establish acts were part of a series). See also *Tait v Redcar and Cleveland Borough Council* [2008] All ER (D) 17 (Apr), EAT (disciplinary action was held to be clearly capable of being classified as an act extending over a period within the meaning of the Employment Rights Act 1996 s 48(4)(a)). See also note 21.

For the purposes of s 48(3)(a), s 207A(3) (extension because mediation in certain European cross-border disputes starts before the time limit expires: see PARA 1454) and s 207B (extension of time limits to facilitate conciliation before institution of proceedings: see PARA 1455) apply: s 48(4A) (added by SI 2011/1133; and amended by the Enterprise and Regulatory Reform Act 2013 s 8, Sch 2 paras 15, 19). As to time limits generally see PARA 1453.

24 Employment Rights Act 1996 s 48(3)(b). See also note 21.

25 Certain expressions used in the Employment Rights Act 1996 s 48 and s 49 (see PARA 626) have the same meaning as in the Agency Workers Regulations 2010, SI 2010/93: see the Employment Rights Act 1996 s 48(6) (added by the Children and Families Act 2014 s 129(2)(f)). Accordingly, as to the meaning of 'agency worker' see PARA 97; definition in the Agency Workers Regulations 2010, SI 2010/93, reg 3, applied by the Employment Rights Act 1996 s 48(6) (as so added).

26 Ie in contravention of the Employment Rights Act 1996 s 47C(5): see PARA 620.

27 As to the meaning of 'temporary work agency' see PARA 97; definition in the Agency Workers Regulations 2010, SI 2010/93, reg 4, applied by the Employment Rights Act 1996 s 48(6) (as added: see note 25).

28 Employment Rights Act 1996 s 48(1AA) (added by the Children and Families Act 2014 s 129(2)(b)). As to the meaning of 'hirer' see PARA 97 note 3; definition in the Agency Workers Regulations 2010, SI 2010/93, reg 2, applied by the Employment Rights Act 1996 s 48(6) (as added: see note 25).

29 Employment Rights Act 1996 s 48(2A) (added by the Children and Families Act 2014 s 129(2)(d)). In the absence of evidence establishing the contrary, a temporary work agency or hirer is to be taken to decide on a failure to act when he does an act inconsistent with doing the failed act or, if he has done no such inconsistent act, when the period expires within which he might reasonably have been expected to do the failed act if it was to be done: see the Employment Rights Act 1996 s 48(4) (amended by the Children and Families Act 2014 s 129(2)(e)).

626. Remedies available on complaint to employment tribunal: employee, worker or agency worker subjected to detriment. Where an employment tribunal[1] finds a complaint that a person, employee[2] or worker[3] has been subjected to a detriment[4] well-founded, it must make a declaration to that effect and may make an award of compensation to be paid by the employer[5] to the complainant in respect of the act or failure to act to which the complaint relates[6]. Similarly, where an employment tribunal finds a complaint that an agency worker[7] has been subjected to a detriment[8] well-founded, the tribunal must make a declaration to that effect, and may make an award of compensation to be paid by the temporary work agency[9] or (as the case may be) the hirer[10] to the complainant in respect of the act or failure to act to which the complaint relates[11].

The amount of the compensation to be awarded is to be such as the tribunal considers just and equitable in all the circumstances, having regard to the infringement to which the complaint relates and any loss[12] which is attributable to the act, or failure to act, which infringed the complainant's right[13].

Where the tribunal finds that the act, or failure to act, to which the complaint relates was to any extent caused or contributed to by action of the complainant, it must reduce the amount of the compensation by such proportion as it considers just and equitable, having regard to that finding[14].

1 As to employment tribunals see PARA 1399 et seq; and as to the procedure on a complaint made to an employment tribunal see PARA 1453 et seq.
2 As to the meaning of 'employee' see PARA 2.
3 As to the meaning of 'worker' for these purposes see PARA 619 note 1.
4 Ie under the Employment Rights Act 1996 s 48(1), (1ZA), (1A), (1B): see PARA 625.
5 As to the meaning of 'employer' for these purposes see PARA 619 note 4.
6 See the Employment Rights Act 1996 s 49(1) (amended by the Employment Rights (Dispute Resolution) Act 1998 s 1(2)(a); and the Children and Families Act 2014 s 129(3)(a)). As to the application of the Employment Rights Act 1996 s 49, so far as relating to s 44 (health and safety cases), see PARA 614; and as to the application of s 49 to complaints under the National Minimum Wage Act 1998 s 24 see PARA 249 note 14.
7 As to the meaning of 'agency worker' for these purposes see PARA 625 note 25.
8 Ie under the Employment Rights Act 1996 s 48(1AA): see PARA 625.
9 As to the meaning of 'temporary work agency' for these purposes see PARA 625 note 27.
10 As to the meaning of 'hirer' for these purposes see PARA 625 note 28.
11 See the Employment Rights Act 1996 s 49(1A) (added by the Children and Families Act 2014 s 129(3)(b)).
12 The loss is to be taken to include: (1) any expenses reasonably incurred by the complainant in consequence of the act, or failure to act, to which the complaint relates (Employment Rights Act 1996 s 49(3)(a)); and (2) loss of any benefit which he might reasonably be expected to have had but for that act or failure to act (s 49(3)(b)). As to the meaning of 'act' for these purposes see PARA 614 note 3. In ascertaining the loss, the tribunal must apply the same rule concerning the duty of a person to mitigate his loss as applies to damages recoverable under the common law of England and Wales: s 49(4). As to the meanings of 'England' and 'Wales' see PARA 2 note 12. As to the common law duty to mitigate loss see **DAMAGES** vol 12(1) (Reissue) PARA 1041 et seq. See also note 6.
13 See the Employment Rights Act 1996 s 49(2) (amended by the Public Interest Disclosure Act 1998 ss 4(1), (2), 18(2); and SI 1998/1833). See also note 6.

However, where: (1) the complaint is made under the Employment Rights Act 1996 s 48(1ZA) (working time cases: see PARA 625) or, as the case may be, s 48(1A) (protected disclosures: see PARA 625); (2) the detriment to which the worker is subjected is the termination of his worker's contract; and (3) that contract is not a contract of employment, then any compensation must not exceed the compensation that would be payable for unfair dismissal under Pt X Ch II (ss 111–132) (remedies: see PARA 804 et seq), if the worker had been an employee and had been dismissed for the reason specified in s 101A (see PARA 788) or, as the case may be, s 103A (see PARA 792): s 49(5A) (added by SI 1998/1833); Employment Rights Act 1996 s 49(6) (added by the Public Interest Disclosure Act 1998 ss 4(1), (3), 18(2)). For these purposes, 'worker's contract', has the extended meaning given by the Employment Rights Act 1996 s 43K (see PARA 69 note 3): see s 47B(3) (added by the Public Interest Disclosure Act 1998 ss 2, 18(2)). As to the meaning of 'contract of employment' see PARA 2. Where the complaint is made under the Employment Rights Act 1996 s 48(1A), and it appears to the tribunal that the protected disclosure was not made in good faith, the tribunal may, if it considers it just and equitable in all the circumstances to do so, reduce any award it makes to the worker by no more than 25%: s 49(6A) (added by the Enterprise and Regulatory Reform Act 2013 s 18(4)).

Where the complaint is made under the Employment Rights Act 1996 s 48(1B) (tax credits: see PARA 625) by a person who is not an employee, and the detriment to which he is subjected is the termination of his contract with the person who is his employer for the purposes of the Tax Credits Act 2002 s 25 (see **WELFARE BENEFITS AND STATE PENSIONS** vol 104 (2014) PARA 358), any compensation must not exceed the compensation that would be payable under the Employment Rights Act 1996 Pt X Ch II if the complainant had been an employee and had been dismissed for the reason specified in s 104B (see PARA 795): s 49(7) (added by Tax Credits Act 2002 Sch 1 para 1(1), (4)).

It has been held that an employment tribunal has power under the Employment Rights Act 1996 s 49 to make awards for injury to feelings in detriment cases under the Employment Rights Act 1996 s 47B (see PARA 619) as there is no reason why they should be treated differently from awards for other forms of discrimination: *Virgo Fidelis Senior School v Boyle* [2004] ICR 1210, [2004] IRLR 268, EAT; applying *Vento v Chief Constable of West Yorkshire Police* [2002] EWCA Civ 1871, [2003] ICR 318, sub nom *Vento v Chief Constable of West Yorkshire Police (No 2)* [2003] IRLR 102. Although *Dunnachie v Kingston-upon-Hull City Council* [2004] UKHL 36, [2005] 1 AC 226, [2004] 3 All ER 1011 (cited in PARA 818 note 3) decided that such compensation cannot be awarded for cases of unfair dismissal generally, the Employment Rights Act 1996 s 49 is distinguished by the reference to a complainant's rights having been infringed.

14 Employment Rights Act 1996 s 49(5). See also note 6.

(17) PROTECTION AFFORDED UPON EMPLOYER'S INSOLVENCY

627. Priority of certain debts under the Insolvency Act 1986. Where an employer who is a company or an individual becomes insolvent, then, for the purposes of the Insolvency Act 1986, the following sums due to employees constitute preferential debts[1]:

(1) so much of any amount as does not exceed so much as may be prescribed by order made by the Secretary of State[2] which is owed by the employer to a person who is or has been an employee of his and payable by way of remuneration in respect of the whole or part of the period of four months next before the relevant date[3];

(2) an amount owed by way of accrued holiday remuneration, in respect of any period of employment before the relevant date, to a person whose employment by the employer has been terminated, whether before, on or after that date[4];

(3) so much of any sum owed in respect of money advanced for the purpose as has been applied for the payment of a debt which, if it had not been paid, would have been a debt falling within either of head (1) or head (2) above[5]; and

(4) so much of any amount as does not exceed such amount as may be prescribed by order made by the Secretary of State which is ordered, whether before or after the relevant date, to be paid by the employer under the Reserve Forces (Safeguard of Employment) Act 1985[6] and is so ordered in respect of a default made by the employer before the relevant date in the discharge of his obligations under that Act[7].

1 See the Insolvency Act 1986 s 386, Sch 6 paras 9–12; and BANKRUPTCY AND INDIVIDUAL INSOLVENCY vol 5 (2013) PARA 591 et seq; COMPANY AND PARTNERSHIP INSOLVENCY vol 17 (2011) PARA 724. As to preferential debts generally see BANKRUPTCY AND INDIVIDUAL INSOLVENCY vol 5 (2013) PARA 591 et seq; COMPANY AND PARTNERSHIP INSOLVENCY vol 17 (2011) PARA 721 et seq.

2 The prescribed amount for the purposes of head (1) in the text is £800: see the Insolvency Proceedings (Monetary Limits) Order 1986, SI 1986/1996, art 4; and BANKRUPTCY AND INDIVIDUAL INSOLVENCY vol 5 (2013) PARA 593; COMPANY AND PARTNERSHIP INSOLVENCY vol 17 (2011) PARA 724. As to the Secretary of State see PARA 5 note 21.

3 See the Insolvency Act 1986 Sch 6 para 9; and BANKRUPTCY AND INDIVIDUAL INSOLVENCY vol 5 (2013) PARA 593; COMPANY AND PARTNERSHIP INSOLVENCY vol 17 (2011) PARA 724. As to the meaning of 'relevant date' see BANKRUPTCY AND INDIVIDUAL INSOLVENCY vol 5 (2013) PARA 591; COMPANY AND PARTNERSHIP INSOLVENCY vol 17 (2011) PARA 1349.

4 See the Insolvency Act 1986 Sch 6 para 10; and BANKRUPTCY AND INDIVIDUAL INSOLVENCY vol 5 (2013) PARA 593; COMPANY AND PARTNERSHIP INSOLVENCY vol 17 (2011) PARA 724.

5 See the Insolvency Act 1986 Sch 6 para 11; and BANKRUPTCY AND INDIVIDUAL INSOLVENCY vol 5 (2013) PARA 593; COMPANY AND PARTNERSHIP INSOLVENCY vol 17 (2011) PARA 724.

6 As to the Reserve Forces (Safeguard of Employment) Act 1985 see ARMED FORCES vol 3 (2011) PARA 370.

7 See the Insolvency Act 1986 Sch 6 para 12; and BANKRUPTCY AND INDIVIDUAL INSOLVENCY vol 5 (2013) PARA 593; COMPANY AND PARTNERSHIP INSOLVENCY vol 17 (2011) PARA 724. The prescribed amount for the purposes of head (4) in the text is £800: Insolvency Proceedings (Monetary Limits) Order 1986, SI 1986/1996, art 4; and BANKRUPTCY AND INDIVIDUAL INSOLVENCY vol 5 (2013) PARA 593; COMPANY AND PARTNERSHIP INSOLVENCY vol 17 (2011) PARA 724.

628. Employee's rights on employer's insolvency. If, on an application made to him in writing[1] by an employee[2], the Secretary of State[3] is satisfied that[4]:

(1) the employer of that employee has become insolvent[5]; and

(2) the employment of the employee has been terminated[6]; and

(3) on the appropriate date[7] the employee was entitled to be paid the whole or part of any specified debt[8],

the Secretary of State must[9] pay the employee out of the National Insurance Fund the amount to which, in the opinion of the Secretary of State, the employee is entitled in respect of the debt[10]. The debts specified for this purpose are[11]:

(a) any arrears of pay[12] in respect of one or more, but not more than eight, weeks[13];

(b) any amount which the employer is liable to pay the employee for the required[14] period of notice or for any failure of the employer to give such period of notice[15];

(c) any holiday pay[16] in respect of a period or periods of holiday not exceeding six weeks in all, and to which the employee became entitled during the 12 months ending with the appropriate date[17];

(d) any basic award of compensation for unfair dismissal[18], or so much of an award under a designated dismissal procedures agreement[19] as does not exceed any basic award of compensation for unfair dismissal to which the employee would be entitled but for the agreement[20];

(e) any reasonable sum by way of reimbursement of the whole or part of any fee or premium paid by an apprentice or articled clerk[21].

Where the amount of any such debt is referable to a period of time, the total amount payable to an employee in respect of that debt is not to exceed £464 in respect of any one week[22], or (in respect of a shorter period) an amount bearing the same proportion to £464 as that shorter period bears to a week[23].

In a case where one of the following officers (a 'relevant officer') has been, or is required to be, appointed in connection with an employer's insolvency, that is to say a trustee in bankruptcy, a liquidator, an administrator, a receiver or manager, or a trustee[24] under a composition or arrangement between the employer and his creditors, or a trustee under a trust deed for his creditors executed by the employer, the Secretary of State must not make any such payment in respect of a debt until he has received a statement from the relevant officer of the amount of that debt which appears to have been owed to the employee on the appropriate date and to remain unpaid[25]; and a relevant officer must, on request by the Secretary of State, provide him as soon as reasonably practicable with such a statement[26]. If, however, the Secretary of State is satisfied that he does not require such a statement in order to determine the amount of a debt which was owed to the employee on the appropriate date and remains unpaid, he may make a payment in respect of the debt without having received such a statement[27].

1 As to the meaning of 'writing' see PARA 2 note 8.

2 As to the meaning of 'employee' see PARA 2. Whether or not a controlling shareholder of the insolvent company can claim as an 'employee' under these provisions is a question of fact, as there is no rule of law preventing such a claim: see *Secretary of State for Trade and Industry v Bottrill* [1999] ICR 592, [1999] IRLR 326, CA; and see *Secretary Of State for Business, Enterprise And Regulatory Reform v Neufeld and Howe* [2009] EWCA Civ 280, [2009] ICR 1183, [2009] IRLR 475 (guidance as to the principles to be applied in the light of previous authority, including *Secretary of State for Trade and Industry v Bottrill*; and especially *Clark v Clark Construction Initiatives Ltd* [2008] ICR 635, [2008] IRLR 364, EAT); and PARA 9.

3 As to the Secretary of State see PARA 5 note 21.

4 See the Employment Rights Act 1996 s 182. As to the right of complaint to an employment tribunal where payment is not made see PARA 629; as to the transfer of rights to the Secretary of State see PARA 630; and as to the Secretary of State's power to obtain information see PARA 631.

Similar protection is afforded by European Parliament and Council Directive (EC) 2008/94 of 22 October 2008 (OJ L283, 28.10.2008, p 36) on the protection of employees in the event of the insolvency of their employer (Codified version) (the 'Insolvency Protection Directive'). Under Council Directive (EEC) 80/987 of 20 October 1980 (OJ L283, 28.10.1980, p 23) on the protection of employees in the event of the insolvency of their employer, which was repealed and replaced by European Parliament and Council Directive (EC) 2008/94 of 22 October 2008 (OJ L283, 28.10.2008, p 36):

(1) where a company incorporated in one member state goes into insolvency in accordance with the laws of that member state, the appropriate guarantee institution for the company's employees in another member state is that of the member state in which they are employed (Case C-198/98 *Everson v Secretary of State for Trade and Industry* [2000] ICR 525, [2000] IRLR 202, ECJ); and

(2) national courts were warned not to compromise the objectives pursued by the directive, which had to be construed narrowly and interpreted in a way compatible with its social purpose, which was to guarantee employees a minimum level of protection across the European Union in the event of an employer's insolvency through payment of outstanding claims resulting from contracts of employment or employment relationships and relating to pay for a specific period (Case C-201/01 *Walcher v Bundesamt fur Soziales und Behindertenwesen Steiermark* [2003] ECR I-8827, [2003] 3 CMLR 534, ECJ).

European Parliament and Council Directive (EC) 2008/94 of 22 October 2008 (OJ L283, 28.10.2008, p 36) does not preclude a provision of national law that excludes an employee from entitlement under the guarantee of payment of employees' outstanding claims on the ground that the employee, within the six months preceding the application for a declaration of insolvency, was the owner of an essential part of the undertaking or business concerned and had had a considerable influence on its activities: Case C-30/10 *Andersson v Staten genom Kronofogdemyndigheten i Jönköping, Tillssynsmyndigheten* [2011] ECR I-513, [2012] ICR 447, CJEU. European Parliament and Council Directive (EC) 2008/94 of 22 October 2008 (OJ L283, 28.10.2008, p 36) must, however, be interpreted as applying to the entitlement of former employees to old-age benefits under a supplementary pension scheme set up by their employer: Case C-398/11 *Hogan v Minister for Social and Family Affairs* [2013] 3 CMLR 746, [2013] IRLR 668, CJEU (it is sufficient that the pension scheme is underfunded as of the date of the employer's insolvency and that, on account of his insolvency, the employer does not have the resources to contribute sufficient money to the pension scheme to enable the pension benefits owned to the beneficiaries of that scheme to be satisfied in full).

5 Employment Rights Act 1996 s 182(a). As to the meaning of 'employer' see PARA 2.

An employer has become insolvent for the purposes of Pt XII (ss 182–190) (insolvency of employers: see also PARAS 629, 630, 631):

(1) where the employer is an individual, if, but only if, s 183(2) is satisfied (s 183(1)(a) (s 183(1)(a), (b) amended, s 183(1)(c), (4) added, by SI 2001/1090));

(2) where the employer is a company, if, but only if, the Employment Rights Act 1996 s 183(3) is satisfied (s 183(1)(b) (as so amended)); and

(3) where the employer is a limited liability partnership, if, but only if, s 183(4) is satisfied (s 183(1)(c) (as so added))).

Accordingly, an employer who is an individual has become insolvent for these purposes in England and Wales if, and only if:

(a) a moratorium period under a debt relief order applies in relation to him (s 183(2)(a)(ai) (added by the Tribunals, Courts and Enforcement Act 2007 Sch 20 Pt 2 para 17));

(b) he has been adjudged bankrupt or has made a composition or arrangement with his creditors (Employment Rights Act 1996 s 183(2)(a)(i)); or

(c) he has died and his estate falls to be administered in accordance with an order under the Insolvency Act 1986 s 421 (insolvent estates of deceased persons: see BANKRUPTCY AND INDIVIDUAL INSOLVENCY vol 5 (2013) PARA 830 et seq) (Employment Rights Act 1996 s 183(2)(a)(ii)).

An employer which is a company has become insolvent for these purposes in England and Wales if, and only if:

(i) a winding-up order has been made or a resolution for voluntary winding up has been passed with respect to the company (s 183(3)(a) (s 183(3)(a) amended, s 183(3)(aa) added, by the Enterprise Act 2002 Sch 17 para 49(1), (3), Sch 26));

(ii) the company is in administration for the purposes of the Insolvency Act 1986 (Employment Rights Act 1996 s 183(3)(aa) (as so added));

(iii) a receiver or a manager of the company's undertaking has been duly appointed, or possession has been taken, by or on behalf of the holders of any debentures secured by a floating charge, of any property of the company comprised in or subject to the charge (s 183(3)(b)); or

(iv) a voluntary arrangement proposed in the case of the company for the purposes of the Insolvency Act 1986 Pt I (ss 1–7B) (see COMPANY AND PARTNERSHIP INSOLVENCY vol 16 (2011) PARA 83 et seq) has been approved under Pt I (Employment Rights Act 1996 s 183(3)(c)).

An employer which is a limited liability partnership has become insolvent for these purposes in England and Wales if, and only if:

(A) a winding-up order, an administration order or a determination for a voluntary winding up has been made with respect to the limited liability partnership (s 183(4)(a) (as so added));

(B) a receiver or a manager of the undertaking of the limited liability partnership has been duly appointed, or possession has been taken, by or on behalf of the holders of any debentures secured by a floating charge, of any property of the limited liability partnership comprised in or subject to the charge (s 183(4)(b) (as so added)); or

(C) a voluntary arrangement proposed in the case of the limited liability partnership for the purposes of Insolvency Act 1986 Pt I has been approved under Pt I (Employment Rights Act 1996 s 183(4)(c) (as so added)).

For these purposes, references to a company are to be read as including references to a charitable incorporated organisation (see CHARITIES vol 8 (2010) PARA 240 et seq), and any reference to the Insolvency Act 1986 in relation to a company is to be read as including a reference to that Act as it applies to charitable incorporated organisations: see the Employment Rights Act 1996 s 183(5) (added by SI 2012/3014). The onus is on an applicant seeking to make a claim against the Secretary of State to adduce direct evidence that one of the events amounting to insolvency listed exhaustively in the Employment Rights Act 1996 s 183(3) (see heads (i)–(iv) above) has taken place: *Secretary of State for Trade and Industry v Walden* [2000] IRLR 168, EAT. A protective award made after liquidation can be recovered from the Secretary of State: see *Haine v Day* [2008] EWCA Civ 626, [2008] ICR 1102, [2008] IRLR 642. It makes no sense, however, to interpret each occasion on which an employer might become insolvent, provided for by the Employment Rights Act 1996 s 183(3), as being a separate occasion, each of which would constitute its own appropriate date: *Secretary of State for Business Innovation and Skills v McDonagh* [2013] ICR 1177, [2013] IRLR 598, EAT (Parliament took a deliberate decision to treat the debts which arrears of pay and holiday pay constituted separately from other debts arising on insolvency, and arrears of pay and holiday pay would be payable only in respect of a time before the date on which the employer became insolvent; employees had continued to work after the employer had entered into a company voluntary arrangement ('CVA'), but before it had been wound up; employers became insolvent when the CVAs were approved). The existence of these statutory rights for employees may be a factor in deciding to make a winding-up order: *Re Eloc Electro-Optieck and Communicatie BV* [1982] Ch 43, [1981] ICR 732. As to the meanings of 'England' and 'Wales' see PARA 2 note 12. As to debt relief orders see BANKRUPTCY AND INDIVIDUAL INSOLVENCY vol 5 (2013) PARA 101 et seq; as to compositions or arrangements with creditors see BANKRUPTCY AND INDIVIDUAL INSOLVENCY vol 5 (2013) PARA 43 et seq; and as to bankruptcy generally see BANKRUPTCY AND INDIVIDUAL INSOLVENCY vol 5 (2013) PARA 129 et seq. As to winding-up orders see COMPANY AND PARTNERSHIP INSOLVENCY vol 16 (2011) PARA

386 et seq. As to voluntary winding-up see COMPANY AND PARTNERSHIP INSOLVENCY vol 17 (2011) PARA 898 et seq. As to administration orders see COMPANY AND PARTNERSHIP INSOLVENCY vol 16 (2011) PARA 158 et seq. As to the appointment of receivers and managers see COMPANY AND PARTNERSHIP INSOLVENCY vol 16 (2011) PARA 340 et seq. As to the taking of possession by or on behalf of the holders of debentures secured by a floating charge see COMPANIES vol 15 (2009) PARA 1333 et seq.

6 Employment Rights Act 1996 s 182(b). As to the meaning of 'employment' see PARA 2.

7 For these purposes, 'appropriate date' means:

(1) in relation to arrears of pay, not being remuneration under a protective award made under the Trade Union and Labour Relations (Consolidation) Act 1992 s 189 (see PARA 1189), and in relation to holiday pay, the date on which the employer became insolvent (Employment Rights Act 1996 s 185(a));

(2) in relation to a basic award of compensation for unfair dismissal and to remuneration under a protective award so made, whichever is the latest of: (a) the date on which the employer became insolvent; (b) the date of the termination of the employee's employment; and (c) the date on which the award was made (see s 185(b)); and

(3) in relation to any other debt to which Pt XII (insolvency of employers: see also PARAS 629, 630, 631) applies, whichever is the later of the date on which the employer became insolvent and the date of the termination of the employee's employment (see s 185(c)).

As to the meaning of 'holiday pay' see note 16.

8 Employment Rights Act 1996 s 182(c). Head (3) in the text refers to a debt to which Pt XII applies (see heads (a) to (e) in the text): see s 182(c).

9 Ie subject to the provisions of the Employment Rights Act 1996 s 186: see the text and notes 22–23. Sums equal to the amount of any expenses incurred by the Secretary of State, or by persons acting on his behalf, in exercising his functions under Pt XII (insolvency of employers: see also PARAS 629, 630, 631) are to be paid out of the National Insurance Fund into the Consolidated Fund: s 237(b). As to the Consolidated Fund see CONSTITUTIONAL AND ADMINISTRATIVE LAW vol 20 (2014) PARA 480 et seq; PARLIAMENT vol 78 (2010) PARAS 1028–1031. As to the National Insurance Fund see WELFARE BENEFITS AND STATE PENSIONS vol 104 (2014) PARA 15.

10 See the Employment Rights Act 1996 s 182.

11 See the Employment Rights Act 1996 s 184(1). The text refers to debts to which Pt XII (insolvency of employers: see also PARAS 629, 630, 631) applies: see s 184(1).

12 For the purposes of head (a) in the text, the following amounts are to be treated as arrears of pay, namely:

(1) a guarantee payment (Employment Rights Act 1996 s 184(2)(a));

(2) any payment for time off under Pt VI (ss 50–63C) (time off work: see PARA 326 et seq) or the Trade Union and Labour Relations (Consolidation) Act 1992 s 169 (payment for time off for carrying out trade union activities: see PARA 1065) (Employment Rights Act 1996 s 184(2)(b));

(3) remuneration on suspension on medical grounds under s 64 (see PARA 596) and remuneration on suspension on maternity grounds under s 68 (see PARA 598) (s 184(2)(c));

(4) remuneration under a protective award made under the Trade Union and Labour Relations (Consolidation) Act 1992 s 189 (see PARA 1189) (s 184(2)(d)).

As to the meaning of 'guarantee payment' see PARA 261.

13 Employment Rights Act 1996 s 184(1)(a). As to the meaning of 'week' see PARA 126 note 13. If appropriate, the employee may choose the eight weeks in question, so as to maximise entitlement: *Mann v Secretary of State for Employment* [1999] ICR 898, [1999] IRLR 566, HL.

14 Ie required by the Employment Rights Act 1996 s 86(1) or (2): see PARA 736.

15 Employment Rights Act 1996 s 184(1)(b). Head (b) in the text refers to the period of notice required by s 86(1): see PARA 736. In spite of the fact that the right to notice in s 86 is backed by the provisions of ss 87–91 (see PARAS 737–742), the employee's right to notice remains essentially contractual, even when enforced against the fund under s 182; and thus the right to claim loss is subject to the normal contractual rules on mitigation of such loss: *Westwood v Secretary of State for Employment* [1985] AC 20, [1985] ICR 209, HL. This means that the Secretary of State may properly deduct from the amount claimed the amount of jobseeker's allowance received by the employee (see WELFARE BENEFITS AND STATE PENSIONS vol 104 (2014) PARA 419 et seq) during the period of statutory notice: *Westwood v Secretary of State for Employment*. Also properly deducted are: (1) wages received from new employment during the notice period; and (2) income tax otherwise payable on the amount due: *Secretary of State for Employment v Cooper* [1987] ICR 766, EAT (applying *British Transport Commission v Gourlay* [1956] AC 185, [1955] 3 All ER 796, HL). In the light of the decision of the House of

Lords in *Westwood v Secretary of State for Employment* above, the prior decision of the Employment Appeal Tribunal in *Secretary of State for Employment v Haynes* [1980] ICR 371, [1980] IRLR 270, EAT (fund's liability limited to amount calculated under what are now the Employment Rights Act 1996 ss 87–91, not the full measure, if greater, of damages at common law) is probably wrong, inasmuch as it suggests that the basis of the employee's claim is statutory, not contractual.

16 For the purposes of head (c) in the text, 'holiday pay' means:
(1) pay in respect of a holiday actually taken by the employee (Employment Rights Act 1996 s 184(3)(a)); or
(2) any accrued holiday pay which under the employee's contract of employment would in the ordinary course have become payable to him in respect of the period of a holiday if his employment with the employer had continued until he became entitled to a holiday (s 184(3)(b)).

As to the meaning of 'contract of employment' see PARA 2.

17 See the Employment Rights Act 1996 s 184(1)(c).

18 As to the basic award see the Employment Rights Act 1996 s 119; and PARA 815.

19 As to the meaning of 'dismissal procedures agreement' see PARA 150 note 9.

20 Employment Rights Act 1996 s 184(1)(d) (amended by the Employment Rights (Dispute Resolution) Act 1998 s 12(4)).

21 Employment Rights Act 1996 s 184(1)(e). A sum is to be taken to be reasonable for the purposes of head (e) in the text in a case where a trustee in bankruptcy or liquidator has been or is required to be appointed, if it is admitted to be reasonable by the trustee in bankruptcy or liquidator under the Insolvency Act 1986 s 348 (effect of bankruptcy on apprenticeships etc: see **BANKRUPTCY AND INDIVIDUAL INSOLVENCY** vol 5 (2013) PARA 720) whether as originally enacted or as applied to the winding up of a company by rules under s 411 (see **COMPANY AND PARTNERSHIP INSOLVENCY** vol 17 (2011) PARA 1002): see the Employment Rights Act 1996 s 184(4)(a).

22 Employment Rights Act 1996 s 186(1)(a) (s 186(1)(a), (b) amended by SI 2014/382). The maximum refers to the employee's gross pay; it is proper, therefore, for the Secretary of State to apply the maximum in an appropriate case and then reduce the amount payable by an amount representing tax and National Insurance contributions: *Morris v Secretary of State for Employment* [1985] ICR 522, [1985] IRLR 297, EAT. See also *Titchener v Secretary of State for Trade and Industry* [2002] ICR 225, [2002] IRLR 195, EAT.

As to the Secretary of State's duty to increase or decrease the amount in the Employment Rights Act 1996 s 186(1) in line with the retail prices index see the Employment Relations Act 1999 s 34(1)(d), (2), (3)(b); and PARA 160. In exercise of the powers so conferred, the Secretary of State made the Employment Rights (Increase of Limits) Order 2014, SI 2014/382. The limit in the Employment Rights Act 1996 s 186(1)(a), (b) has effect as respects any day in respect of which an employee becomes entitled to a basic award on or after 6 April 2014: see the Employment Rights (Increase of Limits) Order 2014, SI 2014/382, arts 3, 4(1). In a case where the appropriate date fell before 6 April 2014, the limits having effect immediately before 6 April 2014 continue to apply (the previous limit having been £450): see art 4(1). As to the meaning of 'appropriate date' see art 4(2).

The Work and Families Act 2006 s 14 also applies to the sum specified in the Employment Rights Act 1996 s 186(1)(a), (b), however: see the Work and Families Act 2006 s 14(1)(a). Accordingly, the Secretary of State may, on one occasion only, by order substitute for the sum specified in the Employment Rights Act 1996 s 186(1)(a), (b) such higher sum as may be specified in the order: Work and Families Act 2006 s 14(2). An order under s 14 must be made by statutory instrument, it may include transitional provision, and it may exclude (on a single occasion specified in the order under s 14) any duty to make an order under the Employment Relations Act 1999 s 34 (indexation of certain amounts etc: see PARA 160), so far as relating to the sum specified in the Employment Rights Act 1996 s 186(1)(a), (b): see the Work and Families Act 2006 s 14(3). Subject to any provision so made, s 14 does not affect the operation of the Employment Relations Act 1999 s 34 in relation to the sum specified in the Employment Rights Act 1996 s 186(1)(a), (b) as so substituted: see the Work and Families Act 2006 s 14(4). No statutory instrument containing an order under s 14 may be made unless a draft of the instrument has been laid before, and approved by a resolution of, each House of Parliament: s 14(5). At the date at which this volume states the law, no such order had been made under s 14.

23 Employment Rights Act 1996 s 186(1)(b). See note 22.

24 For these purposes, 'trustee', in relation to a composition or arrangement, includes the supervisor of a voluntary arrangement proposed for the purposes of, and approved under, the Insolvency Act 1986 Pt I (see **COMPANY AND PARTNERSHIP INSOLVENCY** vol 16 (2011) PARA 83

et seq) or Pt VIII (ss 252–263) (see BANKRUPTCY AND INDIVIDUAL INSOLVENCY vol 5 (2013) PARA 43 et seq): see the Employment Rights Act 1996 s 187(5).
25 See the Employment Rights Act 1996 s 187(1), (4).
26 See the Employment Rights Act 1996 s 187(3).
27 Employment Rights Act 1996 s 187(2).

629. Complaint to employment tribunal: person who has applied for payment of a guaranteed debt. A person who has applied for a payment of a guaranteed debt[1] may present a claim to an employment tribunal that[2]:

(1) the Secretary of State[3] has failed to make any such payment[4]; or
(2) any such payment made by the Secretary of State is less than the amount which should have been paid[5].

An employment tribunal must not consider such a complaint, however, unless it is presented[6]:

(a) before the end of the period of three months beginning with the date on which the decision of the Secretary of State on the application was communicated to the applicant[7]; or
(b) within such further period as the tribunal considers reasonable in a case where it is not reasonably practicable for the complaint to be presented before the end of that period of three months[8].

Where an employment tribunal finds that the Secretary of State ought to make such a payment[9], it must make a declaration to that effect, and it must declare the amount of any such payment which it finds the Secretary of State ought to make[10].

1 Ie under the Employment Rights Act 1996 s 182: see PARA 628.
2 See the Employment Rights Act 1996 s 188(1) (amended by the Employment Rights (Dispute Resolution) Act 1998 s 1(2)(a)). As to employment tribunals see PARA 1399 et seq; and as to the procedure on a complaint made to an employment tribunal see PARA 1453 et seq.
3 As to the Secretary of State see PARA 5 note 21.
4 Employment Rights Act 1996 s 188(1)(a).
5 Employment Rights Act 1996 s 188(1)(b).
6 See the Employment Rights Act 1996 s 188(2) (amended by the Employment Rights (Dispute Resolution) Act 1998 s 1(2)(a)).
7 Employment Rights Act 1996 s 188(2)(a). As to time limits generally see PARA 1453.
8 Employment Rights Act 1996 s 188(2)(b). See note 7.
9 Ie under the Employment Rights Act 1996 s 182: see PARA 628.
10 See the Employment Rights Act 1996 s 188(3) (amended by the Employment Rights (Dispute Resolution) Act 1998 s 1(2)(a)). The tribunal is restricted under s 188(3) to making a declaration as to what is actually payable on the facts as proved; it may not consider possible liabilities on other possible facts: *Secretary of State for Employment v Cooper* [1987] ICR 766, EAT. As to the transfer of rights and remedies to the Secretary of State see PARA 630.

630. Transfer of rights and remedies to the Secretary of State in respect of a debt owed by an employer. Where the Secretary of State[1] makes[2] any payment to an employee[3] in respect of any specified debt[4]:

(1) on the making of the payment, any rights and remedies of the employee in respect of that debt (or, if the Secretary of State has paid only part of it, in respect of that part) become rights and remedies of the Secretary of State[5]; and
(2) any decision of an employment tribunal[6] requiring an employer[7] to pay that debt to the employee has the effect that the debt (or that part of it which the Secretary of State has paid) is to be paid to the Secretary of State[8].

Where a debt (or any part of a debt) in respect of which the Secretary of State has made such a payment constitutes a preferential debt[9], the rights which so become rights of the Secretary of State include any right arising[10] by reason of the status of the debt, or that part of it, as a preferential debt[11].

Any sum recovered by the Secretary of State in exercising any right, or pursuing any remedy, which is his by virtue of these provisions must be paid into the National Insurance Fund[12].

1 As to the Secretary of State see PARA 5 note 21.
2 Ie in pursuance of the Employment Rights Act 1996 s 182: see PARA 628.
3 As to the meaning of 'employee' see PARA 2.
4 See the Employment Rights Act 1996 s 189(1). The text refers to any debt to which Pt XII (ss 182–190) (insolvency of employers: see also PARAS 628, 629, 631) applies: see PARA 628.
5 Employment Rights Act 1996 s 189(1)(a).
6 As to employment tribunals see PARA 1399 et seq; and as to the procedure on a complaint made to an employment tribunal see PARA 1453 et seq.
7 As to the meaning of 'employer' see PARA 2.
8 Employment Rights Act 1996 s 189(1)(b) (amended by the Employment Rights (Dispute Resolution) Act 1998 s 1(2)(a)).
9 Ie within the meaning of the Insolvency Act 1986 for the purposes of any provision of that Act, including any such provision as applied by any order made under that Act, or any provision of the Companies Act 2006: see **BANKRUPTCY AND INDIVIDUAL INSOLVENCY** vol 5 (2013) PARA 591 et seq; **COMPANY AND PARTNERSHIP INSOLVENCY** vol 17 (2011) PARA 721 et seq.
10 Ie under any provision of the Insolvency Act 1986, including any such provision as applied by any order made under that Act, or any provision of the Companies Act 2006.
11 See the Employment Rights Act 1996 s 189(2) (amended by SI 2008/948). In computing for the purposes of any provision referred to in note 9, the aggregate amount payable in priority to other creditors of the employer in respect of:
   (1) any claim of the Secretary of State to be paid in priority to other creditors of the employer by virtue of the Employment Rights Act 1996 s 189(2) (s 189(3)(a)); and
   (2) any claim by the employee to be so paid in his own right (s 189(3)(b)),
   any claim of the Secretary of State to be so paid by virtue of s 189(2) is to be treated as if it were a claim of the employee (see s 189(3)).
12 Employment Rights Act 1996 s 189(5). As to the National Insurance Fund see **WELFARE BENEFITS AND STATE PENSIONS** vol 104 (2014) PARA 15.

631. Power of the Secretary of State to obtain information in respect of a debt owed by an employer. Where an application is made to the Secretary of State[1] in respect of a debt owed by an employer[2], the Secretary of State may require[3]:

(1) the employer to provide him with such information as the Secretary of State may reasonably require for the purpose of determining whether the application is well-founded[4]; and
(2) any person having the custody or control of any relevant records or other documents to produce for examination on behalf of the Secretary of State any such document in that person's custody or under his control which is of such a description as the Secretary of State may require[5].

Any such requirement must be made by notice in writing given to the person on whom the requirement is imposed and may be varied or revoked by a subsequent notice so given[6].

If a person:

(a) refuses or wilfully neglects to furnish any information or produce any document which he has been required to furnish or produce by such a notice, he is guilty of an offence and liable to a penalty[7];
(b) in purporting to comply with a requirement of such a notice, knowingly or recklessly makes any false statement, he is guilty of an offence and liable to a penalty[8].

Where any such offence[9] committed by a body corporate is proved to have been committed with the consent or connivance of, or to be attributable to any neglect on the part of, any director, manager[10], secretary or other similar officer of the body corporate, or any person who was purporting to act in any such capacity, he, as well as the body corporate, is guilty of the offence and liable to be proceeded against and punished accordingly[11].

1 Ie under the Employment Rights Act 1996 s 182: see PARA 628. As to the Secretary of State see PARA 5 note 21.
2 As to the meaning of 'employer' see PARA 2.
3 See the Employment Rights Act 1996 s 190(1).
4 Employment Rights Act 1996 s 190(1)(a).
5 Employment Rights Act 1996 s 190(1)(b).
6 See the Employment Rights Act 1996 s 190(2).
7 Employment Rights Act 1996 s 190(3). The penalty on summary conviction is a fine not exceeding level 3 on the standard scale: see s 190(3). As to the standard scale see **SENTENCING AND DISPOSITION OF OFFENDERS** vol 92 (2010) PARA 142.
8 Employment Rights Act 1996 s 190(4). The penalty on summary conviction is a fine not exceeding level 5 on the standard scale: see s 190(4).
9 Ie an offence under the Employment Rights Act 1996 s 190: see heads (a), (b) in the text.
10 As to the meaning of 'manager' at common law see PARA 40 note 11.
11 Employment Rights Act 1996 s 190(5). Where the affairs of a body corporate are managed by its members, s 190(5) applies in relation to the acts and defaults of a member in connection with his functions of management as if he were a director of the body corporate: s 190(6).

(18) PROTECTION AFFORDED UPON TRANSFER OF UNDERTAKINGS

632. Protection afforded upon the Transfer of Undertakings (Protection of Employment) Regulations 2006. Statutory protection is afforded to employees[1] affected by the transfer from one person to another of an undertaking[2], business, or part of an undertaking[3] or business, situated immediately before the transfer in the United Kingdom[4]. Accordingly, on such a transfer:

(1) the contract of employment[5] of any person employed by the transferor and assigned to the organised grouping of resources or employees that is subject to the relevant transfer, which would otherwise have been terminated by the transfer, continues to have effect after the transfer as if originally made between the person so employed and the transferee[6];
(2) all the transferor's rights, powers, duties and liabilities under or in connection with any such contract transfer to the transferee[7];
(3) any act or omission before the transfer is completed by or in relation to the transferor in respect of any such contract or any such employee is deemed to have been done by or in relation to the transferee[8];
(4) any employee of the transferor or transferee who is dismissed for a reason connected with the transfer is treated as automatically unfairly dismissed, except in special circumstances[9];
(5) any collective agreement made by or on behalf of the transferor with a trade union recognised by the transferor in respect of any employee whose contract of employment is preserved by head (1) above has effect, after the transfer, as if made by or on behalf of the transferee with that trade union[10];
(6) where an independent trade union is recognised to any extent by the transferor in respect of employees of any description who in consequence of the transfer become employees of the transferee, then, after the transfer, the union is deemed to have been recognised by the transferee to the same extent in respect of those employees and any agreement for recognition may be varied or rescinded accordingly[11];

(7) the transferor and transferee are obliged to inform and consult duly appointed employee representatives in relation to any employee (in respect of whom that trade union is recognised) who may be affected by the transfer or by any measures taken in connection with it[12].

Any provision of any agreement, whether a contract of employment or not, is void, in so far as it purports to exclude or limit the operation of the provisions described in heads (1) to (4) or in head (7) above[13].

1 As to the meaning of 'employee' for these purposes see PARA 137 note 8.
2 Ie the Transfer of Undertakings (Protection of Employment) Regulations 2006, SI 2006/246, made by the Secretary of State in exercise of the powers conferred upon him by the European Communities Act 1972 s 2(2) (see **CONSTITUTIONAL AND ADMINISTRATIVE LAW** vol 20 (2014) PARA 156), and the Employment Relations Act 1999 s 38, in order to give effect in the United Kingdom to Council Directive (EC) 2001/23 of 12 March 2001 (OJ L82, 22.03.2001, p 16) on the approximation of the laws of the member states relating to the safeguarding of employees' rights in the event of transfers of undertakings, businesses or parts of undertakings or businesses ('the Acquired Rights Directive'), and for associated purposes: see PARA 136. The Acquired Rights Directive was enacted initially as Council Directive (EC) 77/187 (OJ L161, 5.3.77, p 26): see PARA 136 note 3.
3 As to the meaning of references to the transfer of part of an undertaking see PARA 137 notes 3, 4.
4 See the Transfer of Undertakings (Protection of Employment) Regulations 2006, SI 2006/246, reg 3; and PARA 137. Such a transfer is a 'relevant transfer'; and 'transferor' and 'transferee' are to be construed accordingly: see reg 2(1); and PARA 137. As to the meaning of 'United Kingdom' see PARA 2 note 12.
5 As to the meaning of 'contract of employment' for these purposes see PARA 138 note 5.
6 See the Transfer of Undertakings (Protection of Employment) Regulations 2006, SI 2006/246, reg 4(1); and PARA 139.
7 See the Transfer of Undertakings (Protection of Employment) Regulations 2006, SI 2006/246, reg 4(2)(a); and PARA 139. As to the effect of a relevant transfer on an occupational pension scheme see reg 10; and PARA 141.
8 See the Transfer of Undertakings (Protection of Employment) Regulations 2006, SI 2006/246, reg 4(2)(b); and PARA 139. See also note 7.
9 See the Transfer of Undertakings (Protection of Employment) Regulations 2006, SI 2006/246, reg 7; and PARA 803.
10 See the Transfer of Undertakings (Protection of Employment) Regulations 2006, SI 2006/246, reg 5; and PARA 139 note 24.
11 See the Transfer of Undertakings (Protection of Employment) Regulations 2006, SI 2006/246, reg 6; and PARA 1095.
12 See the Transfer of Undertakings (Protection of Employment) Regulations 2006, SI 2006/246, regs 13–16; and PARAS 1196–1200.
13 See the Transfer of Undertakings (Protection of Employment) Regulations 2006, SI 2006/246, reg 18 which applies the Employment Rights Act 1996 s 203 (see PARA 150) in relation to the Transfer of Undertakings (Protection of Employment) Regulations 2006, SI 2006/246, as if in that Act, except that provision does not apply in so far as the Regulations provide for an agreement (whether a contract of employment or not) to exclude or limit the operation of the regulations: see PARA 137.

3. EMPLOYMENT TRAINING

(1) EMPLOYMENT AND TRAINING; IN GENERAL

633. Dissolution of the Training Commission. All authorisations or directions given to the Training Commission[1] or deemed[2] to have been given under the Employment and Training Act 1973[3] were revoked on 15 September 1988[4] and there were transferred to the Secretary of State[5]:

(1) all property, other than land or any interest in land, held by the Commission on 1 December 1988 in connection with the carrying out by the Commission of any of the revoked functions[6];

(2) all rights and liabilities to which the Commission was entitled or subject, other than any to which it was entitled or subject in connection with an interest in land:

(a) in connection with any property transferred by virtue of head (1) above; or

(b) in connection with the carrying out by the Commission of any of the revoked functions[7].

The Commission was dissolved on 16 November 1989[8] and all the property, rights and liabilities[9] to which the Commission was entitled or subject immediately before that date became, on that date, property, rights and liabilities of the Secretary of State[10].

Anything done by or in relation to the Commission, if in force or effective immediately before 16 November 1989, has effect, so far as may be required for continuing its effect on or after that date, as if done by or in relation to the relevant minister[11]; and anything which immediately before that date was in the process of being done by or in relation to the Commission may be continued on or after that date by or in relation to the relevant minister[12]; but, where anything done by the Commission before 16 November 1989 for the purposes of any provision of the Industrial Training Act 1982[13] required the approval of the Secretary of State, it does not so have effect unless it was done with his approval[14].

Every agreement, whether written[15] or not, and every instrument or other document, which relates to any function, property, right or liability of the Commission has effect, so far as may be required for continuing its effect on or after that date, as if:

(i) where the Commission is a party to it, the relevant minister were substituted as that party;

(ii) for any reference[16] to the Commission there were substituted a reference to the relevant minister;

(iii) for any reference[17] to the chairman or deputy chairman or any member of the Commission there were substituted a reference to such officer or officers as the relevant minister appoints for the purpose; and

(iv) for any reference[18] to the office or place of business of the Commission, there were substituted a reference to the principal office of the relevant minister[19].

1 The former Manpower Services Commission (established under the Employment and Training Act 1973 s 1 (repealed)) was renamed the 'Training Commission' by the Employment Act 1988 s 24(1) (repealed).

2 Ie by virtue of the Employment Act 1988 s 25(2), Sch 2 para 4 (repealed).

3 Ie under the Employment and Training Act 1973 s 2 (as originally enacted) or s 3 (repealed).

4 See the Training Commission (Incidental and Transitional Provisions) Order 1988, SI 1988/1905, art 2, Schedule (made under the Employment Act 1988 s 25(2), Sch 2 paras 6–8 (repealed); and continued in force, in relation to any provision having effect immediately before 16 November 1989, by the Employment Act 1989 s 22(5), Sch 5 para 11). As to the exceptions to the revocation see the Training Commission (Incidental and Transitional Provisions) Order 1988, SI 1988/1905, Schedule paras (a)–(d).

5 As to the Secretary of State see PARA 5 note 21.

6 Training Commission (Incidental and Transitional Provisions) Order 1988, SI 1988/1905, arts 1–3. 'Revoked functions' means the powers and duties which, by virtue of the revocation set out in the Schedule, ceased to apply to the Commission and any activities carried on at any time by the Commission pursuant to those powers and duties: art 2. Anything done or in the process of being done by or in relation to the Commission for the purposes of, or in connection with, the revoked functions is from 1 December 1988 to be treated as having been done by or in relation to the Secretary of State or, as the case may be, may be continued by or in relation to the Secretary of State: art 5. See further art 5(a)–(d).

7 Training Commission (Incidental and Transitional Provisions) Order 1988, SI 1988/1905, art 4.

8 Ie the date on which the Employment Act 1989 was passed.

9 For these purposes, references to property, rights and liabilities of the Commission are references to all such property, rights and liabilities, whether or not capable of being transferred or assigned by the Commission: Employment Act 1989 s 22(6).

10 Employment Act 1989 s 22(1), (2). As to the incorporation of the Secretary of State as a corporation sole, and the effect of documents made or issued by his predecessors, see Sch 5 para 2. As to corporations sole see CORPORATIONS vol 24 (2010) PARAS 314–315.

Any liability in respect of pensions, superannuation allowances or gratuities which, but for the passing of the Employment Act 1989, would have arisen or existed on or after 16 November 1989 as a liability of the Commission to or in respect of the chairman or any former chairman of the Commission, is instead a liability of the Paymaster General (s 22(3)); and any function which, immediately before 16 November 1989, was a function of the Commission in relation to preserved pensions, other than its function of making payments in respect of such pensions, became on that date a function of the Secretary of State (s 22(5), Sch 5 para 5(2)). For these purposes, 'preserved pensions' means pensions, superannuation allowances or gratuities in respect of which liabilities are so transferred to the Paymaster General: Sch 5 para 5(4). As to the Paymaster General see CONSTITUTIONAL AND ADMINISTRATIVE LAW vol 20 (2014) PARA 484.

11 Ie the Secretary of State, although references to the relevant minister in the Employment Act 1989 Sch 5 paras 3, 4, in the application of those provisions in relation to: (1) the Commission's function of making payments in respect of preserved pensions; or (2) any liability in respect of such pensions which is transferred by s 22(3) (see note 10), are to be construed as references to the Paymaster General: see Sch 5 paras 1, 5(3).

12 Employment Act 1989 Sch 5 para 3(1), (2). Schedule 5 para 3 applies in particular to things done by or in relation to the Commission for purposes of, or in connection with, functions which are transferred to the Secretary of State by s 22(4), Sch 4 (amendments to the Industrial Training Act 1982) (see PARA 658 et seq); but the Employment Act 1989 Sch 5 para 3(1) is subject to Sch 5 para 7 (see the text and notes 13–14): Sch 5 para 3(3).

13 See PARA 658 et seq.

14 Employment Act 1989 Sch 5 para 7.

15 As to the meaning of 'writing' see PARA 2 note 8.

16 Ie including any reference which is to be construed as such a reference.

17 Ie however worded and whether express or implied, and including any reference which is to be construed as such a reference.

18 See note 17.

19 Employment Act 1989 Sch 5 para 4(2).

634. Functions and powers of the Secretary of State. The Secretary of State[1] must make such arrangements as he considers appropriate for the purpose of assisting persons to select, train for, obtain and retain employment[2] suitable for their ages and capacities or of assisting persons to obtain suitable employees[3], including partners and other business associates[4]. Arrangements so made may:

(1) include arrangements for providing temporary employment for persons in Great Britain[5] who are without employment[6];

(2) include arrangements for encouraging increases in the opportunities for employment and training that are available to women and girls or to disabled persons[7];
(3) be made[8] in respect of employment and training[9] anywhere in the United Kingdom[10] or elsewhere[11];
(4) include provision for the making of payments by the Secretary of State[12], by way of grant or loan or otherwise, to persons who provide facilities in pursuance of the arrangements, to persons who use those facilities and to other persons specified in or determined under the arrangements[13];
(5) include provision for the making of payments to the Secretary of State[14] by other parties to the arrangements and by persons who use those facilities[15];
(6) include arrangements for securing that assistance in relation to the specified matters[16] is provided by persons other than the Secretary of State[17].

Such arrangements may not include arrangements in respect of employment for sexual purposes[18].

The Secretary of State may:

(a) appoint such persons as he thinks fit for the purpose of advising him with respect to the performance of any of the functions[19] conferred or imposed[20] on him[21]; and
(b) pay to any person appointed in pursuance of head (a) above such subsistence and travelling allowances and such compensation for loss of remunerative time as the Secretary of State may determine with the approval of the Treasury[22]; and
(c) arrange for, or make payments in respect of, research into any matter connected with any of his functions relating to employment, unemployment or training for employment and the dissemination of information derived from such research[23],

but he is not to make any payments in pursuance of head (c) above unless the amounts of the payments and the terms on which they are made are approved by the Treasury[24].

The powers conferred on the Secretary of State by the Employment and Training Act 1973 are in addition to, and not in substitution for, any powers otherwise exercisable by him[25].

1 As to the Secretary of State see PARA 5 note 21. The functions of the Secretary of State under the Employment and Training Act 1973 are, so far as exercisable in relation to Wales, transferred, subject to certain exceptions, to the Welsh Ministers: see the National Assembly for Wales (Transfer of Functions) Order 1999, SI 1999/672, art 2, Sch 1; and PARA 5 note 21. The exceptions are ministerial functions under the Employment and Training Act 1973 s 2, s 4 (see PARA 635), s 5 (see the text and notes 19–24) and s 11 (see PARA 637), which are to be exercisable by the Welsh Ministers concurrently with any Ministers of the Crown by whom they are exercisable, save that the functions exercisable by the Welsh Ministers under s 2 do not include the function of making arrangements for the principal purpose of helping all those, as distinct from a particular section of the population of Wales, without work to find employment and to help employers to fill vacancies, or any function ancillary to that function: National Assembly for Wales (Transfer of Functions) Order 1999, SI 1999/672, art 2, Sch 1. As to the Welsh Ministers see PARA 5 note 21. See also note 13.

2 For these purposes, 'employment' means employment under a contract of service or apprenticeship or a contract for services or otherwise than under a contract; and 'employed' is to be construed accordingly: Employment and Training Act 1973 s 13(1) (amended by the Employment Protection Act 1975 Sch 14 para 6, Sch 18). As to the meanings of 'employment',

'employed', and related expressions in relation to employment rights generally see PARA 2 et seq. As to the meanings of 'contract of service' and 'contract for service' see PARA 1 note 1. As to contracts of apprenticeship see PARA 112.

3 For these purposes 'employee' includes a person engaged under a contract for services; and 'employer' is to be construed accordingly: Employment and Training Act 1973 s 13(1) (amended by the Employment Protection Act 1975 Sch 14 para 6, Sch 18). As to the meaning of 'employee' and related expressions in relation to employment rights generally see PARA 2 et seq.

4 Employment and Training Act 1973 s 2(1) (s 2 substituted by the Employment Act 1988 s 25(1)). A jobcentre, as the provider of a publicly funded service with obligations under the Employment and Training Act 1973, is bound to demonstrate a measure of flexibility in the way in which it operates the service, so as not to deny access to an employer in a discriminatory manner: *R (on the application of Ann Summers Ltd) v Jobcentre Plus* [2003] EWHC 1416 (Admin), [2003] All ER (D) 235 (Jun) (potential difficulties caused by advertisements for job vacancies received from a company which sells lingerie and sex toys outweighed by the potential benefit which jobseekers could obtain by taking up the employment).

Information relating to employment or training which is held by the Secretary of State or by a person providing services to him in connection with the provision of those services may be used and supplied to them for the purposes of, or for any purposes connected with, the exercise of functions in relation to employment or training: see the Social Security Act 1998 s 3; and **WELFARE BENEFITS AND STATE PENSIONS** vol 104 (2014) PARA 546.

As to the provision of information held by the Secretary of State in relation to his functions exercised for the purposes of: (1) the prevention, detection, investigation or prosecution of offences relating to a scheme or arrangement under the Employment and Training Act 1973 s 2; or (2) checking the accuracy of any benefit, payment or advantage in a scheme or arrangement under s 2, see the Proceeds of Crime Act 2002 (Disclosure of Information) Order 2008, SI 2008/1909, Schedule. As to the provision of information about a young person by public bodies for the purposes of the provision of services in Wales under the Employment and Training Act 1973 s 2 see the Learning and Skills Act 2000 s 138; and **EDUCATION** vol 36 (2011) PARA 1344.

5 As to the meaning of 'Great Britain' see PARA 2 note 12.

6 Employment and Training Act 1973 s 2(2)(a) (as substituted: see note 4).

7 Employment and Training Act 1973 s 2(2)(b) (as substituted: see note 4). It is the duty of the Secretary of State, in exercising any power to select disabled persons for courses of training and other courses or any power to submit for engagements the names of disabled persons, to give preference, so far as he considers it consistent with the efficient exercise of that power, to persons of the classes specified in the Disabled Persons (Employment) Act 1944 s 16 (classes of ex-service men and women to whom preference is to be given) (see PARA 610); and for these purposes 'disabled person' has the same meaning as in the Equality Act 2010: Employment and Training Act 1973 s 12(1) (amended by the Employment Act 1988 Sch 2 para 2; the Employment Act 1989 Sch 7 Pt I; the Disability Discrimination Act 1995 Sch 6 para 1; and further amended by the Equality Act 2010 Sch 26 para 3). As to unlawful discrimination, as respects vocational training, on grounds of sex or race see **DISCRIMINATION** vol 33 (2013) PARA 48 et seq. The Secretary of State may by order provide that special treatment afforded to or in respect of lone parents in connection with their participation in any specified arrangements made under the Employment and Training Act 1973 s 2 or any specified class or description of training for employment provided otherwise than in pursuance of the Employment and Training Act 1973 s 2 is not to be regarded for the purposes of the Equality Act 2010 as giving rise to any contravention of Pt 5 (see **DISCRIMINATION** vol 33 (2013) PARA 110 et seq), so far as relating to marriage and civil partnership discrimination (within the meaning of that Act: see **DISCRIMINATION** vol 33 (2013) PARA 60): see the Employment Act 1989 s 8 (amended by the Equality Act 2010 Sch 26 para 14; and SI 2013/630). In exercise of the powers conferred by the Employment Act 1989 s 8, the Sex Discrimination Act 1975 (Exemption of Special Treatment for Lone Parents) Order 1989, SI 1989/2140, and the Sex Discrimination Act 1975 (Exemption of Special Treatment for Lone Parents) Order 1991, SI 1991/2813, have been made.

Marriage of same sex couples is lawful in the law of England and Wales, and such marriages have the same effect as marriages of opposite sex couples: see the Marriage (Same Sex Couples) Act 2013 s 1(1), 11(1); and **MATRIMONIAL AND CIVIL PARTNERSHIP LAW** vol 72 (2009) PARA 1 et seq.

8 Ie subject to the restriction of the Employment and Training Act 1973 s 2(2)(a) (see head (1) in the text) to persons in Great Britain.

9 For these purposes, 'training' includes any education with a view to employment; and cognate expressions are to be construed accordingly: Employment and Training Act 1973 s 13(1).

10 As to the meaning of 'United Kingdom' see PARA 2 note 12.

11 Employment and Training Act 1973 s 2(2)(c) (as substituted: see note 4).
12 The payments for which such arrangements may provide: (1) include the payment to a person by the Secretary of State of an allowance pending a time when payments will be or may be made to that person in respect of his use of facilities which will be or may be made available to him under any such arrangements; (2) do not include the payment of any such allowance to a person for any period: (a) after that person has attained the age of 18 years; or (b) for which child benefit is payable in respect of that person: Employment and Training Act 1973 s 2(3)(a), (b) (as substituted: see note 4). No payments may be made by or on behalf of the Secretary of State by virtue of any power conferred by s 2, other than payments under s 11(3) (see PARA 637) or s 12(4) (see PARA 637) unless the Treasury has approved: (i) the amounts of the payments or the manner of determining those amounts; and (ii) the terms on which they are made or the manner of determining those terms: s 2(5) (as so substituted). For these purposes, 'facilities' includes services: s 13(1). As to the Treasury see CONSTITUTIONAL AND ADMINISTRATIVE LAW vol 20 (2014) PARA 262 et seq. As to the payment of child benefit see WELFARE BENEFITS AND STATE PENSIONS vol 104 (2014) PARA 155 et seq.
13 Employment and Training Act 1973 s 2(2)(d) (as substituted: see note 4). Where a company has: (1) entered into an arrangement with the Secretary of State with a view to receiving payments under s 2(2)(d) in connection with the provision of facilities; (2) before 28 July 2000 (ie before the passing of the Learning and Skills Act 2000) the company has received notice from the Secretary of State that he intends to terminate the arrangement; (3) the company's articles of association are in a form approved by the Secretary of State generally or specifically for purposes connected with such arrangements; and (4) the company's articles of association requires all income and profits to be applied towards the promotion of the company's objects and not to be distributed to members, then, unless the Secretary of State consents in writing, such a company may not after 28 July 2000 take action of a prescribed kind or cause or permit a person to take action of a prescribed kind: s 141(1), (2) (s 141(1) amended by SI 2009/1941). As to the meaning of 'writing' see PARA 2 note 8. For these purposes, 'prescribed' means prescribed by order of the Secretary of State; and the action which may be so prescribed includes, in particular: (a) making a disposal or payment of a prescribed kind or in prescribed circumstances; (b) incurring expenditure of a prescribed kind or in prescribed circumstances; and (c) entering into a transaction of a prescribed kind or in prescribed circumstances: s 141(3). As to the actions prescribed see the Training Programmes (Cessation of Funding) (Prescribed Actions) Order 2000, SI 2000/2170. Where a company fulfils the requirements in heads (1)–(4) above, it must comply with a written direction from the Secretary of State given after 28 July 2000 which requires it to transfer an asset to a specified body or the Secretary of State (Learning and Skills Act 2000 s 141(4)); but before giving such a direction the Secretary of State must consult the company (s 141(5)). Where such a company takes, causes or permits a prescribed action, the High Court may on the application of the Secretary of State make any order which seems to it appropriate (s 141(6)); and such an order may, in particular: (i) provide for a contract or other agreement to be of no effect; (ii) vary the terms of a contract or other agreement; (iii) require money to be paid to the Secretary of State by or on behalf of the company to which this section applies; (iv) require money to be paid to the Secretary of State by or on behalf of any other specified person; (v) require the Secretary of State to pay to a specified person compensation of an amount specified in the order or determined in accordance with the order (s 141(7)). This function is not exercisable in relation to Wales by the Welsh Ministers; but in the application of s 141 to a company which operates in Wales: (A) a reference to the Secretary of State in heads (1) and (2) above must be construed as a reference to the Secretary of State or the Welsh Ministers; (B) the functions conferred or imposed on the Secretary of State by s 141(2)–(6) are exercisable by the Welsh Ministers; and (C) a reference in s 141(2)–(7) to the Secretary of State must be taken as a reference to the Welsh Ministers: s 141(8). As to the meaning of 'Wales' see PARA 2 note 12. As to a company's memorandum and articles of association see COMPANIES vol 14 (2009) PARA 104.
14 The payments for which such arrangements may provide do not include any payment by any person to the Secretary of State, other than a payment for publications issued in pursuance of the arrangements, in respect of the seeking or obtaining for that person of any employment under a contract of service or apprenticeship: Employment and Training Act 1973 s 2(3)(c) (as substituted: see note 4). See also note 12.
15 Employment and Training Act 1973 s 2(2)(e) (as substituted: see note 4).
16 Ie the matters mentioned in the Employment and Training Act 1973 s 2(1): see the text and notes 1–4.
17 Employment and Training Act 1973 s 2(2)(f) (as substituted: see note 4).
18 Employment and Training Act 1973 s 2A(1) (s 2A added by the Welfare Reform Act 2012 s 144). For these purposes, employment is for sexual purposes if (1) it involves the employee

engaging in an activity; and (2) the employee's activity, or the way in which it is performed, may reasonably be assumed to be intended solely or principally to stimulate one or more other persons sexually (by whatever means): Employment and Training Act 1973 s 2A(2) (as so added). The Secretary of State may by order specify exceptions to s 2A(1): see s 2A(3), (4). However, at the date at which this volume states the law, no such order had been made.

19 For these purposes, 'functions' includes powers and duties: Employment and Training Act 1973 s 13(1).

20 Ie by the Employment and Training Act 1973 s 2 (see the text and notes 1–17), s 8 (see PARA 638), s 9 (see PARA 639), s 10 (see PARA 640) and s 12 (see note 7; and PARAS 637, 643). In the appointment of persons, in pursuance of s 5(2)(a), to advise the Secretary of State with respect to the performance of the functions conferred on him by virtue of s 10(6) (see PARA 640), regard is to be had to the desirability of including one or more persons with experience of work among, and the special needs of, young disabled persons and to the person or persons with that experience being or including a disabled person or persons: Chronically Sick and Disabled Persons Act 1970 s 13(2) (amended by the Employment and Training Act 1973 Sch 3 para 11, Sch 4; and the Trade Union Reform and Employment Rights Act 1993 Sch 8 para 3, Sch 10).

21 Employment and Training Act 1973 s 5(2)(a) (amended by the Trade Union Reform and Employment Rights Act 1993 Sch 8 para 5); Transfer of Functions (Minister for the Civil Service and Treasury) Order 1981, SI 1981/1670, art 2(1).

22 Employment and Training Act 1973 s 5(2)(b); Transfer of Functions (Minister for the Civil Service and Treasury) Order 1981, SI 1981/1670, art 2(1).

23 Employment and Training Act 1973 s 5(3) (amended by the Employment and Training Act 1981 Sch 2 para 11, Sch 3; and the Employment Act 1989 Sch 7 Pt I).

24 Employment and Training Act 1973 s 5(4) (amended by the Employment Act 1988 Sch 4).

25 Employment and Training Act 1973 s 13(3).

635. Obtaining and disclosure of information. Nothing in the Statistics of Trade Act 1947[1] prevents or penalises the disclosure by the Secretary of State or the Chancellor of the Exchequer[2]:

(1) to a board[3] of relevant information[4];

(2) of relevant information, consisting of the name and address of any establishment, the numbers of persons of different descriptions employed[5] there and the nature of the activities carried on there, to:

  (a) any person who is or is to be engaged in the carrying out on behalf of the Secretary of State or the Chancellor of the Exchequer of any research or survey relating to matters connected with training for employment[6], with industrial relations or otherwise with employment or unemployment; or

  (b) an officer of any of the specified bodies[7] who is authorised by that body to receive the information;

(3) of statistics compiled wholly or partly from relevant information about the numbers of persons employed in any activity or area[8].

Where, however, the Secretary of State or the Chancellor of the Exchequer discloses information to a board or any other person under head (1) or head (3) above, he must give a notice in writing to that person specifying the purposes for which the information may be used[9].

A person to whom information is so disclosed is not to use the information for a purpose other than:

(i) in a case falling within head (1) or head (3) above, a purpose specified in the notice given[10] with respect to the information;

(ii) in the case of information given to such a person as is mentioned in head (2)(a) above, a purpose related to the carrying out of the research or survey in the carrying out of which that person is or is to be engaged;

(iii) in the case of information given to an officer of a local planning authority, the purposes of the specified functions conferred[11] on the authority;

(iv) in the case of information given to an officer of the National Assembly for Wales, the purposes of specified functions conferred[12] on that body;

(v) in the case of information given to an officer of a development corporation, the purposes of specified functions conferred[13] on the corporation,

and a person who contravenes these provisions is guilty of an offence and liable on summary conviction to a fine[14].

Information relating to employment or training which is held by the Secretary of State or by a person providing services to him in connection with the provision of those services may be used and supplied to them for the purposes of, or for any purposes connected with, the exercise of functions in relation to employment or training[15].

1 Ie the Statistics of Trade Act 1947 s 9 (which restricts the disclosure of information obtained under that Act): see TRADE AND INDUSTRY vol 97 (2010) PARA 1016 et seq.

2 For these purposes, any reference to the Secretary of State or the Chancellor of the Exchequer or a government department includes respectively a reference to an officer of his or of that body: Employment and Training Act 1973 s 4(4) (amended by the Employment and Training Act 1981 Sch 2 para 10(b), Sch 3; the Employment Act 1989 Sch 7 Pt I; and SI 1995/2986). As to the Secretary of State see PARA 5 note 21. Functions under Employment and Training Act 1973 s 4, so far as exercisable by the Chancellor of the Exchequer for the disclosing of information obtained under Employment and Training Act 1973, transferred to the Statistics Board, by the Statistics and Registration Service Act 2007 (Delegation of Functions) (Economic Statistics) Order 2008, SI 2008/792, art 6(c). As to the Statistics Board see the REGISTRATION CONCERNING THE INDIVIDUAL vol 88 (2012) PARA 353 et seq. As to the Chancellor of the Exchequer see CONSTITUTIONAL AND ADMINISTRATIVE LAW vol 20 (2014) PARA 265. As to the exercise of functions under the Employment and Training Act 1973 in relation to Wales see PARA 634 note 1.

3 For these purposes, a 'board' means an industrial training board established under the Industrial Training Act 1964 s 1 (repealed) or the Industrial Training Act 1982 s 1 (see PARA 658); and any reference to such a board includes a reference to an officer of that board and also a reference to any committee appointed by the board, to any officer of such a committee and to any person entitled to take part in the proceedings of the board: Employment and Training Act 1973 s 4(4) (amended by the Industrial Training Act 1982 Sch 3 para 3).

4 For these purposes, 'relevant information' means information obtained under the Statistics of Trade Act 1947: Employment and Training Act 1973 s 4(4).

5 As to the meaning of 'employed' see PARA 634 note 2.

6 As to the meaning of 'employment' see PARA 634 note 2; and as to the meaning of 'training' see PARA 634 note 9.

7 Ie: (1) a local planning authority within the meaning of the Town and Country Planning Act 1990 (see PLANNING vol 81 (2010) PARA 43 et seq); (2) an officer of the National Assembly for Wales (see CONSTITUTIONAL AND ADMINISTRATIVE LAW vol 20 (2014) PARA 351); and (3) a development corporation within the meaning of the New Towns Act 1981 (see PLANNING vol 83 (2010) PARA 1499 et seq).

8 Employment and Training Act 1973 s 4(3) (amended by the Welsh Development Agency Act 1975 s 24(6); the Employment and Training Act 1981 Sch 2 para 10(a)(iii), Sch 3; the Employment Act 1988 s 28(1); the Employment Act 1989 Sch 6 para 9(1), (2), Sch 7 Pt I; the Planning (Consequential Provisions) Act 1990 Sch 2 para 30(a); the Trade Union Reform and Employment Rights Act 1993 Sch 10; the Government of Wales Act 1998 Sch 18; SI 1995/2986; and SI 2005/3226); and see the Interpretation Act 1978 s 17(2)(a).

9 Employment and Training Act 1973 s 4(3A) (added by the Employment Act 1989 Sch 6 para 9(1), (3); and amended by SI 1995/2986). As to the meaning of 'writing' see PARA 2 note 8.

10 Ie in pursuance of the Employment and Training Act 1973 s 4(3A): see the text and note 9.

11 Ie by the Town and Country Planning Act 1990 Pt II (ss 10A–54A) (repealed: see now the Planning and Compulsory Purchase Act 2004). As to the meaning of 'functions' see PARA 634 note 19.

12 Ie by the Welsh Development Agency Act 1975: see TRADE AND INDUSTRY vol 97 (2010) PARA 954 et seq.

13 Ie by the New Towns Act 1981 s 4 (which relates to the laying out and development of new towns): see PLANNING vol 83 (2010) PARA 1500.

14 Employment and Training Act 1973 s 4(5) (amended by the Welsh Development Agency Act 1975 s 24(6); the Development of Rural Wales Act 1976 s 17(2); the Criminal Justice Act 1982 ss 38, 46; the Employment Act 1988 s 28(2); the Employment Act 1989 Sch 6 para 9(1), (4), Sch 7 Pt I; the Planning (Consequential Provisions) Act 1990 Sch 2 para 30(b); the Trade Union Reform and Employment Rights Act 1993 Sch 10; the Government of Wales Act 1998 Sch 18; and SI 2005/3226); and see the Interpretation Act 1978 s 17(2)(a). The penalty is a fine not exceeding level 5 on the standard scale: see the Employment and Training Act 1973 s 4(5) (as so amended). As to the standard scale see SENTENCING AND DISPOSITION OF OFFENDERS vol 92 (2010) PARA 142.

15 See the Social Security Act 1998 s 3; and WELFARE BENEFITS AND STATE PENSIONS vol 104 (2014) PARA 546.

636. Status of trainees etc. Where it appears to the Secretary of State[1] that provision has been made[2] for persons using facilities provided in pursuance of arrangements made by him under the Employment and Training Act 1973[3] to receive payments from any person in connection with their use of those facilities, the Secretary of State may by order provide that:

(1) those persons are, for the purposes and in the cases specified or described in or determined under the order, to be treated in respect of their use of those facilities as being or as not being employed;

(2) where those persons are treated as being employed, they are to be treated as being the employees of the persons so specified, described or determined and of no others;

(3) where those persons are treated as not being employed, they are to be treated as being trained, or are to be treated in such other manner as may be so specified, described or determined; and

(4) those payments are to be treated for the purposes of such enactments[4] and subordinate legislation[5] as may be so specified, described or determined in such manner as may be so specified, described or determined[6].

Where it appears to the Secretary of State that provision has been made for trainees to receive payments from the Secretary of State under the Education Act 2002[7], from the Chief Executive of Skills Funding under the Apprenticeships, Skills, Children and Learning Act 2009[8], or from the Welsh Ministers under the Learning and Skills Act 2000[9], the Secretary of State may by order provide:

(a) that the trainees[10] are, for the purposes and in the cases specified or described in or determined under the order, to be treated in respect of the training as being or as not being employed;

(b) that, where those trainees are treated as being employed, they are to be treated as being the employees of the persons so specified, described or determined and of no others;

(c) that, where those trainees are treated as not being employed, they are to be treated in such other manner as may be so specified, described or determined; and

(d) that those payments are to be treated for the purposes of such enactments and subordinate legislation as may be so specified, described or determined in such manner as may be so specified, described or determined[11].

The power to make an order is exercisable by statutory instrument subject to annulment in pursuance of a resolution of either House of Parliament; and such an order may:

(i) modify[12] any enactment or subordinate legislation;

(ii) make different provision for different purposes and for different cases; and

(iii) contain such incidental, consequential and transitional provision as appears to the Secretary of State to be appropriate[13].

1 As to the Secretary of State see PARA 5 note 21.
2 Ie under the Employment and Training Act 1973 s 2: see PARA 634.
3 See note 2.
4 For these purposes, 'enactment' includes an enactment contained in the Employment Act 1988 or in any Act passed after that Act: Employment Act 1988 s 26(4).
5 For these purposes, 'subordinate legislation' has the same meaning as in the Interpretation Act 1978 (see STATUTES AND LEGISLATIVE PROCESS vol 96 (2012) PARA 609): Employment Act 1988 s 26(4).
6 Employment Act 1988 s 26(1) (amended by the Trade Union Reform and Employment Rights Act 1993 Sch 8 para 38(b)); Employment Act 1988 s 32(1). The power of the Secretary of State to make an order under s 26 includes power to make, in relation to: (1) persons participating in any scheme; and (2) payments received by them by virtue of the Welfare Reform and Pensions Act 1999 s 60(5) (see WELFARE BENEFITS AND STATE PENSIONS vol 104 (2014) PARA 289), provision corresponding to any provision which, by virtue of the Employment Act 1988 s 26(1) or s 26(2) (see the text and notes 12–13), may be made in relation to persons using such facilities, and to such payments received by them, as are mentioned in s 26(1): Welfare Reform and Pensions Act 1999 s 60(8). As from a day to be appointed, s 60 is repealed by the Welfare Reform Act 2009 Sch 7 Pt 3. At the date this volume states the law, no such day had been appointed.
7 Ie under the Education Act 2002 s 14 (see EDUCATION vol 35 (2011) PARA 77).
8 Ie under the Apprenticeships, Skills, Children and Learning Act 2009 s 100(1)(c) or (d) (see EDUCATION vol 36 (2011) PARA 1296).
9 Ie under the Learning and Skills Act 2000 s 34(1)(c) (see EDUCATION vol 36 (2011) PARA 1319).
10 For these purposes, trainees are persons receiving or proposing to receive training: Employment Act 1988 s 26(1B) (as added: see note 8).
11 Employment Act 1988 s 26(1A), (1B) (s 26(1A) substituted and s 26(1B) added by the Education Act 2011 Sch 16 para 7).
12 For these purposes, 'modifications' includes additions, alterations and omissions; and cognate expressions are to be construed accordingly: Employment Act 1988 s 32(1).
13 Employment Act 1988 s 26(2). See also note 6. The consent of the Treasury is required for the making of any such order which contains provision for the manner in which any payment is to be treated for the purposes of the Income Tax Acts: Employment Act 1988 s 26(3). As to the Treasury see CONSTITUTIONAL AND ADMINISTRATIVE LAW vol 20 (2014) PARA 262 et seq. As to the meaning of 'Income Tax Acts' see INCOME TAXATION vol 58 (2014) PARA 24; STATUTES AND LEGISLATIVE PROCESS vol 96 (2012) PARA 1212. In exercise of this power the Secretary of State has made the Social Security (Employment Training: Payments) Order 1988, SI 1988/1409; the Employment Action (Miscellaneous Provisions) Order 1991, SI 1991/1995; the Community Action (Miscellaneous Provisions) Order 1993, SI 1993/1621; the Learning for Work (Miscellaneous Provisions) Order 1993, SI 1993/1949; the Training for Work (Miscellaneous Provisions) Order 1995, SI 1995/1780; the Project Work (Miscellaneous Provisions) Order 1996, SI 1996/1623; the New Deal (Miscellaneous Provisions) Order 1998, SI 1998/217; the New Deal (25 plus) (Miscellaneous Provisions) Order 1999, SI 1999/779; the New Deal (Miscellaneous Provisions) Order 2001, SI 2001/970; the New Deal (Lone Parents) (Miscellaneous Provisions) Order 2001, SI 2001/2915; the Flexible New Deal (Miscellaneous Provisions) Order 2009, SI 2009/1562; and the Community Task Force (Miscellaneous Provisions) Order 2010, SI 2010/349: see WELFARE BENEFITS AND STATE PENSIONS vol 104 (2014) PARA 382. As to the position of apprentices and youth trainees at common law see also PARAS 112, 128–129, 747–754. As to the statutory law on apprenticeships see EDUCATION vol 35 (2011) PARA 682 et seq.

637. Financial provisions. There must be paid out of money provided by Parliament:

(1) any expenses incurred by the Secretary of State[1] for the purposes of the Employment and Training Act 1973; and

(2) any increase attributable to the provisions of that Act in the sum payable under any other Act out of money so provided,

and any sums received by the Secretary of State by virtue of the Employment and Training Act 1973 must be paid into the Consolidated Fund[2].

Where it appears to the Secretary of State or an industrial training board[3] that any person would have been entitled, by reference to an injury or disease developed by him or another person in consequence of attendance at a course provided or approved by or on behalf of the Secretary of State or by the board or in consequence of the use of facilities[4] so provided or approved, to receive any benefit or increase in benefit[5] but for the fact that he or the other person was not at a relevant time an employed earner[6], the Secretary of State or the board may make to him payments equal to the whole or part of the benefit or increase in question[7].

The Secretary of State or an industrial training board may make to any person payments by way of travelling and subsistence allowances and compensation for loss of remunerative time which, in the case of payments by such a board, are approved by the Secretary of State and which the Secretary of State or board considers are appropriate in connection with the person's attendance at any examination connected with a claim for payments from the Secretary of State or board[8].

1 As to the Secretary of State see PARA 5 note 21; and as to the exercise of functions under the Employment and Training Act 1973 in relation to Wales see PARA 634 note 1.
2 Employment and Training Act 1973 s 11(2). As to the Consolidated Fund see CONSTITUTIONAL AND ADMINISTRATIVE LAW vol 20 (2014) PARA 480 et seq; PARLIAMENT vol 78 (2010) PARAS 1028–1031.
3 Ie established under the Industrial Training Act 1964 s 1 (repealed) or the Industrial Training Act 1982 s 1 (see PARA 658).
4 As to the meaning of 'facilities' see PARA 634 note 12.
5 Ie in pursuance of the Social Security Contributions and Benefits Act 1992 Pts II–IV (ss 20–93): see WELFARE BENEFITS AND STATE PENSIONS vol 104 (2014) PARA 409 et seq.
6 As to the meaning of 'employed earner' see the Social Security Contributions and Benefits Act 1992 s 2(1)(a), s 2(3); and WELFARE BENEFITS AND STATE PENSIONS vol 104 (2014) PARA 381.
7 Employment and Training Act 1973 s 11(3) (amended by the Social Security (Consequential Provisions) Act 1975 Sch 2 para 68; the Industrial Training Act 1982 Sch 3 para 3; the Employment Act 1988 Sch 2 para 1, Sch 4; the Social Security (Consequential Provisions) Act 1992 Sch 2 para 10; and the Welfare Reform Act 2012 s 66).
8 Employment and Training Act 1973 s 12(4) (amended by the Employment Act 1988 Sch 2 para 2(3), Sch 4). As to the exercise of the functions of the Secretary of State under the Employment and Training Act 1973 s 12 in relation to Wales by the Welsh Ministers see PARA 634 note 1.

(2) CAREERS SERVICES

638. Secretary of State's duty to ensure provision of career services for school and college students. It is the duty of the Secretary of State[1] to secure the provision of relevant services[2] for assisting persons undergoing relevant education[3] to decide:

(1) what employments, having regard to their capabilities, will be suitable for and available to them when they cease undergoing such education; and
(2) what training or education is or will be required by and available to them in order to fit them for those employments,

and for assisting persons ceasing to undergo relevant education to obtain such employments, training and education[4].

1 As to the Secretary of State see PARA 5 note 21. As to the exercise of the functions of the Secretary of State under the Employment and Training Act 1973 s 8 in relation to Wales see PARA 634 note 1.
2 For these purposes, 'relevant services' means: (1) giving of assistance by collecting, or disseminating or otherwise providing, information about persons seeking, obtaining or offering employment, training and education; (2) offering advice and guidance; and (3) other services calculated to facilitate the provision of any services specified in heads (1) and (2) above: Employment and Training Act 1973 s 8(2) (s 8 substituted by the Trade Union Reform and Employment Rights Act 1993 s 45). As to the meaning of 'employment' see PARA 634 note 2; and as to the meaning of 'training' see PARA 634 note 9.
3 For these purposes, 'relevant education' means: (1) education involving full-time attendance at any educational institution in Great Britain, other than an educational institution within the higher education sector; and (2) education involving part-time attendance at any educational institution in Great Britain, other than an educational institution within the higher education sector, which is education of a description commonly undergone by persons in order to fit them for employment: Employment and Training Act 1973 s 8(3) (as substituted: see note 2). The reference to an educational institution within the higher education sector is to be construed in accordance with the Further and Higher Education Act 1992 s 91(5) (see EDUCATION vol 36 (2011) PARA 809): Employment and Training Act 1973 s 8(4) (as so substituted). As to the meaning of 'Great Britain' see PARA 2 note 12.
4 Employment and Training Act 1973 s 8(1) (as substituted: see note 2). As to the provision of information about a young person by public bodies for the purposes of the provision of services in Wales under s 8 see the Learning and Skills Act 2000 s 138; and EDUCATION vol 36 (2011) PARA 1344.

639. Secretary of State's power to arrange for the provision of careers services for others. The Secretary of State[1] has power to secure the provision of relevant services[2], or any description of relevant services, for assisting persons other than those undergoing relevant education[3], or any description of such persons, to decide:

(1) what employments[4], having regard to their capabilities, are or will be suitable for and available to them; and
(2) what training[5] or education is or will be required by and available to them in order to fit them for those employments,

and for assisting those persons to obtain such employments, training and education[6].

1 As to the Secretary of State see PARA 5 note 21. As to the exercise of the functions of the Secretary of State under the Employment and Training Act 1973 s 9 in relation to Wales see PARA 634 note 1.
2 As to the meaning of 'relevant services' see PARA 638 note 2.
3 As to the meaning of 'relevant education' see PARA 638 note 3.
4 As to the meaning of 'employment' see PARA 634 note 2.
5 As to the meaning of 'training' see PARA 634 note 9.
6 Employment and Training Act 1973 s 9 (substituted by the Trade Union Reform and Employment Rights Act 1993 s 45). As to the provision of information about a young person by public bodies for the purposes of the provision of services in Wales under s 9 see the Learning and Skills Act 2000 s 138; and EDUCATION vol 36 (2011) PARA 1344.

640. Provision of services. The Secretary of State[1] may perform the duty imposed on him to ensure the provision of careers services for school and college students[2], and exercise his power to arrange for the provision of careers services for others[3], by making arrangements with:

(1) local authorities[4];
(2) persons of any other description; or
(3) local authorities and persons of any other description acting jointly,

under which they undertake to provide, or arrange for the provision of, services in accordance with the arrangements; and, in doing so, the Secretary of State must have regard to the requirements of disabled persons[5].

The Secretary of State may also perform the duty imposed on him to ensure the provision of careers services for school and college students, and exercise his power to arrange for the provision of careers services for others, by giving directions to local education authorities requiring them to provide, or arrange for the provision of, services in accordance with the directions; and, in doing so, the Secretary of State must have regard to the requirements of disabled persons[6].

Directions so given may require local authorities to provide services themselves or jointly with other authorities or persons, to arrange for the provision of services by other authorities or persons, or to consult and co-ordinate in the provision, or in the arranging for the provision, of services with other authorities or persons[7].

Arrangements made, and directions given, under the provisions described above:

(a) may include provision for the making of payments by the Secretary of State, whether by way of grant or loan or otherwise, to the persons with whom they are made or to whom they are given[8];

(b) must require the person with whom they are made or to whom they are given:

  (i) to provide, or arrange for the provision, of services in accordance with such guidance of a general character as the Secretary of State may give; and

  (ii) to furnish the Secretary of State, in such manner and at such times as he may specify in the arrangements or directions or in guidance given under head (b)(i) above, with such information and facilities for obtaining information as he may so specify[9].

Arrangements made, and directions given, in exercise of the Secretary of State's power to arrange for the provision of careers services for others[10] may include provision permitting the making of charges for the provision of the services to which they relate[11].

The Secretary of State may give directions to local authorities requiring them to transfer, on such terms as may be specified in the directions, to any persons who are providing, or are to provide, services in accordance with arrangements made, or directions given, under the provisions described above any records of the authorities which may be relevant in the provision of the services[12].

Local authorities have power:

(A) to provide services, or arrange for the provision of services, in accordance with arrangements made, or directions given, under the provisions described above, including services provided outside their areas, by any such means, including by the formation of companies for the purpose, as they consider appropriate; and

(B) to employ officers and provide facilities for and in connection with the provision of services or arranging for the provision of the services,

but where directions are given to local authorities, the power conferred on them by these provisions must be exercised in accordance with the directions[13].

Where services are being provided in pursuance of arrangements made, or directions given, under the provisions described above, the authority with which the arrangements are made or to which the directions have been given has power, with the consent of the Secretary of State, to provide, or arrange for the provision of, more extensive (relevant) services than the arrangements authorise or the directions require and to employ more officers and provide more facilities accordingly[14].

A direction given under these provisions may be revoked or varied by another direction so given[15].

Nothing in the provisions described above is to be taken to limit the arrangements which may otherwise be made[16] by the Secretary of State for the purpose of assisting persons to select, train for, obtain and retain employment[17] suitable for their ages and capacities or of assisting persons to obtain suitable employees[18].

1 As to the Secretary of State see PARA 5 note 21. See also PARA 639 note 1. As to the exercise of the functions of the Secretary of State under the Employment and Training Act 1973 s 10 in relation to Wales see PARA 634 note 1.
2 Ie by the Employment and Training Act 1973 s 8: see PARA 638.
3 Ie by the Employment and Training Act 1973 s 9: see PARA 639.
4 'Local authority' has the meaning given by the Education Act 1996 s 579(1) (see EDUCATION vol 35 (2011) PARA 24 et seq); Employment and Training Act 1973 s 13(1) (definition added by SI 2010/1158).
5 Employment and Training Act 1973 s 10(1) (s 10 substituted by the Trade Union Reform and Employment Rights Act 1993 s 45; Employment and Training Act 1973 s 10(1), (2), (3), (6), (7), (8), (10) amended by SI 2010/1158). Nothing in the Employment and Training Act 1973 s 8, s 9 and s 10 makes it unlawful for a local authority to defray the cost of exercising its powers under s 10 from resources other than payments of the Secretary of State: s 10(10) (as so substituted and amended). As to the provision of information about a young person by public bodies for the purposes of the provision of services in Wales under s 10 see the Learning and Skills Act 2000 s 138; and EDUCATION vol 36 (2011) PARA 1344.
6 Employment and Training Act 1973 s 10(2) (as substituted and amended: see note 5).
7 Employment and Training Act 1973 s 10(3) (as substituted and amended: see note 5).
8 Employment and Training Act 1973 s 10(4) (as substituted: see note 5).
9 Employment and Training Act 1973 s 10(6) (as substituted and amended: see note 5). As to the meaning of 'facilities' see PARA 634 note 12.
10 See note 3.
11 Employment and Training Act 1973 s 10(5) (as substituted: see note 5).
12 Employment and Training Act 1973 s 10(7) (as substituted and amended: see note 5).
13 Employment and Training Act 1973 s 10(8) (as substituted and amended: see note 5).
14 Employment and Training Act 1973 s 10(9) (as substituted: see note 5).
15 Employment and Training Act 1973 s 10(11) (as substituted: see note 5).
16 Ie under the Employment and Training Act 1973 s 2: see PARA 634.
17 As to the meaning of 'employment' see PARA 634 note 2.
18 Employment and Training Act 1973 s 10(12) (as substituted: see note 5).

641. Role of Her Majesty's Chief Inspector of Education, Children's Services and Skills; inspection of careers services in England. Her Majesty's Chief Inspector of Education, Children's Services and Skills[1]:

(1) must, when requested to do so by the Secretary of State[2], inspect and report on the provision of services provided in England[3] in pursuance of the Employment and Training Act 1973[4] by any person or institution[5]; and

(2) may undertake such other inspections of the provision of those services by persons or institutions[6] as he thinks fit[7].

A request under head (1) above may be general or in relation to specific matters, may relate to a specific person or institution providing services or to a specific class of person or institution, and may relate to a specific area[8].

A person carrying out or participating in an inspection under head (1) or head (2) above has the same powers in relation to the right of access to premises, records and documents[9] and to the inspection of computer records[10] as the Chief Inspector has under the Education Act 2005[11]; and the provisions relating to publication of reports under that Act[12] also apply[13]. A person who wilfully obstructs a person in carrying out or participating in the inspection is guilty of an offence and liable on summary conviction to a fine[14].

1 As to Her Majesty's Chief Inspector of Education, Children's Services and Skills see EDUCATION vol 36 (2011) PARA 1359 et seq.
2 As to the Secretary of State see PARA 5 note 21.
3 For these purposes, a reference to the provision of services includes a reference to the management and use of resources in providing services: Employment and Training Act 1973 s 10B(4) (s 10B added by the Learning and Skills Act 2000 s 122).
4 Ie in pursuance of the Employment and Training Act 1973 s 8 (see PARA 638) or s 9 (see PARA 639).
5 Such an inspection (ie under head (1) or (2) in the text) may not relate to services provided for persons who have attained the age of 20: Employment and Training Act 1973 s 10B(3) (as added: see note 3).
6 See note 5.
7 Employment and Training Act 1973 s 10B(1) (s 10B as added (see note 3); s 10B(1) amended by the Education and Inspections Act 2006 Sch 14 para 4, Sch 18 Pt 5).
8 Employment and Training Act 1973 s 10B(2) (as added: see note 3).
9 Ie the power under the Education Act 2005 s 10(1)(a), (d): see EDUCATION vol 36 (2011) PARA 1389.
10 Ie the power under the Education Act 2005 s 58: see EDUCATION vol 36 (2011) PARA 1379.
11 Employment and Training Act 1973 s 10B(5), (6) (s 10B as added (see note 3); s 10B(6) substituted by the Education Act 2005 Sch 9 para 2(1), (2)).
12 Ie under the Education Act 2005 s 11: see EDUCATION vol 36 (2011) PARA 1393.
13 Employment and Training Act 1973 s 10B(5), (7) (s 10B as added (see note 3); s 10B(7) amended by the Education Act 2005 Sch 9 para 2(1), (3)).
14 Employment and Training Act 1973 s 10B(5), (8) (as added: see note 3). The penalty is a fine not exceeding level 4 on the standard scale: see s 10B(5), (8) (as so added). As to the standard scale see SENTENCING AND DISPOSITION OF OFFENDERS vol 92 (2010) PARA 142.

642. Provision of ancillary goods and services. The functions of a local authority[1] include power to enter into agreements for the duly authorised supply of goods[2] or provision of services with any person[3], other than an authority, who provides, or arranges for the provision of, relevant services[4] and is a person duly authorised with whom such arrangements[5] may be made[6].

The supply by an authority of such goods or services to any such person:

(1) is duly authorised only for the purpose of the provision by that person of relevant services[7];

(2) is duly authorised only during the period of two years beginning with the day on which that person first provides relevant services in the area of that authority[8];

(3) is authorised outside as well as within the area of that authority[9].

Goods and services must be supplied on such terms as can reasonably be expected to secure that the full cost of making the supply is recovered by the authority[10].

The provisions described above are without prejudice to the generality of any other enactment conferring functions on local education authorities[11].

1 As to the meaning of 'local authority' see PARA 640 note 4. As to the meaning of 'functions' see PARA 634 note 19.
2 For these purposes, 'goods' includes materials: Employment and Training Act 1973 s 10A(9) (s 10A added by the Trade Union Reform and Employment Rights Act 1993 s 46).
3 Subject to the Employment and Training Act 1973 s 10A(4)–(6) (see the text and notes 7, 8, 10), s 10A authorises:
   (1) the supply by the authority to the person of any goods;
   (2) the provision by the authority for the person of any administrative, professional or technical services;
   (3) the use by the person of any vehicle, plant or apparatus belonging to the authority and,

without prejudice to head (2) above, the placing at the disposal of the person of the services of any person employed in connection with the vehicle or other property in question;

(4) the carrying out by the authority of works of maintenance in connection with land or buildings for the maintenance of which the person is responsible,

and the authority may purchase and store any goods which in its opinion it may require for the purposes of head (1) above: s 10A(3) (as added: see note 2).

4 For these purposes, 'relevant services' has the meaning given by the Employment and Training Act 1973 s 8(2) (see PARA 638 note 2): s 10A(9) (as added: see note 2).

5 The Employment and Training Act 1973 s 10A authorises the making of such arrangements with any person: (1) who, under arrangements, or joint arrangements, made with that person under s 10(1) or (3) (see PARA 640) provides, or arranges for the provision of, the services; (2) who provides the services jointly with an authority under s 10(3) (see PARA 640); (3) who is the means by which, under s 10(8) (see PARA 640), an authority provides, or arranges for the provision of, the services: s 10A(2) (as added: see note 2).

6 Employment and Training Act 1973 s 10A(1) (s 10A as added (see note 2); s 10A(1) amended by SI 2010/1158).

7 Employment and Training Act 1973 s 10A(4) (as added: see note 2).

8 Employment and Training Act 1973 s 10A(5) (as added: see note 2).

9 Employment and Training Act 1973 s 10A(7) (as added: see note 2).

10 Employment and Training Act 1973 s 10A(6) (as added: see note 2).

11 Employment and Training Act 1973 s 10A(8) (as added: see note 2). It is submitted that the reference in the text to local education authorities should be to local authorities within the meaning of Education Act 1996 (see s 579(1); and EDUCATION vol 35 (2011) PARA 24).

643. Control of local authorities by the Secretary of State. It is the duty of each local authority[1]:

(1) to furnish the Secretary of State with such information in its possession[2] as the Secretary of State may specify as being information required by him in connection with the determination of questions relating to the exercise by him of any power[3] to make payments to any persons[4]; and

(2) to furnish the Secretary of State with such information in its possession as the Secretary of State may require as being information required in connection with the determination of questions[5] relating to contributions or benefit[6].

1 As to the meaning of 'local authority' see PARA 640 note 4.

2 Any information falling to be so furnished must be furnished in such form and at such times as the Secretary of State may direct: Employment and Training Act 1973 s 12(1A) (added by the Employment Act 1988 Sch 2 para 2(2)). As to the Secretary of State see PARA 5 note 21. As to the exercise of the functions of the Secretary of State under the Employment and Training Act 1973 s 12A in relation to Wales see PARA 634 note 1.

3 Ie in accordance with the Employment and Training Act 1973.

4 Employment and Training Act 1973 s 12(1A) (as added (see note 2); amended by the Employment Act 1989 Sch 7 Pt I; and SI 2010/1158).

5 Ie under the Social Security Contributions and Benefits Act 1992: see WELFARE BENEFITS AND STATE PENSIONS.

6 Employment and Training Act 1973 s 12(2) (substituted by the Social Security Act 1988 Sch 4 para 2; amended by the Employment Act 1989 Sch 7 Pt I; the Social Security (Consequential Provisions) Act 1992 Sch 2 para 11; and SI 2010/1158). Any information falling to be so furnished must be furnished in such form and at such times as the Secretary of State may direct: Employment and Training Act 1973 s 12(2) (as so substituted and amended). See also note 2.

(3) PARTICIPATION IN EDUCATION OR TRAINING IN ENGLAND

(i) General Obligation in regard to Education or Training

644. Appropriate arrangements to be in place before commencement of employment. As from a day to be appointed, the following provisions have effect[1]. A person must not, as employer, enter into a relevant contract of employment[2] with a person to whom Part 1 of the Education and Skills Act 2008 applies[3] without being satisfied, having taken all such steps as are reasonable to ascertain, that the person has made appropriate arrangements[4] for training or education[5].

In the case of a relevant contract of employment which provides for commencement of the employment to be conditional on the employee's having made such arrangements: (1) the above provisions[6] do not apply; but (2) the employer must not permit the employment to commence, at a time when the employee is a person to whom Part 1 of the Education and Skills Act 2008 applies, without being satisfied, having taken all such steps as are reasonable to ascertain, that the employee has made appropriate arrangements for training or education[7].

Failure to comply with these provisions[8] in relation to a contract of employment is not to be taken to affect the validity of the contract[9].

1 The Education and Skills Act 2008 ss 19–21 are to be brought into force by an order under s 173(4). At the date at which this volume states the law no such day had been appointed. As to the application of ss 19–36 to Wales, see s 67; and EDUCATION vol 35 (2011) PARA 680. As to the meaning of 'Wales' see PARA 2 note 12.

2 In the Education and Skills Act 2008 Pt 1 Ch 3 (ss 19–39) 'relevant contract of employment' means a contract of employment (1) under which the employee is required to work for at least 20 hours per week; (2) which has a fixed term of eight weeks or longer, or does not have a fixed term but can reasonably be expected to be, or has been, in force for at least eight weeks; and (3) under which the place of work, or one of the places where the employee may be required to work, is in England: s 19(1) (not yet in force). See note 1. As to the meaning of 'England' see PARA 2 note 12.

However a contract is not a 'relevant contract of employment' if (a) the employer has undertaken to provide the employee with sufficient relevant training or education in each relevant period; and (b) by virtue of the contract, the employee is in full-time occupation for the purposes of Pt 1 Ch 3: s 19(2) (not yet in force).

3 Ie a person to whom the Education and Skills Act 2008 Pt 1 (ss 1–67) applies. See also EDUCATION vol 35 (2011) PARA 646.

4 For the purposes of the Education and Skills Act 2008 Pt 1 Ch 3 (ss 19–39), a person to whom Pt 1 (ss 1–67) applies has made appropriate arrangements for training or education if (1) the person has enrolled on a course or courses constituting relevant training or education (or arrangements have otherwise been made for the person to receive relevant training or education); or (2) the person is participating in full-time education or training: s 20(1) (not yet in force). See note 1. References in Pt 1 Ch 3 to appropriate arrangements made by the person are to the arrangements (of whatever kind and whether or not made by the person) for the person to receive the training or education in question: s 20(2) (not yet in force).

5 Education and Training Act 2008 s 21(1) (not yet in force). See note 1.

6 Ie the Education and Training Act 2008 s 21(1).

7 Education and Training Act 2008 s 21(2) (not yet in force). See note 1.

8 Ie the Education and Training Act 2008 s 21.

9 Education and Training Act 2008 s 21(3) (not yet in force). See note 1.

645. Financial penalty and penalty notice. As from a day to be appointed, the following provisions have effect[1]. Where a relevant local authority[2] is satisfied that a person (the 'employer') has contravened the provision about having appropriate arrangements in place before employment begins[3], the authority may by notice (a 'penalty notice') require the employer to pay a financial penalty[4]. The amount of the financial penalty is to be determined in accordance with regulations[5].

A penalty notice must state: (1) particulars of the contravention of the above provision[6] in respect of which the penalty is imposed; (2) the amount of the penalty; (3) how payment may be made; (4) the period within which the penalty must be paid (which must be not less than four weeks beginning with the date on which the notice is given); (5) the steps that the employer may take if the employer objects to the giving of the penalty notice, including how the employer may appeal against it; and (6) the consequences of non-payment[7].

1 The Education and Skills Act 2008 s 22 is to be brought into force by an order under s 173(4). At the date at which this volume states the law no such day had been appointed. As to the application of ss 19–36 to Wales, see s 67; and EDUCATION vol 35 (2011) PARA 680. As to the meaning of 'Wales' see PARA 2 note 12.

2 For the purposes of the Education and Skills Act 2008 s 22(1), a local authority is a relevant local authority in relation to a contract of employment under which a person to whom Pt 1 (ss 1–67) applies is employed if (1) the person belongs to the authority's area; or (2) the person's place of work, or one of the places at which the person works, under the contract is in the authority's area: s 22(4) (amended by SI 2010/1158) (not yet in force). See note 1. 'Local authority' has the meaning given by the Education Act 1996 s 579(1) (see EDUCATION vol 35 (2011) PARA 24 et seq); definition applied by Education and Skills Act 2008 s 168(2), (3).

3 Ie the Education and Skills Act 2008 s 21: see PARA 644.

4 Education and Skills Act 2008 s 22(1) (amended by SI 2010/1158) (not yet in force). See note 1.

5 Education and Skills Act 2008 s 22(2) (not yet in force). See note 1. Without prejudice to s 166(6) (see EDUCATION), regulations under s 22(2) may make provision for penalties of different amounts to be payable in different cases or circumstances (including provision for the penalty payable under a penalty notice to differ according to the time by which it is paid): s 22(5) (not yet in force). 'Regulations' means regulations made by the Secretary of State: s 168. As to the Secretary of State see PARA 5 note 21. At the date at which this volume states the law no such regulations had been made.

6 See note 3.

7 Education and Skills Act 2008 s 22(3) (not yet in force). See note 1.

646. Withdrawal or variation of penalty notice following notice of objection. As from a day to be appointed, the following provisions have effect[1]. Where a penalty notice has been given[2] to a person (the 'employer') by a local authority[3], the employer may, by giving notice (a 'notice of objection') to the authority, object to the giving of the penalty notice on either or both of the following grounds: (1) that the employer did not commit the contravention of the provision about having appropriate arrangements in place before employment begins[4] stated in the penalty notice; (2) that the amount of the penalty stated in the penalty notice is too high[5].

A notice of objection (a) may be given to the authority only during the period of two weeks beginning with the day on which the penalty notice was given to the employer; and (b) must state the grounds of the objection and the employer's reasons for objecting on those grounds[6].

A local authority must consider a notice of objection[7] and, by giving notice (a 'determination notice') to the employer (i) withdraw the penalty notice; (ii) if the amount of the penalty determined in accordance with regulations[8] is smaller than the amount stated in the penalty notice, replace the penalty with the smaller amount[9]; or (iii) confirm the penalty notice[10]. The determination notice must be given within the prescribed[11] period beginning with the day on which the notice of objection was given[12].

1 The Education and Skills Act 2008 s 23 is to be brought into force by an order under s 173(4). At the date at which this volume states the law no such day had been appointed.
2 Ie under the Education and Skills Act 2008 s 22: see PARA 645.
3 Education and Skills Act 2008 s 23(1) (amended by SI 2010/1158) (not yet in force). See note 1. As to the meaning of 'local authority' see PARA 645 note 2.
4 Ie the Education and Skills Act 2008 s 21: see PARA 644.
5 Education and Skills Act 2008 s 23(2) (not yet in force). See note 1.
6 Education and Skills Act 2008 s 23(3) (not yet in force). See note 1.
7 Ie given under the Education and Skills Act 2008 s 23(2).
8 Ie regulations made under the Education and Skills Act 2008 s 22(2): see PARA 645.
9 Where, under the Education and Skills Act 2008 s 23(4)(b) (see head (ii) in the text), the amount of a penalty stated in a penalty notice is replaced with a smaller amount, the notice is to have effect as if it had originally stated the smaller amount: s 23(6) (not yet in force). See note 1.
10 Education and Skills Act 2008 s 23(4) (amended by SI 2010/1158) (not yet in force). See note 1. See also PARA 648.
11 'Prescribed' means prescribed by regulations: Education and Skills Act 2008 s 168. As to the meaning of 'regulations' see PARA 645 note 5.
12 Education and Skills Act 2008 s 23(5) (not yet in force). See note 1.

647. Appeal against penalty notice. As from a day to be appointed, the following provisions have effect[1]. Where a penalty notice has been given[2] to a person (the 'employer') and (1) the period during which a notice of objection[3] may be given in relation to the penalty notice has expired; and (2) if a notice of objection has been given in relation to the penalty notice, a determination notice[4] has been given in relation to the notice of objection[5], the employer may appeal to the First-tier Tribunal[6] against the giving of the penalty notice on one or more of the following grounds: (a) that the employer did not contravene provision about having appropriate arrangements in place before employment begins[7] in the way stated in the penalty notice; (b) that the circumstances of the contravention of that provision stated in the penalty notice make the giving of the notice unreasonable[8]; (c) that the amount of the penalty stated in the penalty notice is too high[9].

On such an appeal[10], the First-tier Tribunal may (i) allow the appeal and cancel the penalty notice; (ii) if the amount of the penalty determined in accordance with regulations[11] is smaller than the amount stated in the penalty notice, allow the appeal and replace the penalty with the smaller amount; or (iii) dismiss the appeal[12].

1 The Education and Skills Act 2008 s 24 is to be brought into force by an order under s 173(4). At the date at which this volume states the law no such day had been appointed. As to the application of ss 19–36 to Wales, see s 67; and EDUCATION vol 35 (2011) PARA 680. As to the meaning of 'Wales' see PARA 2 note 12.
2 Ie under the Education and Skills Act 2008 s 22: see PARA 645.
3 In the Education and Skills Act 2008 s 24(1), 'notice of objection' and 'determination notice' have the same meanings as in s 23 (see PARA 646): s 24(5) (not yet in force). See note 1.
4 See note 3.
5 Education and Skills Act 2008 s 24(1) (not yet in force). See note 1.
6 As to First-tier Tribunals see COURTS AND TRIBUNALS vol 24 (2010) PARA 874 et seq.
7 Ie the Education and Skills Act 2008 s 21: see PARA 644.
8 Where, under the Education and Skills Act 2008 s 24(3)(b) (see head (ii) in the text), the amount of a penalty stated in a penalty notice is replaced with a smaller amount, the notice is to have effect as if it had originally stated the smaller amount: s 24(4) (not yet in force). See note 1.
9 Education and Skills Act 2008 s 24(2) (not yet in force). See note 1.
10 Ie an appeal under the Education and Skills Act 2008 s 24.
11 Ie regulations under the Education and Skills Act 2008 s 22(2): see PARA 645.
12 Education and Skills Act 2008 s 24(3) (not yet in force). See note 1.

648. Further provisions on withdrawal and variation of penalty notices. As from a day to be appointed, the following provisions have effect[1]. Where (1) a penalty notice has been given[2] to a person (the 'employer') by a local authority; and (2) any appeal[3] in respect of the penalty notice has not been determined[4], the authority may withdraw the penalty notice by giving notice of the withdrawal to the employer[5].

If a penalty notice is withdrawn[6], any sum already paid or recovered in respect of the penalty notice must be repaid to the employer with interest at the appropriate rate[7] running from the date when the sum was paid or recovered[8].

If the amount of a penalty is reduced[9], any sum already paid or recovered must, to the extent that it was paid or recovered in respect of any amount in excess of the reduced amount, be repaid to the employer with interest at the appropriate rate running from the date when the sum was paid or recovered[10].

1 The Education and Skills Act 2008 ss 25, 26 are to be brought into force by an order under s 173(4). At the date at which this volume states the law no such day had been appointed. As to the application of ss 19–36 to Wales, see s 67; and EDUCATION vol 36 (2011) PARA 680. As to the meaning of 'Wales' see PARA 2 note 12.
2 Ie under the Education and Skills Act 2008 s 22: see PARA 645.
3 Ie made under the Education and Skills Act 2008 s 24: see PARA 647.
4 Education and Skills Act 2008 s 25(1) (amended by SI 2010/1158) (not yet in force). See note 1.
5 Education and Skills Act 2008 s 25(2) (not yet in force). See note 1.
6 Ie under the Education and Skills Act 2008 s 23 (see PARA 646) or s 25 (see the text and notes 1–5).
7 In the Education and Skills Act 2008 s 26, the 'appropriate rate' means the rate that, on the date the sum was paid or recovered, was specified in the Judgments Act 1983 s 17 (see CIVIL PROCEDURE vol 12 (2009) PARA 1149): Education and Skills Act 2008 s 26(3) (not yet in force). See note 1.
8 Education and Skills Act 2008 s 26(1) (not yet in force). See note 1.
9 Ie under the Education and Skills Act 2008 s 23: see PARA 646.
10 Education and Skills Act 2008 s 26(2) (not yet in force). See note 1.

(ii) Employer's Duty to Enable Participation in Education or Training

649. Duty to enable participation: initial arrangements. As from a day to be appointed, the following provisions have effect[1]. Where (1) a person to whom Part 1 of the Education and Skills Act 2008 applies[2] is employed under a relevant contract of employment[3]; and (2) before commencement of the employment the person notified the employer in accordance with heads (a) to (c) below[4] of appropriate arrangements[5] which the person had made[6], the employer must permit the employee to participate in training or education in accordance with those appropriate arrangements[7].

A person notifies an employer (or a prospective employer) of appropriate arrangements[8] by giving a notice which (a) specifies the arrangements; (b) states the times when the person would need to be not at work in order to participate in training or education in accordance with those arrangements; and (c) if so required[9], is given in writing[10].

The above obligation of the employer[11] operates as a requirement, in relation to each of the times specified in the notice under head (b) above which falls during normal working time[12], for the employer (i) if the contract was entered into before the notice was given, to offer to vary the terms and conditions of the contract of employment so as to secure that that time does not fall during normal working time; or (ii) in any case, to permit the employee to take that time off[13].

1 The Education and Skills Act 2008 s 27 is to be brought into force by an order under s 173(4). At the date at which this volume states the law no such day had been appointed. As to the application of ss 19–36 to Wales, see s 67; and EDUCATION vol 35 (2011) PARA 680. As to the meaning of 'Wales' see PARA 2 note 12.
2 Ie a person to whom the Education and Skills Act 2008 Pt 1 (ss 1–67) applies. See also EDUCATION vol 35 (2011) PARA 646.
3 As to the meaning of 'relevant contract of employment' see PARA 644 note 2.
4 Ie the Education and Skills Act 2008 s 27(3).
5 As to the meaning of 'appropriate arrangements' see PARA 644 note 4.
6 Education and Skills Act 2008 s 27(1) (not yet in force). See note 1.
7 Education and Skills Act 2008 s 27(2) (not yet in force). See note 1.
8 Ie in accordance with the Education and Training Act 2008 s 27(3).
9 Ie required by the Education and Skills Act 2008 s 27(4). Such a notice need not be given in writing, but, if it is not, the employer may, on the occasion when the notice is given, require it to be given in writing; and, if the employer does so, the notice is not to be treated as having been given until given in writing: s 27(4) (not yet in force). See note 1.
10 Education and Skills Act 2008 s 27(3) (not yet in force). See note 1.
11 Ie the obligation in the Education and Skills Act 2008 s 27(2): see the text and note 7.
12 In the Education and Skills Act 2008 s 27, 'normal working time', in relation to a contract of employment, means any time when, in accordance with the contract, the employee is required to be at work: s 27(6) (not yet in force). See note 1.
13 Education and Skills Act 2008 s 27(5) (not yet in force). See note 1.

650. Duty to enable participation: arrangements subsequently notified. As from a day to be appointed, the following provisions have effect[1]. Where (1) a person to whom Part 1 of the Education and Skills Act 2008 applies[2] is employed under a relevant contract of employment[3]; and (2) after commencement of the employment the person notifies the employer in accordance with heads (i) to (iii) below[4] of appropriate arrangements[5] which the person has made[6], the employer must, so far as is reasonable having regard to the matters mentioned in heads (a) to (c) below[7], permit the person to participate in training or education in accordance with those appropriate arrangements[8].

The matters referred to above are (a) the needs of the person in order to fulfil the duty to participate in education or training in regard to young persons[9]; (b) the circumstances of the employer's business; (c) the effect of the person's absence from work on the running of that business[10].

A person notifies an employer of appropriate arrangements[11] by giving a notice which (i) specifies the arrangements; (ii) states the times when the employee needs to be not at work in order to participate in education or training in accordance with those arrangements; and (iii) if so required[12], is given in writing[13].

The above obligation of the employer[14] operates as a requirement, in relation to each of the times specified in the notice under head (ii) above which falls during normal working time[15], for the employer (A) to offer to vary the terms and conditions of the contract of employment so as to secure that, so far as is reasonable having regard to the matters mentioned in heads (a) to (c) above, that time does not fall during normal working time; or (B) so far as is reasonable having regard to those matters, to permit the employee to take that time off[16].

1 The Education and Skills Act 2008 s 28 is to be brought into force by an order under s 173(4). At the date at which this volume states the law no such day had been appointed. As to the application of ss 19–36 to Wales, see s 67; and EDUCATION vol 35 (2011) PARA 680. As to the meaning of 'Wales' see PARA 2 note 12.
2 Ie a person to whom the Education and Skills Act 2008 Pt 1 (ss 1–67) applies. See also EDUCATION vol 35 (2011) PARA 646.
3 As to the meaning of 'relevant contract of employment' see PARA 644 note 2.
4 Ie the Education and Skills Act 2008 s 28(4).

5 As to the meaning of 'appropriate arrangements' see PARA 644 note 4.
6 Education and Skills Act 2008 s 28(1) (not yet in force). See note 1.
7 Ie the Education and Skills Act 2008 s 28(3).
8 Education and Skills Act 2008 s 28(2) (not yet in force). See note 1.
9 Ie the duty imposed by the Education and Skills Act 2008 s 2: see EDUCATION vol 35 (2011) PARA 646.
10 Education and Skills Act 2008 s 28(3) (not yet in force). See note 1.
11 Ie in accordance with the Education and Skills Act 2008 s 28(4).
12 Ie required by the Education and Skills Act 2008 s 28(5). Such a notice need not be given in writing but, if it is not, the employer may, on the occasion when the notice is given, require it to be given in writing; and, if the employer does so, the notice is not to be treated as having been given until given in writing: s 28(5) (not yet in force). See note 1.
13 Education and Skills Act 2008 s 28(4) (not yet in force). See note 1.
14 Ie the obligation in the Education and Skills Act 2008 s 28(2): see the text and notes 7, 8.
15 In the Education and Skills Act 2008 s 28, 'normal working time', in relation to a contract of employment, means any time when, in accordance with the contract, the employee is required to be at work: s 28(7) (not yet in force). See note 1.
16 Education and Skills Act 2008 s 28(6) (not yet in force). See note 1.

651. Extension for persons reaching 18. As from a day to be appointed, the following provisions have effect[1]. Where (1) a person to whom Part 1 of the Education and Skills Act 2008 applies[2] is employed under a relevant contract of employment[3]; (2) the person reaches the age of 18; and (3) at that time the person is participating in a course of education or training for the purpose of fulfilling the duty to participate in education or training in regard to young persons[4], the person is to continue to be treated[5] as a person to whom Part 1 applies until one of the following occurs: (a) the course of education or training concludes; (b) the person reaches the age of 19; (c) the person ceases to be resident in England[6]; (d) the person attains a level 3 qualification[7].

1 The Education and Skills Act 2008 s 29 is to be brought into force by an order under s 173(4). At the date at which this volume states the law no such day had been appointed. As to the application of ss 19–36 to Wales, see s 67; and EDUCATION vol 35 (2011) PARA 680. As to the meaning of 'Wales' see PARA 2 note 12.
2 Ie a person to whom the Education and Skills Act 2008 Pt 1 (ss 1–67) applies. See also EDUCATION vol 35 (2011) PARA 646.
3 As to the meaning of 'relevant contract of employment' see PARA 644 note 2.
4 Education and Skills Act 2008 s 29(1) (not yet in force). See note 1. The duty referred to is that imposed by the Education and Skills Act 2008 s 2: see EDUCATION vol 35 (2011) PARA 646.
5 Ie for the purposes of the Education and Skills Act 2008 s 27 (see PARA 649), s 28 (see PARA 650), s 29, ss 30–36 (see PARAS 652–657).
6 As to the meaning of 'England' see PARA 2 note 12.
7 Education and Skills Act 2008 s 29(2) (not yet in force). See note 1. As to a level 3 qualification see EDUCATION vol 35 (2011) PARA 646.

652. Contravention of duties to enable participation and enforcement notice. As from a day to be appointed, the following provisions have effect[1]. Where a person to whom Part 1 of the Education and Skills Act 2008 applies[2] is employed under a relevant contract of employment[3], and where a relevant local authority[4] in England[5] is satisfied that the employer has contravened the provisions on the duties to enable participation[6], the authority may give the employer a notice (an 'enforcement notice')[7].

An enforcement notice means a notice requiring the employer to take such steps as are specified in the notice[8]. The steps that may be specified in the notice are: (1) to offer to vary the terms and conditions of employment in the manner specified in the notice[9]; (2) to permit the employee to take time off during normal working time at the times specified in the notice[10]. However, in the case of an enforcement notice given in respect of a contravention of the provision setting out the duty to enable participation in regard to arrangements subsequently notified[11], any steps specified in the notice must be steps which it would be reasonable for the employer to take having regard to the matters mentioned in that provision[12].

An enforcement notice must also specify: (a) particulars of the contravention of the provisions on the duties to enable participation[13] in respect of which the notice is given; and (b) the consequences of failure to comply with any requirement imposed by it[14].

Where an enforcement notice requires the employer to offer to vary the terms and conditions of employment under head (1) above[15]: (i) the employer must make the offer within the time specified in the notice; (ii) the employer's offer must not be made directly or indirectly conditional on the employee's agreeing to any other variation of the terms and conditions of employment; and (iii) if the employee accepts the employer's offer to vary the terms and conditions of employment, those terms and conditions have effect subject to the variation (but subject to any subsequent variation that may be agreed between the employer and employee)[16].

Where an enforcement notice requires the employer, under head (2) above[17], to permit the employee to take time off at specified times during normal working time, the enforcement notice remains in force until: (A) the last of the times so specified; or (B) if earlier, the termination of the contract of employment[18].

1 The Education and Skills Act 2008 s 30 is to be brought into force by an order under s 173(4). At the date at which this volume states the law no such day had been appointed. As to the application of ss 19–36 to Wales, see s 67; and EDUCATION vol 35 (2011) PARA 680. As to the meaning of 'Wales' see PARA 2 note 12.

2 Ie a person to whom the Education and Skills Act 2008 Pt 1 (ss 1–67) applies. See also EDUCATION vol 35 (2011) PARA 646.

3 Education and Skills Act 2008 s 30(1) (not yet in force). See note 1. As to the meaning of 'relevant contract of employment' see PARA 644 note 2.

4 For the purposes of the Education and Skills Act 2008 s 30(2), a local authority is a relevant local authority in relation to a contract of employment under which a person to whom Pt 1 (ss 1–67) applies is employed if (1) the person belongs to the authority's area; or (2) the person's place of work, or one of the places at which the person works, under the contract is in the authority's area: s 30(9) (amended by SI 2010/1158) (not yet in force). See note 1. As to the meaning of 'local authority' see PARA 645 note 2.

5 As to the meaning of 'England' see PARA 2 note 12.

6 Ie the Education and Skills Act 2008 s 27 (see PARA 649) or s 28 (see PARA 650).

7 Education and Skills Act 2008 s 30(2) (amended by SI 2010/1158) (not yet in force). See note 1.

8 Education and Skills Act 2008 s 30(3) (not yet in force). See note 1.

9 Education and Skills Act 2008 s 30(4)(a) (not yet in force). See note 1. However, any variation specified under s 30(4)(a) (see head (1) in the text) must be a variation only for the purpose of securing that normal working time does not include any time when, in order to be able to participate in education or training in accordance with appropriate arrangements notified to the employer under s 27(1)(b) (see PARA 649 head (2)) or s 28(1)(b) (see PARA 650 head (2)), the employee needs to be not at work: s 30(5)(a) (not yet in force). In s 30, 'normal working time', in relation to a contract of employment, means any time when, in accordance with the contract, the employee is required to be at work: s 30(10) (not yet in force). As to the meaning of 'appropriate arrangements' see PARA 644 note 4.

10 Education and Skills Act 2008 s 30(4)(b) (not yet in force). See note 1. However, any time specified under s 30(4)(b) (see head (2) in the text) must be a time when the employee needs to be not at work in order to participate in education or training in accordance with appropriate arrangements notified to the employer under s 27(1)(b) (see PARA 649 head (2)) or s 28(1)(b) (see PARA 650 head (2)): see s 30(5)(b) (not yet in force).

11 Ie in respect of a contravention of the Education and Skills Act 2008 s 28: see PARA 650.

12 Education and Skills Act 2008 s 30(5)(c) (not yet in force). See note 1. The matters are those mentioned in s 28(3): see PARA 650 heads (a)–(c).

13 See note 6.

14 Education and Skills Act 2008 s 30(6) (not yet in force). See note 1.
15 Ie under the Education and Skills Act 2008 s 30(4)(a).
16 Education and Skills Act 2008 s 30(7) (not yet in force). See note 1.
17 Ie under the Education and Skills Act 2008 s 30(4)(b).
18 Education and Skills Act 2008 s 30(8) (not yet in force). See note 1.

653. Financial penalty for non-compliance with enforcement notice. As from a day to be appointed, the following provisions have effect[1]. Where a local authority has given an enforcement notice to a person (the 'employer')[2], and where the local authority is satisfied: (1) that the employer has failed to comply with the notice; or (2) in the case of an enforcement notice requiring the employer to offer to vary the terms and conditions of employment[3], the employee has agreed to the variation but the employer has failed to give effect to the variation, the authority may by notice (a 'penalty notice') require the employer to pay a financial penalty[4]. The amount of the financial penalty is to be determined in accordance with regulations[5].

A penalty notice must state: (a) particulars of the failure by the employer in respect of which the penalty notice is given; (b) the amount of the penalty; (c) how payment may be made; (d) the period within which the penalty must be paid (which must be not less than four weeks beginning with the date on which the notice is given); (e) the steps that the employer may take if the employer objects to the giving of the penalty notice, including how the employer may appeal against it; and (f) the consequences of non-payment[6].

1 The Education and Skills Act 2008 s 31 is to be brought into force by an order under s 173(4). At the date at which this volume states the law no such day had been appointed. As to the application of ss 19–36 to Wales, see s 67; and EDUCATION vol 35 (2011) PARA 680. As to the meaning of 'Wales' see PARA 2 note 12.
2 Education and Skills Act 2008 s 31(1) (amended by SI 2010/1158) (not yet in force). See note 1. The reference is to an enforcement notice under s 30: see PARA 652. As to the meaning of 'local authority' see PARA 645 note 2.
3 Ie by the Education and Skills Act 2008 s 30(4)(a): see PARA 652.
4 Education and Skills Act 2008 s 31(2) (amended by SI 2010/1158) (not yet in force). See note 1.
5 Education and Skills Act 2008 s 31(3) (not yet in force). See note 1. As to the meaning of 'regulations' see PARA 645 note 5. Without prejudice to s 166(6) (general provisions as to orders and regulations), regulations under s 31(3) may make provision for penalties of different amounts to be payable in different cases or circumstances (including provision for the penalty payable under a penalty notice to differ according to the time by which it is paid): s 31(5) (not yet in force).
6 Education and Skills Act 2008 s 31(4) (not yet in force). See note 1.

654. Withdrawal of enforcement notice. As from a day to be appointed, the following provisions have effect[1]. Where: (1) an enforcement notice has been given to a person (the 'employer') by a local authority[2]; and (2) if a penalty notice has been given in respect of the enforcement notice[3], any appeal made[4] in respect of the penalty notice has not been determined[5], the local education authority may withdraw the enforcement notice by giving notice of the withdrawal to the employer[6].

After the withdrawal, no penalty notice may be given[7] in respect of: (a) any failure to comply with the enforcement notice; or (b) any failure to give effect to any variation of terms and conditions of employment required by the enforcement notice to be offered, which occurred before the enforcement notice was withdrawn[8].

Where an enforcement notice is withdrawn: (i) any penalty notice given[9] in respect of the enforcement notice ceases to have effect; and (ii) any sum paid or recovered in respect of any such penalty notice must be repaid to the employer with interest at the appropriate rate[10] running from the date when the sum was paid or recovered[11].

1 The Education and Skills Act 2008 s 32 is to be brought into force by an order under s 173(4). At the date at which this volume states the law no such day had been appointed.
2 Ie under the Education and Skills Act 2008 s 30: see PARA 652. As to the meaning of 'local authority' see PARA 645 note 2.
3 Ie under the Education and Skills Act 2008 s 31: see PARA 653.
4 Ie under the Education and Skills Act 2008 s 34: see PARA 656.
5 Education and Skills Act 2008 s 32(1) (amended by SI 2010/1158) (not yet in force). See note 1.
6 Education and Skills Act 2008 s 32(2) (amended by SI 2010/1158) (not yet in force). See note 1. Such a notice of withdrawal must state the effect of the withdrawal (but a failure to do so does not make the notice of withdrawal ineffective): s 32(6) (not yet in force).
7 See note 3.
8 Education and Skills Act 2008 s 32(3) (not yet in force). See note 1.
9 See note 3.
10 'Appropriate rate' means the rate that, on the date the sum was paid or recovered, was specified in the Judgments Act 1838 s 17 (see CIVIL PROCEDURE vol 12 (2009) PARA 1149): Education and Skills Act 2008 s 32(5) (not yet in force). See note 1.
11 Education and Skills Act 2008 s 32(4) (not yet in force). See note 1.

655. Withdrawal or variation of penalty notice following notice of objection. As from a day to be appointed, the following provisions have effect[1]. Where a penalty notice has been given to a person (the 'employer') by a local authority[2] in respect of a failure[3] relating to an enforcement notice[4], the employer may, by giving notice (a 'notice of objection') to the authority, object to the giving of the penalty notice on one or more of the following grounds: (1) that the employer did not contravene the provisions on the duties to enable participation[5] in the way stated in the enforcement notice; (2) that the requirements imposed by the enforcement notice were unreasonable; (3) that the employer did not fail in the way stated in the penalty notice; (4) that the amount of the penalty stated in the penalty notice is too high[6].

A notice of objection: (a) may be given to the authority only during the period of two weeks beginning with the day on which the penalty notice was given to the employer; and (b) must set out the grounds of the objection and the employer's reasons for objecting on those grounds[7].

A local authority must consider a notice of objection given under heads (1) to (4) above and, by giving notice (a 'determination notice') to the employer: (i) withdraw the penalty notice; (ii) if the amount of the penalty determined in accordance with regulations[8] is smaller than the amount stated in the penalty notice, replace the penalty with the smaller amount[9]; or (iii) confirm the penalty notice[10]. The determination notice must be given within the prescribed[11] period beginning with the day on which the notice of objection was given[12].

1 The Education and Skills Act 2008 s 33 is to be brought into force by an order under s 173(4). At the date at which this volume states the law no such day had been appointed. As to the application of ss 19–36 to Wales, see s 67; and EDUCATION vol 35 (2011) PARA 680. As to the meaning of 'Wales' see PARA 2 note 12.
2 Ie under the Education and Skills Act 2008 s 31: see PARA 653. As to the meaning of 'local authority' see PARA 645 note 2.
3 Ie a failure of a kind mentioned in the Education and Skills Act 2008 s 31(2): see PARA 653 heads (1), (2).
4 Education and Skills Act 2008 s 33(1) (amended by SI 2010/1158) (not yet in force). See note 1.
5 Ie the Education and Skills Act 2008 s 27 (see PARA 649) or s 28 (see PARA 650).
6 Education and Skills Act 2008 s 33(2) (not yet in force). See note 1.
7 Education and Skills Act 2008 s 33(3) (not yet in force). See note 1.
8 Ie regulations under the Education and Skills Act 2008 s 31(3): see PARA 653.

9 Where, under the Education and Skills Act 2008 s 33(4)(b) (see head (ii) in the text), the amount of a penalty stated in a penalty notice is replaced with a smaller amount, the notice is to have effect as if it had originally stated the smaller amount: s 33(6) (not yet in force). See note 1.
10 Education and Skills Act 2008 s 33(4) (amended by SI 2010/1158) (not yet in force). See note 1.
11 'Prescribed' means prescribed by regulations: Education and Skills Act 2008 s 168. As to the meaning of 'regulations' see PARA 645 note 5.
12 Education and Skills Act 2008 s 33(5) (not yet in force). See note 1.

656. Appeal against penalty notice. As from a day to be appointed, the following provisions have effect[1]. Where a penalty notice has been given to a person[2] in respect of a failure[3] in relation to an enforcement notice and (1) the period during which a notice of objection[4] may be given in relation to the penalty notice has expired; and (2) if a notice of objection has been given in relation to the penalty notice, a determination notice[5] has been given in relation to the notice of objection[6], the person may appeal to the First-tier Tribunal[7] against the giving of the penalty notice on one or more of the following grounds: (a) that the person did not contravene the provisions on the duties to enable participation[8] in the way stated in the enforcement notice; (b) that the circumstances of the contravention of the provisions stated in the enforcement notice make the giving of an enforcement notice[9] unreasonable; (c) that the requirements imposed by the enforcement notice were unreasonable; (d) that the person did not fail in the way stated in the penalty notice; (e) that the circumstances of the failure stated in the penalty notice make the giving of the notice unreasonable; (f) that the amount of the penalty stated in the penalty notice is too high[10].

On an appeal[11], the First-tier Tribunal may (i) allow the appeal and cancel the penalty notice; (ii) if the amount of the penalty determined in accordance with regulations[12] is smaller than the amount stated in the penalty notice, allow the appeal and replace the penalty with the smaller amount[13]; or (iii) dismiss the appeal[14].

1 The Education and Skills Act 2008 s 34 is to be brought into force by an order under s 173(4). At the date at which this volume states the law no such day had been appointed. As to the application of ss 19–36 to Wales, see s 67; and EDUCATION vol 35 (2011) PARA 680. As to the meaning of 'Wales' see PARA 2 note 12.
2 Ie under the Education and Skills Act 2008 s 31: see PARA 653.
3 Ie a failure of a kind mentioned in the Education and Skills Act 2008 s 31(2): see PARA 653 heads (1), (2).
4 In the Education and Skills Act 2008 s 34(1), 'notice of objection' and 'determination notice' have the same meanings as in s 33 (see PARA 655): s 34(5) (not yet in force). See note 1.
5 See note 4.
6 Education and Skills Act 2008 s 34(1) (not yet in force). See note 1.
7 As to First-tier Tribunals see COURTS AND TRIBUNALS vol 24 (2010) PARA 874 et seq.
8 Ie the Education and Skills Act 2008 s 27 (see PARA 649) or s 28 (see PARA 650).
9 Ie under the Education and Skills Act 2008 s 30: see PARA 652.
10 Education and Skills Act 2008 s 34(2) (not yet in force). See note 1.
11 Ie under the Education and Skills Act 2008 s 34.
12 Ie regulations under the Education and Skills Act 2008 s 31(3): see PARA 653.
13 Where, under the Education and Skills Act 2008 s 34(3)(b) (see head (ii) in the text), the amount of a penalty stated in a penalty notice is replaced with a smaller amount, the notice is to have effect as if it had originally stated the smaller amount: s 34(4) (not yet in force). See note 1.
14 Education and Skills Act 2008 s 34(3) (not yet in force). See note 1.

657. Further provisions on withdrawal and variation of penalty notices. As from a day to be appointed, the following provisions have effect[1]. Where (1) a penalty notice has been given to a person (the 'employer') by a local authority[2];

and (2) any appeal made[3] in respect of the penalty notice has not been determined[4], the authority may withdraw the penalty notice by giving notice of the withdrawal to the employer[5].

If a penalty notice is withdrawn[6], any sum already paid or recovered in respect of the penalty notice must be repaid to the employer with interest at the appropriate rate[7] running from the date when the sum was paid or recovered[8].

If the amount of a penalty is reduced[9], any sum already paid or recovered must, to the extent that it was paid or recovered in respect of any amount in excess of the reduced amount, be repaid to the employer with interest at the appropriate rate running from the date when the sum was paid or recovered[10].

1 The Education and Skills Act 2008 ss 35, 36 are to be brought into force by an order under s 173(4). At the date at which this volume states the law no such day had been appointed. As to the application of ss 19–36 to Wales, see s 67; and EDUCATION vol 35 (2011) PARA 680. As to the meaning of 'Wales' see PARA 2 note 12.
2 Ie under the Education and Skills Act 2008 s 31: see PARA 653. As to the meaning of 'local authority' see PARA 645 note 2.
3 Ie made under the Education and Skills Act 2008 s 34: see PARA 656.
4 Education and Skills Act 2008 s 35(1) (amended by SI 2010/1158) (not yet in force). See note 1.
5 Education and Skills Act 2008 s 35(2) (not yet in force). See note 1.
6 Ie under the Education and Skills Act 2008 s 33 (see PARA 655) or s 35 (see the text and notes 1–5).
7 'Appropriate rate' means the rate that, on the date the sum was paid or recovered, was specified in the Judgments Act 1838 s 17 (see CIVIL PROCEDURE vol 12 (2009) PARA 1149): Education and Skills Act 2008 s 36(3) (not yet in force). See note 1.
8 Education and Skills Act 2008 s 36(1) (not yet in force). See note 1.
9 Ie under the Education and Skills Act 2008 s 33: see PARA 655.
10 Education and Skills Act 2008 s 36(2) (not yet in force). See note 1.

(4) INDUSTRIAL TRAINING BOARDS

(i) In general

658. Establishment of industrial training boards. For the purpose of making better provision for the training of persons over compulsory school age[1] for employment[2] in any activities of industry or commerce[3], the Secretary of State[4] may[5] make an order (an 'industrial training order')[6] specifying those activities and establishing a board (an 'industrial training board')[7] to exercise in relation to them the functions conferred[8] on industrial training boards[9].

Before making an industrial training order, the Secretary of State must consult[10]:

(1) such organisations or associations of organisations appearing to him to be representative of substantial numbers of employers[11], and such bodies established for the purpose of carrying on under national ownership any industry or part of an industry or undertaking, as he thinks fit; and
(2) such other organisations, associations or bodies, if any, as he thinks fit[12].

Any consultations required to be so carried out may be in such form and in respect of such matters, whether or not related to the making of a specific order, as the Secretary of State thinks fit[13].

An industrial training order may make provision with respect to:

(a) the tenure of office of the members of the board;
(b) the quorum and[14] the proceedings and meetings of the board;
(c) the execution of instruments by and on behalf of the board and the

proof of documents purporting to be executed, issued or signed by the board or a member, officer or servant thereof,

and any provision made by virtue of head (b) above may enable votes to be cast by proxy[15].

An industrial training board is a body corporate, by such name as may be specified in the industrial training order[16].

1 As to the meaning of 'compulsory school age' see the Education Act 1996 s 8; and EDUCATION vol 35 (2011) PARA 18.
2 For these purposes, 'employment' means employment under a contract of service or apprenticeship or a contract for services or otherwise than under a contract; and 'employed' is to be construed accordingly: Industrial Training Act 1982 s 1(2). As to the meanings of 'employment', 'employed', and related expressions in relation to employment rights generally, see PARA 2 et seq. As to the meanings of 'contract of service' and 'contract for service' see PARA 1 note 1. As to contracts of apprenticeship see PARA 112.
3 As to the meaning of 'activities of industry or commerce' see *Hotel and Catering Industry Training Board v Automobile Pty Ltd* [1969] 2 All ER 582, [1969] 1 WLR 697, HL (the Secretary of State could not make orders purporting to extend to a members' club).
4 As to the Secretary of State see PARA 5 note 21.
5 Ie subject to the Industrial Training Act 1982 s 1(3)–(8): see the text and notes 6, 11–13.
6 For these purposes, 'industrial training order' means an order under the Industrial Training Act 1982 s 1: s 1(2). The power to make such an order is exercisable by statutory instrument, which is subject to annulment in pursuance of a resolution of either House of Parliament: s 1(8). Any such order may provide for any incidental or supplementary matter for which it appears to the Secretary of State to be necessary or expedient to provide, and an order amending or revoking such an order may provide for any incidental, transitional or consequential matter for which it appears to the Secretary of State to be necessary or expedient to provide; and, without prejudice to the generality of the foregoing or to the powers implied in s 3(1)(b) (see PARA 674 head (2)), the matters for which such orders may provide include the amendment or revocation of an order under s 3 (see PARA 674): s 1(7) (amended by the Employment Act 1989 Sch 4 para 1(1), (4)).
7 For these purposes, 'industrial training board' means, subject to the Industrial Training Act 1982 s 20(2) (repealed), a board established under s 1 or the Industrial Training Act 1964 s 1 (repealed): Industrial Training Act 1982 s 1(2).
8 Ie conferred by the Industrial Training Act 1982.
9 Industrial Training Act 1982 s 1(1). By virtue of the Interpretation Act 1978 s 17(2)(b), the Industrial Training (Construction Board) Order 1964, SI 1964/1079, and the Industrial Training (Engineering Board) Order 1964, SI 1964/1086, have effect as if so made; and, in exercise of the powers conferred by the Industrial Training Act 1982 s 1, the Industrial Training (Engineering Construction Board) Order 1991, SI 1991/1305 and the Industrial Training (Film Industry Training Board for England and Wales) Order 2007, SI 2007/3148, have been made.
10 As to the meaning of 'consult' see *Rollo v Minister of Town and Country Planning* [1948] 1 All ER 13, CA; *Agricultural, Horticultural and Forestry Industry Training Board v Aylesbury Mushrooms Ltd* [1972] 1 All ER 280, [1972] 1 WLR 190. For the purposes of the Industrial Training Act 1982 s 1(4) (see the text and notes 11–12), any consultation carried out by the Training Commission in pursuance of s 1(5) (repealed) before 16 November 1989 in connection with a proposed industrial training order is taken to have been carried out by the Secretary of State in connection with that proposed order: Employment Act 1989 s 22(5), Sch 5 paras 1, 9(1). Schedule 5 para 9(1) is without prejudice to the generality of Sch 5 para 3 (see PARA 633): Sch 5 para 9(4). As to the Training Commission see PARA 633.
11 For these purposes, 'employee' includes a person engaged under a contract for services; and 'employer' is to be construed accordingly: Industrial Training Act 1982 s 1(2). See note 2.
12 Industrial Training Act 1982 s 1(4) (substituted by the Employment Act 1989 s 23). The Industrial Training Act 1982 s 1(4) does not apply in relation to the making of any order under s 1 which amends one or more other orders under s 1 and contains a statement that the only amendments made by the order are amendments which appear to the Secretary of State to be necessary or expedient in consequence of the Employment Act 1988 s 29(2) (see PARA 662 note 7): s 29(3).
13 Industrial Training Act 1982 s 1(6) (amended by the Employment Act 1989 Sch 4 para 1(1), (3), Sch 7 Pt I).
14 Ie subject to the Industrial Training Act 1982 s 1(3), Sch 1 para 6 (see PARA 662) and Sch 1 para 7 (see PARAS 662, 663).

15 Industrial Training Act 1982 Sch 1 para 8. See note 9.
16 Industrial Training Act 1982 Sch 1 para 1. See note 9.

659. Grants etc to industrial training boards. The Secretary of State[1] may make grants and loans to an industrial training board[2]; and he may give to an industrial training board such directions as he thinks fit for the purpose of securing:

(1) that the board's expenditure for a purpose specified in the directions does not exceed an amount so specified; and
(2) that the whole or part of any grant or loan made[3] to the board is used only for the purposes specified in the directions,

and it is the duty of the board to comply with the directions[4].

An industrial training board may, with the consent of the Secretary of State or in accordance with the terms of any authority given by him, borrow temporarily from any other person by way of overdraft or otherwise such sums as it may require[5].

An industrial training board may give security for any money borrowed by it[6]; but it must not invest any money otherwise than in such manner as the Secretary of State may approve[7].

1 As to the Secretary of State see PARA 5 note 21.
2 Industrial Training Act 1982 s 17(1) (amended by the Employment Act 1989 Sch 4 para 15(1), (2)). As to the meaning of 'industrial training board' see PARA 658 note 7.
3 Ie in pursuance of the Industrial Training Act 1982 s 17(1): see the text and notes 1, 2.
4 Industrial Training Act 1982 s 17(2) (amended by the Employment Act 1989 Sch 4 para 15(1), (3)).
5 Industrial Training Act 1982 s 17(3) (amended by the Employment Act 1989 Sch 4 para 15(1), (4)).
6 Industrial Training Act 1982 s 17(4).
7 Industrial Training Act 1982 s 17(5) (amended by the Employment Act 1989 Sch 4 para 15(1), (5)).

(ii) Constitution of Industrial Training Boards; Appointment of Committees

660. Membership of the board. The members of an industrial training board[1] must be appointed by the Secretary of State[2]. A board must consist of:

(1) a chairman and, if the Secretary of State thinks fit, a deputy chairman, each of whom must be a person appearing to the Secretary of State to have industrial or commercial experience[3];
(2) such number of persons appointed after the appropriate consultation[4] as the Secretary of State thinks fit[5]; and
(3) such other persons, if any, whom it appears to the Secretary of State to be appropriate to appoint in addition to those appointed by virtue of head (2) above[6].

The Secretary of State may reconstitute the membership of an industrial training board as from any time after 16 November 1989[7]:

(a) by terminating such of the appointments of its existing members as would otherwise expire after that time[8]; and
(b) by making[9] fresh appointments to it, as from that time[10].

1 As to the meaning of 'industrial training board' see PARA 658 note 7.
2 Industrial Training Act 1982 s 1(3), Sch 1 para 2. As to the Secretary of State see PARA 5 note 21.
3 Industrial Training Act 1982 Sch 1 para 3(1)(a) (Sch 1 para 3 substituted by the Employment Act 1989 s 25(1)).

4 For these purposes, the reference to the appropriate consultation is a reference to consultation with such organisations, or associations of organisations, representative of employers engaging in the industry as appear to the Secretary of State to be appropriate: Industrial Training Act 1982 Sch 1 para 3(2) (as substituted: see note 3). 'The industry', in relation to an industrial training board, means the activities in relation to which it exercises functions: s 1(2). Any body established for the purpose of carrying on under national ownership any industry or part of an industry or undertaking is to be treated for these purposes as if it were an organisation representative of employers: Sch 1 para 13. As to the meaning of 'consult' see PARA 658 note 10. As to the meaning of 'employer' for these purposes see PARA 658 note 11.

5 Industrial Training Act 1982 Sch 1 para 3(1)(b) (as substituted: see note 3). A person so appointed must at the time of his appointment be a person appearing to the Secretary of State to be concerned, whether as a director, manager or sole proprietor or otherwise, in the management of the activities, or any of the activities, of an employer engaging in the industry: Sch 1 para 3(2) (as so substituted).

6 Industrial Training Act 1982 Sch 1 para 3(1)(c) (as substituted: see note 3). The Secretary of State must not, however, make any such appointment if to do so would result in the number of persons for the time being appointed by virtue of Sch 1 para 3(1)(c) being equal to, or greater than, the number of persons for the time being appointed by virtue of Sch 1 para 3(1)(b) (see head (2) in the text): Sch 1 para 3(3) (as so substituted).

7 Ie as from any time after the passing of the Employment Act 1989.

8 Employment Act 1989 s 25(2)(a). The termination of a person's appointment to an industrial training board in accordance with s 25(2)(a) does not preclude him from being reappointed to the board in pursuance of s 25(2)(b) (see head (b) in the text): s 25(3).

The power conferred on the Secretary of State by s 25(2) is not exercisable in relation to an industrial training board if all of its members were appointed to it in accordance with the provisions substituted by s 25(1) (see the text and notes 3–6), whether they were so appointed in pursuance of s 25(2)(b) (see head (b) in the text) or otherwise: s 25(4).

9 Ie in accordance with the provisions substituted by the Employment Act 1989 s 25(1): see the text and notes 3–6.

10 Employment Act 1989 s 25(2)(b). See also note 8.

661. Remuneration; appointment of staff. An industrial training board[1] must pay to its chairman[2] such remuneration, if any, as the Secretary of State[3] may from time to time, with the approval of the Treasury[4], determine and may make such arrangements for the payment of pensions, superannuation allowances and gratuities to or in respect of its chairman as the Secretary of State may specify with the approval of the Treasury[5].

Where a person ceases to be the chairman of an industrial training board otherwise than on the expiry of his term of office and it appears to the Secretary of State that there are special circumstances which make it right for him to receive compensation, the board may make him a payment of such amount as the Secretary of State may determine, with the approval of the Treasury[6].

An industrial training board may pay to its members such allowances for loss of remunerative time as the Secretary of State may determine, with the approval of the Treasury, and such travelling, subsistence and other allowances as the board may determine[7].

An industrial training board may appoint such officers and servants, on such terms as to remuneration, pension rights and other conditions of service, as the board may determine[8].

1 As to the meaning of 'industrial training board' see PARA 658 note 7.

2 For these purposes, references to a chairman include a deputy chairman: Industrial Training Act 1982 s 1(3), Sch 1 para 3(4) (substituted by the Employment Act 1989 s 25(1)).

3 As to the Secretary of State see PARA 5 note 21.

4 As to the Treasury see CONSTITUTIONAL AND ADMINISTRATIVE LAW vol 20 (2014) PARA 262 et seq.

5 Industrial Training Act 1982 Sch 1 para 4.

6 Industrial Training Act 1982 Sch 1 para 5.

7 Industrial Training Act 1982 Sch 1 para 12.

8 Industrial Training Act 1982 Sch 1 para 11. The trustees of the Industrial Training Boards' Combined Pension Fund may, with the consent of three-quarters of the number of the industrial training boards whose officers and servants are eligible to benefit from the Fund, make such amendments of the rules of the Fund as they think fit: s 19.

662. Procedure. An industrial training board[1] has the power[2] to regulate its own procedure[3]; and the proceedings of a board are not invalidated by any vacancy in the membership of the board or by any defect in the appointment of any member[4].

Only members appointed[5] by the Secretary of State after the appropriate consultation may vote on any matter relating to the imposition of a levy[6]; and, accordingly, no such matter is to be decided except in accordance with the votes of the majority of the members who were so appointed[7].

The Secretary of State[8], the minister concerned with education in Scotland[9], the ministers concerned with education in England and Wales[10], acting jointly, and, if the Secretary of State thinks fit in a particular case, such other ministers in charge of government departments as he may specify, may each appoint one person to attend the meetings of an industrial training board; and any person so appointed is entitled to take part in the proceedings of the board and receive copies of all documents distributed to its members, but has no vote[11].

1 As to the meaning of 'industrial training board' see PARA 658 note 7.
2 Ie subject to the Industrial Training Act 1982 s 1(3), Sch 1 para 6 (see the text and notes 5–7) and Sch 1 para 7 (see the text and notes 8–11; and PARA 663) and to any provision made by virtue of Sch 1 para 8 (see PARA 658).
3 Industrial Training Act 1982 Sch 1 para 9. As to the proceedings of the Film Industry Training Board for England and Wales, see the Industrial Training (Film Industry Training Board for England and Wales) Order 2007, SI 2007/3148.
4 Industrial Training Act 1982 Sch 1 para 10.
5 Ie members appointed by virtue of the Industrial Training Act 1982 Sch 1 para 3(1)(b): see PARA 660.
6 As to levies see PARA 678.
7 Industrial Training Act 1982 Sch 1 para 6 (substituted by the Employment Act 1988 s 29(2); and amended by the Employment Act 1989 Sch 6 para 29).
8 As to the Secretary of State see PARA 5 note 21.
9 See CONSTITUTIONAL AND ADMINISTRATIVE LAW vol 20 (2014) PARA 69.
10 See EDUCATION vol 35 (2011) PARA 53 et seq. As to the meanings of 'England' and 'Wales' see PARA 2 note 12.
11 Industrial Training Act 1982 Sch 1 para 7(1) (amended by the Employment Act 1989 Sch 4 para 16(1), (2), Sch 7 Pt I).

663. Establishment of committees. An industrial training board[1] may:

(1) appoint committees, which need not include members of the board;

(2) join with one or more other industrial training boards in appointing joint committees consisting of such persons, whether or not members of an industrial training board, as may be determined by the boards,

and delegate to any such committee, to such extent as may be stated in proposals submitted to and approved by the Secretary of State[2], all or any of the functions conferred[3] on the board[4].

An industrial training board may pay or, as the case may be, join in paying:

(a) to the members of such a committee such allowances for loss of remunerative time as the Secretary of State may, with the approval of the Treasury[5], determine and such travelling, subsistence and other allowances as the board or, as the case may be, the boards may determine; and

(b) to the chairman of any such committee to which functions are so delegated such remuneration as the board or, as the case may be, the boards may determine[6].

An industrial training board may make, or as the case may be join in making, such arrangements as the board may determine:

(i) for the payment of pensions, superannuation allowances and gratuities to or in respect of the chairmen of such committees as are mentioned in head (b) above;

(ii) for the payment of compensation to a person who ceases to be such a chairman otherwise than on the expiry of his term of office where it appears to the board that there are special circumstances which make it right for him to receive compensation[7].

Subject to any directions of the board or boards which appointed it, a committee so appointed may regulate its own procedure and fix a quorum for its proceedings[8].

The Secretary of State may appoint one or more persons to attend the meetings of a committee of an industrial training board; and a person so appointed is entitled to take part in the proceedings of the committee and receive copies of all documents distributed to its members, but has no vote[9].

1 As to the meaning of 'industrial training board' see PARA 658 note 7.
2 Ie under the Industrial Training Act 1982 s 5(5): see PARA 664. As to the Secretary of State see PARA 5 note 21.
3 Ie by the Industrial Training Act 1982 s 5 (see PARAS 664, 666, 667) or s 14(5) (see PARA 683).
4 Industrial Training Act 1982 s 2(1) (amended by the Employment Act 1989 Sch 4 para 2).
5 As to the Treasury see CONSTITUTIONAL AND ADMINISTRATIVE LAW vol 20 (2014) PARA 262 et seq.
6 Industrial Training Act 1982 s 2(2).
7 Industrial Training Act 1982 s 2(3).
8 Industrial Training Act 1982 s 2(4).
9 Industrial Training Act 1982 s 1(3), Sch 1 para 7(2) (amended by the Employment Act 1989 Sch 4 para 16(1), (3)).

(iii) Control by the Secretary of State

664. General control by the Secretary of State. An industrial training board[1]:

(1) must from time to time submit to the Secretary of State[2] for his approval proposals for the exercise of functions conferred[3] on the board; and

(2) may from time to time submit to the Secretary of State for his approval proposals for the delegation of all or any of those functions to committees[4],

and the board must exercise its functions in accordance with proposals submitted to the Secretary of State and approved by him[5].

An industrial training board must give to the Secretary of State such information or facilities for obtaining information with regard to the exercise of its functions, in such manner and at such times as the Secretary of State may reasonably require[6].

1 As to the meaning of 'industrial training board' see PARA 658 note 7.
2 As to the Secretary of State see PARA 5 note 21.
3 Ie the functions conferred by the Industrial Training Act 1982 s 5: see also PARAS 666, 667.
4 Ie committees established under the Industrial Training Act 1982 s 2: see PARA 663.
5 Industrial Training Act 1982 s 5(5) (amended by the Employment Act 1989 Sch 4 para 4(1), (3)).
6 Industrial Training Act 1982 s 5(6) (amended by the Employment Act 1989 Sch 4 para 4(1), (2)).

665. Default powers in relation to proposals. The Secretary of State[1] may direct an industrial training board[2] to submit proposals[3] to him within the time specified in the direction; and it is the duty of the board to comply with such a direction[4]. Where proposals so submitted to the Secretary of State appear unsatisfactory to him, he may direct the board to submit fresh proposals within a specified time, stating in the direction in what respect the proposals already submitted appear to him unsatisfactory; and where the fresh proposals also appear unsatisfactory to the Secretary of State, he may make an order (a 'default order') declaring the board to be in default[5]. Where a board has failed to comply with such a direction of the Secretary of State within the time specified in the direction, he may make a default order[6].

1 As to the Secretary of State see PARA 5 note 21.
2 As to the meaning of 'industrial training board' see PARA 658 note 7.
3 Ie under the Industrial Training Act 1982 s 5(5) (see PARA 664), s 11(1) (see PARA 678) or s 13(1) (see PARA 681).
4 Industrial Training Act 1982 s 15(1) (amended by the Employment Act 1989 Sch 4 para 13(1), (2)). For the purposes of the Industrial Training Act 1982 s 15: (1) any direction of the Training Commission given before 16 November 1989 under s 15(1) has effect as if given by the Secretary of State under s 15(1); (2) any direction of the Training Commission given before that date under s 15(2) has effect as if given by the Secretary of State under s 15(2) (see the text and note 5); (3) any proposals submitted to the Training Commission before that date in pursuance of a direction under s 15(1) are to be taken to have been submitted to the Secretary of State in pursuance of a direction under s 15(1); and (4) any proposals submitted to the Training Commission before that date in pursuance of a direction under s 15(2) are to be taken to have been submitted to the Secretary of State in pursuance of a direction given by him under s 15(2): Employment Act 1989 s 22(5), Sch 5 paras 1, 9(3). Schedule 5 para 9(3) is without prejudice to the generality of Sch 5 para 3 (see PARA 633): Sch 5 para 9(4). As to the Training Commission see PARA 633.
5 Industrial Training Act 1982 s 15(2) (substituted by the Employment Act 1989 Sch 4 para 13(1), (3)). See also note 4. A default order may contain such incidental or supplementary provisions as appear to the Secretary of State to be necessary or expedient and may be varied or revoked by a subsequent order: Industrial Training Act 1982 s 15(8).

On the making of a default order, the members of the board must forthwith vacate their office; and the order may contain such provisions as seem to the Secretary of State expedient for authorising any person to act in place of the members of the board during such period, not exceeding six months, as may elapse before new members are appointed: s 15(6). The Secretary of State may out of moneys provided by Parliament defray the expenses of any person so acting in the place of the members of a board and recover from the board any expenses so defrayed: s 15(9).

While a default order is in force with respect to a board, s 1(3), Sch 1 para 3 (see PARA 660) and any provision of the industrial training order made by virtue of Sch 1 para 8(a) (see PARA 658 head (a)) do not apply in relation to it; and accordingly, but without prejudice to any provision made under s 15(8), the provisions of Sch 1 para 6 (see PARA 662) do not apply: s 15(7). As to the meaning of 'industrial training order' see PARA 658 note 6.

The provisions of s 15(5)–(9) also apply in relation to a direction given under s 3A: see PARA 675 note 5.
6 Industrial Training Act 1982 s 15(5) (substituted by the Employment Act 1989 Sch 4 para 13(1), (5)). See also note 4.

(iv) Functions of Industrial Training Boards

A. IN GENERAL

666. Provision and approval of training facilities and advice. For the purpose of encouraging adequate training of persons employed[1] or intending to be employed in the industry[2], an industrial training board[3] may:

(1) provide or secure the provision of such courses and other facilities,

which may include residential accommodation, for the training of those persons as the board considers adequate, having regard to any courses or facilities otherwise available to those persons;

(2) approve such courses and facilities provided by other persons;

(3) from time to time consider such employments[4] in the industry as appear to require consideration and publish recommendations with regard to the nature and length of the training for any such employment and the post-school education[5] to be associated with the training, the persons by and to whom the training ought to be given, the standards to be attained as a result of the training and the methods of ascertaining whether those standards have been attained;

(4) apply or make arrangements for the application of selection tests and of tests or other methods for ascertaining the attainment of any standards recommended by the board and award certificates of the attainment of those standards;

(5) assist persons in finding facilities for being trained for employment in the industry;

(6) carry on or assist other persons in carrying on research into any matter relating to training for employment in the industry; and

(7) provide advice about training connected with the industry[6].

An industrial training board may enter into contracts of service or apprenticeship[7] with persons who intend to be employed in the industry and to attend courses or avail themselves of other facilities provided or approved by the board[8].

An industrial training board may:

(a) at the request of another industrial training board, provide advice for the other board and courses and other facilities for the training of persons employed or intending to be employed in the industry for which that other board is established;

(b) at the request of the Secretary of State[9], provide such other advice, and such other courses and facilities for training, as are mentioned in the request;

(c) at the request of an employer[10] in the industry, provide for him advice about training connected with activities carried on in Northern Ireland or outside the United Kingdom[11] which, if they were carried on in Great Britain, would be included in the industry;

(d) enter into agreements with persons for the making by them of payments to the board in respect of the exercise by the board of any of its functions;

(e) take part in any arrangements[12] for persons to select, train for and obtain suitable employments and to obtain suitable employees;

(f) provide services or arrange for the provision of services in pursuance of arrangements made, or a direction given, under the provisions relating to career services[13],

but any expense incurred by the board in pursuance of head (c) above is not to be defrayed out of sums received by way of levy[14].

1 As to the meaning of 'employed' for these purposes see PARA 658 note 2.
2 As to the meaning of 'the industry' see PARA 660 note 4.
3 As to the meaning of 'industrial training board' see PARA 658 note 7.
4 As to the meaning of 'employment' for these purposes see PARA 658 note 2.
5 For these purposes, 'post-school education' means 'higher education' as defined by the Education Reform Act 1988 (see EDUCATION vol 35 (2011) PARA 23) or 'further education' as

defined by the Education Act 1996 s 1(3)–(5) (see EDUCATION vol 35 (2011) PARA 22): Industrial Training Act 1982 s 5(8)(a) (substituted by the Education Act 1996 Sch 37 para 54).

6 Industrial Training Act 1982 s 5(1) (amended by the Education Reform Act 1988 Sch 12 para 87(1), (2)). The functions conferred by the Industrial Training Act 1982 s 5 which are exercisable outside Great Britain are those which are exercisable under provisions which are applied by s 10(1A) (see PARA 668 note 5) in connection with the training of persons outside Great Britain under s 10: s 5(7) (added by the Industrial Training Act 1986 s 1(2)). As to the meaning of 'Great Britain' see PARA 2 note 12.

As to industrial injuries benefits for accidents in training see the Industrial Training Act 1982 s 18; and WELFARE BENEFITS AND STATE PENSIONS vol 104 (2014) PARA 188.

7 As to the meaning of 'contract of service' see PARA 1 note 1; and as to contracts of apprenticeship see PARA 112.

8 Industrial Training Act 1982 s 5(2).

9 As to the Secretary of State see PARA 5 note 21.

10 As to the meaning of 'employer' for these purposes see PARA 658 note 11.

11 As to the meaning of 'United Kingdom' see PARA 2 note 12.

12 Ie any arrangements made in pursuance of the Employment and Training Act 1973 s 2: see PARA 634.

13 Ie under the Employment and Training Act 1973 s 10: see PARA 640.

14 Industrial Training Act 1982 s 5(3) (amended by the Employment Act 1988 Sch 3 para 14(1); the Employment Act 1989 Sch 4 para 4(1), (2), Sch 7 Pt I; and the Trade Union Reform and Employment Rights Act 1993 Sch 8 para 34, Sch 10). As to levies see PARA 678.

667. Payment for training. An industrial training board[1] may:

(1) pay maintenance and travelling allowances to persons attending courses provided or approved by the board;

(2) make grants or loans to persons providing courses or other facilities approved by the board, to persons who make studies for the purpose of providing such courses or facilities and to persons who maintain arrangements to provide such courses or facilities which are not for the time being in use;

(3) pay fees to persons providing post-school education[2] in respect of persons who receive it in association with their training in courses provided or approved by the board;

(4) make payments to persons in connection with arrangements under which they or employees[3] of theirs make use of courses or other facilities provided or approved by the board[4].

1 As to the meaning of 'industrial training board' see PARA 658 note 7.

2 As to the meaning of 'post-school education' see PARA 666 note 5.

3 As to the meaning of 'employee' for these purposes see PARA 658 note 11.

4 Industrial Training Act 1982 s 5(4) (amended by the Education Reform Act 1988 Sch 12 para 87(1), (2)).

668. Training for employment overseas. An industrial training board[1] may, with the consent of the Secretary of State[2], exercise such functions in connection with training for employment[3] in a similar industry outside Great Britain[4] as are exercisable by it under the relevant provisions[5] in connection with the training of persons employed or intended to be employed in the industry[6] in Great Britain[7].

An industrial training board may delegate any power so exercisable by it to a committee, which need not include members of the board, appointed for that purpose or to any other committee appointed[8] by the board[9].

An industrial training board must keep separate accounts:

(1) with respect to its functions under the provisions described above; and

(2) with respect to its other functions under the Industrial Training Act 1982,

and no money raised by a levy[10] may be carried to an account kept in pursuance of head (1) above[11].

1 As to the meaning of 'industrial training board' see PARA 658 note 7.
2 As to the Secretary of State see PARA 5 note 21.
3 As to the meaning of 'employment' for these purposes see PARA 658 note 2.
4 As to the meaning of 'Great Britain' see PARA 2 note 12.
5 For these purposes, 'relevant provisions' means: (1) in relation to the training of persons in Great Britain, the Industrial Training Act 1982 s 5(1), (3)(d), (4) (see PARAS 666, 667); and (2) in relation to the training of persons outside Great Britain, s 5(1)(a), (c)–(g), (3)(d) (see PARA 666): s 10(1A) (substituted by the Industrial Training Act 1986 s 1(1)).
6 As to the meaning of 'the industry' see PARA 660 note 4.
7 Industrial Training Act 1982 s 10(1) (substituted by the Industrial Training Act 1986 s 1(1); and amended by the Employment Act 1989 Sch 4 para 9, Sch 7 Pt I).
8 Ie under the Industrial Training Act 1982 s 2: see PARA 663.
9 Industrial Training Act 1982 s 10(2).
10 Ie a levy imposed by the Industrial Training Act 1982. As to levies see PARA 678.
11 Industrial Training Act 1982 s 10(3). Any expenses and liabilities incurred by the board under s 10 must be disregarded for the purposes of s 4(2) (see PARA 677) and s 11(1) (see PARA 678): s 10(3).

B. INFORMATION, REPORTS AND ACCOUNTS

669. Power to obtain information from employers. An industrial training board[1] may require employers[2] in the industry[3] to furnish such returns and other information of a kind approved by the Secretary of State[4], and to keep such records of a kind approved by him and produce them for examination on behalf of the board as appear to the board to be necessary for carrying out its functions[5]. If any person fails to comply with any such requirement, he is liable to a fine[6].

If any person:

(1) knowingly or recklessly furnishes[7] any return or information which is false in a material particular; or
(2) wilfully makes a false entry in any record required to be so produced or, with intent to deceive, makes use of any such entry which he knows to be false[8],

he is liable to a penalty[9].

Where such an offence committed by a body corporate is proved to have been committed with the consent or connivance of, or to be attributable to any neglect on the part of, any director, manager[10], secretary or other similar officer of the body corporate, or any person who was purporting to act in any such capacity, he, as well as the body corporate, is guilty of that offence and is liable to be proceeded against and punished accordingly[11].

The Secretary of State may direct an industrial training board to exercise such power (the 'information power') so as to require employers in the industry to furnish to the board, in such form and on such occasions as are specified in the direction, such information as the Secretary of State considers that he needs for the purposes of his functions and as is so specified; and it is the duty of the board to comply with the direction[12].

An industrial training board is not to exercise the information power except:

(a) in pursuance of a direction so given; or
(b) with the approval of the Secretary of State[13] and in accordance with the conditions, if any, of the approval,

and any application by a board for approval in pursuance of head (b) above must be made to the Secretary of State and contain such information as he may require with respect to the proposed exercise of the information power[14].

1 As to the meaning of 'industrial training board' see PARA 658 note 7.
2 As to the meaning of 'employer' for these purposes see PARA 658 note 11.
3 As to the meaning of 'the industry' see PARA 660 note 4.
4 As to the Secretary of State see PARA 5 note 21.
5 Industrial Training Act 1982 s 6(1). As to the exemption from s 6(1) in the case of an establishment situated wholly or mainly within an area designated as an enterprise zone see PARA 670.
6 Industrial Training Act 1982 s 6(5) (amended by the Criminal Justice Act 1982 ss 38, 46). The penalty on summary conviction is a fine not exceeding level 4 on the standard scale: see the Industrial Training Act 1982 s 6(5) (as so amended). As to the standard scale see **SENTENCING AND DISPOSITION OF OFFENDERS** vol 92 (2010) PARA 142.
7 Ie in pursuance of any requirement made under the Industrial Training Act 1982 s 6(1): see the text and notes 1–5.
8 Industrial Training Act 1982 s 6(6)(a), (b).
9 Industrial Training Act 1982 s 6(6). The penalty on conviction on indictment is imprisonment for a term not exceeding two years or a fine, or both, and on summary conviction is imprisonment for a term not exceeding three months or a fine not exceeding the prescribed sum, or both: see s 6(6). For this purpose, the 'prescribed sum' means the prescribed sum within the meaning of the Magistrates' Courts Act 1980 s 32: Industrial Training Act 1982 s 6(7)(a). As to the prescribed sum see **SENTENCING AND DISPOSITION OF OFFENDERS** vol 92 (2010) PARA 141.
10 As to the meaning of 'manager' see PARA 40 note 11.
11 Industrial Training Act 1982 s 6(8).
12 Industrial Training Act 1982 s 7(1) (amended by the Employment Act 1989 Sch 4 para 6(1), (2)).
13 An approval of an application so given by the Secretary of State may be given subject to conditions that the board in question may exercise the information power only for the purpose of requiring the furnishing of information in such forms and on such occasions as are specified in the instrument of approval: Industrial Training Act 1982 s 7(4).
14 Industrial Training Act 1982 s 7(2) (amended by the Employment Act 1989 Sch 4 para 6(1), (3)).

670. Enterprise zones. An employer[1] is not obliged to comply with a requirement to provide information[2] in respect of an establishment or employee[3] if:

(1) at the time the requirement is imposed the establishment is situated wholly or mainly within an area designated as an enterprise zone[4] or, as the case may be, the employee's employment[5] is carried on at or from such an establishment; or

(2) the requirement relates to a period during which the establishment was so situated or, as the case may be, the employee's employment was so carried on[6].

1 As to the meaning of 'employer' for these purposes see PARA 658 note 11.
2 Ie a requirement imposed under the Industrial Training Act 1982 s 6: see PARAS 669, 671.
3 As to the meaning of 'employee' for these purposes see PARA 658 note 11.
4 Ie under the Local Government, Planning and Land Act 1980 s 179, Sch 32: see **PLANNING** vol 83 (2010) PARA 1640 et seq.
5 As to the meaning of 'employment' for these purposes see PARA 658 note 2.
6 Industrial Training Act 1982 s 16(1), (3). The Secretary of State may by order made by statutory instrument provide that s 16 is not to apply in relation to such employees or such establishments as he may specify in the order or is to apply to them with such modifications as he may so specify: s 16(4) (amended by the Employment Act 1989 Sch 4 para 14, Sch 7 Pt I). An order so made is subject to annulment by a resolution of either House of Parliament: Industrial Training Act 1982 s 16(5). At the date at which this volume states the law no such order had been made. As to the Secretary of State see PARA 5 note 21.

671. Prohibition on disclosure of information. Returns and other information furnished under the information power[1] and any information obtained on an examination made thereunder must not, without the consent of the employer[2] to whose business the returns or information relate, be disclosed otherwise than to the Secretary of State[3] or one of his officers, or to an industrial training board[4] or a committee appointed by such a board, or to an officer of such a board or committee or any person entitled to take part in the proceedings of such a board[5].

However, this prohibition does not apply to:

(1) the disclosure of returns or information in the form of a summary of similar returns or information furnished by or obtained from a number of employers, if the summary is so framed as not to enable particulars relating to any individual business to be ascertained from it[6];

(2) any disclosure of information made for the purposes of any legal proceedings pursuant to the Industrial Training Act 1982 or any criminal proceedings[7], or for the purposes of any report of any such proceedings[8].

If any person discloses any information in contravention of the provisions described above[9], he is liable to a penalty[10].

Where such an offence committed by a body corporate is proved to have been committed with the consent or connivance of, or to be attributable to any neglect on the part of, any director, manager[11], secretary or other similar officer of the body corporate, or any person who was purporting to act in any such capacity, he, as well as the body corporate, is guilty of that offence and is liable to be proceeded against and punished accordingly[12].

1 As to the meaning of 'information power' see PARA 669.
2 As to the meaning of 'employer' for these purposes see PARA 658 note 11.
3 As to the Secretary of State see PARA 5 note 21.
4 As to the meaning of 'industrial training board' see PARA 658 note 7.
5 Industrial Training Act 1982 s 6(2) (amended by the Employment Act 1989 Sch 4 para 5, Sch 7 Pt I).
6 Industrial Training Act 1982 s 6(3)(a).
7 Ie whether pursuant to the Industrial Training Act 1982 or not.
8 Industrial Training Act 1982 s 6(3)(b). A certificate purporting to be issued by or on behalf of the Secretary of State and stating that he has approved any kind of information, return or record for the purposes of s 6(1) (see PARA 669) is evidence, in any legal proceedings, of the facts stated in the certificate: s 6(4).
9 Ie the Industrial Training Act 1982 s 6(2): see the text and notes 1–5.
10 Industrial Training Act 1982 s 6(6)(c). The penalty on conviction on indictment is imprisonment for a term not exceeding two years or a fine, or both, and on summary conviction is imprisonment for a term not exceeding three months or a fine not exceeding the prescribed sum, or both: see s 6(6). As to the prescribed sum see SENTENCING AND DISPOSITION OF OFFENDERS vol 92 (2010) PARA 141.
11 As to the meaning of 'manager' see PARA 40 note 11.
12 Industrial Training Act 1982 s 6(8).

672. Reports and accounts. An industrial training board[1] must keep proper accounts and other records in relation to the accounts and prepare in respect of each of its financial years a statement of account in such form as the Secretary of State[2] may, with the approval of the Treasury[3], determine[4].

The accounts of an industrial training board must be audited by auditors appointed by the board[5], except for the accounts of the Construction Industry Training Board and the Engineering Construction Industry Training Board[6], which must each send a copy of its statement of account[7] to the Comptroller and Auditor General[8] as soon as reasonably practicable after the end of the financial year to which each statement relates[9].

An industrial training board must for each of its financial years make a report of its activities to the Secretary of State; and that report must include a statement of the accounts of the board for that year together with a copy of any report made by the auditors on the accounts or, as the case may be, by the Comptroller and Auditor General on the statement[10].

The Secretary of State must lay a copy of every such report before Parliament[11].

1 As to the meaning of 'industrial training board' see PARA 658 note 7.
2 As to the Secretary of State see PARA 5 note 21.
3 As to the Treasury see **CONSTITUTIONAL AND ADMINISTRATIVE LAW** vol 20 (2014) PARA 262 et seq.
4 Industrial Training Act 1982 s 8(1) (amended by the Employment Act 1989 Sch 4 para 7(1), (2)).
5 Industrial Training Act 1982 s 8(2). For these purposes, no person is to be appointed by the board unless he is eligible for appointment as a statutory auditor under the Companies Act 2006 Pt 42 (ss 1209–1264) (see **COMPANIES** vol 15 (2009) PARA 957 et seq): Industrial Training Act 1982 s 8(2) (amended by SI 1991/1997; and SI 2008/948). Where a partnership constituted under the law of England and Wales, or under the law of any other country or territory in which a partnership is not a legal person, is appointed under the Industrial Training Act 1982 s 8(2), the provisions of the Companies Act 2006 Pt 42 (see **COMPANIES** vol 15 (2009) PARA 957 et seq) apply to the appointment in the same way as they apply to the appointment as company auditor of such a partnership: Companies Act 1989 (Eligibility for Appointment as Company Auditor) (Consequential Amendments) Regulations 1991, SI 1991/1997, reg 3; and see the Interpretation Act 1978 s 17(2). As to the meanings of 'England' and 'Wales' see PARA 2 note 12.
6 Ie in respect of financial years ending on or after 31 December 2003: Industrial Training Act 1982 s 8(2A) (s 8(2A)–(2C) added by SI 2003/1326).
7 Ie the statement of account prepared under the Industrial Training Act 1982 s 8(1) (see the text and notes 1–4) in respect of each financial year ending on or after 31 December 2003.
8 As to the Comptroller and Auditor General see **CONSTITUTIONAL AND ADMINISTRATIVE LAW** vol 20 (2014) PARAS 494–496 et seq.
9 Industrial Training Act 1982 s 8(2B) (as added: see note 6). The Comptroller and Auditor General must examine, certify and report on each statement of account so sent to him: Industrial Training Act 1982 s 8(2C) (as so added).
10 Industrial Training Act 1982 s 8(3) (amended by the Employment Act 1989 Sch 4 para 7(1), (3); and SI 2003/1326). As to the publication of information in the report see PARA 673.
11 Industrial Training Act 1982 s 8(4) (amended by the Employment Act 1989 Sch 4 para 7(1), (4)).

673. Publication of information. The Secretary of State[1] may direct an industrial training board[2] to publish in the report made[3] by it, or otherwise as he may direct, such information in the possession of the board as he may specify in the direction[4].

No such direction may, however, require any information which is so framed as to enable particulars relating to any individual employer[5] or establishment of an employer to be ascertained from it to be published without the consent of the employer in question[6].

1 As to the Secretary of State see PARA 5 note 21.
2 As to the meaning of 'industrial training board' see PARA 658 note 7.
3 Ie under the Industrial Training Act 1982 s 8(3): see PARA 672.
4 Industrial Training Act 1982 s 9(1) (amended by the Employment Act 1989 Sch 4 para 8, Sch 7 Pt I).
5 As to the meaning of 'employer' for these purposes see PARA 658 note 11.
6 Industrial Training Act 1982 s 9(2).

(v) Transfer of Activities; Winding Up of Industrial Training Boards

674. Transfer of establishments' activities. If an employer[1] in the industry[2] of an industrial training board[3] requests the Secretary of State[4] in writing[5] to secure that the activities carried on at a particular establishment of the employer are, instead of being included[6] in that industry, to be included[7] in the industry of another industrial training board, the Secretary of State:

(1) must consult both boards in question about the request[8]; and

(2) after such consultation may, if he thinks fit, make an order giving effect to that request[9].

1 As to the meaning of 'employer' for these purposes see PARA 658 note 11.
2 As to the meaning of 'the industry' see PARA 660 note 4.
3 As to the meaning of 'industrial training board' see PARA 658 note 7.
4 As to the Secretary of State see PARA 5 note 21.
5 As to the meaning of 'writing' see PARA 2 note 8.
6 Ie for the purposes of the Industrial Training Act 1982.
7 See note 6.
8 Any consultation carried out in pursuance of the Industrial Training Act 1982 s 3(1) before 16 November 1989 in connection with a request so made is to be taken, for these purposes, to have been carried out by the Secretary of State in connection with that request: Employment Act 1989 s 22(5), Sch 5 paras 1, 9(2). Schedule 5 para 9(2) is without prejudice to the generality of Sch 5 para 3 (see PARA 633): Sch 5 para 9(4).
9 Industrial Training Act 1982 s 3(1) (s 3 substituted by the Employment Act 1989 Sch 4 para 3). The power to make such an order is exercisable by statutory instrument: Industrial Training Act 1982 s 3(2) (as so substituted).

In exercise of the power so conferred the Secretary of State has made the Industrial Training (Transfer of the Activities of Establishments) Order 1990, SI 1990/928. By virtue of the Interpretation Act 1978 s 17(2)(b), the following orders have effect as if so made: the Industrial Training (Transfer of the Activities of Establishments) Order 1974, SI 1974/1154; the Industrial Training (Transfer of the Activities of Establishments) (No 2) Order 1974, SI 1974/1495; the Industrial Training (Transfer of the Activities of Establishments) Order 1975, SI 1975/434; the Industrial Training (Transfer of the Activities of Establishments) (No 2) Order 1975, SI 1975/1157; the Industrial Training (Transfer of the Activities of Establishments) Order 1976, SI 1976/396; the Industrial Training (Transfer of the Activities of Establishments) (No 2) Order 1976, SI 1976/1635; the Industrial Training (Transfer of the Activities of Establishments) (No 3) Order 1976, SI 1976/2110; the Industrial Training (Transfer of the Activities of Establishments) Order 1977, SI 1977/1951; the Industrial Training (Transfer of the Activities of Establishments) Order 1978, SI 1978/448; the Industrial Training (Transfer of the Activities of Establishments) (No 2) Order 1978, SI 1978/1225; the Industrial Training (Transfer of the Activities of Establishments) (No 3) Order 1978, SI 1978/1643; the Industrial Training (Transfer of the Activities of Establishments) Order 1979, SI 1979/793; the Industrial Training (Transfer of the Activities of Establishments) Order 1980, SI 1980/586; the Industrial Training (Transfer of the Activities of Establishments) (No 2) Order 1980, SI 1980/1753; the Industrial Training (Transfer of the Activities of Establishments) Order 1981, SI 1981/1041; and the Industrial Training (Transfer of the Activities of Establishments) Order 1985, SI 1985/1662. Each of the orders treated as so made, except the last one mentioned, include certain transfers between the industries of two industrial training boards which have both been wound up under the Industrial Training Act 1982 s 4 (see PARA 677) and to that extent they may be considered as having become spent.

675. Transfer of assets on revocation or amendment of industrial training order. Where an order has been made[1] which:

(1) revokes an industrial training order[2]; or

(2) amends such an order so as to exclude from the scope of operation of an industrial training board[3] some of the activities in relation to which it exercises functions,

the board concerned:

(a) may with the consent of the Secretary of State[4]; or

(b) must, if he so directs[5],

transfer all or any of its assets to any person on trust to be used for charitable purposes which are related to or connected with training for employment[6].

Any such transfer may be made for a consideration which is less than the market value of the assets transferred or for no consideration; and different assets may be so transferred by a board to different persons[7].

1 Ie under the Industrial Training Act 1982 s 1: see PARA 658.
2 As to the meaning of 'industrial training order' see PARA 658 note 6.
3 As to the meaning of 'industrial training board' see PARA 658 note 7.
4 As to the Secretary of State see PARA 5 note 21.
5 The provisions of the Industrial Training Act 1982 s 15(5)–(9) (see PARA 665) apply in relation to any direction so given as they apply in relation to any direction given under s 15(1) or s 15(2) (see PARA 665): s 3A(4) (s 3A added by the Employment Act 1989 s 24(1)). However, where any such direction is given in a case where an industrial training order is revoked, the provisions of the Industrial Training Act 1982 s 15(5)–(9) apply with the omission from s 15(6) of the words from 'during such period' onwards: s 3A(5) (as so added).
6 Industrial Training Act 1982 s 3A(1) (as added: see note 5). Such a transfer may be made in a case where an industrial training order is revoked even if the assets of the board concerned are, or will be after the transfer, insufficient to meet its liabilities and the expenses of the winding up of the board in pursuance of s 4(1) (see PARA 677): s 3A(3) (as so added). As to the meaning of 'employment' for these purposes see PARA 658 note 2.
7 Industrial Training Act 1982 s 3A(2) (as added: see note 5).

676. Transfer of staff employed by industrial training boards. If arrangements are made[1] for any activities of an industrial training board[2] to be carried on by some other person (the 'transferee') as from a particular date, the following provisions have effect in relation to any employee[3] of the board who, immediately before that date, was employed[4] wholly or mainly in connection with those activities[5].

The statutory protection for employees affected by transfers of undertakings[6] applies in relation to any such employee of the board[7]; and, for the purposes of their application in relation to any such employee, the activities referred to above[8] are to be regarded, whether or not they would otherwise be so regarded:

(1) as constituting an undertaking[9] which is transferred from the board to the transferee on the date referred to above[10]; and
(2) as being so transferred by a transfer to which the statutory protection for employees affected by transfers of undertakings applies[11] and which is completed on that date[12].

1 Ie whether in connection with a transfer of assets under the Industrial Training Act 1982 s 3A(1) (see PARA 675) or otherwise.
2 As to the meaning of 'industrial training board' see PARA 658 note 7.
3 As to the meaning of 'employee' for these purposes see PARA 658 note 11.
4 As to the meaning of 'employed' for these purposes see PARA 658 note 2.
5 Industrial Training Act 1982 s 3B(1) (s 3B added by the Employment Act 1989 s 24(1)). A certificate issued by an industrial training board, in connection with any such arrangements as are referred to in the Industrial Training Act 1982 s 3B(1), to the effect that a person was, immediately before the date referred to therein, employed by the board wholly or mainly in connection with the activities to which the arrangements relate is conclusive evidence of the facts stated in the certificate: s 3B(4) (as so added).
6 Ie the Transfer of Undertakings (Protection of Employment) Regulations 2006, SI 2006/246: see PARA 137 et seq.
7 Industrial Training Act 1982 s 3B(2) (as added (see note 5); and amended by SI 2006/246).
8 Ie the activities referred to in the Industrial Training Act 1982 s 3B(1): see the text and notes 1–5.
9 Ie to which the Transfer of Undertakings (Protection of Employment) Regulations 2006, SI 2006/246, apply: see PARA 137.

10 Ie the date referred to in the Industrial Training Act 1982 s 3B(1) (see the text and notes 1–5).

11 Ie a transfer to which the Transfer of Undertakings (Protection of Employment) Regulations 2006, SI 2006/246, apply: see PARA 137.

12 Industrial Training Act 1982 s 3B(3) (s 3B as added (see note 5); s 3B(3) amended by SI 2006/246).

677. Winding up of industrial training boards. An order[1] revoking an industrial training order[2] (a 'revocation order') must provide for the winding up of the industrial training board[3].

A revocation order may provide:

(1) for the imposition of a levy[4] on employers[5] in the industry[6], whether or not exemption certificates[7] have been issued to them, other than such, if any, as may be exempted by the order, for the purposes of raising the whole or part of any amount by which the assets of the board[8] may be insufficient to meet its liabilities and the expenses of the winding up; and

(2) for any assets of the board which are not required to meet those liabilities and expenses to be transferred to the Secretary of State and for those assets to be applied for purposes specified in the order[9].

A revocation order making provision for the imposition of a levy may:

(a) provide for payments by way of levy to accrue due from day to day over a period specified in the order; and

(b) contain provisions as to the evidence by which a person's liability to the levy or his discharge of that liability may be established and as to the time at which any amount payable by any person by way of levy is, whether or not any period over which that amount accrues due has expired, to become due and recoverable by the board[10].

A person assessed to levy imposed under a revocation order may appeal to an employment tribunal[11]; and a revocation order imposing a levy must make provision as to the time within which such an appeal may be made[12].

1 Ie an order made under the Industrial Training Act 1982 s 1: see PARA 658.

2 As to the meaning of 'industrial training order' see PARA 658 note 6.

3 Industrial Training Act 1982 s 4(1). As to the meaning of 'industrial training board' see PARA 658 note 7. As to orders providing for such winding up see the Industrial Training (Iron and Steel Board) (Revocation) Order 1982, SI 1982/661; the Industrial Training (Clothing and Allied Products Board) (Revocation) Order 1990, SI 1990/2038; the Industrial Training (Hotel and Catering Board) (Revocation) Order 1990, SI 1990/2549; the Industrial Training (Offshore Petroleum Board) (Revocation) Order 1991, SI 1991/263; the Industrial Training (Plastics Processing Board) (Revocation) Order 1991, SI 1991/334; the Industrial Training (Road Transport Board) (Revocation) Order 1992, SI 1992/1895.

Where a revocation order has been made for the winding up of an industrial training board, the Secretary of State may out of moneys provided by Parliament pay: (1) such pension, superannuation allowance or gratuity to or in respect of the former chairman of the board as he may, with the approval of the Treasury, determine; and (2) such sums as he may so determine to the trustees of the Industrial Training Boards' Combined Pension Fund for the purpose of meeting the whole or part of any shortfall in the assets of the Fund referable to the pensions, superannuation allowances and gratuities payable in respect of the former officers and servants of the board: Industrial Training Act 1982 s 4(6). As to the Secretary of State see PARA 5 note 21; and as to the Treasury see CONSTITUTIONAL AND ADMINISTRATIVE LAW vol 20 (2014) PARA 262 et seq.

4 See PARA 678 et seq.

5 As to the meaning of 'employer' for these purposes see PARA 658 note 11.

6 As to the meaning of 'the industry' see PARA 660 note 4.

7 For these purposes, 'exemption certificate' has the meaning assigned to it by the Industrial Training Act 1982 s 13(1) (see PARA 681): s 1(2).

8 For these purposes, any reference to the assets of the board is a reference to the assets, if any, held by it after the making of any transfer or transfers under the Industrial Training Act 1982 s 3A(1) (see PARA 675): s 4(2) (amended by the Employment Act 1989 s 24(2)).
9 Industrial Training Act 1982 s 4(2) (as amended: see note 8). Any expenses and liabilities incurred by the board under s 10 (see PARA 668) are to be disregarded for these purposes: see s 10(3); and PARA 668 note 11.
10 Industrial Training Act 1982 s 4(3).
11 See PARA 1486 et seq.
12 Industrial Training Act 1982 s 4(4) (amended by the Employment Rights (Dispute Resolution) Act 1998 s 1(2)(a)).

(vi) Levies and Levy Orders; Exemption Certificates

A. LEVIES AND LEVY ORDERS

678. Levies. An industrial training board[1] may from time to time submit to the Secretary of State[2] proposals ('levy proposals') for the raising and collection of a levy to be imposed for the purpose of raising money towards meeting the board's expenses[3].

Levy proposals[4] must include:

(1) in relation to each levy period, proposals for exempting from the levy payable in respect of that levy period any employer[5] who, in view of the small number of his employees[6], ought, in the opinion of the board, to be exempted; and the Secretary of State must not make a levy order[7] in pursuance of levy proposals unless they provide, in relation to each levy period, for the exemption of employers who, in view of the small number of their employees, ought in his opinion to be exempted[8];

(2) such information or further information as the Secretary of State directs the board to furnish and any additional information which the board considers appropriate for the purpose of assisting him to reach specified[9] decisions[10].

Levy proposals may:

(a) include, in relation to any levy period, proposals for securing:
 (i) that any exemption certificates[11] issued by the board do not exempt from the whole or a portion of the levy payable in respect of that levy period the employers or some of the employers in the industry[12]; or
 (ii) that no exemption certificates are to be issued by the board[13],

 and the Secretary of State must not make a levy order in pursuance of any levy proposals unless he is satisfied that the proposals published[14] by the board provide for exemption certificates relating to levy[15] in such cases as he considers appropriate[16];

(b) provide for the amendment of a previous levy order and may make different provision in relation to different classes or descriptions of employer[17].

The Secretary of State must not make a levy order in pursuance of any levy proposals unless the amount of levy payable in respect of each levy period which, disregarding any exemption, he estimates would, if the order were made, be payable by virtue of it by any employer in the industry:

(A) does not exceed an amount which the Secretary of State estimates is equal to one per cent of the relevant emoluments in respect of the base period for that levy period[18]; or

(B) does exceed the amount mentioned in head (A) above but is considered by him to be appropriate in the circumstances[19].

1 As to the meaning of 'industrial training board' see PARA 658 note 7.
2 As to the Secretary of State see PARA 5 note 21.
3 Industrial Training Act 1982 s 11(1) (amended by the Employment Act 1989 Sch 4 para 10(1), (2), Sch 7 Pt I). Any expenses and liabilities incurred by the board under the Industrial Training Act 1982 s 10 (see PARA 668) are to be disregarded for these purposes: see s 10(3); and PARA 668 note 11. As to the exemption from levy in the case of establishments situated wholly or mainly in an enterprise zone see PARA 679.
4 For these purposes, 'levy proposals' has the meaning assigned to it by the Industrial Training Act 1982 s 11(1) (see the text to note 3): s 1(2). As to the Secretary of State's powers to direct the submission to him of levy proposals and to make default orders see PARA 665. For the avoidance of doubt, where before 16 November 1989 levy proposals were approved by the Training Commission under s 11(1), the proposals are not, by virtue of the Employment Act 1989 s 22(5), Sch 5 para 3(1) (see PARA 633), to be taken to have been approved by the Secretary of State: Sch 5 para 8(a). As to the Training Commission see PARA 633.

Levy proposals must provide for one or more periods ('levy periods') by reference to which a person's liability to levy is to be established and the levy period or periods must fall within the period of three years beginning with the day on which the levy order giving effect to the proposals is made; levy proposals may not provide for more than three levy periods: Industrial Training Act 1982 s 1(2) (definition added by the Further Education and Training Act 2007 Sch 1 paras 1, 2(c)); Industrial Training Act 1982 s 11(2A) (s 11(2A)–(2E) added by the Further Education and Training Act 2007 s 25(1), (2)). The Industrial and Training Act 1982 s 11(2A) is subject to s 11(2C), (2D) (see below): s 11(2B) (as so added). If the levy order giving effect to levy proposals submitted by an industrial training board would be the first or second levy order giving effect to proposals submitted by the board, the proposals may instead provide for a single levy period that falls within the period of one year starting with the day on which the levy order giving effect to the proposals is made: s 11(2C) (as so added). No levy order may be made in reliance upon s 11(6)(b) (see note 16 head (b)) unless the proposals in pursuance of which the order would be made provide for a single levy period that falls within the period of one year starting with the day on which the levy order giving effect to the proposals is made: s 11(2D) (as so added).

Levy proposals must specify, for each levy period, a period (a 'base period') by reference to which the relevant emoluments are to be calculated: s 1(2) (definition added by the Further Education and Training Act 2007 Sch 1 paras 1, 2(a)); Industrial Training Act 1982 s 11(2E) (as so added).

'Relevant emoluments', in relation to any person, means the aggregate of the emoluments and payments intended to be disbursed as emoluments which are paid and payable by him to or in respect of persons employed in the industry in respect of the period specified in the levy proposals as a base period: s 11(8) (amended by the Further Education and Training Act 2007 ss 24(1), (5), 25(1), (5)).
5 As to the meaning of 'employer' for these purposes see PARA 658 note 11.
6 As to the meaning of 'employee' for these purposes see PARA 658 note 11.
7 For these purposes, 'levy order' has the meaning assigned to it by the Industrial Training Act 1982 s 11(2) (see PARA 680): s 1(2).
8 Industrial Training Act 1982 s 11(3) (amended by the Further Education and Training Act 2007 Sch 1 paras 1, 3(1), (2)).
9 Ie for the purpose of assisting him to decide: (1) in a case where the levy proposals include such proposals as are mentioned in the Industrial Training Act 1982 s 11(4) (see head (a) in the text), whether a levy order made in pursuance of them would fall within s 11(5) (see note 16) and, if so, whether the condition mentioned in s 11(6)(a) (see note 16 head (a)) would be satisfied (see s 12(1)(a)); and (2) whether a levy order made in pursuance of the proposals would fall within s 11(7)(a) or (b) (see heads (A), (B) in the text) (see s 12(1)(b)).

Where a levy order (the 'new levy order') giving effect to levy proposals submitted by an industrial training board will be made (a) after the making of a levy order (the 'earlier levy order') that gives effect to earlier proposals submitted by the board; and (b) within three years or, where the earlier levy order provides for a single levy period in accordance with s 11(2C) or (2D) (see note 4), within one year after the making of the earlier levy order, the proposals for the new levy order must include proposals for securing that no liability to levy is imposed under the earlier levy order by reference to such part of a levy period provided for in the earlier levy order as falls on or after the day on which the new levy order is made: s 12(1A), (1B) (added by the Further Education and Training Act 2007 s 25(6)).

10 Industrial Training Act 1982 s 12(1) (amended by the Employment Act 1989 Sch 4 para 11). A levy order which falls within the Industrial Training Act 1982 s 11(5) in a case where the condition mentioned in s 11(6)(c) (see note 16 head (c)) is satisfied or which falls within s 11(7)(b) must state that fact: s 12(1) (as so amended).

11 As to the meaning of 'exemption certificate' see PARA 677 note 7.

12 Industrial Training Act 1982 s 11(4)(a) (s 11 and s 11(4)(a) amended by the Further Education and Training Act 2007 Sch 1 paras 1, 3(1)(b), 3(3)(a)). As to the meaning of 'the industry' see PARA 660 note 4.

13 Industrial Training Act 1982 s 11(4)(b).

14 Ie under the Industrial Training Act 1982 s 13(5): see PARA 681.

15 Ie other than that payable by virtue of the Industrial Training Act 1982 s 11(4) (see the text and note 16).

16 Industrial Training Act 1982 s 11(4) (amended by the Further Education and Training Act 2007 Sch 1 para 1, 3(3)(c)). If, as a result of such levy proposals: (1) in a case within the Industrial Training Act 1982 s 11(4)(a) (see head (a)(i) in the text), the amount of the levy payable in respect of a levy period from which an exemption certificate will not exempt any person will exceed 0.2% of the relevant emoluments in respect of the base period for that levy period; or (2) in a case within s 11(4)(b) (see head (a)(ii) in the text), the amount of the levy payable by any person in respect of a levy period will exceed that percentage of the relevant emoluments in respect of the base period for that levy period, then the Secretary of State may not make a levy order in pursuance of the levy proposals unless he is satisfied that they are necessary to encourage adequate training in the industry and one of the specified conditions is satisfied: s 11(5) (amended by the Employment Act 1989 Sch 4 para 10(1), (4); and the Further Education and Training Act 2007 Sch 1 paras 1, 3(4)(a), (b)).

The conditions specified above are: (a) that the Secretary of State is satisfied that (i) the board has taken reasonable steps to ascertain the views of persons who the Secretary of State considers are likely to be liable to make payments by way of levy in consequence of the levy proposals; and (ii) a class of persons, who together satisfy the requirements in the Industrial Training Act 1982 s 11(6A) (see below), considers that the proposals are necessary to encourage adequate training in the industry; (b) that the order will be made: (i) after the making of a levy order (the 'earlier levy order') in respect of which the Secretary of State was satisfied that the condition in head (a) above applied; and (ii) within the period described in s 11(6E) (see below), and the condition in s 11(6F) or s 11(6G) (see below) is satisfied; (c) that neither of the conditions mentioned in heads (a), (b) above applies but the proposals are considered by the Secretary of State to be appropriate in the circumstances: Industrial Training Act 1982 s 11(6) (amended by the Further Education and Training Act 2007 ss 24(1), (2), 25(1), (3)).

The requirements referred to head (a) above are that: (A) the class must consist of more than half of those persons who the Secretary of State considers are likely to be liable to make payments by way of levy in consequence of the levy proposals; and (B) the class must include such persons as the Secretary of State considers are together likely to be liable to make payments by way of levy in consequence of the levy proposals which amount to more than half the aggregate amount of those payments: Industrial Training Act 1982 s 11(6A) (s 11(6A)–(6G) added by the Further Education and Training Act 2007 s 24(1), (3), (4)). The Secretary of State may by regulations make provision as to what constitutes 'reasonable steps' for the purposes of head (a) above: Industrial Training Act 1982 s 11(6B) (as so added). Regulations under s 11(6B) may include: provision for ascertaining the views of persons with respect to levy proposals by means of a sample of those persons; provision for treating a person who is represented by an organisation of such description as may be prescribed by the regulations as having the same view as the organisation with respect to levy proposals: s 11(6C) (as so added). Regulations under s 11(6B) must be made by statutory instrument which must be subject to annulment in pursuance of a resolution of either House of Parliament: s 11(6D) (as so added). The period mentioned in head (b)(ii) above is: if the earlier levy order provides for such levy periods as are referred to in s 11(2A) (see note 4), the period beginning with the third anniversary and ending with the fourth anniversary of the making of the earlier levy order; if the earlier levy order provides for such levy period as is referred to in s 11(2C) (see note 4), the period beginning with the first anniversary and ending with the second anniversary of the making of the earlier levy order: s 11(6E) (as so added). The condition in s 11(6F) is that the proposals relating to the earlier levy order included proposals for securing: that no exemption certificates should be issued; or that the exemption certificates to be issued should not exempt employers from any of the levy payable in respect of any levy period: s 11(6F) (as so added). The condition in s 11(6G) is that: the proposals in pursuance of which the earlier levy order was made included proposals for securing that exemption certificates should not exempt employers from a portion of the levy payable in respect of a levy period; and the percentage of the relevant emoluments from which under the current proposals the exemption certificates will not exempt any person will not exceed the percentage of the relevant emoluments in respect of any of the base periods specified in the earlier levy order from which that person was not exempted under that order: s 11(6G) (as so added). As to the meaning of 'relevant emoluments' see note 4. As to regulations made under s 11(6B), (6C) see the Industrial Training Levy (Reasonable Steps) Regulations 2008, SI 2008/1639.

17 Industrial Training Act 1982 s 12(2). In particular: (1) proposals made in pursuance of s 11(3) (see head (1) in the text) may be made in respect of different numbers of employees for different employers or classes of employers and may provide for numbers of employees or for employers or classes of employers to be determined by reference to such factors as are specified in the proposals; and (2) different proposals may be made in pursuance of s 11(4) (see head (a) in the text) as respects different portions of the levy: s 12(2)(a), (b).

18 Industrial Training Act 1982 s 11(7)(a) (s 11(7) and s 11(7)(a) amended by the Further Education and Training Act 2007 Sch 1 paras 1, 3(5)). As to the meaning of 'relevant emoluments' see note 4.

19 Industrial Training Act 1982 s 11(7)(b).

679. Enterprise zones. No employer[1] is liable to any levy[2] in respect of any establishment situated wholly or mainly within an area designated as an enterprise zone[3]; and, for the purposes of any levy order[4], such an establishment is to be treated as if it were not carrying on business[5]. No levy is to be imposed by reference to emoluments paid or payable to an employee[6] whose employment[7] is carried on at or from any such establishment[8].

1 As to the meaning of 'employer' for these purposes see PARA 658 note 11.

2 Ie under the Industrial Training Act 1982: see PARA 678.

3 Ie under the Local Government, Planning and Land Act 1980 s 179, Sch 32: see PLANNING vol 83 (2010) PARA 1640 et seq.

4 As to the meaning of 'levy order' see PARA 678 note 7.

5 Industrial Training Act 1982 s 16(1). As to the power to exclude or modify the application of s 16 in specified cases see PARA 670 note 6.

6 As to the meaning of 'employee' for these purposes see PARA 658 note 11.

7 As to the meaning of 'employment' for these purposes see PARA 658 note 2.

8 Industrial Training Act 1982 s 16(2).

680. Levy orders. A levy to be imposed for the purpose of raising money towards meeting the expenses of an industrial training board[1] must be imposed in accordance with an order made by the Secretary of State[2] (a 'levy order') which must give effect to levy proposals[3] submitted[4] to him and must provide for the levy to be imposed on employers[5] in the industry[6], except in so far as they are exempted from it by the industrial training order[7], the levy order or an exemption certificate[8]; but nothing in the Industrial Training Act 1982 is to be construed as requiring the Secretary of State to make a levy order in a case in which he considers it inexpedient to make one[9].

A levy order may:

(1) provide for payments by way of levy to accrue due from day to day over a levy period;

(2) contain provisions as to the evidence by which a person's liability to the levy or his discharge of that liability may be established and as to the time at which any amount payable by any person by way of the levy is, whether or not any period over which that amount accrues due has expired, to become due and recoverable by the industrial training board[10].

A person assessed to levy imposed under a levy order may appeal to an employment tribunal[11]; and the levy order must make provision as to the time within which such an appeal may be made[12].

1 See PARA 678.
2 As to the Secretary of State see PARA 5 note 21.
3 As to the meaning of 'levy proposals' see PARA 678 note 4.
4 Ie under the Industrial Training Act 1982 s 11(1): see PARA 678.
5 As to the meaning of 'employer' for these purposes see PARA 658 note 11.
6 As to the meaning of 'the industry' see PARA 660 note 4.
7 As to the meaning of 'industrial training order' see PARA 658 note 6.
8 As to the meaning of 'exemption certificate' see PARA 677 note 7.
9 Industrial Training Act 1982 s 11(2) (amended by the Employment Act 1989 Sch 4 para 10(1), (3)). The power to make a levy order is exercisable by statutory instrument, which is subject to annulment in pursuance of a resolution of either House of Parliament unless the instrument contains only an order which includes such a statement as is mentioned in the Industrial Training Act 1982 s 11(1) (see PARA 678); and no levy order which includes such a statement is to be made unless a draft of the order has been approved by a resolution of each House of Parliament: s 12(6). See eg the Industrial Training Levy (Construction Board) Order 2005, SI 2005/546 (superseded by SI 2006/334); the Industrial Training Levy (Engineering Construction Board) Order 2005, SI 2005/2089 (superseded by SI 2006/335); the Industrial Training Levy (Construction Board) Order 2006, SI 2006/334 (superseded by SI 2007/607); the Industrial Training Levy (Engineering Construction Board) Order 2006, SI 2006/335 (superseded by SI 2007/609); the Industrial Training Levy (Construction Industry Training Board) Order 2007, SI 2007/607 (superseded by SI 2008/534); the Industrial Training Levy (Engineering Construction Industry Training Board) Order 2007, SI 2007/609 (superseded by SI 2008/534); the Industrial Training Levy (Construction Industry Training Board) Order 2008, SI 2008/534 (superseded by SI 2009/549); the Industrial Training Levy (Engineering Construction Industry Training Board) Order 2008, SI 2008/535 (superseded by SI 2009/548); the Industrial Training Levy (Engineering Construction Industry Training Board) Order 2009, SI 2009/548; the Industrial Training Levy (Construction Industry Training Board) Order 2009, SI 2009/549; the Industrial Training Levy (Construction Industry Training Board) Order 2012, SI 2012/958; the Industrial Training Levy (Engineering Construction Industry Training Board) Order 2012, SI 2012/959; the Industrial Training Levy (Engineering Construction Industry Training Board) Order 2013, SI 2013/1397; and the Industrial Training Levy (Engineering Construction Industry Training Board) Order 2014, SI 2014/791.
10 Industrial Training Act 1982 s 12(3) (amended by the Further Education and Training Act 2007 Sch 1 para 4). As to orders see note 9.
11 See PARA 1486 et seq.
12 Industrial Training Act 1982 s 12(4) (amended by the Employment Rights (Dispute Resolution) Act 1998 s 1(2)(a)). As to orders see note 9. The courts have no jurisdiction to determine liability for a levy: *Road Transport Industry Training Board v J Wyatt Junior (Haulage) Ltd* [1973] QB 469, [1972] 3 All ER 913.

B. EXEMPTION CERTIFICATES

681. Proposals for exemption certificates. An industrial training board[1] may from time to time, and must[2] always at or before the time when it submits[3] levy proposals[4], submit to the Secretary of State[5] for his approval proposals for the issue of certificates ('exemption certificates') which, while in force, are to exempt from relevant levy[6] employers in the industry who:

(1) make arrangements for the training, or the training and post-school education[7] associated with training, of persons employed[8] or to be employed in the industry; and
(2) satisfy the board by reference to criteria[9] specified in the proposals that the arrangements are adequate and are to a material extent being implemented[10].

However, an industrial training board is not obliged to submit proposals for the issue of exemption certificates to any category of employer at or before the time when it submits levy proposals in respect of a levy on those employers which include:

(a) proposals that no exemption certificates will be issued by the board to employers in that category; or

(b) proposals by virtue of which the levy payable in respect of each levy period[11] by any employer in that category, disregarding any exemptions, will not exceed 0.2 per cent of the relevant emoluments[12] in respect of the base period[13] for that levy period; or

(c) proposals[14] by virtue of which any exemption certificates issued to those employers will not exempt them from any of the levy payable by virtue of the resulting levy order[15].

If the Secretary of State approves proposals submitted to him by a board and informs the board of his approval, the board must arrange for them to be published as soon as practicable in a manner approved by the Secretary of State[16].

1 As to the meaning of 'industrial training board' see PARA 658 note 7.

2 Ie subject to the Industrial Training Act 1982 s 13(2): see the text and notes 11–15.

3 Ie under the Industrial Training Act 1982 s 11: see PARA 678.

4 As to the meaning of 'levy proposals' see PARA 678 note 4.

5 As to the Secretary of State see PARA 5 note 21.

6 For these purposes, 'relevant levy' means levy which, apart from any exemption certificate, is payable to the board in question by virtue of the Industrial Training Act 1982 by employers in the industry, other than levy which the levy order authorising it provides is to be payable notwithstanding any exemption certificate: s 13(1). As to the meaning of 'employer' for these purposes see PARA 658 note 11; and as to the meaning of 'the industry' see PARA 660 note 4.

7 For these purposes, 'post-school education' has the same meaning as in the Industrial Training Act 1982 s 5 (see PARA 666 note 5): s 13(1) (amended by the Education Reform Act 1988 Sch 12 para 88).

8 As to the meaning of 'employed' for these purposes see PARA 658 note 2.

9 The criteria must relate to the quality or amount of training, or training and education, provided for by the arrangements, but need not relate solely to the needs of establishments of the employers; and the proposals may specify different criteria as respects arrangements made by different categories of employers: Industrial Training Act 1982 s 13(3). The Secretary of State may issue guidance concerning the criteria which are to be specified in proposals submitted: s 13(4) (amended by the Employment Act 1989 Sch 4 para 12(1), (3), Sch 7 Pt I).

10 Industrial Training Act 1982 s 13(1) (amended by the Education Reform Act 1988 Sch 12 para 88; and the Employment Act 1989 Sch 4 para 12(1), (2)). Proposals made by a board:

(1) must include proposals as to the arrangements for the reconsideration of decisions in pursuance of the Industrial Training Act 1982 s 14(5) (see PARA 683); and

(2) may include proposals for altering or cancelling any previous proposals made by the board in pursuance of s 13(1),

but proposals made by virtue of head (2) above do not affect the operation of any exemption certificates issued in pursuance of previous proposals: s 13(6). As to the Secretary of State's powers to direct the submission to him of proposals for exemption certificates, and to make default orders, see PARA 665.

11 As to the meaning of 'levy period' see PARA 678 note 4.

12 As to meaning of 'relevant emoluments' see PARA 678 note 4, definition applied by the Industrial Training Act 1982 s 13(2) (amended by the Further Education and Training Act 2007 Sch 1 paras 1, 5(4)).

13 As to the meaning of 'base period' see PARA 678 note 4.

14 Ie proposals within the Industrial Training Act 1982 s 11(4)(a): see PARA 678.

15 Industrial Training Act 1982 s 13(2) (amended by the Further Education and Training Act 2007 Sch 1 paras 1, 5(1), (2), (3)).

16 Industrial Training Act 1982 s 13(5) (substituted by the Employment Act 1989 Sch 4 para 12(1), (4)). For the avoidance of doubt, where before 16 November 1989 proposals for the issue of exemption certificates were approved by the Training Commission under the Industrial Training Act 1982 s 13, the proposals are not, by virtue of the Employment Act 1989 s 22(5), Sch 5 para 3(1) (see PARA 633) to be taken to have been approved by the Secretary of State: Sch 5 para 8(b). As to the Training Commission see PARA 633.

682. Exemption certificates. Where an industrial training board[1] is satisfied, on an application made in writing[2] to the board by an employer[3] otherwise liable[4] to pay to the board any levy from which exemption may be conferred on him by an exemption certificate[5], that the arrangements made by him for the training, or the training and post-school education[6] associated with training, of persons employed[7] or to be employed in the industry[8] are such that, in accordance with proposals published[9] by the board, an exemption certificate falls to be issued to him in respect of any establishment of his, it is the duty of the board to issue such a certificate to him[10].

A person to whom an exemption certificate is issued (the 'holder') is exempt, while the certificate is in force, from levy payable to the board[11] in respect of persons employed at the establishment to which the certificate relates, other than levy which the levy order authorising it provides is to be payable notwithstanding any exemption certificate[12].

An exemption certificate:

(1) may require the holder to comply with such conditions relating to the training, or the training and education, of persons employed or to be employed in the industry, including, in particular, conditions as to the inspection on behalf of the relevant board of the arrangements for the training or the training and education, as are specified in the certificate and are in accordance with the proposals mentioned[13] above[14];

(2) must specify the date on which the certificate is to come into force[15];

(3) must specify the period, not exceeding three years beginning with that date, at the expiration of which it ceases to be in force, unless it has previously ceased[16] to be in force[17];

(4) may provide that the certificate is to be deemed to have been in force for such period before the date on which it comes into force as is specified in the certificate, which may not begin before the period of one year ending with the date on which the board received the application in pursuance of which it issues the certificate[18],

and any levy paid to the board by a person for a period in respect of which, by virtue of head (4) above, it becomes not payable is repayable by the board to that person[19].

An exemption certificate issued by an industrial training board ceases to be in force if the board gives notice in writing to the holder stating that, in the opinion of the board, he has failed to comply with conditions specified in the certificate and mentioned in the notice; but a notice so given must be disregarded[20] if the board subsequently informs the person to whom it was given that the notice is withdrawn[21].

1 As to the meaning of 'industrial training board' see PARA 658 note 7.
2 As to the meaning of 'writing' see PARA 2 note 8.
3 As to the meaning of 'employer' for these purposes see PARA 658 note 11.
4 Ie apart from the Industrial Training Act 1982 s 14.
5 As to the meaning of 'exemption certificate' see PARA 677 note 7.
6 For these purposes, 'post-school education' has the same meaning as in the Industrial Training Act 1982 s 5 (see PARA 666 note 5): s 14(1A) (added by the Education Reform Act 1988 Sch 12 para 89).
7 As to the meaning of 'employed' for these purposes see PARA 658 note 2.
8 As to the meaning of 'the industry' see PARA 660 note 4.
9 Ie in pursuance of the Industrial Training Act 1982 s 13: see PARA 681.
10 Industrial Training Act 1982 s 14(1) (amended by the Education Reform Act 1988 Sch 12 para 89).
11 Ie by virtue of the Industrial Training Act 1982.

12 Industrial Training Act 1982 s 14(2).
13 Ie mentioned in the Industrial Training Act 1982 s 14(1).
14 Industrial Training Act 1982 s 14(3)(a).
15 Industrial Training Act 1982 s 14(3)(b).
16 Ie by virtue of the Industrial Training Act 1982 s 14(4): see the text and notes 20–21.
17 Industrial Training Act 1982 s 14(3)(c).
18 Industrial Training Act 1982 s 14(3)(d).
19 Industrial Training Act 1982 s 14(3).
20 Ie for the purposes of the Industrial Training Act 1982 s 14(1)–(3): see the text and notes 1–19.
21 Industrial Training Act 1982 s 14(4).

C. REFERENCES

(A) In general

683. Right to make a reference. If a person who is liable, apart from any exemption certificate[1], to pay an industrial training board levy[2], from which exemption may be conferred by an exemption certificate, is dissatisfied with the decision of the board:

(1) to refuse to issue to him an exemption certificate relating to such levy in respect of a particular establishment; or
(2) to refuse to include in an exemption certificate issued to him authorised provisions[3]; or
(3) to include in an exemption certificate provisions requiring him to comply with conditions; or
(4) to give a notice of non-compliance[4] to him,

and requests the board in writing[5] to reconsider the decision, it is the duty of the board to reconsider it or to secure that it is reconsidered by a committee authorised[6] to deal with such requests; and if, on reconsidering the decision, the board or committee decides not to alter it, or not to alter it in a manner which the person who made the request considers is satisfactory, that person may refer the decision to a body established[7] by regulations made by the Secretary of State[8].

No appeal lies to an employment tribunal in respect of such a decision[9].

1 As to the meaning of 'exemption certificate' see PARA 677 note 7.
2 As to industrial training board levies see PARA 678 et seq. As to the meaning of 'industrial training board' see PARA 658 note 7.
3 Ie provisions or different provisions authorised by the Industrial Training Act 1982 s 14(3)(b) (see PARA 682) or s 14(3)(d) (see PARA 682).
4 Ie a notice given to him in pursuance of the Industrial Training Act 1982 s 14(4): see PARA 682.
5 As to the meaning of 'writing' see PARA 2 note 8.
6 Ie authorised by virtue of the Industrial Training Act 1982 s 2(1): see PARA 663.
7 Ie established in pursuance of the Industrial Training Act 1982 s 14(6): see PARA 684.
8 Industrial Training Act 1982 s 14(5). As to the Secretary of State see PARA 5 note 21. For the purpose of hearing and determining references under s 14(5), referees must be established in accordance with the Industrial Training (Levy Exemption References) Regulations 1974, SI 1974/1335, which have effect in relation to such references as if made under the Industrial Training Act 1982, s 14(6), (7) (see PARA 684).
9 Industrial Training Act 1982 s 14(9) (amended by the Employment Rights (Dispute Resolution) Act 1998 s 1(2)(a)).

684. Regulations. It is the duty of the Secretary of State[1] to make regulations establishing a body to which decisions relating to exemption certificates are to be referred[2]; and regulations so made may include provisions as to the powers and procedure of the body and such other provisions, including provisions for defraying the body's expenses out of moneys provided by Parliament or otherwise, as the Secretary of State considers appropriate for the purpose of facilitating the exercise by the body of its functions[3].

Regulations so made may[4]:

(1) require an industrial training board[5] to draw the attention of a person to his right to refer a decision to the body;

(2) authorise the body to direct a board whose decision is referred to the body to alter the decision in a manner specified in the direction; and

(3) require the board to comply with the direction and provide for any case in which it fails to do so[6].

1 As to the Secretary of State see PARA 5 note 21.
2 Ie in pursuance of the Industrial Training Act 1982 s 14(5): see PARA 683.
3 Industrial Training Act 1982 s 14(6). Such regulations must be made by statutory instrument which is subject to annulment in pursuance of a resolution of either House of Parliament: s 14(8). At the date at which this volume states the law no such regulations had been made but, by virtue of the Interpretation Act 1978 s 17(2)(b), the Industrial Training (Levy Exemption References) Regulations 1974, SI 1974/1335 (see PARA 685 et seq) have effect as if so made.
4 Ie without prejudice to the generality of the Industrial Training Act 1982 s 14(6): see the text and notes 1–3.
5 As to the meaning of 'industrial training board' see PARA 658 note 7.
6 Industrial Training Act 1982 s 14(7).

(B) Procedure

(a) The Referees; Secretary to the Referees

685. Establishment of the referees. For the purpose of hearing and determining references[1] concerning decisions of industrial training boards, there must be established referees in accordance with the following provisions[2].

The referees are to consist of the following persons:

(1) a person appointed by the Secretary of State[3] to be the President[4] together with such number of persons as the Secretary of State sees fit to appoint to be chairmen;

(2) such number of persons as the Secretary of State sees fit to appoint to be members, being persons so appointed after consultation with organisations representing employers; and

(3) such number of persons as the Secretary of State sees fit to appoint to be members, being persons so appointed after consultation with organisations representing employees[5].

The expenses of the referees must be defrayed by the Secretary of State out of moneys provided by Parliament; and the Secretary of State may out of such moneys pay to the President, chairmen, members and to any assessors such remuneration and allowances, including allowances for loss of remunerative time, as he may determine with the approval of the Treasury[6].

The President, chairmen and members so appointed hold and must vacate office under the terms of the instruments under which they are appointed, but they may resign office by notice in writing[7] to the Secretary of State; and any such person who ceases to hold office is eligible for reappointment[8].

If the President is for any reason unable to act, or during a vacancy in his office, his functions may be discharged by a person nominated for that purpose by the Secretary of State[9].

The referees sit in divisions[10] and two or more such divisions may sit at the same time[11].

1 Ie under the Industrial Training Act 1982 s 14(5): see PARA 683. The Industrial Training (Levy Exemption References) Regulations 1974, SI 1974/1335, have effect in relation to such references as if made under the Industrial Training Act 1982, s 14(6), (7) (see PARA 684); and the rules of procedure that are contained in Schedule (see also PARA 686 et seq) have effect specifically in relation to such references (see reg 6).

2 Industrial Training (Levy Exemption References) Regulations 1974, SI 1974/1335, reg 3(1); Interpretation Act 1978 s 17(2)(a). For these purposes, 'referees' means the referees so established and, in relation to a particular reference, the division to whom that reference has been assigned: Industrial Training (Levy Exemption References) Regulations 1974, SI 1974/1335, reg 2(1).

Any act, other than the hearing of a reference (see PARA 696) and the determination of a reference (see PARA 697), required or authorised to be done by the referees may be done by, or on the direction of, the chairman of the referees to whom a reference has been assigned or by the President: Schedule r 10(4). As to the meaning of 'President' see note 4; and as to the meaning of 'chairman' see PARA 689 note 5.

3 As to the Secretary of State see PARA 5 note 21.

4 For these purposes, 'President' means the President of the referees or the person nominated by the Secretary of State to discharge for the time being the functions of the President: Industrial Training (Levy Exemption References) Regulations 1974, SI 1974/1335, reg 2(1).

5 Industrial Training (Levy Exemption References) Regulations 1974, SI 1974/1335, reg 3(3).

6 Industrial Training (Levy Exemption References) Regulations 1974, SI 1974/1335, reg 3(4); Transfer of Functions (Minister for the Civil Service and Treasury) Order 1981, SI 1981/1670, art 2(2). As to the Treasury see CONSTITUTIONAL AND ADMINISTRATIVE LAW vol 20 (2014) PARA 262 et seq.

7 As to the meaning of 'writing' see PARA 2 note 8.

8 Industrial Training (Levy Exemption References) Regulations 1974, SI 1974/1335, reg 3(5).

9 Industrial Training (Levy Exemption References) Regulations 1974, SI 1974/1335, reg 3(6).

10 Ie in accordance with the Industrial Training (Levy Exemption References) Regulations 1974, SI 1974/1335, reg 5: see PARA 689.

11 Industrial Training (Levy Exemption References) Regulations 1974, SI 1974/1335, reg 3(2).

686. Secretary to the referees. The Secretary of State[1] must appoint a secretary to the referees[2] and may appoint such other persons as he thinks fit to be assistant secretaries[3]; and it is the duty of the secretary[4] and any assistant secretaries to make all necessary arrangements for the proper and expeditious determination of references[5].

The secretary and any assistant secretaries must carry out their duties in accordance with the general and special directions of the President[6].

1 As to the Secretary of State see PARA 5 note 21.

2 As to the meaning of 'referees' see PARA 685 note 2.

3 Industrial Training (Levy Exemption References) Regulations 1974, SI 1974/1335, reg 4(1).

4 For these purposes, 'secretary' means the secretary to the referees for the time being; and references to 'the secretary' are to be taken to include an assistant secretary: Industrial Training (Levy Exemption References) Regulations 1974, SI 1974/1335, reg 2(1).

5 Industrial Training (Levy Exemption References) Regulations 1974, SI 1974/1335, reg 4(2).

6 Industrial Training (Levy Exemption References) Regulations 1974, SI 1974/1335, reg 4(3). As to the meaning of 'President' see PARA 685 note 4.

(b) Preliminary Procedure

687. Reference of decision. Within six months from the date on which he receives from the board[1] notice of its determination not to alter its decision or not to alter it to the satisfaction of the applicant[2], the applicant must refer the decision to the referees by sending a notice to the secretary[3] setting out:

(1) the name and address of the applicant; and

(2) the grounds of the reference and, in particular, in what respects the decision of the board is alleged to be unsatisfactory[4].

If they think fit, the referees may dismiss the reference if the applicant at any time gives notice of the abandonment of his reference[5].

1 For these purposes, the 'board' means, in relation to a reference, the respondent industrial training board: Industrial Training (Levy Exemption References) Regulations 1974, SI 1974/1335, reg 2(1). As to the meaning of 'industrial training board' see PARA 658 note 7.
2 For these purposes, the 'applicant' means, in relation to a reference, the person who, having applied for or being the holder of an exemption certificate, refers the relevant decision of the board under the Industrial Training Act 1982 s 14(5) (see PARA 683) for determination by the referees: Industrial Training (Levy Exemption References) Regulations 1974, SI 1974/1335, reg 2(1); Interpretation Act 1978 s 17(2)(a). As to the meaning of 'referees' see PARA 685 note 2. As to the meaning of 'exemption certificate' see PARA 677 note 7.
3 As to the meaning of 'secretary' see PARA 686 note 4.
4 Industrial Training (Levy Exemption References) Regulations 1974, SI 1974/1335, reg 6, Schedule r 1.
5 Industrial Training (Levy Exemption References) Regulations 1974, SI 1974/1335, Schedule r 10(1)(c).

688. Registration of reference. On receiving a notice[1], the secretary[2] must enter particulars of the reference in the register of references[3] and must forthwith send a copy of the notice to the board[4] and must inform the board and the applicant[5] in writing[6] of the number of the reference entered in the register which thereafter constitutes the title of the reference[7].

On receiving the copy of the notice, the board must forthwith send to the secretary and to the applicant a copy of the minute of the decision together with a statement of the reasons for that decision and the facts relied on to support it[8].

1 Ie under the Industrial Training (Levy Exemption References) Regulations 1974, SI 1974/1335, reg 6, Schedule r 1: see PARA 687.
2 As to the meaning of 'the secretary' see PARA 686 note 4.
3 For these purposes, the 'register of references' means the register of references kept in pursuance of the Industrial Training (Levy Exemption References) Regulations 1974, SI 1974/1335: reg 2(1). As to references see PARA 687.
4 As to the meaning of 'board' see PARA 687 note 1.
5 As to the meaning of 'applicant' see PARA 687 note 2.
6 As to the meaning of 'writing' see PARA 2 note 8.
7 Industrial Training (Levy Exemption References) Regulations 1974, SI 1974/1335, Schedule r 2(1).
8 Industrial Training (Levy Exemption References) Regulations 1974, SI 1974/1335, Schedule r 2(2).

689. Assignment of references. A reference[1] must be assigned by the secretary[2] to a division of the referees[3] consisting of:

(1) the President[4] or a chairman[5] who must preside;
(2) one member selected from those appointed[6] by the Secretary of State after consultation with organisations representing employers; and
(3) one member selected from those appointed[7] by the Secretary of State after consultation with organisations representing employees[8].

If for any reason it becomes necessary, the secretary may at any time make such substitutions as respects the persons to whom a reference has been assigned as may be appropriate[9].

With the consent of both parties, a reference may be heard in the absence of any one member of the division other than the President or, as the case may be, the chairman; and in such a case the division is deemed to be properly constituted[10].

1 Ie a reference under the Industrial Training (Levy Exemption References) Regulations 1974, SI 1974/1335, reg 6, Schedule r 1: see PARA 687.

2 As to the meaning of 'secretary' see PARA 686 note 4.
3 As to the meaning of 'referees' see PARA 685 note 2.
4 As to the meaning of 'President' see PARA 685 note 4.
5 For these purposes, a 'chairman' means the President or a person appointed to be a chairman; and, in relation to a reference which has been assigned to a division of the referees under the Industrial Training (Levy Exemption References) Regulations 1974, SI 1974/1335, reg 5, means the President or the chairman of that division, as the case may require: reg 2(1).
6 Ie under the Industrial Training (Levy Exemption References) Regulations 1974, SI 1974/1335, reg 3(3)(b): see PARA 685 head (2).
7 Ie under the Industrial Training (Levy Exemption References) Regulations 1974, SI 1974/1335, reg 3(3)(c): see PARA 685 head (3).
8 Industrial Training (Levy Exemption References) Regulations 1974, SI 1974/1335, reg 5(1).
9 Industrial Training (Levy Exemption References) Regulations 1974, SI 1974/1335, reg 5(2).
10 Industrial Training (Levy Exemption References) Regulations 1974, SI 1974/1335, reg 5(3). The reference must otherwise be heard by a full division: see Schedule r 10(4); and PARA 685 note 2.

690. Notices etc. Any notice required[1] must be in writing[2], and all notices and documents required or authorised[3] to be sent or given to any person may be sent by the recorded delivery service[4] or delivered:

(1) in the case of a document directed to the secretary[5], to the office of the referees[6];
(2) in the case of a document directed to a board[7], to the office of the board;
(3) in the case of a document directed to the applicant[8], to his address for service specified in any notice given[9], or to his last known address or place of business in the United Kingdom[10] or, if the applicant is a company, to the company's registered office[11],

and, if sent or given to the authorised representative of the applicant or the board, is deemed to have been sent or given to him or the board, as the case may be[12].

The applicant may at any time by notice to the secretary, to the referees and to the board change his address for service[13].

1 Ie by the Industrial Training (Levy Exemption References) Regulations 1974, SI 1974/1335, reg 6, Schedule: see PARAS 685 et seq, 691 et seq.
2 As to the meaning of 'writing' see PARA 2 note 8.
3 See note 1.
4 As to the recorded delivery service see **POSTAL SERVICES** vol 85 (2012) PARA 203.
5 As to the meaning of 'secretary' see PARA 686 note 4.
6 As to the meaning of 'referees' see PARA 685 note 2.
7 As to the meaning of 'board' see PARA 687 note 1.
8 As to the meaning of 'applicant' see PARA 687 note 2.
9 Ie under the Industrial Training (Levy Exemption References) Regulations 1974, SI 1974/1335.
10 As to the meaning of 'United Kingdom' see PARA 2 note 12.
11 As to a company's registered office see **COMPANIES** vol 14 (2009) PARA 129.
12 Industrial Training (Levy Exemption References) Regulations 1974, SI 1974/1335, Schedule r 12(1).
13 Industrial Training (Levy Exemption References) Regulations 1974, SI 1974/1335, Schedule r 12(2).

(c) Interim Matters

691. Further particulars. The President[1], or a chairman[2] to whom a reference[3] has been assigned[4], may at any time direct either party to the reference to furnish any further particulars which appear to him to be requisite for the determination of the reference; and the party so directed must send the particulars to the secretary[5] and to the other party within 14 days of the receipt of the direction[6].

1 As to the meaning of 'President' see PARA 685 note 4.
2 As to the meaning of 'chairman' see PARA 689 note 5.
3 Ie a reference under the Industrial Training (Levy Exemption References) Regulations 1974, SI 1974/1335, reg 6, Schedule r 1: see PARA 687.
4 As to the assignment of references see PARA 689.
5 As to the meaning of 'secretary' see PARA 686 note 4.
6 Industrial Training (Levy Exemption References) Regulations 1974, SI 1974/1335, reg 6, Schedule r 3.

692. Extension of time; directions. If they think fit, the referees[1] may extend the time appointed[2] for doing any act, notwithstanding that the time appointed may have expired[3].

An application to the referees for such an extension of time must be addressed to the secretary[4] and may be made by a party either before or after the expiration of the time so appointed[5].

Either party may at any time apply to the referees for directions on any matter arising in connection with a reference[6].

An application under these provisions[7] or for an extension of the time for referring a decision of the board[8] must be made by sending to the secretary in duplicate a notice which, where appropriate, must state the title of the reference and must set out the grounds of the application[9].

1 As to the meaning of 'referees' see PARA 685 note 2.
2 Ie under the Industrial Training (Levy Exemption References) Regulations 1974, SI 1974/1335, reg 6, Schedule: see PARAS 685 et seq, 693 et seq.
3 Industrial Training (Levy Exemption References) Regulations 1974, SI 1974/1335, Schedule r 10(1)(a).
4 As to the meaning of 'secretary' see PARA 686 note 4.
5 Industrial Training (Levy Exemption References) Regulations 1974, SI 1974/1335, Schedule r 11(1). As to the service of notices etc see PARA 690.
6 Industrial Training (Levy Exemption References) Regulations 1974, SI 1974/1335, Schedule r 11(2). References are made under reg 6, Schedule r 1: see PARA 687.
7 Ie under the Industrial Training (Levy Exemption References) Regulations 1974, SI 1974/1335, Schedule r 11(1) or (2): see the text and notes 1–6.
8 As to the meaning of 'board' see PARA 687 note 1.
9 Industrial Training (Levy Exemption References) Regulations 1974, SI 1974/1335, Schedule r 11(3).

693. Time and place of hearing. On the directions of the President[1], the secretary[2] must fix the date, time and place of the hearing[3] of a reference and must, not less than 14 days before the date so fixed, send to the applicant[4] and to the board[5] a notice stating the date, time and place[6].

If they think fit, the referees may postpone the date or time fixed for, or adjourn the hearing of, any reference[7].

1 As to the meaning of 'President' see PARA 685 note 4.
2 As to the meaning of 'secretary' see PARA 686 note 4.
3 For these purposes, 'hearing' means a sitting of the referees duly constituted for the purpose of receiving evidence, hearing addresses and witnesses or doing anything lawfully requisite to enable the referees to determine a reference: Industrial Training (Levy Exemption References) Regulations 1974, SI 1974/1335, reg 2(1). As to the making of such references see reg 6, Schedule r 1; and PARA 687. See also PARA 689. As to the meaning of 'referees' see PARA 685 note 2.
4 As to the meaning of 'applicant' see PARA 687 note 2.
5 As to the meaning of 'board' see PARA 687 note 1.
6 Industrial Training (Levy Exemption References) Regulations 1974, SI 1974/1335, Schedule r 4. As to the service of notices etc see PARA 690.
7 Industrial Training (Levy Exemption References) Regulations 1974, SI 1974/1335, Schedule r 10(1)(b).

(d) Hearing; Determination

694. Appointment of assessors. The President[1], or a chairman[2] to whom a reference[3] has been assigned, may, in any case in which he considers it appropriate, appoint a person or persons having special knowledge or experience in relation to the subject matter of the reference to sit with the referees[4] as assessor or assessors[5].

1 As to the meaning of 'President' see PARA 685 note 4.
2 As to the meaning of 'chairman' see PARA 689 note 5.
3 Ie a reference under the Industrial Training (Levy Exemption References) Regulations 1974, SI 1974/1335, reg 6, Schedule r 1: see PARA 687.
4 As to the meaning of 'referees' see PARA 685 note 2.
5 Industrial Training (Levy Exemption References) Regulations 1974, SI 1974/1335, Schedule r 5.

695. The hearing. The hearing[1] of a reference[2] must take place in public, unless the referees[3] determine, at the request of the applicant[4] or of the board[5], to hear the reference in private[6].

If the applicant or the board desires to submit representations in writing[7] for consideration at the hearing, the party concerned must send the representations to the secretary[8] not less than seven days before the hearing and must at the same time send a copy of them to the other party[9].

The applicant may appear at the hearing and may be heard in person or be represented by counsel or solicitor or by any other person[10].

The board may appear at the hearing and may be represented by any of its members or officers or by counsel or solicitor[11].

1 As to the meaning of 'hearing' see PARA 693 note 3.
2 Ie a reference under the Industrial Training (Levy Exemption References) Regulations 1974, SI 1974/1335, reg 6, Schedule r 1: see PARA 687.
3 As to the meaning of 'referees' see PARA 685 note 2.
4 As to the meaning of 'applicant' see PARA 687 note 2.
5 As to the meaning of 'board' see PARA 687 note 1.
6 Industrial Training (Levy Exemption References) Regulations 1974, SI 1974/1335, Schedule r 6(1) (amended by SI 2008/2683).
7 As to the meaning of 'writing' see PARA 2 note 8.
8 As to the meaning of 'secretary' see PARA 686 note 4.
9 Industrial Training (Levy Exemption References) Regulations 1974, SI 1974/1335, Schedule r 6(2). As to the service of notices etc see PARA 690.
10 Industrial Training (Levy Exemption References) Regulations 1974, SI 1974/1335, Schedule r 7(1).
11 Industrial Training (Levy Exemption References) Regulations 1974, SI 1974/1335, Schedule r 7(2).

696. Procedure at hearing. The referees[1] may regulate[2] their own procedure[3]; and, in sitting to hear any reference[4], the referees must seek to avoid formality in their proceedings, so far as it appears to them to be appropriate to do so[5].

The applicant[6] and the board[7] are entitled to make opening statements, to call witnesses, to cross-examine any witnesses called by the other party and to address the referees[8].

If he so desires, the applicant may give evidence on his own behalf[9].

If either or both parties fail to appear or to be represented at the time and place fixed for the hearing[10] of a reference, the referees may dispose of the reference in the absence of such party or parties or may adjourn the hearing to a later date[11]. Before so disposing of a reference in the absence of either or both parties, the referees must, however, consider any representations submitted[12] by such party or parties[13].

The referees may require any witness to give evidence on oath or affirmation, and for that purpose may administer an oath or affirmation in due form[14].

1 As to the meaning of 'referees' see PARA 685 note 2.
2 Ie subject to the provisions of the Industrial Training (Levy Exemption References) Regulations 1974, SI 1974/1335, reg 6, Schedule: see PARAS 687 et seq, 697.
3 Industrial Training (Levy Exemption References) Regulations 1974, SI 1974/1335, Schedule r 10(3).
4 Ie a reference under the Industrial Training (Levy Exemption References) Regulations 1974, SI 1974/1335, Schedule r 1: see PARA 687.
5 Industrial Training (Levy Exemption References) Regulations 1974, SI 1974/1335, Schedule r 10(2).
6 As to the meaning of 'applicant' see PARA 687 note 2.
7 As to the meaning of 'board' see PARA 687 note 1.
8 Industrial Training (Levy Exemption References) Regulations 1974, SI 1974/1335, Schedule r 8(1).
9 Industrial Training (Levy Exemption References) Regulations 1974, SI 1974/1335, Schedule r 8(2).
10 As to the meaning of 'hearing' see PARA 693 note 3.
11 Industrial Training (Levy Exemption References) Regulations 1974, SI 1974/1335, Schedule r 8(3).
12 Ie under the Industrial Training (Levy Exemption References) Regulations 1974, SI 1974/1335, Schedule r 6(2): see PARA 695.
13 Industrial Training (Levy Exemption References) Regulations 1974, SI 1974/1335, Schedule r 8(3) proviso.
14 Industrial Training (Levy Exemption References) Regulations 1974, SI 1974/1335, Schedule r 8(4).

697. Determination of referees; correction of errors; appeals. If the applicant[1] and the board[2] agree in writing[3] on the terms of a decision to be made by the referees[4], the referees may, if they think fit, decide accordingly[5].

The determination of the referees may be made by a majority and, if the referees are constituted of two persons only[6], the chairman has a second or casting vote[7].

The determination of the referees must be recorded in a document signed by the chairman which must contain the reasons for the decision and must, where appropriate, include a direction requiring the board to alter its decision in such manner as may be specified in the direction; and it is the duty of the board to comply with the direction[8].

The clerk to the referees[9] must transmit the document signed by the chairman to the secretary who must, as soon as may be, enter it in the register of references[10] and must send a copy of the entry to each of the parties[11].

The register of references must be kept at the office of the referees and must be open to the inspection of any person without charge at all reasonable hours[12].

A chairman has power by certificate under his hand to correct any clerical mistake or error in a determination of the referees arising from any accidental slip or omission[13]. A copy of any decision so corrected must be sent with the certificate of the chairman to the secretary who must thereupon enter the correction in the register of references and must send a copy of the correct entry to each of the parties[14].

A person who is dissatisfied on a point of law with a decision of the referees may appeal to the High Court[15].

1 As to the meaning of 'applicant' see PARA 687 note 2.

2 As to the meaning of 'board' see PARA 687 note 1.
3 As to the meaning of 'writing' see PARA 2 note 8.
4 As to the meaning of 'referees' see PARA 685 note 2.
5 Industrial Training (Levy Exemption References) Regulations 1974, SI 1974/1335, reg 6, Schedule r 10(1)(d).
6 Ie in accordance with the Industrial Training (Levy Exemption References) Regulations 1974, SI 1974/1335, reg 5(3): see PARA 689.
7 Industrial Training (Levy Exemption References) Regulations 1974, SI 1974/1335, Schedule r 9(1).
8 Industrial Training (Levy Exemption References) Regulations 1974, SI 1974/1335, Schedule r 9(2).
9 For these purposes, the 'clerk to the referees' means the person appointed by the secretary to act in that capacity at one or more hearings: Industrial Training (Levy Exemption References) Regulations 1974, SI 1974/1335, reg 2(1). As to the meaning of 'secretary' see PARA 686 note 4. As to the meaning of 'hearing' see PARA 693 note 3.
10 As to the meaning of 'register of references' see PARA 688 note 3.
11 Industrial Training (Levy Exemption References) Regulations 1974, SI 1974/1335, Schedule r 9(3). As to the service of notices etc see PARA 690.
12 Industrial Training (Levy Exemption References) Regulations 1974, SI 1974/1335, Schedule r 9(4).
13 Industrial Training (Levy Exemption References) Regulations 1974, SI 1974/1335, Schedule r 9(5).
14 Industrial Training (Levy Exemption References) Regulations 1974, SI 1974/1335, Schedule r 9(6).
15 See PARA 1531.

4. DISCIPLINARY AND GRIEVANCE PROCEDURES

(1) IN GENERAL

698. Former and revised systems. Previously when an employer[1] contemplated dismissing an employee[2], or taking disciplinary action against an employee short of dismissal[3], he had to follow an established procedure whose minimum requirements were set out in statute[4]. Similar requirements applied where an employee wished to pursue a grievance by making a formal complaint against his employer[5]. A failure to follow the statutory dismissal, disciplinary and grievance procedures, where they applied, could have a number of legal implications for the parties. For instance, employment tribunals[6] could find any dismissal so made automatically unfair[7].

These procedures were supplemented by the employer's own regime so long as it was consistent with these requirements[8].

The Advisory, Conciliation and Arbitration Service (ACAS)[9] also issued a Code of Practice on Disciplinary and Grievance Procedures[10] which offered guidance on:

(1) the statutory requirements relating to disciplinary and grievance issues[11];

(2) what constituted reasonable behaviour when dealing with disciplinary and grievance issues[12];

(3) producing and using disciplinary and grievance procedures[13]; and

(4) a worker's right to bring a companion to grievance and disciplinary hearings[14].

The statutory provisions referred to above were repealed from 6 April 2009[15] and a revised shorter ACAS code of practice was issued[16]. This was part of a new approach to disciplinary and grievance procedures which involves less emphasis on mechanics and statutory requirements and more emphasis on flexibility and non-statutory and non-mandatory guidance.

1 As to the meaning of 'employer' see PARA 700 note 3.

2 As to the meaning of 'employee' see PARA 700 note 4. As to dismissal see PARA 733 et seq.

3 Eg suspension without pay or demotion.

4 See the Employment Act 2002 s 29, Sch 2; and the Employment Act 2008 (Commencement No 1, Transitional Provisions and Savings) Order 2008, SI 2008/3232, and PARA 700). Note that the Employment Act 2002 (Dispute Resolution) Regulations 2004, SI 2004/752 were made under the Employment Act 2002 ss 31(6), 32(7), 33 (all repealed) and s 51(1) (see PARA 700). See also PARA 700 note 1.

5 See notes 4, 10.

6 As to the establishment and constitution of employment tribunals see PARA 1399 et seq; and as to proceedings before employment tribunals see PARA 1453 et seq.

7 As to unfair dismissal see PARA 755 et seq. Even where the relevant procedure was followed, the dismissal could still be unfair if the employer had not acted reasonably in all the circumstances; however, if an employer could show that a failure in any element of his own disciplinary and dismissal procedures which went beyond the minimum statutory requirement would have made no difference to the decision to dismiss, that would not of itself caused the dismissal to be unfair: see PARA 767.

8 See the Employment Act 2002 s 30(2) (repealed); and PARA 700 note 6.

9 As to the constitution and powers of ACAS see PARA 1213 et seq.

10 See the Code of Practice on Disciplinary and Grievance Procedures (ACAS/CP01) (September 2004), which was issued by ACAS under the Trade Union and Labour Relations (Consolidation) Act 1992 ss 199, 200 (see PARA 1223) and came into effect on 1 October 2004: Employment Code of Practice (Disciplinary and Grievance Procedures) Order 2004, SI 2004/2356, art 2 (now

spent on the coming into force of ACAS Code of Practice 1: Disciplinary and Grievance Procedures (2009)). As to ACAS Codes of Practice generally see PARAS 1223–1224. See also PARA 700 et seq.

11 See notes 4, 10.

12 See notes 4, 10. The standard of reasonable behaviour had an obvious relevance to unfair dismissal cases: see PARA 767.

13 See notes 4, 10.

14 See PARA 717 et seq. See note 15.

15 See the Employment Act 2008 ss 1, 20, Schedule Pt 1. Amongst the provisions repealed are the Employment Act 2002 ss 31(6), 32(7), 33 (see PARA 700 note 6) under which the Employment Act 2002 (Dispute Resolution) Regulations 2004, SI 2004/752, were made: see note 4. See the Employment Act 2008 (Commencement No 1, Transitional Provisions and Savings) Order 2008, SI 2008/3232 (C 146), art 2. As to the transitional provisions and savings in art 3, Schedule see PARA 700 note 1. Note also that the statutory provisions relating to the right to be accompanied to disciplinary and grievance hearings under the Employment Relations Act 1999 ss 10–15 (see head (4) in the text) are unaffected: see PARA 717 et seq.

16 See the Code of Practice 1 on Disciplinary and Grievance Procedures (2009), ACAS/CP01) (April 2009), which was issued by ACAS under the Trade Union and Labour Relations (Consolidation) Act 1992 ss 199, 200 (see PARA 1223) and came into effect on 6 April 2009: Employment Code of Practice (Disciplinary and Grievance Procedures) Order 2009, SI 2009/771, art 2. See PARA 700 et seq.

699. Contractual basis for disciplinary powers. Although certain disciplinary measures may lie within the employer's discretion, such as withholding a discretionary bonus[1], most serious forms of disciplining are capable of affecting an employee's normal rights and expectations under the contract of employment, and, therefore, the employer needs contractual authority in order to impose any such measure lawfully[2]. This may be done by including disciplinary powers expressly into the contract[3], or by the device of a written disciplinary procedure incorporated into the contract[4] or referred to in the obligatory written statement[5].

Suspension with pay is normally lawful[6], being within the employer's discretion, since the employer is continuing to discharge his obligation by paying the employee[7]; but measures such as suspension without pay or a disciplinary demotion are likely to be breaches of contract unless provided for in the contract[8]. If the employer imposes a disciplinary sanction which is neither within managerial discretion nor permitted by the contract, the employee may sue the employer for breach of contract[9] or may leave his employment and claim to have been constructively dismissed[10]. It is particularly important that any power to fine and/or withhold wages already earned has contractual authority[11], since otherwise an unauthorised fine could be both a breach of contract and an unlawful deduction from wages, contrary to the Employment Rights Act 1996[12]. Contractual authority to dismiss, in the sense that a contractual disciplinary procedure lays down grounds for dismissal that cover the particular misconduct by the employee, does not necessarily make a dismissal fair, though breach by the employee of known rules may be important evidence[13].

Even if an employer has contractual authority to impose a particular sanction, if he does so in a manner or to a degree out of all proportion to the employee's offence, that may be considered a breach of contract by the employer, at least for the purposes of permitting the employee to terminate the employment and claim constructive dismissal[14].

1 If the bonus is a contractual right, with the only discretion being as to qualification, the employee may be able to sue on the basis of work actually performed: *Powell v Braun* [1954] 1 All ER 484, [1954] 1 WLR 401, CA. See also *Clark v Nomura International plc* [2000] IRLR

766 (employer withheld discretionary bonus on basis of behaviour which did not merit a warning; employer's exercise of discretion was perverse and irrational and was in breach of contract). See further PARA 828 et seq.

2 The disciplinary procedure itself may be contractually binding, so that failure to abide by it may be a breach of contract: *Dietmann v Brent London Borough Council* [1988] ICR 842, sub nom *Dietman v Brent London Borough Council* [1988] IRLR 299, CA. See also *Saeed v Royal Wolverhampton Hospitals NHS Trust* [2001] ICR 903, CA. As to the possibility of enforcement of a binding procedure see PARA 826. Whether or not a disciplinary procedure is contractually binding is, however, of much less significance in an unfair dismissal action: *Westminster City Council v Cabaj* [1996] ICR 960, [1996] IRLR 399, CA.

3 See PARA 826. Where the contract provides for external procedures to apply, eg in cases involving issues of 'professional' conduct or competence, it is for the employer to decide, in accordance with the terms of the contract, which of the disciplinary procedures to follow: *Saeed v Royal Wolverhampton Hospitals NHS Trust* [2001] ICR 903, CA (decision involved construing contract; public law issues not involved).

4 As to the incorporation of terms see PARA 116.

5 See PARA 120.

6 In cases where a period of suspension with pay is considered necessary, this period should be as brief as possible, should be kept under review and it should be made clear that this suspension is not considered a disciplinary action: see ACAS Code of Practice 1: Disciplinary and Grievance Procedures (2009), para 8. As to the ACAS Code of Practice see PARAS 700, 701; and as to ACAS Codes of Practice generally see PARAS 1223–1224.

The court has the power to grant an injunction to stay a suspension of employment if it judged it right to do so considering the circumstances: *Mezey v South West London and St George's Mental Health NHS Trust* [2007] EWCA Civ 106, [2007] IRLR 244, (2007) 94 BMLR 25. It is not permissible to enforce disciplinary proceedings against a doctor where lack of knowledge or ability has not been shown and it is possible to get an injunction so as to prevent the employer from bringing disciplinary proceedings in such a case: *Mezey v South West London and St George's Mental Health NHS Trust* [2010] EWCA Civ 293, [2010] IRLR 512. See also *West London Mental Health NHS Trust v Chhabra* [2013] UKSC 80, [2014] 1 All ER 943, [2014] ICR 194, [2014] IRLR 227, for guidance on the operation of disciplinary procedures for doctors.

7 See PARA 22. There is usually no obligation on the employer to provide work for the employee to do: see PARA 30.

8 *Hanley v Pease & Partners Ltd* [1915] 1 KB 698.

9 *Gorse v Durham County Council* [1971] 2 All ER 666, [1971] 1 WLR 775.

10 See PARA 763. As to unfair dismissal generally see PARA 755 et seq.

11 Ie either as part of the original contract or as a separate agreement. For the purposes of the Employment Rights Act 1996 Pt II (ss 13–27) (see PARA 254 et seq), any such ad hoc agreement must be in writing and have taken effect before the conduct on account of which the deduction is imposed: see s 13(1)(b); and PARA 255.

12 See PARA 255.

13 *Laws Stores Ltd v Oliphant* [1978] IRLR 251, EAT; *Taylor v Parsons Peebles NEI Bruce Peebles Ltd* [1981] IRLR 119, EAT; *Ladbroke Racing Ltd v Arnott* [1983] IRLR 154, Ct of Sess. An ambiguous rule on dismissal may, however, make a dismissal for a first offence unfair: *Trusthouse Forte (Catering) Ltd v Adonis* [1984] IRLR 382, EAT.

14 *BBC v Beckett* [1983] IRLR 43, EAT; *Cawley v South Wales Electricity Board* [1985] IRLR 89, EAT. *Quaere* whether this 'proportionality' limitation would be applied in a common law claim for breach of contract.

(2) FORMER STATUTORY DISMISSAL AND DISCIPLINARY AND GRIEVANCE PROCEDURES

700. Statutory dispute resolution procedures and their application. Until 5 April 2009[1], every contract of employment[2] was to have effect to require the employer[3] and employee[4] to comply, in relation to any matter to which a statutory procedure[5] applies, with the requirements of that procedure[6]. Until 5 April 2009, the statutory dismissal, disciplinary and grievance procedures[7] applied only to employees as defined in the Employment Act 2002. For other employees, and for disputes that have followed the statutory procedures but have not been resolved, the Code of Practice on Disciplinary and Grievance Procedures, issued by the Advisory, Conciliation and Arbitration Service (ACAS), applied[8].

On 6 April 2009, the statutory provisions relating to statutory procedures, and the Code of Practice on Disciplinary and Grievance Procedures, were replaced by a new ACAS Code of Practice on Discipline and Grievance Procedure[9] and a guidance booklet which complements the new code[10].

1 The provisions of the Employment Act 2002 ss 29–33 and the definition of 'statutory procedure' in s 40 (see note 5) were repealed from 6 April 2009 by the Employment Act 2008 s 20, Schedule Pt 1. The provisions of the Employment Act 2002 s 30(1), (2) had never actually been brought into force before this repeal.

The above repeal, like other provisions, is subject to the transitional provisions in the Employment Act 2008 (Commencement No 1, Transitional Provisions and Savings) Order 2008, SI 2008/3232 (C 146), art 3, Schedule (see below).

The following amendments and repeals made by the Employment Act 2008 have effect subject to the provisions of the Employment Act 2008 (Commencement No 1, Transitional Provisions and Savings) Order 2008, SI 2008/3232, Schedule Pt 1 paras 2, 3 (see below): (1) the repeal of the Employment Act 2002 ss 29–33, s 34(2) (adding the Employment Rights Act 1996 s 98A: see PARA 768), and of the definition of 'statutory procedure' in the Employment Act 2002 s 40 (see note 5), and the repeal of Schedules 2–4; (2) the repeal of the Employment Rights Act 1996 s 98A (see PARA 768), and of the words 'or 98A(1)' in s 112(5)(a) (see PARA 810) and s 120(1A)(a) (repealed); (3) the amendments to the Trade Union and Labour Relations (Consolidation) Act 1992 (see PARAS 1026, 1028, 1234); and (4) the amendment to the Employment Rights Act 1996 s 124A (see PARAS 818, 821): Employment Act 2008 (Commencement No 1, Transitional Provisions and Savings) Order 2008, SI 2008/3232, Schedule Pt 1 para 1.

The amendments and repeals referred to in the Schedule Pt 1 para 1 (see above) do not have effect where on or before 5 April 2009 the standard dismissal and disciplinary procedure or the modified dismissal procedure applies by virtue of the Employment Act 2002 (Dispute Resolution) Regulations 2004, SI 2004/752, reg 3 and on or before that date the employer has complied with the requirements of the Employment Act 2002 Sch 2 para 1, 2 or 4; taken relevant disciplinary action against the employee; or dismissed the employee: Employment Act 2008 (Commencement No 1, Transitional Provisions and Savings) Order 2008, SI 2008/3232, Schedule Pt 1 para 2(1). For the purposes of the Schedule Pt 1 para 2(1) the employer is treated as having complied with the Employment Act 2002 Sch 2 para 1 where that employer has complied with Sch 2 para 1(1), and sent the statement or a copy of it to the employee; with Sch 2 para 2 where the employee attends a meeting with the employer and the employee is informed that the employer is contemplating dismissing or taking disciplinary action against them; with Sch 2 para 4, where that employer has complied with Sch 2 para 4(a)(i), (ii) and Sch 2 para 4(b): Employment Act 2008 (Commencement No 1, Transitional Provisions and Savings) Order 2008, SI 2008/3232, Schedule Pt 1 para 2(2).

The amendments and repeals referred to in the Schedule Pt 1 para 1 (see above) do not have effect where the standard grievance procedure or the modified grievance procedure applies by virtue of the Employment Act 2002 (Dispute Resolution) Regulations 2004, SI 2004/752, reg 6, and the action about which the employee complains (by complying with the Employment Act 2002 Sch 2 para 6 or Sch 2 para 9, or presenting a complaint to an employment tribunal) occurs wholly before 6 April 2009: Employment Act 2008 (Commencement No 1, Transitional Provisions and Savings) Order 2008, SI 2008/3232, Schedule Pt 1 para 3(1). The amendments and repeals referred to in the Schedule Pt 1 para 1 (see above) do not have effect where the standard grievance procedure or the modified grievance procedure applies by virtue of the Employment Act 2002 (Dispute Resolution) Regulations 2004, SI 2004/752, reg 6 and the action which forms the basis of a grievance begins on or before 5 April 2009 and continues beyond that date; and the employee presents a complaint to the employment tribunal or complies with the Employment Act 2002 Sch 2 para 6 or Sch 2 para 9 in relation to the grievance (a) on or before 4 July 2009 under a jurisdiction listed in the amendments and repeals referred to in the Employment Act 2008 (Commencement No 1, Transitional Provisions and Savings) Order 2008, SI 2008/3232, Schedule Pt 2 (see below) and the Trade Union and Labour Relations (Consolidation) Act 1992 s 238 (see PARA 1351) does not apply; (b) on or before 4 October 2009 under a jurisdiction so listed (see below) and s 238 applies; (c) on or before

4 October 2009 under a jurisdiction listed in the Employment Act 2008 (Commencement No 1, Transitional Provisions and Savings) Order 2008, SI 2008/3232, Schedule Pt 3 (see below): Schedule Pt 1 para 3(2).

The terms 'action'; 'dismissed'; 'grievance', 'modified dismissal procedure'; 'modified grievance procedure'; 'relevant disciplinary action'; 'standard dismissal and disciplinary procedure'; and 'standard grievance procedure', have the same meaning in the Employment Act 2008 (Commencement No 1, Transitional Provisions and Savings) Order 2008, SI 2008/3232, as they have in the Employment Act 2002 (Dispute Resolution) Regulations 2004, SI 2004/752: Employment Act 2008 (Commencement No 1, Transitional Provisions and Savings) Order 2008, SI 2008/3232, Schedule Pt 1 para 4.

The tribunal jurisdictions in the Schedule Pt 2 referred to in heads (a), (b) above are: the Sex Discrimination Act 1975 s 63 (discrimination in the employment field); the Race Relations Act 1976 s 54 (discrimination in the employment field); the Trade Union and Labour Relations (Consolidation) Act 1992 s 145A (inducements relating to union membership or activities) (see PARA 1051), s 145B (inducements relating to collective bargaining) (see PARA 1052), s 146 (detriment in relation to union membership and activities) (see PARA 1048), Sch A1 para 156 (detriment in relation to union recognition rights) (see PARA 1169); the Disability Discrimination Act 1995 s 17A (discrimination in the employment field); the Employment Rights Act 1996 s 23 (unauthorised deductions and payments) (see PARA 259), s 48 (detriment in employment) (see PARA 625), s 111 (unfair dismissal) (see PARA 804); the National Minimum Wage Act 1998 s 24 (detriment in relation to national minimum wage); the Working Time Regulations 1998, SI 1998/1833, reg 30 (breach of regulations) (see PARA 319); the Transnational Information and Consultation of Employees Regulations 1999, SI 1999/3323, reg 32 (detriment relating to European Works Councils) (see PARA 1278); the Employment Equality (Religion or Belief) Regulations 2003, SI 2003/1660, reg 28 (discrimination in the employment field); the Employment Equality (Sexual Orientation) Regulations 2003, SI 2003/1661, reg 28 (discrimination in the employment field); the European Public Limited-Liability Company (Employee Involvement) (Great Britain) Regulations 2009, SI 2009/2401, reg 31 (detriment in employment) (see PARA 1334); the Information and Consultation of Employees Regulations 2004, SI 2004/3426, reg 33 (detriment in employment) (see PARA 1313); the Occupational and Personal Pension Schemes (Consultation by Employers and Miscellaneous Amendment) Regulations 2006, SI 2006/349, Schedule para 8 (detriment in employment) (see **PERSONAL AND OCCUPATIONAL PENSIONS** vol 80 (2013) PARA 486); the Employment Equality (Age) Regulations 2006, SI 2006/1031, reg 36 (discrimination in the employment field); the European Co-operative Society (Involvement of Employees) Regulations 2006, SI 2006/2059, reg 33 (detriment in relation to involvement in a European Co-operative Society) (see PARA 1338); the Companies (Cross-Border Mergers) Regulations 2007, SI 2007/2974, reg 51 (detriment in relation to special negotiating body or employee participation) (see **COMPANIES** vol 15 (2009) PARA 1451); and the Cross-border Railways Services (Working Time) Regulations 2008, SI 2008/1660, reg 17 (breach of regulations).

The tribunal jurisdictions in the Employment Act 2008 (Commencement No 1, Transitional Provisions and Savings) Order 2008, SI 2008/3232, Schedule Pt 3 referred to in head (c) above are: the Equal Pay Act 1970 s 2 (equality clauses); and the Employment Rights Act 1996 s 163 (redundancy payments) (see PARA 886).

2 For these purposes, 'contract of employment' has the same meaning as in the Employment Rights Act 1996 (see PARA 2): Employment Act 2002 s 30(4) (now repealed). See note 1.

3 For these purposes, 'employer' has the same meaning as in the Employment Rights Act 1996 (see PARA 2): Employment Act 2002 s 40.

4 For these purposes, 'employee' has the same meaning as in the Employment Rights Act 1996 (see PARA 2): Employment Act 2002 s 40.

5 For the purposes of the Employment Act 2002 Pt III (ss 29–40), 'statutory procedure' means a procedure set out in s 29(1), Sch 2: s 40. See note 1. The procedure set out in Sch 2 applies both to dismissal and disciplinary procedures and to grievance procedures, involving a three step 'standard' procedure or a short 'modified' procedure.

6 See the Employment Act 2002 ss 29–33, Sch 2–4 (repealed). See note 1.

7 Ie the procedures set out in the Employment Act 2002: see PARA 700.

8 See the Code of Practice on Disciplinary and Grievance Procedures (ACAS/CP01) (September 2004), which was issued by ACAS under the Trade Union and Labour Relations (Consolidation) Act 1992 ss 199, 200 (see PARA 1223) and came into effect on 1 October 2004: Employment Code of Practice (Disciplinary and Grievance Procedures) Order 2004, SI 2004/2356, art 2. As to ACAS Codes of Practice generally see PARAS 1223–1224; and as to the constitution and powers of ACAS see PARA 1213 et seq. See also PARAS 698, 701 et seq.

9 See the ACAS Code of Practice 1: Disciplinary and Grievance Procedures (2009), issued under the Trade Union and Labour Relations (Consolidation) Act 1992 ss 199, 200: Employment Code of Practice (Disciplinary and Grievance Procedures) Order 2009, SI 2009/771, art 2.

10 See Discipline and Grievances at work: The ACAS guide (September 2014). The guidance booklet provides good practice advice for dealing with discipline and grievances in the workplace.

(3) REVISED NON-STATUTORY DISCIPLINARY AND GRIEVANCE PROCEDURES

(i) Introduction

701. Approach adopted from 6 April 2009. The Advisory, Conciliation and Arbitration Service (ACAS)[1] issued a revised code of practice on disciplinary and grievance procedures which has effect from 6 April 2009[2]. This code is non-mandatory and replaces the Employment Act 2002 (Dispute Resolution) Regulations 2004[3] which introduced the concept of 'statutory' disciplinary and grievance procedures based on a three-step process. The 2004 Regulations were supported by the former ACAS code[4] and failure to follow the demanding procedures could result in automatically unfair dismissal and automatic award of compensation to the dismissed employee[5]. However the previous system, despite its laudable aims to reduce the number of cases going to tribunals and to encourage discussion between employers and employees, proved inappropriately inflexible and prescriptive. The revised ACAS code of practice is drafted as basic practical guidance for employers, employees and their representatives and sets out principles for handling disciplinary and grievance situations in the workplace.

The code does not apply to dismissals due to redundancy or the non-renewal of fixed-term contracts on their expiry[6].

A failure to follow any part of the ACAS Code of Practice does not, in itself, render a person or organisation liable to proceedings[7]. However, in any proceedings before an employment tribunal[8] or the Central Arbitration Committee[9] the ACAS Code of Practice is admissible in evidence; and any of its provisions which appears to the tribunal or the Central Arbitration Committee to be relevant to any question arising in the proceedings is taken into account in determining that question[10]. Compliance with the ACAS Code of Practice is particularly important in the context of unfair dismissal[11]. Failure to follow the code will not make the employer liable for unfair dismissal but tribunals may increase any award by up to 25 per cent if they consider that the employer failed unreasonably to follow the code's guidance or can decrease it by the up to the same percentage if they consider that the employee unreasonably failed to follow it[12]. However, failure to comply with it does not necessarily render a dismissal unfair since there may be good reason in a particular case for non-compliance[13].

Under the revised code the mandatory three-step process goes although guidance on appropriate conduct of a disciplinary or dismissal procedure remains similar. The new system is intended to be more flexible and user-friendly although it will remain important that both sides have taken part in the procedures leading up to dismissal. Employees are to be given opportunity to improve performance before being dismissed and in general the tribunals will be given back more power, being able to take a wider view of claims and more discretion in regard to compensation[14].

The revised code of practice is supported by an enhanced ACAS helpline, a free ACAS early conciliation service available through that helpline and a revised non-statutory guidance booklet providing supplementary information on handling discipline and grievances in the workplace[15].

1 As to the constitution and powers of ACAS see PARA 1213 et seq.

2 See the revised ACAS Code of Practice 1: Disciplinary and Grievance Procedures (2009); and PARA 702 et seq. The Code is issued under the Trade Union and Labour Relations (Consolidation) Act 1992 ss 199, 200 (see PARA 1223); and came into effect by order of the Secretary of State on 6 April 2009: Employment Code of Practice (Disciplinary and Grievance Procedures) Order 2009, SI 2009/771, art 2. As to the Secretary of State see PARA 5 note 21.

3 Ie the Employment Act 2002 (Dispute Resolution) Regulations 2004, SI 2004/752, made under the Employment Act 2002 s 31(6) (repealed), s 32(7) (repealed), s 33 (repealed), s 51(1) (see PARA 85 note 2). As to transitional provisions in regard to the relevant statutory provisions: see PARAS 698, 700 note 1.

4 See note 3.

5 See PARAS 755 et seq, 768, 814 et seq.

6 See ACAS Code of Practice 1: Disciplinary and Grievance Procedures (2009) Foreword. Guidance on handling proposed redundancies of 20 or more is contained in the ACAS booklet *Handling large-scale redundancies* (April 2014), which, at the date at which this volume states the law, is available at *http://www.acas.org.uk*. As to the ACAS Code of Practice see PARAS 700, 701; and as to ACAS Codes of Practice generally see PARAS 1223–1224.

7 See the Trade Union and Labour Relations (Consolidation) Act 1992 s 207(1); and PARA 1224. See also the ACAS Code of Practice 1: Disciplinary and Grievance Procedures (2009) Foreword,

8 As to the establishment and constitution of employment tribunals see PARA 1399 et seq; and as to proceedings before employment tribunals see PARA 1453 et seq.

9 As to the Central Arbitration Committee see PARA 1226 et seq.

10 See the Trade Union and Labour Relations (Consolidation) Act 1992 s 207(2); and PARA 1224.

11 As to unfair dismissal see PARA 755 et seq; and as to the importance of procedural fairness see PARA 768. The continuing importance of the ACAS Code of Practice was reaffirmed in *Lock v Cardiff Rly Co Ltd* [1998] IRLR 358, EAT. See *Spence v Manchester United plc* [2004] All ER (D) 241 (Nov), EAT (tribunal misdirected itself in law in not having regard to the Code of Practice). See also *East Hertfordshire District Council v Boyten* [1977] IRLR 347, EAT (following a jointly agreed procedure is important evidence on an employer's behalf in an unfair dismissal case).

12 See the Trade Union and Labour Relations (Consolidation) Act 1992 s 207A; and PARA 1234. See also ACAS Code of Practice 1: Disciplinary and Grievance Procedures (2009) Foreword.

13 *Lewis Shops Group v Wiggins* [1973] ICR 335, [1973] IRLR 205, NIRC; *Retarded Children's Aid Society Ltd v Day* [1978] 1 WLR 763, [1978] ICR 437, CA.

14 See ACAS Code of Practice 1: Disciplinary and Grievance Procedures (2009) Foreword.

15 See Discipline and Grievances at work: The ACAS guide (September 2014). See also PARA 702.

702. General principles. The revised Code of Practice on Disciplinary and Grievance Procedures from the Advisory, Conciliation and Arbitration Service (ACAS)[1] advises that employers and employees should always seek to resolve disciplinary[2] and grievance situations[3] in the workplace[4]. Where this is not possible the Code suggests that they should consider using an independent third party to help resolve the problem[5].

Although many potential disciplinary or grievance issues can be resolved informally, where this is not possible then they may be pursued formally; and the Code sets out the basic requirements of fairness that will be applicable in most cases and is intended to provide the standard of reasonable behaviour in most instances[6].

More comprehensive advice and guidance on dealing with disciplinary and grievance situations is contained in the ACAS non-statutory supplementary guide which also contains sample disciplinary and grievance procedures[7]. Although employment tribunals[8] must follow the Code they are not required to have regard to the guidance booklet which however provides more detailed advice and guidance that employers and employees are likely to find helpful both in general terms and in individual cases[9].

Fairness and transparency are promoted by developing and using rules and procedures for handling disciplinary and grievance situations[10]. These should be set down in writing, be specific and clear; and employees and, where appropriate, their representatives should be involved in the development of rules and procedures[11]. It is also important to help employees and managers understand what the rules and procedures are, where they can be found and how they are to be used[12].

Where some form of formal action is needed, what action is reasonable or justified will depend on all the circumstances of the particular case[13]. Employment tribunals will take the size and resources of an employer into account when deciding on relevant cases and it may sometimes not be practicable for all employers to take all of the steps set out in the Code[14].

However whenever a disciplinary or grievance process is being followed it is important to deal with issues fairly and there are the following elements to this: (1) employers and employees should raise and deal with issues promptly and should not unreasonably delay meetings, decisions or confirmation of those decisions; (2) employers and employees should act consistently; (3) employers should carry out any necessary investigations, to establish the facts of the case[15]; (4) employers should inform employees of the basis of the problem and give them an opportunity to put their case in response before any decisions are made[16]; (5) employers should allow employees to be accompanied at any formal disciplinary or grievance meeting[17]; (6) employers should allow an employee to appeal against any formal decision made[18].

1 As to the constitution and powers of ACAS see PARA 1213 et seq.

2 Disciplinary situations include misconduct and/or poor performance; if employers have a separate capability procedure they may prefer to address performance issues under this procedure. If so, however, the basic principles of fairness set out in the Code should still be followed, although they may need to be adapted: ACAS Code of Practice 1: Disciplinary and Grievance Procedures (2009) para 1. As to the ACAS Code of Practice see PARAS 700, 701; and as to ACAS Codes of Practice generally see PARAS 1223–1224.

3 Grievances are concerns, problems or complaints that employees raise with their employers: ACAS Code of Practice 1: Disciplinary and Grievance (2009) para 1.

4 See ACAS Code of Practice 1: Disciplinary and Grievance Procedures (2009) Foreword. See also generally PARA 701.

5 The third party need not come from outside the organisation but could be an internal mediator, so long as they are not involved in the disciplinary or grievance issue; and in some cases, an external mediator might be appropriate: see ACAS Code of Practice 1: Disciplinary and Grievance Procedures (2009) Foreword.

6 Employers would be well advised to keep a written record of any disciplinary or grievances cases they deal with; and organisations may wish to consider dealing with issues involving bullying, harassment or whistleblowing under a separate procedure: see ACAS Code of Practice 1: Disciplinary and Grievance Procedures (2009) Foreword.

7 See Discipline and Grievances at work: The ACAS guide (September 2014), in particular Appendix 2).

8 As to the establishment and constitution of employment tribunals see PARA 1399 et seq; and as to proceedings before employment tribunals see PARA 1453 et seq.

9 See ACAS Code of Practice 1: Disciplinary and Grievance Procedures (2009) Foreword. In *McMillan v Airedale NHS Foundation Trust* [2014] EWCA Civ 1031, [2014] IRLR 803, it was accepted that, while the ACAS guidance in itself does not have the formal status of a Code of Practice, it is so closely tied into the actual Code, fleshing out the deliberately shortened principles set out in it, that they should be read together.

10 ACAS Code of Practice 1: Disciplinary and Grievance Procedures (2009) para 2.

11 ACAS Code of Practice 1: Disciplinary and Grievance Procedures (2009) para 2. Where a policy is in place dealing in a bespoke way with a particular issue at work, especially so when it has been agreed by trade unions, it should be used: *Blackburn with Darwen Borough Council v Stanley* [2005] All ER (D) 135 (May), EAT (agreed dignity at work policy encompassed accusations of bullying).
12 ACAS Code of Practice 1: Disciplinary and Grievance Procedures (2009) para 2.
13 ACAS Code of Practice 1: Disciplinary and Grievance Procedures (2009) para 3.
14 ACAS Code of Practice 1: Disciplinary and Grievance Procedures (2009) para 3.
15 This is particularly important in cases of suspected misconduct, especially theft: *British Home Stores Ltd v Burchell* [1980] ICR 303n, [1978] IRLR 379, EAT; and see *ILEA v Gravett* [1988] IRLR 497, EAT. See also *Steele v William Hill Organisation Ltd* [2008] All ER (D) 80 (Aug), EAT; *Rees v Makro Self Service Wholesalers* [2008] All ER (D) 96 (Aug), EAT. As to investigation see PARA 703.
16 See PARA 704.
17 Where a trade union representative accompanies the employee, this does not mean per se that the employer recognises the union: *Union of Shop, Distributive and Allied Workers v Sketchley Ltd* [1981] ICR 644, [1981] IRLR 291, EAT; and see PARA 1094. As to the statutory right to be accompanied at a disciplinary hearing see PARA 717 et seq.
18 ACAS Code of Practice 1: Disciplinary and Grievance Procedures (2009) para 4. See PARA 708.

(ii) Keys to Handling Disciplinary Issues

703. Establishing the facts of the case. It is important to carry out necessary investigations of potential disciplinary matters without unreasonable delay to establish the facts of the case[1]. In some cases this will require the holding of an investigatory meeting with the employee before proceeding to any disciplinary hearing[2]. In others, the investigatory stage will be the collation of evidence by the employer for use at any disciplinary hearing[3].

In misconduct cases, where practicable, different people should carry out the investigation and disciplinary hearing[4].

If there is an investigatory meeting this should not by itself result in any disciplinary action[5]. Although there is no statutory right for an employee to be accompanied at a formal investigatory meeting, such a right may be allowed under an employer's own procedure[6].

In cases where a period of suspension with pay is considered necessary, this period should be as brief as possible, should be kept under review and it should be made clear that this suspension is not considered a disciplinary action[7].

1 ACAS Code of Practice 1: Disciplinary and Grievance Procedures (2009) para 5. As to the ACAS Code of Practice see PARAS 700, 701; and as to ACAS Codes of Practice generally see PARAS 1223–1224. As to investigations see also the guidelines laid down in *Linfood Cash and Carry Ltd v Thomson* [1989] ICR 518 at 522–523, [1989] IRLR 235 at 237, EAT, per Wood P; and as to the guidance given therein regarding the anonymity of witnesses see *Ramsey v Walkers Snack Foods Ltd* [2004] IRLR 754, EAT (departure from the guidelines justified where the fear of retribution and reprisal was real and informants refused to sign detailed statements or be exposed to further questioning which would risk revealing their identities).
2 ACAS Code of Practice 1: Disciplinary and Grievance Procedures (2009) para 5.
3 ACAS Code of Practice 1: Disciplinary and Grievance Procedures (2009) para 5.
4 ACAS Code of Practice 1: Disciplinary and Grievance Procedures (2009) para 6. Where there is some ambiguity or confusion about the correct procedures to use, it is for the management to operate the disciplinary procedure properly: *Clarke v Trimoco Motor Group Ltd* [1993] ICR 237, [1993] IRLR 148, EAT (it is not enough to say that an aggrieved employee could have used the grievance procedure instead).
5 ACAS Code of Practice 1: Disciplinary and Grievance Procedures (2009) para 7.
6 ACAS Code of Practice 1: Disciplinary and Grievance Procedures (2009) para 7.
7 ACAS Code of Practice 1: Disciplinary and Grievance Procedures (2009) para 8. An unreasonable and/or hasty suspension may breach the implied term of trust and respect (see PARA 48): *Gogay v Hertfordshire County Council* [2000] IRLR 703, CA.

704. Informing the employee of the problem. If it is decided that there is a disciplinary case to answer, the employee should be notified of this in writing[1]. It would normally be appropriate to provide copies of any written evidence, which may include any witness statements, with the notification[2].

The notification should also give details of the time and venue for the disciplinary meeting and advise the employee of his right to be accompanied at the meeting[3].

1 ACAS Code of Practice 1: Disciplinary and Grievance Procedures (2009) para 9. As to the ACAS Code of Practice see PARAS 700, 701; and as to ACAS Codes of Practice generally see PARAS 1223–1224. This notification should contain sufficient information about the alleged misconduct or poor performance and its possible consequences to enable the employee to prepare to answer the case at a disciplinary meeting: para 9. See *Knight v Robert Bates Wrekin Landscapes Ltd* [2014] All ER (D) 262 (Feb), EAT (procedure had clearly been defective, since the employee had not had the advance information and the opportunity to properly represent himself, to the point where it had been procedurally unfair).

2 ACAS Code of Practice 1: Disciplinary and Grievance Procedures (2009) para 9.

3 ACAS Code of Practice 1: Disciplinary and Grievance Procedures (2009) para 10. As to the statutory right to be accompanied see PARA 717 et seq.

705. Holding a meeting with the employee to discuss the problem. The meeting should be held without unreasonable delay whilst allowing the employee reasonable time to prepare his case[1].

Employers and employees (and their companions) should make every effort to attend the meeting[2]. At the meeting the employer should explain the complaint against the employee and go through the evidence that has been gathered[3]. The employee should be allowed to set out his case and answer any allegations that have been made; and he should also be given a reasonable opportunity to ask questions, present evidence and call relevant witnesses[4]. The employee should also be given an opportunity to raise points about any information provided by witnesses[5].

1 ACAS Code of Practice 1: Disciplinary and Grievance Procedures (2009) para 11. As to the ACAS Code of Practice see PARAS 700, 701; and as to ACAS Codes of Practice generally see PARAS 1223–1224.

2 ACAS Code of Practice 1: Disciplinary and Grievance Procedures (2009) para 12.

3 ACAS Code of Practice 1: Disciplinary and Grievance Procedures (2009) para 12.

4 ACAS Code of Practice 1: Disciplinary and Grievance Procedures (2009) para 12. See *Salim v London United Busways Ltd* [2008] All ER (D) 137 (Aug), EAT (where the employee unsuccessfully (on appeal by the employer) argued for unfair dismissal on the basis that he had been given insufficient time to consider his response before the meeting).

5 ACAS Code of Practice 1: Disciplinary and Grievance Procedures (2009) para 12. Where an employer or employee intends to call relevant witnesses they should give advance notice that they intend to do this: para 12.

706. Allowing the employee to be accompanied at the meeting. Workers have a statutory right to be accompanied by a companion where the disciplinary meeting could result in (1) a formal warning being issued; or (2) the taking of some other disciplinary action; or (3) the confirmation of a warning or some other disciplinary action (appeal hearings)[1].

The chosen companion may be a fellow worker, a trade union representative, or an official employed by a trade union[2].

To exercise the statutory right to be accompanied workers must make a reasonable request[3].

The companion should be allowed to address the hearing to put and sum up the worker's case, respond on behalf of the worker to any views expressed at the meeting and confer with the worker during the hearing[4]. The companion does not, however, have the right to answer questions on the worker's behalf, address the hearing if the worker does not wish it or prevent the employer from explaining his case[5].

1 ACAS Code of Practice 1: Disciplinary and Grievance Procedures (2009) para 13. As to the ACAS Code of Practice see PARAS 700, 701; and as to ACAS Codes of Practice generally see PARAS 1223–1224. As to the statutory right to be accompanied see PARA 717 et seq.

2 ACAS Code of Practice 1: Disciplinary and Grievance Procedures (2009) para 14. A trade union representative who is not an employed official must have been certified by their union as being competent to accompany a worker: para 14.

3 ACAS Code of Practice 1: Disciplinary and Grievance Procedures (2009) para 15. What is reasonable will depend on the circumstances of each individual case, but it would not normally be reasonable for workers to insist on being accompanied by a companion whose presence would prejudice the hearing nor would it be reasonable for a worker to ask to be accompanied by a companion from a remote geographical location if someone suitable and willing was available on site: para 15. See, however, *Toal v GB Oils Ltd* [2013] IRLR 696, EAT (ACAS Code of Practice 1: Disciplinary and Grievance Procedures (2009) para 15 suggests that 'it would not normally be reasonable for workers to insist on being accompanied by a companion whose presence would prejudice the hearing ...' but the word 'reasonable' in this context applies only to the request to be accompanied and does not attach also to the choice of representative); and *Roberts v GB Oils Ltd* [2014] ICR 462, [2014] All ER (D) 229 (Jan), EAT (the conclusions that the EAT had reached in *Toal v GB Oils Ltd* had been right and proper for the reasons that the EAT had given); and see further PARA 717 note 6.

4 ACAS Code of Practice 1: Disciplinary and Grievance Procedures (2009) para 16.

5 ACAS Code of Practice 1: Disciplinary and Grievance Procedures (2009) para 16.

707. Deciding on appropriate action. After the meeting the employer must decide whether or not disciplinary or any other action is justified and inform the employee accordingly in writing[1].

Where misconduct is confirmed or the employee is found to be performing unsatisfactorily it is usual to give the employee a written warning; and a further act of misconduct or failure to improve performance within a set period would normally result in a final written warning[2].

If an employee's first misconduct or unsatisfactory performance is sufficiently serious, it may be appropriate to move directly to a final written warning[3].

A first or final written warning should set out the nature of the misconduct or poor performance and the change in behaviour or improvement in performance required (with the appropriate timescale)[4]. The employee should be told how long the warning will remain current, and should be informed of the consequences of further misconduct, or failure to improve performance, within the set period following a final warning[5].

A decision to dismiss should only be taken by a manager who has the authority to do so[6]. The employee should be informed as soon as possible of the reasons for the dismissal, the date on which the employment contract will end, the appropriate period of notice and his right of appeal[7].

Some acts, termed gross misconduct, are so serious in themselves or have such serious consequences that they may call for dismissal without notice for a first offence[8]. Disciplinary rules should give examples of acts which the employer regards as acts of gross misconduct[9].

As the existence of warnings is not a legal requirement, but rather a factor to be considered when applying the overall test of fairness[10], there may be cases where it is fair to dismiss without a warning[11]; these include cases[12] where:

(1) the employee's attitude makes a warning or further warning fruitless[13];
(2) disciplinary rules themselves act as an unambiguous warning of dismissal for breach of them[14];
(3) the consequences of a single failure are disastrous[15];

(4) the employee is grossly incompetent or obviously unsuitable[16]; or
(5) the employee is in a senior position, knowing clearly what is required of him[17].

Where an employee is persistently unable or unwilling to attend a disciplinary meeting without good cause the employer should make a decision on the evidence available[18].

1 ACAS Code of Practice 1: Disciplinary and Grievance Procedures (2009) para 17. As to the ACAS Code of Practice see PARAS 700, 701; and as to ACAS Codes of Practice generally see PARAS 1223–1224.
2 ACAS Code of Practice 1: Disciplinary and Grievance Procedures (2009) para 18. Although warnings may be most obviously applicable to cases of misconduct by the employee, they may also be relevant in a case of incapability: *Winterhalter Gastronom Ltd v Webb* [1973] ICR 245, [1973] IRLR 120, NIRC; *Grant v Ampex Great Britain Ltd* [1980] IRLR 461, EAT; and see PARAS 773–775.
3 ACAS Code of Practice 1: Disciplinary and Grievance Procedures (2009) para 19. This might occur where the employee's actions have had, or are liable to have, a serious or harmful impact on the organisation: para 19.
4 ACAS Code of Practice 1: Disciplinary and Grievance Procedures (2009) para 20. A warning, particularly a final warning, should be unambiguous (see *Trusthouse Forte (Catering) Ltd v Adonis* [1984] IRLR 382, EAT; *McCall v Castleton Crafts* [1979] IRLR 218, EAT (written warning unnecessary when clear verbal warning given), although a series of warnings normally relates to one particular ground of unsatisfactory behaviour, the existence of warnings on other grounds could be taken into account when deciding whether to dismiss, if reasonable to do so in the circumstances).
5 ACAS Code of Practice 1: Disciplinary and Grievance Procedures (2009) para 20. For example, that it may result in dismissal or some other contractual penalty such as demotion or loss of seniority: para 20. A record of the warning should be kept, but it should be disregarded for disciplinary purposes after a specified period (eg, six months): Discipline and Grievances at work: The ACAS guide (September 2014), p 29; see also *Charles v Science Research Council* (1977) 12 ITR 208, EAT. If there is no express lapse provision, whether it is to be inferred depends on the circumstances: *Kraft Foods Ltd v Fox* [1978] ICR 311, [1977] IRLR 431, EAT. It is unreasonable for an employer to treat an expired warning as a determining factor in deciding to dismiss an employee: *Diosynth Ltd v Thomson* [2006] CSIH 5, [2006] IRLR 284. However this does not mean that *no* use can be made of an expired warning: see *Webb v Airbus UK Ltd* [2008] EWCA Civ 49, [2008] ICR 561, [2008] IRLR 309 (where *Diosynth Ltd v Thomson* above was narrowly construed, the employer in that case accepting that the employee would not have been dismissed at all but for the expired warning).
6 ACAS Code of Practice 1: Disciplinary and Grievance Procedures (2009) para 21.
7 ACAS Code of Practice 1: Disciplinary and Grievance Procedures (2009) para 21.
8 ACAS Code of Practice 1: Disciplinary and Grievance Procedures (2009) para 22. However a fair disciplinary process should always be followed, before dismissing for gross misconduct: para 22.
9 ACAS Code of Practice 1: Disciplinary and Grievance Procedures (2009) para 23. Such acts may vary according to the nature of the organisation and what it does, but might include things such as theft or fraud, physical violence, gross negligence or serious insubordination: para 23. See also Discipline and Grievances at work: The ACAS guide (September 2014), p 31.
10 See PARA 768. The issue of warnings should be a proportionate response to the situation: see *Sheridan v Stanley Cole (Wainfleet) Ltd* [2003] ICR 297, [2003] IRLR 52, EAT; affd but without mentioning this point [2003] EWCA Civ 1046, [2003] 4 All ER 1181, [2003] ICR 1449 (a final written warning was a disproportionate response to the employee's conduct in absenting herself from work for a short period without permission after an altercation with another employee).
11 Eg in cases falling short of summary dismissal for gross misconduct, where there is no requirement of a warning: see PARAS 743–746.
12 Heads (1)–(5) in the text do not constitute an exhaustive list.
13 *James v Waltham Holy Cross UDC* [1973] ICR 398, [1973] IRLR 202, NIRC; *Atkin v Enfield Group Hospital Management Committee* [1975] IRLR 217, CA; *Retarded Children's Aid Society Ltd v Day* [1978] 1 WLR 763, [1978] ICR 437, CA; *Grant v Ampex (Great Britain) Ltd* [1980] IRLR 461, EAT.
14 *Dalton v Burton's Gold Medal Biscuits Ltd* [1974] IRLR 45, NIRC; *Elliot Bros (London) Ltd v Colverd* [1979] IRLR 92, EAT; *Hoover Ltd v Forde* [1980] ICR 239, EAT; *Dairy Produce*

Packers Ltd v Beverstock [1981] IRLR 265, EAT; *Rowe v Radio Rentals Ltd* [1982] IRLR 177, EAT. To have this effect, the rule in question must be unambiguous, known to the employee and consistently applied: *Meridian Ltd v Gomersall* [1977] ICR 597, [1977] IRLR 425, EAT (but cf *Elliot Bros (London) Ltd v Colverd* above); *Meyer Dunmore International Ltd v Rogers* [1978] IRLR 167, EAT; *W Brooks & Son v Skinner* [1984] IRLR 379, EAT. The existence of a clear rule does not, however, relieve a tribunal from the need to apply the overall test of fairness, and a dismissal for breach of a clear rule is not automatically fair: see PARA 767.

15 *Alidair Ltd v Taylor* [1978] ICR 445, sub nom *Taylor v Alidair Ltd* [1978] IRLR 82, CA; *Turner v Pleasurama Casinos Ltd* [1976] IRLR 151; cf *ILEA v Lloyd* [1981] IRLR 394, CA.

16 *James v Waltham Holy Cross UDC* [1973] ICR 398, [1973] IRLR 202, NIRC; *AJ Dunning & Sons (Shopfitters) Ltd v Jacomb* [1973] ICR 448, [1973] IRLR 206, NIRC; *Littlewoods Organisation Ltd v Egenti* [1976] ICR 516, [1976] IRLR 334, EAT.

17 *James v Waltham Holy Cross UDC* [1973] ICR 398, [1973] IRLR 202, NIRC; *Winterhalter Gastronom Ltd v Webb* [1973] ICR 245, [1973] IRLR 120, NIRC; *Littlewoods Organisation Ltd v Egenti* [1976] ICR 516, [1976] IRLR 334, EAT; *Cook v Thomas Linnell & Sons Ltd* [1977] ICR 770, [1977] IRLR 132, EAT; cf *McPhail v Gibson* [1977] ICR 42, [1976] IRLR 254, EAT.

18 ACAS Code of Practice 1: Disciplinary and Grievance Procedures (2009) para 24.

708. Providing employees with an opportunity to appeal. Where an employee feels that disciplinary action taken against him is wrong or unjust he should appeal against the decision[1]. Appeals should be heard without unreasonable delay and ideally at an agreed time and place[2]. Employees should let employers know the grounds for their appeal in writing[3].

The appeal should be dealt with impartially and wherever possible, by a manager who has not previously been involved in the case[4]. The opportunity to appeal against a disciplinary decision is essential to natural justice[5]. The rules of natural justice[6] must, however, be applied realistically[7]. In particular, there is no absolute right for the employee to be present at all stages of an investigation[8] or to challenge or cross-examine witnesses[9]; and it will not necessarily be a procedural breach for the same manager to be involved at more than one stage in the procedure[10]. What matters is whether a generally fair procedure was adopted[11]. In a case of suspected misconduct, reasonable investigation is of the essence[12]. However, for the purposes of unfair dismissal[13], the failure by an employer to follow any element of his own disciplinary and dismissal procedure is not by itself unreasonable if it can be shown that the procedural lapse would have made no difference to the decision to dismiss[14].

An internal appeal is an important and integral part of a disciplinary procedure[15]. Further evidence coming to light at an appeal may be taken into consideration by the employer[16]. It used to be thought that a fair appeal would only cure a bad hearing if the appeal took the form of a complete rehearing (not just a review) but that was disapproved as a rule of law; the proper test is whether the appeal was conducted in a fair and open-minded way[17].

Workers have a statutory right to be accompanied at appeal hearings[18].

Employees should be informed in writing of the results of the appeal hearing as soon as possible[19].

1 ACAS Code of Practice 1: Disciplinary and Grievance Procedures (2009) para 25. As to the ACAS Code of Practice see PARAS 700, 701; and as to ACAS Codes of Practice generally see PARAS 1223–1224. An employee should be given an opportunity to be heard on each matter: *Budgen & Co v Thomas* [1976] ICR 344, [1976] IRLR 174, EAT; cf *Parker v Clifford Dunn Ltd* [1979] ICR 463, [1979] IRLR 56, EAT.

2 ACAS Code of Practice 1: Disciplinary and Grievance Procedures (2009) para 25. An appeal procedure should specify a time-limit within which the appeal should be lodged (five working days is commonly felt appropriate although this may be extended in particular circumstances). As to the appeals procedure see Discipline and Grievances at work: The ACAS guide (September 2014), p 34.

Where contractual provision is made for an internal appeal following a procedure which results in dismissal, the employee may be regarded in the period between the initial notification and the outcome of the appeal either as standing dismissed with the possibility of reinstatement or suspended with the possibility of the proposed dismissal not being confirmed and the suspension being ended. As to the 'dismissal' approach, where the fact that the employee has been pursuing an internal appeal does not, if the appeal fails and he remains dismissed, advance the effective date of termination (see PARA 764), nor amount per se to a good reason to extend the three-month limit (see PARA 804) for bringing an action for unfair dismissal, see *J Sainsbury Ltd v Savage* [1981] ICR 1, [1980] IRLR 109, CA, approved in *West Midlands Co-operative Society Ltd v Tipton* [1986] AC 536, [1986] ICR 192, HL; *Palmer v Southend-on-Sea Borough Council* [1984] 1 All ER 945, [1984] ICR 372, CA. See also *Roberts v West Coast Trains Ltd* [2004] EWCA Civ 900, [2005] ICR 254, [2004] IRLR 788 (where an appeal under contractual disciplinary procedure results in a penalty of dismissal being reduced to a demotion, the employee's contract of employment is resurrected and there is no dismissal in law; accordingly, unfair dismissal proceedings lodged before the outcome of the appeal is known cannot be heard). *Roberts v West Coast Trains Ltd* above was distinguished in *Saminaden v Barnet, Enfield and Haringey NHS Trust* [2008] All ER (D) 286 (Nov), EAT (where the employee has not given written agreement to the downgrading he could contend that it was more than a mere variation and that he had been dismissed or constructively dismissed by the unilateral imposition of the downgrading). As to the 'suspension' approach, where the effective date of termination falls when the appeal is dismissed, see *Drage v Governors of Greenford High School* [2000] ICR 899, [2000] IRLR 314, CA, distinguishing *J Sainsbury Ltd v Savage* above. The terms of the letter giving notice of dismissal are likely to be of great importance, but not necessarily determinative, in determining which approach applies: *Drage v Governors of Greenford High School*.

3 ACAS Code of Practice 1: Disciplinary and Grievance Procedures (2009) para 25.

4 ACAS Code of Practice 1: Disciplinary and Grievance Procedures (2009) para 26.

5 Appeals may be raised by employees on any number of grounds, for instance new evidence, undue severity or inconsistency of the penalty. The appeal may either be a review of the disciplinary sanction or a re-hearing depending on the grounds of the appeal: Discipline and Grievances at work: The ACAS guide (September 2014), p 33.

6 See JUDICIAL REVIEW vol 61 (2010) PARA 629 et seq.

7 *Rowe v Radio Rentals Ltd* [1982] IRLR 177, EAT; *R v Chief Constable of South Wales, ex p Thornhill* [1987] IRLR 313, CA (a judicial review case: see PARA 827). A similar approach is taken to the application of the rules of natural justice to expulsions from trade unions: see PARAS 1026–1028. It may be particularly difficult to attack a dismissal on the grounds of breach of natural justice if the employer has followed a procedure jointly agreed with the relevant union or unions: see *East Hertfordshire District Council v Boyten* [1977] IRLR 347, EAT; *Khanum v Mid-Glamorgan Area Health Authority* [1979] ICR 40, [1978] IRLR 215, EAT.

8 *Ayanlowo v IRC* [1975] IRLR 253, CA; *Gray Dunn & Co Ltd v Edwards* [1980] IRLR 23, EAT; and see *ILEA v Gravett* [1988] IRLR 497, EAT.

9 *Khanum v Mid-Glamorgan Area Health Authority* [1979] ICR 40, [1978] IRLR 215, EAT; *Ulsterbus Ltd v Henderson* [1989] IRLR 251, NI CA. See also *Santamera v Express Cargo Forwarding (t/a IEC Ltd)* [2003] IRLR 273, EAT (fairness did not require a forensic or quasi-judicial investigation; sufficient for employer to have conducted an investigation which was fair and proportionate to his capacity and resources).

10 *Rowe v Radio Rentals Ltd* [1982] IRLR 177, EAT; *Slater v Leicestershire Health Authority* [1989] IRLR 16, CA. Wherever possible, it is desirable to have separate levels of management dealing with the different stages: *Sartor v P & O European Ferries (Felixstowe) Ltd* [1992] IRLR 271, CA; *Byrne v BOC Ltd* [1992] IRLR 505, EAT. Moreover, it may be unfair if a manager who is a witness to the employee's alleged misconduct also sits in judgment on him: *Moyes v Hylton Castle Working Men's Social Club and Institute Ltd* [1986] IRLR 482, EAT. A chief constable can properly adjudicate in disciplinary proceedings against an officer in his force despite being the respondent to proceedings in an employment tribunal brought by the same officer: see *R v Chief Constable of Merseyside Police, ex p Bennion* [2001] EWCA Civ 638, [2002] ICR 136, [2001] IRLR 442; and POLICE AND INVESTIGATORY POWERS vol 84 (2013) PARA 206 et seq.

11 *Hussain v Elonex plc* [1999] IRLR 420, CA (dismissal still fair in all the circumstances, even though witness statements not disclosed to the employee). In *R v Chief Constable of the Thames Valley Police, ex p Cotton* [1990] IRLR 344, CA, it was held, on an application for judicial review to quash a dismissal, that a challenge based on breach of natural justice will succeed only if the applicant can show: (1) a breach of procedure; and (2) that that breach probably affected the outcome of the employer's decision. See also *Spink v Express Foods Group Ltd* [1990] IRLR

320, EAT; and PARA 768. There may be cases where it is reasonable to dispense with the procedures: *Hollister v National Farmers' Union* [1979] ICR 542, [1979] IRLR 238, CA; *Bailey v BP Oil (Kent Refinery) Ltd* [1980] ICR 642, [1980] IRLR 287, CA. See also *Abbey National plc v Fairbrother* [2007] IRLR 320, EAT (defects in early stages of grievance procedure cured as the procedure progressed). *Abbey National plc v Fairbrother* was applied in *Claridge v Daler Rowney Ltd* [2008] ICR 1267, [2008] IRLR 672, EAT.

12 *British Home Stores Ltd v Burchell* [1980] ICR 303n, [1978] IRLR 379, EAT; and see PARAS 776, 777. See also *Steele v William Hill Organisation Ltd* [2008] All ER (D) 80 (Aug), EAT; *Rees v Makro Self Service Wholesalers* [2008] All ER (D) 96 (Aug), EAT.

13 As to unfair dismissal see PARA 755 et seq.

14 See the Employment Rights Act 1996 s 98A(2) (repealed); and PARA 768. This provision adopts the approach taken in *British Labour Pump Co Ltd v Byrne* [1979] ICR 347, [1979] IRLR 94, EAT (no unfair dismissal, in spite of procedural lapse, if it in fact made no difference to the end result), which had been overruled in *Polkey v AE Dayton Services Ltd* [1988] AC 344, [1988] ICR 142, HL. As to procedural fairness generally see PARA 768.

15 Even if there is no contractual right to an appeal, it may be reasonable for the employer to arrange an ad hoc procedure: *Whitbread & Co plc v Mills* [1988] ICR 776 at 789, [1988] IRLR 501 at 507, EAT, per Wood P. The ACAS advice is to provide for the appeal to be heard where possible by a person who was not involved in the original meeting or decision and who is senior in authority to the person who took the disciplinary decision: Discipline and Grievances at work: The ACAS guide (September 2014), p 34. See note 1. Fundamental unfairness may result if evidence taken into consideration at an original hearing is not disclosed at the internal appeal hearing: *Pratt v Trustees of the Grace Eyre Foundation* [2004] All ER (D) 06 (Sep), EAT.

16 This may not, however, be done in such a way as to increase the penalty at appeal stage, unless there is a very clear contractual power to do so: *McMillan v Airedale NHS Foundation Trust* [2014] EWCA Civ 1031. If, therefore, new facts are disclosed which show substantially greater culpability, it will normally be necessary to re-charge the employee with the greater offence and operate the disciplinary procedure again (although in *McMillan v Airedale NHS Foundation Trust* at [70]–[74] per Underhill LJ, it was emphasised that, bearing in mind the practical realities of the employment relationship, formal compliance with procedures may give way if it can be seen that substantial fairness had been observed).

17 *Taylor v OCS Group Ltd* [2006] EWCA Civ 702, [2006] ICR 1602, [2006] IRLR 613, disapproving on this point *Whitbread & Co plc v Mills* [1988] ICR 776, [1988] IRLR 501, EAT.

18 ACAS Code of Practice 1: Disciplinary and Grievance Procedures (2009) para 27. As to the statutory right to be accompanied see PARA 717 et seq.

19 ACAS Code of Practice 1: Disciplinary and Grievance Procedures (2009) para 28.

709. Special cases. Where disciplinary action is being considered against an employee who is a trade union representative the normal disciplinary procedure should be followed[1]. Depending on the circumstances, however, it is advisable to discuss the matter at an early stage with an official employed by the union, after obtaining the employee's agreement[2].

If an employee is charged with, or convicted of a criminal offence this is not normally in itself reason for disciplinary action[3]. Consideration needs to be given to what effect the charge or conviction has on the employee's suitability to do the job and his relationship with his employer, work colleagues and customers[4].

1 ACAS Code of Practice 1: Disciplinary and Grievance Procedures (2009) para 29. As to the ACAS Code of Practice see PARAS 700, 701; and as to ACAS Codes of Practice generally see PARAS 1223–1224.

2 ACAS Code of Practice 1: Disciplinary and Grievance Procedures (2009) para 29.

3 ACAS Code of Practice 1: Disciplinary and Grievance Procedures (2009) para 30.

4 ACAS Code of Practice 1: Disciplinary and Grievance Procedures (2009) para 30.

(iii) Keys to Handling Grievances

710. Letting the employer know the nature of the grievance. If it is not possible to resolve a grievance informally employees should raise the matter formally and without unreasonable delay with a manager who is not the subject of the grievance[1]. This should be done in writing and should set out the nature of the grievance[2].

1 ACAS Code of Practice 1: Disciplinary and Grievance Procedures (2009) para 31. As to the ACAS Code of Practice see PARAS 700, 701; and as to ACAS Codes of Practice generally see PARAS 1223–1224.
2 ACAS Code of Practice 1: Disciplinary and Grievance Procedures (2009) para 31.

711. Holding a meeting with the employee to discuss the grievance. Employers should arrange for a formal meeting to be held without unreasonable delay after a grievance is received[1].

Employers, employees and their companions should make every effort to attend the meeting[2]. An employee should be allowed to explain his grievance and how he thinks it should be resolved[3]. Consideration should be given to adjourning the meeting for any investigation that may be necessary[4].

1 ACAS Code of Practice 1: Disciplinary and Grievance Procedures (2009) para 32. As to the ACAS Code of Practice see PARAS 700, 701; and as to ACAS Codes of Practice generally see PARAS 1223–1224.
2 ACAS Code of Practice 1: Disciplinary and Grievance Procedures (2009) para 33. As to the statutory right to be accompanied see PARA 717 et seq.
3 ACAS Code of Practice 1: Disciplinary and Grievance Procedures (2009) para 33.
4 ACAS Code of Practice 1: Disciplinary and Grievance Procedures (2009) para 33.

712. Allowing the employee to be accompanied at the meeting. Workers have a statutory right to be accompanied by a companion at a grievance meeting which deals with a complaint about a duty owed by the employer to the worker[1]. This would apply where the complaint is, for example, that the employer is not honouring the worker's contract, or is in breach of legislation[2].

The chosen companion may be a fellow worker, a trade union representative or an official employed by a trade union[3].

To exercise the right to be accompanied a worker must first make a reasonable request[4].

The companion should be allowed to address the hearing to put and sum up the worker's case, respond on behalf of the worker to any views expressed at the meeting and confer with the worker during the hearing[5]. The companion does not however, have the right to answer questions on the worker's behalf, address the hearing if the worker does not wish it or prevent the employer from explaining their case[6].

1 ACAS Code of Practice 1: Disciplinary and Grievance Procedures (2009) para 34. As to the ACAS Code of Practice see PARAS 700, 701; and as to ACAS Codes of Practice generally see PARAS 1223–1224. As to the statutory right to be accompanied see PARA 717 et seq.
2 ACAS Code of Practice 1: Disciplinary and Grievance Procedures (2009) para 34.
3 ACAS Code of Practice 1: Disciplinary and Grievance Procedures (2009) para 35. A trade union representative who is not an employed official must have been certified by their union as being competent to accompany a worker: para 35.
4 ACAS Code of Practice 1: Disciplinary and Grievance Procedures (2009) para 36. What is reasonable will depend on the circumstances of each individual case, but it would not normally be reasonable for workers to insist on being accompanied by a companion whose presence would prejudice the hearing nor would it be reasonable for a worker to ask to be accompanied by a companion from a remote geographical location if someone suitable and willing was available on site: para 36.
5 ACAS Code of Practice 1: Disciplinary and Grievance Procedures (2009) para 37.
6 ACAS Code of Practice 1: Disciplinary and Grievance Procedures (2009) para 37.

713. Deciding on appropriate action. Following the meeting the employer should decide on what action, if any, to take[1]. Decisions should be communicated to the employee, in writing, without unreasonable delay and, where appropriate, should set out what action the employer intends to take to resolve the grievance[2]. The employee should be informed that he can appeal if he is not content with the action taken[3].

1 ACAS Code of Practice 1: Disciplinary and Grievance Procedures (2009) para 38. As to the ACAS Code of Practice see PARAS 700, 701; and as to ACAS Codes of Practice generally see PARAS 1223–1224.
2 ACAS Code of Practice 1: Disciplinary and Grievance Procedures (2009) para 38.
3 ACAS Code of Practice 1: Disciplinary and Grievance Procedures (2009) para 38.

714. Allowing the employee to take the grievance further if not resolved. Where an employee feels that his grievance has not been satisfactorily resolved he should appeal[1]. He should let the employer know the grounds for his appeal without unreasonable delay and in writing[2].

Appeals should be heard without unreasonable delay and at a time and place which should be notified to the employee in advance[3].

The appeal should be dealt with impartially and wherever possible by a manager who has not previously been involved in the case[4].

Workers have a statutory right to be accompanied at any such appeal hearing[5].

The outcome of the appeal should be communicated to the employee in writing without unreasonable delay[6].

1 ACAS Code of Practice 1: Disciplinary and Grievance Procedures (2009) para 39. As to the ACAS Code of Practice see PARAS 700, 701; and as to ACAS Codes of Practice generally see PARAS 1223–1224.
2 ACAS Code of Practice 1: Disciplinary and Grievance Procedures (2009) para 39.
3 ACAS Code of Practice 1: Disciplinary and Grievance Procedures (2009) para 40.
4 ACAS Code of Practice 1: Disciplinary and Grievance Procedures (2009) para 41.
5 ACAS Code of Practice 1: Disciplinary and Grievance Procedures (2009) para 42. As to the statutory right to be accompanied see PARA 717 et seq.
6 ACAS Code of Practice 1: Disciplinary and Grievance Procedures (2009) para 43.

715. Overlapping grievance and disciplinary cases. Where an employee raises a grievance during a disciplinary process the disciplinary process may be temporarily suspended in order to deal with the grievance[1]. Where the grievance and disciplinary cases are related it may be appropriate to deal with both issues concurrently[2].

1 ACAS Code of Practice 1: Disciplinary and Grievance Procedures (2009) para 44. As to the ACAS Code of Practice see PARAS 700, 701; and as to ACAS Codes of Practice generally see PARAS 1223–1224. As to the disciplinary process see PARA 703 et seq.
2 ACAS Code of Practice 1: Disciplinary and Grievance Procedures (2009) para 44.

716. Collective grievances. The provisions of the ACAS Code of Practice on Disciplinary and Grievance Procedures do not apply to grievances raised on behalf of two or more employees by a representative of a recognised trade union or other appropriate workplace representative[1]. These grievances should be handled in accordance with the organisation's collective grievance process[2].

1 ACAS Code of Practice 1: Disciplinary and Grievance Procedures (2009) para 45.
2 ACAS Code of Practice 1: Disciplinary and Grievance Procedures (2009) para 45.

(4) RIGHT TO BE ACCOMPANIED AT DISCIPLINARY AND GRIEVANCE HEARINGS

717. Right to be accompanied. Where a worker[1] is required or invited by his employer[2] to attend a disciplinary[3] or grievance[4] hearing and reasonably[5] requests to be accompanied at the hearing, the employer must permit the worker to be accompanied at the hearing by a single companion who:

(1) is chosen by the worker and is of a specified description[6];

(2) must be permitted by the employer to address the hearing in order to do any or all of the following:

   (a) put the worker's case;

   (b) sum up that case;

   (c) respond on the worker's behalf to any view expressed at the hearing[7], and

must also be permitted by the employer to confer with the worker during the hearing[8].

If a worker has such a right to be accompanied at a hearing and his chosen companion will not be available at a time proposed for the hearing by the employer, but the worker proposes an alternative time[9], the employer must postpone the hearing to the time proposed by the worker[10].

An employer must permit a worker to take time off during working hours for the purpose of accompanying another of the employer's workers in accordance with a request under the provisions described above[11].

1 As to the meaning of 'worker' for these purposes see PARA 718.

2 As to the meaning of 'employer' see PARA 700 note 3.

3 For these purposes, a disciplinary hearing is a hearing which could result in: (1) the administration of a formal warning to a worker by his employer; (2) the taking of some other action in respect to a worker by his employer (eg suspension without pay, demotion or dismissal); or (3) the confirmation of a warning issued or some other action taken (eg an appeal hearing): Employment Relations Act 1999 s 13(4). As to the right to be accompanied at a disciplinary meeting see also ACAS Code of Practice 1: Disciplinary and Grievance Procedures (2009) paras 13–16; and PARA 706. As to the statutory right to be accompanied by a companion at a grievance meeting see also ACAS Code of Practice 1: Disciplinary and Grievance Procedures (2009) paras 34–37; and PARA 712. As to the ACAS Code of Practice see PARAS 700, 701; and as to ACAS Codes of Practice generally see PARAS 1223–1224. Where the purpose of a meeting is simply to inform the employee that he is to be dismissed on the ground of redundancy, it is not a disciplinary hearing for the purposes of the Employment Relations Act 1999 ss 10, 13(4) and he has no right to be accompanied: *Heathmill Multimedia Asp Ltd v Jones* [2003] IRLR 856, EAT. In *London Underground Ltd v Ferenc-Batchelor* [2003] ICR 656, [2003] IRLR 252, EAT, it was held that an informal oral warning issued to employees under the employer's disciplinary or attendance at work procedure can be, in effect, a formal warning in terms of the Employment Relations Act 1999 s 13(4) (see head (1) above). However, this decision was later held to have been made in excess of the Employment Appeal Tribunal's jurisdiction: see *Refreshment Systems Ltd (t/a Northern Vending Services) v Wolstenholme* (2004) Times, 2 March, [2004] All ER (D) 185 (Mar), EAT.

The Employment Relations Act 1999 ss 10, 13 are to be treated as part of the Employment Rights Act 1996 Pt V (ss 44–49A) (protection from suffering detriment in employment) (see PARA 614 et seq) for the purposes of s 203(1), (2)(e), (f), (3), (4) (restrictions on contracting out) (see PARAS 150, 151) and the Employment Tribunals Act 1996 s 18(1)(b) (ACAS conciliation) (see PARA 152 note 1): Employment Relations Act 1999 s 14(a), (b) (amended by SI 2014/431). The Employment Relations Act 1999 ss 10, 13 do not apply in relation to a person employed for the purposes of the Security Service, the Secret Intelligence Service or the Government Communications Headquarters: s 15. As to the Security Service, the Secret Intelligence Service, and the Government Communications Headquarters, see CONSTITUTIONAL AND ADMINISTRATIVE LAW vol 20 (2014) PARAS 243–245.

4 For these purposes, a grievance hearing is a hearing which concerns the performance of a duty by an employer in relation to a worker: Employment Relations Act 1999 s 13(5). This means a

legal duty arising from statute or common law, eg contractual commitments: Discipline and Grievances at work: The ACAS guide (September 2014), p 47. See note 3. However, an individual's request for a pay rise is unlikely to fall within the definition unless specifically provided for in the contract or the request raises an issue about equal pay. Equally, most employers will be under no legal duty to provide their workers with car parking facilities and thus a grievance about such facilities would carry no right to be accompanied, although if the worker were disabled and needed a car to get to and from work he would be entitled to a companion at a grievance hearing, as an issue might arise as to whether the employer was meeting their obligations under the Equality Act 2010 (DISCRIMINATION vol 33 (2013) PARA 1 et seq): see p 47, 48.

5 It will be for the courts and tribunals to decide which requests are reasonable in all the circumstances: Discipline and Grievances at work: The ACAS guide (September 2014), p 48. See note 3. However, in making their choice of companion, workers should bear in mind that it would not be reasonable to insist on being accompanied by a colleague whose presence would prejudice the hearing or who might have a conflict of interest; nor would it be sensible for a worker to request accompaniment by a colleague from a geographically remote location when someone suitably qualified was available on site: see p 48. The request to be accompanied does not have to be in writing; and it is good practice to allow workers to be accompanied at a formal grievance meeting even when the statutory right does not apply: see p 48. There is, however, doubt as to the validity of the part of the advice concerning a colleague whose presence would prejudice the hearing: see *Toal v GB Oils Ltd* [2013] IRLR 696, EAT; *Roberts v GB Oils Ltd* [2014] ICR 462, [2014] All ER (D) 229 (Jan), EAT; and note 6.

6 Employment Relations Act 1999 s 10(1), (2A) (s 10(2A)–(2C) added by the Employment Relations Act 2004 s 37(1)). See note 3. The chosen companion must be: (1) employed by a trade union of which he is an official (within the meaning of the Trade Union and Labour Relations (Consolidation) Act 1992 ss 1, 119: see PARA 1018); (2) an official of a trade union (within that meaning) whom the union has reasonably certified in writing as having experience of, or as having received training in, acting as a worker's companion at disciplinary or grievance hearings; or (3) another of the employer's workers: Employment Relations Act 1999 s 10(3). The certification referred to in head (2) above may take the form of a card or letter: Discipline and Grievances at work: The ACAS guide (September 2014), p 24. See note 3. Workers may ask an official from any trade union to accompany them at a disciplinary or grievance hearing regardless of whether the union is recognised or not. Trade unions should ensure that their officials are trained in the role of acting as a worker's companion and, even when a trade union official has experience of acting in the role, there may still be a need for periodic refresher training. Fellow workers or trade union officials do not have to accept a request to accompany a worker and no pressure should be brought to bear on a person to do so: see p 25.

Workers may have contractual rights to be accompanied by persons other than those listed in heads (1) and (2) above, eg a partner, spouse or legal representative; and if workers are disabled, employers should consider whether it might be reasonable to allow them to be accompanied because of their disability: Discipline and Grievances at work: The ACAS guide (September 2014), pp 24, 25. Reasonable adjustment may be needed for a worker with a disability (and possibly for their companion if they are disabled): see p 25. Before the hearing takes place, the worker should tell the employer whom he has chosen as a companion: see p 25. In certain circumstances (eg when the companion is an official of a non-recognised trade union), it can be helpful for the companion and employer to make contact before the hearing: see p 25.

See *Toal v GB Oils Ltd* [2013] IRLR 696, EAT (concerning the construction and application of the Employment Relations Act 1999 s 10: Parliament had legislated for the choice of companion to be that of the worker, subject only to the safeguards set out in s 10(3) as to the identity or the class of person who might be available to be a companion; ACAS Code of Practice 1: Disciplinary and Grievance Procedures (2009) para 15 (see PARA 706) suggests that 'it would not normally be reasonable for workers to insist on being accompanied by a companion whose presence would prejudice the hearing ...' but the word 'reasonable' in this context applies only to the request to be accompanied and does not attach also to the choice of representative); and *Roberts v GB Oils Ltd* [2014] ICR 462, [2014] All ER (D) 229 (Jan), EAT (on the proper construction of the Employment Relations Act 1999 s 10, the conclusions that the EAT had reached in *Toal v GB Oils Ltd* had been right and proper for the reasons that the EAT had given, in particular regarding the safeguards for an employer set out in the Employment Relations Act 1999 s 10(3); the appropriate weight given to ACAS Code of Practice 1: Disciplinary and Grievance Procedures (2009) para 15 and the Trade Union and Labour Relations (Consolidation) Act 1992 s 207 (see PARA 1224) did not have sufficient force to displace a clear conclusion as to the proper construction of the relevant words in the statute).

As to the possible extra-territorial effect of the Employment Relations Act 1999 s 10 see *CreditSights Ltd v Dhunna* [2014] EWCA Civ 1238, [2014] All ER (D) 140 (Sep); and PARA 757 note 4.

As to whether there is a requirement under the Convention for the Protection of Human Rights and Fundamental Freedoms (Rome, 4 November 1950; TS 71 (1953); Cmd 8969) art 6 (right to a fair trial: see RIGHTS AND FREEDOMS vol 88A (2013) PARA 243 et seq) to allow legal representation in internal disciplinary proceedings in the employment field see *R (on the application of G) v Governors of X School* [2011] UKSC 30, [2012] 1 AC 167, [2011] 4 All ER 625, [2011] ICR 1033, [2011] IRLR 756; and see also JUDICIAL REVIEW vol 61 (2010) PARA 642.

7 Employment Relations Act 1999 s 10(1), (2B)(a) (s 10(2B) as added: see note 6). It is good practice to allow the companion to address the hearing to put and sum up the worker's case, respond on behalf of the worker to any views expressed at the meeting and confer with the worker during the hearing: ACAS Code of Practice 1: Disciplinary and Grievance Procedures (2009) paras 16, 37. See note 3. However, the right of the companion to address and confer given by the Employment Relations Act 1999 s 10(2B) does not require the employer to permit the workers' companion to: (1) answer questions on the worker's behalf; (2) address the hearing if the worker indicates that he does not wish his companion to do so; or (3) use the powers so conferred in a way that prevents the employer from explaining his case or prevents any other person at the hearing from making his contribution to it: s 10(1), (2C) (s 10(2C) as so added). See note 3.

8 Employment Relations Act 1999 s 10(1), (2B)(b) (s 10(2B) as added: see note 6). See also note 3. Informal discussions, counselling sessions or investigatory meetings do not attract the right to be accompanied. Meetings to investigate an issue are not disciplinary meetings. If it becomes apparent that formal disciplinary action may be needed then this should be dealt with at a formal meeting at which the employee will have the statutory right to be accompanied: Discipline and Grievances at work: The ACAS guide (September 2014), p 24.

Where possible, the employer should allow a companion to have a say in the date and time of a hearing. If the companion cannot attend on a proposed date, the worker can suggest an alternative time and date so long as it is reasonable and it is not more than five working days after the original date: Discipline and Grievances at work: The ACAS guide (September 2014), p 25.

9 An alternative time must be reasonable and must fall before the end of the period of five working days beginning with the first working day after the day proposed by the employer: Employment Relations Act 1999 s 10(5). See note 3. For these purposes, in relation to a part of Great Britain, a working day is a day other than a Saturday or a Sunday, Christmas Day or Good Friday, or a day which is a bank holiday under the Banking and Financial Dealings Act 1971 (see TIME vol 97 (2010) PARA 321) in that part of Great Britain: Employment Relations Act 1999 s 13(6). As to the meaning of 'Great Britain' see PARA 2 note 12.

10 Employment Relations Act 1999 s 10(4). See note 3.

11 Employment Relations Act 1999 s 10(6). For these purposes, the provisions of the Trade Union and Labour Relations (Consolidation) Act 1992 ss 168(3), (4), 169, 171–173 (time off for carrying out trade union duties) (see PARAS 349, 1065, 1068) apply in relation to the Employment Relations Act 1999 s 10(6) as they apply in relation to the Trade Union and Labour Relations (Consolidation) Act 1992 s 168(1) (see PARA 1065): Employment Relations Act 1999 s 10(7). See note 3.

A worker who has agreed to accompany a colleague employed by the same employer is entitled to a reasonable amount of paid time off to fulfil this responsibility. The time off should not only cover the hearing but should also allow a reasonable amount of time for the companion to familiarise himself with the case and confer with the worker before and after the hearing: Discipline and Grievances at work: The ACAS guide (September 2014), pp 25, 49. A lay trade union official is permitted to take a reasonable amount of paid time off to accompany a worker at a hearing, so long as the worker is employed by the same employer; but time off for a lay official to accompany a worker at another employer is a matter for agreement by the parties concerned: pp 25, 49.

718. Meaning of 'worker'. For the purposes of the right to be accompanied at a disciplinary or grievance hearing[1], 'worker' means an individual who is:

(1) a worker within the meaning of the Employment Rights Act 1996[2];

(2) an agency worker[3];

(3) a home worker[4];

(4) a person in Crown employment[5], other than a member of the naval, military, air or reserve forces of the Crown; or

(5) employed as a relevant member[6] of the House of Lords staff or the House of Commons staff[7].

1 Ie for the purposes of the Employment Relations Act 1999 ss 10–12: see also PARAS 717, 719–721.

2 Ie within the meaning of the Employment Rights Act 1996 s 230(3): see PARA 5.

3 For these purposes, 'agency worker' means an individual who:
(1) is supplied by a person (the 'agent') to do work for another (the 'principal') by arrangement between the agent and the principal;
(2) is not a party to a worker's contract (within the meaning of the Employment Rights Act 1996 s 230(3): see PARA 5) relating to that work; and
(3) is not a party to a contract relating to that work under which he undertakes to do the work for another party to the contract whose status is, by virtue of the contract, that of a client or customer of any professional or business undertaking carried on by the individual,

and, for these purposes, both the agent and the principal are employers of an agency worker: Employment Relations Act 1999 s 13(2).

Section 13 is to be treated as part of the Employment Rights Act 1996 Pt V (ss 44–49A) (protection from suffering detriment in employment) (see PARA 614 et seq) for the purposes of s 203(1), (2)(e), (f), (3), (4) (restrictions on contracting out) (see PARAS 150, 151) and the Employment Tribunals Act 1996 s 18(1)(b) (ACAS conciliation) (see PARA 152 note 1): Employment Relations Act 1999 s 14(a), (b). As to regulations made in relation to agency workers, see PARA 11.

Section 13 does not apply in relation to a person employed for the purposes of the Security Service, the Secret Intelligence Service or the Government Communications Headquarters: s 15. As to the Security Service, the Secret Intelligence Service, and the Government Communications Headquarters, see CONSTITUTIONAL AND ADMINISTRATIVE LAW vol 20 (2014) PARAS 243–245.

4 For these purposes, 'home worker' means an individual who:
(1) contracts with a person, for the purposes of the person's business, for the execution of work to be done in a place not under the person's control or management; and
(2) is not a party to a contract relating to that work under which the work is to be executed for another party to the contract whose status is, by virtue of the contract, that of a client or customer of any professional or business undertaking carried on by the individual,

and, for these purposes, the person mentioned in head (1) above is the home worker's employer: Employment Relations Act 1999 s 13(3).

5 Ie within the meaning of the Employment Rights Act 1996 s 191: see PARA 163.

6 Ie within the meaning of the Employment Rights Act 1996 s 194(6) (see PARA 164 note 3) or s 195(5) (see PARA 165 note 3).

7 Employment Relations Act 1999 s 13(1).

719. Complaint to employment tribunal. A worker[1] may present a complaint to an employment tribunal[2] that his employer[3] has failed, or threatened to fail, to comply with the obligation to allow the worker to be accompanied by a companion at a disciplinary or grievance hearing[4], to permit the worker's companion to address such a hearing or to confer with the worker during such a hearing[5], or to postpone[6] the time of the hearing[7].

A tribunal must not consider such a complaint in relation to a failure or threat unless it is presented:

(1) before the end of the period of three months beginning with the date of the failure or threat; or

(2) within such further period as the tribunal considers reasonable in a case where it is satisfied that it was not reasonably practicable for the complaint to be presented before the end of that period of three months[8].

Where a tribunal finds that such a complaint is well-founded, it must order the employer to pay compensation to the worker of an amount not exceeding two weeks' pay[9].

1 As to the meaning of 'worker' for these purposes see PARA 718.
2 As to the establishment and constitution of employment tribunals see PARA 1399 et seq; and as to proceedings before employment tribunals see PARA 1453 et seq.
3 As to the meaning of 'employer' see PARA 700 note 3.
4 Ie under the Employment Relations Act 1999 s 10(2A): see PARA 717.
5 Ie under the Employment Relations Act 1999 s 10(2B): see PARA 717.
6 Ie under the Employment Relations Act 1999 s 10(4): see PARA 717.
7 Employment Relations Act 1999 s 11(1) (amended by the Employment Relations Act 2004 s 37(2)). The Employment Relations Act 1999 s 11 is to be treated as part of the Employment Rights Act 1996 Pt V (ss 44–49A) (protection from suffering detriment in employment) (see PARA 614 et seq) for the purposes of s 203(1), (2)(e), (f), (3), (4) (restrictions on contracting out) (see PARAS 150, 151) and the Employment Tribunals Act 1996 s 18(1)(b) (ACAS conciliation) (see PARA 152 note 1): Employment Relations Act 1999 s 14(a), (b) (amended by SI 2014/431). The Employment Relations Act 1999 s 11 does not apply in relation to a person employed for the purposes of the Security Service, the Secret Intelligence Service or the Government Communications Headquarters: s 15. As to the Security Service, the Secret Intelligence Service, and the Government Communications Headquarters, see CONSTITUTIONAL AND ADMINISTRATIVE LAW vol 20 (2014) PARAS 243–245.
8 Employment Relations Act 1999 s 11(2). See note 7. As to time limits generally see PARA 1453. The Employment Rights Act 1996 s 207A(3) (extension because of mediation in certain European cross-border disputes) (see PARA 1454) and s 207B (extension of time limits to facilitate conciliation before institution of proceedings) (see PARA 1455) apply for the purposes of head (1) in the text: s 11(2A) (s 11(2A), (2B) added by the Enterprise and Regulatory Reform Act 2013 Sch 2 para 40). The Employment Relations Act 1999 s 11(2), (2A) are to be treated as provisions of the Employment Rights Act 1996 for the purposes of ss 207A, 207B (extension of time limits: see PARAS 1454, 1455): Employment Relations Act 1999 s 11(2B) (as so added).
9 Employment Relations Act 1999 s 11(3). See note 7. Compensation under the Employment Relations Act 1999 s 11(3) is not a penalty or a fine; it is recompense for a loss or detriment suffered: *Toal v GB Oils Ltd* [2013] IRLR 696, EAT (wording 'shall order the employer to pay compensation' suggests that the tribunal does not have the right to order that no compensation should be payable so that, in a case in which it is satisfied that no loss or detriment has been suffered by an employee, the tribunal should feel constrained to make an award of nominal compensation only, either in the traditional sum now replacing 40 shillings, £2 or in some other small sum of that order).

The Employment Rights Act 1996 Pt XIV Ch II (ss 220–229) (calculation of a week's pay) (see PARA 143 et seq) applies for the purposes of the Employment Relations Act 1999 s 11(3) (s 11(4)); and the limit on the maximum amount of a week's pay in the Employment Rights Act 1996 s 227(1) (see PARA 147) applies for the purposes of the Employment Relations Act 1999 s 11(3) (s 11(5)). In applying the Employment Rights Act 1996 Pt XIV Ch II, the calculation date is to be taken to be: (1) in the case of a claim which is made in the course of a claim for unfair dismissal, the date on which the employer's notice of dismissal was given or, if there was no notice, the effective date of termination; (2) in any other case, the date on which the relevant hearing took place, or was to have taken place: Employment Relations Act 1999 s 11(4)(a), (b).

Workers whose employers fail to comply with a reasonable request to be accompanied may present a complaint to an employment tribunal. Workers may also complain to a tribunal if employers fail to re-arrange a hearing to a reasonable date proposed by the worker when a companion cannot attend on the date originally proposed. The tribunal may order compensation of up to two weeks' pay: Discipline and Grievances at work: The ACAS guide (September 2014), pp 26, 50.

720. Right not to be subjected to detriment. A worker[1] has the right not to be subjected to any detriment by any act, or any deliberate failure to act, by his employer[2] done on the ground that:

(1) he exercised or sought to exercise the right: (a) to be accompanied by a companion at a disciplinary or grievance hearing[3]; (b) for his

companion to address such a hearing or to confer with him during such a hearing[4]; or (c) to postpone[5] the time of the hearing; or

(2) he accompanied or sought to accompany another worker, whether of the same employer or not, pursuant to a request to be accompanied at a disciplinary or grievance hearing[6].

1 As to the meaning of 'worker' for these purposes see PARA 718.
2 As to the meaning of 'employer' see PARA 700 note 3.
3 Ie under the Employment Relations Act 1999 s 10(2A): see PARA 717.
4 Ie under the Employment Relations Act 1999 s 10(2B): see PARA 717.
5 Ie under the Employment Relations Act 1999 s 10(4): see PARA 717.
6 Employment Relations Act 1999 s 12(1) (amended by the Employment Relations Act 2004 s 37(3)(a)). Employers should be careful not to disadvantage workers for using their right to be accompanied or for being companions, as this is against the law and could lead to a claim to an employment tribunal: Discipline and Grievances at work: The ACAS guide (September 2014), pp 26, 50.

The Employment Rights Act 1996 s 48 (complaint to employment tribunal) (see PARA 625) applies in relation to contraventions of the Employment Relations Act 1999 s 12(1) as it applies in relation to contraventions of certain other provisions of the Employment Rights Act 1996: Employment Relations Act 1999 s 12(2).

The Employment Relations Act 1999 s 12 is to be treated as part of the Employment Rights Act 1996 Pt V (ss 44–49A) (protection from suffering detriment in employment) (see PARA 614 et seq) for the purposes of s 203(1), (2)(e), (f), (3), (4) (restrictions on contracting out) (see PARAS 150, 151) and the Employment Tribunals Act 1996 s 18(1)(b) (ACAS conciliation) (see PARA 152 note 1): Employment Relations Act 1999 s 14(a), (b) (amended by SI 2014/431). The Employment Relations Act 1999 s 12 does not apply in relation to a person employed for the purposes of the Security Service, the Secret Intelligence Service or the Government Communications Headquarters: s 15. As to the Security Service, the Secret Intelligence Service, and the Government Communications Headquarters, see **CONSTITUTIONAL AND ADMINISTRATIVE LAW** vol 20 (2014) PARAS 243–245.

721. Unfair dismissal. A worker[1] who is dismissed is to be regarded for the purposes of the law of unfair dismissal[2] as unfairly dismissed if the reason (or, if more than one, the principal reason) for the dismissal is that:

(1) he exercised or sought to exercise the right: (a) to be accompanied by a companion at a disciplinary or grievance hearing[3]; (b) for his companion to address such a hearing or to confer with him during such a hearing[4]; or (c) to postpone[5] the time of the hearing; or

(2) he accompanied or sought to accompany another worker[6], whether of the same employer[7] or not, pursuant to a request to be accompanied at a disciplinary or grievance hearing[8].

1 As to the meaning of 'worker' for these purposes see PARA 718. For these purposes, in the application of the Employment Rights Act 1996 Pt X Ch II (ss 111–132) (remedies for unfair dismissal) (see PARA 804 et seq) in relation to the Employment Relations Act 1999 s 12(3), a reference to an employee is to be taken as a reference to a worker: s 12(6).
2 Ie for the purposes of the Employment Rights Act 1996 Pt X (ss 94–134A): see PARA 757 et seq.
3 Ie under the Employment Relations Act 1999 s 10(2A): see PARA 717.
4 Ie under the Employment Relations Act 1999 s 10(2B): see PARA 717.
5 Ie under the Employment Relations Act 1999 s 10(4): see PARA 717.
6 As to the meaning of 'employer' see PARA 700 note 3.
7 References in the Employment Relations Act 1999 s 12 to a worker having accompanied or sought to accompany another worker include references to his having exercised or sought to exercise any of the powers conferred by s 10(2A) or s 10(2B) (see PARA 717): s 12(7) (added by the Employment Relations Act 2004 s 37(3)(b)).
8 Employment Relations Act 1999 s 12(3) (amended by the Employment Relations Act 2004 s 37(3)(a)). The Employment Rights Act 1996 s 108 (qualifying period of employment) (see PARA 758) does not apply in relation to the Employment Relations Act 1999 s 12(3) (see s 12(4)); but the Employment Rights Act 1996 ss 128–132 (interim relief) (see PARA 805 et seq) apply in relation to dismissal for the reason specified in the Employment Relations Act 1999

s 12(3)(a) or (b) (see heads (1), (2) in the text) as they apply in relation to dismissal for a reason specified in the Employment Rights Act 1996 s 128(1)(b) (see PARA 805) (Employment Relations Act 1999 s 12(5)).

Section 12 is to be treated as part of the Employment Rights Act 1996 Pt V (ss 44–49A) (protection from suffering detriment in employment) (see PARA 614 et seq) for the purposes of s 203(1), (2)(e), (f), (3), (4) (restrictions on contracting out) (see PARAS 150, 151) and the Employment Tribunals Act 1996 s 18(1)(b) (ACAS conciliation) (see PARA 152 note 1): Employment Relations Act 1999 s 14(a), (b) (amended by SI 2014/431). The Employment Relations Act 1999 s 12 does not apply in relation to a person employed for the purposes of the Security Service, the Secret Intelligence Service or the Government Communications Headquarters: s 15. As to the Security Service, the Secret Intelligence Service, and the Government Communications Headquarters, see **CONSTITUTIONAL AND ADMINISTRATIVE LAW** vol 20 (2014) PARAS 243–245.

INDEX

Employment

References are to paragraph numbers; superior figures refer to notes

Words and Phrases

Words in parentheses indicate the context in which the word or phrase is used

Fifth Edition volumes:

1 (2008), 2 (2008), 3 (2011), 4 (2011), 5 (2013), 6 (2011), 7 (2008), 8 (2010), 9 (2012), 10 (2012), 11 (2009), 12 (2009), 13 (2009), 14 (2009), 15 (2009), 16 (2011), 17 (2011), 18 (2009), 19 (2011), 20 (2014), 21 (2011), 22 (2012), 23 (2013), 24 (2010), 25 (2010), 26 (2010), 27 (2010), 28 (2010), 30 (2012), 31 (2012), 32 (2012), 33 (2013), 34 (2011), 35 (2011), 36 (2011), 37 (2013), 38 (2013), 38A (2013), 39 (2014), 40 (2014), 41 (2014), 41A (2014), 42 (2011), 43 (2011), 44 (2011), 45 (2010), 46 (2010), 47 (2014), 47A (2014), 48 (2008), 49 (2008), 50 (2008), 51 (2013), 52 (2014), 53 (2014), 54 (2008), 55 (2012), 56 (2011), 57 (2012), 58 (2014), 58A (2014), 59 (2014), 59A (2014), 60 (2011), 61 (2010), 62 (2012), 63 (2012), 64 (2012), 65 (2008), 66 (2009), 67 (2008), 68 (2008), 69 (2009), 70 (2012), 71 (2013), 72 (2009), 73 (2009), 74 (2011), 75 (2013), 76 (2013), 77 (2010), 78 (2010), 79 (2014), 80 (2013), 81 (2010), 82 (2010), 83 (2010), 84 (2013), 84A (2013), 85 (2012), 86 (2013), 87 (2012), 88 (2012), 88A (2013), 89 (2011), 90 (2011), 91 (2012), 92 (2010), 93 (2008), 94 (2008), 95 (2013), 96 (2012), 97 (2010), 97A (2014), 98 (2013), 99 (2012), 100 (2009), 101 (2009), 102 (2010), 103 (2010), 104 (2014)

Fourth Edition volumes (bold figures represent reissues):

12(**1**)

Additional Materials:

Sentencing and Disposition of Offenders (*Release and Recall of Prisoners*) containing vol **92** (2010) paras 761–820; *Tort* (*Conversion and Wrongful Interference with Goods*) containing vol **45**(**2**) (Reissue) paras 542–686

Fourth and Fifth Edition volumes:

2014 Consolidated Index (A–E), 2014 Consolidated Index (F–O), 2014 Consolidated Index (P–Z), 2015 Consolidated Table of Statutes, 2015 Consolidated Table of Statutory Instruments, etc, 2014 Consolidated Table of Cases (A–G), 2014 Consolidated Table of Cases (H–Q), 2014 Consolidated Table of Cases (R–Z, ECJ Cases)

Updating and ancillary materials:

2014 Annual Cumulative Supplement; Monthly Current Service; Annual Abridgments 1974–2013

November 2014